DIFFERENTIAL EQUATIONS

DIFFERENTIAL EQUATIONS

RALPH PALMER AGNEW

Professor of Mathematics
Cornell University

SECOND EDITION

McGRAW-HILL BOOK COMPANY, INC.

New York Toronto London

1960

DIFFERENTIAL EQUATIONS

 Library of Congress Catalog Card Number 59-13927

THE MAPLE PRESS COMPANY, YORK, PA.

II

00599

PREFACE

This book has been prepared to serve as a textbook for students taking a first course in differential equations, and as a reference book for those who have completed such a course. It is designed for students having a reasonable working knowledge of algebra, trigonometry, and elementary calculus. It undertakes to cultivate thorough understandings of basic ideas, facts, and techniques that have greatest interest and importance in pure and applied mathematics. Moreover, it gives valuable preliminary glimpses of many things encountered in advanced undergraduate or graduate work in mathematics and other sciences. For example, the problems of the first chapter reveal substantial information usually reserved for more advanced courses. Thus, from the beginning, attention is directed toward things scientists must know, and students are provided opportunities to make great strides toward scientific competence.

The book provides much more lengthy, detailed, and accurate discussions of problems than are customary in elementary textbooks on calculus and differential equations. It is expected that the number of pages covered by an assignment will usually be much greater than the number to which students become accustomed in more elementary courses. This involves a significant shift of emphasis in the students' work. Assignments no longer involve looking hastily at an "example" solved in "the book" and then spending two hours performing laborious manipulations essentially like those in the example. On the contrary, a considerable portion of the students' time is to be spent reading and answering questions that arise in the course of the reading. Many of these questions can be answered without use of pencil, paper, and eraser; many others require all three. A homely analogy may illustrate this point. If we were teaching our students to dig ditches, we would not put them to work with only picks and shovels and expect them to become masters of the trade by using their own ingenuities to surmount the difficulties provided by rocks and by roots of nearby trees. We would insist that they study and use more modern equipment because we prefer to turn out students who know about mechanical diggers and blasting powder. These better-trained students will surely be the ones who will supervise the efforts of their brethren who, for one reason or another, never studied instructive material but only used picks and shovels.

The book contains ample material for a full year course. Those taking shorter courses will find that whole chapters at the end of the book, and portions of others as well, will not be covered in classroom discussions. Such material is always available for study and reference, and experience with Edition 1 shows that this material is interesting to students both when courses are in progress and after they have been completed. Chapter 8 on Numerical Methods and Chapter 9 on Laplace Transforms, which did not appear in the first edition, should be welcomed by those who wish a comprehensive but nevertheless relatively brief exposition of these subjects.

The subject matter of this second edition is organized in such a way that it is easy to select appropriate material for a course covering about 40 classroom lessons. Moreover, the new arrangement makes possible a greater degree of flexibility. This affords opportunities to focus greatest emphasis upon material selected in accordance with personal preferences. The addition of a greatly expanded collection of problems provides enough problems to suit individual tastes, as well as permit assignment of different sets of problems in different years. Particularly in schools where several classes must follow essentially identical assignment schedules to prepare for a single final examination for all students, it is often necessary to prepare a chart, such as the accompanying one,

Suggested Assignment Chart

Lessons	*Sections*	*Lessons*	*Sections*
1–3	1.1–1.6	26–27	6.4
4–5	2.0–2.1	28	6.5
6–7	2.2–2.3	29	6.6
8–10	2.4–2.5	30	6.7
11–12	3.0–3.1	31–32	6.8
13–14	3.2–3.9	33	6.88
15	4.0–4.8	34–35	6.96
16–17	5.0–5.1	36	7.0–7.3
18	5.3	37	7.4
19–20	6.0–6.08	38	7.6–7.7
21–22	6.1	39–40	7.8
23	6.2	41	7.9
24–25	6.3		

which requires, for example, that three classroom lessons be devoted to Sections 1.1–1.6. It is reasonable that most, but not necessarily all, of the questions on preliminary and final examinations should be closely related to material for which the schedule provides adequate time for extensive classroom discussions. The only claim made for this schedule chart is that students who read the first seven chapters of this book, who solve the problems assigned by their teachers in the lessons of the chart, and who participate in class discussions of the text and problems, will have an excellent short course sure to promote their general intellectual as well as scientific development. Modifications, and even drastic modifications, of this assignment chart may be made. For example, those responsible for supplying intellectual respectability to their students may require the reading of some or all of Chapter 8 and the solution of at least a few problems.

Finally, the author wishes to emphasize the view of Chapter 4 expressed in the introduction to that chapter. Everybody should read it, but in a short course nobody should dwell very long upon it because time can be more profitably spent studying linear combinations, independence, sinusoids, complex exponentials, transients, stability, and other fundamentally important topics in Chapter 6.

Ralph Palmer Agnew

Mathematics Department
Cornell University
Ithaca, New York

CONTENTS

CHAPTER 1

INTRODUCTION TO DIFFERENTIAL EQUATIONS

1.1. Preliminary Remarks; Definitions. Many fundamental problems in pure and applied mathematics are solved by determining how one quantity depends upon one or more other quantities. Such problems are often solved by means of differential equations.

A *differential equation* is an equation involving derivatives. Derivatives usually are (and always can be) interpreted as rates. For example, the *ordinary derivative* dy/dx is the rate of change of y with respect to x, and the *partial derivative* $\partial u/\partial x$ is the rate of change of u with respect to x when all independent variables except x are given fixed values. Derivatives of higher orders are interpreted as rates of rates, as accelerations, and so on. Hence it is proper to say that a differential equation is an equation involving rates.

The "law" which states that the time rate of change of the amount x of radium in a portion of matter is proportional to the amount x is expressed by the differential equation

$$\frac{dx}{dt} = kx. \tag{1.11}$$

This law is discussed in detail in Sections 3.5 and 3.55. One who specializes in applied mathematics or in such subjects as engineering, physics, chemistry, and biology learns that many physical laws are expressed by differential equations. We shall meet several illustrations later.

Some examples of differential equations are

$$\frac{dy}{dx} = 3x^2 \tag{1.121}$$

$$x + y\frac{dy}{dx} = 0 \tag{1.122}$$

$$\frac{d^2y}{dx^2} + 4y = 0 \tag{1.123}$$

$$\frac{d^2y}{dx^2} = \frac{m}{H}\sqrt{1 + \left(\frac{dy}{dx}\right)^2} \tag{1.124}$$

$$\frac{d^2y}{dx^2} + \frac{g}{l}\sin y = 0 \tag{1.125}$$

$$\frac{\partial^2 u}{\partial x^2} + \frac{\partial^2 u}{\partial y^2} = 0. \tag{1.126}$$

The *order* of a differential equation is the order of the highest derivative involved. The first and second equations above are of the first order, and the others are of the second order.

A differential equation is *linear* when it is of the first degree in the dependent variable (or variables) and the derivatives. For example, the equation

$$2\frac{d^2y}{dx^2} + 3\frac{dy}{dx} + 4y = \sin x \tag{1.13}$$

is linear and of the second order. The coefficients 2, 3, and 4 in (1.13) are constants. Each linear differential equation of the second order with a single independent variable x and dependent variable y can be written in the form

$$f_1(x)\frac{d^2y}{dx^2} + f_2(x)\frac{dy}{dx} + f_3(x)y = f_4(x) \tag{1.14}$$

where $f_1(x), \ldots, f_4(x)$ are functions of x. This definition shows that the van der Pol (1889–1959) equation

$$\frac{d^2y}{dx^2} - \epsilon(1 - y^2)\frac{dy}{dx} + y = 0 \tag{1.15}$$

is nonlinear when $\epsilon > 0$. The equations

$$\frac{d^2y}{dx^2} = y^2, \qquad y\frac{dy}{dx} = \sin x \tag{1.151}$$

are also nonlinear.

An *ordinary differential equation* is one containing ordinary derivatives of one or more functions with respect to a single independent variable. Each of the equations heretofore given except (1.126) is an ordinary differential equation. So also is each of the two equations

$$a\frac{dx}{dt} + b\frac{dy}{dt} = c \tag{1.161}$$

$$d\frac{dx}{dt} + e\frac{dy}{dt} = f. \tag{1.162}$$

A *partial differential equation* is one involving partial derivatives of one or more dependent variables with respect to one or more of the independent variables. For example, (1.126) is a partial differential equation; it is known as the *Laplace* (1749–1827) *equation* and it is the most prevalent of all partial differential equations. The Laplace equation is often written in the form $\nabla^2 u = 0$ where, in three-dimensional rectangular, cylindrical, and spherical coordinates respectively of Fig. 5.82,

(1.171) $$\nabla^2 u = \frac{\partial^2 u}{\partial x^2} + \frac{\partial^2 u}{\partial y^2} + \frac{\partial^2 u}{\partial z^2}$$

(1.172) $$\nabla^2 u = \frac{\partial^2 u}{\partial \rho^2} + \frac{1}{\rho}\frac{\partial u}{\partial \rho} + \frac{1}{\rho^2}\frac{\partial^2 u}{\partial \phi^2} + \frac{\partial^2 u}{\partial z^2}$$

(1.173) $$\nabla^2 u = \frac{\partial^2 u}{\partial r^2} + \frac{2}{r}\frac{\partial u}{\partial r} + \frac{1}{r^2}\frac{\partial^2 u}{\partial \theta^2} + \frac{\cos\theta}{r^2 \sin\theta}\frac{\partial u}{\partial \theta} + \frac{1}{r^2 \sin^2\theta}\frac{\partial^2 u}{\partial \phi^2}.$$

We do not try to remember these formulas; the important thing is to remember that we have seen them and know that the index tells us where to find things we have seen. In addition to the Laplace equation $\nabla^2 u = 0$, the *heat equation* $a^2\nabla^2 u = \partial u/\partial t$ and the *wave equation* $a^2\nabla^2 u = \partial^2 u/\partial t^2$ are important. Many useful partial differential equations are more complicated than these, and many are simpler. A simpler one is

(1.18) $$\frac{\partial u}{\partial x} = 0.$$

1.19. Explanation of Numbering System. Nearly all books in pure and applied mathematics facilitate reference to chapters, sections, figures, theorems, equations, problems, etc., by numbers attached to some or all of these items. There are in current use many different numbering systems. The system used in this book is growing in popularity. Each number, such as 2.37, is to be thought of as a positive number represented in decimal form. The number before the decimal point gives the number of the chapter. The first digit after the decimal point (except for a few cases where the first two serve) gives the number of the section. The remaining digits complete the identification of one of the numbered items.

Except for a few instances where page make-up necessitates slight displacement of illustrations and footnotes, the numbers form an increasing sequence from the front to the back of the book. All numbered items have numbers in this single sequence. The number (5.17) identifies an equation in Chapter 5, Section 1. If one is looking at (5.17) and wishes to find Fig. 5.121, one turns toward the front of the book since $5.121 < 5.17$. Finding a numbered item in the book is much like finding a word in the dictionary, one uses the natural order of numbers instead of the alphabetical order of words. The fact that some numbers contain more digits than others and that some numbers fail to represent numbered items causes no more difficulty than the fact that some words are longer than others and that some combinations of letters fail to make words.

1.2. Explicit, Implicit, and Formal Solutions.*

A function $y(x)$ is said to be an *explicit solution* or simply a *solution* of a differential equation involving x, y, and derivatives of y with respect to x if substitution of $y(x)$ and its derivatives reduces the differential equation to an identity in

* An appreciation of the ways in which the words *explicit, implicit,* and *formal* are used in the calculus and other branches of mathematics shows why these words are used here. The equation $y = x + 1$ states *explicitly* that y is $x + 1$. The equation $x - y - 1 = 0$ does not state explicitly that y is $x - 1$ but only *implies* that y is $x - 1$ and hence states *implicitly* that y is $x - 1$. The word *formal* is used with the meaning "having the form but not necessarily the substance."

x. The function $y(x)$ is said to be a *solution over an interval I* if the identity holds for each x in the interval I. For example, the function

$$(1.21) \qquad y = e^{-x} + \sin x$$

is a solution of the equation

$$(1.211) \qquad \frac{d^2y}{dx^2} + y = 2e^{-x}$$

since substitution of (1.21) in (1.211) gives the identity

$$(1.212) \qquad (e^{-x} - \sin x) + (e^{-x} + \sin x) = 2e^{-x}.$$

Likewise, if c is a positive constant, the two functions $y = (c^2 - x^2)^{\frac{1}{2}}$ and $y = -(c^2 - x^2)^{\frac{1}{2}}$ are both* solutions of the equation

$$(1.23) \qquad x + y\frac{dy}{dx} = 0$$

over the interval $-c < x < c$ since substitution yields

$$(1.24) \qquad x + [\pm(c^2 - x^2)^{\frac{1}{2}}][\mp x(c^2 - x^2)^{-\frac{1}{2}}] = 0 \qquad -c < x < c.$$

When a problem is solved by means of differential equations, a solution of the differential equation either furnishes or leads to the solution of the problem. It is usually true that an explicit solution is sought and that implicit and formal solutions are irksome evils to be avoided when possible. However there are some problems, notably those in which it turns out that x and y are related by the equation of a conic section, when it is not always desirable to express y in terms of x.

An equation $f(x, y) = 0$ is said *to furnish a solution* or, briefly, *to be an implicit solution* of a differential equation involving x, y, and derivatives of y with respect to x, if (*a*) the differential equation is satisfied by each function $y(x)$ for which these derivatives exist and $f(x, y(x)) = 0$ and (*b*) at least one such function $y(x)$ exists. It should of course be recognized that, if the equation $f(x, y) = 0$ can be solved for y in terms of x,

* Insofar as real variables are concerned, the symbols $\sqrt{Q}$ and $Q^{\frac{1}{2}}$ are defined only when Q is a nonnegative real number, and each is the nonnegative number whose square is Q. Thus $\sqrt{0} = 0$, $\sqrt{4} = 2$, and $-\sqrt{4} = -2$. It should be known that $\sqrt{R^2} = R$ if $R \geqq 0$ and that $\sqrt{R^2} = -R$ if $R \leqq 0$. If R is real, $\sqrt{R^2}$ is always $|R|$. Those who enjoy sad stories should be interested in the following: It is said that an electrical-engineering student was delayed a year in obtaining an advanced degree because his experiments and theory refused to "jibe." The unfortunate victim of the delay thought that the formula

$$(1.22) \qquad \sqrt{1 - \sin^2 x} = \cos x$$

held for all x. Actually it holds only when x lies in the first or fourth quadrant.

the result consists of one or more functions $y(x)$ such that $f(x, y(x)) = 0$. An example may serve to clarify the meaning of implicit solutions. If c is a positive constant, then the equation $x^2 + y^2 - c^2 = 0$, which we may write in the form

$$x^2 + y^2 = c^2, \tag{1.25}$$

is an implicit solution of (1.23) since solving (1.25) for y yields two functions, namely, $(c^2 - x^2)^{\frac{1}{2}}$ and $-(c^2 - x^2)^{\frac{1}{2}}$, each of which is a solution of (1.23).

Before giving the definition of *formal solution* (something having the form but not necessarily the substance of a solution), we consider a simple example. If c is a constant and we assume that the equation

$$x^2 + y^2 = c \tag{1.26}$$

is satisfied by a differentiable function $y = y(x)$, then we can differentiate to obtain

$$2x + 2y\frac{dy}{dx} = 0 \tag{1.27}$$

and we conclude that (1.26) is a solution (implicit) of (1.27). If c is negative, say $c = -10$, the assumption that (1.26) determines y as a differentiable function of x is unjustified when one is working (as we are here) with real functions of real variables; for there does not exist a single pair of real values of x and y for which (1.26) holds. Hence, when $c \leqq 0$, (1.26) is neither an explicit nor implicit solution of (1.27); but (1.26) is a formal solution of (1.27) in accordance with the following definition.

An equation $f(x, y) = 0$ is said to be a *formal solution* of a differential equation involving x, y, and derivatives of y with respect to x if the conclusion that $y(x)$ is an explicit solution of the differential equation can be drawn from (*a*) the hypothesis that $y(x)$ possesses these derivatives, (*b*) $f(x, y(x)) = 0$, and (*c*) formulas obtained by differentiation of $f(x, y(x))$. This terminology enables us to assert that, for each constant c, the equation $x^2 + y^2 = c$ is a formal solution of $x + y(dy/dx) = 0$ and that (insofar as real variables are concerned) the formal solution becomes an implicit solution which yields explicit solutions only when $c > 0$. The necessity for discussing implicit and formal solutions arises because some methods for solving differential equations lead directly to them.

1.3. Some Remarks on Solving Differential Equations. It is easy to give examples of differential equations having no solutions; for example,

$$\left|\frac{dy}{dx}\right| + |x| + |y| + 1 = 0 \tag{1.31}$$

is such an equation. The equation

$$\left|\frac{dy}{dx}\right| + |y| = 0 \tag{1.32}$$

has just one solution, namely, $y = 0$. Nevertheless, one who takes a course in elementary differential equations and then uses differential equations in the solution of problems in pure and applied mathematics learns to expect that each differential equation he meets in the course of his work will have many solutions. To solve a problem frequently (or usually) requires that one find the solution or solutions of a differential equation satisfying one or more supplementary conditions such as boundary conditions, initial conditions, etc. A standard method of solving such a problem is first to find all the solutions of the differential equation and then to pick out the particular solution or solutions satisfying the supplementary conditions.

This explains why it is desirable to be able to find *all* solutions of a differential equation and why solving a differential equation means finding all solutions of the differential equation.

Many attempts to solve differential equations start with an assumption that $y(x)$ is a function which, for at least some range of values of x, satisfies the differential equation. Then, by some method or other, it is proved that $y(x)$ must have a certain form or at least that $y(x)$ must satisfy a relation of the form $F(x, y) = 0$. This proof does not necessarily imply that the differential equation has any solutions whatever; in particular, it does not imply that each function having this certain form must be a solution of the differential equation, and it does not imply that each differentiable function $y(x)$ for which $F(x, y(x)) = 0$ is a solution of the differential equation.

One way to solve a differential equation is to prove two things, as follows: (i) If $y(x)$ is a solution of the differential equation, then $y(x)$ must have a certain form. (ii) If $y(x)$ has this certain form, then $y(x)$ is a solution of the differential equation.

Working the following problems gives practice in the art of differentiating and helpful preliminary ideas about differential equations, as well as about other things of great importance in mathematics and the sciences. The *rules of our game* must be thoroughly understood. We work some of the problems and read all of them. Working a problem is like cutting down a tree and reading a problem is like looking at a tree. We spend part of our time swinging axes to develop our muscles, and we spend part of our time looking around to keep us from being dolts. The mathematical and scientific forests really are interesting, and we should all enjoy chopping and looking at the scenery.

Problem 1.33

Assuming that $a, b, c, c_0, c_1, \ldots$ are constants, show that each function or equation on the left satisfies the differential equation written opposite it. Remember that we differentiate and substitute.

(a) $y = c_0 + c_1x + c_2x^2 + c_3x^3$ $\qquad \dfrac{d^4y}{dx^4} = 0$

(b) $y = \sin 2x + c$ $\qquad \dfrac{dy}{dx} = 2\cos 2x$

(c) $y = ce^{ax}$ $\qquad \dfrac{dy}{dx} = ay$

(d) $y = ce^{bx} - \dfrac{a}{b}x - \dfrac{a}{b^2}$ $\qquad \dfrac{dy}{dx} = ax + by$

(e) $y = c_1e^{ax} + c_2e^{-ax}$ $\qquad \dfrac{d^2y}{dx^2} - a^2y = 0$

(f) $y = c_1 \cos ax + c_2 \sin ax$ $\qquad \dfrac{d^2y}{dx^2} + a^2y = 0$

(g) $y = e^{ax} \sin bx$ $\qquad \dfrac{d^2y}{dx^2} - 2a\dfrac{dy}{dx} + (a^2 + b^2)y = 0$

(h) $y = x(c - \cos x)$ $\qquad x\dfrac{dy}{dx} - y = x^2 \sin x$

(i) $y - c^2 = 2c(x - c)$ $\qquad \dfrac{1}{4}\left(\dfrac{dy}{dx}\right)^2 - x\dfrac{dy}{dx} + y = 0$

(j) $y = x^2$ $\qquad \dfrac{1}{4}\left(\dfrac{dy}{dx}\right)^2 - x\dfrac{dy}{dx} + y = 0$

(k) $y = \sin(x - c)$ $\qquad \dfrac{d^2y}{dx^2} + \epsilon\left[1 - y^2 - \left(\dfrac{dy}{dx}\right)^2\right]\dfrac{dy}{dx} + y = 0$

(l) $y = cx + f(c)$ $\qquad y = x\dfrac{dy}{dx} + f\left(\dfrac{dy}{dx}\right)$

(m) $(x - c_1)^2 + (y - c_2)^2 = a^2$ $\qquad a\left|\dfrac{d^2y}{dx^2}\right| = \left[1 + \left(\dfrac{dy}{dx}\right)^2\right]^{\frac{3}{2}}$

(n) $y^2 = ce^{2x} - x^2$ $\qquad x + y\dfrac{dy}{dx} = x^2 + y^2$

(o) $y + \tan^{-1} y = x + \tan^{-1} x + c$ $\qquad \dfrac{dy}{dx} = \dfrac{1 + y^2}{1 + x^2}\,\dfrac{2 + x^2}{2 + y^2}$

(p) $xy - \log y = c$ $\qquad \dfrac{dy}{dx} = \dfrac{y^2}{1 - xy}$

(q) $y = c + \dfrac{x}{c}$ $\qquad x\left(\dfrac{dy}{dx}\right)^2 - y\dfrac{dy}{dx} + 1 = 0$

(r) $u = \log(x^2 + y^2)^{\frac{1}{2}}$ $\qquad \dfrac{\partial^2u}{\partial x^2} + \dfrac{\partial^2u}{\partial y^2} = 0$

(s) $u = \tan^{-1}\dfrac{y}{x}$ $\qquad \dfrac{\partial^2u}{\partial x^2} + \dfrac{\partial^2u}{\partial y^2} = 0$

(t) $y = \dfrac{e^{ax} + e^{-ax}}{2a} + c$ $\qquad \dfrac{d^2y}{dx^2} = a\sqrt{1 + \left(\dfrac{dy}{dx}\right)^2}$

Problem 1.341

Everyone must know about i, the famous fellow whose square is -1, and must know that if $z = x + iy$, then

$$z^2 = x^2 - y^2 + i2xy.$$

Show that $x^2 - y^2$ (the real part of z^2) and $2xy$ (the imaginary part of z^2) as well as z^2 itself satisfy the Laplace equation (1.126). *Remark:* The number i is so important that we must not neglect opportunities to use it and see how it can be made to work for us.

Problem 1.342

We have heard about i and we have heard about the chain-rule formulas

$$\frac{\partial}{\partial x} u^k = k u^{k-1} \frac{\partial u}{\partial x}, \qquad \frac{\partial}{\partial y} u^k = k u^{k-1} \frac{\partial u}{\partial y}.$$

Use the fact (it *is* a fact) that these formulas hold when k is a positive integer and $u = z = x + iy$ to prove that if k is a positive integer then $(x + iy)^k$ satisfies the Laplace equation. Without using this result, show that the real part of z^3 is $x^3 - 3xy^2$ and that this satisfies that Laplace equation.

Problem 1.343

We have heard about i and we have heard about the chain-rule formula

$$\frac{d}{dx} e^u = e^u \frac{du}{dx}.$$

Section 6.3 will give an official introduction to e^{ix} and will show that the above formula works when $u = ix$. Show that e^{ix}, $\cos x$, and $\sin x$ are all solutions of the equation

$$\frac{d^2y}{dx^2} + y = 0.$$

[When we have learned about linear differential equations and the *Euler* (1707–1783) *formula*

(1.3431) $$e^{ix} = \cos x + i \sin x,$$

this will be quite unmysterious.]

Problem 1.344

Prove that if

(1.3441) $$J_0(x) = 1 - \frac{x^2}{2^2} + \frac{x^4}{2^2 4^2} - \frac{x^6}{2^2 4^2 6^2} + \frac{x^8}{2^2 4^2 6^2 8^2} - \cdots$$

then

(1.3442) $$\frac{d}{dx} xJ_0'(x) = -xJ_0(x)$$

and hence

(1.3443) $$xJ_0''(x) + J_0'(x) + xJ_0(x) = 0.$$

This problem involves the simplest *Bessel* (1784–1846) *function* and *equation.* The series is not frightening; it is a power series in x which converges for all values of x and can therefore be differentiated termwise just as polynomials can be.

Problem 1.345

Prove that if $v(x)$ is defined by the formulas

(1.3451) $$v(x) = \sqrt{x}\, J_0(x), \qquad J_0(x) = \frac{v(x)}{\sqrt{x}}$$

then

$$\frac{d^2v}{dx^2} + \left(1 + \frac{1}{4x^2}\right)v = 0. \tag{1.3452}$$

Remark: Try to decide whether it is best to use (1.3441) or (1.3443).

Problem 1.346

Show that if

$$y = x - \frac{x^3}{3!} + \frac{x^5}{5!} - \frac{x^7}{7!} + \cdots$$

then $y''(x) + y(x) = 0$. Does this ring any bells?

Problem 1.351

Show that the system of differential equations

$$\frac{dy}{dx} - \frac{dz}{dx} = y, \qquad 2\frac{dy}{dx} - \frac{dz}{dx} = z$$

is satisfied by the pair of functions

$$y = c_1 \cos x + c_2 \sin x, \qquad z = (c_2 + c_1)\cos x + (c_2 - c_1)\sin x.$$

Problem 1.352

For what values of the constant c is there a differentiable function $y(x)$ satisfying the equation

$$x^2 + y^2 + 2x + 2y = c,$$

and hence also the equations

$$2x + 2y\frac{dy}{dx} + 2 + 2\frac{dy}{dx} = 0$$

and

$$\frac{dy}{dx} = -\frac{x+1}{y+1},$$

when x is properly restricted? *Ans.:* $c > -2$.

Remark 1.353

Partly because of the theory of harmonic analysis given in Section 6.7, the results of the next two problems are of great interest. Numerous results like them appear in mathematical physics.

Problem 1.36

Supposing that all letters except u, x, and t represent constants and that

$$u(x, t) = \sum_{k=0}^{n} \left(A_k \cos\frac{k\pi a}{L}t + B_k \sin\frac{k\pi a}{L}t\right)\sin\frac{k\pi}{L}x, \tag{1.361}$$

show that $u(x, t)$ satisfies the *wave equation*

$$a^2\frac{\partial^2 u}{\partial x^2} = \frac{\partial^2 u}{\partial t^2}, \tag{1.362}$$

the boundary conditions $u(0, t) = u(L, t) = 0$, and the initial conditions

$$u(x, 0) = \sum_{k=0}^{n} A_k \sin \frac{k\pi}{L} x, \qquad u_t(x, 0) = \sum_{k=0}^{n} \frac{k\pi a}{L} B_k \sin \frac{k\pi}{L} x.$$

Supposing that $0 \leqq x \leqq \pi$ and taking the simple case in which

$$u(x, t) = \cos at \sin x,$$

sketch graphs of $u(x, t)$ versus x when $t = 0$, $t = \pi/2a$, $t = \pi/a$, $t = 3\pi/2a$, and $t = 2\pi/a$. [These graphs are snapshots of a particular vibrating string which has ends fixed at $x = 0$ and $x = \pi$ in an (x, u) plane.]

Problem 1.37

Supposing that all letters except u, x, and t represent constants and that

$$u(x, t) = \sum_{k=1}^{n} C_k e^{-\frac{k^2\pi^2a^2}{L^2}t} \sin \frac{k\pi}{L} x, \tag{1.371}$$

show that $u(x, t)$ satisfies the *heat equation*

$$a^2 \frac{\partial^2 u}{\partial x^2} = \frac{\partial u}{\partial t},$$

the initial condition

$$u(x, 0) = \sum_{k=1}^{n} C_k \sin \frac{k\pi}{L} x,$$

and the boundary conditions $u(0, t) = u(L, t) = 0$. Supposing that $0 \leqq x \leqq \pi$ and taking the simple case in which

$$u(x, t) = e^{-a^2t} \sin x,$$

sketch rough graphs of $u(x, t)$ versus x when $t = 0$, $t = 1/a^2$, and $t = 10/a^2$. Show that if $C_k = 1/k^2$ and $t = t_1 = L^2/\pi^2a^2$, then (1.371) reduces to

$$u(x, t_1) = \sum_{k=1}^{n} \frac{1}{k^2} e^{-k^2} \sin \frac{k\pi}{L} x. \tag{1.372}$$

What can be said about the relative magnitudes of the terms in (1.372) for which $k = 1$ and $k = 10$? [Under appropriate circumstances, $u(x, t)$ is the temperature at time t at the point with coordinate x in a rod occupying the interval $0 \leqq x \leqq L$.]

Problem 1.38

Problem 6.383, which could be read now, shows that the Bessel function $J_0(x)$ defined by (1.3441) can be put in the form

$$J_0(x) = \frac{1}{\pi} \int_0^\pi \cos (x \cos t)dt. \tag{1.381}$$

It is good to recognize that things like the right side of this formula really are functions of x and can be managed. Using the fact that, in the present circumstance, derivatives of the integral are integrals of the derivatives, show that

$$J_0'(x) = \frac{-1}{\pi}\int_0^{\pi} \cos t \sin (x \cos t)dt$$

$$J_0''(x) = \frac{-1}{\pi}\int_0^{\pi} \cos^2 t \cos (x \cos t)dt.$$

It is not immediately clear that the Bessel equation (1.3443) is satisfied. However, integrate the formula for $J_0'(x)$ by parts and show that it is so. *Remark:* The problem of sketching rough graphs of the integrands in (1.381) and estimating $J_0(x)$ for various values of x is a nice little challenge. The case in which x is very large is particularly interesting, and there is much to be learned. We should all carry copies of (1.381) so we can entertain ourselves the next time we get stranded in an airport or a jail. Some rough approximations to $J_0(x)$ are $J_0(0) = +1$, $J_0(\pi/2) = +0.47$, $J_0(\pi) = -0.30$, $J_0(3\pi/2) = -0.27$, $J_0(2\pi) = +0.22$, $J_0(3\pi) = -0.18$, $J_0(4\pi) = +0.17$, $J_0(5\pi) = -0.12$, and $J_0(x) \to 0$ *as* $x \to \infty$.

Problem 1.39

In Section 6.3 we will learn that, when $z = x + iy$, the series in

(1.3901) $$e^z = 1 + z + \frac{z^2}{2!} + \frac{z^3}{3!} + \cdots$$

converges to a number which is denoted by e^z. Since Problem 1.342 shows that each term in the series satisfies the Laplace equation, it is easy to guess that e^z must also do so. Because of (1.3431), it is easy to write the formula

(1.3902) $$e^z = e^{x+iy} = e^x e^{iy} = e^x(\cos y + i \sin y)$$

which looks right and is right; it is proved in Section 6.3. Check up on this little story by showing that $e^x \cos y$ and $e^x \sin y$ really do satisfy the Laplace equation (1.126).

Problem 1.391

We must see figures and formulas more than once and must work with them in order to become familiar with them. Look at Fig. 2.503 and observe that $z = re^{i\theta}$. Since $\log ab = \log a + \log b$ and $\log e^c = c$, it is easy to write the formula

$$\log z = \log r + i\theta.$$

At least when x is positive, we can put this in the form

$$\log z = \log \sqrt{x^2 + y^2} + i \tan^{-1} \frac{y}{x}.$$

Find out whether the real and imaginary parts of $\log z$ satisfy the Laplace equation (1.126). *Remark:* One who feels that these formulas are complicated need not be disturbed; automobiles are much more complicated and we use them.

Problem 1.392

Read and solve Problem 14.72.

1.4. Mechanical Oscillators. We continue this introductory chapter with a careful examination of the steps in a derivation of one of the most important of these differential equations. The equation is

$$\frac{d^2y}{dt^2} + \frac{\delta}{m}\frac{dy}{dt} + \frac{\sigma}{mL_0}y = \frac{1}{m}f(t). \tag{1.41}$$

Among other things, it governs the motion of a body or physical mass which oscillates at the bottom of the spring in Fig. 1.42.

A force in the spring tends to pull the body upward (at least when the body is far enough down to keep the spring stretched), and gravitational force tends to pull it down. If the body is moving in air (or in a partial vacuum or in water or in molasses) then there is an additional *damping force* pushing down on the body when it is moving up and pushing up on the body when it is moving down; the tendency of the damping force is to reduce, or *damp,* the motion. In addition to these fundamental forces, there may be an *impressed force* applied by some external mechanism; for example, one may push downward with some constant force during the first half of each second and upward during the second half. The various forces acting on the body engage in a tug of war to produce the observable motion of the body. It turns out that examination of these forces leads to the differential equation we are seeking.

It is intended that the derivation should be thoroughly understood by everyone, and that those who are unfamiliar with the elementary principles of physics which we use will learn the principles from the derivation. All of the details should be closely scrutinized by everyone. In particular, algebraic signs and directions of forces must be carefully determined by the mighty as well as by the humble. It is only by thoroughly understanding easy problems to see how hard they really are that one may reasonably hope to progress toward a thorough understanding of harder problems to see how easy they really are. If it is necessary to read this section several times and to sketch figures over and over again, so be it. This investment of time pays handsome dividends.

A spring of *natural length* L_0 is suspended from a ceiling as in Fig. 1.42. Then a body having mass m is hung on the bottom and, while the body is at rest (or motionless) in the *neutral position,* we measure the *static stretched length* L. To study the motion of the body after it has been displaced from the neutral position, let y be a coordinate which represents the displacement of the body from the neutral position. Let y be positive or 0 or negative according as the body is above, or at, or below the neutral position so that the kinds of graphs of y versus t that we ordinarily draw will give correct information about the location of the body at time t. The y shown in Fig. 1.42 is therefore negative, and the distance u from the body to the ceiling is $L - y$ (not $L + y$). Let U denote a vertical unit vector, that is, a vector one unit (a foot or a centimeter) long, having the direction of increasing y. To say of a force F_1 that $F_1 = 6U$ then means that the force has magnitude 6 and is directed upward; and to say that $F_2 = -mgU$ means that the force has magnitude mg but is directed downward. According to the *Hooke* (1635–1703) *law*, there is a *spring constant* σ such that the force F_sU, which the spring having natural length L_0 exerts upon the body when the spring is stationary and stretched to length $L - y$, is

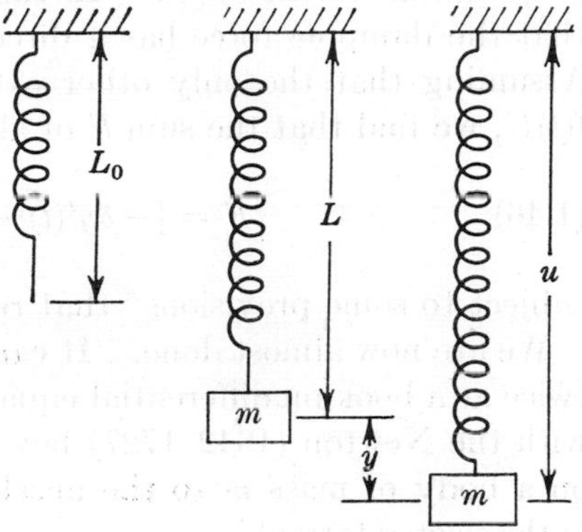

FIG. 1.42

$$F_sU = \sigma \frac{L - y - L_0}{L_0} U \tag{1.43}$$

provided the stretching is well within elastic limits. The number $L - y - L_0$, the *elongation* of the spring, depends upon y; and the law says simply that the magnitude of the force is proportional to the elongation. Engineers and physicists, and perhaps even mathematicians, should know that if the spring is not a spiral, but is a straight uniform elastic steel wire, then $\sigma = EA$ where E is the *Young* (Thomas, 1773–1829) *modulus* of the steel, and A is the area of a cross section of the wire. The gravitational force on the body is simply $-wU$ or $-mgU$ where w is the weight of the body and g is the acceleration of gravity. Actually g changes by imperceptible amounts as the body moves and changes its distance from the center of the earth, but we simplify matters by assuming that g is constant, say 32 feet per second per second or 980 centimeters per second per second. Since the gravitational force $-mgU$ on the body just balances the spring force when $y = 0$, we can put $y = 0$ in (1.43) to obtain

$$-mgU = -\sigma \frac{L - L_0}{L_0} U. \tag{1.44}$$

The damping force F_dU is 0 when the body is not moving, and its magnitude increases as the speed $|y'(t)|$ increases. Experiments show that there is a positive *damping constant* δ such that

$$F_dU = -\delta y'(t) U \tag{1.45}$$

whenever the speed is not too great. This formula really says two things. In the first place, it says that the magnitude of the damping force is proportional to the speed. In the second place, because $\delta > 0$, it says that the damping force has a direction opposite to that of the velocity. Assuming that the only other external force acting upon the body is $f(t)U$, we find that the sum F of all of the external forces is

$$F = [-\delta y'(t) - \frac{\sigma}{L_0} y(t) + f(t)]U \tag{1.46}$$

subject to some provisions* that really should not be overlooked.

We are now almost done. It can be expected that anybody who looks twice at a book on differential equations has at least a little acquaintance with the Newton (1642–1727) law which relates the net external force F on a body of mass m to the acceleration a of the body. The formula is the vector formula

$$F = ma, \tag{1.47}$$

of which the vector formula

$$-wU = -mgU \tag{1.471}$$

is a special case and the scalar formula

$$w = mg \tag{1.472}$$

is a consequence. The law will be discussed in a moment. When the body always lies on a line as in our problem and has coordinate $y(t)$ at time t, where $y(t)$ is a function of t having two derivatives, its velocity and acceleration are defined by

$$v = y'(t)U, \qquad a = y''(t)U, \tag{1.473}$$

and (1.46) becomes

* One proviso is that speeds should not be so great that (1.44) fails to hold. Another is that $|y(t)|$ should never be so great that the oscillating body hits the ceiling or tears the spring apart, for in such cases (1.43) could not be valid. Finally, we consider a more subtle proviso. The formula (1.46) will be quite untrustworthy unless the formula (1.43) holds, not only when the spring is stationary, but also *when the spring is in motion.* One who has not thought about the matter may consider this to be a silly remark, but a little thought shows that the remark is not silly and that there is real trouble here. Problem 6.486 will show this very simply, but the following argument may be convincing. When a body at the bottom of the spring is in motion, the part of the spring near the body (and the rest of it too) must be in motion and must be accelerated along with the body. If the mass of an ordinary spring is m_0 and the mass of the body is $m_0/10^{10}$, most of the forces in the spring will be busy accelerating the spring and all of the forces on the microscopic body will be microscopically small. It is only when the mass m of the oscillating body is large in comparison to the total mass m_0 of the spring that we can neglect the forces required to accelerate the spring and can claim that (1.43) is accurate enough to produce useful results.

(1.474) $$F = my''(t)U.$$

Comparing (1.46) and (1.474) gives the vector equation

(1.475) $$\left[y''(t) + \frac{\delta}{m}y'(t) + \frac{\sigma}{mL_0}y(t)\right]U = \frac{1}{m}f(t)U.$$

This gives the scalar equation

(1.476) $$y''(t) + \frac{\delta}{m}y'(t) + \frac{\sigma}{mL_0}y(t) = \frac{1}{m}f(t).$$

Except for the difference in the symbols used to denote derivatives, this is identical with (1.41) and is the differential equation we have been seeking.

If the laws used and the assumptions made are correct, and if the constants L_0, m, σ, and δ and the signed magnitude $f(t)$ of the force are determined exactly, then the displacement $y(t)$ must satisfy (1.41). In this case, information about $y(t)$ can be obtained by solving (1.41). If some or all of the laws, assumptions, and measurements are false but nevertheless involve only errors that are small in some sense, we can still hope that a solution of (1.41) will give results of sufficient accuracy to meet practical needs. In particular if the damping force is very small, it is very much worth while to see how the system would behave if there were no damping.

1.48. The Newton Law F = ma. Except for some strange exceptions which commonly appear in elementary calculus and when motions on lines are being considered, everybody always understands that forces, velocities, and accelerations are vectors.* Suppose we are interested in a body which moves around in Euclid (*c.* 330 B.C.–275 B.C.) space of 1 or more dimensions, and that 0 is a fixed point or origin in the space. Let $W(t)$ denote the vector running from the origin to the position of the body at time t. If, for a given value of t, the limit in

(1.481) $$v(t) = W'(t) = \lim_{\Delta t \to 0} \frac{W(t + \Delta t) - W(t)}{\Delta t}$$

exists, then the limit is (by two simultaneous definitions which can never be separated by more than pedagogical convenience) called the derivative

* It is easy to see how these strange exceptions appear. When a body lies on an x axis and has the numerical (scalar) coordinate $x(t)$ at the time t, the vector running from the origin to the body is $x(t)U$ where U is a unit vector in the direction of increasing x. The honest velocity is then the vector $x'(t)U$; but the scalar coefficient $x'(t)$, which may be negative and which can be called the *signed magnitude of the velocity* or the *scalar velocity*, is often referred to as the velocity. It can be claimed that this confusion is introduced to simplify the lives of young scientists, but confusion is not always desirable.

$W'(t)$ of $W(t)$ and the velocity $v(t)$ of the body at the given time. Similarly if the limit in

$$(1.482) \qquad a(t) = v'(t) = W''(t) = \lim_{\Delta t \to 0} \frac{W'(t + \Delta t) - W'(t)}{\Delta t}$$

exists, then the limit is the *second derivative* of $W(t)$, the first derivative of $v(t)$, and the *acceleration* $a(t)$ of the body at the given time. In terms of these vectors, we can give a version of the Newton law that is often needed.

Suppose that we are interested in the motion of a body over a time interval $t_1 \leqq t \leqq t_2$. Suppose that the body has mass $m(t)$ where $m(t)$ may depend upon t but has a continuous derivative. Suppose that the net external force on the body is $F(t)$ where $F(t)$ need not be continuous but is required to be integrable over the interval $t_1 \leqq t \leqq t_2$. Then $W(t)$ and $W'(t)$ will be continuous (in fact, absolutely continuous) over $t_1 \leqq t \leqq t_2$, $W''(t)$ will exist whenever $F(t)$ is continuous, and the formula

$$(1.483) \qquad F(t) = \frac{d}{dt}\, m(t)W'(t)$$

will hold whenever $F(t)$ is continuous.

The vector quantity $m(t)W'(t)$ is called the *momentum* of the body; Newton phrased his law in terms of momentum. In some cases, $m(t)$ is different at different times; this happens when the body is a rocket consisting partly of fuel which burns and disappears behind the rocket. In case $m(t)$ is a constant m, the formula (1.483) is equivalent to

$$(1.484) \qquad F(t) = m\frac{d^2W}{dt^2} = ma(t)$$

and the law involving (1.483) becomes a law involving (1.484).

Problem 1.49

Sketch Fig. 1.42 and then, with the positive y axis and unit vector U directed downward (instead of upward), derive the differential equation governing the motion. Repeat the process until you can do it easily and naturally without aid of the text. *Remark:* Scientists, like professional golfers and piano players, should sometimes concentrate upon a task until they can perform it with professional skill.

Problem 1.491

Suppose that the oscillator is unforced; *i.e.*, $f(t) = 0$. Try to guess what the motion would be and try to graph y versus t when (a) there is very little damping, as when the body is in air, and (b) there is heavy damping, as when the body is in molasses. *Remark:* It is better to have ideas that are not quite right than to have no ideas at all.

Problem 1.492

A body of mass m is falling in air with no forces upon it except a constant gravitational force and a resistance proportional to the speed. Let $s(t)$ be a coordinate of the body which increases as the body falls earthward. Show that

$$\frac{d^2s}{dt^2} + \frac{\delta}{m}\frac{ds}{dt} = g. \tag{1.4921}$$

Remark: Sometimes people contribute to their intellectual and scientific developments by just looking at differential equations and thinking a little. Notice that (1.4921) really is trying to tell us about the (scalar) velocity and acceleration of a falling body. Suppose a body is projected downward with velocity $v_0 = mg/\delta$ which makes $(\delta/m)v_0 = g$. Then d^2s/dt^2 will be 0 and (1.4921) will be satisfied. Possibly (1.4921) is trying to tell us that if a body starts falling with velocity mg/δ, then it will continue to fall with this velocity. The next step is easier. Suppose the body starts to fall with velocity 0. The acceleration will then be g, but the acceleration must decrease as the velocity increases. Why? Try to eke out more information. Quantitative information appears in Section 3.8.

Problem 1.493

A body of mass m is thrown vertically upward from the surface of the earth with no forces upon it except a constant gravitational force and a resistance proportional to the speed. This time let $s(t)$ be a coordinate of the body which increases as the body rises. Show that the equation

$$\frac{d^2s}{dt^2} + \frac{\delta}{m}\frac{ds}{dt} = -g$$

holds when the body is going up and when it is coming back down.

Problem 1.494

Suppose everything is as in Problem 1.493 except that the resistance is proportional to the square of the speed. Show that

$$\frac{d^2s}{dt^2} + \frac{\delta}{m}\left(\frac{ds}{dt}\right)^2 = -g$$

when the body is going up and

$$\frac{d^2s}{dt^2} - \frac{\delta}{m}\left(\frac{ds}{dt}\right)^2 = -g$$

when the body is coming back down.

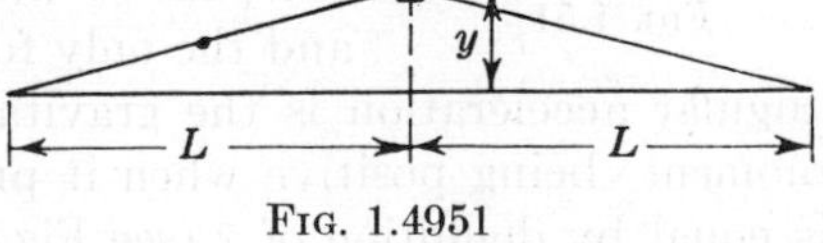

FIG. 1.4951

Problem 1.495

A horizontal elastic steel wire having length $2L_0$ and spring constant σ is stretched to length $2L$, as in Fig. 1.4951. A body, having a mass m much greater than the mass of the wire, is tied to the center of the wire and is put in motion on a vertical line through the center of the wire. Supposing that the only forces on the body are produced by tension in the wire [no gravity, no damping, no $f(t)$], show that the differential equation

$$\frac{d^2y}{dt^2} + \frac{2\sigma}{m}\frac{(L^2 + y^2)^{\frac{1}{2}} - L_0}{L_0(L^2 + y^2)^{\frac{1}{2}}}y = 0 \tag{1.4952}$$

governs the motion. *Remark:* In case y is small in comparison to L, the approximation

$$\frac{d^2y}{dt^2} + \frac{2\sigma}{m}\frac{L - L_0}{LL_0}y = 0 \tag{1.4953}$$

is used. Would you know why?

Problem 1.496

This problem is the same as the preceding except that the body moves to the right or left so that its displacement from the neutral position is x. Show that the equation

$$\frac{d^2x}{dt^2} + \frac{2\sigma}{mL_0}x = 0 \tag{1.4961}$$

governs the motion.

1.5. Motion of a Pendulum. We now consider the motion of a pendulum which swings (or rotates) in a vertical plane. All forces except gravitational forces will be disregarded, and the pendulum will be considered inelastic. Thus it may be said that we are going to find what the motion of a pendulum would be if there were no friction and if the pendulum were inelastic. Since some friction and elasticity are always present when a physical pendulum swings, our results can at best give an approximate description of the motion of a physical pendulum. Our first step is to derive a differential equation which governs the motion of the pendulum.

Let m and I denote the mass of the pendulum and its moment of inertia about the axis which passes through the point of suspension O (see Fig. 1.51) and is perpendicular to the plane of the paper. Let l (the effective length of the pendulum) denote the distance from O to the centroid (or center of gravity) C of the pendulum. Let θ, measured positive in a counterclockwise direction, be the angular displacement of the line OC from the vertical line drawn downward from O. Under our assumptions, the point C must move on a circle with center at O, and the only force having a moment which produces angular acceleration is the gravitational force on the pendulum. This moment, being positive when it produces positive angular acceleration, is equal by definition of $\bar{x}$ (see Fig. 1.51) to $-mg\bar{x}$ and hence is equal to $-mgl \sin \theta$.

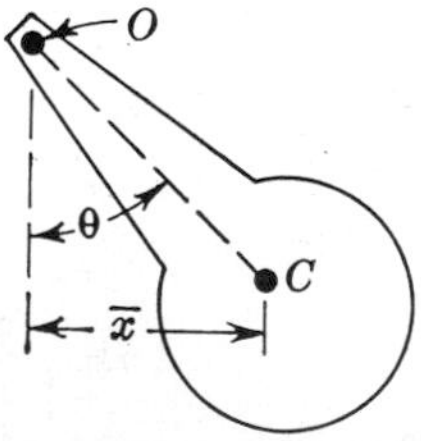

FIG. 1.51

We are now in a position to use the formula

$$(\text{Moment of inertia}) \times (\text{angular acceleration}) = \text{moment},$$

which governs angular acceleration in the same way that the formula

$$\text{Mass} \times \text{acceleration} = \text{force}$$

governs linear acceleration, to obtain

$$I\frac{d^2\theta}{dt^2} = -mgl \sin \theta; \tag{1.52}$$

this is the differential equation we sought.

In case the pendulum consists of a small bob at the end of a relatively light wire, it is a standard trick to neglect the mass of the wire, to regard the bob as concentrated at a point C, and to use ml^2 as an approximation for I. The equation (1.52) then becomes

$$\frac{d^2\theta}{dt^2} + \frac{g}{l}\sin \theta = 0. \tag{1.53}$$

This equation is nonlinear. In case the pendulum swings through short arcs, $\sin \theta$ and θ always have the same order of magnitude because

$$\frac{\sin \theta}{\theta} = 1 - \frac{\theta^2}{3!} + \frac{\theta^4}{5!} + \cdots,$$

and solutions of the equation

$$\frac{d^2\theta}{dt^2} + \frac{g}{l}\theta = 0 \tag{1.54}$$

are used as approximations to solutions of (1.53).

1.6. History. From time to time we shall learn bits of history, and this is a very modest beginning. Leibniz* (1646–1716) and Newton (1642–1727) invented the calculus and initiated use of differential equations in solving problems. The incomparable Euler (1707–1783) developed theories and applications in an amazing number of ways. It is easy to put the origins of our subject in their historical place. Everything centers around Euler. Euler was young when Leibniz and Newton were old. Euler was old when the United States were being united.

* The full name is Gottfried Wilhelm Leibniz. The Latin spelling "Leibnitz," which appeared in his scientific publications, is sometimes used.

CHAPTER 2

APPLICATIONS OF PRINCIPLES OF CALCULUS

2.0. Introduction. Considerable parts of first courses in the calculus are devoted to the problem of finding elementary expressions for functions $y(x)$, for which the first and hence the second of the formulas

$$(2.01) \qquad \frac{dy}{dx} = f(x), \qquad y = \int f(x)dx$$

hold when $f(x)$ is a given elementary function. Examples such as

$$(2.011) \qquad \frac{dy}{dx} = 3x^2, \qquad y = \int 3x^2\,dx = x^3 + c$$

are completely familiar and completely satisfying. An example such as

$$(2.02) \qquad \frac{dy}{dx} = \frac{\sin x}{1 + x^2}, \qquad y = \int \frac{\sin x}{1 + x^2}\,dx$$

is more awkward. One who cannot find an elementary expression for y, and who is unacquainted with theory which covers such matters, simply does not know whether the equations in (2.02) have any solutions.

The theory we need now, and will need many times in the future, is contained in the following *fundamental theorem of the calculus;* it involves integration of derivatives and differentiation of integrals.

THEOREM 2.03. *If $f(x)$ is continuous over the interval $x_1 < x < x_2$ and if $x_1 < a < x_2$, then each function $y(x)$ for which*

$$(2.031) \qquad \frac{dy}{dx} = f(x), \qquad x_1 < x < x_2,$$

can be put in the form

$$(2.032) \qquad y(x) = y(a) + \int_a^x f(t)dt, \qquad x_1 < x < x_2.$$

Moreover, for each value of the constant $y(a)$, the function $y(x)$ defined by (2.032) *satisfies* (2.031).

While there are other options, the integral in (2.032) may be considered to be a Riemann (1826–1866) integral, this being the particular brand of definite integral which some elementary calculus books call *the* definite integral. Riemann integrals are limits of Riemann sums and can be interpreted as areas when the integrands are positive. Each solution of (2.02) can be put in the form

$$y(x) = y(0) + \int_0^x \frac{\sin t}{1 + t^2}\, dt, \tag{2.04}$$

the integral being a perfectly explicit function of x which can be tabulated and studied as thoroughly as occasions demand.

It is a consequence of Theorem 2.03 that if f is continuous, then

$$\frac{d}{dx}\int_a^x f(t)dt = f(x). \tag{2.05}$$

We shall use this fact very often. Anyone who feels that this formula is somewhat mysterious should sketch graphs in which integrals represent areas, note the change in the integral that occurs when x is increased a little, and think about the matter until it ceases to be mysterious. We want to know what we are doing. Some uses of the formula involve application of the chain rule for differentiating a function of a function. If, for example, v is a function of x and other variables, then

$$\frac{\partial}{\partial x}\int_a^v f(t)dt = \left[\frac{d}{dv}\int_a^v f(t)dt\right]\frac{\partial v}{\partial x} = f(v)\,\frac{\partial v}{\partial x}. \tag{2.051}$$

In addition to Riemann integrals, we shall sometimes use *Cauchy* (1789–1857) *integrals* which are Cauchy extensions of Riemann integrals and are sometimes given "defamatory" names (improper integrals) in elementary calculus textbooks. For example, if $f(x)$ is Riemann integrable over $a \leqq x \leqq b$ whenever $b > a$, and if the limit in

$$\int_a^\infty f(x)dx = \lim_{b\to\infty}\int_a^b f(x)dx \tag{2.06}$$

exists, then the left member is a Cauchy integral which is defined by the formula. For another example, if $f(x)$ is Riemann integrable over $h \leqq x \leqq b$ whenever $a < h < b$ and if the limit in

$$\int_a^b f(x)dx = \lim_{h\to a+}\int_h^b f(x)dx \tag{2.061}$$

exists, then the left member is another Cauchy integral which is defined by the formula.

A more comprehensive account of these matters is given in Chapter 13 which can be read at any time, which should be read more than once, and which can be consulted whenever the occasion demands.

Problem 2.07

+

Show that if a and C are positive constants, the function $u(x, t)$ defined for $x > 0$ and $t > 0$ by the formula

$$u(x, t) = \int_0^{x/\sqrt{t}} Ce^{-s^2/4a^2}\, ds \tag{2.08}$$

is a solution of the heat equation

$$a^2 \frac{\partial^2 u}{\partial x^2} = \frac{\partial u}{\partial t}. \tag{2.081}$$

One who has completed the required task may feel that this problem is finished, but it is not. On this occasion, as on many others, we cultivate the habit of attempting to understand the meaning and significance of formulas that appear in our work. Without such attempts, we are in intellectual and scientific doldrums.

Our present situation is far from simple, but we shall think a little about an application involving an infinitely long insulated rod which is strung out along a whole positive x axis. At time $t = 0$, the rod had a constant temperature 100°C and the end at $x = 0$ was suddenly brought to temperature 0°C and is maintained at temperature 0°C at all times $t \geqq 0$. At all times after $t = 0$, heat is flowing from the hot rod to the cold end in a manner that depends upon the conductivity constant a in our formulas. Draw a picture of the rod and think about this. Heat is flowing out of the rod and its temperature should go down, but the rod is so long and contains so much heat that we do not know what to expect. However, the formula does. When the constant C is given the appropriate value, the right side of (2.08) is a formula (well known in mathematical physics) for the temperature $u(x, t)$ of the point in the rod having coordinate x at time t. We now look at the formula to see what it says. It says that, if x and t are positive, then $u(x, t)$ is the integral of the function

$$G(s) = Ce^{-s^2/4a^2} \tag{2.082}$$

over the interval from $s = 0$ to $s = x/\sqrt{t}$.

Without going into details, we note that $G(s)$ is, except for the size of the constant C, one of those *Gauss* (1777–1855) or *normal probability functions* that statisticians use all over the place. Whenever C and a are positive, the graph of $G(s)$ has the form shown in Fig. 2.084, and, for our problem, the value of C is determined so that

$$\int_0^\infty G(s)ds = 100. \tag{2.083}$$

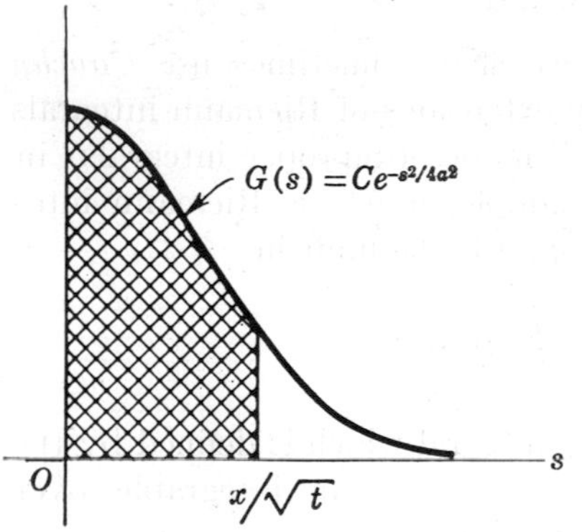

FIG. 2.084

The value of the function $u(x, t)$ determined from (2.08) is then precisely the area of the region shaded in Fig. 2.084. This enables us to see that, for each fixed positive value of t, $u(x, t) \to 0$ as $x \to 0$ and $u(x, t) \to 100$ as $x \to \infty$. Similarly, for each fixed positive value of x, $u(x, t) \to 0$ as $t \to \infty$ and $u(x, t) \to 100$ as $t \to 0$. If s_0 is determined such that

$$\int_0^{s_0} G(s)ds = 50, \tag{2.085}$$

then $u(x, t) = 50$ when $x/\sqrt{t} = s_0$ or $x = s_0\sqrt{t}$. This shows that, as t increases, the place where the temperature is 50°C moves to the right more and more slowly. The formula gives us all the answers. When the numerical values of a and C are known, probability (or statistics) tables can be used to calculate $u(x, t)$ whenever x and t are positive. It is easy to calculate the temperature gradient $\partial u/\partial x$ and to show that, if x is not large, $\partial u/\partial x$ is small when t is large. This is fortunate for us because otherwise heat would come from inside the earth so fast it would make the surface too hot for us. The fact that the Gauss probability function appears in (2.08) is quite appropriate. Studies of random motions of molecules show that probability and statistics do enter into determinations of temperatures and into other problems involving diffusion processes. We can conclude with the remark that it is not always easy to give reasonable interpretations to statements involving probabilities. Ordinary formulas involving temperature give only results that are very likely to be very closely approximated. They do not preclude the logical possibility that we may all freeze tonight because molecules happen to bounce in such a way that only slowly moving ones remain near us.

Problem 2.09

If $f(x) = \operatorname{sgn} x$ (pronounced "signum x"), that is, $f(x) = -1$ when $x < 0, f(0) = 0$, and $f(x) = 1$ when $x > 0$ as in Fig. 2.0901, draw a graph of

$$y(x) = \int_{-1}^{x} f(t)dt.$$

For what values of x is it true that $y'(x) = f(x)$? *Ans.:* $x \neq 0$.

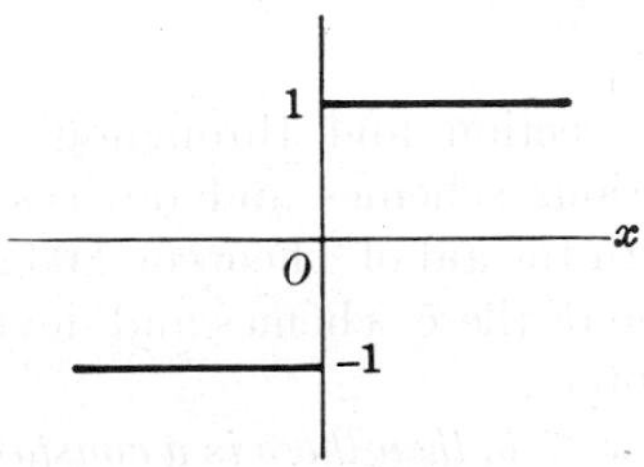

FIG. 2.0901

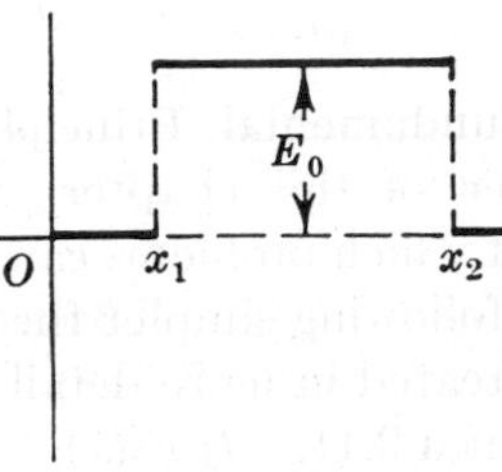

FIG. 2.0902

Remark: One whose training has been such as to make him skeptical of the value of the discontinuous signum function may take a few minutes to show that the graph of the function

$$y = \tfrac{1}{2}E_0[\operatorname{sgn}(x - x_1) - \operatorname{sgn}(x - x_2)]$$

has, when $0 < x_1 < x_2$, the form shown in Fig. 2.0902 and to read Section 3.9 through equation (3.94). One who still feels that the function sgn x is too simple and undignified to be worthy of notice may be impressed by the formula

$$\operatorname{sgn} x = \frac{1}{\pi}\int_{-\infty}^{\infty} \frac{\sin xt}{t}\, dt, \tag{2.0903}$$

the integral on the right being the *Dirichlet* (1805–1859) *discontinuous integral* which occurs in many phases of mathematical analysis.

Problem 2.091

Show that

$$\int_0^\infty e^{-x}\,dx = 1; \qquad \int_0^1 \log x\,dx = -1.$$

Problem 2.092

Determine, for each of the two integrals

$$\int_1^\infty t^p\,dt, \qquad \int_0^1 t^p\,dt,$$

the values of the exponent p for which the integrals exist. *Ans.*: $p < -1$; $p > -1$.

Problem 2.093

Show that the solution $y(x)$ of the equation

$$\frac{dy}{dx} = \frac{\sin x}{1 + x^2}$$

for which $y(x) \to 0$ as $x \to \infty$ is

$$y = -\int_0^\infty \frac{\sin t}{1 + t^2}\,dt + \int_0^x \frac{\sin t}{1 + t^2}\,dt$$

or

$$y = -\int_x^\infty \frac{\sin t}{1 + t^2}\,dt.$$

2.1. Fundamental Principles. In this section and throughout the remainder of this chapter, we study various schemes and devices by means of which problems can be solved with the aid of Theorem 2.03 and the two following simpler theorems. Some of these schemes and devices will be treated in more detail in later chapters.

THEOREM 2.11. *If $F'(x) = 0$ when $a \leqq x \leqq b$, then there is a constant c such that $F(x) = c$ when $a \leqq x \leqq b$.*

THEOREM 2.12. *If $F'(x) = g(x)$ and $G(x)$ is a function for which $G'(x) = g(x)$ when $a \leqq x \leqq b$, then there is a constant c such that*

$$F(x) = G(x) + c$$

when $a \leqq x \leqq b$.

The first of these theorems is sometimes proved in elementary calculus and is always proved in advanced calculus; besides, everybody who has never seen a proof of it thinks it is obviously true. In any case, it is true and we shall use it. Meanwhile, we show that the two theorems are equivalent; that is, if one of the theorems is true, then we can prove the other by use of it. The first theorem is a corollary of the second, as we can see by putting $g(x) = G(x) = 0$. On the other hand, the second theorem is a corollary of the first, because if we set, $H(x) = F(x) - G(x)$, then $H'(x) = F'(x) - g(x) = 0$; so, by the first theorem, $H(x) = c$ and $F(x) = G(x) + c$. Thus the two theorems are equivalent. Moreover they are corollaries of Theorem 2.03; we have stated them separately because they are simpler and easier to apply.

It is quite correct to view Theorem 2.12 as being a precise and perhaps ponderous way of saying that if

$$F'(x) = g(x), \tag{2.121}$$

then integration gives

$$F(x) = \int g(x)dx, \tag{2.122}$$

provided $G(x)$ is a particular function whose derivative is $g(x)$ and $\int g(x)dx$ stands for $G(x) + c$. When a formula for a solution of a differential equation is to be thrown into a wastebasket, the right member of (2.122) is as good as any other. However when the formula is being obtained to serve some useful purpose, it is better to replace (2.122) by

$$F(x) = \int_a^x g(t)dt + c \tag{2.123}$$

in case it is not possible to give a simpler expression for $G(x)$. Of course it is inelegant to present an answer in the form

$$F(x) = \int_a^x 2t\,dt + c_1 \tag{2.124}$$

when it is so easy to present it in the more useful form $F(x) = x^2 + c_2$. On this account, those who wish to produce meaningful results which are not to be thrown into wastebaskets should observe the following rule. When (2.121) appears and $g(x)$ is a given elementary function that can be integrated by use of tables of integrals in heads or books, write (2.122) and proceed to evaluate the integral. When (2.121) appears and $g(x)$ does not have this simple nature, write (2.123).

The following problems lead us more or less gently to an understanding of standard methods by which differential equations are solved and information is obtained. The importance of thoroughly understanding the first ones cannot be overemphasized. Moreover, we must never forget the rules of our game.

Problem 2.13

Prove that if y is a function of x such that

$$\frac{d}{dx}\frac{y}{x^2} = 0$$

when $x > 0$, then there is a constant c such that $y = cx^2$ when $x > 0$. [Note that if y is a function of x then (provided $x > 0$) y/x^2 is another one which we may denote by $F(x)$. Tell precisely how your result is obtained.]

Problem 2.131

Prove that if y is a function of x for which $y(2) = 3$ and

$$\frac{d}{dx}\frac{y}{x^2} = \frac{\sin x}{1 + x^2}$$

then

$$y = x^2\left[\frac{3}{4} + \int_2^x \frac{\sin t}{1 + t^2}\,dt\right].$$

Problem 2.132

Prove that if y is a function of x for which $y(2) = 3$ and

$$\frac{d}{dx}\frac{y}{x^2} = \frac{1}{x^2}$$

when $x > 0$, then $y = \frac{5}{4}x^2 - x$.

Problem 2.14

Show that if y is a function of x for which

$$\frac{d}{dx}\,e^{ax}y = 0,$$

then there is a constant c such that $y = ce^{-ax}$. [Note that if y is a function of x, then $e^{ax}y$ is another one which can be denoted by $F(x)$. Tell precisely how your result is obtained.]

Problem 2.141

Find a function $y(x)$ such that $y(0) = 0$ and

$$\frac{d}{dx}\,e^{-x}y = e^{-x}.$$

Check your answer.

Problem 2.142

Estimate $y(10)$ if $y(0) = 0$ and

(2.1421) $$\frac{d}{dx}\,e^{-x^2/2}y = e^{-x^2/2}.$$

Solution: The first step is to obtain the formula

$$y(x) = \int_0^x e^{(x^2-t^2)/2}\,dt$$

and notice that

(2.1422) $$y(10) = \int_0^{10} e^{50-t^2/2}\,dt.$$

Once again we are required to learn something about a formula, and we look at it. Everybody should know that e^{50} is very large. Everybody should know or learn that e^3 is about 20, so e^{48} is about 20^{16} or $2^{16} \times 10^{16}$. Now 2^{10} is about 10^3 so $e^{48} > 6 \times 10^{20}$. A look at the integrand shows that it is positive and decreasing over the interval

$0 \leqq t \leqq 10$. If we keep only the integral from 0 to 1, we will throw away a lot but we will retain much more than a tenth of $y(10)$. Hence the estimate

$$y(10) > \int_0^1 e^{50-t^2/2}\,dt$$

is thoroughly informative. Over the interval $0 \leqq t \leqq 1$, the integrand lies between $e^{49.5}$ and e^{50}. Hence $y(10) > e^{49.5}$. This shows that $y(10)$ is big. Take a quick look at (2.1422) and see that $y(10) < 10e^{50}$. *Remark:* It is not implied that we could not work harder and get more information. It is, however, implied that we should understand our formulas and should develop the art of extracting information from them.

Problem 2.143

Show that if y is a function of x for which $x > 0$ and

$$x\frac{dy}{dx} + y = 2x,$$

then there is a constant c for which

$$y = x + \frac{c}{x}.$$

[Note that if y is a function of x, then xy is another one which may be denoted by $F(x)$.]

Problem 2.144

Solve the equation

$$x\frac{dy}{dx} - y = x^2 \sin x$$

and check your answer by differentiation and substitution. *Hint:* When the equation is divided by x^2, the new LHS (left hand side) becomes the derivative of a simple quotient.

Problem 2.145

If

(2.1451) $$\frac{dy}{dx} + y = e^{-x} \sin x$$

show that

(2.1452) $$\frac{d}{dx} e^x y = \sin x$$

and hence that $y = (c - \cos x)e^{-x}$. What is the value of c if $y(0) = 0$?

Problem 2.146

If $y(0) = 0$ and

$$\frac{dy}{dx} + y = f(x)$$

where $f(x)$ is a given continuous function, find $y(x)$ by the method of the previous problem. *Ans.:* $y(x) = e^{-x}\int_0^x e^t f(t)dt.$

Problem 2.147

Prove that if $y(0) = 0$ and

$$\frac{dy}{dx} + y = f(x)$$

where $f(x)$ is a given continuous function for which $|f(x)| \leqq M$ when $x \geqq 0$, then $|y(x)| < M$ when $x > 0$. *Solution:* Using the result of the previous problem, we find that

$$|y(x)| \leqq e^{-x} \int_0^x e^t |f(t)| dt$$
$$\leqq e^{-x} \int_0^x e^t M \, dt = Me^{-x}(e^x - 1) < M.$$

Problem 2.148

Prove that if y is a function of x for which $y(2) = 3$ and

$$\frac{d}{dx} \frac{y}{x^2} = \frac{\sin^2 x}{1 + x^2},$$

then $y(x) < \left(\frac{3}{4} + \frac{\pi}{2} - \tan^{-1} 2\right) x^2$ when $x > 2$.

Problem 2.15

If $u(x, y)$ is a function of x and y and y is a function of x such that

(2.1501) $$\frac{du}{dx} = g(x)$$

where $g(x)$ is continuous, then

(2.1502) $$u(x, y) = c + \int_0^x g(t) dt.$$

Why? It follows that if

(2.1503) $$\frac{\partial u}{\partial x} + \frac{\partial u}{\partial y} \frac{dy}{dx} = g(x),$$

then (2.1502) holds. Why? If a given equation

(2.1504) $$M(x, y) + N(x, y) \frac{dy}{dx} = Q(x, y)$$

is multiplied by a factor $\mu(x, y)$ and thereby thrown into the form (2.1501) or (2.1503), then the multiplier $\mu(x, y)$ is called an *integrating factor* of (2.1504). Sometimes it is easy to see integrating factors and solve equations by using them. Tell why e^x is an integrating factor of (2.1451).

Problem 2.151

Keeping in mind the notation and terminology of the previous problem, find an integrating factor of the equation

$$y - x \frac{dy}{dx} = \frac{y^2}{1 + x^2}$$

and solve the equation. *Ans.:* An integrating factor is $1/y^2$ and the solutions have the form $y = x/(c + \tan^{-1} x)$.

Problem 2.152

Solve the equation

$$x + y\frac{dy}{dx} = x^2 + y^2,$$

which might not be so easy if the terms were all transposed to the left side and we were not thinking about integrating factors. *Ans.*: $y^2 = Ae^{2x} - x^2$.

Problem 2.153

Look over all of the preceding problems in this list to see which ones were given in the form (2.1501) and which ones required use of an integrating factor.

Problem 2.16

Prove that if $u(x, y)$ is a function of x and y for which $\partial u/\partial x = 0$, then there is a function $f(y)$ such that $u(x, y) = f(y)$. Prove that if $v(x, y)$ is a function of x and y such that $\partial v/\partial x = y$, then there must be a function $g(y)$ such that

$$v(x, y) = xy + g(y).$$

Solution (second part): For each fixed y, the derivative with respect to x of $v - xy$ is 0. Hence, for each fixed y, the value of $v - xy$ is independent of x and must have a constant value, say $g(y)$, which can depend upon y. Thus $v - xy = g(y)$ and the result follows from this.

Problem 2.17

It can be shown that if $u(x, t)$ is a function which has continuous partial derivatives of second order and satisfies the *wave equation*

$$a^2\frac{\partial^2 u}{\partial x^2} = \frac{\partial^2 u}{\partial t^2}$$

in which a is a positive constant, and if two new variables ξ and η are defined by the formulas $\xi = x + at$ and $\eta = x - at$, then

$$\frac{\partial^2 u}{\partial \eta\, \partial \xi} = 0.$$

Use this fact to show existence of functions f and g such that $u = f(\xi) + g(\eta)$ and accordingly

$$u = f(x + at) + g(x - at).$$

Remark: This result has a vivid meaning to mathematical physicists.

Problem 2.18

Let $u(x, y)$ be a function of x and y having continuous partial derivatives. The function is said to be *homogeneous of degree n in x and y* if n is a constant and

$$u(tx, ty) = t^n u(x, y) \qquad (2.181)$$

whenever $t > 0$. For example, $x^2 + y^2$ is homogeneous of degree 2. By use of the formula

$$\frac{d}{dt} F(\alpha, \beta) = \frac{\partial F}{\partial \alpha}\frac{d\alpha}{dt} + \frac{\partial F}{d\beta}\frac{d\beta}{dt}, \tag{2.182}$$

show that differentiating (2.181) with respect to t when x and y are fixed gives the formula

$$xu_x(tx, ty) + yu_y(tx, ty) = nt^{n-1}u(x, y) \tag{2.183}$$

in which the subscripts denote partial derivatives. Show that putting $t = 1$ gives

$$x\frac{\partial u}{\partial x} + y\frac{\partial u}{\partial y} = nu. \tag{2.184}$$

We have proved part of the important *Euler* (1707–1783) *theorem on homogeneous functions* which says that u satisfies this partial differential equation if and only if it is homogeneous of degree n in x and y. It happens that a little trick enables us to prove the remainder of the theorem. Suppose u satisfies (2.184). When x and y are fixed and $t > 0$, let

$$f(t) = \frac{u(tx, ty)}{t^n}. \tag{2.185}$$

Prove that $f'(t) = 0$ so that $f(t) = f(1)$ when $t > 0$ and u must be homogeneous of degree n in x and y. *Hint:* When you calculate $f'(t)$, use partial derivative notation like that in (2.183) so that you can see what you are doing.

Problem 2.19

This problem illustrates a principle. We do not always use differential equations to find functions. Sometimes, when functions are defined by infinite series or otherwise, differential equations are used to obtain information about the functions.

Let two functions $c(x)(= \cos x)$ and $s(x)(= \sin x)$ be defined by

$$c(x) = 1 - \frac{x^2}{2!} + \frac{x^4}{4!} - \frac{x^6}{6!} + \cdots \tag{2.191}$$

$$s(x) = x - \frac{x^3}{3!} + \frac{x^5}{5!} - \frac{x^7}{7!} + \cdots \tag{2.192}$$

and let

$$f(x) = [c(x)]^2 + [s(x)]^2. \tag{2.193}$$

By differentiating (2.191) and (2.192), show that $c'(x) = -s(x)$ and $s'(x) = c(x)$. Use this result and (2.193) to show that $f'(x) = 0$. Calculate $f(0)$ and show that $f(x) = 1$ for each x. This gives the familiar formula

$$\cos^2 x + \sin^2 x = 1 \tag{2.194}$$

which is by no means an obvious consequence of (2.191) and (2.192). Prove the formula

$$s(y) = s(x)c(y - x) + c(x)s(y - x) \tag{2.195}$$

by proving that the derivative with respect to x of the right side is 0 and that the right side reduces to $s(y)$ when $x = y$. Show that putting $y = x + z$ in (2.195) gives the familiar formula

$$\sin(x + z) = \sin x \cos z + \cos x \sin z, \tag{2.196}$$

and then differentiating this (with respect to what?) gives

$$\cos(x + z) = \cos x \cos z - \sin x \sin z. \tag{2.197}$$

Problem 2.198

Letting $y(x)$ denote the function in the right member of (2.192), show that $y(0) = 0$, $y'(0) = 1$, and

$$\frac{d^2y}{dx^2} + y = 0.$$

The remainder of this problem involves careful reasoning and anyone who undertakes to do it does it at his own peril. The problem is (i) to use only the properties of $y(x)$ listed above, (ii) to use fundamental facts involving increase and decrease of functions and their derivatives, (iii) to prove that there is a least positive number x_0 for which $y(x_0) = 0$, and (iv) to prove that $y'(x_0) < 0$. If this is done and x_0 is called π, the results of Problem 2.19 can be used to show that $y(x)$ has period 2π, and much more trigonometry is derived by use of differential equations.

2.2. Variables Separable or Separated. It often happens that a differential equation of first order appears in one or another of the forms

$$\frac{dy}{dx} = \phi(x, y) \tag{2.21}$$

$$M(x, y) + N(x, y)\frac{dy}{dx} = 0 \tag{2.211}$$

$$M(x, y)dx + N(x, y)dy = 0, \tag{2.212}$$

and it is possible to divide by a function of x or y or both to put the equation in the forms

$$g(y)\frac{dy}{dx} = f(x) \tag{2.22}$$

$$g(y)dy = f(x)dx. \tag{2.221}$$

In such cases the variables in (2.21), (2.211), and (2.212) are said to be *separable* and the variables in (2.22) and (2.221) are said to be *separated.* Passing from the first state to the second is called *separating* the variables. If a function is not 0, we can multiply by it by dividing by its reciprocal.

One way to try to dispose of (2.221) is to claim that if (2.221) holds, then integration gives

$$\int g(y)dy = \int f(x)dx + c \tag{2.23}$$

and, conversely, if (2.23) holds then differentiation gives (2.221); hence (2.23) "gives" all solutions and only solutions of (2.221). This attempt to dispose of (2.22) and (2.221) is characterized by admirable brevity, but some discussion is required to explain it and show how it is used.

We suppose that $g(y)$ and $f(x)$ are continuous. Then, when a and b

are constants,

$$G(y) = \int_b^y g(t)dt, \qquad F(x) = \int_a^x f(t)dt \tag{2.231}$$

exist. If $y(x)$ is a differentiable function satisfying (2.22), then

$$\frac{d}{dx}[G(y) - F(x)] = g(y)\frac{dy}{dx} - f(x) = 0 \tag{2.232}$$

and there must be a constant c such that

$$G(y) = F(x) + c. \tag{2.24}$$

Thus each solution of (2.22) must satisfy (2.24), and of course (2.24) is nothing more or less than an informative way of writing (2.23) in those cases where $f(x)$ and $g(y)$ do not have elementary indefinite integrals. Conversely, (2.24) is at least a formal solution of (2.22) because if $y(x)$ is assumed to be a differentiable function for which (2.24) holds, then differentiating (2.24) gives (2.22).

Thus, when $f(x)$ and $g(y)$ are continuous, matters are very simple. If $u(x)$ is a function for which

$$g(y)dy = f(x)dx \tag{2.25}$$

then *the formula*

$$\int g(y)dy = \int f(x)dx + c \tag{2.251}$$

obtained by integrating the left side with respect to y and the right side with respect to x must be satisfied by $y(x)$. Do not forget, however, that we want limits of integration on the integrals if we are unable to evaluate the integrals in terms of elementary functions.

When variables are separated by division by a function, the results are valid over intervals where the divisor is not 0. If, for example, we want to divide by x we confine attention to intervals over which $x > 0$ or, alternatively, to intervals over which $x < 0$. Sometimes, as in part (*d*) of Problem 2.27, investigation of the solution shows that it is valid for values of x for which division is impossible. Note also that $y = 0$ is a solution of part (*e*) and that this solution is completely missed if we fail to consider the possibility that y may be 0.

Remark 2.26

We have called attention to the fact that if $f(x)$ is continuous for all values of x, then there are functions $y(x)$ for which

$$\frac{dy}{dx} = f(x) \qquad -\infty < x < \infty \tag{2.261}$$

and that formulas for these functions can be given in terms of Riemann integrals.

It would be easy to suppose that if $g(x, y)$ is a simple continuous function of x and y, then there would also be functions $y(x)$ for which

$$\frac{dy}{dx} = g(x, y) \qquad -\infty < x < \infty. \tag{2.262}$$

It is, however, easy to show that life is not that simple, and we shall do it. Let us suppose that $y(x)$ is a function which satisfies the equation

$$\frac{dy}{dx} = 1 + y^2 \tag{2.263}$$

over some interval, and see what we can discover. Since $1 + y^2$ can never be 0, we can separate the variables in (2.263) to obtain

$$\frac{1}{1 + y^2}\, dy = dx. \tag{2.264}$$

Integration gives $\tan^{-1} y = x - c$ and hence

$$y(x) = \tan(x - c), \tag{2.265}$$

where c is a constant that depends upon the particular solution with which we started. We now call upon our knowledge of trigonometry and look at Fig. 2.266. If $x = c$, then $y(x) = \tan 0 = 0$. If $x \to c + \pi/2$, then $y(x) \to \infty$ and the graph of $y(x)$ runs off the map. If $x \to c - \pi/2$, then $y(x) \to -\infty$ and again the graph runs off the map. We are forced to the conclusion that there simply is no interval of length greater than π over which $y(x)$ can satisfy (2.263). If, however, $c - \pi/2 < x < c + \pi/2$, then the function $y(x)$ defined by (2.265) does satisfy (2.263) because

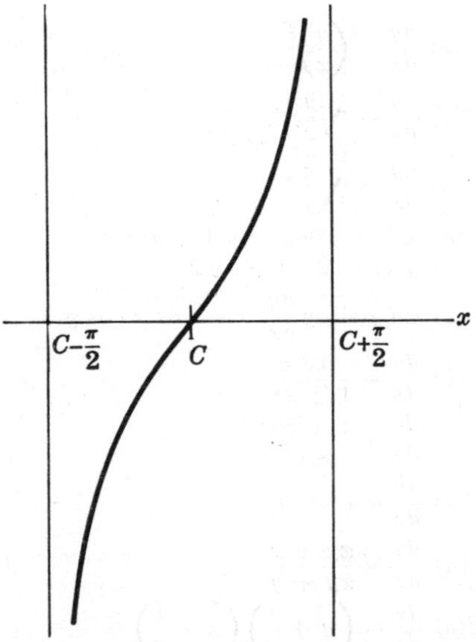

FIG. 2.266

$$\frac{dy}{dx} = \sec^2(x - c) = 1 + \tan^2(x - c) = 1 + y^2. \tag{2.267}$$

Thus when we undertake to solve (2.263), the best we can do is give the answer (2.265); for each constant c the resulting function satisfies the equation over the interval $c - \pi/2 < x < c + \pi/2$, but this interval is certainly not the whole infinite interval $-\infty < x < \infty$.

All this could make us wonder whether equations like $dy/dx = g(x, y)$ always have solutions over even small intervals. This brings us to the subject of existence theorems. Everybody should have considerable experience with problems such as the following ones before seriously attacking Chapter 15 where existence theorems are stated and proved. Section 5.1, which is much simpler, throws a little light upon the subject; it can be read any time and might even be read more than once. Meanwhile, it is not illegal to read Theorem 15.62 and to observe that if $g(x, y)$ is a continuous function having a continuous partial derivative with respect to y, then the equation does determine a reasonable family of solutions $y(x)$ satisfying the equation over intervals which are short in some cases and long in others.

Problem 2.27

Solve the following, giving explicit solutions whenever possible and not too inconvenient. Suppose that $x > 0$ when this is convenient.

(*a*) $y\,dy = -x\,dx$ — *Ans.:* $y = \pm(c - x^2)^{\frac{1}{2}}$

(*b*) $dy = -x\,dx$ — *Ans.:* $y = c - \dfrac{x^2}{2}$

(*c*) $dy = y\,dx$ — *Ans.:* $y = Ae^x$

(*d*) $x\dfrac{dy}{dx} = y$ — *Ans.:* $y = cx$

(*e*) $\dfrac{dy}{dx} = \left(\dfrac{y}{x}\right)^2$ — *Ans.:* $y = \dfrac{x}{1 + cx}$

(*f*) $\dfrac{dy}{dx} = \sqrt{\dfrac{y}{x}}$ — *Ans.:* $y = (\sqrt{x} + c)^2$

(*g*) $\dfrac{dy}{dx} = \sqrt{\dfrac{x}{y}}$ — *Ans.:* $y = (x^{\frac{3}{2}} + c)^{\frac{2}{3}}$

(*h*) $x(1 + y^2)dy = y(1 + x^2)dx$ — *Ans.:* $y^2 + 2\log y = x^2 + 2\log x + c$

(*i*) $y\,dy = 2(xy + x)dx$ — *Ans.:* $y - \log(1 + y) = x^2 + c$

(*j*) $\sin x \sin y \dfrac{dy}{dx} = -\cos x \cos y$ — *Ans.:* $\cos y = c \sin x$

(*k*) $\dfrac{dy}{dx} = \dfrac{\cos^2 y}{1 + x^2}$ — *Ans.:* $y = \tan^{-1}(c + \tan^{-1} x)$

(*l*) $\dfrac{dy}{dx} = \dfrac{1 + \cos x}{\sec^2 y}$ — *Ans.:* $y = \tan^{-1}(c + x + \sin x)$

(*m*) $\dfrac{dy}{dx} = e^{-(x+y)}$ — *Ans.:* $y = \log(c - e^{-x})$

(*n*) $\dfrac{dy}{dx} = \dfrac{xy + x}{xy + y}$ — *Ans.:* $y - \log(y + 1) = x - \log(x + 1) + c$

(*o*) $\dfrac{dy}{dx} = \left(y + \dfrac{1}{y}\right)\left(x + \dfrac{1}{x}\right)$ — *Ans.:* $y^2 + 1 = cx^2e^{x^2}$

(*p*) $\dfrac{dy}{dx} = \dfrac{y^3 + y}{2x}$ — *Ans.:* $y^2 = \dfrac{x}{c - x}$

(*q*) $\dfrac{dy}{dx} = \dfrac{xy}{x^2 - 1}$ — *Ans.:* $\dfrac{x^2}{1^2} - \dfrac{y^2}{c} = 1$

(*r*) $2x\dfrac{dy}{dx} + y = 0$ — *Ans.:* $y = \dfrac{c}{\sqrt{x}}$

(*s*) $\dfrac{dy}{dx} = 2x - 2xy$ — *Ans.:* $y = 1 + ce^{-x^2}$

(*t*) $\sin x \dfrac{dy}{dx} = 2y \cos x$ — *Ans.:* $y = c \sin^2 x$

(*u*) $\dfrac{dy}{dx} = |y|$ — *Ans.:* $y = ce^{x \operatorname{sgn} c}$

Problem 2.28

The problems in this list, as well as some preceding ones, are special *Riccati* (1705–1775) *equations*. Note the ways in which c appears in the answers. Note that replacing c by $1/c$ converts answers from one form to another. Note that, in at least some cases, taking limits as $c \to \infty$ yields solutions which we may call solutions for which $c = \infty$. Note that, in at least some cases, solutions for which $c = 0, 1, \infty$ are obvious solutions of the given equation. The index cites this and other occurrences of Riccati equations, and it is sometimes a good idea to look around.

(a) $\dfrac{dy}{dx} = \dfrac{y^2 + 1}{x^2 + 1}$ *Ans.:* $y = \dfrac{c + x}{-cx + 1}$ or $y = \dfrac{cx + 1}{c - x}$

(b) $\dfrac{dy}{dx} = -\dfrac{y^2 + 1}{x^2 + 1}$ *Ans.:* $y = \dfrac{c - x}{cx + 1}$

(c) $\dfrac{dy}{dx} = \left(\dfrac{y + 1}{x + 1}\right)^2$ *Ans.:* $y = \dfrac{cx - x - 1}{c + x + 1}$

(d) $\dfrac{dy}{dx} = a(b^2 - y^2)$ *Ans.:* $y = b\,\dfrac{ce^{2abx} - 1}{ce^{2abx} + 1}$

(e) $\dfrac{dy}{dx} = \dfrac{(y - 1)(y - 2)}{x}$ *Ans.:* $y = \dfrac{cx - 2}{cx - 1}$

(f) $\dfrac{dy}{dx} = \dfrac{(y - 1)(y - 2)}{(x - 1)(x - 2)}$ *Ans.:* $y = \dfrac{c(x - 2) - 2(x - 1)}{c(x - 2) - (x - 1)}$

(g) $\dfrac{dy}{dx} = \dfrac{(y - a)^2}{x}$ *Ans.:* $y = \dfrac{ca + a\log x - 1}{c + \log x}$

(h) $\dfrac{dy}{dx} = \dfrac{(y - a)(y - b)}{x}$, $x > 0$, $a \neq b$ *Ans.:* $y = \dfrac{cax^{b-a} - b}{cx^{b-a} - 1}$

(i) $\dfrac{dy}{dx} = p(x)(y - a)(y - b)$ where $a \neq b$ and $p(x)$ is continuous at $x = 1$

Ans.: $y = \dfrac{caf(x) - b}{cf(x) - 1}$ where $f(x) = e^{(b-a)\int_1^x p(t)d}$

Problem 2.281

Let $y(x)$ be the function for which $y(0) = 0$ and

$$\frac{dy}{dx} = \frac{1}{(1 + x^2)(1 + y^2)}.$$

Before solving the equation, look at it. Tell why y is an increasing function of x. Find $y'(0)$ and discuss the behavior of $y'(x)$ as x increases. Show that, when $x > 0$,

$$y(x) = \int_0^x \frac{1}{[1 + t^2][1 + y(t)^2]}\,dt < \int_0^x \frac{1}{1 + t^2}\,dt = \tan^{-1} x < \frac{\pi}{2}.$$

Therefore (since $y(x)$ is a bounded increasing function) there must be a number L such that

$$\lim_{x \to \infty} y(x) = L.$$

Why is it true that $L \leqq \pi/2 = 1.5708$? Now solve the equation and find L.
Ans.: $y^3 + 3y - 3\tan^{-1} x = 0.$
Hence $L^3 + 3L - 4.7124 = 0$ and $L = 1.11$ approximately.

Problem 2.282

Solve the equation

(2.2821) $$\frac{dp}{dh} = -k\left(\frac{R}{R + h}\right)^2 p$$

in which k and R are positive constants. [For a physical interpretation of this equation, see (3.46).] Show that if $p(0) = A$, then

$$p = Ae^{-k\frac{Rh}{R+h}}. \tag{2.2822}$$

Observe that

$$\lim_{h\to\infty} p(h) = Ae^{-kR}. \tag{2.2823}$$

Problem 2.283

Solve the equation

$$(1 + x^2)\frac{d^2u}{dx^2} = 1 + \left(\frac{du}{dx}\right)^2$$

by letting $y = du/dx$ and finding y and then u.

Ans.: $y = A + Bx - (1 + B^2)\log(x + B)$.

Problem 2.284

The variables in the equation

$$\frac{dy}{dx} = \frac{-2xy}{(x^2 + y^2)^2 + y^2 - x^2}$$

+

are far from separable. Show that introducing polar coordinates by setting $x = r\cos\theta$ and $y = r\sin\theta$ leads to the equation

$$(r^2 + 1)\sin\theta\, dr + r(r^2 - 1)\cos\theta\, d\theta = 0$$

with solutions

$$\left(r - \frac{1}{r}\right)\sin\theta = c, \qquad y - \frac{y}{x^2 + y^2} = c.$$

Problem 2.285

Sometimes it is convenient to use the fact that if y is a differentiable function of x and $y'(x) \neq 0$, then the coordinates (X, Y) of points on the tangent and normal to the graph of $y(x)$ at the point (x, y) satisfy the equations

$$Y - y = y'(x)(X - x)$$

and

$$Y - y = -\frac{1}{y'(x)}(X - x).$$

With or without the aid of this idea, find equations of curves C such that when P lies on C the normal to C at P meets the x and y axes at points Q and R for which Q lies midway between P and R.

Ans.: $\dfrac{x^2}{2c^2} + \dfrac{y^2}{c^2} = 1$.

Problem 2.286

Find equations of curves C such that if P lies on C then the tangent to C at P lies at unit distance from the foot of the perpendicular from P to the x axis.

Ans.: $y = \pm\frac{1}{2}[e^{x+c} + e^{-(x+c)}] = \pm\cosh(x + c)$.

Problem 2.287

Find equations of other curves C which share with the graph of $y = x$, $x \geqq 0$ the following property. The curve C lies in the first quadrant and has an end at the origin. Whenever P is on C, the interior of the rectangle R, bounded by the coordinate axes and lines through P parallel to them, is separated into two parts by C. When the part adjacent to the x axis is rotated about the x axis and the part adjacent to the y axis is rotated about the y axis, two solids of equal volumes are generated.

Ans.: $y = \dfrac{x}{1 + cx}$ with $x \geqq 0$ when $c \geqq 0$ and $0 \leqq x < 1/|c|$ when $c < 0$.

Problem 2.288

Calculus textbooks give the formula

$$R = \frac{[1 + (dy/dx)^2]^{\frac{3}{2}}}{|d^2y/dx^2|}$$

for *radius of curvature.* It should be, and is, possible to suppose that R is a constant and solve this equation to obtain $(x - c_1)^2 + (y - c_2)^2 = R^2$. Do it.

Problem 2.289

Solve the equation

$$\frac{dy}{dx} = -\frac{x + h \operatorname{sgn} y}{y}$$

in which $\operatorname{sgn} y = 1$ when $y > 0$, $\operatorname{sgn} 0 = 0$, and $\operatorname{sgn} y = -1$ when $y < 0$.

Ans.: See Problem 4.192.

Problem 2.29

The *pendulum equation* (1.52) can be put in the form

$$\frac{d^2\theta}{dt^2} = -a^2 \sin \theta$$

where $a > 0$ and $a^2 = mgl/I$. Multiply this by $2\, d\theta/dt$ and obtain

$$\left(\frac{d\theta}{dt}\right)^2 = c + 2a^2 \cos \theta.$$

Supposing that $\theta = 0$ and $d\theta/dt = \omega_0 > 0$ when $t = 0$, show that

$$\left(\frac{d\theta}{dt}\right)^2 = \omega_0^2 \left(1 - k^2 \sin^2 \frac{\theta}{2}\right)$$

where

$$k = \frac{2a}{\omega_0} = \frac{2}{\omega_0}\sqrt{\frac{mlg}{I}}.$$

In case $k < 1$, show that

$$\frac{d\theta}{dt} = \omega_0 \sqrt{1 - k^2 \sin^2 \frac{\theta}{2}} \geqq \omega_0 \sqrt{1 - k^2}$$

and hence that the pendulum rotates completely and repeatedly around its point of suspension and has minimum angular velocity when it goes over the top.

In case $k = 1$, show that $d\theta/dt = \omega_0 \cos \theta/2$ and hence that

$$\theta = -\pi + 4 \tan^{-1} e^{-(\omega_0/2)t};$$

this says that the pendulum continually climbs toward the vertical position which it approaches as $t \to \infty$.

In case $k > 1$, show that the pendulum will swing with increasing θ until θ reaches the acute angle θ_0 for which $d\theta/dt = 0$ and $\sin \frac{1}{2}\theta_0 = 1/k$. Show that

$$t = \frac{1}{\omega_0} \int_0^\theta \frac{1}{\sqrt{1 - k^2 \sin^2 \dfrac{u}{2}}} du$$

when $0 \leqq \theta \leqq \theta_0$. This is not an elementary integral. It can be shown that changing the variable of integration by setting $k \sin \frac{1}{2}u = \sin x$ gives the more agreeable integral

$$t = \sqrt{\frac{I}{mlg}} \int_0^{\sin^{-1}(k \sin \frac{1}{2}\theta)} \frac{1}{\sqrt{1 - (1/k)^2 \sin^2 x}} dx$$

in which $1/k < 1$. This is an incomplete elliptic integral; the complete elliptic integral is the integral over the whole interval $0 \leqq x \leqq \pi/2$. The latter integral is the time required for the pendulum to swing from its lowest to its highest position and is a quarter of the period T. Thus

$$T = 4 \sqrt{\frac{I}{mlg}} \int_0^{\pi/2} \frac{1}{\sqrt{1 - (1/k)^2 \sin^2 x}} dx.$$

When θ_0 is small and hence k is large, the integrand is everywhere near 1 and we obtain the approximation $T = 2\pi \sqrt{I/mlg}$ which reduces to the more familiar formula $T = 2\pi \sqrt{l/g}$ when $I = ml^2$.

Problem 2.291

A function $y(x)$ for which $y(1) = 1$ satisfies the differential equation $y' = y^2$ over an interval J. Find how large the interval J may be, and sketch a graph of $y(x)$. Solve the corresponding problem with the boundary condition $y(0) = 0$.

Problem 2.292

Show that for each constant c the function $y(x)$ defined by

$$\begin{aligned} y(x) &= 0 && x < c \\ &= (x - c)^2 && x \geqq c \end{aligned}$$

is a solution of the differential equation

$$\frac{dy}{dx} = 2\sqrt{y}.$$

Find more solutions, or prove that there are no more.

2.3. A Snowplow Problem. In this section we propose and solve a problem which illustrates a way in which differential equations are used. It is not a "pure" mathematical problem, *i.e.*, one that provides all the hypotheses required for determination of an answer. Rather, it is of a type most frequently encountered by applied mathematicians: to solve it, one is forced to make what may be called a *physical assumption*. To anyone who may object to making assumptions, we can say that much of the progress in science is due to men who have the courage to make assumptions, the good sense to make reasonable assumptions, and the ability to draw correct conclusions from the assumptions. It will appear later in this book that many problems may be solved by means of differential equations which are consequences of physical assumptions. Our present problem is as follows:

One day it started snowing at a heavy and steady rate. A snowplow started out at noon, going 2 miles the first hour and 1 mile the second hour. What time did it start snowing?

Our first task is to try to recover from the shock of being asked to solve such a problem, by attempting to analyze the problem. In the first place, the data of the problem are in agreement with the idea that the plow will move slower as the snow gets deeper. This idea is, however, not sufficiently precise to enable us to solve the problem; we must make some assumption involving the rate at which the plow clears snow from the road. Without pretending to determine whether different assumptions may be equally good or perhaps better, we assume that the plow clears snow at a constant rate of k cubic miles per hour. Let t be time measured in hours from noon, let x denote the depth in miles of the snow at time t, and let y denote the distance the plow has moved at time t. Then dy/dt is the velocity of the plow, and our assumption gives

$$wx\frac{dy}{dt} = k \tag{2.311}$$

where w is the width of the plow. To find how x depends on t, let t_0 be the number of hours before noon when it started snowing, and let s be the constant rate (in miles per hour) at which the depth of the snow increases; then, when $t > -t_0$,

$$x = s(t + t_0) \tag{2.312}$$

and we obtain the differential equation

$$\frac{dy}{dt} = \frac{k}{ws}\frac{1}{t + t_0}. \tag{2.313}$$

This differential equation has the form $dy/dt = f(t)$, and we see that

$$y = \frac{k}{ws}[\log(t + t_0) + c] \tag{2.314}$$

where c is a constant. It may be suspected (or expected) that knowledge of enough pairs of values of y and t will enable us to determine t_0 and thus obtain a solution of our problem. Since $y = 0$ when $t = 0$, we find from (2.314) that $c = -\log t_0$ and hence

$$y = \frac{k}{ws}\log\left(1 + \frac{t}{t_0}\right). \tag{2.315}$$

Next we use the fact that $y = 2$ when $t = 1$ and $y = 3$ when $t = 2$ to obtain

$$\left(1 + \frac{2}{t_0}\right)^2 = \left(1 + \frac{1}{t_0}\right)^3. \tag{2.316}$$

Expanding the powers and simplifying give the equation

$$t_0^2 + t_0 - 1 = 0. \tag{2.317}$$

Since $t_0 > 0$, we obtain $t_0 = (-1 + \sqrt{5})/2 = 0.618$ hours $= 37 +$ minutes. Hence, it started snowing about 11:23 A.M.

2.32. The Big Noise. Read the following problem and then draw a rough figure showing the path of the pilot. Mark the point P on the path which the pilot reaches at time t, and consider what must happen if the noise he makes at that time is heard at O simultaneously with the noise made when $t = 0$. Study the problem and your figure until you can decide what to do.

Problem 2.33

The pilot of a supersonic jet airplane wishes to make a big noise at a point O by flying around O in a path such that all of the noise he makes is heard simultaneously at O. His *Mach* (1838–1916) *number* is M, which means that his speed is Mc where c is the speed of sound, and $M > 1$ because the speed is supersonic. Letting O be the origin of a plane with polar coordinates θ and r, and supposing that the pilot starts at time $t = 0$ from the point $\theta = 0$, $r = a$ and flies around point O in the positive direction, find the simplest equation of the path. *Outline of solution:* The nature and statement of the problem suggest that we should let $\theta(t)$ and $r(t)$ denote the polar coordinates of the airplane at time t. Then $t + r/c = a/c$ so that $dr/dt = -c$. Also, as we can show with or without the aid of the rectangular coordinates $x = r\cos\theta$, $y = r\sin\theta$, we have

$$M^2c^2 = \left(\frac{dx}{dt}\right)^2 + \left(\frac{dy}{dt}\right)^2 = \left(\frac{dr}{dt}\right)^2 + \left(r\frac{d\theta}{dt}\right)^2. \tag{2.331}$$

In case $r > 0$ and $d\theta/dt > 0$, we obtain $r^{-1}\,dr/d\theta = -(M^2 - 1)^{-\frac{1}{2}}$ so that $\log r = C - (M^2 - 1)^{-\frac{1}{2}}\theta$ and $r = a\exp[-(M^2 - 1)^{-\frac{1}{2}}\theta]$. This path is a spiral. It is easy to imagine that a pilot could follow this spiral so long as r is sufficiently great. It is not so clear that the pilot and airplane could accomplish and survive the operation of making an infinite set of turns around P to reach P when $t = a/c$.

2.4. Assorted Problems. This section includes several subsections containing problems of various sorts. All are solved by separation of variables. Several problems are worked out in the text because they involve nonmathematical ideas or principles with which not everyone is familiar. The problems are important because they give ideas about origins and uses of differential equations. The rules of our game apply here; we work some of the problems and read everything.

2.41. Evaporation. Suppose it has been observed that a mothball of radius $\frac{1}{2}$ inch evaporates to leave a ball of radius $\frac{1}{4}$ inch at the end of 6 months. Express the radius of the ball as a function of the time.

This problem is not a pure mathematical problem; to solve the problem, one is forced to make a physical assumption. Since evaporation occurs at the surface of the ball, it is reasonable to assume that the time rate at which the volume V decreases is proportional to the area S of surface exposed at time t; that is,

$$\frac{dV}{dt} = -kS \tag{2.4101}$$

where k is some positive constant. Denoting the radius of the ball at time t by r, we can use the formulas $V = \frac{4}{3}\pi r^3$ and $S = 4\pi r^2$ to obtain, when $r > 0$,

$$\frac{dr}{dt} = -k. \tag{2.4102}$$

(Could this equation have been surmised in the first place without arguments involving volume and area?) From (2.4102) we obtain

$$r = c - kt \tag{2.4103}$$

where c is a constant of integration. Taking the radius to be $\frac{1}{2}$ when $t = 0$ shows that $c = \frac{1}{2}$; hence, $r = \frac{1}{2} - kt$. Setting $r = \frac{1}{4}$ and $t = 6$ (time being measured in months) shows that $k = \frac{1}{24}$; hence we obtain

$$r = \frac{1}{2} - \frac{t}{24} \tag{2.4104}$$

as the answer to our problem. A graph of $r = r(t)$ shows precisely how the radius changes as t increases. Is $r = -\frac{1}{2}$ when $t = 24$? Is $r = 1$ when $t = -12$?

Problem 2.411

At time $t = 0$, a layer of volatile material of thickness y_0 suddenly appears all over the bottom of a sealed box or room whose base has area B^2 and whose height is H. At later times t, when the thickness of the layer is y or $y(t)$, molecules leave the layer at a constant rate and return at a rate proportional to the amount evaporated. Show that, with appropriate positive constants a and b,

$$\frac{dy}{dt} = -a + b(y_0 - y)$$

and

$$y = y_0 - \frac{a}{b}[1 - e^{-bt}]$$

so long as $y \geqq 0$. Discuss the cases in which $y_0 > a/b$, $y_0 = a/b$, and $y_0 < a/b$.

Problem 2.412

Suppose that numerical values of the constants a and b in Problem 2.411 have been determined. Use them to find a formula for $y(t)$ when the layer of volatile material covers only p per cent of the bottom of the container.

Ans.: $y = y_0 - \dfrac{100a}{bp}[1 - e^{-b(p/100)t}]$.

Problem 2.413

In terms of these same constants a and b, obtain the differential equation governing the radius $r(t)$ of a volatile sphere at initial radius r_0 which suddenly appears at time $t = 0$ in the sealed container of Problem 2.411. *Ans.:* $\dfrac{dr}{dt} = -a + \dfrac{4\pi b}{3B^2}(r_0^3 - r^3)$

Remark: In case the evaporation causes relatively little reduction in the radius of the sphere, the identity

$$r_0^3 - r^3 = (r_0^2 + rr_0 + r^2)(r_0 - r)$$

provides an excuse for writing the approximation

$$\frac{dr}{dt} = -a + \frac{4\pi r_0^2}{B^2} b(r_0 - r)$$

and this merits some discussion.

2.42. Flow of Liquid through Orifices. When an object, starting from rest, falls a distance h feet with only a little friction, it acquires a speed of about $\sqrt{2gh}$ feet per second where $g = 32$. Hence it seems reasonable that water would escape about $A\sqrt{2gh}$ cubic feet per second from an orifice of area A which lies h feet below the surface of the water; h is called the *head* of the water. However, friction and contraction of the stream near the orifice reduce the rate of flow to $qA\sqrt{2gh}$ where $0 < q < 1$. Thus

$$\frac{dV}{dt} = -qA\sqrt{2gh}, \qquad f(h)\frac{dh}{dt} = -qA\sqrt{2gh}$$

when $V(h)$ and $f(h)$ denote the volume of water in a container and the area of the upper surface of the water when the head is h. The negative sign is required because V and h decrease as t increases. It should be expected that q depends in a very complicated way upon the sizes and shapes of the container and orifice and upon the head h. Nevertheless, reasonable answers to many problems are obtained from the simplifying assumption that q is the constant 0.6.

Problem 2.421

A cylindrical tank 4 feet high stands on its circular base of radius 3 feet. At noon, when the tank was full of water, a plug was removed from a circular orifice of radius $\frac{1}{2}$ inch in the bottom of the tank and the tank was thereby drained. Find the times at which the tank was one-half full, one-quarter full, and empty.

Outline of solution: Let units be feet and seconds, with $t = 0$ at noon. If $h(t)$ is the head and $V(t)$ is the volume at time t, then $9\pi h = V$; so

$$9\pi \frac{dh}{dt} = \frac{dV}{dt} = -0.6\pi \left(\frac{0.5}{12}\right)^2 \sqrt{64h} = \frac{-\pi}{120} \sqrt{h}.$$

Division by 9π and by $2\sqrt{h}$ gives

$$\frac{d}{dt} h^{\frac{1}{2}} = \frac{1}{2} h^{-\frac{1}{2}} \frac{dh}{dt} = -\frac{1}{2{,}160}$$

so $\sqrt{h} = c - t/2{,}160$. Since $h = 4$ when $t = 0$, we see that $c = 2$ and, hence, that $t = 2{,}160(2 - \sqrt{h})$. The tank was one-half full when $t = 1{,}265$ (about 12:21 P.M.), one-quarter full when $t = 2{,}160$ (12:36 P.M.), and empty when $t = 4{,}320$ (1:12 P.M.).

Problem 2.422

A conical funnel of height H and base radius R has a small hole of area A at the bottom. Using the factor 0.6 as in the previous problem, find the time T required to empty a full funnel.

Ans.: $T = \pi R^2 H^{\frac{1}{2}}/12A$ seconds when the dimensions are measured in feet.

Problem 2.423

A sphere of radius R is full of water. Holes of area A are put at the top and bottom to let air in and water out. Using $q = 0.6$ as above, find the numbers T_1 and T_2 of seconds required for half and all of the water to run out.

Ans.: $T_1 = \dfrac{\pi}{18A}\left(1 - \dfrac{7}{\sqrt{128}}\right)(2R)^{\frac{5}{2}}, \qquad T_2 = \dfrac{\pi}{18A}(2R)^{\frac{5}{2}}.$

Problem 2.424

Same as Problem 2.423, except that the tank is a right circular cylinder of length L and radius R whose axis is horizontal. *Ans.:* $T_1 = \dfrac{L}{3.6A} R^{\frac{3}{2}}, \qquad T_2 = \dfrac{L}{3.6A}\sqrt{8}\, R^{\frac{3}{2}}.$

Problem 2.425

An empty rectangular tank of base area B^2 has a hole of area A in the bottom. At time $t = 0$, water starts running into the tank E cubic feet per second. Using $q = 0.6$

as above, show that the height h of the water is related to t by the formula

$$t = \frac{2}{a}\left[b \log \frac{b}{b - \sqrt{h}} - \sqrt{h} \right],$$

where $a = 4.8A/B^2$ and $b = E/4.8A$, at least until the tank is filled. Show that if the tank has height H, it will never be filled unless $E > 4.8A\sqrt{H}$. *Hint:* Integrals such as $\int (a - \sqrt{h})^{-1}\, dh$ are simplified by the substitution $x = \sqrt{h}$.

Problem 2.426

A rectangular tank of base area B^2 and height H contains two holes, one of area A in the bottom and the other of the same area A half way up a side of the tank. Starting with the tank full of water and using $q = 0.6$, find how long water will run out the upper hole. *Ans.:* $B^2 \dfrac{\sqrt{H}}{3.6A}$ seconds.

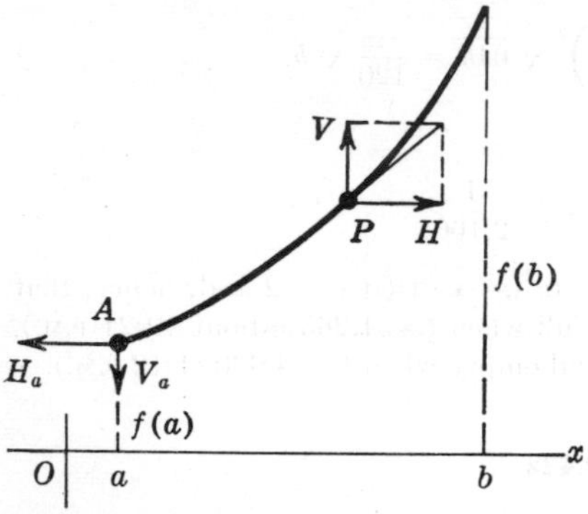

FIG. 2.431

2.43. A Hanging Cable. We are going to determine the shape of a flexible inextensible cable hanging with its ends fastened at points $(a, f(a))$ and $(b, f(b))$ in a vertical plane. Let $y = y(x)$ be the equation of the curve, and let $P \equiv P(x, y)$ be a point on the curve. The forces acting on the part of the cable between A and P are gravitational forces and those represented by arrows at A and P in Fig. 2.431. The resultant of the forces at P lies along the tangent at P so that $y' = V/H$. But $H = H_a$, and V is the sum of V_a and the weight of the cable. Thus, letting w represent the weight per unit length of the cable, we have

$$V = V_a + w \int_a^x \{1 + [y'(t)]^2\}^{\frac{1}{2}} dt$$

so that

$$y'(x) = \frac{V_a}{H} + \frac{w}{H} \int_a^x \{1 + [y'(t)]^2\}^{\frac{1}{2}} dt. \tag{2.432}$$

Our hypothesis that the cable is flexible is now interpreted to mean that $y'(t)$ is continuous. Hence, by the fundamental theorem of the calculus, we can differentiate to obtain

$$y''(x) = k\{1 + [y'(x)]^2\}^{\frac{1}{2}}$$

where $k = w/H > 0$. We can make this equation look simpler (do not forget this trick) by setting $p(x) = y'(x)$, $p'(x) = y''(x)$ to obtain

$p' = k(1 + p^2)^{\frac{1}{2}}$. This can be written in the form

$$(1 + p^2)^{-\frac{1}{2}}dp - k\,dx = 0$$

in which the variables are separated so that

$$\log (p + \sqrt{1 + p^2}) - kx = kc$$

where the constant of integration is called kc for convenience. From this we obtain

$$p = \tfrac{1}{2}[e^{k(x+c)} - e^{-k(x+c)}]$$

and

(2.433) $$y = \frac{1}{k}[e^{k(x+c)} + e^{-k(x+c)}] + c_1.$$

Since a *catenary* is by definition a curve whose equation has the form (2.433), it follows that the cable must hang in the form of a catenary. The function $y(x)$ in (2.433) has a minimum at the only point $x = -c$ where $p(x) = y'(x) = 0$. If the origin of the coordinate system is chosen so that the minimum of $y(x)$ occurs for $x = 0$ and if $y = 1/k$ when $x = 0$, then $c = c_1 = 0$ and (2.433) takes the standard form

(2.434) $$y = \frac{1}{2k}[e^{kx} + e^{-kx}]$$

of the equation of a catenary.

Remark 2.435

The formula (2.433) contains three constants k, c, and c_1 which can be determined to make the hanging cable pass through two prescribed points and satisfy an additional condition which may involve (i) the length of the part of the cable between the two points, or (ii) the sag of the cable, that is, the difference between the elevations of the lowest point on the cable and the lowest end of the cable, or (iii) the tensions at the ends of the cable. In most cases the equations which determine the constants are not algebraic and numerical methods (interpolation and successive approximation, for example) are required to solve them. Anyone who works very long with problems of this nature should use the *hyperbolic functions* defined by

$$\cosh u = \frac{e^u + e^{-u}}{2}, \qquad \sinh u = \frac{e^u - e^{-u}}{2},$$

and $\tanh u = \sinh u/\cosh u$ and should use properties and tables of these functions. This puts (2.433) in the form

$$y = \frac{1}{k}\cosh k(x + c) + c_1,$$

and differentiation gives $y' = \sinh k(x + c)$. Most of the difficulties in determining k, c, and c_1 disappear when the ends of the cable have the same horizontal level and the y axis is midway between them so that $y'(0) = 0$ and $c = 0$. In this case the equation takes the much simpler form

$$y = \frac{1}{k} \cosh kx + c_1,$$

but determining k and c_1 can still be a nontrivial task.

Everybody should think a little about the next three problems, and perhaps somebody should assign numerical values to the constants and work out numerical answers.

Problem 2.4361

A cable hangs from two points at the same horizontal level and a distance $2D$ apart. Find the equation of the cable (i) when the sag in the cable is S, and (ii) when the length of the cable is L.

Problem 2.4362

A chain of length $2L$ is draped over two small pulleys or smooth rods at the same horizontal level a distance $2D$ apart. Find conditions under which the chain is in equilibrium with its ends hanging straight down from the supports and its middle sagging between the supports.

Problem 2.4363

A chain of length L has one end welded to the origin of a vertical plane and is draped over a pulley at the point (b, h) where b and h are constants with $b > 0$. Find conditions for equilibrium.

Problem 2.437

One side of a footbridge 100 feet long is supported by a hanging cable. The ends of the cable are 25 feet above the ends of the bridge, and the center of the cable is 5 feet above the center of the bridge. The bridge is fastened to the cable by closely and equally spaced vertical rods each of which carries a weight of w pounds. Find a good approximation to the equation of the cable. *Ans.*: Neglecting the weight of the cable, assuming a uniform horizontal loading, and taking the origin at the center of the bridge, one obtains $y = 0.008x^2 + 5$.

Problem 2.438

A container partly filled by a liquid is rotated about a vertical axis with constant angular velocity ω. Show that the "free" surface of the liquid is a part of a paraboloid of revolution. *Hint:* A particle of mass m at the free surface is subject to a gravitational force mg and to a centrifugal force $mr\omega^2$ where r is the distance from the axis to the particle; the resultant of these forces is orthogonal to the free surface.

2.44. Law of Mass Action. Chemists observe that, in certain cases, when two substances are mixed, a compound is formed at a rate which is proportional to the product of the weights of the untransformed parts of the two substances. In such cases, the *law of mass action* applies, good chemists knowing when and why. Let a grams of a substance A and b grams of a substance B be mixed, and let a compound X be formed from m parts by weight of A and n parts by weight of B. When x grams of X has been formed, $a - [m/(m+n)]x$ grams of A remains and $b - [n/(m+n)]x$ grams of B remains. Hence, when the law of mass action applies,

$$\frac{dx}{dt} = k\left(a - \frac{m}{m+n}x\right)\left(b - \frac{n}{m+n}x\right). \tag{2.441}$$

This equation looks somewhat better when we write it in the form

$$\frac{dx}{dt} = \frac{kmn}{(m+n)^2}\left[\frac{a(m+n)}{m} - x\right]\left[\frac{b(m+n)}{n} - x\right] \tag{2.442}$$

and set

$$k_1 = \frac{kmn}{(m+n)^2}, \qquad a_1 = \frac{a(m+n)}{m}, \qquad b_1 = \frac{b(m+n)}{n} \tag{2.443}$$

to obtain

$$\frac{dx}{dt} = k_1(a_1 - x)(b_1 - x). \tag{2.444}$$

This is an equation in which the variables are separable; the solutions take different forms according as $a_1 = b_1$ or $a_1 \neq b_1$.

Problem 2.445

Show that, if $a_1 = b_1$, the differential equation (2.444), together with the initial condition $x(0) = 0$, implies that

$$x = a_1\left[1 - \frac{1}{1 + a_1k_1t}\right] = \frac{a(m+n)}{m}\,\frac{aknt}{m + n + aknt} \tag{2.4451}$$

and that $x \to a(m+n)/m$ as $t \to \infty$. If x attains 50 per cent of the limiting value in 1 hour, how long is required for it to attain 90 per cent of the limiting value?

Ans.: 9 hours.

Problem 2.446

If $a_1 \neq b_1$, we can suppose that the names A and B are assigned to the substances in such a way that $a_1 < b_1$. Show that the solutions of (2.444) are, in this case,

$$\log\frac{b_1 - x}{a_1 - x} = (b_1 - a_1)k_1t + c; \tag{2.4461}$$

use the condition $x(0) = 0$ to determine c; and then solve for x to obtain

$$x = a_1b_1\,\frac{e^{(b_1-a_1)k_1t} - 1}{b_1e^{(b_1-a_1)k_1t} - a_1}. \tag{2.4462}$$

Show that $x \to a_1$ as $t \to \infty$.

Problem 2.447

It can be shown that, if a_1, k_1, and t are fixed, then the limit as $b_1 \to a_1$ of the right member of (2.4462) is the second member of (2.4451). Can you give mathematical or chemical justification (or both) for this assertion?

Remark 2.448

Because of problems like the following two, it is useful to know that

$$k(a - x)(b - x) = k_f(C - x)^2 - k_r x^2$$

when

$$k_f = k\,\frac{(a + b)^2}{4ab}, \qquad k_r = k\,\frac{(a - b)^2}{4ab}, \qquad C = \frac{2ab}{a + b}.$$

Problem 2.4481

A chemist wants a formula to enable him to calculate k_f and k_r, the forward and reverse reaction constants, for a particular reaction which involves acetic acid and ethyl alcohol. He knows that the equilibrium constant K is 4 and hence that $k_f/k_r = 4$. He knows that $x(0) = 0$ and that

$$\frac{dx}{dt} = k_f(a - x)^2 - k_r x^2$$

where a is a known positive constant, and he has experimentally determined x for a single positive value of t. Show that

$$k_f = \frac{1}{at}\log\frac{2a - x}{2a - 3x}.$$

Show also that

$$x = \frac{2a}{3}\,\frac{1 - e^{-ak_f t}}{1 - (\frac{1}{3})e^{-ak_f t}}.$$

Problem 2.4482

In the formula

$$\frac{dx}{dt} = k_f(a - x)^2 - k_r\left(\frac{x}{2}\right)^2,$$

$x(t)$ represents an amount of dissociated hydrogen iodide produced from an original amount a of hydrogen iodide. For study of the dissociation process at a fixed high temperature, we want formulas for k_f and k_r. We suppose that the equilibrium amount b, such that $x = b$ when $dx/dt = 0$, has already been determined. Show that

$$k_r = \frac{4(a - b)^2}{b^2}k_f.$$

Then, supposing that $x(0) = 0$, show that

$$k_f = \frac{b}{2a(a - b)t}\log\frac{ab + (a - 2b)x}{a(b - x)}.$$

Problem 2.4483

At time $t = 0$ a tank of solute contains A grams of a soluble material of which x_0 grams is already in solution, and M grams in solution yields a saturated solution. Circumstances are such that the number x of grams of material in solution increases at a rate jointly proportional to the number of grams undissolved and the number of grams that can still be dissolved. Thus

$$\frac{dx}{dt} = k(A - x)(M - x).$$

Suppose that A and M are known and that $A \neq M$, but that k is unknown. Show that

$$x = \frac{M(A - x_0) - A(M - x_0)e^{k(M-A)t}}{A - x_0 - (M - x_0)e^{k(M-A)t}}.$$

Show that if $x = x_1$ when $t = t_1$, then

$$k = \frac{1}{(M - A)t_1} \log \frac{(M - x_1)(A - x_0)}{(A - x_1)(M - x_0)}.$$

Problem 2.4484

At time $t = 0$ a tank of solute contains A grams of a soluble material of which y_0 grams is undissolved, and M grams in solution yields a saturated solution. Circumstances are such that the number y of grams of undissolved material decreases at a rate jointly proportional to the number of grams undissolved and the number of grams that can still be dissolved. Thus

$$\frac{dy}{dt} = -ky[M - (A - y)].$$

Suppose that A and M are known and that $A \neq M$, but that k is unknown. Show that

$$y = \frac{y_0(A - M)}{y_0 - (M - A + y_0)e^{k(M-A)t}}.$$

Show that if $y = y_1$ when $t = t_1$, then

$$k = \frac{1}{(M - A)t_1} \log \frac{y_0(M - A + y_1)}{y_1(M - A + y_0)}.$$

Problem 2.449

Suppose that the Society for the Promotion of Studies of Societies starts at time $t = 0$ with x_0 charter members. The members are avid recruiters and, except for one sad circumstance, the membership would doubtless increase at a rate proportional to the membership. The sad fact is that the world contains only M persons who can be induced to join, and the Society grows slowly when the membership is near M because it is not easy to find recruits. The Society studies itself and presumes that the membership $x(t)$ should grow in such a way that

$$\frac{dx}{dt} = kx(M - x)$$

where k and M are unknown positive constants. Show that this presumption implies that

$$x = \frac{M}{1 + \dfrac{M - x_0}{x_0} e^{-kMt}}$$

where k and M are still unknown constants. After t_1 years, the membership has grown to x_1. Use this to obtain the formula

$$k = \frac{1}{Mt_1} \log \frac{x_1(M - x_0)}{x_0(M - x_1)}$$

which would determine k if we knew M. Suppose finally that $x = x_2$ when $t = t_2$ and derive the formula

$$\frac{M - x_0}{M - x_2} \left[\frac{x_0(M - x_1)}{x_1(M - x_0)}\right]^{t_2/t_1} = \frac{x_0}{x_2}$$

which determines M.

2.45. A Pursuit Problem. A point A starts from the origin of an xy plane and moves in the direction of the positive x axis; and, at the same time, a point P starts at the point $(0, a)$ and moves (at the end of a towrope or otherwise) always in the direction of A in such a way that the distance from P to A is always the constant a. The path of P is called a *tractrix;* its equation may be found as follows:

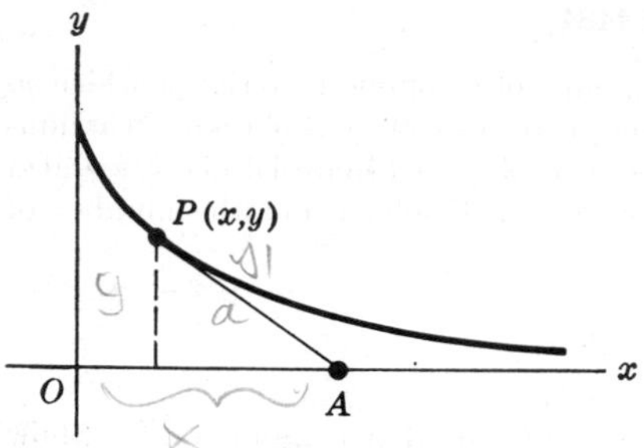

FIG. 2.451

The tangent to the path at a point $P(x, y)$ for which $x > 0$ and $0 < y < a$ meets the x axis at the point $(x - y/y', 0)$; but this point must be the point A, and hence, according to Pythagoras (ca. 580 B.C.–500 B.C.),

$$\left(\frac{y}{y'}\right)^2 = a^2 - y^2. \tag{2.452}$$

Since $0 < y < a$ and $y' < 0$, taking positive square roots gives

$$\frac{-y}{y'} = (a^2 - y^2)^{\frac{1}{2}}$$

and we can separate the variables to obtain

$$dx + \frac{(a^2 - y^2)^{\frac{1}{2}}}{y}\, dy = 0. \tag{2.453}$$

Integration (by means of a trigonometric substitution or use of a table of integrals) and determination of the constant of integration from the condition $y(0) = a$ give

$$x + (a^2 - y^2)^{\frac{1}{2}} - a \log \frac{a + (a^2 - y^2)^{\frac{1}{2}}}{y} = 0. \tag{2.454}$$

It is a simple matter to solve (2.454) for x to obtain $x = \phi(y)$; but to obtain $y = \psi(x)$ by methods of elementary algebra is impossible. If

$x = \phi(y)$ were used to obtain a table of corresponding values of x and y, then interpolation in this table would furnish approximate values of $\psi(x)$. The table of values of $x = \phi(y)$ could be used to construct a graph of $x = \phi(y)$ which would be at the same time a graph of $y = \psi(x)$.

Problem 2.455

This problem requires us to think about pursuit problems. An object or target moves in a plane in such a way that its rectangular coordinates x and y at time t are $X(t)$ and $Y(t)$. A second object or pursuer is said to follow or pursue the target if it moves in the direction of the target at all times. Show that if the coordinates of the pursuer at time t are $x(t)$ and $y(t)$, then

$$Y - y = \frac{dy}{dx}(X - x) \tag{2.4551}$$

over each time interval over which y is a differentiable function of x. Note that if X and Y are known functions of x and y, then (2.4551) is an equation of first order which gives information about the path of the pursuer. In case the pursuer always remains the same distance a behind the target, we obtain the helpful equation

$$(X - x)^2 + (Y - y)^2 = a^2.$$

Without performing the difficult steps, tell how to find the path of a pursuer that starts at the origin and pursues, at distance $\sqrt{2}$, a target which starts at the point (1, 1) and moves along the hyperbola $xy = 1$ or the parabola $y = x^2$. Tell why these problems are more difficult than the problem in which the target follows the path $y = 0$.

Problem 2.456

A pursuer P starts at the point $(0, a)$ in a plane and pursues, with speed p, a target T which starts at the origin and moves, with speed q, in the direction of the positive x axis. Find the path of P. If P hits T, tell where. Finally, for the case in which $p = q$, calculate the limiting distance from P to T. *Outline of Solution:* Solving the first of the equations

$$\frac{dy}{dx} = \frac{-y}{qt - x}, \qquad \left(\frac{dx}{dt}\right)^2 + \left(\frac{dy}{dt}\right)^2 = p^2$$

for t, differentiating with respect to y, and using the second equation gives

$$y\frac{du}{dy} = r\sqrt{u^2 + 1}$$

where $r = q/p$ and $u = dx/dy$. Hence

$$\frac{dx}{dy} = \frac{1}{2}\left[\left(\frac{y}{a}\right)^r - \left(\frac{y}{a}\right)^{-r}\right].$$

In case $p \neq q$ and hence $r \neq 1$, the answer is

$$x = \frac{a}{2}\left[\frac{1}{1+r}\left(\frac{y}{a}\right)^{1+r} - \frac{1}{1-r}\left(\frac{y}{a}\right)^{1-r}\right] + \frac{ar}{1-r^2}.$$

If $p < q$ and hence $r > 1$, then $x \to \infty$ as $y \to \infty$ and P lags behind T. If $p > q$ and hence $r < 1$, then $x = ar/(1 - r^2)$ when $y = 0$ and P hits T at this point. In case $p = q$ and hence $r = 1$, the equation of the path is

$$x = \frac{1}{2}\left[a \log \frac{a}{y} - \frac{a^2 - y^2}{2a}\right].$$

2.46. Parasites. The following problem provides an introduction to a phase of mathematical biology.

Problem 2.461

When a parasite population x lives on a host population y, the rate of change of x with respect to time t depends upon both x and y; and when the parasites affect the hosts (being beneficial in some cases and detrimental in others), the rate of change of y with respect to t also depends upon both x and y. Since the product xy represents the number of ways of pairing a parasite with a host, it may be expected that this product appears in equations. In many cases, $x(t)$ and $y(t)$ may be regarded (as in the radium problem of Sections 3.5 and 3.55) as solutions of the equations

$$\frac{dx}{dt} = ax + bxy, \qquad \frac{dy}{dt} = cy + dxy \tag{2.462}$$

in which a, b, c, and d are constants, not necessarily positive, and $b \neq 0$, $d \neq 0$. Using these equations, find a formula for dy/dx (which holds whenever $dx/dt \neq 0$), and proceed to show that x and y must be related as in the formula

$$by + a \log y = dx + c \log x + k \tag{2.463}$$

in which k is a constant.

Even when a, b, c, d have known values, say $a = b = c = 1$, $d = -1$ so that (2.463) becomes

$$y + \log y = -x + \log x + k, \tag{2.464}$$

the equation does not look good to a biologist. Solving these equations for y in terms of x is not a simple algebraic process. By the method given in the next section, it is possible to "solve" (2.463) for y and to exhibit a graph of $y(x)$ when a, b, c, d, and k are known.

Problem 2.465

The previous problem seems to have dodged the problem of finding x and y in terms of t. What can be said about that?

2.47. Graphic Solution of G(y) = F(x) + c. We do not propose to consider the general problem of determining conditions under which an equation of the form $G(y) = F(x) + c$, in which c is fixed, is satisfied by a differentiable function $y(x)$. Sometimes elementary algebraic manipulation produces one or more such functions $y(x)$, and sometimes no such function exists. We are now working with real functions of real variables, and there is no $y(x)$ for which $\sin y = \sin x + 25$.

We shall see how graphs can be used to indicate whether the equation

$$G(y) = F(x) + c \tag{2.471}$$

has a solution and to obtain an approximation to one when it exists. The first step is to draw graphs of $G(u)$ and $F(u)$ in a (u, v) plane, as shown in Fig. 2.472. Naturally there is no reason why the letters u and v must be used; the point is that confusion is eliminated by choosing letters different from x and y. The value of the constant c being given, we are now ready to hunt pairs of values of x and y for which (2.471) holds.

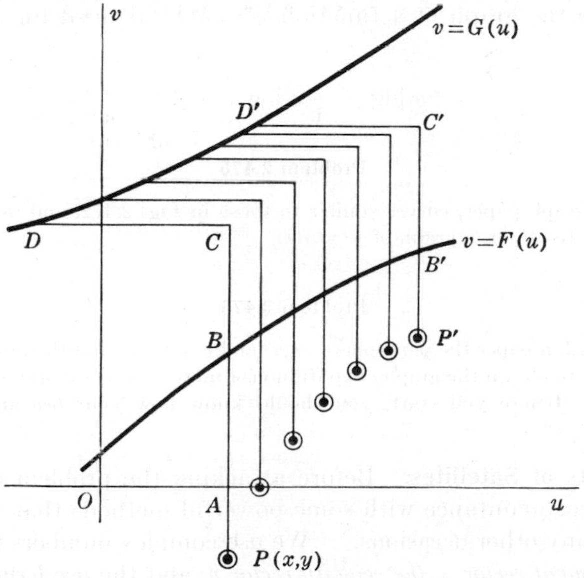

FIG. 2.472

Starting with a fixed x (which we could call x_0, but we omit the subscript), we determine the point A with coordinates $(x, 0)$ in the figure. The vertical line through A meets the graph of $F(u)$ at the point B with coordinates $(x, F(x))$. If $c > 0$, we find the point C with coordinates $(x, F(x) + c)$ by running up a distance c from B; if $c \leqq 0$, we find C by running down or staying at B. If by good luck, as in Fig. 2.472, the horizontal line through C meets the graph of $G(u)$ at D, we may call the u coordinate of D by the name y so that D has coordinates $(y, F(x) + c)$. We now have a pair of values of x and y for which (2.471) holds. Moreover we can now plot a point $P(x, y)$ on the graph of the function $y(x)$; the abscissa of D is simply the ordinate of P. When D has been found, we can find P by running on a vertical line from D to a point E (not shown in the figure) on the line through the origin having slope 1 and then running on a horizontal line from E to the vertical line through A. When the process is understood, it is seen to be very simple. More pairs (x, y) and points $P(x, y)$ can be speedily obtained. The segments from B' to C' to D' determine another pair, it being unnecessary to think of all the details of the method when new pairs and points are being found.

The problem of finding a function $y = y(x)$ such that

$$G(y) = G(x) + c \tag{2.473}$$

is amusing in that the drawing of only one curve $v = G(u)$ prepares the way for determination of pairs (x, y). It would not take long to approximate the graph of a function $y = y(x)$, defined for $x > 0$, such that

$$y \log y = x \log x + 1. \tag{2.474}$$

Problem 2.475

Sketch, on graph paper, curves similar to those in Fig. 2.472, and use the method of this section to obtain a graph of $y = y(x)$.

Problem 2.476

Sketch on graph paper the parabolas $v = u^2$ and $v = -u^2$, and then use the method of this section to obtain the graph of continuous functions $y(x)$ satisfying the equation $x^2 + y^2 = 1$. (Before you start, you should know how your *two* answers should look.)

2.5. Orbits of Satellites. Before attacking the problem of the title, we start an acquaintance with some powerful methods that will be very useful on many other occasions.* We use complex numbers to represent the *displacement vector* z, *the velocity vector* v, and the *acceleration vector* a of a point moving in a plane. For present purposes, we need only a little information about vectors and complex numbers. We need to know that, when i is the so-called imaginary unit for which $i^2 = -1$, the complex exponential $e^{i\theta}$ is defined in such a way that the Euler (1707–1783) formula

$$e^{i\theta} = \cos\theta + i\sin\theta \tag{2.501}$$

is valid. More information about this matter is given in Section 6.3; we do not need it now, but Section 6.3 can be read at any time and it is not illegal to read it more than once. When we are concerned with a plane in which a point has rectangular coordinates (x, y) and polar coordi-

* In defense of this strategy, we can note that beavers who spend all of their time chewing down trees attack only little ones while humans who spend part of their time making axes and saws can cut down everything.

nates (θ, r) with $r \geqq 0$, so that $x = r \cos \theta$ and $y = r \sin \theta$, it is very often convenient to set

(2.502) $$z = x + iy = r(\cos \theta + i \sin \theta) = re^{i\theta}.$$

Sometimes we think of z as being a *complex number*. Sometimes it is useful to think of z as being a *vector* running from the origin to the point having rectangular coordinates (x, y) and polar coordinates (θ, r).

All this is easily remembered in terms of the simple Fig. 2.503 which should be drawn and looked at until it becomes thoroughly familiar. When we think of z as being a number, x and y are called the *real* and *imaginary parts* of z; and when we think of z as being a vector, x and iy

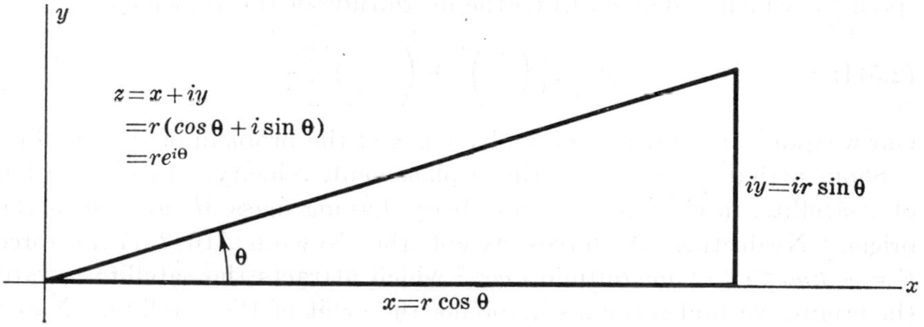

FIG. 2.503

are the horizontal and vertical *components* of z. When $z = re^{i\theta}$, the *absolute value* or *length* or *magnitude* $|z|$ of z is r, so

(2.504) $$|z| = r = (x^2 + y^2)^{\frac{1}{2}}.$$

When $r > 0$, the vector $e^{i\theta}$ is a *unit vector* (vector of unit length) having the direction of z, and the vector $-e^{i\theta}$ is a unit vector whose direction is opposite to that of z. When $z = 0$, it does not make sense to talk about the direction of z; θ is completely undetermined. Finally, we need the fact that the rules for calculating with complex numbers and exponentials are the same as the rules for calculating with real numbers and exponentials; in particular

(2.505) $$(x_1 + iy_1) + (x_2 + iy_2) = (x_1 + x_2) + i(y_1 + y_2)$$

(2.506) $$(x_1 + iy_1)(x_2 + iy_2) = (x_1x_2 - y_1y_2) + i(x_1y_2 + x_2y_1)$$

(2.507) $$e^{z_1+z_2} = e^{z_1}e^{z_2}, \qquad e^{x+iy} = e^x e^{iy}$$

and

(2.508) $$\frac{d}{dt}\, e^{q\theta} = qe^{q\theta}\, \frac{d\theta}{dt}$$

whenever q is a real or complex constant and θ is a differentiable function of t.

When $z(t)$, $r(t)$, and $\theta(t)$ are related by the first of the three formulas:

$$z = re^{i\theta} \tag{2.511}$$

$$v = \frac{dz}{dt} = \left[\frac{dr}{dt} + ir\frac{d\theta}{dt}\right] e^{i\theta} \tag{2.512}$$

and

$$a = \frac{dv}{dt} = \frac{d^2z}{dt^2} = \left[\frac{d^2r}{dt^2} - r\left(\frac{d\theta}{dt}\right)^2 + 2i\frac{d\theta}{dt}\frac{dr}{dt} + ir\frac{d^2\theta}{dt^2}\right] e^{i\theta}, \tag{2.513}$$

when θ and r are functions of t having two derivatives, differentiation gives* the next two. This is very important; everybody must know how to differentiate products and must check the details carefully. The speed $|v|$, which is defined to be the magnitude of the velocity, is

$$|v| = \left[\left(\frac{dr}{dt}\right)^2 + \left(r\frac{d\theta}{dt}\right)^2\right]^{\frac{1}{2}}. \tag{2.514}$$

Our weapons are now forged, and we attack the problem of the satellite.

Suppose that z, v, and a are the displacement, velocity, and acceleration of a satellite, having mass m, of a body, having mass M, located at the origin. Neglecting all forces except the Newton (1642–1727) force $F = -kmr^{-2}e^{i\theta}$ of magnitude kmr^{-2} which attracts the satellite toward the origin, we find formulas involving the orbit of the satellite. Note† that $k = gR^2$. Using the Newton law $ma = F$ gives

$$\frac{d^2z}{dt^2} = -kr^{-2}e^{i\theta}. \tag{2.52}$$

This and (2.513) give

$$\frac{d^2r}{dt^2} + 2i\frac{d\theta}{dt}\frac{dr}{dt} - r\left(\frac{d\theta}{dt}\right)^2 + ir\frac{d^2\theta}{dt^2} = -kr^{-2}. \tag{2.521}$$

* Those familiar with ordinary vector analysis should realize that we can let i_0 and j_0 denote unit orthogonal vectors in the directions of the x and y axes and write the vector formula

$$z = (r\cos\theta)i_0 + (r\sin\theta)j_0. \tag{2.509}$$

Differentiating this gives formulas equivalent to, but much more complicated than, (2.512) and (2.513). As science develops, engineers, physicists, and mathematicians are rapidly learning that many problems are greatly simplified by use of complex exponentials.

† The Newton law of universal gravitation says that two sphericial bodies of masses M and m are attracted toward each other by a force of magnitude GMm/r^2 where r is the distance between their centers and G is a universal gravitational constant whose value depends only upon the units used. We have set $k = GM$, so the force has magnitude km/r^2. When r is the radius R of the earth, the magnitude of the force is the weight mg of the satellite so $mg = km/R^2$ and $k = gR^2$. The constant g is the acceleration of gravity. When feet and seconds are used for units, the approximations $g = 32$ and $R = 4{,}000 \times 5{,}280$ are useful.

This is the differential equation which governs the motion of the satellite, and the first phase of our work is already ended. Our next task is to extract information from (2.521).

Equating the coefficients of i in the two members of this equation and multiplying the result by r give

$$\frac{d}{dt} r^2 \frac{d\theta}{dt} - r^2 \frac{d^2\theta}{dt^2} + 2r \frac{dr}{dt}\frac{d\theta}{dt} = 0. \tag{2.522}$$

Hence, for some real constant c_1,

$$r^2 \frac{d\theta}{dt} = c_1. \tag{2.523}$$

It is easy to see that this is an analytic statement of the famous law of Kepler (1571–1630) which says that the satellite moves in an orbit such that the vector from the central body to the satellite sweeps over regions of equal areas in equal time intervals. The *areal velocity* is $c_1/2$.

Considering only the case in which $c_1 > 0$, which means that the satellite rotates in the positive direction, we use (2.523) to remove the variable r from (2.52) and obtain

$$\frac{d^2z}{dt^2} = \frac{k}{c_1} e^{i\theta} \frac{d\theta}{dt}. \tag{2.524}$$

Integrating this gives

$$\frac{dz}{dt} = \frac{ik}{c_1} e^{i\theta} + ic_2 e^{i\theta_0} \tag{2.525}$$

where c_2 and θ_0 are real constants and $c_2 \geqq 0$. There are several ways in which the above formulas can be combined to obtain others. For example, we can equate the right members of (2.512) and (2.525) and multiply the result by $e^{-i\theta}$ to obtain

$$\frac{dr}{dt} + ir\frac{d\theta}{dt} = \frac{ik}{c_1} + ic_2 e^{-i(\theta-\theta_0)}. \tag{2.526}$$

Equating real and imaginary parts gives the two equations

$$\frac{dr}{dt} = c_2 \sin(\theta - \theta_0) \tag{2.527}$$

$$r\frac{d\theta}{dt} = \frac{k}{c_1} + c_2 \cos(\theta - \theta_0). \tag{2.528}$$

Eliminating $d\theta/dt$ from (2.523) and (2.528) gives

$$r = \frac{c_1^2}{k + c_1 c_2 \cos(\theta - \theta_0)}. \tag{2.53}$$

Depending upon the position and velocity of the satellite at some particular time, say $t = 0$, the orbit of the satellite is all or a part of the graph of this ordinary polar coordinate equation. Supposing, for simplicity, that the axes are oriented so that $\theta_0 = 0$, we can put this equation in the form

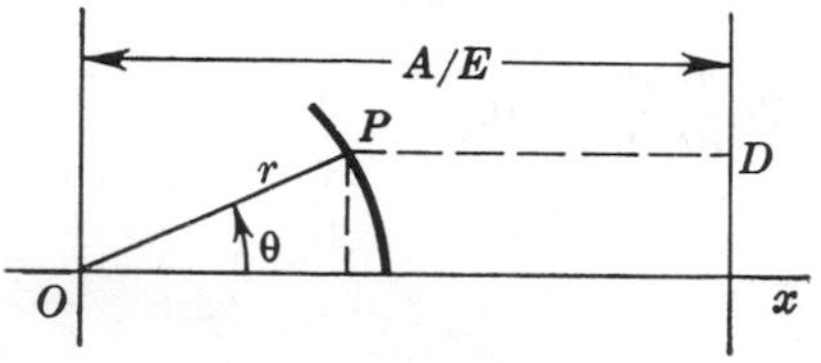

FIG. 2.532

$$(2.531) \qquad r = \frac{A}{1 + E \cos \theta}$$

where

$$A = c_1^2/k > 0 \text{ and } E = c_1c_2/k \geqq 0.$$

When $E = 0$, the orbit is a circle. When $E > 0$, the graph of (2.531) is the locus of points P (Fig. 2.532) with rectangular coordinates (x, y) and polar coordinates (θ, r), such that $x < A/E$ and $OP = E \times PD$ where OP is the distance r from the origin to P and PD is the distance $A/E - r \cos \theta$ from P to the line $x = A/E$. Thus, when $E > 0$, the graph of (2.531) is a conic having eccentricity E, the origin for a focus, and the line $x = A/E$ for a directrix. The conic is an ellipse when $0 < E < 1$, a parabola when $E = 1$, and half of a hyperbola when $E > 1$.

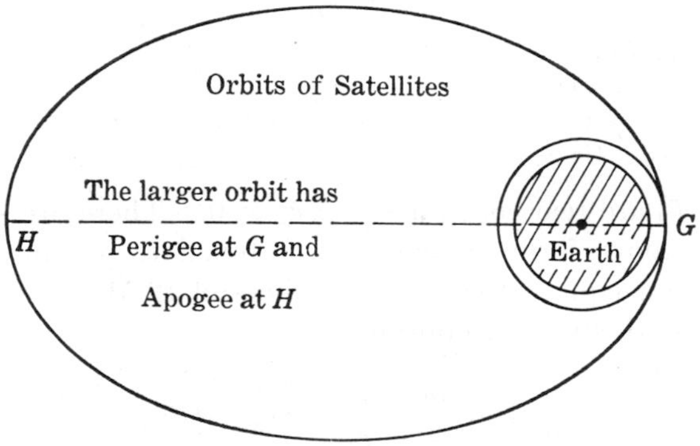

FIG. 2.533

Various of the above formulas are useful for various purposes. For example, if the numerical values of the constants c_1, c_2, and θ_0 in (2.523) and (2.527) are known, and if the values of θ and r are known at some time t_0, then computers can use (2.523) and (2.527) to find numerical approximations to θ and r at later times. Numerical methods are required because, except when the orbit is a circle or parabola, θ and r are not elementary functions of t. In order to solve the following problems, it is necessary to use some of the above formulas, but it is not necessary to be able to derive them with facility.

Problem 2.54

Of the above formulas use appropriate ones to determine the constants c_1, c_2, and θ_0 when the satellite is a satellite of the earth which is released, at time $t = 0$ by the last of a battery of rockets, with $\theta = 0$, $r = r_0$, $d\theta/dt = \omega_0$, and $dr/dt = \Omega_0$. Use your result to determine the conditions under which the orbit will be a circle. *Ans.:* The formulas needed are (2.523), (2.527), (2.528), and $k = gR^2$. These give $c_1 = r_0^2\omega_0$,

$$c_2 = \left[\Omega_0^2 + \left(r_0\omega_0 - \frac{gR^2}{r_0^2\omega_0}\right)^2\right]^{\frac{1}{2}}, \tag{2.541}$$

and, in case $c_2 \neq 0$, θ_0 is then determined from the two formulas

$$\sin\theta_0 = -\frac{\Omega_0}{c_2}, \qquad \cos\theta_0 = \frac{r_0\omega_0 - gR^2/r_0^2\omega_0}{c_2}. \tag{2.542}$$

In case $c_2 = 0$, the orbit is a circle and θ_0 is both irrelevant and undetermined. The orbit will be a circle if and only if $\Omega_0 = 0$ and $r_0^3\omega_0^2 = gR^2$.

Problem 2.543

Find the number of minutes required for a satellite to complete a circuit of a circular orbit 300 miles above the surface of the earth. *Solution:* When feet and seconds are used for units, the angular velocity in radians per second is constant and is the ω_0 in the last formula of the previous problem. Hence

$$\omega_0 = (g/r_0)^{\frac{1}{2}}(R/r_0). \tag{2.544}$$

Taking $g = 32$, $R = 4{,}000 \times 5{,}280$, and $r_0 = 4{,}300 \times 5{,}280$ gives $\omega_0 = 1.1 \times 10^{-3}$. This is equivalent to 910 seconds per radian or 5,700 seconds per revolution or 95 minutes per revolution. History records that the first sputnik, fired back in 1957, completed a circuit of its elliptic but nearly circular orbit in 96 minutes.

Problem 2.55

Suppose that, in the previous problems, $\Omega_0 = 0$. If $\omega_0 > 0$ and $r_0^3\omega_0^2 < gR^2$, show that $\theta_0 = \pi$, that

$$r = \frac{r_0^4\omega_0^2}{gR^2 - |r_0^3\omega_0^2 - gR^2|\cos\theta}, \tag{2.551}$$

that the *apogee* of the orbit (the point on the orbit farthest from the earth) is the point from which the satellite is released, that the satellite will not sail around the center of the earth without striking the surface of the earth unless

$$r_0^3\omega_0^2 > \frac{2gR^3}{R + r_0}, \tag{2.552}$$

and that if (2.552) holds then the distance from the center of the earth to the *perigee* of the orbit (the point on the orbit nearest the earth) is

$$\frac{r_0^4\omega_0^2}{2gR^2 - r_0^3\omega_0^2}. \tag{2.553}$$

Problem 2.56

Suppose, as before, that $\Omega_0 = 0$. If $\omega_0 > 0$ and $r_0^3\omega_0^2 > gR^2$, show that $\theta_0 = 0$, that

$$r = \frac{r_0^4\omega_0^2}{gR^2 + |r_0^3\omega_0^2 - gR^2| \cos\theta}, \tag{2.561}$$

that the perigee of the orbit is the point from which the satellite is released, and that the distance from the center of the earth to the apogee of the orbit is

$$\frac{r_0^4\omega_0^2}{2gR^2 - r_0^3\omega_0^2} \tag{2.562}$$

provided the denominator is positive. Show that if $r_0^3\omega_0^2 \geqq 2gR^2$, then the orbit has no apogee and the projectile is not a satellite because it has become a space traveller which is never destined to return to the neighborhood of the earth. Finally, show that in the special case when $r_0^3\omega_0^2 = 2gR^2$ the initial speed s of the projectile is given by the formula

$$s = r_0\omega_0 = (2gR^2/r_0)^{\frac{1}{2}} \tag{2.563}$$

and that using the approximation $r_0 = R$ gives the well-known formula $s = (2gR)^{\frac{1}{2}}$ for the *escape speed,* and that $s = 7$ miles per second.

Problem 2.57

Everybody should know some history. Before the heyday of Newton, Kepler deduced his famous laws with the aid of many remarkable observations of the planets (satellites of the sun) made and carefully recorded by Tycho Brahe (1546–1601). The first Kepler law says that the orbits of the planets are ellipses with the sun at a focus. The second is the law involving areal velocities. The third, which we do not need now, will appear later in Problem 2.58. Thus Newton knew about the formulas

$$r = \frac{A}{1 + E\cos\theta}, \qquad r^2\frac{d\theta}{dt} = c_1. \tag{2.571}$$

From these formulas, Newton derived the inverse-square law which describes the forces which the sun exerts upon its satellites. The result led Newton to originate his law of universal gravitation. It is now our task to see how Newton might have extracted information from (2.571) if he had known about complex exponentials. Start with

$$z = re^{i\theta}, \tag{2.572}$$

differentiate with respect to t, and make appropriate uses of (2.571) to obtain

$$v = \frac{dz}{dt} = \frac{c_1 i}{A}e^{i\theta} + \frac{c_1 iE}{A}. \tag{2.573}$$

Continue the work to obtain

$$a = \frac{d^2z}{dt^2} = -\frac{c_1^2}{A}\frac{1}{r^2}e^{i\theta}. \tag{2.574}$$

Thus the satellite is accelerated toward the origin, and the magnitude of the acceleration is inversely proportional to the square of the distance from the origin to the satellite. This is the fundamental discovery of Newton. *Remark:* It is said that Newton delayed publication of his theory of attraction (or gravitation) for 20 years because he was dissatisfied with his theory until he was able to prove the following fact. Two spheres which are radially homogeneous—*i.e.*, homogeneous in the sense that their densities depend only upon distances from their centers—attract each other as though their total masses were concentrated at their centers.

Problem 2.58

We now work out the third Kepler law, which gives the period T of a satellite whose orbit is an ellipse. Supposing that $0 < c_1c_2 < k$ and that the coordinate system is oriented so that $\theta_0 = 0$, show that the rectangular coordinate equation of the orbit (2.53) is

(2.5801)
$$\frac{(x+h)^2}{a^2} + \frac{y^2}{b^2} = 1$$

where

(2.5802)
$$h = \frac{c_1^3c_2}{k^2 - c_1^2c_2^2}, \qquad a = \frac{c_1^2k}{k^2 - c_1^2c_2^2}, \qquad b = \frac{c_1^2}{(k^2 - c_1^2c_2^2)^{\frac{1}{2}}}.$$

Show that

(2.5803)
$$\frac{b}{a} = \left(1 - \frac{c_1^2c_2^2}{k^2}\right)^{\frac{1}{2}}$$

and hence that $0 < b < a$. Thus a is the length of the major semiaxis of the ellipse. The area A of the ellipse is, as is shown in the calculus,

(2.5804)
$$A = \pi ab = \pi \frac{c_1^4k}{(k^2 - c_1^2c_2^2)^{\frac{3}{2}}}.$$

Since the radius vector from the origin to the satellite sweeps out an area at the constant rate $c_1/2$, the number T of units of time it takes the satellite to complete one circuit of the elliptic orbit must be $T = 2A/c_1$. Use this fact, (2.5804), and (2.5802) to show that

(2.5805)
$$T = \frac{2\pi}{k^{\frac{1}{2}}}\left(\frac{c_1^2k}{k^2 - c_1^2c_2^2}\right)^{\frac{3}{2}} = \frac{2\pi}{k^{\frac{1}{2}}} a^{\frac{3}{2}}.$$

Hence

(2.5806)
$$T^2 = \frac{4\pi^2}{k} a^3.$$

The constant k depends only upon the mass of the central body and upon the units used. The points on an elliptic orbit at minimum and maximum distances from a focus lie on the major axis, and the sum of these two distances is $2a$, the length of the major axis. The average a of these two distances is called the *mean distance* of the orbit. Thus (2.5806) gives the following third Kepler law involving the periods of satellites which sail around a central body in elliptic orbits: *The squares of the periods are proportional to the cubes of the mean distances.*

Problem 2.581

The last of a battery of rockets discharges a satellite of the earth into an elliptic orbit which lies effectively outside the atmosphere of the earth. Letting r_0 denote the distance from the center of the earth and λ the speed at the moment of discharge, show that the mean distance a of the orbit is given by the first of the equivalent formulas

$$a = \frac{gR^2}{2(gR^2/r_0) - \lambda^2}, \qquad \lambda^2 = gR^2\left(\frac{2}{r_0} - \frac{1}{a}\right). \tag{2.5811}$$

Remark: This shows that a depends only upon r_0 and λ, being independent of the direction in which the satellite is discharged. This and the third Kepler law imply that if the members of a family of satellites are simultaneously projected from the same place with equal speeds but with different directions, there will be a reunion $[4\pi^2a^3/(gR^2)^{\frac{1}{2}}]^{\frac{1}{2}}$ seconds later. *Hint:* The formula (2.5802) gives a in terms of quantities appearing in Problem 2.54. Do not forget that (2.514) gives a formula for speed.

Remark 2.582

It has been said that the gravitational pull of the moon should provide very substantial assistance in sending a spaceship to the moon. This remark is for those who wish to invest a moment to see that this is not true. We suppose that the earth and moon are stationary spheres of masses M and $M/81$, that R is the radius of the earth, and that the distance from the earth to the moon is $60R$.

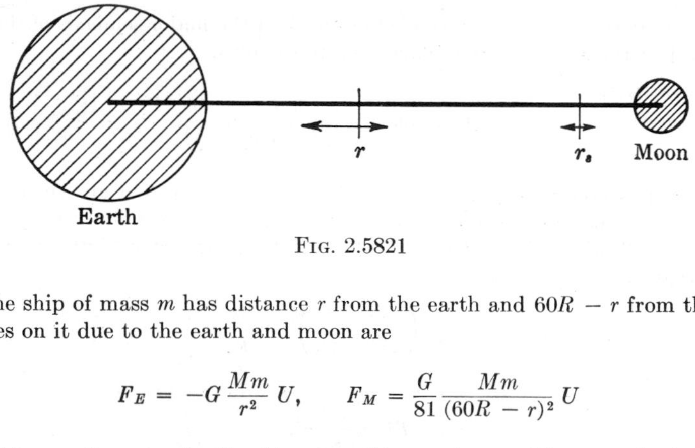

FIG. 2.5821

When the ship of mass m has distance r from the earth and $60R - r$ from the moon the forces on it due to the earth and moon are

$$F_E = -G\frac{Mm}{r^2}U, \qquad F_M = \frac{G}{81}\frac{Mm}{(60R - r)^2}U$$

where U is a unit vector in the direction of increasing r. The magnitudes of these forces are equal at the *stagnation point* for which $r = r_s = 54R$. The work done against the attraction of the earth in taking the ship from the surface of the earth to the stagnation point is

$$\int_R^{54R} |F_E|dr = GMm\left[\frac{1}{R} - \frac{1}{54R}\right].$$

The assistance received from the moon during this operation has magnitude (measured in work)

$$\int_R^{54R} |F_M| dr = GMm\left[\frac{1}{486R} - \frac{1}{4779R}\right].$$

The net amount of work required to get the ship to the stagnation point is therefore only 2 per cent less than the work GMm/R required to overcome all of the attraction of the earth and only 0.4 per cent less than the work to send the ship to the moon without benefit of the attraction of the moon. Even after the stagnation point has been passed, the attraction of the moon is not completely helpful to passengers who do not want to hit the moon too hard.

Problem 2.59

Suppose that, instead of (2.52), we have

$$\frac{d^2z}{dt^2} = f(\theta, r)e^{i\theta} \tag{2.5901}$$

where $f(\theta, r)$ is a given real function of θ and r. This means that, whenever $f(\theta, r) \neq 0$, points are accelerated toward the origin or away from the origin. The forces producing this acceleration are called *central forces*. Using the method by which (2.523) was derived, prove that the Kepler formula

$$r^2\frac{d\theta}{dt} = c_1 \tag{2.5902}$$

must hold. [When you have done this, you have proved the following very reasonable theorem: Central forces acting upon a particle of unit mass cannot change the central angular momentum (sometimes called moment of momentum because that is what it is) of the particle.]

Problem 2.591

A smuggler in a boat is known to have started from the well-known origin at time $t = 0$ and to have sped away with speed k_1 in an unknown direction. Our speed k_2 exceeds k_1 and we want to catch him, but unfortunately we have no radar or sonar and the visibility is so bad that we cannot see him until we are much closer to him. What shall we do? *Hint:* It is clear that we should find and navigate a part of a path such that our distance from O is k_1t. Our position vector z is then

$$z = k_1te^{i\theta(t)}$$

where $\theta(t)$ is a real function of t to be determined in such a way that our speed will be k_2. *Ans.:* We go to and follow a path for which

$$z = k_1te^{i(\lambda \log t + c)}$$

where c is a real constant and $\lambda = (k_2^2/k_1^2 - 1)^{\frac{1}{2}}$. Putting $r = k_1t$ and $\theta = \lambda \log t + c$ yields $r = k_1e^{(\theta - c)/\lambda}$ for the ordinary polar equation of the path.

Problem 2.592

Solve Problem 2.33 by use of complex exponentials, obtaining full information comparable to that given in Problem 2.591.

Problem 2.593

Discuss the derivation and an application of the formulas

$$a = \frac{d^2z}{dt^2} = -ig$$

$$v = \frac{dz}{dt} = -igt + c_1 + ic_2,$$

$$x + iy = z = -\tfrac{1}{2}igt^2 + (c_1 + ic_2)t + (c_3 + ic_4),$$

$$x = c_1t + c_3,$$

$$y = -\tfrac{1}{2}gt^2 + c_2t + c_4,$$

where the c's are real constants. What is the reason, if any, for starting with $-ig$ instead of g in the right-hand side of the first equation? When $c_1 \neq 0$, describe the result of eliminating t from the last two equations.

CHAPTER 3

LINEAR EQUATIONS OF FIRST ORDER

3.0. Introduction. In this chapter we solve successively the linear differential equations of the forms

$$y' = ky, \qquad y' = ky + a, \qquad y' + py = q$$

in which k and a are constants and p and q are functions of x. Then we discuss several problems designed to illustrate various methods by which differential equations are derived (or perhaps conjured up) and used.

3.01. Solution of y′ = ky. If k is a constant, if $y(x)$ is a solution of the equation

$$\frac{dy}{dx} = ky, \tag{3.011}$$

and if we know that $y(x) > 0$ for each x, then we can separate the variables to obtain

$$\frac{1}{y}\frac{dy}{dx} = k \tag{3.012}$$

or

$$\frac{d}{dx} \log y = k$$

so that $\log y = kx + c$ and $y = e^{kx+c} = e^{kx}e^c$; if we put $A = e^c$, then

$$y = Ae^{kx}. \tag{3.013}$$

Similarly, if $y(x)$ is a solution of (3.011) and we know that $y(x) < 0$ for each x, then we can obtain the results of replacing y by $-y$ in (3.012) and (3.013) and can conclude that $y = -Ae^{kx}$. All this shows that if $y(x)$ is a solution of (3.011) which never vanishes (*i.e.*, is never zero), then there must be a nonzero constant B such that $y = Be^{kx}$. Conversely, if $y = Be^{kx}$, then differentiation and substitution show that y satisfies (3.011).

If $y(x)$ is known to be a solution of $y' = ky$ and we do not know that $y(x) \neq 0$ for all x, then the preceding method of determining $y(x)$ cannot be used. To divide by $y(x)$ would violate the *fundamental commandment of mathematics* which prohibits division by zero.*

We now assume merely that $y(x)$ is a solution of $y' = ky$ and determine the form of $y(x)$ by an impeccable process which does not involve division by $y(x)$. The first step is to write the equation in the standard form

$$\frac{dy}{dx} - ky = 0. \tag{3.014}$$

The next step is the key step in the process. We multiply by the *integrating factor* e^{-kx} to obtain

$$e^{-kx}\left(\frac{dy}{dx} - ky\right) = 0. \tag{3.015}$$

This is equivalent to

$$\frac{d}{dx}\, e^{-kx}y = 0, \tag{3.016}$$

the left side of (3.016) being the same as the left side of (3.015). Everybody who knows how to differentiate products and exponentials must check this carefully, and everybody else better learn how to differentiate products and exponentials and then check this carefully. After (3.016) has been reached, we have very clear sailing. From (3.016) we conclude that there must be a constant c for which $e^{-kx}y = c$ and hence

$$y = ce^{kx}. \tag{3.017}$$

Therefore each solution of (3.015) must have the form ce^{kx}; and it is easy to see that, if c is a constant (positive, negative, or 0) then $y = ce^{kx}$ is a solution of (3.015). Since e^{kx} never vanishes, it follows that each solution of $y' = ky$ is either always zero (if $c = 0$) or never zero (if $c \neq 0$).

3.02. Solution of $y' = ky + a$. The method of solving the equation $y' = ky$ can be applied to solve the equation

$$\frac{dy}{dx} = ky + a \tag{3.021}$$

when k and a are constants and $k \neq 0$. The trick is to transpose the term ky and multiply by e^{-kx} to write (3.021) in the form

$$e^{-kx}\left(\frac{dy}{dx} - ky\right) = ae^{-kx}. \tag{3.022}$$

* It is not unreasonable to suppose that the reader learned while studying arithmetic or some more advanced subject that one writes $x = b/a$ when and only when there is exactly one number x such that $ax = b$. If $a \neq 0$, the equation $ax = b$ has exactly one solution, and this is b/a. If $a = 0$ and $b \neq 0$, there is *no* number x such that $ax = b$; so b/a is meaningless. If $a = b = 0$, then *every* number x satisfies the equation; so again b/a is meaningless. If $a \neq 0$, the equation $ax = ay$ implies $x = y$; but the equation $0 \cdot 2 = 0 \cdot 3$ does *not* imply that $2 = 3$.

Again e^{-kx} is an integrating factor. The equation (3.022) is equivalent to

$$\frac{d}{dx} e^{-kx}y = ae^{-kx} \tag{3.023}$$

and

$$e^{-kx}y = A - \frac{a}{k} e^{-kx} \tag{3.024}$$

and

$$y = Ae^{kx} - \frac{a}{k}. \tag{3.025}$$

Thus the functions y obtained by giving different values to the constant A in (3.025) are solutions (and the only solutions) of (3.021).

Problem 3.026

Show that if $y(x)$ is a solution of (3.021) for which $ky + a$ never vanishes, then it is possible to separate the variables and derive (3.025).

Problem 3.027

Solve (3.021) for the case in which $k = 0$, and notice that the solutions look quite different from (3.025). One who has a little time and skill at his disposal should enjoy proving and interpreting the following: If, for each fixed k, $y(k, x)$ is the solution of (3.021) which is equal to 1 when x is 0, then

$$\lim_{k \to 0} y(k, x) = y(0, x).$$

3.03. Solution of Linear Equations of First Order. By a linear differential equation of the first order, we mean an equation of the form

$$\alpha(x) \frac{dy}{dx} + \beta(x)y = \gamma(x) \tag{3.031}$$

where $\alpha(x)$, $\beta(x)$, and $\gamma(x)$ are given functions of x. If there is no interval of values of x over which $\alpha(x) \neq 0$, we shun the equation. Otherwise we select an interval over which $\alpha(x) \neq 0$ and divide by $\alpha(x)$ to put the equation in the standard form

$$\frac{dy}{dx} + p(x)y = q(x). \tag{3.032}$$

We suppose that x is confined to an interval over which $p(x)$ and $q(x)$ are continuous, and that x_0 is a point of this interval.

The very important equation (3.032) can be solved by a method that must be both thoroughly understood and remembered. The first step is to find a function $P(x)$ whose derivative with respect to x is $p(x)$. If $p(x)$ is, as it often is in specific elementary applications, an innocent elementary function for which $\int p(x)dx$ can be evaluated, then

$$P(x) = \int f(x)dx.$$

In every case, we can put

$$P(x) = \int_{x_0}^{x} p(t)dt. \tag{3.033}$$

The essential point to remember when solving problems is the following: *When the equation*

$$\frac{dy}{dx} + p(x)y = q(x) \tag{3.034}$$

is multiplied by the integrating factor $e^{P(x)}$, *it becomes*

$$\frac{d}{dx} e^{P(x)}y = e^{P(x)}q(x) \tag{3.035}$$

and use of fundamental ideas then gives $y(x)$. Be very sure that there is no mystery about this; differentiate the product $e^{P(x)}y$ and see that everything is as stated.

In very many important applications, it is very easy to employ this ritual to obtain simple formulas for the solutions (and all the solutions) of (3.034). It is clear that the final formulas will be simplest when the given function $p(x)$ is a constant or some other nice little elementary function of x for which $\int p(x)dx$ is also a nice elementary function and the right side of (3.035) is easy to integrate. Many examples appear in this chapter, and the wide world contains many others. There is much to be learned by solving many important special problems one by one. There is also much to be learned by solving many problems all at once. For the latter reason, we plunge into a section which should be read before special problems are solved and should sometimes be thought about when problems are being solved.

3.1. Theory, Inputs, Outputs. We start with the equation

$$\frac{dy}{dx} + p(x)y = q(x) \tag{3.11}$$

where $p(x)$ and $q(x)$ are given functions which are continuous over some interval of values of x which contains x_0. This equation and more or less similar equations of higher order often appear in applied mathematics in situations where x represents time, $q(x)$ represents an applied mechanical or electromotive force which engineers call an *input*, and $y(x)$ represents a response which engineers call an *output*. In fact whenever such equations occur we can always give the variables and functions the interpretations they have in a problem involving currents and charges in an electrical network; this is the principle upon which analog computers work. The engineering terminology is so neat and helpful that we adopt it. Thus $q(x)$ is the *input* of the differential equation (3.11), and $y(x)$ is the *output*. Now we are getting somewhere. Input and output are related like cause (or partial cause) and effect. Scientists, and perhaps even philosophers, should cultivate abilities to discover relationships between causes and effects. Hence we should get busy and attack (3.11) to see whether or how inputs $q(x)$ determine outputs $y(x)$.

According to Section 3.03, the first step is to obtain a function $P(x)$ for which $P'(x) = p(x)$. Since we cannot now give a simple elementary formula for $P(x)$, we put it in the form

$$P(x) = \int_{x_0}^{x} p(s)ds. \tag{3.12}$$

Using the integrating factor $e^{P(x)}$, which can never be 0, we see that (3.11) holds iff (if and only if)*

$$e^{P(x)}\left[\frac{dy}{dx} + p(x)y\right] = q(x)e^{P(x)}. \tag{3.13}$$

Again comes practice of the art of differentiating a product to show that (3.13) holds iff

$$\frac{d}{dx}\, e^{P(x)}y = q(x)e^{P(x)}. \tag{3.14}$$

By the fundamental theorem of the calculus (Theorem 2.03) this holds iff

$$e^{P(x)}y = A + \int_{x_0}^{x} q(t)e^{P(t)}\, dt \tag{3.15}$$

where A is a constant. Putting $x = x_0$ in (3.15), and using (3.12) which shows that $P(x_0) = 0$, gives the relation $y(x_0) = A$. Hence $y(x)$ satisfies (3.11) iff

$$e^{P(x)}y = y(x_0) + \int_{x_0}^{x} q(t)e^{P(t)}\, dt. \tag{3.16}$$

Finally, since $e^{P(x)}$ is never 0, $y(x)$ satisfies (3.11) iff

$$y(x) = y(x_0)e^{-P(x)} + e^{-P(x)} \int_{x_0}^{x} q(t)e^{P(t)}\, dt. \tag{3.17}$$

Thus (3.11) is thoroughly and completely solved.

This formula packs a tremendous amount of information. In the first place, it tells us that if $p(x)$ and $q(x)$ are continuous over an interval I (finite or infinite) containing a point x_0, then to each number y_0 there corresponds one and only one function $y(x)$ defined over I such that $y(x_0) = y_0$ and the equation (3.11) is satisfied over I. Moreover it gives an explicit formula for $y(x)$; there are no implicit function jumbles like those that often appear when equations are solved by separation of variables.

* This convenient abbreviation "iff," standing for "if and only if," will be used throughout the book.

If we think of $y(x)$ as being a number which tells where we will be at a time x following a time x_0, (3.17) is thoroughly enlightening. It says that the place we will occupy at time x depends upon x_0, x, and just three other things: (i) the place we occupy at time x_0, this being $y(x_0)$; (ii) the amount of kicking around we get in the time interval $x_0 \leqq t \leqq x$, the thing giving this information being $q(t)$; and (iii) a function $p(x)$ which determines $P(x)$, this being some kind of a personal function that depends upon us alone and not upon the forces which a capricious world brings to bear upon us. You can look at (3.17) all day and still fail to find anything else there. Moreover (3.17) tells us exactly how $y(x)$ depends upon these three things. It is all very remarkable; in particular the formula is educated enough to know that our position at time x does not depend upon the buffetings that occur at later times.

We now look at (3.17) to see what it says about inputs and outputs. In order to simplify our discussion, we shall suppose that $p(x)$ remains a fixed given function; in applications, $p(x)$ is determined by knowledge of the mechanical or electrical hardware involved. Thus $P(x)$ is to be regarded as a fixed known function. Then (3.17) tells us that, whatever the input $q(t)$ may be, the output $y(t)$ is the sum of two terms which we can call partial outputs. The first depends only upon the output at time x_0, and is completely independent of the input. By setting $q(t) = 0$, we can see that this is the output that results when there is no input. Those who are familiar with trees, or L-R-C oscillators, or banks, or such things should see how there can be outputs when there are no inputs. A tree which is swaying at time x_0 will continue to sway for a while even when no breezes are present; a charged capacitor can make electrons slosh to and fro in the oscillator even when no external electromotive force is applied; and an interest-earning account can exist and continue to grow even when no deposits are being made. The second term is 0 when $x = x_0$, is completely independent of the output when $x = x_0$, and depends only upon the input $q(t)$ over the range $x_0 \leqq t \leqq x$. We shall hear a great deal more about these matters in Chapter 6.

One of the important features of a function y is its behavior for large values of x. Borrowing another term from engineering, we will say that y is a *transient* if $y(x) \to 0$ as $x \to \infty$. Observe that the first term in the right member of (3.17) is always a transient if $P(x) \to \infty$ as $x \to \infty$.

3.18. Problems. In spite of the great importance of the formula (3.17), it is not necessary to learn it; we can hunt it up in the book when we want to use it. Even when (3.17) is temporarily (or perhaps permanently) learned, it is not a good idea to use it to obtain solutions of problems in which $p(x)$ has an elementary integral $P(x)$. It is more informative, more pleasant, and perhaps even quicker to employ integrating factors as directed in the statement involving (3.034).

Problem 3.181

Verify each of the steps in the solution of the equation

$$L \frac{dy}{dt} + Ry = E_0 e^{kt} \tag{3.1811}$$

in which L, R, E_0, and k are constants for which $L \neq 0$ and $R + kL \neq 0$. Dividing by L and using the integrating factor $e^{(R/L)t}$ gives

$$\frac{d}{dt} e^{(R/L)t}y = \frac{E_0}{L} e^{(R/L+k)t},$$

$$e^{(R/L)t}y = c + \frac{E_0}{R + kL} e^{(R/L+k)t}$$

and hence we obtain the solution

$$y = ce^{-(R/L)t} + \frac{E_0}{R + kL} e^{kt}. \tag{3.1812}$$

Observe that the first term of the right member is a transient when L and R are positive. It is only the last term which depends upon the input E_0e^{kt}.

Problem 3.182

Solve some of the following problems by use of integrating factors.

(a) $\frac{dy}{dx} + ay = 0$ — *Ans.:* $y = ce^{-ax}$

(b) $\frac{dy}{dx} + ay = k$ — *Ans.:* $y = \frac{k}{a} + ce^{-ax}$

(c) $\frac{dy}{dx} = ax + by$ — *Ans.:* $y = ce^{bx} - \frac{a}{b}x - \frac{a}{b^2}$

(d) $\frac{dy}{dx} + xy = 0$ — *Ans.:* $y = ce^{-x^2/2}$

(e) $\frac{dy}{dx} + xy = x$ — *Ans.:* $y = 1 + ce^{-x^2/2}$

(f) $\frac{dy}{dx} + my = e^{kx}\ (m + k \neq 0)$ — *Ans.:* $y = \frac{1}{k + m} e^{kx} + ce^{-mx}$

(g) $\frac{dy}{dx} + my = e^{-mx}$ — *Ans.:* $y = xe^{-mx} + ce^{-mx}$

(h) $\frac{dy}{dx} + \frac{1}{x} y = 12x$ — *Ans.:* $y = 4x^2 + \frac{c}{x}$

(i) $\frac{dy}{dx} + \frac{2}{x} y = 12$ — *Ans.:* $y = 4x + \frac{c}{x^2}$

(j) $x\frac{dy}{dx} + (1 + x)y = e^x$ — *Ans.:* $y = \frac{e^x + ce^{-x}}{2x}$

(k) $\frac{dy}{dx} + (\tan x)y = 0$ — *Ans.:* $y = c \cos x$

(l) $\frac{dy}{dx} + (\sin x)y = kx$ — *Ans.:* $y = ce^{\cos x} + ke^{\cos x} \int_0^x te^{-\cos t}\,dt$

(m) $\frac{dy}{dx} + \frac{2x}{x^2 + 1} y = x$ — *Ans.:* $y = \frac{x^4 + 2x^2 + c}{4(x^2 + 1)}$

(n) $(1 - x^2)\dfrac{dy}{dx} + xy = kx$ *Ans.:* $y = k + c\sqrt{1 - x^2}$

(o) $\dfrac{dy}{dx} = 2x - 2xy$ *Ans.:* $y = 1 + ce^{-x^2}$

(p) $\dfrac{dy}{dx} + \dfrac{kx}{1 + x^2}y = 0$ *Ans.:* $y = c(1 + x^2)^{-k/2}$

Problem 3.183

Show that, if m is a constant and $q(x)$ is continuous, the solution of the equation

$$\frac{dy}{dx} + my = q(x)$$

for which $y(x_0) = A$ can be written in the form

$$y(x) = Ae^{-m(x-x_0)} + \int_{x_0}^{x} e^{-m(x-t)}q(t)dt.$$

If $m = 2$, $x_0 = 0$, and $A = 100$, give the range of values of x for which $q(x)$ must be known before $y(10)$ can be computed.

Problem 3.184

Find all continuous functions $y(x)$ for which

$$y(x) = 1 + \int_0^x y(t)dt.$$ *Ans.:* $y = e^x$.

Hint: Start by differentiating the given equation with respect to x.

Problem 3.1841

Supposing that M and k are positive constants, find the functions $s(x)$, if any, for which

$$M = Ms(x) + k\int_0^x s(x - t)dt.$$

Hint: The integral can be replaced by $\int_0^x s(t)dt$ and differentiation yields a linear differential equation which $s(x)$ must satisfy. *Ans.:* $s(x) = e^{-(k/M)x}$.

Problem 3.185

Find, for each equation below, all functions $y(x)$ satisfying the equation over $-\infty < x < \infty$.

(a) $x\dfrac{dy}{dx} + y = 2x$ *Ans.:* $y = x$

(b) $x\dfrac{dy}{dx} + 2x^2y = 1$ *Ans.:* None

Problem 3.1851

Show that the outputs of the equation $y'(x) + p(x)y(x) = 0$ are all transients iff

$$\lim_{x \to \infty} \int_{x_0}^{x} p(t)dt = \infty.$$

Problem 3.186

This is a chance to gain more familiarity with complex exponentials. In (3.1811), let L, R, and E_0 be positive constants, let $k = i\omega$ where ω is a real constant, and let $y = J + iI$ where J and I are real functions of t. With the aid of the Euler formula (2.501), show that (3.1811) can be written

$$L\frac{dJ}{dt} + RJ + i\left[L\frac{dI}{dt} + RI\right] = E_0 \cos \omega t + iE_0 \sin \omega t. \tag{3.1861}$$

Show that

$$\frac{E_0}{R + i\omega L} = E_0 \frac{R - i\omega L}{(R + i\omega L)(R - i\omega L)} = E_0 \frac{R - i\omega L}{R^2 + \omega^2 L^2}$$

and hence that (3.1812) can be written

$$J + iI = c_1 e^{-(R/L)t} + ic_2 e^{-(R/L)t} + E_0 \frac{R - i\omega L}{R^2 + \omega^2 L^2} e^{i\omega t} \tag{3.1862}$$

where c_1 and c_2 are real constants. In Chapter 6, we shall learn to handle these things very neatly. Meanwhile, show that equating the coefficients of i in (3.1861) and (3.1862) gives

$$L\frac{dI}{dt} + RI = E_0 \sin \omega t \tag{3.1863}$$

and

$$I = c_2 e^{-(R/L)t} + E_0 \frac{R \sin \omega t - \omega L \cos \omega t}{R^2 + \omega^2 L^2}. \tag{3.1864}$$

Show that if ϕ is the angle (there is just one) between 0 and $\pi/2$ for which $\tan \phi = \omega L/R$ and accordingly

$$\cos \phi = \frac{R}{(R^2 + \omega^2 L^2)^{\frac{1}{2}}}, \qquad \sin \phi = \frac{\omega L}{(R^2 + \omega^2 L^2)^{\frac{1}{2}}} \tag{3.1865}$$

then (3.1864) can be put in the more attractive form

$$I = c_2 e^{-(R/L)t} + \frac{E_0}{(R^2 + \omega^2 L^2)^{\frac{1}{2}}} \sin (\omega t - \phi). \tag{3.1866}$$

The first term on the right is a transient, and the last term is a sinusoidal output. We shall learn more about these things later.

Problem 3.187

By use of an integrating factor and using only real functions, solve (3.1863) and obtain the solution (3.1864). *Remark:* A formula for the unpleasant integral

$$\int e^{-(R/L)t} \sin \omega t \, dt$$

is required. It can be derived by integration by parts provided that one knows or devises the proper trick. It is in every respectable integral table. This is the only time you will be asked to bother with such integrals; complex exponentials will eliminate them.

Problem 3.1871

A tapered concrete column h feet high is to be designed to support a load of W pounds distributed uniformly over the top. A building code forbids pressures exceeding P pounds per square foot, and concrete weighs k pounds per cubic foot. Supposing that no concrete is wasted, find the area $A(y)$ of the cross section of the column at height y above the base. *Hint:* Sketch a figure and show that the problem requires that

$$PA(y) = W + \int_y^h kA(t)dt.$$

The derivative with respect to y of the last term is $-kA(y)$.

Ans.: $A(y) = (W/P)e^{(k/P)(h-y)}$.

Problem 3.1872

This is a very simple problem in renewal theory. It is known that

$$y'(x) + p(x)y(x) = q(x)$$

where $p(x)$ is a given function. Let M be a given constant. We want to determine an input (or renewal function) $q(x)$ so that if $y(0) = M$, then $y(x)$ must be M whenever $x > 0$. Investigate this.

Problem 3.188

Find an equation in Section 1.1 which shows that if u satisfies the Laplace equation in spherical coordinates and if u depends only upon r, then

$$\frac{d^2u}{dr^2} + \frac{2}{r}\frac{du}{dr} = 0.$$

Show that in any such situation (where u could be the electrical potential between two concentric charged spherical shells, or the steady-state temperature in a homogeneous isotropic material between two concentric spherical surfaces which are maintained at constant temperatures) there must be constants c_1 and c_2 such that

$$u = c_2 + \frac{c_1}{r}.$$

Show that if $u(r_1) = u_1$ and $u(r_2) = u_2$, then

$$u = u_1 + \frac{u_2 - u_1}{\dfrac{1}{r_2} - \dfrac{1}{r_1}}\left(\frac{1}{r} - \frac{1}{r_1}\right).$$

Show that if A is the area of a sphere of radius r, then

$$A\frac{du}{dr} = 4\pi\frac{u_2 - u_1}{\dfrac{1}{r_1} - \dfrac{1}{r_2}}.$$

Hint: Start by finding du/dr which can be called $y(r)$. *Remark:* If k is (in appropriate units) the thermal conductivity of the material noted above, then $-kA\ du/dr$ is the rate [measured in calories or Btu (British thermal units)] at which heat flows outward over the spherical surface of radius r.

Problem 3.1881

Find an equation in Section 1.1 which shows that if u satisfies the Laplace equation in cylindrical coordinates and if u depends only upon ρ, then

$$\frac{d^2u}{d\rho^2} + \frac{1}{\rho}\frac{du}{d\rho} = 0.$$

Show that in any such situation (where u could be the electrical potential between two coaxial charged cylindrical shells or the steady-state temperature in a homogeneous isotropic material between two coaxial cylindrical surfaces which are maintained at constant temperatures) there must be constants c_1 and c_2 such that

$$u = c_2 + c_1 \log \rho.$$

Show that if $u(\rho_1) = u_1$ and $u(\rho_2) = u_2$, then

$$u = u_1 + \frac{u_2 - u_1}{\log \rho_2 - \log \rho_1}(\log \rho - \log \rho_1).$$

Show that if A is the area of a cylinder of radius ρ and length L, then

$$A\frac{du}{d\rho} = 2\pi L \frac{u_2 - u_1}{\log \rho_2 - \log \rho_1}.$$

Hint: Start by finding $du/d\rho$. *Remark:* If k is the thermal conductivity of the material noted above, then $-kA\ du/d\rho$ is the rate at which heat flows outward over a section of length L of the cylindrical surface of radius ρ. This is, as it should be, independent of ρ. Handbooks and some textbooks for chemists, engineers, and physicists give numerical values of k for various useful materials. Suppose distances are measured in centimeters, time in seconds, temperatures in degrees centigrade, and quantities of heat in calories. The values of k used are shown in Table 3.18812. If Q denotes

TABLE 3.18812. THERMAL CONDUCTIVITY OF USEFUL MATERIALS

air	0.000056	glass	0.0016
brick	0.0015	glass wool	0.00009
concrete	0.0022	iron	0.11
copper	0.92	water	0.0014

the flow of heat in calories per second across a surface of area A and in the direction of increasing x, then

$$Q = -kA\frac{du}{dx}$$

where u is the temperature and x is a coordinate measured on a line orthogonal to the surface. These formulas are very useful, but it is easy to get very bad answers by making false assumptions about the temperatures on the two sides of a glass window that separates a warm room from a frigid world.

Problem 3.1882

Find an equation in Section 1.1 which shows that if u satisfies the Laplace equation in rectangular coordinates and if u depends only upon x, then

$$\frac{d^2u}{dx^2} = 0.$$

Show that, in any such situation, there exist constants c_1 and c_2 such that $u = c_1 + c_2x$. Show that if $u(x_1) = u_1$ and $u(x_2) = u_2$, then

$$u = u_1 + \frac{u_2 - u_1}{x_2 - x_1}(x - x_1).$$

Make remarks similar to those of the two preceding problems.

Problem 3.1883

The temperatures on the two sides of a concrete wall 25 centimeters thick are $-10°$C and 20°C. Find the number of calories of heat lost per hour through a square meter of the wall. *Ans.:* 95,000 calories.

Problem 3.1884

Insulation on a steam pipe has inner and outer radii 10 cm and 12 cm and has inner and outer temperatues 100°C and 20°C. To what thickness must the insulation be increased to eliminate 90 per cent of the heat loss? *Ans.:* 62 centimeters.

Problem 3.1885

A circular pipe of length L and outer radius ρ_0 is covered by n layers of insulation having known thermal conductivities $k_1, k_2, \ldots, k_n$ and known outer radii $\rho_1, \rho_2, \ldots, \rho_n$. Let u_j be the temperature at distance ρ_j from the axis. Suppose that u_0 and u_n are known constants, and let Q be the steady rate (say calories per second or Btu per hour) at which heat flows outward over the cylindrical surfaces within the insulation. Show that, for each $j = 1, 2, \ldots, n$,

$$-2\pi Lk_j \frac{u_j - u_{j-1}}{\log \rho_j - \log \rho_{j-1}} = Q.$$

Use this to show that

$$u_n - u_0 = -Q \sum_{j=0}^{n} \frac{\log \rho_j - \log \rho_{j-1}}{2\pi Lk_j},$$

and note that division gives Q in terms of known quantities. Finally, tell how to find $u_1, u_2, \ldots, u_{n-1}$ from these formulas.

3.19. Remarks. If y' is interpreted as the rate of change of y with respect to x, the equation

$$\frac{dy}{dx} = ky \tag{3.191}$$

can be read either, "The rate of change of y with respect to x is proportional to y," or "The rate of change of y with respect to x is a constant times y." Of course, the two readings mean the same thing. (It may perhaps be true that the first reading is sometimes preferred because it is less likely to cause some unpleasant person to ask what the constant is.)

In the remainder of this chapter we consider several problems solvable by means of the differential equation $y' = ky$ and more general linear equations. A student who wants to learn where differential equations come from and how they are used should pay careful attention to the problems. To solve a great many problems rapidly and thoughtlessly is a waste of time.

If in connection with some of these problems a student begins to feel that solving problems in applied mathematics involves so many approximations that the whole business is utter nonsense, he is to be congratulated. He is perhaps approaching a point where he may begin to learn something about the manner in which mathematics is used in the sciences.

3.2. Problems in Temperature. A steel ball is heated to temperature 100°C and placed at time $t = 0$ in a medium which is maintained at temperature 40°C. Heat flows so rapidly within the ball that at each time the temperature is essentially the same at all points of the ball. At the end of 2 minutes, the temperature of the ball is reduced to 80°C. We shall find the time at which the temperature of the ball will be 43°C.

It is common knowledge that the ball will lose heat most rapidly and that the temperature u of the ball will fall most rapidly when the temperature difference $u - 40$ is greatest. One may guess (and experiments will show) that the rate of change of u with respect to t is roughly proportional to $u - 40$, and we suppose that there is a constant k for which

$$\frac{du}{dt} = -k(u - 40). \tag{3.21}$$

This is an application of *Newton's law of cooling*. The negative sign in (3.21) is inserted so that k will turn out to be positive; if $-k$ were replaced by k in (3.21), then k would be negative. If one is willing to *assume* that u always remains, for $t \geqq 0$, greater than 40, then we may divide (3.21) by $u - 40$ to obtain

$$\frac{d}{dt} \log (u - 40) = -k$$

so that $\log (u - 40) = -kt + c$ and

$$u = 40 + Ae^{-kt}. \tag{3.22}$$

If one wishes to *prove* rather than *assume* that $u > 40$, he can multiply (3.21) by e^{kt} to obtain

$$\frac{d}{dt} e^{kt}(u - 40) = 0$$

and then (3.22). The fact that $u = 100$ when $t = 0$ implies that $A = 60$; hence,

$$u = 40 + 60e^{-kt}. \tag{3.221}$$

The fact that $u = 80$ when $t = 2$ implies that $e^{-2k} = \frac{2}{3}$, $e^{2k} = 1.5$, and hence

$$k = \tfrac{1}{2} \log 1.5 = 0.2027. \tag{3.222}$$

If one has no table of natural logarithms, he may write

$$2k \log_{10} e = \log_{10} 1.5$$

and then use a table of logarithms with base 10 to obtain k. Thus,

$$u = 40 + 60e^{-0.2027t}. \tag{3.23}$$

This formula enables us to find u for each given $t > 0$ and to find t for each $u > 40$. If $u = 43$, then (3.23) gives $e^{0.2027t} = 20$; using a table of natural logarithms, we find

$$t = \frac{1}{0.2027} \log 20 = \frac{2.9957}{0.2027} = 14.8; \tag{3.24}$$

the equation $0.2027t \log_{10} e = \log_{10} 20$ and a table of logarithms with base 10 can be used to find t. Thus 14.8 minutes is the time required for the ball to reach a temperature of 43°C.

It is possible to base the derivation of the differential equation (3.21) on experiments less complicated than that of measuring a rate of change of temperature. It may be verified by experiment that if the ball and the surrounding medium are maintained at temperatures u and u_0, respectively, then the number ΔH of calories of heat which flow from the ball to the medium in Δt minutes is proportional to $u - u_0$ and to Δt so that

$$\Delta H = k_1(u - u_0)\Delta t \tag{3.25}$$

where k_1 is a constant depending on the physical properties of the ball and the medium but k_1 is independent of $u - u_0$ and Δt. Let us now assume that the temperature u of the ball is initially greater than u_0, that no heat is added to the ball, and that the temperature of the ball decreases continuously as time passes. Let $H = H(t)$ denote the number of calories of heat lost by the ball in the first t minutes after $t = 0$. Then, when $t_1 < t_2$, $u_1 = u(t_1)$, $u_2 = u(t_2)$, we have $u_2 < u_1$. Hence the number ΔH of calories of heat passing from the ball to the medium in the time interval from t_1 to t_2 satisfies the inequality

$$k_1(u_2 - u_0)(t_2 - t_1) < \Delta H < k_1(u_1 - u_0)(t_2 - t_1). \tag{3.251}$$

Since the temperature u changes steadily as t increases from t_1 to t_2, we can choose a time t' between t_1 and t_2 such that

$$\Delta H = k_1[u(t') - u_0](t_2 - t_1). \tag{3.252}$$

Setting $\Delta t = t_2 - t_1$ and dividing by Δt give

$$\frac{\Delta H}{\Delta t} = k_1[u(t') - u_0]. \tag{3.253}$$

If we give t_1 a fixed value t and let $t_2 \to t_1$ (or give t_2 the fixed value t and let $t_1 \to t_2$), then t', which lies between t_1 and t_2, must approach t and, since $u(t)$ was assumed continuous, $u(t')$ must approach $u(t)$. Thus the right side of (3.253) has a limit as $\Delta t \to 0$; hence also the left and by definition of derivative

$$\frac{dH}{dt} = k_1(u - u_0) \tag{3.254}$$

where u on the right stands for $u(t)$. We have still to make the connection between calories of heat lost by the ball and temperature of the ball. It is a physical fact that (at least for ordinary temperatures) temperature scales are so adjusted that the decrease in temperature of an object is proportional to the number of calories of heat lost by the object; that is,

$$u(t) - u(t_1) = -k_2[H(t) - H(t_1)]$$

where $k_2 > 0$. Thus $du/dt = -k_2dH/dt$ so that setting $k = k_1k_2$ and using (3.254) give

$$\frac{du}{dt} = -k(u - u_0). \tag{3.255}$$

Problem 3.26

A ball having temperature 80°C was put into a pint of stirred ice water at 0°C and after 10 minutes the two temperatures were 60°C and 20°C. The ball was then transferred to a new pint of ice water. In each case, the only exchanges of heat are between the ball and the water. Find the temperature of the ball at the end of another 10-minute interval. *Ans.*: 15°C.

Problem 3.27

The ball of the previous problem was reheated to 80°C and put into 2 pints of ice water. Find the temperature of the ball after 20 minutes has elapsed. *Ans.*: 43.9°C.

Problem 3.28

A chemist wants a jug of chemical cooled to 80°C. Ten minutes ago he set the jug, with the temperature of the chemical 120°, in a vat of water at temperature 40°. Since that time he has been busy stirring both the chemical and the water and observing that the only appreciable transfer of heat is from the chemical to the water. The temperature of the chemical is now 100°, and that of the water is 55°. How long must he continue to stir? *Ans.*: When time $t = 0$ represents the instant 10 minutes after stirring started and $u = u(t)$ is the temperature of the chemical at time t, $u = \frac{520}{7} + Ae^{-k_1t}$. Determination of constants gives $u = \frac{1}{7}[520 + 180e^{-.0575t}]$, and $u = 80$ when $t = 26.1$ minutes. The total time of the stirring is 36.1 minutes.

Problem 3.29

How long would it take to cool the chemical in Problem 3.28 from 120° to 80° if the water is maintained at temperature 40°? Explain why your answer is wrong if you get more than 36.2 minutes.

Remark 3.291

According to the law of Stefan (1835–1893) and Boltzmann (1844–1906), a body at absolute [Kelvin (1824–1907)] temperature U radiates energy of a given frequency at a rate proportional to U^4. If, instead of the Newton law (3.255), we assume the law

$$\frac{dU}{dt} = -k_1(U^4 - U_0^4),$$

matters seem quite different. However we can put this in the form

$$\frac{dU}{dt} = -q(U - U_0),$$

where $q = k_1(U^2 + U_0^2)(U + U_0)$, and observe that, when U and U_0 are both of the order of magnitude of 300, a reasonable approximation is obtained by supposing that q is a constant k.

3.3. A Window Problem. A certain type of glass is such that a slab 1 inch thick absorbs one quarter of the light which starts to pass through it. How thin must a pane be made to absorb only 1 per cent of the light?

Let t be a variable representing thicknesses of panes of glass, and let $x = x(t)$ denote the fractional part of entering light which passes through a pane of thickness t. Then obviously x decreases as t increases. Since a pane of thickness 0 means no pane at all and accordingly no absorption of light, we have $x(0) = 1$; and, by the statement of the problem, $x(1) = \frac{3}{4}$. We are required to determine t such that $x(t) = 0.99$.

Let $t \geqq 0$ be fixed; let $\Delta t > 0$; and consider two panes, the first of thickness t and the second, of thickness $t + \Delta t$, obtained by adding a layer of thickness Δt to the right side of the first. Of L units of light entering the first pane at the left, xL units emerge from the first pane to enter the layer, and $(x + \Delta x)L$ units emerge from the layer. The homogeneity of the glass used indicates that there is a constant k (depending only on the type of glass used and the kind of light considered) such that, if xL units of light enter a "thin" pane of thickness Δt, then the amount $(-\Delta x)L$ of light absorbed by the thin pane will be roughly $kxL\,\Delta t$; using the symbol $\sim$ to mean "is roughly equal to," we may express this idea by writing

$$-\Delta xL \sim kxL\,\Delta t. \tag{3.31}$$

This idea may be expressed otherwise by saying that the amount of light absorbed by a "thin" pane is roughly proportional to the amount entering and to the thickness of the pane. The idea is an extension to other factors of the idea that, if one doubles (or halves) the amount of entering light, then one will also double (or halve) the amount of absorbed light; and that, if one doubles (or halves) the thickness of a thin pane, one will roughly double (or halve) the amount of light absorbed. The reason why one must say "roughly double" instead of "double" lies in the fact that, if light passes through two thin panes each of thickness Δt, then the first pane which the light reaches will absorb slightly more than the second because the amount of light which enters the first pane is slightly greater than the amount which enters the second pane.

If we write (3.31) in the form

$$\frac{\Delta x}{\Delta t} \sim -kx \tag{3.32}$$

and make the natural assumption that the error in the approximation decreases and approaches 0 as the thickness Δt approaches zero, then we can let Δt approach 0 to obtain (by definition of derivative)

$$\frac{dx}{dt} = -kx. \tag{3.33}$$

Solving (3.33) gives $x = Ae^{-kt}$. Since $x(0) = 1$, we can put $t = 0$ and $x = 1$ to find that $A = 1$, and $x = e^{-kt}$. Since $x(1) = \frac{3}{4}$, we can set $x = \frac{3}{4}$ and $t = 1$ to obtain

$$k = -\log \tfrac{3}{4} = 0.288;$$

or if no table of logarithms with base e is available, we can solve the equation $\log_{10} \frac{3}{4} = -k \log_{10} e$ to find k. Hence,

$$x = e^{-0.288t}. \tag{3.34}$$

Setting $x = 0.99$ and solving for t by one or the other of the equations

$$-0.288t = \log 0.99 = -0.010, \qquad -0.288t \log_{10} e = \log_{10} 0.99$$

gives $t = 0.035$ inch as the thickness of a pane which allows 99 per cent of the light to pass through and therefore absorbs 1 per cent.

Problem 3.35

That water absorbs light is attested by the fact that it is dark in the ocean depths. If 10 feet of water absorbs 40 per cent of the light which strikes the surface, at what depth would the light at noonday be the same as bright moonlight which is 1/300,000 that of noonday sunlight? *Ans.:* About 247 feet.

3.4. Atmospheric Pressures. It is well known that atmospheric pressure as measured by a barometer at a given place on the earth is not constant, but is a function of the time; the barometer, invented in 1643, has long been used in weather forecasting. It is also well known that atmospheric pressure p decreases as distance h above sea level increases. We propose to disregard pressure changes which depend on the time and, assuming the earth to be surrounded by a motionless gas to which we may apply fundamental gas laws, to try to determine how p depends on h.

We begin by assuming that $p(h)$ is a continuous function which decreases as h increases. Let a rectangular parallelepiped be constructed whose lower base is 1 unit square and h_1 units above sea level and whose upper base is h_2 units above sea level. (The reader should draw a figure and amplify it as the discussion proceeds.) Then $p(h_1)$ is the magnitude of the upward force which would be exerted on the lower base if it were a part of the surface of a tank from which all air has been pumped, and $p(h_2)$ is the magnitude of the smaller downward force similarly determined for the upper base. Let $\Delta h = h_2 - h_1$ and $\Delta p = p(h_2) - p(h_1)$. Since the air in the parallelepiped moves neither up nor down, the pressure difference $-\Delta p$ must be equal to the weight Δw of the air within the parallelepiped.

To put ourselves in a position to estimate Δw, let us think about the weight of the air in a tank. If air is pumped from the tank, then the pressure decreases and the weight of the air in the tank decreases; if air is pumped into the tank, both pressure and weight increase. If the tank is sealed and heated or cooled, then pressure is increased or decreased but the weight of the air in the tank does not change. These considerations indicate that pressure, temperature, and weight are interrelated and that we may be able to use the *fundamental gas law*, one form of which is the following: if N molecules of a gas at pressure p and absolute temperature T are confined in a volume v, then

$$N = \frac{k_1 pv}{T} \tag{3.41}$$

where k_1 is an absolute constant depending only on the units used. Since the mass, which we denote by Δm, of the gas is proportional to the number of molecules, we obtain

$$\Delta m = \frac{k_2 pv}{T}. \tag{3.42}$$

Our first observation, when we come to apply (3.42) to obtain the mass of the air in the rectangular parallelepiped, is that neither (3.42) nor the fundamental formula (3.41) from which it is obtained takes into account the very fact which gives rise to our problem, namely, the fact that pressure is different at different distances h above sea level. Likewise, formulas (3.41) and (3.42) do not take into account the fact that the temperature T may be different at different points. (Dependence of T on h will be discussed later.) Let us meet these difficulties by making the assumption that (3.42) will hold if p and T are taken, respectively, to be the pressure and temperature at two properly chosen points of the rectangular parallelepiped. The volume v is easily obtained, for the base has unit area and the altitude is Δh; thus $v = \Delta h$. Hence, if h' and h'' are properly chosen such that $h_1 < h' < h_2$ and $h_1 < h'' < h_2$, then the mass of the air in the rectangular parallelepiped is

$$(3.43) \qquad \Delta m = k_2 \frac{p(h')\Delta h}{T(h'')}.$$

To make the connection between the weight Δw and the mass Δm, we recall that, if the mass Δm is situated at sea level, then $\Delta w = g\,\Delta m$ where g is the acceleration of gravity but that, if Δm is a height h above sea level, one must use the more general formula $F = k_3 m_1 m_2/d^2$ where F is force, m_1 and m_2 are masses, d is the distance between the masses, and k_3 is a constant. Using the more general formula, we obtain

$$(3.44) \qquad \Delta w = k_4 \frac{p(h')\Delta h}{(R + h''')^2 T(h')}$$

where R is the radius of the earth and h''' is properly chosen so that $h_1 < h''' < h_2$. Since $\Delta p = -\Delta w$, we obtain

$$(3.441) \qquad \frac{\Delta p}{\Delta h} = -k_4 \frac{p(h')}{(R + h''')^2 T(h'')}.$$

If we assume that $T(h)$ as well as $p(h)$ is a continuous function of h, then we can give h_1 a fixed value h and let h_2 approach h (or let $h_2 = h$, and let h_1 approach h); then h', h'', and h''' which all lie between h_1 and h_2 must approach h, and we obtain

$$(3.45) \qquad \frac{dp}{dh} = -k_4 \frac{p(h)}{(R + h)^2 T(h)}.$$

The differential equation (3.45) involves not only the function $p(h)$ we are trying to determine but also a temperature function $T(h)$. That the absolute temperature T does depend on h is indicated by the fact that, although the temperature may be 311°K (about 38°C or 100°F) at sea level, the temperature is about 251°K (about −55°C or −67°F) at all altitudes from 6 to 20 miles. If a graph of $T(h)$ is known and $p(0)$, the atmospheric pressure at sea level, is known, then it is possible to obtain approximations to $p(h)$ by methods appearing later.

Assuming that we do not know enough about the function $T(h)$ to enable us to use (3.45) to determine $p(h)$, we make progress by application of a time honored method which often brings valuable results in applied mathematics. This method consists in making an assumption known to be absolutely and unequivocally false. In the present application, we assume that T is independent of h. The virtue of this assumption is that (3.45) can now be written in the simpler form

$$\frac{dp}{dh} = -k_5 \frac{p}{(R+h)^2} = -k\left(\frac{R}{R+h}\right)^2 p. \tag{3.46}$$

Having degraded ourselves by making one false assumption, we find it easy to make another. Noticing that if h is "small as compared with R" then $[R/(R+h)]^2$ is near 1, we omit the factor and write simply

$$\frac{dp}{dh} = -kp. \tag{3.47}$$

Solving (3.47) gives

$$p = Ae^{-kh}. \tag{3.471}$$

If h is measured in feet and p in pounds per square inch, then $p(0) = 14.7$ so that $A = 14.7$ and $p = 14.7e^{-kh}$. Assuming that $p(4{,}500) = 12.5$, we obtain $k = 0.000037$ so that

$$p = 14.7e^{-0.000037h}. \tag{3.48}$$

Having obtained formula (3.48), the question arises whether or not it is useful. If (3.48) were actually correct, then it could be used to find pressure at a given height or to find the height at which the pressure has an assigned value. But it must be remembered that (3.48) is not correct unless by accident the errors resulting from false assumptions happen to cancel.

Finally we wish to point out, in language which is at best exceedingly vague, that there is a sense in which (3.48) may be useful. If the range of values of h is such that $R/(R+h)$ is nearly 1 and the temperature T is nearly constant over the range, then the deduction (3.48) from the false assumptions may be sufficiently accurate for practical purposes.

Problem 3.49

What do you make out of the result (2.2823) that we get if we try to obtain a more accurate approximation to $p(h)$ by solving the equation (3.46) which does not involve the assumption that h is always small in comparison to R?

Problem 3.491

The pressure $p(y)$ at depth y beneath the surface of an ocean is greater than it would be if water were not compressible. Let units be pounds and feet. Suppose, as is very nearly true, that a cubic foot of water under pressure p weighs $w(1 + kp)$ pounds where

$w = 64$ and $k = 2 \times 10^{-8}$. Show that

$$p(y) = \frac{e^{wky} - 1}{wky} wy. \tag{3.4911}$$

Note that the pressure at depth y would be wy if the water were not compressible. Note that, when wky is small, the quotient in (3.4911) is appraised most easily by use of the power series expansion of e^{wky}. Show that when $y = 3 \times 10^4$ feet (about six miles) the quotient is 1.0195. This shows that, even at great depths, the relative increase in pressure due to compressibility is unexciting.

Problem 3.492

A long steel rod is lying on the ground. Its length is a feet, it weighs w pounds per linear foot, and k is a constant (in fact, the product of Young's modulus and the area of a cross section of the rod) such that within elastic limits the force required to stretch or compress the rod to length b is $k(b - a)/a$. Let $u(x)$ be the function such that, when the rod hangs motionless from one end, the point which was x feet from that end will be $u(x)$ feet from the end. Draw figures and present an argument to show that

$$w(a - x) \sim k \frac{u(x + \Delta x) - u(x) - \Delta x}{\Delta x}$$

where "$\sim$" means "is approximately equal to." Make the necessary steps to obtain

$$u(x) = x + \frac{w}{2k} [a^2 - (a - x)^2]. \tag{3.4921}$$

Can you see any connection between the fact that $u(a) = a + wa^2/2k$ and the fact that, when the rod is lying on the ground, a force equal to the weight of the rod stretches it to length $a + wa^2/k$?

Problem 3.493

Show that if the rod of the preceding problem is made to stand, as a vertical column, on one end, then a point which was x feet from that end will be

$$v(x) = x - \frac{w}{2k} [a^2 - (a - x)^2] \tag{3.4931}$$

feet from the base.

Problem 3.494

Using the result of the previous problem, show that a steel rod whose length is the height of the Empire State Building would be compressed 1.05 inches when it is stood on one end. Assume that the steel weighs 0.3 pounds per cubic inch, that Young's modulus for the steel is $32 \cdot 10^6$ when units are pounds and inches, and that the height of the building is 15,000 inches (1,250 feet).

3.5. Radioactive Decay. Everyone who has had a course in physics, and nearly everyone else who finds himself studying differential equations, knows that unstable elements exist in nature and are manufactured. Since it is easy to adapt the ideas to other situations, we consider radioactive decay of radium. Alpha particles are radiated from matter containing radium and, as time passes, the amount of radium decreases. Let x denote the number of grams of radium in a given portion of matter, and let t denote time measured in years; we propose to find how x depends on t.

It is reasonable to guess (and certain physical considerations lead one to believe) that the rate at which the amount of radium decreases is proportional to the amount present. This statement is expressed in mathematical terms by the differential equation

$$\frac{dx}{dt} = -kx \tag{3.51}$$

where k is a constant. Solving gives $x = Ae^{-kt}$. If x_0 represents the weight of the radium at time $t = 0$, then setting $t = 0$ shows that $A = x_0$ so that

$$x = x_0e^{-kt}. \tag{3.52}$$

If the value of k is known, then formula (3.52) enables us to compute the value of x for each given t, or the value of t for each given $x > 0$. The value of k has been computed from results of different observations; its value turns out to be about 0.00041. Thus we obtain as the solution of our problem

$$x = x_0e^{-0.00041t}. \tag{3.53}$$

If t_1 is the number of years required to reduce the amount of radium in a portion of matter by one-half, then $0.5 = e^{-0.00041t_1}$ so that $t_1 = 1{,}700$ years. The graph of the function in (3.53) is shown in Fig. 3.531.

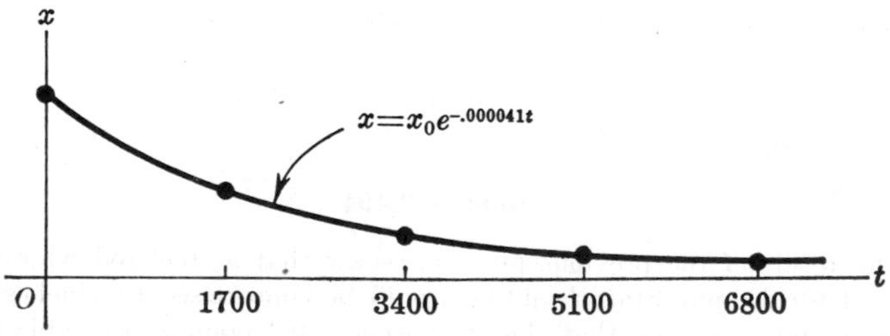

FIG. 3.531

The solution (3.53) of our problem involves a formula which is simple and elegant, which was obtained by a seemingly rigorous method, and which is useful. Hence, it is appropriate that one who wants only superficial knowledge of many problems should pass to another problem. However, there are reasons why a serious-minded student of either mathematics or physics should view the formula with grave suspicion.

To bring these reasons to the fore, we begin afresh to consider the problem.

A physicist who has appropriate training and apparatus can see the "tracks" of radiated particles and can count them one by one as they are radiated. If we know (or assume) that the weight x of the radium suddenly decreases when a particle is radiated and remains constant over time intervals in which there is no radiation, we have immediately a contradiction of (3.53). For if $x(t)$ is constant over some interval, then $x'(t) = 0$ over that interval. This implies that (3.53) cannot be true; for if (3.53) is true, then $x'(t) = -kx_0e^{-kt} \neq 0$ for all t. The graph of $x(t)$ which a physicist would construct to cover a time interval a few seconds long may be illustrated by Fig. 3.532 or by Fig. 3.533, depending

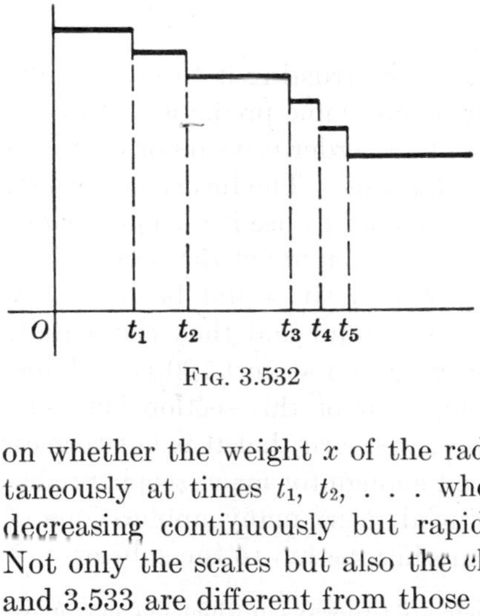

FIG. 3.532

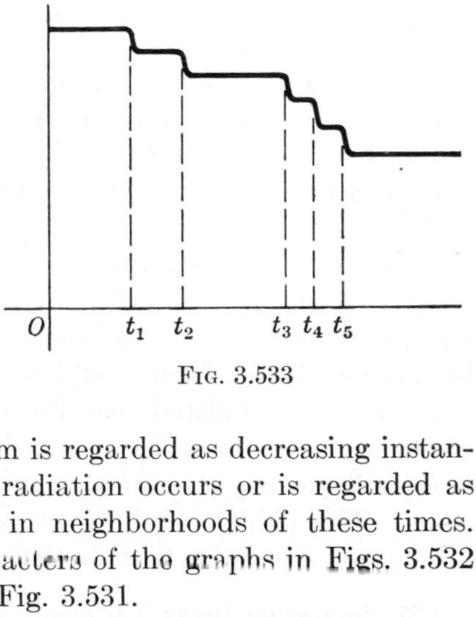

FIG. 3.533

on whether the weight x of the radium is regarded as decreasing instantaneously at times $t_1, t_2, \ldots$ when radiation occurs or is regarded as decreasing continuously but rapidly in neighborhoods of these times. Not only the scales but also the characters of the graphs in Figs. 3.532 and 3.533 are different from those of Fig. 3.531.

We are now in a predicament. We have apparently used good mathematics and physics to show that (3.53) is true and then used equally good mathematics and physics to show that (3.53) is not true.

The data and graphs obtained by experimental physicists must be accepted as accurate, and we must conclude that it is definitely not true that there is a constant k such that $dx/dt = -kx$ and $x = x_0e^{-kt}$; the function $x(t)$ is far more capricious. In fact, the data and observations of experimental physicists leave one in doubt as to whether $x(t)$ is differentiable; in particular, if it is not continuous, then it certainly is not differentiable. Thus we are driven to conclude that our pleasant attempt to foist the differential equation $dx/dt = -kx$ and the solution $x = x_0e^{-kt}$ on the public was not so innocent as it appeared to be; unfortunately, the formulas are not correct.

There is still the possibility that the function $\xi(t)$ defined by

$$\xi = x_0 e^{-kt} \tag{3.54}$$

is a good approximation to the function $x(t)$ which we are seeking. We know that, if $\xi(t)$ and $x(t)$ are plotted with scales so adjusted that time differences of the order of seconds and weight differences of the order of the weight of a radiated particle are displayed, then the graphs of $\xi(t)$ and $x(t)$ will be very different; but if we are optimistic, we can hope that, if $\xi(t)$ and $x(t)$ are plotted (as in Fig. 3.531) so that time differences of the order of centuries and weight differences of the order of grams are displayed, then the "kinks" in the graph of $x(t)$ will not be visible and the graphs of $\xi(t)$ and $x(t)$ will appear to coincide. Thus, *if* the optimism is justified, we can use the equation

$$x = x_0 e^{-kt}, \tag{3.541}$$

knowing that it is false but at the same time trusting it to give results which may be regarded as accurate for macroscopic predictions, that is, for predictions involving time intervals of the order of years or centuries and weights of the order of grams or milligrams. The incorrect formula (3.541) is certainly objectionable when one tries to use it for microscopic predictions, that is, for predictions involving weights of the order of the weight of an atom of radium. In particular, it would be obviously ridiculous to start with a single atom of radium and then claim that, because of (3.541), there would be exactly half an atom 1,700 years later.

It must be admitted that the development of this section has been surprising; we get the formula $x = x_0 e^{-kt}$, we learn that it is not correct, and finally we say that we *hope* it is good enough for macroscopic predictions. The points involved are so crucial in so many applications of differential equations that we devote another section to the subject.

3.55. Radioactive Decay (*Continued*). There are two ways in which one may guess that a solution of the differential equation $dx/dt = -kt$ will furnish a formula for $x(t)$ which is sufficiently accurate for macroscopic applications. One takes macroscopic observations for its starting point, and the other takes microscopic observations for its starting point. We indicate below the natures of the ideas on which the two methods are based. The first may or may not be convincing. The second, when accurately presented, involves so much mathematics (probability, statistics, etc.) that it is certainly impressive and perhaps convincing.

The first method depends on an assumption which is false, and hence the results obtained are at least open to suspicion; but there is nevertheless the possibility that our conclusions will be correct. We argue that, if the weight x of the radium were decreased by a suitable steady flow of weight instead of by radiation of discrete particles, then $x(t)$ would be equal to a function $\xi(t)$ such that the rate of change of ξ with respect to t is proportional to ξ so that $\xi'(t) = -k\xi$ and $\xi = x_0 e^{-kt}$; and since macroscopic weight does not depend essentially on whether the weight decreases steadily or by jumps, we conclude that $x(t)$ is essentially $\xi(t)$ and hence that the formula

$$x(t) = x_0e^{-kt} \tag{3.56}$$

is essentially true insofar as macroscopic measurements are concerned. A logician may insist that the reasoning leading to (3.56) was idiotic. But at least we made a good guess and got a useful answer. Moreover, we can remind the logician that the real pioneers in physics (and other sciences) are those who make correct guesses; after correct guesses are made, mathematicians and physicists construct whole theories to prove that the guesses are correct.

The second method begins with a guess. It is entirely reasonable to guess that if N is the number of particles radiated by x grams of radium in a reasonably short time interval Δt, then N is at least roughly proportional to x and to the time interval Δt; we express this by writing

$$N \sim k_1x\,\Delta t. \tag{3.57}$$

It may then be expected that a physicist who can count radiated particles should experiment with different weights x and different time intervals Δt to validate (3.57), the limits of error being those involved in measuring time intervals and weights of radium. The physicist who tries to verify (3.57) observes a fact which does not contribute to simple and easy exposition of the subject. The particles do not come from the radium at a steady regular rate as ticks come from a good watch; the number of particles radiated in a given short time interval may be none or one or several, depending simply on the number of particles which happened to receive the urge to escape during that time interval. But in spite of the "randomness" of emission of particles, it seems to be true that there is a constant k_1 such that $N/\Delta t$ is usually roughly k_1x provided that Δt is "large" enough to make N large but at the same time not large enough to produce an appreciable change in x. This statement of experimental results is quite analogous to the following statement: In spite of the randomness with which heads and tails appear when a coin is tossed, it seems to be true that there is a constant p $(= \frac{1}{2})$ such that the number H of heads divided by the total number T of throws is usually roughly p provided that T is large. Each one of these statements must be made much more precise and intelligible before it can be accepted as a part of a satisfactory theory of probability and statistics, and it is not the intention of the author to expect the reader to understand something unintelligible. If we know (or make the reasonable assumption) that the increase Δx (which is negative) in x during the time Δt is proportional to the number N of particles radiated during the time Δt, we obtain $\Delta x = -k_2N$ so that setting $k = k_1k_2$ gives, by use of (3.57),

$$\frac{\Delta x}{\Delta t} \sim -kx. \tag{3.58}$$

It is usually true in pure (but not applied) mathematics that the relationship expressed in (3.58) indicates roughly that $\Delta x/\Delta t$ is near $-kx$ when Δt is small and indicates precisely that $\lim \Delta x/\Delta t = -kx$ or (by definition of derivative) that $dx/dt = -kx$. But in the present instance the meaning of (3.58) is much more complicated. It is clear that nothing is obtained in the present instance by allowing Δt to approach zero. For if Δt is very small, then $\Delta x/\Delta t$ will be 0 if none of the capricious particles were radiated in the time interval Δt; and $\Delta x/\Delta t$ will be numerically large if one or more particles happened to be radiated during the time interval. In particular, it is definitely not true that $dx/dt = -kx$.

We shall not explain the manner in which the vague notion that "$\Delta x/\Delta t$ is usually roughly $-kx$ when Δt is neither too small nor too large" can be made more precise;

such explanations belong to statistics and statistical mechanics. But it may be helpful to think of its meaning something like this: If Δt is 1 year, then the probability (chance) that $\Delta x/(-kx\,\Delta t)$ will differ from 1 by more than .01 is equal to the probability (chance) of throwing 10^{20} consecutive heads when throwing a normal coin.

Let us think of constructing a graph of $x(t)$ on ordinary graph paper, showing t ranging from 0 to 5,000 years and x ranging downward from 1 grain at $t = 0$ to a fractional part of a grain when $t = 5{,}000$. A time interval Δt appearing to the eye to represent a "small" time interval would represent several years, and the corresponding Δx would be a small fractional part of x; hence, it is extremely unlikely that $\Delta x/\Delta t$ would differ much from $-kx$. This situation leads us to guess that it is likely that the graph of $x(t)$ would not differ appreciably from the graph of a function $\xi(t)$, satisfying the differential equation $d\xi/dt = -k\xi$, and hence from x_0e^{-kt}.

We have arrived finally at the following meaning which experts in atomic physics attach to the formula

$$x = x_0e^{-kt} \tag{3.59}$$

as applied to radioactive substances: The formula (3.59) is absolutely useless insofar as predictions involving microscopic weights of the order of weights of atoms are concerned; but insofar as predictions involving macroscopic weights of the order of grams or milligrams are concerned, it is extremely unlikely that physical observations will differ by measurable amounts from the predictions.

Problem 3.591

Growing tissues, both plant and animal, are partly constructed from carbon taken from CO_2 (carbon dioxide) in the air around us. This carbon is mostly C^{12} but contains a small fixed percentage of unstable radioactive carbon C^{14} produced by cosmic radiation. It turns out that the ratio $|C^{14}|/|C^{12}|$ of the amount of C^{14} to the amount of C^{12} in a fragment of living tissue is essentially the same small constant for all fragments. When the tissue dies, no more C^{14} is received and $|C^{14}|$ slowly decreases in such a way that its half-life is 5,550 years. Letting x denote the number of grams of C^{14} in a gram of tissue t years after death of the tissue, show that

$$x = x_0e^{-t/8{,}007}, \qquad t = 8{,}007 \log \frac{x_0}{x}$$

where $x = x_0$ when $t = 0$. These formulas are used to determine the dates at which trees and other things lived. Pieces of wood or charcoal found in ancient caves and tombs, or covered by glaciers, or volcanic eruptions give fundamental information in history and geology. For example, charcoal from the famous prehistoric cave of Lascaux in France contained 14.5 per cent of the original C^{14} content. Show that the wood grew about 15,500 years ago.

3.6. Dilution Problems. At time $t = 0$, fresh water starts running g gallons per minute into a tank of volume v which is filled with a salt solution containing s pounds of salt. The solution is stirred to keep the contents of the tank homogeneous, and dilute solution flows out g gallons per minute. The problem is to find the amount x of salt in the tank at time t.

At time t, the number of pounds of salt per gallon is x/v, and the number of gallons of brine flowing out in Δt minutes is $g\,\Delta t$. If Δt is so small that the concentration x/v changes only a little in the time between t and $t + \Delta t$, but at the same time Δt is not so small as to clash with observations of molecule counters, the change Δx in x will be approximately $-(x/v)g\,\Delta t$. Thus

$$\frac{\Delta x}{\Delta t} \sim -kx \tag{3.61}$$

where $k = g/v$ and the symbol $\sim$ has a significance much like that in Section 3.55. This leads us to expect that the function $x(t)$ which we are seeking will be (insofar as measurements involving weights of the order of pounds can determine) equal to a function $x(t)$ for which

$$\frac{dx}{dt} = -kx. \tag{3.62}$$

Thus $x = Ae^{-kt}$; and since $x(0) = s$, we obtain

$$x = se^{-kt} \tag{3.63}$$

for our answer.

Problem 3.64

If $k = g/v = 0.01$, how long will it take to wash 99 per cent of the salt out of the tank?

Problem 3.65

How much credence would you put in the formula (3.63) if the tank, instead of containing s pounds of salt, had contained s tiny separate pieces of sponge where (*a*) $s = 1{,}000{,}000$ (*b*) $s = 12$, and (*c*) $s = 1$?

Problem 3.651

Should (3.63) be accepted to support a contention that it would be impossible to run the salt-free water long enough to wash every molecule of salt out of the tank?

Remark 3.652

Observe that our formulas do not tell us what *must* happen. They tell us only what is very likely to almost happen. These dilution problems, like problems involving flow of heat, involve random motions of individual molecules.

Problem 3.66

A tank, only half filled, contains 100 gallons of pure water. Brine containing 2 pounds of salt per gallon flows in at the rate of 5 gallons per minute, and the diluted but well-mixed mixture flows out at the rate of 3 gallons per minute. How many pounds of salt will the tank contain when it is full? *Ans.*: $x = 375$ pounds.

Problem 3.661

How much brine was in the tank of the preceding problem when the brine contained one pound of salt per gallon? *Ans.*: 127 gallons.

Problem 3.662

At time $t = 0$, a huge number N of dollar bills or fish circulate in an appropriate medium. These are continuously caught in banks or nets at the rate of n per day and, after alterations (which could be replacements by new varieties), are returned to circulation. Assuming that the altered and unaltered items are always well mixed, find the number x of altered items as a function of t. Find the number T of days required to alter k per cent of the items.

Ans.: $x = N[1 - e^{-(n/N)t}]$, $\quad T = \frac{N}{n} \log \frac{100}{100 - k}$.

Problem 3.663

Two identical bathtubs are full of ice water at temperature 0°C. Half of the water in the first tub is allowed to run down the drain. Then hot water, having temperature 80°C, is allowed to run into the first tub until it is full. At the same time and at the same rate, hot water having temperature 80°C runs into the second tub and a well-stirred mixture of the hot and cold water runs down the drain. Find the final temperatures of the water in the two tubs. *Ans.*: 40° and 31.5°C.

Problem 3.664

If the tubs of the previous problem have volume V, how much hot water must be put through the second tub to bring the temperature to 40°C? *Ans.*: $0.693\ V$.

Problem 3.67

Two tanks in a chemical plant each contain about 50,000 gallons of liquid A. To each tank there should be added 5 gallons of liquid B; but through an accident all 10 gallons are put in one tank. Stirring apparatus keeps the tanks well stirred, and pumps which circulate liquid through the two tanks at the rate of 100 gallons per minute are part of the plant equipment. How long must the pumps be operated before the numbers of gallons of liquid B in the two tanks are 5.5 and 4.5?

Ans.: About 9.6 hours.

Problem 3.68

The first tank in a row contains a mixture of $G - g$ gallons of liquid A and g gallons of liquid B; each other tank contains G gallons of liquid A. From time $t = 0$, liquid A is pumped into the first tank at the rate of r gallons per minute, and a mixture of A and B is thus forced from each tank to the next at the same rate. Assume that the tanks are perfectly stirred. Letting $x_0(t)$, $x_1(t)$, $x_2(t)$, . . . denote the amounts of liquid B in the successive tanks at time t, show that

$$x_n = \frac{g}{n!}\left(\frac{r}{G}\right)^n t^n e^{-(r/G)t} \qquad n = 0, 1, 2, \ldots. \tag{3.69}$$

Show that, when $n > 0$, $x_n(t)$ increases until $t = nG/r$ and thereafter decreases and that the maximum value M_n of $x_n(t)$ is

$$M_n = g\frac{n^n e^{-n}}{n!} \qquad n = 1, 2, 3, \ldots . \tag{3.691}$$

[The right side of (3.691) can of course be used to compute M_n for any desired value of n; but it is an interesting fact that obvious properties of M_n give some information about the right side of (3.691). The obvious fact that the amount of liquid B in one tank can never exceed g implies that $n^n e^{-n}/n! \leqq 1$ and hence that

$$n! \geqq n^n e^{-n}. \tag{3.692}$$

By use of the *Stirling* (1692–1770) *formula*

$$n! = \sqrt{2n\pi}\, n^n e^{-n} e^{\theta_n/12n} \tag{3.693}$$

in which θ_n represents a sequence for which $0 < \theta_n < 1$, it is easy to show that M_n is approximately $g/\sqrt{2n\pi}$ (in the sense that the ratio is near 1) when n is large. Stirling's formula (3.693) has many important applications in many phases of pure and applied mathematics. Its proof is difficult.]

3.7. Compound Interest. If A dollars draws interest at rate k (where k may be, for example, 0.04 or 4 per cent) per year compounded annually, then the total amount of principal and interest will be $A(1 + k)$ at the end of 1 year, $A(1 + k)^2$ at the end of 2 years, and, in general, $A(1 + k)^n$ at the end of n years. If the money is loaned at rate k per year compounded monthly, then the total amount is $A(1 + k/12)$ at the end of 1 month, $A(1 + k/12)^2$ at the end of 2 months, $A(1 + k/12)^r$ at the end of r months, and $A(1 + k/12)^{12n}$ at the end of n years. In general, if the rate is k per year compounded m times a year, then the amount at the end of n years will be

$$A\left(1 + \frac{k}{m}\right)^{mn} = A\left[\left(1 + \frac{k}{m}\right)^m\right]^n. \tag{3.71}$$

Let k and n be fixed, and consider how this amount behaves as m becomes infinite and accordingly the length $1/m$ of a conversion interval approaches 0. The answer to this question is provided by the fact that

$$\lim_{m\to\infty}\left(1 + \frac{k}{m}\right)^m = e^k. \tag{3.72}$$

It thus appears that, when the conversion interval approaches 0, the amount at the end of n years approaches $y(n) = Ae^{kn}$. This analysis motivates the following definition: Money is said to increase at annual rate k *compounded continuously* if an amount A at a stated time increases to the amount

$$y(t) = Ae^{kt} \tag{3.73}$$

during the first t years after the stated time. The number t is not restricted to integer values; and when A and k are positive, the amount $y(t)$ increases continuously as t increases.

We have seen that (3.73) holds if and only if

$$\frac{dy}{dt} = ky; \tag{3.74}$$

hence, the condition that y *increases at rate* k *per year compounded continuously* implies and is implied by (3.74).

Problem 3.75

What rate of interest, compounded annually, is equivalent to 6 per cent compounded continuously? *Ans.:* 6.18 per cent.

Problem 3.76

A man has \$40,000 in a fund paying interest at the rate of 4 per cent per year compounded continuously. If he withdraws money continuously at the rate of \$2,400 per year, how long will the fund last? *Ans.:* 27+ years.

Problem 3.77

When a certain food product is produced, the number of organisms of a certain kind in a package is estimated to be N. In 60 days, the number of organisms is estimated to be $1{,}000N$. The "safe" number of organisms is $200N$. You are the Board of Health. What do you do to justify your salary and position?

3.8. Falling Bodies; Terminal Speeds. In this section, we consider the speed of a body of mass m falling toward the earth, on a vertical line, in the dense part of our atmosphere. During such falls, the distance from the center of the earth changes relatively little, and we may suppose that the gravitational force is mgU where g is a constant (32 feet per second per second) and U is a unit vector directed downward. In case no other forces are present (as when the body falls in a vacuum or air resistance is neglected) the formulas

$$a = gU, \qquad v = (gt + c_1)U, \qquad s = \tfrac{1}{2}gt^2 + c_1t + c_2$$

involving acceleration a, velocity v, and coordinate s are thoroughly familiar and are obtained by simple integration.

When air resistance is taken into account, it is quite impossible to work out exact formulas giving a, v, and s in terms of t. In addition to the gravitational force, there is a resistive force whose magnitude increases as the speed increases and, moreover, increases as the body enters more dense atmosphere nearer the surface of the earth. This resistive force is the reason why speeds of aviators descending by parachute keep within reasonable bounds. It is the reason why bombs dropped from great heights do not hit the earth appreciably harder than bombs dropped from a few thousand feet. Attempts to compute speeds of falling bodies depend upon experimental results which show how resistance depends upon speed and density, and how density depends upon distance from the surface of the earth. It is all quite complicated, and in such cases we start making progress by considering simple cases with simplifying approximations.

Henceforth we confine attention to falls over intervals over which the density of the atmosphere can be considered to be constant. Without going into details, we can remark that attempts have been made to determine positive constants k_1, k_2, and k_3 such that the magnitude $|R|$ of the resistance R and the magnitude (speed) $|v|$ of the velocity v are related by the formula $|R| = k_1|v|$ when $|v|$ is "not too great," by the formula $|R| = k_2|v|^2$ when $|v|$ is "great," and by the formula $|R| = k_3|v|^3$ when $|v|$ is "very great." If, within a given range of velocities, the formula $|R| = k|v|^n$ is valid, it is easy to work out the equation of motion of the body which falls earthward with coordinate s increasing as t increases so $v = |v|U = (ds/dt)U$ and $|v| = ds/dt \geq 0$. The gravitational force is mgU, the resistive force R is $-k(ds/dt)^nU$, and the Newton law $ma = F$ gives

$$m\frac{d^2s}{dt^2}U = mgU - k\left(\frac{ds}{dt}\right)^n U \tag{3.81}$$

or

$$\frac{d^2s}{dt^2} + \frac{k}{m}\left(\frac{ds}{dt}\right)^n = g. \tag{3.82}$$

Whether n is an integer or not, this equation can be attacked by methods to be described later.

In case $n = 1$, the equation for the scalar velocity v becomes

$$\frac{dv}{dt} + \frac{k}{m}v = g \tag{3.83}$$

so that

$$v = \frac{mg}{k} + ce^{-(k/m)t}. \tag{3.831}$$

On letting $v(0) = v_0$, we can put this in the form

$$v(t) = \frac{mg}{k} + \left(v_0 - \frac{mg}{k}\right)e^{-(k/m)t}. \tag{3.84}$$

It follows from this that if $v_0 = mg/k$ or $v_0 < mg/k$ or $v_0 > mg/k$, then, respectively, $v = mg/k$ or $v < mg/k$ or $v > mg/k$ for each t; and that, in each case, $v(t) \to mg/k$, as t increases. This limiting scalar velocity mg/k, which we better call speed when we summarize results, is called the *terminal speed* of the falling body.

Problem 3.85

When a parachutist jumps with his parachute closed, k is relatively near 0 and the speed increases toward a corresponding terminal speed; when the parachute opens, the resistance factor k suddenly increases to a much larger value and the speed decreases toward a new terminal speed. Sketch a rough graph to exhibit the speed $|v(t)|$ of the falling parachutist.

Problem 3.86

Compare the descents of two identical men who jump with identical parachutes, the first carrying no extra weight, and the second carrying military equipment which weighs as much as the man and parachute, but which is so compact that it does not appreciably change the resistance factors.

Problem 3.87

A baseball of mass m is thrown vertically upward from the surface of the earth with initial speed v_0. Let s be the coordinate of the ball at time t, with $s = 0$ at the surface of the earth and $s > 0$ above the earth. Assume no forces upon the ball except a constant gravitational force mg and an air resistance of magnitude $k|v|$ where v is the scalar velocity. Show that

$$v = -\frac{mg}{k} + \left(v_0 + \frac{mg}{k}\right) e^{-(k/m)t},$$

find the time at which the ball reaches its greatest height H, and show that

$$H = \frac{mv_0}{k} - \frac{m^2g}{k^2} \log\left(1 + \frac{kv_0}{mg}\right).$$

Note that calculating H is least palatable when k/m is small, but it is just when k/m is small that we can make most effective use of the good old series

$$\log(1 + x) = x - \frac{x^2}{2} + \frac{x^3}{3} - \cdots.$$

Use this to obtain

$$H = \frac{v_0^2}{g}\left[\frac{1}{2} - \frac{1}{3}\frac{kv_0}{mg} + \frac{1}{4}\left(\frac{kv_0}{mg}\right)^2 - \frac{1}{5}\left(\frac{kv_0}{mg}\right)^3 + \cdots\right].$$

Note that this formula, unlike its parent, is meaningful and correct when $k = 0$ and is easy to use when kv_0/mg is small.

Problem 3.88

We want to find the constant k of the previous problem. We drop the ball from rest and find that it falls H feet in T seconds. Show that k must satisfy the equation

$$k^2H - kgmT + gm^2[1 - e^{-(k/m)T}] = 0.$$

Problem 3.89

Assuming the simple resistance law $|R| = k|v|$, derive the equation or equations governing the flight of a projectile of mass m in an (x, y) plane whose positive y axis is above the origin. Consider the short-range case in which the only forces on the projectile are a resistance whose direction is always exactly opposite to that of the velocity and a constant gravitational force which always has the direction of the negative y axis. Use complex numbers as in Section 2.5. *Solution:* Let the vector running from the origin to the position of the projectile at time t be

$$z(t) = x(t) + iy(t).$$

The velocity v and acceleration a are then $z'(t)$ and $z''(t)$. The gravitational force is $-img$. The resistance R is

$$R = |R|\left(\frac{-v}{|v|}\right) = k|v|\left(\frac{-v}{|v|}\right) = -kv = -kz'(t).$$

The Newton Law $ma = F$ then gives

$$m\frac{d^2z}{dt^2} = -img - k\frac{dz}{dt}.$$

This is equivalent to the two equations

$$m\frac{d^2x}{dt^2} + k\frac{dx}{dt} = 0$$
$$m\frac{d^2y}{dt^2} + k\frac{dy}{dt} = -mg$$

involving only real quantities.

3.9. A Simple Electric Circuit. In this section we consider the problem of determining, as a function of the time t, the electric *current* I in a circuit (Fig. 3.91) containing a *resistor* (resistance R) an *inductor* (inductance L), and an applied (or impressed) *electromotive force* E.

One who is not familiar with such terms as electric current, resistance, inductance, and electromotive force should not be disturbed. It serves our present purpose to think of electricity as being stuff which flows; of an electromotive force as being something which, depending on direction or sign attached, tends to increase or decrease flow of electricity; of a resistor as being something which always tends to diminish flow of electricity; and of an inductor as being something which tends to keep electricity flowing at a constant rate by opposing both increase and decrease in rate of flow. With proper adjustment of units and under general conditions which good electrical engineers must know about, the resistor produces an electromotive force equal to RI, and the inductor produces force equal to $L\,dI/dt$.

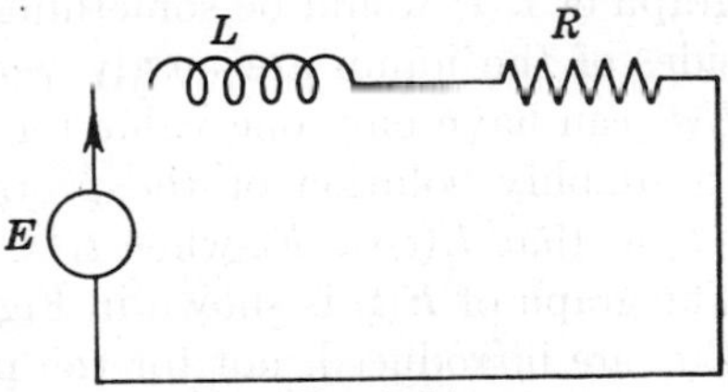

Fig. 3.91

By use of rules for attaching signs to and equating electromotive forces, one obtains the differential equation

$$L\frac{dI}{dt} + RI = E \tag{3.92}$$

which governs the flow $I(t)$ in the circuit. The resistance R and inductance L are always positive; in this discussion they are regarded as constants.

The electromotive force E may be either constant, say E_0, or variable, say $E(t)$. A constant electromotive force E_0 may, for example, be obtained by keeping a battery attached at the spot marked E in Fig. 3.91. A variable electromotive force $E(t) = E_0 \sin \omega t$ may be obtained by hooking up ordinary alternating "house" current.

Another way to get a nonconstant electromotive force $E(t)$ is to operate a switch in such a way that a battery is attached and detached over alternate intervals.* If the switch is closed at time t_1, the electromotive force $E(t)$ may rise very quickly (but continuously) from the value 0 at

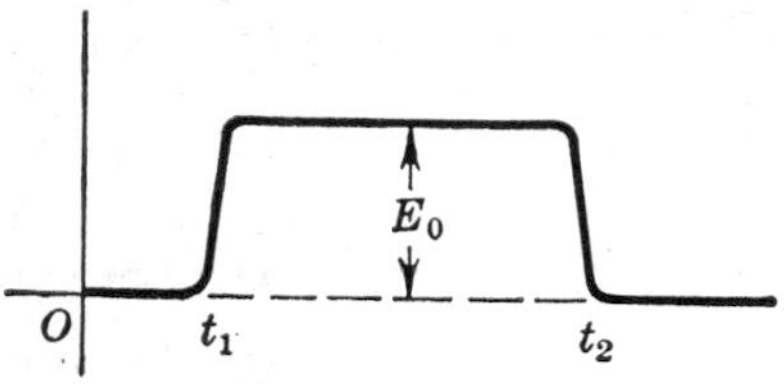

Fig. 3.93

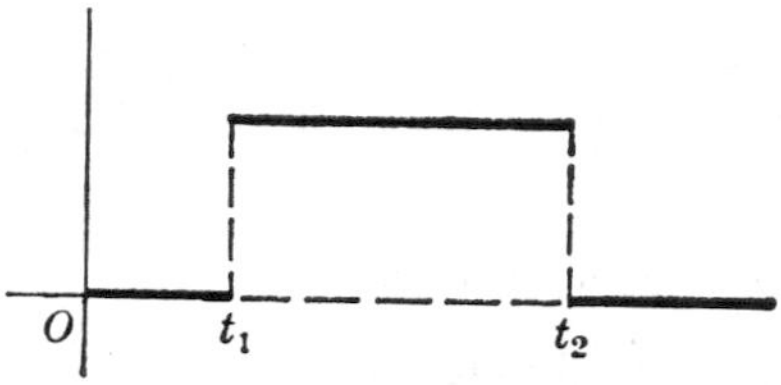

Fig. 3.931

t_1 to a value very nearly equal to E_0; and if the switch is opened at a later time t_2, the electromotive force may fall very quickly (but continuously) from the value E_0 at t_2 to a value very nearly 0. Then the true graph of $E(t)$ would be something like that shown in Fig. 3.93 where the sides of the hump are nearly vertical but, of course, not vertical since $E(t)$ can have only one value for each t. In such cases, it is customary to simplify solution of the problem by *assuming* that $E(t) = 0$ when $t \leqq t_1$, that $E(t) = E_0$ when $t_1 < t \leqq t_2$, and that $E(t) = 0$ when $t > t_2$. The graph of $E(t)$ is shown in Fig. 3.931. Thus discontinuous functions $E(t)$ are introduced, not for the purpose of complicating a simple world but, on the contrary, for the purpose of simplifying a complicated world.† With the admission of discontinuous impressed electromotive forces, it becomes necessary to revise the requirement that the differential equation

* Much electrical equipment is operated in this way, and much attention has been given to the engineering problem of constructing switches which operate so as to give "clean makes and breaks."

† Of course, it is not the world that is changed; it is the description of the world that is changed from a very complicated description which is exact to a very simple description which is sufficiently exact for practical purposes.

(3.92) hold for all values of t. (Why?) Accordingly we revise the statement concerning the differential equation as follows:

The current $I(t)$ is a continuous function of t such that

$$L\frac{dI}{dt} + RI = E(t) \tag{3.94}$$

*for each value of t for which $E(t)$ is continuous.**

The equation (3.94) is linear, and the method of Section 3.1 is used to solve it. Dividing (3.94) by L and multiplying by the integrating factor $e^{(R/L)t}$ give

$$\frac{d}{dt}\, e^{(R/L)t}I(t) = \frac{1}{L}\, e^{(R/L)t}E(t).$$

This holds if and only if

$$e^{(R/L)t}I(t) = c + \frac{1}{L}\int_{t_0}^{t} e^{(R/L)u}E(u)du.$$

Letting $I_0 = I(t_0)$, we see that $c = e^{(R/L)t_0}I_0$ and hence that

$$I(t) = I_0e^{-(R/L)(t-t_0)} + \frac{1}{L}\, e^{-(R/L)t}\int_{t_0}^{t} e^{(R/L)u}E(u)du. \tag{3.95}$$

This is the solution of our problem.

Since $R/L > 0$, the first term

$$I_0e^{-(R/L)(t-t_0)} \tag{3.96}$$

in the right member of (3.95) approaches 0 as t increases, and measurable effects of this current disappear as t increases; for this reason this current is called a *transient current* or simply a *transient*. The ratio R/L tells how rapidly the transient fades.

Problem 3.97

If $E(t)$ is a constant E_0, show that

$$I(t) = \frac{E_0}{R} + \left(I_0 - \frac{E_0}{R}\right)e^{-(R/L)(t-t_0)}.$$

Draw graphs for cases in which (i) $I_0 > E_0/R$, (ii) $I_0 < E_0/R$, and (iii) $I_0 = E_0/R$.

* If this book were written for experts in modern analysis, we should require merely that $E(t)$ be Lebesgue integrable over each finite interval and that $I(t)$ be an absolutely continuous function satisfying the differential equation for all t except possibly a set of measure 0. For present purposes, it suffices to suppose that $E(t)$ is bounded and has at most a finite set of discontinuities in each finite interval; the above requirement is then appropriate.

Problem 3.98

Show that, when $E(t)$ is the electromotive force whose graph is shown in Fig. 3.931, the graph of $I(t)$ must have the form shown in Fig. 3.981. Show that for values of t

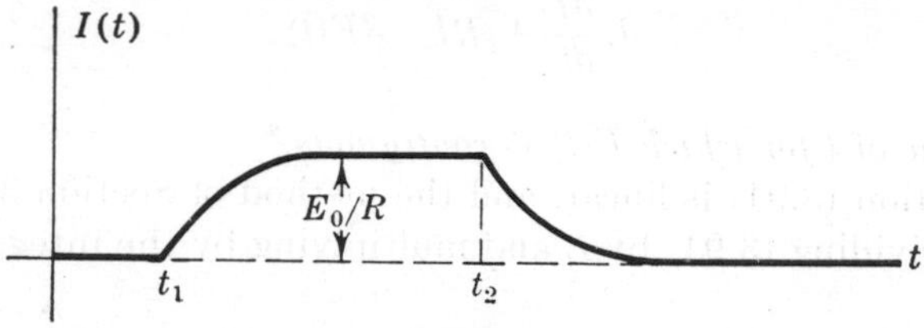

FIG. 3.981

just a little greater than t_1, the slope of the curve is nearly E_0/L. Discuss this slope as a function of L. One who objects to the term "just a little greater than" may show that

$$\lim_{t \to t_1+} I'(t) = \frac{E_0}{L} \tag{3.982}$$

where the + sign after t_1 indicates that only values of t greater than t_1 are considered [Assume that both $E(t)$ and $I(t)$ are 0 when $t \leqq t_1$.]

Remark 3.983

The important case in which $E = E_0 \sin \omega t$ has been treated in Problems 3.186 and 3.187 and will be treated later.

3.99. Survival Functions; Renewal Theory. This section involves ideas that are very important in many practical problems and can be of interest to everybody. Suppose that we start at time $x = 0$ with a huge number $y(0)$ of infant moths in a fur coat or new electronic tubes in a digital computer or new windshield wipers on automobiles or new television sets or new toothbrushes. Suppose that, by use of appropriate theories or observations, we have determined or could determine a *survival function* $s(x)$ such that $y(0)s(x)$ of these survive at time x when $x > 0$. In typical situations $s(0) = 1$, $0 \leqq s(x) \leqq 1$ when $x > 0$, $s(x_2) \leqq s(x_1)$ when $x_2 > x_1$, and $s(x) \to 0$ as $x \to \infty$.

We now introduce a *renewal function* $r(x, y)$ which is sometimes a given function and is sometimes an unknown function which we wish to determine to produce desired results. To see how this function is used, let $x > 0$, and let the interval $0 \leqq t \leqq x$ be separated into subintervals (x_{k-1}, x_k) by points $x_0, x_1, \ldots, x_n$ for which

$$0 = x_0 < x_1 < \cdots < x_n = x.$$

For each $k = 1, 2, \ldots, n$, let $x_{k-1} \leqq t_k \leqq x_k$. Suppose that, at time t_k,

$$r(t_k, y(t_k))(x_k - x_{k-1}) \tag{3.9901}$$

new items are added to the population so that, in the jargon of the trade, the population is renewed. Supposing that these new items are governed by the same survival function that governed the original ones, we find that the number of these surviving at time x (that is, the number surviving $x - t_k$ units of time later) is

$$r(t_k, y(t_k))s(x - t_k)(x_k - x_{k-1}). \tag{3.9902}$$

The total population $y(x)$ at time x, due to the original population $y(0)$ and the n renewals at times $t_1, t_2, \ldots, t_n$, is therefore

$$y(x) = y(0)s(x) + \sum_{k=1}^{n} r(t_k, y(t_k))s(x - t_k)(x_k - x_{k-1}). \tag{3.9903}$$

Under the assumption that $r(x, y)$ and $s(x)$ are reasonably decent functions (continuity is sufficient but not necessary), the hypothesis that the numbers $x_k - x_{k-1}$ are all small leads, by the definition of the Riemann integral, to the conclusion that there is little difference between the function $y(x)$ in (3.9903) and the function $y(x)$ in

$$y(x) = y(0)s(x) + \int_0^x r(t, y(t))s(x - t)dt. \tag{3.9904}$$

This $y(x)$ is the population at time x resulting from the initial population $y(0)$ and continuous renewals at rate $r(x, y(x))$. As can easily be imagined, these ideas and formulas have many swarms of applications, and large books can be written about special swarms. Many useful applications involve special renewal functions $r(x, y)$ that are independent of y and hence can be denoted by $r(x)$. In this case (3.9904) takes the much simpler form

$$y(x) = y(0)s(x) + \int_0^x r(t)s(x - t)dt. \tag{3.9905}$$

Problem 3.991

Determine those survival functions $s(x)$, if any, for which the population $y(x)$ in (3.9904) always maintains the constant value $y(0)$ when the renewal function $r(x, y)$ always has the constant value k. *Ans.*: See Problem 3.1841.

Problem 3.992

Can we determine a constant renewal function, say $r(x, y) = k$, such that the population $y(x)$ in (3.9904) will grow in such a way that, for a given positive constant λ, $y(x) = y(0)(1 + \lambda x)$? *Ans.*: Only when the survival function $s(x)$ has a very special form which can be determined.

Problem 3.993

For what survival functions $s(x)$, assumed to satisfy the condition $0 \leqq s(x) \leqq 1$, can we be sure that the population $y(x)$ in (3.9904) will be bounded whenever the renewal function $r(x, y)$ is bounded? *Ans.*: Those for which $\int_0^\infty s(x)dx$ exists.

Problem 3.994

A population of P items is said to have the *age density function* $\delta(x)$ if $\delta(x) \geqq 0$, if $\int_0^\infty \delta(x)dx = 1$, and if the number of items with ages between a and b is $P \int_a^b \delta(x)dx$ whenever $0 \leqq a < b$. Show that if a population has the survival function $s(x)$, if $\delta(t_k) > 0$, and if $P\delta(t_k)(x_k - x_{k-1})$ items have age t_k, then $s(t_k) > 0$ and the number of these items surviving to age $t_k + x$ is, when $x > 0$,

$$P\delta(t_k)\,\frac{s(t_k + x)}{s(t_k)}\,(x_k - x_{k-1}).$$

Use these ideas to show that if we start at time $x = 0$ with $y(0)$ items having age density function $\delta(x)$ and survival function $s(x)$, then the number of these items surviving at a later time x is the first term in the right member of the formula

$$y(x) = y(0)\int_0^\infty \delta(t)\,\frac{s(t + x)}{s(t)}\,dt + \int_0^x r(t, y(t))s(x - t)dt. \tag{3.9941}$$

This formula then gives the number of survivors at time x when we start with the population having age density function $\delta(x)$ and survival function $s(x)$, and supply renewals as in the derivation of (3.9904).

Some problems involving (3.9941) can be very complicated, but the formula will show us something if we tinker with it. Suppose

$$\int_0^\infty s(t)dt = I$$

where I is a positive constant. Then we can set $\delta(t) = s(t)/I$ and $r(x, y) = y(0)/I$. Substitution in (3.9941) then gives

$$y(x) = \frac{y(0)}{I}\left[\int_x^\infty s(t)dt + \int_0^x s(t)dt\right]$$

and hence $y(x) = y(0)$. What could be simpler? This tells us how to choose an initial age density function and a constant renewal rate in order to make $y(x)$ have at all times the initial value $y(0)$.

Problem 3.995

Suppose that the Cayuga Rock Salt Mines have been continuously lit for many years by N light bulbs that have the survival function $1/(1 + a^2x^2)$ where a is a positive constant and x is measured in years. Show that replacements must be made at the rate of $2aN/\pi$ per year.

Problem 3.996

Read the first paragraph of Section 3.99 and think about it. We can easily imagine that a huge collection of new electric clocks possesses a survival function $s(x)$. However, if we start at time $x = 0$ with 25 new clocks, it is absurd to claim that exactly 25 $s(x)$ of them will survive at a later time x; different samples would surely exhibit different phenomena. To handle this situation, and hordes of more or less similar ones, we need the theories of probability and statistics.

CHAPTER 4

FAMILIES OF CURVES; EQUATIONS OF HIGHER DEGREE

4.0. Introduction. It is the opinion of the author that students taking a short course in our subject should read all of this chapter rather casually and then pass on to other topics. The chapter contains ideas that everybody should have but relatively few people should dwell upon very long. Since the topics covered sound quite geometrical, the author must emphasize the fact that this view does not cast aspersions upon modern geometry; there is little if any modern geometry in it.

4.1. Families of Curves. For each constant $c > 0$, the equation

$$x^2 + y^2 = c \tag{4.11}$$

is the equation of the circle with center at the origin and radius $\sqrt{c}$. The constant c is called a *parameter*, and the totality of circles obtained for positive values of c is called a *one-parameter family* of curves. Likewise, if m is fixed, the equation

$$y = mx + b \tag{4.12}$$

furnishes, for different values of the parameter b, the one-parameter family of curves which consists of the set of parallel lines having slope m; if b is fixed, the equation furnishes, for different values of m, the one-parameter family of curves which consists of all lines through the point $(0, b)$ except the vertical line through $(0, b)$. If neither m nor b is fixed and both m and b are regarded as parameters, then (4.12) represents the *two-parameter family* of curves consisting of all nonvertical lines. If $f(x)$ is a differentiable function of x, then

$$y - f(c) = f'(c)(x - c) \tag{4.13}$$

represents the one-parameter family of tangents to the graph of the function $y = f(x)$.

When parameters enter into an equation in such a way that different values of the parameters do not yield different equations, it is often desirable to reduce the number of parameters. For example,

$$y = x + a + b \tag{4.14}$$

gives the same equation when $a = 3$, $b = 4$ as when $a = 4$, $b = 3$; and the family of lines (4.14) is the same as the family

$$y = x + c \tag{4.141}$$

where c is a single parameter. Similar reduction is possible if $y = ae^{x+b}$ since $y = ae^be^x = ce^x$ where $c = ae^b$. A more troublesome example is that of the family

$$\alpha y = \beta x + \gamma \tag{4.15}$$

where α, β, and γ are three parameters and α and β are not both zero. The family (4.15) consists of all lines in the plane; but $\alpha = 2, \beta = 3, \gamma = 4$ give the same line as $\alpha = 4, \beta = 6, \gamma = 8$. It is natural to try to reduce the number of parameters by dividing by α, setting $m = \beta/\alpha$, setting $b = \gamma/\alpha$, and writing (4.15) in the form

$$y = mx + b \tag{4.151}$$

so that there are now two parameters and different pairs of values of m and b always give different lines. But of course division by α is impossible when $\alpha = 0$, and hence the lines in (4.15) for which $\alpha = 0$ (*i.e.*, the vertical lines) are not included in the family (4.151). In this case, reduction of the number of parameters resulted in the loss of all vertical lines.

It may be true that there is no subject in mathematics upon which more unintelligible nonsense has been written than that of families of curves.* The following example illustrates a difficulty confronting anyone who hopes to classify families of curves according to the number of parameters appearing in the equation of the family. If c is a real nonnegative number, then c can be written in exactly one way in the form

$$c = \cdots c_{-3}c_{-2}c_{-1}c_0.c_1c_2c_3 \cdots \tag{4.16}$$

where the central dot is a decimal point; each c_n is one of the digits $0, 1, \ldots, 9$; $c_{-n} = 0$ for all sufficiently great n; c_n may be but is not necessarily 0 for all sufficiently great n; and there is no number N such that $c_n = 9$ whenever $n > N$. For example,

$$\begin{aligned} \tfrac{1}{8} &= \cdots 000.125000 \cdots \\ \tfrac{4}{3} &= \cdots 001.333333 \cdots \\ \pi &= \cdots 003.14159\ 26535\ 89793 \cdots \\ 1{,}000e &= \cdots 002{,}718.28182\ 84590\ 45 \cdots. \end{aligned}$$

* A biography of Thomas Gray (1716–1771) says that he withdrew from Cambridge, without taking a degree, because of his dislike of mathematics. Perhaps Gray was thinking of families of curves when he wrote his famous lines

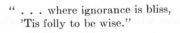

"... where ignorance is bliss,
'Tis folly to be wise."

Let four functions $f_1(c)$, $f_2(c)$, $f_3(c)$, and $f_4(c)$ be defined for $c \geqq 0$ by the formulas

$$(4.171) \qquad f_1(c) = \cdots c_{-12}c_{-8}c_{-4}.c_0c_4c_8c_{12} \cdots$$
$$(4.172) \qquad f_2(c) = \cdots c_{-11}c_{-7}c_{-3}.c_1c_5c_9c_{13} \cdots$$
$$(4.173) \qquad f_3(c) = \cdots c_{-10}c_{-6}c_{-2}.c_2c_6c_{10}c_{14} \cdots$$
$$(4.174) \qquad f_4(c) = \cdots c_{-9}c_{-5}c_{-1}.c_3c_7c_{11}c_{15} \cdots$$

Then, for each $c \geqq 0$, the equation

$$(4.18) \qquad y = [f_1(c) - f_2(c)]x + [f_3(c) - f_4(c)]$$

is the equation of a nonvertical line. Moreover, it is easy to see that each nonvertical line is obtained for an infinite set of values of c. For example, the line

$$y = 2x - \tfrac{3}{2}$$

is obtained by setting

$$f_1(c) = 3, \qquad f_2(c) = 1, \qquad f_3(c) = 0.5, \qquad f_4(c) = 2$$

and hence by setting

$$c = 31{,}020.05.$$

Therefore the two-parameter family (4.151) of lines is exactly the same as the one-parameter family (4.18).

If n is an integer greater than 1 and we have an n-parameter family of functions

$$(4.181) \qquad y = f(x, c_1, c_2, \ldots, c_n)$$

involving n parameters $c_1, c_2, \ldots, c_n$, we can employ the same method to show that the family is the same as a one-parameter family

$$(4.182) \qquad y = F(x, c).$$

We start with

$$(4.183) \qquad f_1(c) = \cdots c_{-4n}c_{-2n}.c_0c_{2n}c_{4n}c_{8n} \cdots$$

and define $2n$ functions instead of the 4 which begin with (4.171). On this account, it is easy to enter the realm of fantasy when making general statements about n-parameter families of functions and their graphs. With this disturbing remark, we pass to the next section, hoping that some interesting or useful ideas (but no bad ones) can be gleaned from it.

Problem 4.19

Find what lines are representable in the form

$$y = f_1(c)x + f_2(c)$$

where (4.16) holds and

$$f_1(c) = \cdots c_{-4}c_{-2}.c_0c_2c_4 \cdots$$
$$f_2(c) = \cdots c_{-3}c_{-1}.c_1c_3c_5 \cdots.$$

Problem 4.191

Considering positive values of x, prove that if $A \neq 0$ and y is a continuous function of x for which

$$Ay^2 + Bxy + Cx^2 = 0,$$

then there is a constant k such that $y = kx$.

Problem 4.192

This problem involves an amazing family F of fancy curves. It should be illegal to print a figure showing the curves; everyone should earn the right to see it by drawing it for himself. Let h be a fixed positive constant. Each curve C in the family F is composed partly of *upper semicircles* which lie in upper half of an (x, y) plane and have their centers at $(-h, 0)$, and partly of *lower semicircles* which lie in the lower half of the plane and have their centers at $(h, 0)$. The upper and lower semicircles are joined at points on the x axis at which C has vertical tangents. Only two of the curves in the family have end points, and the figure becomes more vivid when these are colored red and green. Show that the slope dy/dx of C at a point (x, y) on C for which $y \neq 0$ is given by

$$\frac{dy}{dx} = -\frac{x + h \operatorname{sgn} y}{y} \tag{4.1921}$$

where, as usual, sgn y is 1 when $y > 0$, is 0 when $y = 0$, and is -1 when $y < 0$. *Remark:* We have done some engineering. We have stumbled upon the solutions of (4.1921), which, according to Problem 5.183, is the *phase-plane equation* of the equation

$$\frac{d^2x}{dt^2} + h \operatorname{sgn} \frac{dx}{dt} + x = 0. \tag{4.1922}$$

The x and y of our problem are the displacement and velocity (or electrical charge and current) in an undamped oscillator which has an input of constant magnitude and of sign always opposite to that of the scalar velocity (or current). In the mechanical case, such inputs (or forces) are produced by *Coulomb* (1736–1806) *friction.* The index refers to other occurrences of phase planes, and anyone who is interested in physics or engineering or electronic computers should not miss opportunities to learn about these planes.

4.2. Differential Equations of Families of Curves. We begin with examples. For each positive constant c, the graph of the equation

$$x^2 + y^2 = c^2 \tag{4.21}$$

is a circle. Equations of the top and bottom semicircles can be put in the form $y = y(x)$, and equations of the right and left semicircles can be put in the form $x = x(y)$. The simplest explicit equations of the circle are the parametric equations $x = c \cos t$, $y = c \sin t$, the circle being traced once by the point (x, y) as t increases over an interval of length 2π. We shall therefore think of the x and y appearing in (4.21) as being differentiable functions of a parameter t where we may, if we wish to confine attention to a part of the circle, let $t = x$ or $t = y$. Differentiating (4.21) gives the differential equation

$$x\frac{dx}{dt} + y\frac{dy}{dt} = 0. \tag{4.211}$$

This is a (or perhaps *the*) differential equation of the family (4.21), or of the family of graphs of (4.21).

If c is a real constant, the graph of

$$(x - c)^2 + y^2 = 1 \tag{4.22}$$

is a circle with center at $(c, 0)$ and radius 1. After introducing t, as before, we can differentiate (4.22) to obtain

$$(x - c)\frac{dx}{dt} + y\frac{dy}{dt} = 0. \tag{4.221}$$

The next step is to eliminate c from (4.22) and (4.221), and we try to learn something by making the pretense that the problem is difficult. By a result of eliminating c from (4.22) and (4.221), we mean an equation which (i) involves no quantities other than those appearing in (4.22) and (4.221), (ii) does not involve c, and (iii) is satisfied whenever both (4.22) and (4.221) are satisfied. There is no one single form that such a result must have, and some results may be much better than others. Sometimes there is a result which everybody agrees is a best one, and it seems that nearly everybody is quite happy when this is called *the* result. On the other hand, there is *always* a worst result; the differential equation

$$0x + 0y + 0\frac{dx}{dt} + 0\frac{dy}{dt} = 0 \tag{4.222}$$

always meets the requirement and is always completely useless as a source of information about $x(t)$ and $y(t)$ because it is satisfied whenever $x(t)$ and $y(t)$ are differentiable functions. Getting back to (4.22) and (4.221), we eliminate c to obtain the equation

$$\left(y\frac{dy}{dt}\right)^2 + \left(y\frac{dx}{dt}\right)^2 = 1 \tag{4.223}$$

which is a (and perhaps even *the*) differential equation of the family (4.22). Putting $t = x$ gives the equation

$$\left(y\frac{dy}{dx}\right)^2 + y^2 = 1 \tag{4.224}$$

which holds whenever y is a differentiable function of x and c is a constant for which (4.22) holds.

It is thoroughly essential to observe that terminology which makes (4.223) and (4.224) differential equations of the family (4.22) does not imply that the *only* functions satisfying the differential equation are functions satisfying (4.22). Such an implication would clash violently with the obvious fact that the function y for which $y(x) = 1$ when $-\infty < x < \infty$ satisfies (4.224) while there is no c for which (4.22) is satisfied. If, for purposes of argument, we agree that (4.222) is a bad differential equation of the family (4.22) because too many functions satisfy it, then we are stuck. The best differential equations may be bad too; it is all a matter of the magnitude of the sins.

Perhaps we should recognize the fact that some philosophers do not like bad eggs and claim that the only eggs are the best eggs. These poor fellows take a dim view of (4.222) and create for themselves the impossible task of proving that there is always a best formula obtainable by eliminating c from two formulas containing c.

Problem 4.23

Show that, if (4.22) is solved for c and the resulting equation is differentiated, the differential equation (4.222) will result.

We now begin what a charitable person might call a general theory. The results are summed up in the paragraph containing (4.27). Each of the equations (4.21) and (4.22) has, when all terms are transposed to the left side, the form $f(x, y, c) = 0$. Hence our discussion of the two equations motivates the following terminology. If, for some range of values of t, $x(t)$ and $y(t)$ are differentiable functions of t for which

$$f(x, y, c) = 0, \tag{4.241}$$

if we can differentiate with respect to t to obtain

$$\phi(x, y, x'(t), y'(t), c) = 0 \tag{4.242}$$

and if we eliminate c from (2.241) and (2.242) to obtain

$$F(x, y, x'(t), y'(t)) = 0, \tag{4.243}$$

then (4.243) is called a differential equation of the family (4.241).

Suppose now we start with an equation

$$f(x, y, c_1, c_2) = 0 \tag{4.25}$$

in which two parameters appear in some way or other. Suppose differentiation gives

$$\phi(x, y, x'(t), y'(t), c_1, c_2) = 0. \tag{4.251}$$

Except in cases which may sometimes be called trivial, it is not possible to obtain a useful formula by eliminating c_1 and c_2 from (4.25) and (4.251).

In many cases it is possible to differentiate again to obtain

$$\psi(x, y, x'(t), y'(t), x''(t), y''(t), c_1, c_2) = 0 \tag{4.252}$$

and eliminate c_1 and c_2 from the three equations to obtain

$$F(x, y, x'(t), y'(t), x''(t), y''(t)) = 0. \tag{4.253}$$

This is then called a differential equation of the family (4.25).

The general case, which includes the preceding ones, is the following. When n is a positive integer and the function f in

$$f(x, y, c_1, c_2, \ldots, c_n) = 0 \tag{4.26}$$

has appropriate partial derivatives, we can eliminate $c_1, c_2, \ldots, c_n$, from this formula and the n formulas obtained by differentiating n times with respect to t to obtain

$$F(x, y, x'(t), y'(t), \ldots, x^{(n)}(t), y^{(n)}(t)) = 0. \tag{4.261}$$

This equation is then called a differential equation of the family (4.27). If the best equation obtainable is one like (4.222), so be it. Sometimes it is possible to obtain useful equations. Sometimes there is a best equation which everybody is willing to call *the* differential equation of the family. The nature of the results obtained depends upon the nature of the function f in the equation with which we started. What we have said is about all that can be said when the nature of f is completely unknown.

Problem 4.27

Find differential equations of the following families in which a, b, c, and d are parameters:

(a) $y = ax + b$ — *Ans.:* $y'' = 0$

(b) $y = cx + c^2$ — *Ans.:* $y = y'x + y'^2$

(c) $y = a \cos x + b \sin x$ — *Ans.:* $y'' + y = 0$

(d) $y = c \sin (x + d)$ — *Ans.:* $y'' + y = 0$

(e) $y = a + b \cos x$ — *Ans.:* $y'' \sin x - y' \cos x = 0$

(f) $\sin x + \sin y = c$ — *Ans.:* $y' \cos y + \cos x = 0$

(g) $y = \tan (x + c)$ — *Ans.:* $y' = 1 + y^2$

(h) $y = ce^x$ — *Ans.:* $y' = y$

(i) $y = e^{ax}$ — *Ans.:* $xy' = y \log y$

(j) $y = \sin ax$ — *Ans.:* $xy' = \sqrt{1 - y^2} \sin^{-1} y$

(k) $y = ae^x + b \sin x$

Ans.: $(\sin x + \cos x)\dfrac{d^2y}{dx^2} - 2 \sin x \dfrac{dy}{dx} + (\sin x - \cos x)y = 0$

(l) $y^2 = \dfrac{x^3}{a - x}$ — *Ans.:* $\dfrac{dy}{dx} = \dfrac{y(y^2 + 3x^2)}{2x^3}$

The graphs are *cissoids*.

Problem 4.28

Assuming a to be a fixed constant (not a parameter), show that a differential equation of the family of curves

$$\frac{x^2}{c^2} + \frac{y^2}{c^2 - a^2} = 1 \tag{4.281}$$

is

$$xyy'^2 + (x^2 - y^2 - a^2)y' - xy = 0. \tag{4.282}$$

[*Remark:* The graphs of (4.281) are confocal conics with foci at $(-a, 0)$ and $(a, 0)$; see Problem 4.79 and Section 5.6.]

Problem 4.29

There are different ways of approaching the problem of finding differential equations of the family

$$ax^2 + 2bxy + y^2 + 2dx + 2ey + f = 0.$$

Show that solving for y gives

$$y = -(bx + e) \pm \sqrt{px^2 + 2qx + r}$$

where p, g, r are constants and then show that

$$((y'')^{-\frac{2}{3}})''' = 0$$

and

$$9(y'')^2y^v - 30y''y^{iv} + 40y''' = 0.$$

Problem 4.291

Show that the differential equation of the family

$$y = \frac{cf_1(x) + f_2(x)}{cf_3(x) + f_4(x)}, \tag{4.2911}$$

in which f_1, f_2, f_3, f_4 are differentiable functions with nonzero determinant

$$\Delta = \begin{vmatrix} f_1 & f_2 \\ f_3 & f_4 \end{vmatrix} = f_1f_4 - f_2f_3,$$

is

$$\Delta y' = \begin{vmatrix} f_3 & f_4 \\ f_3' & f_4' \end{vmatrix} y^2 + \left[\begin{vmatrix} f_2 & f_3 \\ f_2' & f_3' \end{vmatrix} - \begin{vmatrix} f_1 & f_4 \\ f_1' & f_4' \end{vmatrix}\right] y + \begin{vmatrix} f_1 & f_2 \\ f_1' & f_2' \end{vmatrix}.$$

Division by the coefficient of y' gives a *Riccati* (1707–1775) *equation*

$$y'(x) = P(x)[y(x)]^2 + Q(x)y(x) + R(x). \tag{4.2912}$$

Remark: One reason for interest in (4.2911) is its close relation to cross ratios. If y_1, y_2, y_3, y_4 are four different functions for which

$$y_k(x) = \frac{c_kf_1(x) + f_2(x)}{c_kf_3(x) + f_4(x)} \qquad k = 1, 2, 3, 4, \tag{4.2913}$$

a little simplification of quotients shows that, for each x,

$$\frac{y_4 - y_1}{y_3 - y_1} \div \frac{y_4 - y_2}{y_3 - y_2} = \frac{c_4 - c_1}{c_3 - c_1} \div \frac{c_4 - c_2}{c_3 - c_2}, \tag{4.2914}$$

that is, the *cross ratio* of the four functions is independent of x. On the other hand, if the left member of (4.2914) is a constant λ, then solving for y_4 shows that the relation

$$y = \frac{cy_2(y_3 - y_1) - y_1(y_3 - y_2)}{c(y_3 - y_1) - (y_3 - y_2)}$$

is valid when $y = y_4$ and $c = \lambda$. Moreover it is easily checked that the right side is y_1 when $c = 0$, is y_3 when $c = 1$, and converges to y_2 as $c \to \infty$. This shows that there exist functions f_1, f_2, f_3, f_4 such that each of the four functions y_1, y_2, y_3, y_4 is representable in the form (4.2911) for some c or as a limit as $c \to \infty$. Problem 6.194 will show that, in ordinary circumstances, each solution of the Riccati equation (4.2912) has the form (4.2911).

Remark 4.292

Sometimes, as in the preceding and following problems, we should know at least a little about *determinants*. They can be defined by the formulas

$$\Delta_2 = \begin{vmatrix} a_{11} & a_{12} \\ a_{21} & a_{22} \end{vmatrix} = a_{11}a_{22} - a_{21}a_{12}$$

$$\Delta_3 = \begin{vmatrix} a_{11} & a_{12} & a_{13} \\ a_{21} & a_{22} & a_{23} \\ a_{31} & a_{32} & a_{33} \end{vmatrix} = a_{11}\Delta_{11} - a_{21}\Delta_{21} + a_{31}\Delta_{31}$$

$$\Delta_4 = \begin{vmatrix} a_{11} & a_{12} & a_{13} & a_{14} \\ a_{21} & a_{22} & a_{23} & a_{24} \\ a_{31} & a_{32} & a_{33} & a_{34} \\ a_{41} & a_{42} & a_{43} & a_{44} \end{vmatrix} = a_{11}\Delta_{11} - a_{21}\Delta_{21} + a_{31}\Delta_{31} - a_{41}\Delta_{41},$$

et cetera, where Δ_{rs} is in each case the determinant obtained by deleting the row and column containing a_{rs} from the array or *matrix* on the left side. In each case, the sign before the term $a_{rs}\Delta_{rs}$ is $(-1)^{r+s}$. The right sides of the above formulas are the Laplace expansions involving the first columns of the matrices. The theory of determinants shows that we can use any other row or column. For example, use of the bottom rows shows that

$$\begin{aligned} \Delta_2 &= -a_{21}a_{12} + a_{22}a_{11} \\ \Delta_3 &= a_{31}\Delta_{31} - a_{32}\Delta_{32} + a_{33}\Delta_{33} \\ \Delta_4 &= -a_{41}\Delta_{41} + a_{42}\Delta_{42} - a_{43}\Delta_{43} + a_{44}\Delta_{44}. \end{aligned}$$

The principal uses of determinants appear in applications of the following two theorems and their obvious modifications that apply to systems involving two or more than three linear algebraic equations.

THEOREM 4.2921. *In order that the system of equations*

$$\begin{aligned} a_{11}c_1 + a_{12}c_2 + a_{13}c_3 &= 0 \\ a_{21}c_1 + a_{22}c_2 + a_{23}c_3 &= 0 \\ a_{31}c_1 + a_{32}c_2 + a_{33}c_3 &= 0 \end{aligned}$$

have a nontrivial solution for c_1, c_2, c_3 *(i.e., be satisfied by three numbers* c_1, c_2, c_3 *not all* 0), *it is necessary and sufficient that the determinant of their coefficients* (Δ_3 *above*) *be* 0.

Theorem 4.2922. *In order that the system of equations*

$$\begin{aligned} a_{11}c_1 + a_{12}c_2 + a_{13}c_3 &= d_1 \\ a_{21}c_1 + a_{22}c_2 + a_{23}c_3 &= d_2 \\ a_{31}c_1 + a_{32}c_2 + a_{33}c_3 &= d_3 \end{aligned}$$

have a unique solution for c_1, c_2, c_3 (i.e., be satisfied by one and only one set of three numbers c_1, c_2, c_3), it is necessary and sufficient that the determinant of their coefficients (Δ_3 above) be different from 0. If $\Delta_3 = 0$, then (depending upon the numbers d_1, d_2, d_3) the system has either no solutions or many solutions.

We complete this remark by showing how a system of linear algebraic equations with numerical coefficients, such as the system

$$\begin{aligned} y_1 - 2y_2 + 3y_3 &= x_1 \\ 2y_1 - 3y_2 + 4y_3 &= x_2 \\ y_1 + 3y_2 - 6y_3 &= x_3, \end{aligned} \tag{2.2923}$$

should be solved for y_1, y_2, and y_3. The method is particularly valuable when the system involves many equations. We suppose that the determinant of the coefficients of the y's is not 0. This guarantees that the equations have a unique solution, but we do not use determinants to find the solution. The first trick is to think of the given system as being written in the form

$$\begin{aligned} 1y_1 - 2y_2 + 3y_3 &= 1x_1 + 0x_2 + 0x_3 \\ 2y_1 - 3y_2 + 4y_3 &= 0x_1 + 1x_2 + 0x_3 \\ 1y_1 + 3y_2 - 6y_3 &= 0x_1 + 0x_2 + 1x_3, \end{aligned}$$

but it is not necessary to write these equations when the method is understood. The next trick is to write the matrix

$$\begin{pmatrix} 1 & -2 & 3 & 1 & 0 & 0 \\ 2 & -3 & 4 & 0 & 1 & 0 \\ 1 & 3 & -6 & 0 & 0 & 1 \end{pmatrix}$$

of coefficients and to think of each row as representing a linear equation involving the y's and x's. If the element a_{11} in the upper left corner is 0, we can add the elements of a lower row to the elements of the first row to bring a nonzero coefficient to this position. Then if $a_{11} \neq 1$ we can divide each element of the first row by a_{11} to bring a 1 into the upper left corner. After having done this (when it is required) we multiply the elements of the first row by -2 and add the products to the elements of the second row and, similarly, multiply the elements of the first row by -1 and add the products to the elements of the last row. This gives the new matrix

$$\begin{pmatrix} 1 & -2 & 3 & 1 & 0 & 0 \\ 0 & 1 & -2 & -2 & 1 & 0 \\ 0 & 5 & -9 & -1 & 0 & 1 \end{pmatrix}$$

which corresponds to a system of equations equivalent to the given system* (2.4923).

* To really appreciate what we have done, we should notice two things. In the first place, our work is like synthetic (or abridged) division in algebra and arithmetic because we write only the coefficients and do not bother to write the variables. In the second place, we started with a system of three equations in three unknowns and, by the old familiar process of successive elimination of variables, have obtained a system of two equations in two unknowns.

If the second element of the second row were 0, we would add the elements of a lower row to the elements of the second row to bring a nonzero coefficient to this position. Division puts a 1 in the position. Multiplying the elements of the second row by 2 and adding the products to the elements of the first row and, similarly, multiplying the elements of the second row by -5 and adding to the elements of the third row gives the matrix

$$\begin{pmatrix} 1 & 0 & -1 & -3 & 2 & 0 \\ 0 & 1 & -2 & -2 & 1 & 0 \\ 0 & 0 & 1 & 9 & -5 & 1 \end{pmatrix}$$

A repetition of the procedure brings the matrix

$$\begin{pmatrix} 1 & 0 & 0 & 6 & -3 & 1 \\ 0 & 1 & 0 & 16 & -9 & 2 \\ 0 & 0 & 1 & 9 & -5 & 1 \end{pmatrix}$$

and our problem is solved because this matrix corresponds to the system of equations

$$\begin{aligned} y_1 &= 6x_1 - 3x_2 + x_3 \\ y_2 &= 16x_1 - 9x_2 + 2x_3 \\ y_3 &= 9x_1 - 5x_2 + x_3. \end{aligned}$$

This standard procedure for solving systems of linear algebraic equations (and, what amounts to the same thing, finding inverses of matrices) is very clean and efficient and is easily programmed for electronic digital computers. A system of n equations is solved in n steps. Ordinarily we do not bother to find out whether the determinant of the coefficients is 0; if it is 0, the fact will be revealed by the impossibility of always getting a 1 for the kth element of the kth row.

Problem 4.293

Look over the following derivation of a differential equation of the family (4.2932) and then derive a differential equation of the family

(4.2931) $$y(x) = c_1y_1(x) + c_2y_2(x) + c_3y_3(x).$$

Suppose

(4.2932) $$y(x) = c_1y_1(x) + c_2y_2(x)$$

where c_1 and c_2 are constants and y_1 and y_2 each have two derivatives. Then the three equations

$$\begin{aligned} c_0y + c_1y_1 + c_2y_2 &= 0 \\ c_0y' + c_1y_1' + c_2y_2' &= 0 \\ c_0y'' + c_1y_1'' + c_2y_2'' &= 0 \end{aligned}$$

hold when $c_0 = -1$ and hence have a nontrivial solution, that is, a solution for c_0, c_1, c_2 for which c_0, c_1, c_2 are not all 0. Therefore the determinant of the coefficients of the c's must be 0, that is,

$$\begin{vmatrix} y & y_1 & y_2 \\ y' & y_1' & y_2' \\ y'' & y_1'' & y_2'' \end{vmatrix} = 0.$$

Hence, the functions (4.2932) satisfy the equation

(4.2933) $$\begin{vmatrix} y_1 & y_2 \\ y_1' & y_2' \end{vmatrix} y'' - \begin{vmatrix} y_1 & y_2 \\ y_1'' & y_2'' \end{vmatrix} y' + \begin{vmatrix} y_1' & y_2' \\ y_1'' & y_2'' \end{vmatrix} y = 0.$$

This is a linear homogeneous differential equation of order 2 when the coefficient of y'' is not 0. This coefficient is the *Wronskian* of y_1 and y_2; the index tells where it will appear later. All this can easily be extended to the case in which y is a linear combination of n functions $y_1, y_2, \ldots, y_n$.

Remark 4.294

Perhaps we should look at some examples that would be very troublesome if we had not been rather careful in formulating statements about families of curves. We begin by working out formulas for the derivatives of some special functions. Let n be a positive integer for which $n \geqq 2$ and, when x is real, let $f(x)$ be defined by the first of the formulas

$$f(x) = x^{n-1}|x|, \qquad f'(x) = nx^{n-2}|x|. \tag{4.2941}$$

We now prove the second. If $x > 0$, then $f(x) = x^n$ so $f'(x) = nx^{n-1}$ and the result is correct. If $x < 0$, then $f(x) = -x^n$ so $f'(x) = -nx^{n-1}$ and the result is correct. Finally

$$f'(0) = \lim_{h\to 0} \frac{f(h) - f(0)}{h} = \lim_{h\to 0} \frac{h^{n-1}|h|}{h} = 0,$$

and the result is correct when $x = 0$. Thus our formula for $f'(x)$ is correct for all real values of x.

We now consider the two-parameter family of functions $y(x)$ defined by

$$y(x) = c_1x^n + c_2x^{n-1}|x| \tag{4.2942}$$

where n is fixed positive integer for which $n \geqq 3$. Note that (4.2932) reduces to this example when $y_1(x) = x^n$ and $y_2(x) = x^{n-1}|x|$. For this example, we have $y_1'(x) = nx^{n-1}$, $y_1''(x) = n(n-1)x^{n-2}$, $y_2'(x) = nx^{n-2}|x|$, and $y_2''(x) = n(n-1)x^{n-3}|x|$. Substituting in the honorable equation (4.2933) shows that the functions in (4.2942) satisfy the equation

$$0y'' + 0y' + 0y = 0. \tag{4.2943}$$

This result is obviously correct, but it is also completely useless. See the next problem.

Problem 4.295

Show that both c_1 and c_2 are easily eliminated from (4.2942) and the result of differentiating it once, and thus obtain the differential equation $xy' = ny$ of first order.

4.3. General Solutions; Singular Solutions. It frequently happens that a differential equation of order n has an n-parameter family of solutions expressed by

$$y(x) = f(x, c_1, c_2, \ldots, c_n) \tag{4.31}$$

or by

$$g(x, y, c_1, c_2, \ldots, c_n) = 0 \tag{4.32}$$

and that these are the only solutions of the differential equation. In such cases, (4.31) or (4.32) is known as a *general solution* of the differential equation. We have seen that this is true for the equation $y' = f(x)$ if $f(x)$ is continuous, the general solution being $y = \int f(x)dx + c_1$, and for $y' = ky$, the general solution being $y = c_1 e^{kx}$. We shall see later that the differential equation

$$\frac{d^2y}{dx^2} + a^2y = 0, \tag{4.33}$$

in which a is a positive constant, has a two-parameter family of solutions

$$y = c_1 \cos ax + c_2 \sin ax \tag{4.331}$$

and that these are the only solutions of (4.33). Thus (4.331) is a general solution of (4.33).

The remainder of this section consists of two remarks. The first involves a differential equation having many solutions whose graphs are quite easily described. The second involves an attempt to start with a differential equation of order n whose nature is completely unspecified and then separate the family of all solutions into two parts, the first consisting of "the general solution" and the second consisting of "singular solutions."

Remark 4.34

As we shall see, the equation

$$\left(\frac{dy}{dx}\right)^2 + y^2 = 1 \tag{4.341}$$

has vast hordes of real solutions. The equation is so simple that we can easily solve it and see what we are doing. Suppose that $y(x)$ is real and satisfies the equation over the infinite interval $-\infty < x < \infty$. Then, clearly, $-1 \leqq y(x) \leqq 1$. If I is an interval over which $-1 < y < 1$, we can solve the equation for y' and separate the variables to obtain

$$y = \sin (x + C_I) \tag{4.342}$$

when x lies in I, the constant C_I being a constant that may depend upon I. Conversely, if (4.342) holds when x is in I, then (4.341) holds when x is in I. If J is an interval over which $y = 1$ or $y = -1$, we cannot divide by $1 - y^2$ but we can notice that the differential equation is satisfied. It remains for us to consider various cases and put things together to learn about $y(x)$.

In case there is no interval J over which $y = 1$ or $y = -1$, matters are very simple; there must be a constant c such that $y = \sin (x + c)$ for all values of x. This gives a one-parameter family of solutions. In case $y = 1$ (or $y = -1$) over the whole infinite interval, we obtain another solution $y = 1$ (or $y = -1$). Another one-parameter family of solutions is that for which $y = -1$ when $x \leqq c$,

$$y = \sin (x - c - \pi/2) \tag{4.343}$$

when $c \leqq x \leqq c + \pi$, and $y = 1$ when $x \geqq c + \pi$. Another one-parameter family of solutions is obtained by replacing these solutions by their negatives.

Figure 4.344 shows the graph of a typical member of a two-parameter family of solutions. Here a and b are parameters for which $a \leqq b + \pi$, and $y(x)$ is defined by the formulas $y = -1$ when $x \leqq a$, $y = \sin(x - a - \pi/2)$ when $a \leqq x \leqq \pi/2$, $y = 1$ when $a + \pi < x \leqq b$, $y = \sin(x - b + \pi/2)$ when $b \leqq x \leqq b + \pi$, and $y = -1$ when $x \geqq b + \pi$. Another two-parameter family of solutions is obtained by replacing these solutions by their negatives.

Graphs of more solutions are obtained by amplifying Fig. 4.344 by putting in more humps to the right or left (or both) of the one already drawn. The set of humps can be finite or infinite; the only thing we are required to do is keep the humps from overlapping. As before, the negatives of solutions are also solutions.

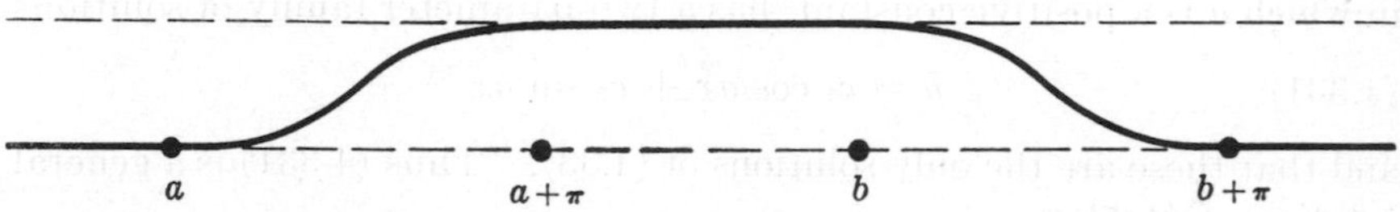

FIG. 4.344

All this shows that the family of solutions of (4.341) really is extensive; we can write formulas for solutions that contain as many parameters as we please. It could be expected that a person who is clever enough, and really wanted to do it, could express the members of the family of all solutions in terms of a single parameter c.

Remark 4.35

It could be supposed that mathematics, being the queen of the sciences, is and always has been free from myths such as the aether and phlogiston of physics and chemistry. Since we are going to pour some acid upon the foundations of the theory of differential equations and look at a gigantic mathematical myth, we pause to see that myths can interfere with scientific progress. H. A. Lorentz (1853–1928), the great Dutch physicist, came very close to developing the theory of relativity before Einstein (1879–1955) did, and it is said that he would have done so if his devotion to aether had been less dogmatic. Unlike the aether, dull stuff that physicists happily pushed into oblivion, our mathematical myth is far from extinct. Survival of our myth, as a pedagogical device in elementary textbooks, is prolonged even by some who do it apologetically and with quite explicit statements that it is done because it is customary.

As we have seen, the equation (1.31) has no solutions, and (4.341) has vast hordes of them. These facts and others lead inevitably to the conclusion that it is not easy to make meaningful and informative statements about the family of solutions of an equation of order n when we know nothing about the equation except that it is an equation of order n. All significant works on our subject, from the most elementary textbooks to the most advanced research, deal with more or less special classes of equations with which one may hope to do something interesting or useful or both.

This is a situation which some of our ancestors failed to recognize when they wrote their elementary textbooks. These mathematical medicine men found a medieval cure-all and, seeing the confusion and lack of clarity in it, can make us wonder how often we can be swindled when we study the sciences. These medicine men undertook to do everything with the aid of myths, undefined terms, and proof by intimidation. They promoted the view that to each differential equation of order n there corresponds an important family of solutions from which all other solutions (*singular solutions*, if any) are obtainable by use of appropriate hocus-pocus involving envelopes and some more complicated things. It was essential that this family of solutions should have a name (this is the start of the intimidation) which would immediately convince everybody that it existed and was important. With dubious regard for appropriateness of terminology, this family was called "the general solution" of the given equation. Great progress has already been made but we must be able to tell when we have found "the general solution." Suppose we start with a given differential equation of order n and succeed in finding a family of solutions $y(x)$ determined explicitly or implicitly by one of the formulas

$$y = f(x, c_1, c_2, \ldots, c_k) \tag{4.36}$$

$$g(x, y, c_1, c_2, \ldots, c_k) = 0. \tag{4.361}$$

The family is then "the general solution" if and only if (4.36), or (4.361) as the case may be, contains exactly n essential constants. It may be unclear whether this is a theorem or a definition or merely a collection of words, but we are now in a realm where nearly everything is unclear. One thing, however, is clear. No meaning has been attached to the statement that a formula contains n essential constants. This gives the good old lecturer a chance to practice the art of proof by intimidation. He shouts that the a and b in the formula

$$y = x + a + b \tag{4.37}$$

are obviously not essential constants because they can be replaced by a single constant c, and concludes with a pound upon the table that (4.37) contains exactly one essential constant. This sounds so reasonable that we give up and concede the point; intimidation has replaced logic. Next the lecturer shouts that the formula

$$y = mx + b \tag{4.38}$$

obviously contains two essential constants because it is obviously impossible to replace m and b by a single constant c. This time, however, it will not do the lecturer any good to pound upon the table. We know that the two-parameter family (4.38) is precisely the same as the one-parameter family (4.18) just as positively as the two-parameter family $y = x + a + b$ is precisely the same as the one-parameter family $y = x + c$. Since no meaning has been attached to the statement that a formula contains n essential constants, our situation is so bad that it is impossible to determine whether it is possible for a formula to contain more than one essential constant. It is clear that myths, undefined terms, and proof by intimidation are not providing a satisfactory basis for development of a theory of differential equations. The trouble with the ancestors we have mentioned is that they tried to do everything with equipment that is too shabby for use even in simple problems.

It is a consequence of all this that the term *general solution* has been and is so confused and abused that it can be a source of serious misunderstandings. Except in the above discussion and another place or two where we use it *with quotation marks*, we always use it with the meaning given in connection with (4.31). Perhaps we should end all difficulties by applying the term *admiral solution* to the family of all solutions and should allow the general solutions to wallow in their own confusion, but the author does not have quite enough courage to do it.

4.4. Degree of a Differential Equation. When the members of a differential equation are polynomials in the derivatives, the greatest exponent appearing on the derivative of highest order is called the *degree* of the equation. The equation

$$\rho(x) = \frac{[1 + (dy/dx)^2]^{3/2}}{d^2y/dx^2} \tag{4.41}$$

does not have a degree; but the equation (which is definitely a different equation)

$$(4.42)\qquad [\rho(x)]^2\left(\frac{d^2y}{dx^2}\right)^2 = 1 + 3\left(\frac{dy}{dx}\right)^2 + 3\left(\frac{dy}{dx}\right)^4 + \left(\frac{dy}{dx}\right)^6,$$

obtained from (4.41) by obvious algebraic processes, is of the second degree. Each equation of the first order and second degree with independent and dependent variables x and y has the form

$$(4.43)\qquad f_1(x, y)\left(\frac{dy}{dx}\right)^2 + f_2(x, y)\frac{dy}{dx} + f_3(x, y) = 0,$$

and each equation of the first order and first degree has the form

$$(4.44)\qquad f_1(x, y)\frac{dy}{dx} + f_2(x, y) = 0.$$

It should be carefully noted that the terms *linear differential equation* and *first-degree differential equation* are not equivalent. Each linear equation, as

$$(4.45)\qquad x^2\frac{d^2y}{dx^2} - x\frac{dy}{dx} + (\alpha^2 - x^2)y = 0,$$

is of the first degree; but the first-degree equations

$$(4.46)\qquad \frac{d^2y}{dx^2} + \left(\frac{dy}{dx}\right)^2 + xy = 0$$

and

$$(4.47)\qquad \frac{dy}{dx} = x^2 + y^2$$

are not linear.

Problem 4.48

Let a be a fixed positive constant. By differentiation and elimination of parameters, show that the equation

$$(4.481)\qquad a^2\left(\frac{d^2y}{dx^2}\right)^2 = \left[1 + \left(\frac{dy}{dx}\right)^2\right]^3$$

is satisfied by the family of circles $(x - h)^2 + (y - k)^2 = a^2$ of radius a. Show also that $x = h + a\cos t$ and $y = k + a\sin t$ are parametric equations of the circles, and that

$$(4.482)\qquad \left(\frac{dx}{dt}\right)^2 + \left(\frac{dy}{dt}\right)^2 = a^2.$$

What pairs of constants c_1 and c_2 are such that (4.482) holds when $x = c_1t$ and $y = c_2t$? What is the geometric significance of this result?

4.5. Equations of Second Degree. Equations of second degree can arise quite naturally. For example, when $f(y)$ is continuous function of y which does not have the form $Ay + B$, a standard method of attacking the *Newton* (1642–1727) *equation*

$$\frac{d^2y}{dx^2} = f(y) \tag{4.51}$$

is to multiply both sides by $2dy/dx$ to put the equation in the form

$$\frac{d}{dx}\left(\frac{dy}{dx}\right)^2 = 2f(y)\,\frac{dy}{dx}. \tag{4.511}$$

Letting F be a function whose derivative is f then gives

$$\left(\frac{dy}{dx}\right)^2 = F(y) + c. \tag{4.512}$$

The next steps involve taking square roots, separating variables, and obtaining solutions in the backhanded form $\phi(y) = x + c$. The best-known example is the simple inelastic pendulum problem involving elliptic integrals whose inverses are elliptic functions (see Problem 2.29). We shall not pursue this matter, but we shall solve a little problem which shows that the problem of finding all of the solutions of an equation of second degree can be tricky.

A careless attempt to find all of the solutions of the equation

$$y'^2 = x^2 \tag{4.52}$$

consists in asserting that the equation holds if and only if $y' = x$ or $y' = -x$ and hence that the solutions are given by

$$y = \tfrac{1}{2}x^2 + c \qquad -\infty < x < \infty \tag{4.53}$$

$$y = -\tfrac{1}{2}x^2 + c \qquad -\infty < x < \infty. \tag{4.531}$$

Graphs of these solutions are easily sketched. The graphs of (4.53) form a family of parabolas opening upward, and the graphs of (4.531) form a family of parabolas opening downward. Through each point (a, b) of the plane there passes exactly one parabola of each family.

Let us now solve equation (4.52), paying careful attention to what we are doing. Assuming that $y(x)$ is a solution of (4.52), we can transpose and factor to obtain

$$[y'(x) - x][y'(x) + x] = 0. \tag{4.54}$$

It is a fundamental fact of arithmetic that, if the product of two numbers A and B is 0, then at least one of A and B must be 0. Hence it is true that, for each x, at least one of the two factors in (4.54) must be 0; but (4.54) definitely does not imply that either the first factor is 0 for all values of x or the second factor is 0 for all values* of x. All one can

* An assumption to the contrary is as silly as the assumption that, if two men A and B keep a pump going continuously, then either A pumps all the time or B pumps all the time. All that can be concluded is that B must be pumping at least when A is not pumping.

conclude from (4.54) is that the first factor must be 0 for some set of values of x and the second must be 0 for all other values of x. Let E (the initial letter of the French word *ensemble* which means *set*) denote the set of x for which the first factor is 0. The nature of the set E is determined by the function $y(x)$; so far as we know at present it may contain no values of x, it may contain all values of x, or it may be any set containing some but not all values of x. Then

$$\begin{aligned} y'(x) &= x && x \text{ in } E \\ &= -x && x \text{ not in } E. \end{aligned}$$

The character of the set E can be determined by use of Rolle's theorem as follows: If $0 < a < b$ and $y(a) = y(b)$, then Rolle's theorem would imply existence of a point c between a and b such that $y'(c) = 0$; but this is impossible since

$$|y'(x)| = |x| \neq 0$$

when $a < x < b$. Therefore $y(a) \neq y(b)$ when $0 < a < b$. Since $y(x)$ is continuous, this implies that $y(x)$ must be an increasing function of x for $x > 0$ or $y(x)$ must be a decreasing function of x for $x > 0$. In the first case, $y'(x) \geqq 0$ so that $y'(x) = x$ for $x > 0$; and in the second case, $y'(x) \leqq 0$ so that $y'(x) = -x$ for $x > 0$. It can be shown in the same way that $y'(x) = x$ for $x < 0$ or $y'(x) = -x$ for $x < 0$. Moreover, (4.52) implies that $y'(0) = 0$. Therefore there are just four possible cases: (i) $y'(x) = x$ for all x; (ii) $y'(x) = -x$ for all x; (iii) $y'(x) = x$ for $x \geqq 0$ and $y'(x) = -x$ for $x \leqq 0$; and (iv) $y'(x) = -x$ for $x \leqq 0$ and $y'(x) = x$ for $x \geqq 0$. In case (i) we have $y(x) = \frac{1}{2}x^2 + c$ as in (4.53); in case (ii) we have $y(x) = -\frac{1}{2}x^2 + c$ as in (4.531); in case (iii) we have

$$\begin{aligned} y(x) &= \tfrac{1}{2}x^2 + c && x \geqq 0 \\ &= -\tfrac{1}{2}x^2 + c && x \leqq 0; \end{aligned} \tag{4.55}$$

and in case (iv) we have

$$\begin{aligned} y(x) &= -\tfrac{1}{2}x^2 + c && x \geqq 0 \\ &= \tfrac{1}{2}x^2 + c && x \leqq 0. \end{aligned} \tag{4.551}$$

Thus each solution of $y'^2 = x^2$ must have one of the four forms. It is easy to show that each such function satisfies $y'^2 = x^2$ and the problem is solved. The natures of the graphs of the solutions in (4.55) and (4.551) should be observed.

In retrospect, we may remark that the careless solution of $y'^2 = x^2$ was very simple but gave incomplete results. The careful solution was a little more difficult, but it gave complete results.

Problem 4.56

By showing that the functions $y(x)$ given by (4.55) and (4.551) do not have second derivatives at $x = 0$, or by some other method, prove that the only solutions of $y'^2 = x^2$ which have second derivatives are the functions given in (4.53) and (4.531).

Problem 4.57

Solve the equation

$$\left(\frac{dy}{dx}\right)^2 = y.$$

Be sure that you find *all* solutions. Sketch graphs of typical solutions.

Problem 4.58

Show that, if

$$\left(y\frac{dy}{dx}\right)^2 + y^2 = 1 \tag{4.5801}$$

and

$$0 < y(x) < 1$$

over an interval $x_1 < x < x_2$, then there is a constant c such that

$$(x - c)^2 + y^2 = 1 \qquad x_1 < x < x_2.$$

Show that if (4.5801) holds then $|y(x)| \leqq 1$; and that if $y(x) = +1$ or $y(x) = -1$ over an interval $x_3 < x < x_4$ then (4.5801) holds.

Problem 4.581

Find all solutions of the equation

$$\left(y\frac{dy}{dx}\right)^2 + y^2 = 1.$$

The graph of one of the solutions which you should obtain is shown in Fig. 4.5811, the range of definition of the function being $c_1 - 1 < x < c_2 + 1$.

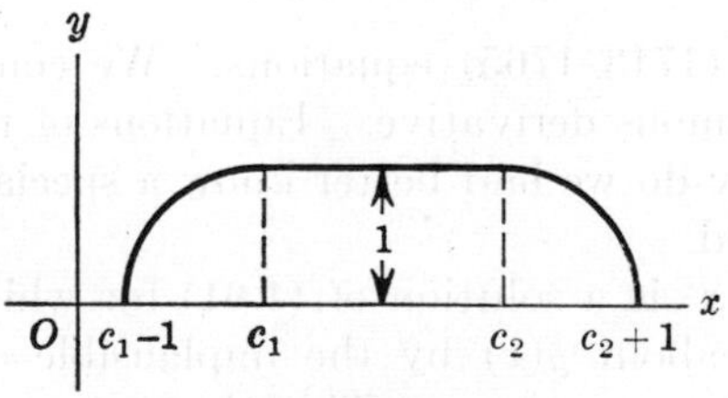

FIG. 4.5811

Problem 4.582

A family F of curves in the xy plane has the following property: If C is a curve of the family and P is a point on C, then the curve C has a normal (and hence also a tangent since a normal is, by definition, a perpendicular to a tangent) at P and at least one of the two points on the normal at a distance 1 from P lies on the x axis. Show that, if $y = y(x)$ is an equation of a part of a curve C for which $y'(x)$ exists, then

$$\left(y\frac{dy}{dx}\right)^2 + y^2 = 1. \tag{4.5821}$$

Show that the circle with equation

$$(x - c)^2 + y^2 = 1 \tag{4.5822}$$

belongs to the family F even though, at the two points where the circle meets the x axis, the tangent is vertical, dy/dx does not exist, and equation (4.5821) therefore fails to hold. Show that the family F contains each curve C which is composed of arcs of circles of the form (4.5822) and segments of the lines $y = 1$ and $y = -1$. Sketch an assortment of curves belonging to the family F.

Problem 4.59

The equation

$$y\frac{d^2y}{dx^2} = 1$$

looks quite simple, and it has a solution $y_1(x)$ for which $y_1(0) = 1$ and $y_1'(0) = 0$. Show that $y_1''(0) = 1$ and that $y'(x) < 0$ when $x < 0$ and $y'(x) > 0$ when $x > 0$. Now put the equation in the form (4.51) and use the trick mentioned there to learn some more.

Problem 4.591

Supposing that n is a positive integer, apply the Newton method [see (4.51)] to the equation

$$\frac{d^2y}{dx^2} + y^n = 0$$

and see whether you get information about solutions $y(x)$ for which $y(0) = 0$ and $y'(0) = 1$.

4.6. Clairaut Equations. Differential equations of the form

$$y = xy' + f(y') \tag{4.61}$$

are called Clairaut (1713–1765) equations. We consider only cases in which f has a continuous derivative. Equations of this type sometimes arise, and when they do we had better know a special method by which they can be attacked.

Assuming that $y(x)$ is a solution of (4.61) for which $y''(x)$ exists, we obtain information about $y(x)$ by the implausible operation of differentiating (4.61) with respect to x. This gives

$$y'(x) = y'(x) + xy''(x) + f'(y'(x))y''(x)$$

and we suddenly see the light when we see that this reduces to

$$y''(x)[x + f'(y'(x))] = 0. \tag{4.62}$$

From (4.62) we can conclude only that for each x at least one of the two factors must vanish. To cover all cases one must consider the possibilities that (i) the first factor may vanish for all x, (ii) the second factor may vanish for all x, and (iii) the first factor may vanish for some but not all values of x while the second factor vanishes for the remaining values of x.

If the solution $y(x)$ happens to be such that the first factor in (4.62) vanishes for all x, then $y''(x) = 0$ so that $y'(x) = c$ and we can use (4.61) to obtain

$$y = cx + f(c). \tag{4.63}$$

That (4.63) is, for each c, a solution of (4.61) is easily shown by differentiation and substitution. Thus (4.63) furnishes a one-parameter family of solutions of the given Clairaut equation. The graph of each function in this family is a line.

The problem of finding *all* of the solutions of a given Clairaut equation is more complex. In particular, it must be observed that if $y(x)$ is a solution for which $y''(x)$ does not exist, then the above method of obtaining information about $y(x)$ is inapplicable. Moreover the possibilities (ii) and (iii) mentioned in the paragraph following (4.62) sometimes lead to vast families of solutions and sometimes to none.

We now find some (but not necessarily all) solutions of the particular Clairaut equation

$$y = xy' - \tfrac{1}{4}y'^2 \tag{4.64}$$

in which the coefficient $-\frac{1}{4}$ is used because it leads to a neat graph. If $y(x)$ is a solution for which $y''(x)$ exists, then differentiation gives

$$y''(x - \tfrac{1}{2}y') = 0. \tag{4.65}$$

While we could start with simpler cases, it might be fun to run down the consequences of the hypothesis that c is a real constant, that $y''(x) = 0$ when $x \leqq c$, and $x - \frac{1}{2}y' = 0$ when $x \geqq c$. There must be a constant k such that $y'(x) = k$ when $x \leqq c$, and (4.64) implies that

$$y(x) = kx - \tfrac{1}{4}k^2 \tag{4.66}$$

when $x \leqq c$. When $x \geqq c$, we have $y'(x) = 2x$ and hence $y(x) = x^2 + c_1$ for some constant c_1. Substitution in (4.64) shows that $c_1 = 0$ and hence that $y(x) = x^2$ when $x \geqq x_1$. Hence $y(c) = c^2$, and putting this in (4.66) shows that $k = 2c$. Thus we obtain

$$\begin{aligned} y(x) &= 2cx - c^2 \qquad & x \leqq c \\ y(x) &= x^2 \qquad & x \geqq c. \end{aligned} \tag{4.67}$$

Our hypothesis has led us to (4.67), and we should now find out whether we have landed a solution of (4.64). Substitution shows that we have. Thus (4.67) is a one-parameter family of solutions of (4.64). Therefore, according to terminology involving (4.36), the family of solutions (4.67) must constitute "the general solution" of (4.64) and all other solutions must be "singular solutions."

It remains for us to run down some "singular solutions." The possibility that the first factor is 0 for all values of x leads to the one-parameter family of "singular solutions"

$$y(x) = cx + \tfrac{1}{4}c^2 \qquad -\infty < x < \infty. \tag{4.671}$$

It could be remarked that some people like to get these solutions first and claim that theirs constitute "the general solution" and that ours are "singular solutions." The possibility that the second factor is 0 for all values of x leads to the solution

$$y(x) = x^2 \qquad -\infty < x < \infty. \tag{4.672}$$

The equation of the tangent to the graph of $y = x^2$ at the point $(c/2, c^2/4)$ is (4.66). Figure 4.68 shows graphs of these things. A look at the

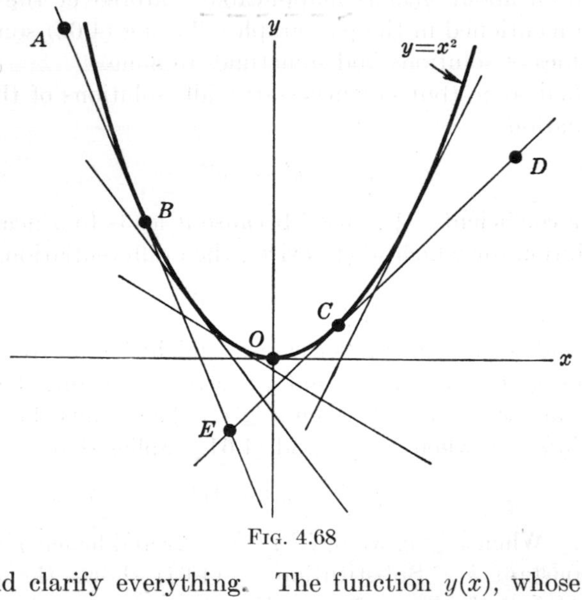

Fig. 4.68

figure should clarify everything. The function $y(x)$, whose graph runs along a tangent from A to B, and then along the parabola from B to C, and then along a tangent from C to D, is a solution for which the second factor in (4.65) vanishes over a central interval and the first factor vanishes elsewhere. Taking the central interval to be the interval $c_1 \leqq x \leqq c_2$ gives a perfectly respectable two-parameter family of solutions.

Problem 4.69

Let $h_3(x)$ be the function whose graph (Fig. 4.68) consists of the part of the line ABE to the left of E, the point E itself, and the part of the line ECD to the right of E. Is $h_3(x)$ a solution of $y = y'x - \frac{1}{4}y'^2$?

Problem 4.691

Without neglecting the possibility that $y(x)$ may be 0 all the time or sometimes, find solutions of the equation

$$\frac{dy}{dx} = 3y^{\frac{2}{3}}.$$

4.7. Orthogonal Trajectories. The family $x^2 + y^2 = c$ of circles with center at the origin and the family $y = mx$ of lines through the origin have an interesting property: wherever a curve of one family intersects a curve of the other family, the two are *perpendicular* or *normal* or *orthogonal*. Whenever two families of curves have this property, each family is said to be the family of *orthogonal trajectories* of the other.

Orthogonal families are of interest in applied mathematics where the curves of one family are called *lines of flow, lines of force, streamlines,* etc., and the curves of the other family are called *level lines, equipotential lines, isothermal lines,* etc.

Let $\phi_1(x, y, c) = 0$ represent a one-parameter family of curves such that through each point (x, y) of a region R of the plane (which may be the entire plane) there passes one and only one curve of the family, the curve having a tangent at (x, y) which is neither vertical nor horizontal. If $f(x, y)$ denotes the slope of the tangent at the point (x, y), then the slope of a line through (x, y) orthogonal to the curve of the family will be $-1/f(x, y)$. Accordingly, if $y(x)$ exists such that

$$\frac{dy}{dx} = -\frac{1}{f(x, y)}, \tag{4.71}$$

then the curve $y = y(x)$ will be orthogonal to the curves of the family $\phi_1(x, y, c) = 0$; and if $\phi_2(x, y, c) = 0$ represents a family of curves for which (4.71) holds, then the family $\phi_2(x, y, c) = 0$ is orthogonal to the family $\phi_1(x, y, c) = 0$ insofar as the region R is concerned.

Let us see whether the process outlined above for trying to find orthogonal trajectories will enable us to find the orthogonal trajectories of the family of lines

$$y - cx = 0, \tag{4.72}$$

c being a parameter. Through each point of the plane not on the coordinate axes there passes a curve of the family (4.72) with slope different from 0, the slope being found by differentiating (4.72) to obtain

$$\frac{dy}{dx} - c = 0, \tag{4.73}$$

and then eliminating c from (4.72) and (4.73) to obtain

$$\frac{dy}{dx} = \frac{y}{x}. \tag{4.74}$$

Accordingly, each solution of the differential equation

$$\frac{dy}{dx} = -\frac{x}{y} \tag{4.75}$$

is an orthogonal trajectory of the system of lines (4.72). But if $y(x)$ satisfies (4.75), then

$$\frac{d}{dx}(x^2 + y^2) = 2x + 2y\frac{dy}{dx} = 0$$

and accordingly

$$x^2 + y^2 = c \tag{4.76}$$

and, conversely, (4.76) satisfies (4.75). Thus we have been able to solve an easy problem of which we knew the answer in advance.

Very often the simplest way to get the differential equation of a family of curves such as

$$x^2 + (y - c)^2 = a^2 + c^2$$

is to start by solving the equation for c to obtain an equation such as

$$\frac{x^2 + y^2 - a^2}{y} = 2c.$$

Differentiation then gives the differential equation of the family.

Perhaps honesty requires calling attention to the fact that families of orthogonal trajectories appear effortlessly in the theory of analytic functions of a complex variable, and that the method involving (4.71) is not used as much as it otherwise would be.

Problem 4.77

Sketch a rough graph of $y = e^x$ and put in graphs of more equations of the family $y = ce^x$. Then sketch curves that look like their orthogonal trajectories. Finally, find the equations of the latter trajectories and see how things check out.

Ans. (partial): The trajectories have equations $y^2 = 2(x + c)$.

Problem 4.771

Sketch curves $xy = c$, sketch trajectories, and find trajectories.

Ans.: Trajectories are $y^2 - x^2 = c$.

Problem 4.78

Find the orthogonal trajectories of the following families of curves

(*a*) $y^2 = 4cx$ *Ans.:* $\dfrac{x^2}{c^2} + \dfrac{y^2}{2c^2} = 1$

(*b*) $y = \log x + c$ *Ans.:* Parts of $y = -\dfrac{x^2}{2} + c$

(*c*) $y^2 = cx^3$ *Ans.:* $\dfrac{x^2}{3c} + \dfrac{y^2}{2c} - 1$

(*d*) $y = ce^{-x^2}$ *Ans.:* $x = ce^{y^2}$

(*e*) $e^x \cos y = c$ *Ans.:* $e^x \sin y = c$

Problem 4.781

Sketch several curves of the family F_1 of circles which pass through two fixed points $(-a, 0)$ and $(a, 0)$ of the plane. Sketch some curves of the orthogonal family F_2 and try to guess whether they are circles. Show that the equation of the member of F_1 having its center at $(0, c)$ is

(4.7811) $$x^2 + (y - c)^2 = c^2 + a^2$$

and that the differential equation of the family F_2 is

(4.7812) $$2xy\frac{dy}{dx} = a^2 + y^2 - x^2.$$

We will solve this equation in Section 5.5. Meanwhile, show that F_2 is a family of circles by showing that the differential equation of the family

(4.7813) $$(x - c)^2 + y^2 = c^2 - a^2$$

is (4.7812).

Problem 4.782

Find the differential equation of the family F_2 of circles tangent to the y axis at the origin, find the differential equation of the orthogonal trajectories, and show that interchanging x and y in one of the differential equations gives the other. What does this imply about orthogonal trajectories of F_2? Sketch graphs.

Problem 4.783

A little theory of functions of a complex variable shows that if $u + iv = z + 1/z$ so that, in polar coordinates

$$u + iv = \left(r + \frac{1}{r}\right)\cos\theta + i\left(r - \frac{1}{r}\right)\sin\theta$$

and in rectangular coordinates

$$u + iv = x + \frac{x}{x^2 + y^2} + i\left(y - \frac{y}{x^2 + y^2}\right),$$

then the graphs of the equations $u = c$ are orthogonal trajectories of the graphs of the equations $v = c$. Work out the differential equations of the two families and verify the orthogonality (see Problem 2.284). *Remark:* Graphs of the equations $v = c$ are *stream curves* which show how breezes and fluids stream past circular cylinders when viscosity is negligible.

Problem 4.79

Let a be a fixed positive constant. For each constant c for which $c > a^2$, the graph of

$$\frac{x^2}{c} + \frac{y^2}{c - a^2} = 1 \tag{4.791}$$

is a member of the family E of confocal ellipses having foci at the points $(-a, 0)$ and $(a, 0)$. For each constant c for which $0 < c < a^2$, the graph is a member of the family H of confocal hyperbolas having the same foci. The union of the two families E and H is a family of *confocal conics*. Show that if $P \equiv (x, y)$ is a given point in the plane for which $x \neq 0$ and $y \neq 0$, then there are exactly two values of c for which (4.791) holds, namely,

$$c_E = \frac{(a^2 + x^2 + y^2) + [(a^2 + x^2 + y^2)^2 - 4a^2x^2]^{\frac{1}{2}}}{2}, \tag{4.792}$$

$$c_H = \frac{(a^2 + x^2 + y^2) - [(a^2 + x^2 + y^2)^2 - 4a^2x^2]^{\frac{1}{2}}}{2}. \tag{4.793}$$

Show that $c_E > a$ and hence that setting $c = c_E$ in (4.791) gives the equation of an ellipse through P. Show that $0 < c_H < a$ and hence that setting $c = c_H$ in (4.791) gives the equation of a hyperbola through P. Differentiate (4.792) to obtain the differential equation

$$\frac{dy}{dx} = \frac{a^2 + y^2 - x^2 - [(a^2 + y^2 - x^2)^2 + 4x^2y^2]^{\frac{1}{2}}}{2xy} \tag{4.794}$$

satisfied by (4.791) when $c > a$. This is a differential equation whose solutions are confocal ellipses. Differentiate (4.793) to obtain the differential equation

$$\frac{dy}{dx} = \frac{a^2 + y^2 - x^2 + [(a^2 + y^2 - x^2)^2 + 4x^2y^2]^{\frac{1}{2}}}{2xy} \tag{4.795}$$

satisfied by (4.791) when $0 < c < a$. This is a differential equation whose solutions are confocal hyperbolas. Show that the derivatives in (4.794) and (4.795) are negative reciprocals of each other, and hence that the hyperbolas are orthogonal trajectories of the ellipses. Show finally that the derivatives in (4.794) and (4.795) both satisfy the second-degree equation (4.282).

4.8. Parabolic Reflectors. A well-known problem is that of determining a plane curve such that light or sound striking it from a point source in the same plane is reflected in a given direction. Let the point source be the origin, and let the given direction be that of the positive x axis. Let us assume that $y = y(x)$, defined for some range of values of x, is a differentiable function whose graph is a part or all of the desired curve.

At a point $P \equiv P(x, y)$ on the curve the incident ray OP and the reflected ray BP make equal angles α with the tangent at P, and the

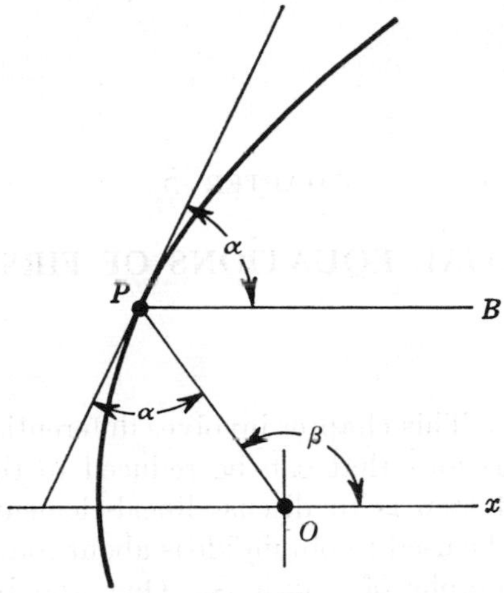

FIG. 4.81

identity $\tan \alpha = \tan (\beta - \alpha)$ gives, when $x \neq 0$,

$$y' = \frac{(y/x) - y'}{1 + (y/x)y'},$$

or

$$y = 2y'x + yy'^2. \tag{4.82}$$

A neat way of solving this equation is to multiply by y and to set $v = y^2$ and $v'(x) = 2y(x)y'(x)$ to obtain

$$v = v'x + \tfrac{1}{4}v'^2. \tag{4.83}$$

This is a Clairaut equation with so-called "general solution" $v = cx + \frac{1}{4}c^2$ and singular solution $v = -\frac{1}{4}x^2$. The "general solution" gives

$$y^2 = c(x + \tfrac{1}{4}c). \tag{4.84}$$

For each $c > 0$, (4.84) is the equation of a parabola with vertex at the point $(-\frac{1}{4}c, 0)$ and focus at the origin; and it can be shown that this is a solution of our problem. Do $c = 0$ and $c < 0$ furnish solutions of the problem? Does the singular solution $v = -x^2/4$ furnish a solution of the problem?

Problem 4.85

Show that equation (4.82) can be written in the form

$$y\,dy + x\,dx = \pm\sqrt{x^2 + y^2}\,dx,$$

and proceed to solve the equation by use of an integrating factor.

CHAPTER 5

DIFFERENTIAL EQUATIONS OF FIRST ORDER

5.0. Introduction. This chapter involves differential equations of first order and some equations that can be reduced to them by changes of variables. Our first step is to discuss lineal-element diagrams and to show how they may be used to obtain ideas about solutions and to sketch approximations to graphs of solutions. One who is interested in the question of existence of solutions can find his *pièce de résistance* in Chapter 15; but we do not suggest that Chapter 15 be read at this time.

5.1. Lineal-element Diagrams. The equation

$$M(x, y)dx + N(x, y)dy = 0$$

can, when $N(x, y) \neq 0$, be written in the form

$$\frac{dy}{dx} = f(x, y) \tag{5.11}$$

where $f(x, y) = -M(x, y)/N(x, y)$. Through each of "several" points (x, y) of the plane, we can draw a "short" line segment with slope $f(x, y)$. By calling the line segment *short*, we mean merely that it is only as long as is necessary to indicate clearly its direction. Each short line segment is called a *lineal element*, and the totality of lineal elements is called a *lineal-element diagram*. If $f(x, y)$ is continuous, then the slope of the lineal elements changes steadily (*i.e.*, without jumps) as one passes continuously over points of the plane. A good lineal-element diagram contains enough lineal elements to indicate the direction at or "near" each point of the region of the plane in which one is interested; but of course it is futile to draw so many lineal elements that the figure becomes completely black and obliterates everything.

A little experimentation with paper and pencil will convince you that, if you draw a smooth curve with a continuously turning tangent (for example, a parabola) and draw through each of a set of closely spaced points on the curve a short line-segment tangent to the curve, then the totality of lineal elements thus obtained will appear to the eye to be simply the curve with which you started. Hence such a curve may be regarded (so far as eyesight is concerned) as a succession of lineal elements.

This implies that a family of curves in the plane (such as a set of concentric circles) may be regarded (so far as eyesight is concerned) as a lineal-element diagram.

This procedure suggests at least the possibility of being able to start with a given lineal-element diagram and then sketch curves each of which appears to the eye to be made up of a succession of lineal elements.

In many cases a lineal-element diagram enables one to make correct guesses involving existence and properties of solutions of $y' = f(x, y)$ and indeed to sketch approximate graphs of solutions. We illustrate this for the differential equation $x\,dy - 2y\,dx = 0$. (After making the guesses, we shall solve the differential equation and verify the guesses.) When $x \neq 0$, the differential equation can be written

$$\frac{dy}{dx} = \frac{2y}{x}. \tag{5.12}$$

If (x, y) is a point not on the y axis, then we can compute the slope of, and draw, the lineal element through (x, y). Hence, we can construct a lineal-element diagram as in Fig. 5.121.

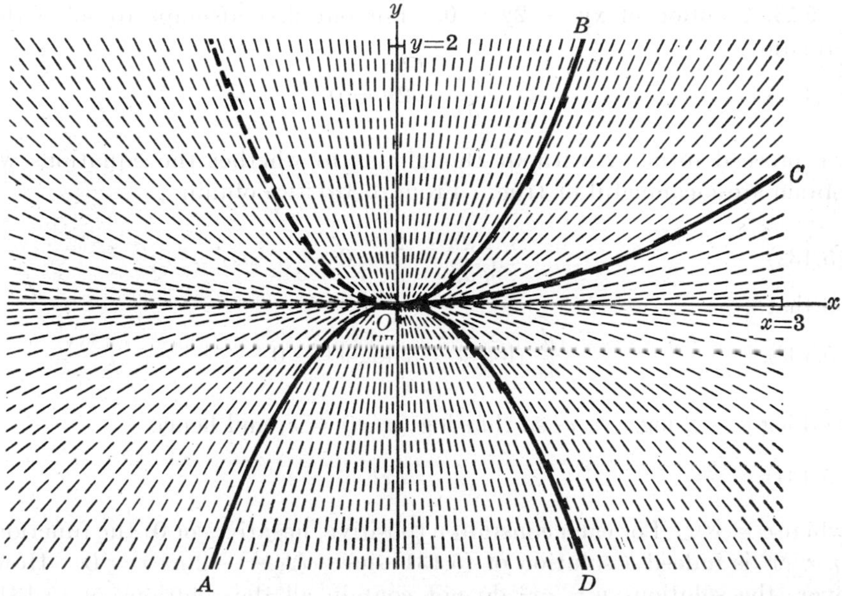

FIG. 5.121

Study of Fig. 5.121 seems to indicate that, if (x_0, y_0) is a point not on the y axis, then enough lineal elements could be added to the diagram to give a succession of lineal elements which form (so far as eyesight is concerned) a smooth curve running from (x_0, y_0) at least as far as the origin in one direction and running outward in the opposite direction.

The question as to how and whether such a curve extends through the origin is more delicate. The differential equation $y' = 2y/x$ does not furnish a lineal element corresponding to the origin since $0/0$ has no meaning. If, however, we add to the lineal-element diagram a lineal element through the origin with slope 0, then it appears that the curve through (x_0, y_0) can be extended through the origin not only in one way but actually in many different ways so that the curve appears to be a succession of lineal elements.

If a curve appears to be a succession of lineal elements, we should expect it to be the graph of a solution of $xy' = 2y$. For y' is the slope of the curve which is the slope of the tangent which is the slope of the lineal element which is $2y/x$ when $x \neq 0$; and the equation $xy' = 2y$ is satisfied when $x = y = y' = 0$. Thus we are led to guess that AOB, AOC, AOX, and AOD are graphs of four of the solutions of $xy' = 2y$ and, of course, that there are many more similar solutions. If these guesses turn out to be in accordance with the facts, we may conclude that in at least some cases we can look at a good lineal-element diagram and "see" the solutions of $y' = f(x, y)$.

5.13. Solution of $xy' - 2y = 0$. For our first attempt to solve the equation

$$x\frac{dy}{dx} - 2y = 0 \tag{5.131}$$

we proceed formally without thought as to whether the equations we obtain are meaningful or true. From (5.131) we obtain

$$\frac{1}{y}\frac{dy}{dx} - \frac{2}{x} = 0 \tag{5.132}$$

so that

$$\frac{d}{dx}(\log y - 2\log x) = 0 \tag{5.133}$$

and $\log y - 2 \log x = c_1$ so that $\log (y/x^2) = c_1$ and hence

$$y = cx^2 \tag{5.134}$$

where $c = e^{c_1}$. For each constant c (positive, negative, or 0) the function $y = cx^2$ is indeed a solution of (5.131) since $x(2cx) - 2(cx^2) = 0$. However, the solutions $y = cx^2$ do not contain all the solutions of (5.131) which we "saw" in Section 5.1. What is the matter?

In the first place, (5.132) can be obtained from (5.131) only for values of x and y different from 0. In the second place, (5.133) is meaningless, insofar as real variables are concerned, except when x and y are both positive, since only positive numbers have real logarithms.

Our first attempt to solve the differential equation $xy' - 2y = 0$ was so discouraging that we start afresh by a different method. Let us assume that $y = y(x)$ is a function defined over $-\infty < x < \infty$ such that

$$x\frac{dy}{dx} - 2y = 0 \tag{5.14}$$

and find by impeccable methods the form which $y(x)$ must have. We can divide by x whenever x is not 0; but we cannot divide by y unless or until we know that y is not 0. Considering first the range of values of x for which $x > 0$, we can divide (5.14) by x to obtain

$$\frac{dy}{dx} - \frac{2}{x}y = 0. \tag{5.141}$$

This is a linear differential equation with integrating factor

$$\exp \int(-2/x)dx = x^{-2},$$

where $\exp Q$ means e^Q. Hence, as in Section 3.1, we are led to write

$$\frac{d}{dx}x^{-2}y = x^{-2}\frac{dy}{dx} - 2x^{-3}y = 0; \tag{5.142}$$

accordingly, there is a constant c_1 such that

$$y = c_1x^2 \qquad x > 0. \tag{5.15}$$

Similar consideration of the range of values of x for which $x < 0$ leads to a constant c_2 such that

$$y = c_2x^2 \qquad x < 0. \tag{5.16}$$

The value of $y(0)$ has not yet been determined, but it is easy to determine it. Since $y(x)$ was assumed to satisfy (5.14) for $-\infty < x < \infty$, it follows that $y(x)$ must be continuous and hence that $y(0) = \lim_{x\to 0} y(x)$. From (5.15) and (5.16) it follows that $\lim_{x\to 0} y(x) = 0$ and therefore $y(0) = 0$. Thus we have shown that *if* $y(x)$ *satisfies* (5.14), *then constants* c_1 *and* c_2 *must exist such that*

$$\begin{aligned} y(x) &= c_1x^2 \qquad x \geqq 0 \\ &= c_2x^2 \qquad x \leqq 0. \end{aligned} \tag{5.17}$$

This, of course, does not imply that the functions in (5.17) are solutions of (5.14). (It may be possible to show that each horse on the Double Diamond ranch is an animal with four legs, but from this it does not follow that each animal with four legs is a horse on the Double Diamond ranch.) However, it is easy to show by direct substitution that the functions in (5.17) are all solutions of (5.14).

Thus the differential equation $xy' - 2y = 0$ is accurately solved, and the results are in complete agreement with those we "saw" by means of the lineal-element diagram (Fig. 5.121). For example, setting $c_1 = -1$, $c_2 = 1$ in (5.17) furnishes the solution AOB of Fig. 5.121; setting $c_1 = -1$, $c_2 = \frac{1}{2}$ furnishes AOC; setting $c_1 = -1$, $c_2 = 0$ furnishes AOX; and setting $c_1 = c_2 = -1$ furnishes AOD.

Problem 5.18

Very often the easiest way to get a collection of lineal elements for the equation $y' = f(x, y)$ is to select a constant p, sketch the graph C_p of $f(x, y) = p$, and then draw *isoclines* (lineal elements all having the same slope p) through points of C_p. Different choices of p give different collections of isoclines. Construct lineal element diagrams for some of the equations

(a) $y' = 2x$ (b) $y' = x + y$

(c) $\dfrac{dy}{dx} = \dfrac{1}{x} + \dfrac{1}{y}$ (d) $\dfrac{dy}{dx} = \dfrac{xy}{x^2 - 1}$

(e) $y' = \max (x, y)$ (f) $y' = x^2 + y^2$

(g) $y' = \log \sqrt{x^2 + y^2}$ (h) $y' = \sqrt{2 \log |y|} \operatorname{sgn} xy$

(i) $y' = (y - x)^2$ (j) $y' = \sqrt{|y|}$

(k) $\dfrac{dy}{dx} = \sqrt{x^2 - y^2}$ (l) $\dfrac{dy}{dx} = -\dfrac{\sqrt{1 - y^2} + x}{y}.$

Problem 5.181

Solve the equation

$$\frac{dy}{dx} = e^{x-y}$$

and sketch rough graphs of some of the solutions.

Ans. (partial): The solutions are $y = \log (e^x + c)$.

Problem 5.182

Several persons with considerable knowledge of differential equations became interested in the equation

$$\frac{dy}{dx} = e^{-2xy}$$

which arose in a physics problem. It was believed that the solutions were not elementary functions. Obtain, by use of a lineal-element diagram or otherwise, some information about the behavior of the graphs of the solutions.

Problem 5.183

In accordance with terminology of the next problem, the equation

$$\frac{d^2x}{dt^2} + f\left(\frac{dx}{dt}\right) + x = 0 \tag{5.1831}$$

has the phase-plane equation

$$\frac{dy}{dx} = -\frac{x + f(y)}{y}. \tag{5.1832}$$

This is important enough to warrant exposition of the *Liénard* (1869–) *method* for construction of lineal elements. First, draw a graph G of $x = -f(y)$. To find the lineal element at $P(x, y)$, run horizontally from P to meet G at A and then run vertically from A to meet the x axis at F. The lineal element at P is then orthogonal to FP. With the aid of a compass, lineal elements can be found very rapidly and where they are desired. Sketch figures and show how and why this works. Apply the method to the case in which $f(y) = h \operatorname{sgn} y$ and obtain the result which was stumbled upon in Problem 4.192. See also Problems 2.289 and 6.069.

Problem 5.191

This problem requires us to think a little about one of the sources of interest in lineal element diagrams. Numerous important nonlinear equations have the form

$$F\left(\frac{d^2x}{dt^2}, \frac{dx}{dt}, x\right) = 0. \tag{5.1911}$$

A standard method of seeking information about solutions of these equations involves *phase-plane diagrams*. The first step is to set

$$\frac{dx}{dt} = y, \qquad \frac{d^2x}{dt^2} = \frac{dy}{dx}\frac{dx}{dt} = y\frac{dy}{dx} \tag{5.1912}$$

so that (5.1911) becomes

$$F\left(y\frac{dy}{dx}, y, x\right) = 0. \tag{5.1913}$$

When this equation can be nicely solved for dy/dx, we get

$$\frac{dy}{dx} = f(x, y). \tag{5.1914}$$

A phase-plane diagram is either a lineal-element diagram formed for (5.1914) or a chart showing graphs of enough solutions of (5.1914) to indicate the natures of the graphs of other solutions. When problems have such natures that information is not readily obtainable by simpler methods, these diagrams are valuable. If $x(t)$ is a solution of (5.1911), then as t increases, the point $(x(t), y(t))$ traverses a curve C in the phase plane; moreover, since $y = dx/dt$, the curve C is traversed in the direction which makes x increase when $y > 0$ and decrease when $y < 0$. If $x(t)$ is periodic, then so also is $y(t)$, and it follows that periodic solutions of (5.1911) correspond to closed curves C in the phase plane. For this and other reasons, information about phase-plane diagrams provides information about solutions of (5.1911).

Show that for the van der Pol equation

$$\frac{d^2x}{dt^2} - \epsilon(1 - x^2)\frac{dx}{dt} + x = 0 \tag{5.1915}$$

the phase-plane equation is

$$\frac{dy}{dx} = \epsilon(1 - x^2) - \frac{x}{y} \tag{5.1916}$$

and that for the equation

$$\frac{d^2x}{dt^2} - \epsilon\left[1 - x^2 - \left(\frac{dx}{dt}\right)^2\right]\frac{dx}{dt} + x = 0 \tag{5.1917}$$

the phase-plane equation is

$$\frac{dy}{dx} = \epsilon(1 - x^2 - y^2) - \frac{x}{y}. \tag{5.1918}$$

The natures of the lineal-element diagrams depend upon ϵ, which is not necessarily small in applications. Nobody could work very long with phase-plane diagrams for (5.1918) without stumbling upon the "obvious" fact that (5.1918) is satisfied when $x^2 + y^2 = 1$. Show that this leads to the "obvious" periodic solution

$$y = \sin (t + c) \tag{5.1919}$$

of (5.1917). Remember that we got (5.1919) from just one of the many solutions of (5.1918). There is much more to be done.

Problem 5.192

Show that the phase-plane equation of the equation

$$\frac{d^2x}{dt^2} + x = 0 \tag{5.1921}$$

is

$$y\frac{dy}{dx} + x = 0.$$

By plotting lineal elements or graphs of solutions of the phase-plane equation, whichever is easier, show that the solutions of (5.1921) are all periodic.

Problem 5.193

Modify the work of the previous problem to fit the equation

$$\frac{d^2x}{dt^2} + \operatorname{sgn} x = 0. \tag{5.1931}$$

Then, considering first an interval I over which $x > 0$ and $\operatorname{sgn} x = 1$, attack (5.1931) directly to find out how x depends upon t. Finally, show how this new information compares with information obtained from the phase plane. *Remark:* Let us make the rather reasonable assumption that (5.1931) looks like a foolish equation to bother with, and that we have heard the word *servomechanism* but we have no idea what such a thing is or does. Let us see what we can see.

Putting (5.1931) in the form

$$\frac{d^2x}{dt^2} = -\operatorname{sgn} x \tag{5.1932}$$

gives an equation which is, except for a few differences, exactly like (1.41). It makes no difference whether a coordinate measuring displacement from 0 is x or y, so this difference is inconsequential. However (5.1932) involves no damping ($\delta = 0$) and no force pulling x toward 0 ($\sigma = 0$), and this is consequential. Moreover the right member of (1.41) is a function of t, the independent variable, while the right member of (5.1932) is a function of x, the dependent variable; and this difference is important.

Because of all this, we can view (5.1932) as being an equation which governs the motion of a particle of unit mass which moves on the x axis with no forces acting upon it except a force of unit magnitude which pushes the particle to the left when it is on the right side of the origin and pushes the particle to the right when it is on the left side of the origin. Thus the force always pushes the particle toward the origin.

If we want a particle to be at the origin, it would seem desirable to have a gadget that would keep an eye on the particle and would push the particle toward the origin whenever the gadget (or its simple or complex mind) perceives that the particle is not at the origin. Such a gadget is an example of a servomechanism. Thus (5.1932) and (5.1931) govern a particularly simple application of a particularly nimble servomechanism. The equation

$$a\frac{d^2x}{dt^2} + b\frac{dx}{dt} + cx = -\operatorname{sgn} x$$

involves a less simple application of the same servo. It is easy to imagine that problems grow more difficult when the servo is a less agile one that cannot perceive minute displacements from 0 and cannot instantaneously produce forces when it does perceive need for them. Problems could be still more complex if the servo is smart enough to realize that it is not a good idea to push the particle toward the origin when it is already near the origin and going so fast that it is about to skid far over to the other side.

5.2. Local Behavior of Solutions. A substantial part of the theory of differential equations is concerned with equations of the form

$$\frac{dy}{dx} = \frac{F(x, y)}{G(x, y)} = \frac{a_1x + a_2y + a_3x^2 + a_4xy + a_5y^2 + \cdots}{b_1x + b_2y + b_3x^2 + b_4xy + b_5y^2 + \cdots} \tag{5.21}$$

where the numerator $F(x, y)$ and the denominator $G(x, y)$ are power series in the two variables x and y which converge when (x, y) lies within some circle with center at the origin $(0, 0)$. One fundamental problem is that of determining the natures, in small neighborhoods of the origin, of the graphs of solutions of these equations. Suppose first that a_1 and a_2 are not both 0 and that b_1 and b_2 are not both 0. When x and y are both near 0, it is easy to say that the terms following the linear terms in the numerator and denominator are so small in comparison to the linear terms that graphs of solutions of (5.21) should practically coincide with graphs of solutions of the equation

$$\frac{dy}{dx} = \frac{a_1x + a_2y}{b_1x + b_2y}. \tag{5.22}$$

Even though the argument about relative smallness breaks down for values of x and y for which $a_1x + a_2y = 0$ or $b_1x + b_2y = 0$ or both, and matters are not as simple as they might seem, a thorough study of equations of the form (5.22) furnishes a very good introduction to study of more general equations of the form (5.21). In case the four constants a_1, a_2, b_1, b_2 in (5.21) are all 0, a study of the equation

$$\frac{dy}{dx} = \frac{a_3x^2 + a_4xy + a_5y^2}{b_3x^2 + b_4xy + b_5y^2} \tag{5.23}$$

becomes appropriate. In the next section we shall introduce a method by which (5.22), (5.23), and many other important equations can be solved.

Remark 5.24

In this book, we shall not undertake to classify the types of configurations that represent graphs of families of solutions of equations of the forms given above. Much information and several relevant references involving solutions of these equations are given in Kaplan's textbook "Ordinary Differential Equations."* It is quite possible to hold the view that the textbooks of Agnew and Kaplan (Wilfred, 1915–) are both good textbooks and that a student studying from one of them is well advised to spend an occasional hour reading the other.

5.3. Homogeneous Functions; Equations Homogeneous in x and v. A function $F(x, y)$ is called *homogeneous of degree n in x and y* if

$$F(tx, ty) = t^n F(x, y). \tag{5.31}$$

The numerator and denominator in (5.22) are both homogeneous of degree 1, and the equation can be written in the form

$$\frac{dy}{dx} = \frac{a_1 + a_2(y/x)}{b_1 + b_2(y/x)}. \tag{5.311}$$

The numerator and denominator in (5.23) are both homogeneous of degree 2, and the equation can be written in the form

$$\frac{dy}{dx} = \frac{a_3 + a_4(y/x) + a_5(y/x)^2}{b_3 + b_4(y/x) + b_5(y/x)^2}. \tag{5.312}$$

The right members of these equations have the form $\phi(y, x)$, and the same is true of each quotient of functions which are homogeneous of the same degree. We could also put them in the form $\psi(x/y)$.

Because of this, a differential equation $y' = f(x, y)$ is said to be *homogeneous in x and y* if it can be written in one of the forms

$$\frac{dy}{dx} = \phi\left(\frac{y}{x}\right), \qquad \frac{dy}{dx} = \psi\left(\frac{x}{y}\right) \tag{5.32}$$

or

$$\phi_1\left(\frac{y}{x}\right) dx + \phi_2\left(\frac{y}{x}\right) dy = 0. \tag{5.33}$$

It is easy to see, *and should be remembered*, that these equations are reduced to an equation with separable variables by retaining the variable x and introducing a new variable z defined by $z = y/x$. In terms of the

* Wilfred Kaplan, "Ordinary Differential Equations," chap. 11, pp. 414–470, Addison-Wesley Publishing Company, Reading, Mass., 1958.

new variables, we have $y = xz$ and

$$\frac{dy}{dx} = x\frac{dz}{dx} + z \tag{5.331}$$

so (5.32) becomes

$$x\frac{dz}{dx} + z = \phi(z). \tag{5.34}$$

Formal separation of variables and integration give

$$\frac{1}{z - \phi(z)}\,dz = \frac{1}{x}\,dx, \qquad G(z) = \log x + c \tag{5.341}$$

when $x > 0$. Thus

$$G\left(\frac{y}{x}\right) = \log x + c \tag{5.342}$$

is, when $x > 0$, a formal solution of our problem.

When there is hope of obtaining a useful result, equations homogeneous in x and y should be attacked by means of the substitution $z = y/x$ and separation of variables; there should be no attempt to remember or substitute in formulas for solutions. There are cases in which the substitution $z = x/y$ works better than $z = y/x$. Sometimes efforts produce only fodder for wastebaskets; sometimes efforts pay off very handsomely. In any case, results obtained for values of x which make denominators vanish must be viewed with suspicion. The function $f(z)$ is not always elementary.

We apply the method to the homogeneous equation

$$(a_1x + b_1y)dx + (a_2x + b_2y)dy = 0 \tag{5.35}$$

in which a_1, b_1, a_2, b_2 are constants such that $a_1b_2 - a_2b_1 \neq 0$. Dividing by x and setting $z = y/x$ give

$$\frac{1}{x}\,dx + \frac{a_2 + b_2z}{b_2z^2 + (b_1 + a_2)z + a_1}\,dz = 0 \tag{5.36}$$

for ranges of values of x in which the denominators are different from 0. The results obtained from (5.36) are of several very different types, depending on the constants a_1, b_1, a_2, and b_2; for example, the character of (5.36) when $b_2 = 0$ is entirely different from that when $b_2 \neq 0$.

Problem 5.37

Solve the following equations by the method of this section, even though some of them may be solved more easily by other methods.

(a) $x\,dx + y\,dy = 0$ Ans.: $x^2 + y^2 = c$

(b) $y\,dx + x\,dy = 0$ Ans.: $xy = c$

(c) $(x + y)dx + x\,dy = 0$ Ans.: $2xy + y^2 = c$

(d) $(x + y)dx + y\,dy = 0$ Ans.: $\log (x^2 + xy + y^2) - \dfrac{2}{\sqrt{3}} \tan^{-1} \dfrac{x + 2y}{\sqrt{3}\,x} = c$

(e) $\dfrac{dy}{dx} = \dfrac{y - \sqrt{x^2 + y^2}}{x}$ Ans.: $y = c - \dfrac{x^2}{4c}$

(f) $\dfrac{dy}{dx} = \dfrac{xy - y^2}{x^2}$ Ans.: $y = \dfrac{x}{c + \log x}$

(g) $\dfrac{dy}{dx} = \dfrac{x + y}{x}$ Ans.: $y = x \log cx$

(h) $\dfrac{dy}{dx} = \dfrac{y + 2x}{2y - x}$ Ans.: $y^2 - xy - x^2 = c$

(i) $\dfrac{dy}{dx} = \dfrac{x^2 + 2xy - y^2}{x^2 - 2xy - y^2}$ Ans.: $x + y = c(x^2 + y^2)$

(j) $\dfrac{dy}{dx} = \dfrac{y(y^2 + 3x^2)}{2x^3}$ Ans.: $y^2 = \dfrac{x^3}{a - x}$

The graphs are *cissoids.*

Problem 5.38

Starting with the ideas of Problem 5.19, show that the phase-plane equations of the equation

(5.381) $$\frac{d^2x}{dt^2} + 2\frac{dx}{dt} + x = 0$$

are

(5.382) $$\frac{dy}{dx} = -2 - \frac{x}{y}, \qquad x + y = ce^{-\frac{x}{x+y}}.$$

In the next chapter, we will learn that the general solution of (5.381) is

(5.383) $$x = (A + Bt)e^{-t}.$$

Use (5.383) and the formula $y = dx/dt$ to obtain both of the formulas (5.382).

5.4. The Equation $\dfrac{dy}{dx} = f\left(\dfrac{a_1x + b_1y + c_1}{a_2x + b_2y + c_2}\right)$.

Equations of this form, in which $a_1, b_1, c_1, a_2, b_2, c_2$ are given constants for which a_2, b_2, c_2 are not all 0, can be simplified by appropriate substitutions. Setting

(5.41) $$\bar{x} = x - h, \qquad \bar{y} = y - k,$$

where h and k are constants, puts the equation in the form

(5.42) $$\frac{d\bar{y}}{d\bar{x}} = f\left(\frac{a_1\bar{x} + b_1\bar{y} + a_1h + b_1k + c_1}{a_2\bar{x} + b_2\bar{y} + a_2h + b_2k + c_2}\right).$$

In case $a_1b_2 - a_2b_1 \neq 0$, the constants h and k can be determined such that

(5.43) $$a_1h + b_1k + c_1 = 0, \qquad a_2h + b_2k + c_2 = 0;$$

the resulting equation (5.42) is then homogeneous in $\bar{x}$ and $\bar{y}$ and Section 5.3 is applicable. In case $b_1 = b_2 = 0$, the variables are separable. In case $a_1b_2 - a_2b_1 = 0$ but $b_1 \neq 0$ or $b_2 \neq 0$, at least one of the two substitutions $z = a_1x + b_1y$ and $z = a_2x + b_2y$ can be used to reduce the given equation to one in which the variables are separable.

In particular, the equation

$$\frac{dy}{dx} = f(ax + by + c) \tag{5.44}$$

is, when $b \neq 0$, reduced by the substitution $z = ax + by + c$ to an equation with separable variables.

Problem 5.45

Solve the following:

(a) $\frac{dy}{dx} = (y - x)^2$ *Ans.:* $y = x + \frac{1 + ce^{2x}}{1 - ce^{2x}}$

(b) $\frac{dy}{dx} = \frac{x + y}{x + y + 2}$ *Ans.:* $y + \log (x + y + 1) = x + c$

(c) $\frac{dy}{dx} = \frac{x + y + 1}{x - y}$ *Ans.:* $\tan^{-1} \frac{y + \frac{1}{2}}{x + \frac{1}{2}} - \frac{1}{2} \log \left[\left(x + \frac{1}{2}\right)^2 + \left(y + \frac{1}{2}\right)^2\right] = c$

(d) $\frac{dy}{dx} = \frac{1}{x + y}$ *Ans.:* $x = -y - 1 + ce^y$

(e) $\frac{dy}{dx} = \cos (x + y)$ *Ans.:* $y = 2 \tan^{-1} (x + c) - x$

5.5. Changes of Variables. In the two previous sections, and occasionally before that, we have simplified differential equations by introducing new variables defined in some way in terms of the original ones. This and the next three sections are devoted to the subject, and our information will come from close scrutiny of only a few examples. The general procedure for changing variables in the equation

$$M(x, y)dx + N(x, y)dy = 0 \tag{5.51}$$

looks ponderous, but most useful applications are quite simple. When s and t are related to x and y by formulas

$$s = f(x, y), \qquad t = g(x, y) \tag{5.511}$$

$$x = F(s, t), \qquad y = G(s, t) \tag{5.512}$$

involving functions having continuous partial derivatives, we use (5.512) to convert (5.51) into a new equation involving s and t. If we can solve the new equation, we do so and then use (5.511) to get back to the original variables. If we are unable to solve the new equation, there are two possibilities. The new equation may look worse than the first, in which case we feed the wastebasket. The new equation may look better than the first, and in this case we can hunt for another change of variables that will bring additional simplification. In many cases there is no guarantee whatever that there exist manageable changes of variables that simplify the equation. Nevertheless if a person is sufficiently interested in a problem, he may spend odd hours or weeks or months or years hunting for some that will. The two variables are sometimes simultaneously changed as they are when we convert from rectangular to polar coordinates or from polar to rectangular. Very often variables are changed one at a time.

For a simple illustration of the ideas, we solve the equation

$$2xy\frac{dy}{dx} = a^2 + y^2 - x^2 \tag{5.52}$$

which arose in Problem 4.781. Of course we do not imply that (5.52) cannot be solved by other methods; in fact we can solve (5.52) in a hurry if we are clever enough to write it in the form obtained by solving (4.7813) for c and differentiating the result.

We begin as usual by assuming that y stands for a function $y(x)$ for which (5.52) holds.

The fact that y appears in the equation only in combinations y^2 and $2y\,dy/dx$ suggests that one introduce a new variable v defined by $v = y^2$; to be more precise, $v(x) = [y(x)]^2$. Then $dv/dx = 2y\,dy/dx$, and (5.52) can be written in the form

$$x\frac{dv}{dx} = a^2 + v - x^2. \tag{5.53}$$

Since setting $v = y^2$ was a good trick, we try setting $u = x^2$. Then

$$x\frac{dv}{dx} = x\frac{dv}{du}\frac{du}{dx} = 2x^2\frac{dv}{du} = 2u\frac{dv}{du}$$

so that (5.53) can be written in the form

$$2u\frac{dv}{du} = a^2 + v - u. \tag{5.531}$$

This equation would be simpler if the term a^2 were absent, and so we eliminate it by setting $w = a^2 + v$; then $dw/du = dv/du$, and (5.531) takes the form

$$2u\frac{dw}{du} = w - u. \tag{5.54}$$

This is an equation which we can handle; it is linear, and it is homogeneous in the sense of Section 5.3.

Let us now consider positive values of x; values of x for which $x < 0$ can be handled similarly. Then $u > 0$ since $u = x^2$, and we can write (5.54) in the form

$$\frac{dw}{du} - \frac{1}{2u} w = -\frac{1}{2}. \tag{5.541}$$

An integrating factor of this equation is $e^{P(u)}$ where

$$P(u) = -\frac{1}{2} \int \frac{1}{u}\, du = -\frac{1}{2} \log u = \log u^{-\frac{1}{2}};$$

thus an integrating factor is $u^{-\frac{1}{2}}$, and we obtain $(u^{-\frac{1}{2}}w)' = -\frac{1}{2}u^{-\frac{1}{2}}$ so that

$$u^{-\frac{1}{2}}w = 2c - u^{\frac{1}{2}} \tag{5.542}$$

where, for convenience, the constant has been called $2c$. Since we are considering positive values of x, $u^{-\frac{1}{2}} = x^{-1}$ and $w = v + a^2 = y^2 + a^2$ so that (5.542) gives

$$y^2 + a^2 = x(2c - x). \tag{5.543}$$

This equation looks better when written in the standard form of the equation of a circle:

$$(x - c)^2 + y^2 = c^2 - a^2. \tag{5.544}$$

From (5.543) we see that $c > 0$; this fact, together with (5.544), implies that $c > a$.

For negative values of x we obtain (5.544) with $c < 0$ and $|c| > a$.

Remark 5.55

The *Bernoulli (James, 1654–1705) equation*

$$\frac{dy}{dx} + p(x)y = q(x)y^n, \tag{5.551}$$

in which n is a constant different from 0 and 1, is a classic example of an equation which is simplified by a little trick. Each solution of (5.551) must, in each interval over which $y(x) > 0$, satisfy the equation

$$(1 - n)y^{-n}\frac{dy}{dx} + (1 - n)p(x)y^{1-n} = (1 - n)q(x) \tag{5.552}$$

and hence also the equation

$$\frac{d}{dx} y^{1-n} + (1 - n)p(x)y^{1-n} = (1 - n)q(x). \tag{5.553}$$

On setting $z(x) = [y(x)]^{1-n}$, we obtain a linear equation determining the form of $z(x)$ and therefore that of $y(x)$.

Problem 5.56

Solve the Bernoulli equation

$$\frac{dy}{dx} + xy = \sqrt{y}.$$

$$Ans.: y = \tfrac{1}{4}e^{-x^2/2}\left(\int_0^x e^{t^2/4}\,dt + c\right)^2.$$

Try to manufacture some Bernoulli equations of which the solutions are elementary functions.

Problem 5.57

Prove that if $y_1(x)$ satisfies the *Riccati* (1707–1775) *equation*

$$\frac{dy}{dx} = P(x) + Q(x)y + R(x)y^2, \tag{5.571}$$

then each solution must have the form $y = y_1 + u$ where u is a solution of the Bernoulli equation

$$\frac{du}{dx} - (Q + 2Ry_1)u = Ru^2. \tag{5.572}$$

Show further that putting $u = 1/v$ gives $y = y_1 + 1/v$ where

$$\frac{dv}{dx} + (Q + 2Ry_1)v = -R.$$

Show finally that the solutions of this equation have the form $v = cv_1 + v_2$ and that

$$y = \frac{cv_1y_1 + v_2y_1 + 1}{cv_1 + v_2}. \tag{5.573}$$

See Problem 2.28.

5.6. Elliptic Reflectors; Confocal Conics. A well-known problem, a brother of the parabolic-reflector problem of Section 4.8, is that of determining a plane curve such that light or sound striking it from a fixed point source is reflected to a second fixed point. Let the two fixed points be taken as the points $(a, 0)$ and $(-a, 0)$ of a rectangular coordinate system (see Fig. 5.61).

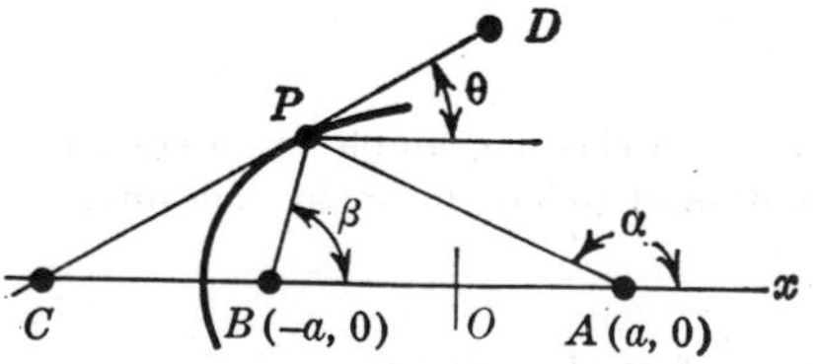

FIG. 5.61

Let $y(x)$ be a differentiable function whose graph is at least a part of the required curve, and let CPD be the tangent to the graph at $P(x, y)$. The angles APD and BPC at which rays of light from A and B meet the tangent must be equal. This implies that

$$\alpha + \beta = 2\theta + \pi$$

where $\tan\theta = y'$. Equating the tangents of these angles and simplifying the result give

$$xyy'^2 + (x^2 - y^2 - a^2)y' - xy = 0. \tag{5.62}$$

This is (see Problems 4.29 and 4.79) the differential equation of the family of conics with foci $(\pm a, 0)$. The following is a method by which we can solve (5.62) when solutions are not known in advance: Multiplying (5.62) by $4y$ and setting $v(x) = [y(x)]^2$, $v' = 2yy'$, we obtain the simpler equation

$$xv'^2 + 2(x^2 - v - a^2)v' - 4xv = 0 \tag{5.63}$$

to solve for $v(x)$. Since the substitution $v = y^2$ simplified (5.62), we may hope that the substitution $t = x^2$ will simplify (5.63). To set $t = x^2$ is to change the independent variable in a differential equation, and this operation requires more thought than change of dependent variable. If $t = x^2$ and $x > 0$, then $v(x) = v(t^{\frac{1}{2}})$ and we may set

$$V(t) = v(t^{\frac{1}{2}}) = v(x).$$

Then $v'(x) = V'(t)(dt/dx) = 2xV'(t) = 2\sqrt{t}\,V'(t)$, and substitution in (5.63) gives

$$tV'^2 + (t - V - a^2)V' - V = 0 \tag{5.64}$$

where the prime on V means differentiation with respect to t. Solutions of (5.64) for which $V''(t)$ exists must satisfy the equation obtained by differentiating with respect to t, that is,

$$V''(2tV' + t - V - a^2) = 0. \tag{5.65}$$

The possibility that $V''(t) = 0$ for all t leads to $V' = c_1$ and hence to the possibility that $tc_1^2 + (t - V - a^2)c_1 - V = 0$ or

$$(c_1^2 + c_1)t - (c_1 + 1)V = a^2c_1 \tag{5.66}$$

is a solution of (5.64) and hence to the possibility that

$$(c_1^2 + c_1)x^2 - (c_1 + 1)y^2 = a^2c_1 \tag{5.67}$$

is a solution of (5.62). If we set $c^2 = a^2/(c_1 + 1)$, then (5.67) takes the more familiar form

$$(c^2 - a^2)x^2 + c^2y^2 = c^2(c^2 - a^2). \tag{5.68}$$

That (5.68) does in fact furnish solutions of (5.62) was shown in Problem 4.29. If $c > a$, then (5.68) furnishes an ellipse which is a curve with the required light-reflection property. If $0 < c < a$, then (5.68) furnishes a hyperbola which does not have the required light-reflection property.

Problem 5.69

Does the result of eliminating V' from (5.64) and the equation obtained by setting the second factor in (5.64) equal to 0 give a solution of (5.64) which in turn leads to a solution of (5.62)?

5.7. Courses of Airplanes in Wind. We consider two methods by which an airplane, with speed v in still air, may attempt to fly from the point $A \equiv (a, 0)$ on the x axis to the origin O of an xy plane in which wind is blowing with speed w in the direction of the positive y axis. If $v > w$ and the airplane points in a shrewdly chosen fixed direction, then the airplane will fly a straight course from A to O. If, however, a naïve pilot keeps his airplane always pointed toward his destination O, then he will be blown from the line OA and the airplane will follow a course which we now determine.

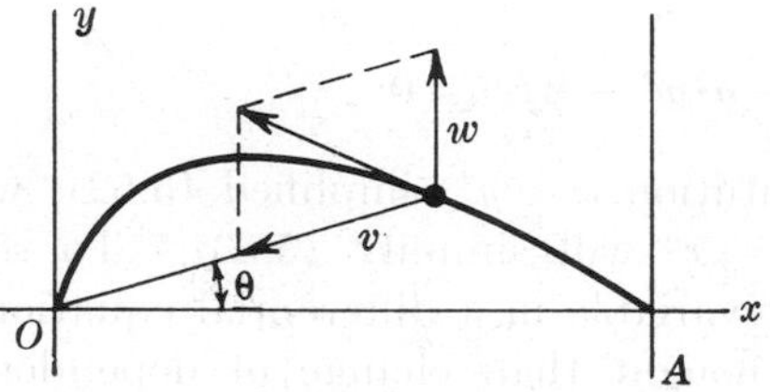

FIG. 5.71

Letting $x = x(t)$ and $y = y(t)$ denote the coordinates of the airplane at time t (and using the angle θ in Fig. 5.71), we obtain, when $0 < x \leqq a$,

$$x'(t) = -v \cos \theta = -vx(x^2 + y^2)^{-\frac{1}{2}} \tag{5.72}$$

$$y'(t) = w - v \sin \theta = w - vy(x^2 + y^2)^{-\frac{1}{2}} \tag{5.721}$$

and

$$\frac{dy}{dx} = \frac{y'(t)}{x'(t)} = \frac{vy - w(x^2 + y^2)^{\frac{1}{2}}}{vx}. \tag{5.73}$$

The analysis up to this point would be valid even if v and w were functions of x, y, and t; we now consider the case in which v and w are constants and set $k = w/v$ to simplify writing. The equation (5.73) is homogeneous, and after making the substitution $y = zx$ we separate the variables to obtain

$$(1 + z^2)^{-\frac{1}{2}}dz + kx^{-1}\,dx = 0. \tag{5.731}$$

Hence,

$$\log\,[z + (1 + z^2)^{\frac{1}{2}}] + k \log x = c$$

where $c = k \log a$ since $z = y = 0$ when $x = a$. Therefore,

$$z + (1 + z^2)^{\frac{1}{2}} = \left(\frac{x}{a}\right)^{-k},$$

and solving for z gives

$$z = \frac{1}{2}\left[\left(\frac{x}{a}\right)^{-k} - \left(\frac{x}{a}\right)^{k}\right]$$

so that

$$y = \frac{a}{2}\left[\left(\frac{x}{a}\right)^{1-k} - \left(\frac{x}{a}\right)^{1+k}\right]. \tag{5.74}$$

Problem 5.75

Show that, if $0 < k < 1$,

$$\lim_{x\to 0} y(x) = 0, \qquad \lim_{x\to 0} y'(x) = \infty; \tag{5.751}$$

that, if $k = 1$,

$$\lim_{x\to 0} y(x) = \frac{a}{2}, \qquad \lim_{x\to 0} y'(x) = 0; \tag{5.752}$$

that, if $k > 1$,

$$\lim_{x\to 0} y(x) = \infty, \qquad \lim_{x\to 0} y'(x) = -\infty; \tag{5.753}$$

and interpret these results by graphs and discussion.

Problem 5.76

One who wishes to study further the courses of airplanes in wind may try to decide which of the following problems are easily solved.

5.761. Find the functions $x = x(t)$ and $y = y(t)$ which give the coordinates of the naïve pilot at time t.

5.762. Find the time required for the naïve pilot to fly from A to O, and compare the result with the time required by a pilot who follows the line AO.

5.763. Give a complete discussion of the problem for the case in which the direction of the wind makes an angle ϕ with the positive x axis.

5.764. Find the path of a submarine crossing from A to O in Fig. 5.71 if (i) the submarine is steered so as to point toward O and (ii) the lines $x = 0$ and $x = a$ are banks of a river in which water is flowing in the direction of the y axis with a speed proportional to the distance from the nearer bank, the speed being w_0 at the center of the river.

5.8. Transformations of the Laplace Operator ∇^2. The problem of obtaining (1.172) and (1.173) from (1.171) is one of the most useful and interesting exercises involving changes of variables in derivative expressions. Supposing that u is a function of three rectangular coordinates x, y, z which is continuous and has continuous partial derivatives of first and second orders, we can define ∇^2 by the formula

$$\nabla^2 u = \frac{\partial^2 u}{\partial x^2} + \frac{\partial^2 u}{\partial y^2} + \frac{\partial^2 u}{\partial z^2}. \tag{5.81}$$

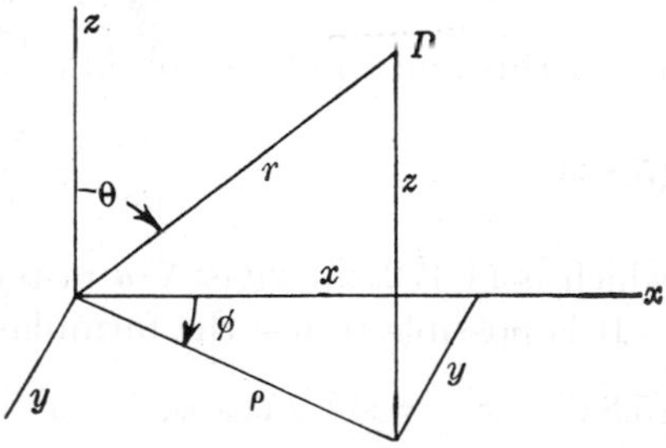

FIG. 5.82

Our problem is to express $\nabla^2 u$ in terms of the *cylindrical coordinates* (ϕ, ρ, z) and the *spherical coordinates* (θ, ϕ, z) shown in Fig. 5.82. As the figure shows, the rectangular and cylindrical coordinates are related by the formulas

$$x = \rho \cos \phi, \qquad y = \rho \sin \phi, \qquad z = z \tag{5.83}$$

and

$$\phi = \tan^{-1}\frac{y}{x}, \qquad \rho = \sqrt{x^2 + y^2}, \qquad z = z.$$

With the aid of the formulas

$$\frac{\partial u}{\partial x} = \frac{\partial u}{\partial \rho}\frac{\partial \rho}{\partial x} + \frac{\partial u}{\partial \phi}\frac{\partial \phi}{\partial x}$$

and

$$\frac{\partial \rho}{\partial x} = \cos\phi, \qquad \frac{\partial \rho}{\partial y} = \sin\phi, \qquad \frac{\partial \phi}{\partial x} = \frac{-\sin\phi}{\rho}, \qquad \frac{\partial \phi}{\partial y} = \frac{\cos\phi}{\rho}$$

we obtain, when $\rho > 0$,

(5.831) $$\frac{\partial u}{\partial x} = \cos\phi\,\frac{\partial u}{\partial \rho} - \frac{\sin\phi}{\rho}\frac{\partial u}{\partial \phi}.$$

With the aid of these formulas and the formula

$$\frac{\partial^2 u}{\partial x^2} = \left[\frac{\partial}{\partial \rho}\frac{\partial u}{\partial x}\right]\frac{\partial \rho}{\partial x} + \left[\frac{\partial}{\partial \phi}\frac{\partial u}{\partial x}\right]\frac{\partial \phi}{\partial x}$$

we obtain, when $\rho > 0$,

$$\frac{\partial^2 u}{\partial x^2} = \cos^2\phi\,\frac{\partial^2 u}{\partial \rho^2} - \frac{2\sin\phi\cos\phi}{\rho}\frac{\partial^2 u}{\partial \rho\,\partial \phi} + \frac{\sin\phi\cos\phi}{\rho^2}\frac{\partial u}{\partial \phi} + \frac{\sin^2\phi}{\rho}\frac{\partial u}{\partial \rho} + \frac{\sin^2\phi}{\rho^2}\frac{\partial^2 u}{\partial \phi^2} + \frac{\sin\phi\cos\phi}{\rho^2}\frac{\partial u}{\partial \phi}.$$

Adding to this a similar expression for $\partial^2 u/\partial y^2$ gives the fundamental identity

(5.832) $$\frac{\partial^2 u}{\partial x^2} + \frac{\partial^2 u}{\partial y^2} = \frac{\partial^2 u}{\partial \rho^2} + \frac{1}{\rho}\frac{\partial u}{\partial \rho} + \frac{1}{\rho^2}\frac{\partial^2 u}{\partial \phi^2}.$$

From this and (5.81) we obtain

(5.833) $$\nabla^2 u = \frac{\partial^2 u}{\partial \rho^2} + \frac{1}{\rho}\frac{\partial u}{\partial \rho} + \frac{1}{\rho^2}\frac{\partial^2 u}{\partial \phi^2} + \frac{\partial^2 u}{\partial z^2}$$

which is (1.172); it gives $\nabla^2 u$ in terms of cylindrical coordinates.

It is possible to use the formulas

(5.84) $$x = r\sin\theta\cos\phi, \qquad y = r\sin\theta\sin\phi, \qquad z = r\cos\theta$$

to convert $\nabla^2 u$ directly from rectangular to spherical coordinates.* It is, however, very much simpler to use (5.833) and the formulas

(5.85) $$z = r\cos\theta, \qquad \rho = r\sin\theta, \qquad \phi = \phi$$

* Doing this can make you forget your troubles the next time you have a toothache at an airport and are informed that your plane is 3 hours late.

relating cylindrical and spherical coordinates. It is both amusing and helpful to observe that, except for the names of the variables involved, the transformation (5.85) from cylindrical to spherical coordinates is exactly the same as the transformation (5.83) from rectangular to cylindrical coordinates. This fact and (5.832) give, without making new calculations like those leading to (5.832), the formula

$$(5.851) \qquad \frac{\partial^2 u}{\partial \rho^2} + \frac{\partial^2 u}{\partial z^2} = \frac{\partial^2 u}{\partial r^2} + \frac{1}{r}\frac{\partial u}{\partial r} + \frac{1}{r^2}\frac{\partial^2 u}{\partial \theta^2}$$

for the sum of the first and last terms of the right member of (5.833). Moreover

$$\frac{\partial u}{\partial \rho} = \sin\theta \frac{\partial u}{\partial r} + \frac{\cos\theta}{r}\frac{\partial u}{\partial \theta}$$

and hence, because $\rho = r \sin \theta$,

$$(5.852) \qquad \frac{1}{\rho}\frac{\partial u}{\partial \rho} = \frac{1}{r}\frac{\partial u}{\partial r} + \frac{\cos\theta}{r^2 \sin\theta}\frac{\partial u}{\partial \theta},$$

these formulas being valid when $r > 0$ and $0 < \theta < \pi$. From (5.833), (5.851), (5.852), and the fact that $\rho = r \sin \theta$, we obtain the formula (1.173) which gives $\nabla^2 u$ in spherical coordinates.

5.86. A More Complicated Example. We invest a little time to see that successions of changes of variables can sometimes be applied to solve difficult problems. Research in analytic number theory led J. B. Rosser (1907–) to the implausible equation

$$(5.87) \qquad x^2 y'' + (3x - x^2)y' + (1 - x - e^{2x})y = 0$$

and he wanted an explicit formula for solutions of it. After breaking his equation (5.87), Rosser cheerfully admitted that it took him several weeks to do it. He found that, for each positive number x_0, the function

$$y(x) = x^{-1}e^{\phi(x)},$$

where

$$\phi(x) = \int_{x_0}^{x} u^{-1}e^{u}\, du,$$

is a solution of (5.87) over the interval $x > 0$ that interested him. This enabled him to obtain the information he was seeking.

We shall not illustrate the long process of trying assorted changes of variables that fail to simplify (5.87), but we shall show a sequence of useful changes. Let $y(x)$ be a function satisfying (5.87) and let x be confined to an interval over which $x \neq 0$ and $xy(x) > 0$. Setting $v = xy$, $y = v/x$, we obtain the simpler equation

$$(5.871) \qquad x^2 v'' + (x - x^2)v' - e^{2x}v = 0.$$

Setting $w = \log v$, so that $v = e^w$, we obtain

$$(5.872) \qquad x^2 w'' + (x - x^2)w' + x^2 w'^2 = e^{2x}.$$

This equation may appear at first glance to be no better than (5.871), but it has a redeeming feature. Though w' and w'' appear in the equation, there is no w and we can make (5.872) look like a first-order equation by making the change of variable $z = w'$. We thus obtain

(5.873) $$x^2z' + (x - x^2)z + x^2z^2 = e^{2x}.$$

Setting $u = xz$ and $z = u/x$, we obtain the simpler equation

(5.874) $$xu' - xu + u^2 = e^{2x}.$$

Setting $s = e^{-x}u$ and $u = e^x s$, we obtain

(5.875) $$xs' = e^x(1 - s^2).$$

Thus, after several successive substitutions, we have arrived at the equation (5.875) which is easily solved.

Before solving (5.875), let us see how $y(x)$ is related to the function $s(x)$. Using the formulas $u = e^x s$, $z = u/x$, and $w' = z$, we find that when $s(x)$ is continuous [and whether $s(x)$ satisfies (5.875) or not]

$$w' = z = \frac{e^x s(x)}{x}$$

and hence that

$$w = c_1 + \int_{x_0}^{x} \frac{e^\alpha s(\alpha)}{\alpha}\, d\alpha$$

where x_0 is a point of the interval considered and c_1 is a constant. Using the formulas $v = e^w$ and $y = v/x$, we then find

(5.876) $$y = c_2 x^{-1} \exp \int_{x_0}^{x} \frac{e^\alpha s(\alpha)}{\alpha}\, d\alpha$$

where $c_2 = \exp c_1$ and, as usual, $\exp Q$ means e^Q. Thus we have shown that, if $y(x)$ is a solution of (5.87) over an interval where $xy(x) > 0$, then there is a function $s(x)$ satisfying (5.875) for which (5.876) holds. In an interval in which $x \neq 0$ and $xy < 0$, the same would be true except that c_2 would then be negative. The steps in the above argument can be reversed to show that, if $s(x)$ satisfies (5.875), then the function $y(x)$ defined by (5.876) satisfies (5.87) when $x \neq 0$.

We now solve (5.875). Before dividing by $x(1 - s^2)$ to separate the variables, we contemplate the possibility that $1 - s^2$ may be 0. Actually the functions $s(x) = 1$ and $s(x) = -1$ are solutions of (5.875) and, for our present purposes, by far the most important solutions of (5.875). They lead by means of (5.876) to very satisfactory formulas for two solutions of (5.87); the theory of Chapter 6 may then be applied.

If $s(x)$ is a solution of (5.875) and x is confined to an interval where $x \neq 0$ and $s(x) \neq \pm 1$, we can separate the variables in (5.875) to obtain

(5.877) $$\frac{1}{1 - s^2}\, ds = \frac{e^x}{x}\, dx$$

and integrate to obtain

(5.878) $$\frac{1}{2} \log \frac{1 + s}{1 - s} = c_3 + \int_{x_0}^{x} \frac{e^\alpha}{\alpha}\, d\alpha.$$

Denoting the integral on the right by $H(x)$ and using the definition

(5.88) $$\tanh A = \frac{e^A - e^{-A}}{e^A + e^{-A}}$$

of the hyperbolic tangent, we find

(5.881) $$s(x) = \tanh\,(c_3 + H(x)).$$

Insertion of these functions $s(x)$ in (5.876) leads to complicated formulas for solutions of (5.87).

Problem 5.89

Prove that if $s'(x)$ exists, then [whether $s(x)$ satisfies (5.875) or not] the result of substituting the function $y(x)$, defined by (5.876), in the left member of (5.87) is

$$c_2(xs' + e^x s^2 - e^x)e^x x^{-1} \exp \int_{x_0}^{x} \frac{e^\alpha s(\alpha)}{\alpha}\, d\alpha.$$

5.9. Exact Derivatives. This section contains a brief account of a topic which really belongs to advanced calculus where matters involving integration of derivatives and differentiation of integrals receive more attention than we can give them. When $f(x, y)$ and $y(x)$ are given functions satisfying appropriate conditions, the formula

$$\frac{d}{dx} f(x, y) = u(x, y) + v(x, y) \frac{dy}{dx} \tag{5.91}$$

is valid when

$$u(x, y) = \frac{\partial f}{\partial x}, \qquad v(x, y) = \frac{\partial f}{\partial y}. \tag{5.92}$$

The problem of this section involves a completely different approach to the two formulas (5.91) and (5.92). We suppose that $u(x, y)$ and $v(x, y)$ are two given functions and we ask whether one or more functions $f(x, y)$ exist such that (5.91) and (5.92) are valid and, furthermore, we ask how we can find an f if one does exist. Some weird terminology must be learned. If f exists such that (5.91) and (5.92) hold, then the right side of (5.91) is (exactly) the derivative of a function f and the right side of (5.91) is said to be an *exact derivative* and is said to be *exact*. If no such f exists, then the right side of (5.91) is said to be *inexact* because it is not (hence is not exactly) the derivative of a function $f(x, y)$. The relevance of the problem to the theory of differential equations is apparent; if tho left side of the equation

$$u(x, y) + v(x, y) \frac{dy}{dx} = 0 \tag{5.93}$$

is exact and if we can find f, then the formula $f(x, y) = c$ is a formal solution of (5.93). We can recall from Problem 2.15 that if (5.93) is not necessarily exact but the result of multiplying by $\mu(x, y)$ is exact, then $\mu(x, y)$ is called an *integrating factor* of (5.93).

We simplify matters by supposing that $u(x, y)$ and $v(x, y)$ are two functions which are continuous and have continuous partial derivatives over a rectangle R containing the point (x_0, y_0) in its interior. Moreover we consider only the problem involving functions f which are continuous and have continuous partial derivatives of first and second orders so that, as is shown in advanced calculus, the second members of the two equations

$$(5.931) \qquad \frac{\partial u}{\partial y} = \frac{\partial^2 f}{\partial y\, \partial x}, \qquad \frac{\partial v}{\partial x} = \frac{\partial^2 f}{\partial x\, \partial y}$$

are equal. Now we can go to work.

If

$$(5.94) \qquad u(x, y) + v(x, y)\frac{dy}{dx}$$

is exact, then there must exist an f for which (5.92) holds and we can differentiate to obtain (5.931) and conclude that

$$(5.95) \qquad \frac{\partial u}{\partial y} = \frac{\partial v}{\partial x}.$$

Thus (5.95) is a necessary condition for exactness of (5.94).

We give an efficient proof that (5.95) is also sufficient for exactness of (5.94) by exhibiting functions $f(x, y)$ for which (5.92) is valid when (5.95) holds. For each constant c, let

$$(5.96) \qquad f(x, y) = \int_{x_0}^{x} u(t, y)dt + \int_{y_0}^{y} v(x_0, u)du + c.$$

Then giving y a fixed value and differentiating with respect to x give

$$\frac{\partial f}{\partial x} = u(x, y).$$

This is the first of the required formulas, and f must have continuous derivatives of second order because u has continuous derivatives of first order. Giving x a fixed value and differentiating (5.96) with respect to y gives, with the aid of (5.95) and some advanced calculus,

$$(5.97) \qquad \begin{aligned} \frac{\partial f}{\partial y} &= \int_{x_0}^{x} u_y(t, y)dt + v(x_0, y) \\ &= \int_{x_0}^{x} v_x(t, y)dt + v(x_0, y) \\ &= v(x, y) - v(x_0, y) + v(x_0, y) = v(x, y). \end{aligned}$$

This is the second of the required formulas and the proof is finished. It is possible to see where the formula (5.96) came from by reversing the order of the steps in the above formulas.

It is sometimes worth while to apply the test (5.95) to see whether a given equation is exact. If the given equation is exact (or has been made exact by use of an integrating factor, as can sometimes be done), then a function f for which (5.91) holds can be obtained by substituting in (5.96). Substituting is sometimes a worthy endeavor, and it might even be worth while to learn more tedious ways of getting answers when the functions are all easily integrated. However we cannot spend 4 hours in every village, and so we pass on.

CHAPTER 6

LINEAR DIFFERENTIAL EQUATIONS

6.0. Definitions and Theorems. This chapter contains an account of basic ideas and applications involving linear differential equations. A *linear differential equation* of order n is defined to be an equation of the form

$$(6.01) \qquad a_0 \frac{d^n y}{dx^n} + a_1 \frac{d^{n-1} y}{dx^{n-1}} + \cdot \cdot \cdot + a_{n-1} \frac{dy}{dx} + a_n y = f(x)$$

where $a_0, a_1, \ldots, a_n$ and $f(x)$ are given functions of x; an important special case is that in which the a's are constants. The equation

$$(6.02) \qquad a_0 \frac{d^n y}{dx^n} + a_1 \frac{d^{n-1} y}{dx^{n-1}} + \cdot \cdot \cdot + a_{n-1} \frac{dy}{dx} + a_n y = 0,$$

which is the same as (6.01) except that the right member has been replaced by 0, is called the *homogeneous equation* corresponding to (6.01).

Linear differential equations are extremely important in many phases of pure and applied mathematics. Indeed, they are so important that many persons with few mathematical interests know enough about them to be able to use them in the solution of problems. In many applictions of (6.01), x is time t (measured in suitable units) and $f(x)$ is a mechanical or electromotive force which is applied to or fed into a system composed of mechanical or electrical hardware. In such situations it is customary to call $f(x)$ the input and $y(x)$ the output of the system. As was remarked in Section 3.1, this terminology is so neat and helpful that we make it available for use at all times by calling $f(x)$ the *input* and $y(x)$ the *output* of the differential equation. Studies of (6.01) then become studies of the manner in which outputs depend upon inputs and other things. Engineers often borrow mathematics to help them understand engineering, and it is only fair that mathematicians should borrow engineering to help them understand mathematics. In view of the importance of the subject to everybody, it is highly gratifying that the fundamental Theorems 6.03 and 6.04, which we shall state presently, have been proved. Proofs appear in Chapter 16.

Before looking at these theorems, it is helpful to have a rough idea what they are all about. Theorem 6.03 says that the output is completely determined by the input and the state of the output (that is, the value of the output and some of its derivatives) at a particular time x_0. The first part of Theorem 6.04 says that, even when the input is zero, there are many possible outputs and gives precise information about these possible outputs. The last part of Theorem 6.04 gives similar information when the input is not zero. The results are extensions of the ideas of Section 3.1 to equations of order n. In order to understand Theorem 6.04, it is necessary to know about linear combinations and independence.

Our program is the following. We learn these theorems, which are really not as fearsome as they look, and then start on a campaign to learn what they mean and what they are good for. As in the case for the fundamental theorem of algebra, which is stated at the end of this section, it is quite appropriate that these theorems should be thoroughly understood and used by persons who have not seen (and perhaps never will see) proofs of them.

THEOREM 6.03. *If $a_0(x), a_1(x), \ldots, a_n(x)$ and $f(x)$ are functions of x continuous when x lies in an interval I and if $a_0(x) \neq 0$ when x is in I, then corresponding to each point x_0 of I and each set of n constants $k_1, k_2, \ldots, k_n$ there is one and only one function $y(x)$ satisfying the boundary conditions.*

$$(6.031) \qquad y(x_0) = k_1, \qquad y'(x_0) = k_2, \qquad \ldots, \qquad y^{(n-1)}(x_0) = k_n,$$

and the differential equation

$$(6.032) \qquad a_0 \frac{d^n y}{dx^n} + a_1 \frac{d^{n-1}y}{dx^{n-1}} + \cdots + a_{n-1}\frac{dy}{dx} + a_n y = f(x)$$

over the interval I.

THEOREM 6.04. *If $a_0(x), a_1(x), \ldots, a_n(x)$ and $f(x)$ are functions of x continuous when x lies in an interval I and if $a_0(x) \neq 0$ when x lies in I, then the homogeneous equation*

$$(6.041) \qquad a_0 \frac{d^n y}{dx^n} + a_1 \frac{d^{n-1}y}{dx^{n-1}} + \cdots + a_{n-1}\frac{dy}{dx} + a_n y = 0$$

has n independent solutions. If $y_1(x), y_2(x), \ldots, y_n(x)$ are n independent solutions of (6.041), *then*

$$(6.042) \qquad y = c_1y_1(x) + c_2y_2(x) + \cdots + c_ny_n(x)$$

is a solution of (6.041) *for each set of constants $c_1, c_2, \ldots, c_n$; and, conversely, each solution of* (6.041) *can be represented in the form* (6.042) *by making appropriate choices of the constants $c_1, c_2, \ldots, c_n$. If $Y(x)$ is a solution of the nonhomogeneous equation*

$$(6.043) \qquad a_0 \frac{d^n y}{dx^n} + a_1 \frac{d^{n-1}y}{dx^{n-1}} + \cdots + a_{n-1}\frac{dy}{dx} + a_n y = f(x)$$

and $y_1(x), \ldots, y_n(x)$ *denote as before* n *independent solutions of the homogeneous equation* (6.041), *then*

$$y = Y(x) + c_1y_1(x) + c_2y_2(x) + \cdots + c_ny_n(x) \tag{6.044}$$

is a solution of (6.043) *for each set of constants* $c_1, c_2, \ldots, c_n$; *and, conversely, each solution of* (6.043) *can be represented in the form* (6.044) *by making appropriate choices of the constants* $c_1, c_2, \ldots, c_n$.

In contrast to nonlinear equations which may have families of solutions in which arbitrary constants (or parameters) enter in all manner of complicated ways and which may have additional "singular" solutions of complicated and unpleasant kinds, the linear equations are very simple. So long as x is restricted to an interval in which $a_0(x) \neq 0$ and all the a's and f are continuous, the linear differential equations (6.041) and (6.043) have general solutions (6.042) and (6.044), respectively, into which the c's enter in a simple way.

The function $y(x)$ in (6.042) is called a *linear combination with constant coefficients* or, briefly, a *linear combination* of the functions $y_1(x), y_2(x), \ldots, y_n(x)$. The function $Y(x)$, which can be any single special solution of (6.043) that one is able to find, is called a *particular solution* of (6.043). Thus the general solution of the nonhomogeneous equation (6.043) is the sum of any particular solution of (6.043) and the general solution of the corresponding homogeneous equation (6.041).

The fundamental theorem of algebra, which was mentioned above and which is ordinarily proved in courses in the theory of functions of a complex variable, may be stated as follows:

THEOREM 6.05. *If* $n \geqq 1$, *if* $a_0, a_1, \ldots, a_n$ *are constants (real or complex) for which* $a_0 \neq 0$, *and if*

$$Z(m) = a_0m^n + a_1m^{n-1} + \cdots + a_{n-1}m + a_n, \tag{6.051}$$

then there exist n *constants* $m_1, m_2, \ldots, m_n$ *(which may be complex even when* $a_0, a_1, \ldots, a_n$ *are real) such that*

$$Z(m) = a_0(m - m_1)(m - m_2) \cdots (m - m_n). \tag{6.952}$$

The numbers $m_1, m_2, \ldots, m_n$ are *zeros* of $Z(m)$, and $Z(m)$ has no other zeros. In physical and engineering applications, these numbers are always or nearly always distinct; that is, no two are equal. In case two or more of the numbers m_k are equal, $Z(m)$ is said to have multiple zeros. In this case, (6.052) takes the form

$$Z(m) = a_0(m - m_1)^{p_1}(m - m_2)^{p_2} \cdots (m - m_r)^{p_r} \tag{6.053}$$

where r and $p_1, p_2, \ldots, p_r$ are positive integers for which

$$p_1 + p_2 + \cdots + p_r = n.$$

The *multiplicity* of m_k is p_k. In every case, $Z(m)$ has at least one zero, has at most n zeros, and has exactly n zeros when multiplicities are counted.

Sometimes the letter m appearing in Theorem 6.05 and other parts of this chapter should be replaced by the letter s to make the notation agree with the representations $s = \sigma + it$ and $s = \sigma + j\omega$ of complex numbers that are fashionable in parts of pure and applied mathematics. However, throughout most of this chapter, it seems best to use the letter that looks least like a variable. It is easy to replace the neutral letter m by another whenever this is desirable.

Problem 6.061

Let k be a positive constant. Show, by differentiation and substitution, that $\cos kx$ and $\sin kx$ are both solutions of the equation

$$y'' + k^2y = 0. \tag{6.0611}$$

As we shall soon learn, $\cos kx$ and $\sin kx$ are independent. What conclusion can now be drawn from Theorem 6.04? *Ans.:* The general solution of $y'' + k^2y = 0$ is

$$y = c_1 \cos kx + c_2 \sin kx. \tag{6.0612}$$

Remark: The part of the conclusion which says that each function of the form (6.0612) is a solution of $y'' + k^2y = 0$ is important and is easily proved by differentiation and substitution. The part of the conclusion which says that each solution of $y'' + k^2y = 0$ has the form (6.0612) is important and is not so easy to prove when we do not have Theorem 6.04 to help do the chores. It is, in this case, easier to catch some fish than to prove that we have caught them all.

Problem 6.062

Theorem 6.03 implies that there is a unique function $y(x)$ for which $y(0) = y'(0) = 1$ and $y'' + y = 0$. Find it and check your answer. *Hint:* The result of the previous problem is useful.

Problem 6.063

When k and A are constants and $k > 0$, a quick glance at the equation

$$y'' + k^2y = A \tag{6.0631}$$

shows that it will be satisfied if y is an appropriately chosen constant. Find this constant. Now what theorem implies what? *Ans.:* Theorem 6.04 implies that the general solution of (6.0631) is

$$y = A/k^2 + c_1 \cos kx + c_2 \sin kx.$$

Problem 6.064

Determine m so that the function e^{mx} satisfies $y'' - y = 0$. Tell precisely what conclusion you could draw from this and Theorem 6.04 if you knew that e^x and e^{-x} are independent. (They are independent.)

Problem 6.065

Find a solution of the equation

$$y'' - y = x - 1 \tag{6.0651}$$

having the form $y = ax + b$. Then, with the aid of the preceding problem, find the general solution of (6.0651). *Ans.*: $y = c_1e^x + c_2e^{-x} - x + 1$.

Problem 6.066

What familiar conclusion results from the hypothesis that 1, x, and x^2 are independent solutions of $d^3y/dx^3 = 0$?

Problem 6.067

Using (1.476) with $\delta = 0$ and $f(t) = 0$, show that the displacement y of the bob on an undamped, unforced mechanical oscillator is given in terms of t by the formula

$$y = c_1 \cos \sqrt{\frac{\sigma}{mL_0}}\, t + c_2 \sin \sqrt{\frac{\sigma}{mL_0}}\, t.$$

The period T of the motion is the number of seconds that t must increase to make $\sqrt{\sigma/mL_0}\, t$ increase from 0 to 2π, and the frequency ν (Greek letter nu, the number of oscillations per second) is $1/T$. Show that

$$T = 2\pi \sqrt{\frac{mL_0}{\sigma}}, \qquad \nu = \frac{1}{2\pi} \sqrt{\frac{\sigma}{mL_0}}.$$

Problem 6.068

Using the approximation in (1.54), show that the angular displacement θ of a swinging pendulum is given in terms of t by the formula

$$\theta = c_1 \cos \sqrt{\frac{g}{l}}\, t + c_2 \sin \sqrt{\frac{g}{l}}\, t.$$

Show that the period and frequency are

$$T = 2\pi \sqrt{\frac{l}{g}}, \qquad \nu = \frac{1}{2\pi} \sqrt{\frac{g}{l}}.$$

Using the approximations $g = 32$ and $\pi^2 = 10$, show that the length of a pendulum which (with small oscillations) beats seconds is 0.8 feet. Show that the length of a pendulum which reaches an extreme position once each second is 3.2 feet.

Problem 6.069

Problem 6.063 implies that if h is a positive constant and

$$\frac{d^2x}{dt^2} + x = -h \tag{6.0691}$$

over each interval of values of t for which $dx/dt > 0$, then to each such interval there correspond constants c_1 and c_2 such that

$$x = -h + c_1 \cos t + c_2 \sin t. \tag{6.0692}$$

Letting $y = dx/dt$, show that to each such interval there corresponds a constant λ such that

$$[x(t) + h]^2 + [y(t)]^2 = \lambda^2 \tag{6.0693}$$

and hence that, as t increases over this interval, the point $(x(t), y(t))$ moves clockwise over the upper half of a circle with center at $(-h, 0)$ in the (x, y) plane. Tell what can be added to this story if we know that

$$\frac{d^2x}{dt^2} + x = +h \tag{6.0694}$$

over each interval of values of t for which $dx/dt < 0$. *Remark:* The two equations (6.091) and (6.094) are equivalent to the single nonlinear equation

$$\frac{d^2x}{dt^2} + f\left(\frac{dx}{dt}\right) + x = 0 \tag{6.0695}$$

where $f(u) = h \operatorname{sgn} u$. The (x, y) plane is a *phase plane*. With the aid of the information obtained above and a compass that will draw arcs of circles, we can easily become authorities on functions $x(t)$ that satisfy (6.0695) and given initial conditions. See Problems 4.192 and 5.183.

Problem 6.07

A rectangular raft, composed of solid wood having density δ, is L feet square and h feet thick. It is floating peacefully in still water with a motionless swimmer of mass S and weight Sg poised at each corner. At time $t = 0$, the swimmers step quietly into the water and leave an unloaded bobbing raft for us to investigate. The problem is to determine the vertical motion of the raft. *Solution:* The total mass m of the raft is volume times mass per unit volume and hence $m = L^2h\delta\rho$ where ρ is the mass of a cubic foot of the water. Let P be a point in the raft which is at the level of the surface of the water when the unloaded raft is floating motionless, and construct a vertical y axis with origin at this point and with y positive when P is above the origin. When $y \neq 0$, the gravitational and buoyant forces no longer balance. Let g be the acceleration of gravity, and let U be a unit vector directed upward. When $y < 0$ there is, according to Archimedes (287 B.C.–212 B.C.), a net upward force F whose magnitude is equal to the weight $L^2(-y)\rho g$ of the additional water displaced and hence $F = -L^2y\rho gU$. When $y > 0$, there is a net downward force F whose magnitude is equal to the weight $L^2y\rho g$ of the water formerly but not now displaced, and again $F = -L^2y\rho gU$. Using the Newton law $ma = F$ in the form $ma - F = 0$ then gives

$$L^2h\delta\rho \frac{d^2y}{dt^2} + L^2h\rho g y = 0. \tag{6.071}$$

This is equivalent to

$$y''(t) + \omega^2 y(t) = 0 \tag{6.072}$$

where $\omega > 0$ and $\omega^2 = g/\delta$. In formulating our problem, we have neglected all forces except the gravitational and buoyant forces. Our results will therefore give a good description of the motion of the raft only until frictional or other forces have time to significantly affect the motion. From Problem 6.061 we obtain the conclusion that there must be constants c_1 and c_2 such that

$$y = c_1 \cos \omega t + c_2 \sin \omega t. \tag{6.073}$$

We are now coming very close to precise information about the motion of our raft. According to the statement of our problem, the raft was below the equilibrium position but was at rest at time $t = 0$. Differentiating (6.073) gives the formula

$$y'(t) = -c_1\omega \sin \omega t + c_2\omega \cos \omega t.$$

Putting $t = 0$ gives the formula $0 = c_2\omega$, so $c_2 = 0$. Therefore

$$y(t) = c_1 \cos \omega t. \tag{6.074}$$

When we have determined c_1, we will be finished. Putting $t = 0$ shows that $c_1 = y(0)$. We must therefore find $y(0)$. We know that $-y(0)$ is the distance the weight of the four swimmers forced the raft below its equilibrium position. Hence $y(0)$ is determined from the formula

$$4Sg = L^2[-y(0)]\rho g$$

in which the left side is the weight of the four swimmers and the right side is the buoyant force on a submerged section of height $[-y(0)]$ of the raft. Thus

$$c_1 = y(0) = -\frac{4S}{L^2\rho}.$$

Putting this and the value of ω in (6.074) gives

$$y = -\frac{4S}{L^2\rho} \cos \sqrt{\frac{g}{\delta}}\, t \tag{6.075}$$

for the solution of our problem.

The period T of the oscillations is the time required for ωt to increase from 0 to 2π so that $\omega T = 2\pi$ and $T = 2\pi/\omega$. Thus, in our case, taking $g = 32.2$ gives

$$T = 2\pi \sqrt{\frac{\delta}{g}} = 1.11 \sqrt{\delta} \tag{6.076}$$

seconds. This is a very curious result. Since 1.11 happens to be a little greater than 1, we can see that T will be about 1 whenever δ is a little less than 1. This shows that if something will be kind enough to (i) float in water with most of it submerged, (ii) have, like the raft, uniform cross sections parallel to the surface of the water, and (iii) bob up and down with damping small enough to allow us to observe several times at which it is in its highest position—if a thing does all these, then it serves as a timekeeper. With only a small relative error, the thing will appear in its highest position once each second. It is quite easy to check all this by observing the periods of rods of wood that are weighted at ends so they will float in vertical positions. The periods will be what the differential equation requires them to be, but if the rods are slender the amplitudes of the oscillations will damp down very quickly.

6.08. Linearity. Since it becomes tedious to write the left members of (6.032), (6.041), and (6.043) very often, we sometimes abbreviate them by the symbol $L_a y$ so that

$$L_a y = a_0 \frac{d^n y}{dx^n} + a_1 \frac{d^{n-1}y}{dx^{n-1}} + \cdots + a_{n-1}\frac{dy}{dx} + a_n y \tag{6.081}$$

and think of L_a as being an *operator* which transforms a function $y(x)$ having n derivatives into the right side of (6.081). Thus the equations become $L_a y = 0$ and $L_a y = f$. More information about operators is given in Section 6.8, but we do not need it now.

If k is a positive integer, c_1 and c_2 are constants, and $y_1(x)$ and $y_2(x)$ are two functions having k derivatives, then

$$\frac{d^k}{dx^k}[c_1 y_1(x) + c_2 y_2(x)] = c_1 \frac{d^k y_1(x)}{dx} + c_2 \frac{d^k y_2(x)}{dx}.$$

Because of this fact, we can put $y = c_1 y_1 + c_2 y_2$ in (6.081) to obtain the very important formula

$$(6.082) \qquad L_a(c_1 y_1 + c_2 y_2) = c_1 L_a y_1 + c_2 L_a y_2.$$

Because this is true, we say that L_a is a *linear operator*. The L in L_a is to keep us remembering that it is linear, and the a indicates that it depends upon $a_0, a_1, \ldots, a_n$. Putting $c_1 = c_2 = 1$ gives the special formula

$$(6.083) \qquad L_a(y_1 + y_2) = L_a y_1 + L_a y_2.$$

Because of this, we say that L_a is an *additive* operator, the idea being that we can get the result of applying L_a to a sum by adding the results of applying L_a to the terms of the sum. Some engineers sometimes call (6.083) the *principle of superposition*.

One service of the notation L_a and the idea of linearity is to make fundamental results seem very simple and easy to prove. Use the notation and the idea in solving the following problems.

Problem 6.091

Prove that if y_1 and y_2 are both solutions of the homogeneous equation (6.041), and if k_1 and k_2 are constants, then $k_1 y_1 + k_2 y_2$ is also a solution of (6.041).

Problem 6.092

Prove that if y satisfies (6.041) and Y satisfies (6.043) then $y + Y$ satisfies (6.043).

Problem 6.093

Prove that if Y_1 and Y_2 satisfy (6.043), then $Y_1 - Y_2$ satisfies (6.041).

Problem 6.094

Prove that if

$$L_a Y_k = f_k \qquad k = 1, 2, \ldots, p,$$

then

$$L_a(Y_1 + Y_2 + \cdots + Y_p) = f_1 + f_2 + \cdots + f_p.$$

Tell precisely what this means in terms of inputs and outputs of (6.043).

6.1. Independence. In order to understand Theorem 6.04, and for other purposes, it is necessary to know about independence. The task of constructing and understanding a theory of independence (which used to be and sometimes still is called linear independence*) is simplified by introduction of a little terminology that everyone ought to know about. Suppose that v_1, v_2, and v_3 are three nonzero vectors issuing from the origin in ordinary three-dimensional Euclid (*c*.330 B.C.–275 B.C.) space. The set of vectors representable in the form $c_1v_1 + c_2v_2$, where c_1 and c_2 are real numerical constants, is called the *span* of v_1 and v_2. If there exist constants c_1 and c_2 not both 0 for which

$$c_1v_1 + c_2v_2 = 0 \tag{6.11}$$

then $v_1 = (-c_2/c_1)v_2$ provided $c_1 \neq 0$ and $v_2 = (-c_1/c_2)v_1$ provided $c_2 \neq 0$; hence the vectors v_1 and v_2 are colinear and the span of v_1 and v_2 is the same as the span of v_1. In this case the two vectors v_1 and v_2 are said to be *dependent*. On the other hand if (6.11) holds only when $c_1 = c_2 = 0$, then v_1 and v_2 are not colinear and the span of v_1 and v_2 is the whole set of vectors running from the origin to points in the plane determined by v_1 and v_2. In this case the two vectors are said to be *independent*. Similarly, if there exist three constants c_1, c_2, c_3 not all zero such that

$$c_1v_1 + c_2v_2 + c_3v_3 = 0, \tag{6.12}$$

then some one of the three vectors v_1, v_2, v_3 belongs to the span of the other two and the three vectors are said to be dependent. On the other hand if (6.12) holds only when $c_1 = c_2 = c_3 = 0$, then no one of the three vectors belongs to the span of the other two and the three vectors are said to be independent. In this case, the span of v_1, v_2, v_3 is the whole three-dimensional space. As is easily seen by drawing appropriate figures showing vectors v_1, v_2, v_3, this gives vivid geometrical interpretations to the notion of independence. Sometimes it is desirable to replace the statement that v_1, v_2, v_3 are independent by the more ponderous statement that v_1, v_2, v_3 constitute an independent set. A set consisting of just one vector v_1 is an independent set if and only if v_1 is not the zero vector. There are times, in the theory of differential equations and elsewhere, when it is helpful to recognize that a set of functions can be treated just like a set of vectors. We may have this fact in mind when we formulate the following definition and study its consequences.

DEFINITION 6.13. *The functions $y_1(x)$, $y_2(x)$, . . . , $y_n(x)$ are independent over an interval I if the only constants c_1, c_2, . . . , c_n for which*

$$c_1y_1(x) + c_2y_2(x) + \cdots + c_ny_n(x) = 0 \tag{6.131}$$

* Perhaps we should call attention to the fact that there exist notions of *rational independence, algebraic independence, functional independence,* and *statistical independence* with which we shall not be concerned.

when x is in I are the constants for which

$$c_1 = c_2 = \cdots = c_n = 0. \tag{6.132}$$

In the contrary case, the functions are said to be *dependent*. It is easy to prove that when $n > 1$ the functions are independent if and only if no one of them is a linear combination of the others, that is, if no one of them belongs to the span of the others. In particular, two functions are independent if and only if neither is a constant multiple of the other. Everyone fortunate enough to have had even a little experience with trigonometry must now see that $\cos x$ and $\sin x$ are independent; obviously neither is a constant multiple of the other. Clearly e^x and e^{-x} are independent because neither is a constant multiple of the other. One who knows the meaning of independence must have woefully little information about two functions if he does not know whether they are independent. When more than two functions are involved, matters can be more delicate. We could wonder how we would know that the functions

$$\cos x, \qquad \sin x, \qquad \sin (x + \pi/4) \tag{6.133}$$

are not independent if we were short on information about the sine of a sum. The standard way of proving that given functions $y_1, y_2, \ldots, y_n$ are independent is to assume (6.131) and prove (6.132). Functions picked up here and there are very likely to be independent, but accidents can happen.

The following fundamental theorem on independence has many important applications.

THEOREM 6.14. *If n is a positive integer and $y_1(x), y_2(x), \ldots, y_n(x)$ are independent over an interval I, then it is impossible to find $n - 1$ functions $u_1(x), u_2(x), \ldots, u_{n-1}(x)$ such that each function y representable in the form*

$$y(x) = c_1y_1(x) + c_2y_2(x) + \cdots + c_ny_n(x) \tag{6.141}$$

is also representable in the form

$$y(x) = d_1u_1(x) + d_2u_2(x) + \cdots + d_{n-1}u_{n-1}(x). \tag{6.142}$$

We prove the result for the case in which $n = 3$; when $n > 3$ the proof is more difficult and we omit it. Let $n = 3$. Intending to establish a contradiction of our hypothesis that y_1, y_2, and y_3 are independent, we assume that two functions u_1 and u_2 exist such that each linear combination of y_1, y_2, y_3 is also a linear combination of u_1, u_2. Then there exist constants a_{nk} such that

$$y_1(x) = a_{11}u_1(x) + a_{12}u_2(x) \tag{6.143}$$
$$y_2(x) = a_{21}u_1(x) + a_{22}u_2(x) \tag{6.144}$$
$$y_3(x) = a_{31}u_1(x) + a_{32}u_2(x) \tag{6.145}$$

for each x in I. From (6.143) and (6.144) we obtain

$$\begin{aligned} ku_1(x) &= a_{22}y_1(x) - a_{12}y_2(x), \\ ku_2(x) &= -a_{21}y_1(x) + a_{11}y_2(x), \end{aligned} \tag{6.146}$$

where $k = a_{11}a_{22} - a_{12}a_{21}$. The four constants a_{11}, a_{12}, a_{21}, a_{22} cannot all be zero because if they are then (6.143) and (6.144) would imply that y_1 and y_2 are not independent. This and (6.146) imply that $k \neq 0$, because if $k = 0$ then the right sides of the equations in (6.146) are 0 and again y_1 and y_2 are not independent. Since $k \neq 0$, we can solve (6.146) for u_1 and u_2 and put the results in (6.145) to see that y_3 belongs to the span of y_1 and y_2. This contradicts the hypothesis that y_1, y_2, y_3 are independent and completes the proof of our result.

It is a consequence of the above theorem that if two independent sets $y_1, y_2, \ldots, y_n$ and $u_1, u_2, \ldots, u_p$ have the same span, then $p = n$. On this account, it makes sense to count the functions (or vectors) in an independent set and, if there are n of them, to say that the set spans an n-dimensional space. Suppose now that two independent sets $y_1, y_2, \ldots, y_n$ and $u_1, u_2, \ldots, u_n$ have the same span. For each $j = 1, 2, \ldots, n$ we see that y_j belongs to the span of $y_1, y_2, \ldots, y_n$ and hence also to the span of $u_1, u_2, \ldots, u_n$; so there exist constants a_{jk} such that the first formula in

$$y_j = \sum_{k=1}^{n} a_{jk}u_k, \qquad u_j = \sum_{k=1}^{n} b_{jk}y_k \tag{6.147}$$

holds. Moreover, for each $j = 1, 2, \ldots, n$, we see that u_j belongs to the span of $u_1, u_2, \ldots, u_n$ and hence also to the span of $y_1, y_2, \ldots, y_n$; so there exist constants b_{jk} such that the last formula in (6.147) holds. In algebra, quantum mechanics, electrical engineering, and other places where matrices are studied for pleasure or business, or both, it is shown that (a_{jk}) and (b_{jk}) are inverse matrices and there are many further developments for which a thorough understanding of the material of this section is absolutely essential.

Some of the following problems give results which are important in the theory of differential equations and elsewhere. When no interval I is mentioned, we may assume that the interval is the whole infinite interval $-\infty < x < \infty$ or any other interval we wish to choose.

Problem 6.15

Prove that if $y_1(x), y_2(x), \ldots, y_n(x)$ are independent, then no function $y(x)$ is representable in more than one way in the form $y(x) = \Sigma c_k y_k(x)$. In other words, prove that if $y(x) = \Sigma c_k y_k(x)$ and $y(x) = \Sigma d_k y_k(x)$, then $c_k = d_k$ for each k.

Problem 6.151

Prove that if $n > 1$ and $v_1, v_2, \ldots, v_n$ are not independent, then there exist $n - 1$ functions $u_1, u_2, \ldots, u_{n-1}$ such that each function y representable in the form

$$y(x) = c_1v_1(x) + c_2v_2(x) + \cdots + c_nv_n(x) \tag{6.1511}$$

is also representable in the form

$$y(x) = d_1u_1(x) + d_2u_2(x) + \cdots + d_{n-1}u_{n-1}(x). \tag{6.1512}$$

Hint: We may suppose that the n given functions are called $v_1, v_2, \ldots, v_n$ in such a way that v_n belongs to the span of $v_1, v_2, \ldots, v_{n-1}$.

Problem 6.152

With the hypotheses and aid of Theorem 6.04, prove that if each solution of (6.041) has the form

$$y = c_1v_1(x) + c_2v_2(x) + \cdots + c_nv_n(x), \tag{6.1521}$$

then the functions $v_1, v_2, \ldots, v_n$ must be independent. *Solution:* If we suppose that $v_1, v_2, \ldots, v_n$ are not independent, then Problem 6.151 shows that each solution of (6.041) belongs to the span of $(n - 1)$ functions $u_1, u_2, \ldots, u_{n-1}$. This is impossible because (6.041) has n independent solutions.

Problem 6.153

Let $y_1(x), y_2(x), \ldots, y_n(x)$ be the solutions of (6.041) for which

$$\begin{aligned}
y_1(x_0) &= 1, \; y_1'(x_0) = 0, \; y_1''(x_0) = 0, \; \ldots, \; y_1^{(n-1)}(x_0) = 0\\
y_2(x_0) &= 0, \; y_2'(x_0) = 1, \; y_2''(x_0) = 0, \; \ldots, \; y_2^{(n-1)}(x_0) = 0\\
y_3(x_0) &= 0, \; y_3'(x_0) = 0, \; y_3''(x_0) = 1, \; \ldots, \; y_3^{(n-1)}(x_0) = 0\\
&\cdots\cdots\cdots\cdots\cdots\cdots\cdots\cdots\cdots\cdots\\
y_n(x_0) &= 0, \; y_n'(x_0) = 0, \; y_n''(x_0) = 0, \; \ldots, \; y_n^{(n-1)}(x_0) = 1.
\end{aligned}$$

Prove that these functions are independent. *Solution:* Suppose

$$c_1y_1(x) + c_2y_2(x) + c_3y_3(x) + \cdots + c_ny_n(x) = 0.$$

Putting $x = x_0$ shows that $c_1 = 0$. Differentiating once and putting $x = x_0$ shows that $c_2 = 0$. Differentiating once more and putting $x = x_0$ shows that $c_3 = 0$, and so on. *Remark:* The above solutions constitute the *fundamental set* of solutions of (6.041). This chapter would be much shorter if there were an easy way of getting useful formulas for these functions.

Problem 6.161

It is an elementary fact that $d^ny/dx^n = 0$ if and only if there exist n constants $c_1, c_2, \ldots, c_n$ such that

$$y = c_1 + c_2x + c_3x^2 + \cdots + c_nx^{n-1}. \tag{6.1611}$$

Show that this fact and Problem 6.152 imply that the functions $1, x, x^2, \ldots, x^{n-1}$ are independent.

Problem 6.162

Show, without the aid of the above theory, that if n is a positive integer and $a < b$, then the functions $1, x, \ldots, x^n$ are independent over $a \leqq x \leqq b$. *Solution:* The following is one of many possible ways of solving the problem. Let

$$a_0 + a_1x + a_2x^2 + \cdots + a_nx^n = 0 \tag{6.1621}$$

when $a \leqq x \leqq b$. Suppose $a_n \neq 0$. Then, by the fundamental theorem of algebra, the equation (6.1621) can have at most n roots and the left member cannot be 0 when $a \leqq x \leqq b$. Hence $a_n = 0$. Continuation of the argument shows that $a_1 = a_2 = \cdots = a_n = 0$. Therefore $a_0 = 0$, and the result follows from the definition of independence.

Problem 6.17

Show that if $m_1, m_2, \ldots, m_n$ are n different constants, then the functions

$$e^{m_1x}, e^{m_2x}, \ldots, e^{m_nx} \tag{6.171}$$

are independent. *Solution:* We prove this by induction on n. The result is clearly valid when $n = 1$. Supposing that the result is valid for a given n and that

$$c_1e^{m_1x} + c_2e^{m_2x} + \cdots + c_ne^{m_nx} + c_{n+1}e^{m_{n+1}x} = 0 \tag{6.172}$$

where $m_1, m_2, \ldots, m_n, m_{n+1}$ are different constants, we must show that $c_1 = c_2 = \cdots = c_n = c_{n+1} = 0$. Multiplying (6.172) by $e^{-m_{n+1}x}$ and setting $q_k = m_k - m_{n+1}$ gives

$$c_1e^{q_1x} + c_2e^{q_2x} + \cdots + c_ne^{q_nx} + c_{n+1} = 0 \tag{6.173}$$

where the numbers $q_1, q_2, \ldots, q_n$ are different from each other and from 0. Differentiating (6.173) gives

$$c_1q_1e^{q_1x} + c_2q_2e^{q_2x} + \cdots + c_nq_ne^{q_nx} = 0. \tag{6.174}$$

Therefore $c_1q_1 = c_2q_2 = \cdots = c_nq_n = 0$ and hence $c_1 = c_2 = \cdots = c_n = 0$. It then follows from (6.173) that $c_{n+1} = 0$.

Problem 6.175

Show that if $m_1, m_2, \ldots, m_n$ are n different constants and if $P_1(x), P_2(x), \ldots, P_n(x)$ are n polynomials or constants of which no one is identically zero, then the functions

$$P_1(x)e^{m_1x}, P_2(x)e^{m_2x}, \ldots, P_n(x)e^{m_nx}$$

are independent. *Solution:* The proof is very similar to that of Problem 6.17. Replacing c_k by $c_kP_k(x)$ in (6.172) and (6.173) gives

$$c_1P_1(x)e^{q_1x} + c_2P_2(x)e^{q_2x} + \cdots + c_nP_n(x)e^{q_nx} + c_{n+1}P_{n+1}(x) = 0.$$

Differentiating this often enough gives

$$c_1Q_1(x)e^{q_1x} + c_2Q_2(x)e^{q_2x} + \cdots + c_nQ_n(x)e^{q_nx} = 0$$

where $Q_1, \ldots, Q_n$ are polynomials in x which are not identically 0; so $c_1 = c_2 = \cdots = c_n = 0$ and hence $c_{n+1} = 0$.

Problem 6.176

Prove that if $m_1, m_2, \ldots, m_n$ are nonzero constants such that no one is equal to another or to the negative of another, then the functions

$$(6.1761) \qquad 1, \cos m_1x, \sin m_1x, \cos m_2x, \sin m_2x, \ldots, \cos m_nx, \sin m_nx$$

are independent. *Solution:* Suppose

$$(6.1762) \qquad A_0 + \sum_{k=1}^{n} (A_k \cos m_kx + B_k \sin m_kx) = 0.$$

Because complex exponentials are more tractable than trigonometric functions, we now use the fact that the first of the Euler formulas

$$(6.1763) \qquad e^{i\theta} = \cos\theta + i\sin\theta, \qquad e^{-i\theta} = \cos\theta - i\sin\theta$$

$$(6.1764) \qquad \cos\theta = \frac{1}{2}[e^{i\theta} + e^{-i\theta}], \qquad \sin\theta = \frac{1}{2i}[e^{i\theta} - e^{-i\theta}]$$

implies the other three. To get the second we replace θ by $-\theta$ in the first formula, and to get the last we solve the first two for $\cos\theta$ and $\sin\theta$. With the aid of (6.1764), we put (6.1762) in the form

$$(6.1765) \qquad A_0e^{im_0x} + \sum_{k=1}^{n}\left(\frac{A_k}{2} + \frac{B_k}{2i}\right)e^{im_kx} + \sum_{k=1}^{n}\left(\frac{A_k}{2} - \frac{B_k}{2i}\right)e^{-im_kx} = 0$$

where $m_0 = 0$. Our hypotheses imply that the numbers $im_0, im_1, -im_1, \ldots, im_k, -im_k$ are all different. Hence the result of Problem 6.17 shows that $A_0 = 0$ and the coefficients in parentheses in (6.1765) are all 0. Hence $A_k = B_k = 0$ for each k.

Problem 6.177

Show that if $m_1 = 0$ or $m_2 = -m_1$, then the functions in (6.1761) are not independent.

Problem 6.181

Suppose that $y_1(x), y_2(x), \ldots, y_n(x)$ are dependent, and each has $n - 1$ derivatives, over an interval I to which x is confined. Then there exist n constants $c_1, c_2, \ldots, c_n$, not all 0, such that the first of the n equations

$$(6.1811) \qquad \begin{aligned} c_1y_1(x) &+ c_2y_2(x) + \cdots + c_ny_n(x) = 0 \\ c_1y_1'(x) &+ c_2y_2'(x) + \cdots + c_ny_n'(x) = 0 \\ &\cdots\cdots\cdots\cdots\cdots\cdots \\ c_1y_1^{(n-1)}(x) &+ c_2y_2^{(n-1)}(x) + \cdots + c_ny_n^{(n-1)}(x) = 0 \end{aligned}$$

holds. Differentiation then gives the rest of them. Since the system (6.1811) has a nontrivial solution for $c_1, c_2, \ldots, c_n$, it follows from the theory of such systems (see Remark 4.292) that the determinant of the coefficients of the c's must be 0. Thus $W(x, y_1, y_2, \ldots, y_n) = 0$ where this is the *Wronskian* (or Wronski determinant) defined by

$$(6.1812) \qquad W(x, y_1, y_2, \ldots, y_n) = \begin{vmatrix} y_1(x) & y_2(x) & \cdots & y_n(x) \\ y_1'(x) & y_2'(x) & \cdots & y_n'(x) \\ \cdots & \cdots & \cdots & \cdots \\ y_1^{(n-1)}(x) & y_2^{(n-1)}(x) & \cdots & y_n^{(n-1)}(x) \end{vmatrix}.$$

This implies that *if* $W(x, y_1, y_2, \ldots, y_n) \neq 0$ *for at least one* x *in* I, *then* $y_1, y_2, \ldots, y_n$ *must be independent over* I.

Now comes the problem of showing that a set of functions can be independent even when their Wronskian is identically zero. Let n be an integer for which $n \geqq 2$ and let $y_1(x) = x^n$ and $y_2(x) = x^{n-1}|x|$ when $-\infty < x < \infty$. Show that $y_1(x)$ and $y_2(x)$ are independent and that their Wronskian is identically zero. *Hint:* If assistance is needed, use Remark 4.294.

Remark 6.182

The following theorem removes some of the mystery from the fact that two functions $y_1(x)$ and $y_2(x)$ can be independent over an interval I even when their Wronskian vanishes identically over I.

THEOREM 6.1821. *If* $y_1(x)$ *and* $y_2(x)$ *are two functions for which*

$$W(x, y_1, y_2) = \begin{vmatrix} y_1 & y_2 \\ y_1' & y_2' \end{vmatrix} = y_1y_2' - y_1'y_2 = 0 \tag{6.1822}$$

for each x *in an interval* I, *then each subinterval* I_1 *of* I *contains a subinterval* I_2 *over which* $y_1(x)$ *and* $y_2(x)$ *are dependent.* *Proof:* Let I_1 be a subinterval of I. If $y_1(x) = 0$ for each x in I_1, then $y_1(x)$ and $y_2(x)$ must be dependent over I_1 because $c_1y_1(x) + c_2y_2(x) = 0$ when $c_1 = 1$ and $c_2 = 0$. In the alternative case, we must have $y_1(x_0) \neq 0$ for some x_0 in I_1. Since $y_1(x)$ must be differentiable and hence continuous, we can choose a subinterval I_2 of I_1 such that $y_1(x) \neq 0$ when x is in I_2. When x is in I_2, use of (6.1822) gives

$$\frac{d}{dx}\frac{y_2}{y_1} = \frac{y_1y_2' - y_1'y_2}{y_1^2} = 0$$

so $y_2/y_1 = c$, so $y_2(x) = cy_1(x)$, and therefore y_1 and y_2 are dependent over I_2. This completes the proof.

The proof shows that to each interval over which $y_1(x) \neq 0$ there corresponds a constant c such that $y_2(x) = cy_1(x)$ when x lies in the interval. However different intervals can require different values of c, so $y_1(x)$ and $y_2(x)$ may fail to be dependent over the whole interval I.

Problem 6.183

Let $y_1(x), y_2(x), \ldots, y_n(x)$ and $z_1(x), z_2(x), \ldots, z_n(x)$ be two sets of functions defined over $a \leqq x \leqq b$ and such that the integrals in

$$I_{j,k} = \int_a^b y_j(x)z_k(x)dx \qquad j, k = 1, 2, \ldots, n \tag{6.1831}$$

all exist. Modify the work of the previous problem to show that if

$$\begin{vmatrix} I_{11} & I_{12} & \cdots & I_{1n} \\ I_{21} & I_{22} & \cdots & I_{2n} \\ \cdots & \cdots & \cdots & \cdots \\ I_{n1} & I_{n2} & \cdots & I_{nn} \end{vmatrix} \neq 0, \tag{6.1832}$$

then $y_1(x), y_2(x), \ldots, y_n(x)$ must be independent over I. Use this to show that if $I_{jk} = 0$ when $j \neq k$ and $I_{k,k} \neq 0$ for each k, then $y_1(x), y_2(x), \ldots, y_n(x)$ must be independent. *Remark:* Suppose that the determinant in (6.1832) is 0. Then there exist constants $c_1, c_2, \ldots, c_n$, not all 0, such that

$$\sum_{j=1}^{n} c_j I_{jk} = 0 \qquad k = 1, 2, \ldots n.$$

Multiplying these equations by $d_1, d_2, \ldots, d_n$ and adding give

$$\sum_{k=1}^{n} \sum_{j=1}^{n} c_j d_k I_{jk} = 0$$

or

$$\int_a^b \left[\sum_{j=1}^{n} c_j y_j(x) \right] \left[\sum_{k=1}^{n} d_k z_k(x) \right] dx = 0. \tag{6.1833}$$

In case

$$d_k = \bar{c}_k, \qquad z_k(x) = \overline{y_k(x)}, \tag{6.1834}$$

(where the bars can be ignored when c_k and $y_k(x)$ are real; see Section 6.3) this reduces to

$$\int_a^b |c_1 y_1(x) + c_2 y_2(x) + \cdots + c_n y_n(x)|^2 \, dx = 0. \tag{6.1835}$$

Provided $y_1(x), y_2(x), \ldots, y_n(x_1)$ are continuous, this implies that $\Sigma c_k y_k(x) = 0$ everywhere over $a \leqq x \leqq b$ and that $y_1, y_2, \ldots, y_n$ are dependent. For the case in which $z_k(x) = \overline{y_k(x)}$, the determinant in (6.1832) was investigated by Gram (1850–1916) and is called the *Grammian* of $y_1, y_2, \ldots, y_n$. Our work shows that n continuous functions $y_1, y_2, \ldots, y_n$ are independent if and only if their Grammian is different from 0.

Remark 6.184

The remaining problems in this list involve linear differential equations of order 2. Let us not be misled by the fact that linear equations of order 1 were quickly and thoroughly solved in Section 3.1 by use of integrating factors for which explicit formulas are easily found. When n is 2 or more, we are in another garden. Except for special cases, which include linear homogeneous equations having constant coefficients, there exists no convenient ritual for obtaining useful formulas for solutions of linear equations of order n. Whether the problems are difficult can be a matter of opinion, but everybody should know that they give useful information about difficult equations.

Problem 6.19

This problem gives us a real opportunity to think about our theories and, in addition, gives a useful result. Suppose $p(x)$ and $q(x)$ are given continuous functions and we want the general solution of the equation

$$y'' + py' + qy = 0. \tag{6.1901}$$

What kind of equation is this and what can be said about its solutions? Suppose that $y_1(x)$ is a known solution and $y_1(x_0) \neq 0$. Are there any more solutions? Now we go to work. We know that

$$y_1'' + py_1' + qy_1 = 0. \tag{6.1902}$$

Let the y in (6.1901) stand for any old solution of (6.1901) and we will see what we can learn. Multiply (6.1901) and (6.902) by y_1 and $-y$ respectively and then add to obtain

$$(y_1y'' - y_1''y) + p(y_1y' - y_1'y) = 0. \tag{6.1903}$$

This may look like a silly thing to do but it is not, because the first quantity in parentheses happens to be the derivative of the second. Check this and show that

$$\frac{d}{dx}(y_1y' - y_1'y) + p(y_1y' - y_1'y) = 0. \tag{6.1904}$$

What kind of equation is this? We may pause to note that the quantity in parentheses is the Wronskian* W of y_1 and y so that

$$W = y_1(x)y'(x) - y_1'(x)y(x) = \begin{vmatrix} y_1(x) & y(x) \\ y_1'(x) & y'(x) \end{vmatrix}. \tag{6.1905}$$

Show that letting $P(x) = \int_{x_0}^{x} p(t)\,dt$ and solving (6.1904) in the usual way by means of an integrating factor gives

$$y_1y' - y_1'y = c_2e^{-P(x)}. \tag{6.1906}$$

This is the *Abel* (1802–1829) *formula* for the Wronskian, and this could make us wonder whether Wronski invented the Wronskian. Since $y_1(x_0) \neq 0$ and y_1 is continuous (it must be because it is differentiable) we can choose an interval I which contains x_0 and is such that $y_1(x) \neq 0$ when x is in I. Henceforth, let x be in I. Then we can divide (6.1906) by y_1^2 to obtain

$$\frac{d}{dx}\frac{y(x)}{y_1(x)} = c_2\frac{e^{-P(x)}}{[y_1(x)]^2}. \tag{6.1907}$$

Integrating and then multiplying by $y_1(x)$ give

$$y(x) = c_1y_1(x) + c_2y_1(x)\int_{x_0}^{x}\frac{e^{-P(s)}}{[y_1(s)]^2}\,ds. \tag{6.1908}$$

Let the function multiplying c_2 be denoted by $y_2(x)$. There are two ways to show that $y_2(x)$ satisfies (6.1901). One way is to substitute in (6.1901) and see that this is so; this is a good little exercise. An easier way is to let the $y(x)$ in (6.1908) be a solution of (6.1901) which is not a constant multiple of $y_1(x)$. Then $c_2 \neq 0$. Moreover $c_2y_2(x)$, being the difference of solutions of (6.1901), must be a solution of (6.1901). Hence $y_2(x)$ itself must be a solution of (6.1901). The two solutions $y_1(x)$ and $y_2(x)$ must be independent, since otherwise (6.1908) would imply that each solution is a constant multiple of one function and (6.1901) could not have two independent solutions as Theorem 6.04 requires. Therefore, according to Theorem 6.04, (6.1908) is the general solution of (6.1901).

A look at (6.1908) gives an important result. *Two solutions y and y_1 of the homogeneous equation* (6.1901) *are independent if and only if their Wronskian is never zero.* This is true because y and y_1 are independent if and only if $c_2 \neq 0$ and the result follows from (6.1906) and the fact that the exponential function is never 0. Note that

* It is named after Wronski (1778–1853) who is said to have begun life as an army officer, redeemed himself by becoming a mathematician, fallen from grace by becoming a philosopher, and completed his downfall by going insane.

everything fits the theory, and that *we have learned how to find the general solution of* (6.1901) *when we have found one nontrivial solution.*

Problem 6.1909

There is another way, slightly more tedious, in which (6.1908) can be obtained. Let $y_1(x)$ be a known function which satisfies (6.1901) and is different from 0 over an interval I containing x_0, and let $y(x)$ be a solution of (6.1901). Then, when x is in I, we can set $v(x) = y(x)/y_1(x)$ so that $y = y_1 v$. Substitution in (6.1901) gives

$$y_1 v'' + (2y_1' + py_1)v' + (y_1'' + py_1' + qy_1)v = 0.$$

Since the coefficient of v in this equation is 0, this is a linear equation of first order in v'. Solve for v' and then v and finally $y(x)$. The formula (6.1908) is your answer. This method is worth remembering.

Problem 6.191

In this problem *we learn how to find a particular solution of the nonhomogeneous equation*

$$y'' + py' + qy = f \tag{6.1911}$$

when two independent solutions $y_1(x)$ *and* $y_2(x)$ *of the homogeneous equation*

$$y'' + py' + qy = 0 \tag{6.1912}$$

have been found. Suppose that f as well as p and q are continuous functions of x. Keep the methods of Problem 6.19 in mind. Supposing that y satisfies (6.1911) and y_1 satisfies (6.1912), show how to obtain the equation

$$\frac{d}{dx}(y_1 y' - y_1' y) + p(y_1 y' - y_1' y) = f y_1$$

and solve this to obtain

$$e^{P(x)}[y_1 y' - y_1' y] = A + \int_{x_0}^{x} y_1(t) f(t) e^{P(t)}\, dt. \tag{6.1913}$$

Note that using the same procedure with y_2 in place of y_1 gives

$$e^{P(x)}[y_2 y' - y_2' y] = B + \int_{x_0}^{x} y_2(t) f(t) e^{P(t)}\, dt. \tag{6.1914}$$

The next thing to notice is that we can eliminate y' from (6.1913) and (6.1914) by introducing the multipliers $y_2(x)$ and $-y_1(x)$ and adding. Show that this gives

$$\begin{aligned} e^{P(x)}[y_1(x)y_2'(x) - y_1'(x)y_2(x)]y(x) &= Ay_2(x) - By_1(x) \\ &+ \int_{x_0}^{x} [y_1(t)y_2(x) - y_2(t)y_1(x)] f(t) e^{P(t)}\, dt. \end{aligned} \tag{6.1915}$$

From the Abel formula (6.1906) for the Wronskian of two solutions of the homogeneous equation, we see that there must be a constant C for which

$$y_1(x)y_2'(x) - y_1'(x)y_2(x) = Ce^{-P(x)}. \tag{6.1916}$$

Since y_1 and y_2 were assumed to be independent, it follows from a result of Problem

6.19 that $C \neq 0$. Use all this to show that

$$(6.1917) \quad y(x) = c_1y_1(x) + c_2y_2(x) + \frac{1}{C}\int_{x_0}^{x} [y_1(t)y_2(x) - y_2(t)y_1(x)]f(t)e^{P(t)}\,dt.$$

Tell what theorem predicted that each solution of (6.1911) would have such a form.

Problem 6.1918

Show that, when one knows a solution $y_1(x)$ of the homogeneous equation which is different from 0 when x lies in an interval J, then the substitution $y = y_1v$ reduces the problem of solving the equation

$$y'' + p(x)y' + g(x)y = f(x)$$

to the problem of solving a linear nonhomogeneous differential equation of first order. *This furnishes an excellent method of solving problems when the integrals are easily evaluated.* Use the method to solve, when $x > 0$, the equation

$$x^2y'' + xy' - y = 1,$$

starting with the fact that the homogeneous equation is satisfied when $y = x$.

Ans.: $y = c_1x + c_2x^{-1} - 1$.

This method can be used to derive (6.1917), but the details are more involved than those of the derivation given above.

Problem 6.192

The function $y_1(x) = x$ is a solution of each of the following equations:

(a) $$x^2y'' + xy' - y = 0$$
(b) $$x^3y'' + xy' - y = 0$$
(c) $$y'' + xy' - y = 0.$$

Find the general solutions, and check your answers by differentiation and substitution.

Remark 6.193

Before leaving the subject of independence and Wronskians, we should learn about the zeros of real solutions of (6.1901). The zeros of $\sin x$ are $0, \pm\pi, \pm 2\pi, \pm 3\pi, \ldots$, and the zeros of $\cos x$ are $\pm\pi/2, 2\pi \pm \pi/2, 4\pi \pm \pi/2, \ldots$. The zeros of $\sin x$ and $\cos x$ are *distinct* in the sense that a zero of one function is not a zero of the other function. The zeros of $\sin x$ and $\cos x$ *interlace* in accordance with the following definition: The zeros of two functions interlace if between each pair of zeros of one function there is a zero of the other function.

The following theorem is known as the *Sturm* (1803–1855) *separation theorem.*

THEOREM 6.1931. *If $p(x)$ and $q(x)$ are continuous and $y_1(x)$ and $y_2(x)$ are real independent solutions of*

$$(6.1932) \quad y'' + p(x)y' + q(x)y = 0,$$

then the zeros of $y_1(x)$ and $y_2(x)$ are distinct and interlace.

To prove this theorem, we use Abel's formula

$$(6.1933) \quad y_1y_2' - y_1'y_2 = Ce^{-P(x)},$$

where $C \neq 0$ since y_1 and y_2 are assumed independent. If $y_1(x_0) = 0$ for some x_0, then $y_2(x_0)$ cannot be 0 since otherwise the equality (6.1933) could not hold when $x = x_0$. This proves that the zeros of y_1 and y_2 are distinct. Now suppose x_1 and x_2, where $x_1 < x_2$, are two zeros of $y_1(x)$; we show that $y_2(x)$ must have at least one zero between x_1 and x_2. Since $y_1(x_1) = y_1(x_2) = 0$, we know that $y_2(x_1) \neq 0$ and $y_2(x_2) \neq 0$. If it were true that $y_2(x) \neq 0$ over $x_1 < x < x_2$, then we would have $y_2(x) \neq 0$ over $x_1 \leqq x \leqq x_2$ and therefore

$$\frac{d}{dx}\frac{y_1}{y_2} = \frac{y_2y_1' - y_1y_2'}{[y_2(x)]^2} = -\frac{Ce^{-P(x)}}{[y_2(x)]^2} \neq 0 \qquad x_1 \leqq x \leqq x_2.$$

This contradicts the Rolle (1652–1719) theorem since the function $f(x) \equiv y_1(x)/y_2(x)$ vanishes at x_1 and x_2 and is differentiable. Hence between each pair of zeros of y_1 there must be at least one zero of y_2. Since y_1 and y_2 enter into our hypothesis in exactly the same way, it follows that between each pair of zeros of y_2 there must be at least one zero of y_1 and Theorem 6.1931 is proved.

Problem 6.194

We now use information about linear differential equations to obtain information about Riccati nonlinear equations; see Problem 4.291. Let $P(x)$, $Q(x)$, and $R(x)$ be continuous functions for which $P'(x)$ is continuous and $P(a) \neq 0$, and consider the *Riccati equation*

(6.1941) $$y'(x) = P(x)[y(x)]^2 + Q(x)y(x) + R(x)$$

with x confined to an interval, containing a, over which $P(x) \neq 0$. Let functions $u(x)$ and $y(x)$ be related by the formulas

(6.1942) $$u(x) = e^{-\int_a^x P(t)y(t)\,dt}, \qquad y(x) = \frac{-1}{P(x)}\frac{u'(x)}{u(x)}.$$

Show that (6.1941) holds iff (if and only if) $u(a) = 1$ and

$$-\frac{Puu'' - P'uu' - Pu'^2}{P^2u^2} = \frac{1}{P}\frac{u'^2}{u^2} - \frac{Q}{P}\frac{u'}{u} + R$$

and hence iff $u(a) = 1$ and

(6.1943) $$Pu'' - (P' + PQ)u' + P^2Ru = 0.$$

Letting $U_1(x)$ and $U_2(x)$ be the fundamental solutions of (6.1943) for which $U_1(a) = 0$, $U_1'(a) = 1$, $U_2(a) = 1$, $U_2'(a) = 0$, show that (6.1941) holds iff for some constant c

(6.1944) $$u(x) = cU_1(x) + U_2(x).$$

Thus (6.1941) holds iff

(6.1945) $$y(x) = \frac{-1}{P(x)}\frac{cU_1'(x) + U_2'(x)}{cU_1(x) + U_2(x)}.$$

Show that $c = u'(a) = -y(a)P(a)$. This shows that each solution of (6.1941) has the form

(6.1946) $$y = \frac{cf_1(x) + f_2(x)}{cf_3(x) + f_4(x)}.$$

Observe that if we start with the linear equation

$$(6.1947) \qquad u''(x) - Q(x)u'(x) + R(x)u(x) = 0,$$

we can put this in the form (6.1943) by setting $P(x) = 1$; hence, when $P(x) = 1$, (6.1942) sets up a one to one correspondence between solutions of (6.1947) for which $u(a) = 1$ and solutions of the Riccati equation (6.1941).

Show that if $y_1(x)$ and $y_2(x)$ are two different solutions of (6.1941), then the functions $u_1(x)$ and $u_2(x)$ determined from (6.1942) satisfy the equations

$$u_1(x) = u_1'(a)U_1(x) + U_2(x)$$
$$u_2(x) = u_2'(a)U_1(x) + U_2(x)$$

and, moreover, these equations determine U_1 and U_2 and hence the general solution (6.1945) of (6.1941).

Problem 6.195

Everyone should know enough about Chapter 4 to know that it is not always easy to determine *the* differential equation satisfied by each function $y(x)$ in a given family. Show that if $y_1(x)$ and $y_2(x)$ are two given functions which are independent and satisfy the equation

$$(6.1951) \qquad y''(x) + p(x)y'(x) + q(x)y(x) = 0$$

over an interval I, then $p(x)$ and $q(x)$ are uniquely determined by the given functions. *Hint:* Do not try to use Chapter 4. Just substitute in (6.1951) and solve for p and q, using Problem 6.19 at a crucial place.

6.2. Linear; Homogeneous; Constant Coefficients. In this and following sections, we study the simplest and most important applications of Theorem 6.04. This section involves the linear homogeneous equation

$$(6.21) \qquad a_0\frac{d^ny}{dx^n} + a_1\frac{d^{n-1}y}{dx^{n-1}} + \cdots + a_{n-1}\frac{dy}{dx} + a_ny = 0$$

where $a_0, a_1, \ldots, a_n$ are constants and $a_0 \neq 0$. These constants are real in most applications, but our results apply even when they are complex.

There are several methods by which (6.21) can be successfully attacked. The simplest method is based upon the observation that if m is a constant and $y = e^{mx}$, then the right members of

$$(6.22) \quad y = e^{mx}, \quad \frac{dy}{dx} = me^{mx}, \quad \frac{d^2y}{dx^2} = m^2e^{mx}, \ldots, \frac{d^ny}{dx^n} = m^ne^{mx}$$

all have the factor e^{mx} and putting $y = e^{mx}$ in (6.21) gives

$$(6.221) \qquad (a_0m^n + a_1m^{n-1} + \cdots + a_{n-1}m + a_n)e^{mx} = 0;$$

hence e^{mx} is a solution of (6.21) whenever m is a zero of the polynomial

$$(6.23) \qquad Z(m) = a_0m^n + a_1m^{n-1} + \cdots + a_{n-1}m + a_n.$$

In case $Z(m)$ has n distinct zeros $m_1, m_2, \ldots, m_n$ (see Theorem 6.05

and the remark which follows it), the solutions e^{m_1x}, e^{m_2x}, . . . , e^{m_nx} are independent (see Problem 6.17) and it follows from Theorem 6.04 that

$$y = c_1e^{m_1x} + c_2e^{m_2x} + \cdots + c_ne^{m_nx} \tag{6.24}$$

is the general solution of (6.21).

What we have just proved is so important that we must discuss the accomplishment. The polynomial $Z(m)$, which appears in (6.23) and plays a central role in the theory of the equation (6.21), is called the *impedance* of the equation. This terminology is particularly pleasing to electrical engineers and is good for everyone else.* The notation $Z(m)$, which prevails in electrical engineering, is also highly appropriate because m and $Z(m)$ are complex numbers (which are real only in special cases) and Z makes everybody think of a complex number. What we have proved can now be stated in the form in which it should be remembered.

THEOREM 6.25. *If the impedance*

$$Z(m) = a_0m^n + a_1m^{n-1} + \cdots + a_{n-1}m + a_n \tag{6.251}$$

of the equation

$$a_0\frac{d^ny}{dx^n} + a_1\frac{d^{n-1}y}{dx^{n-1}} + \cdots + a_{n-1}\frac{dy}{dx} + a_ny = 0 \tag{6.252}$$

has n distinct zeros $m_1, m_2, \ldots, m_n$, then the general solution of (6.252) *is*

$$y = c_1e^{m_1x} + c_2e^{m_2x} + \cdots + c_ne^{m_nx}. \tag{6.253}$$

The impedance $Z(m)$ is obtained by simply copying the left member of (6.252) with d^ky/dx^k replaced by m^k and y replaced by 1. In some situations we think of m as having a fixed complex value, which is sometimes denoted by s or $\sigma + j\omega$, so that $Z(m)$ represents a single complex constant. In other situations we think of m as being a variable, in which case $Z(m)$ is a polynomial in m. As soon as the zeros of $Z(m)$, regarded as a polynomial in m, have been found and are seen to be distinct, the general solution (6.252) should be written as rapidly as we can write legibly. This situation provides an opportunity to see a difference between pure science and applied science. In pure science, we denote the zeros of $Z(m)$ by $m_1, m_2, \ldots, m_n$ and write our answer. In applied science, approximations to the numerical values of $a_0, a_1, \ldots, a_n$ are given in decimal form, and we must find decimal approximations to $m_1, m_2, \ldots, m_n$. When $n = 2$, the quadratic formula gives m_1 and m_2. When $n > 2$ and $m_1, m_2, \ldots, m_n$ are not real, the problem is

* It is customary to think of the electric circuit rather than of the differential equation as *having* the impedance. The question whether the impedance belongs to the differential equation or to the electric circuit is as trivial as the question whether a shoelace belongs to a shoe or to the person who owns the shoe.

much more difficult and advice should be obtained from books or research papers or individuals that retail information about numerical methods for approximating zeros of polynomials. Electrical engineers have the greatest need and the best facilities for finding these zeros.

It must of course be observed that Theorem 6.25 covers only the important case in which $Z(m)$ has n distinct zeros. The following theorem covers the less important and more tedious cases in which $Z(m)$ has multiple zeros. The theorem will be proved in Section 6.8 where the equations are attacked with the aid of operators.

THEOREM 6.26. *If the impedance*

$$Z(m) = a_0m^n + a_1m^{n-1} + \cdots + a_{n-1}m + a_n \tag{6.261}$$

of the equation

$$a_0\frac{d^ny}{dx^n} + a_1\frac{d^{n-1}y}{dx^{n-1}} + \cdots + a_{n-1}\frac{dy}{dx} + a_ny = 0 \tag{6.262}$$

has zeros $m_1, m_2, \ldots, m_n$, then the general solution of (6.262) *is*

$$y = c_1e^{m_1x} + c_2e^{m_2x} + \cdots + c_ne^{m_nx} \tag{6.263}$$

if the m's are distinct; the solution is

$$y = (c_0 + c_1x + c_2x^2 + \cdots + c_nx^{n-1})e^{m_1x} \tag{6.264}$$

if the m's are all equal to m_1; and it is

$$y = [c_0^{(1)} + c_1^{(1)}x + \cdots + c_{h_1-1}^{(1)}x^{h_1-1}]e^{m_1x} + \cdots + [c_0^{(k)} + c_1^{(k)}x + \cdots + c_{h_k-1}^{(k)}x^{h_k-1}]e^{m_kx} \tag{6.265}$$

if h_1 of the m's are equal to m_1, h_2 of the m's are equal to m_2, and so on, until finally h_k of the m's are equal to m_k, where the numbers $m_1, m_2, \ldots, m_k$ are distinct.

The third case of this theorem, which is not as bad as it sounds, reduces to the first case covered by Theorem 6.25 when the m's are distinct and to the second case when the m's are all equal. The fundamental thing to remember is that each solution of a homogeneous linear differential equation of order n with constant coefficients is a linear combination of n terms of the form x^pe^{qx} where p is 0 or a positive integer and q is a constant. The rest comes easily after the zeros of the impedance have been found. The theorem reduces the amount of work involved in solving (6.262) to an irreducible minimum. Obviously one cannot write the solution before the zeros are found, and as soon as the zeros are found, we write the solution.

For example, when m_1, m_2, m_3, are distinct complex numbers, the general solution of the equation with impedance

$$(m - m_1)(m - m_2)^2(m - m_3)^4 \tag{6.266}$$

is the sum of three batches of terms: $c_1e^{m_1x}$ which comes from the first factor, $(c_2 + c_3x)e^{m_2x}$ which comes from the second factor, and $(c_4 + c_5x + c_6x^2 + c_7x^3)e^{m_3x}$ which comes from the last factor. The impedance $Z(m)$ is sometimes called the characteristic polynomial of (6.252), the equation $Z(m) = 0$ is sometimes called the characteristic equation of (6.252), and the zeros of $Z(m)$ are sometimes called the characteristic roots of (6.252). In preparing problems and examinations on the above material, teachers (including the author) must use some restraint. It is not reasonable to expect students in this course to have computing skill and equipment necessary for efficient solving of equations such as

$$(6.267)\quad 4.317\frac{d^4y}{dx^4} + 2.179\frac{d^3y}{dx^3} + 1.416\frac{d^2y}{dx^2} + 1.295\frac{dy}{dx} + 3.169y = 0.$$

On the other hand the author and teachers should expect that students will not fool around all day solving the equation $y'' - 4y = 0$. The impedance is $m^2 - 4$, the zeros are 2 and -2, and the general solution is $y = c_1e^{2x} + c_2e^{-2x}$. For the equation $y'' + 4y = 0$, the impedance is $m^2 + 4$, the zeros are $2i$ and $-2i$, and the general solution is $c_1e^{2ix} + c_2e^{-2ix}$. We leave answers in terms of exponentials unless we encounter a problem which clearly makes it desirable to use an Euler formula (which should always be remembered; otherwise hunt or consult the index) to convert complex exponentials to trigonometric functions.

Problem 6.27

Write the general solutions of the following equations and check by differentiation and substitution.

(a) $y'' - y = 0$ (b) $y'' + y = 0$
(c) $y'' + 3y' + 2y = 0$ (d) $y'' - 3y' + 2y = 0$
(e) $y''' + y = 0$ (f) $y''' - y = 0$
(g) $y' - iy = 0$ (h) $y' + iy = 0$
(i) $\frac{d^2y}{dx^2} + \frac{dy}{dx} = 0$ (j) $\frac{d^3y}{dx^3} = 0$
(k) $\frac{d^2y}{dx^2} + 2\frac{dy}{dx} + y = 0$ (l) $\frac{d^4y}{dx^4} + \frac{d^3y}{dx^3} = 0$
(m) $y''' + y'' + y' + y = 0$

Problem 6.28

Write the general solutions of the equations whose impedances are

(a) $(m - 1)(m - 2)$ *Ans.*: $c_1e^x + c_2e^{2x}$
(b) $m^2(m + 1)$ *Ans.*: $c_1 + c_2x + c_3e^{-x}$
(c) $m(m + 1)^2$ *Ans.*: $c_1 + (c_2 + c_3x)e^{-x}$
(d) $(m + 1)(m + 2)(m^2 + 4)$ *Ans.*: $c_1e^{-x} + c_2e^{-2x} + c_3e^{2ix} + c_4e^{-2ix}$
(e) $(m^2 + 1)^2$ *Ans.*: $(c_1 + c_2x)e^{ix} + (c_3 + c_4x)e^{-ix}$

Problem 6.281

Supposing that $a > 0$ and $b^2 - 4ac = h^2$ where $h > 0$, solve the equation

$$a\frac{d^2y}{dx^2} + b\frac{dy}{dx} + cy = 0. \tag{6.2811}$$

Ans.: The impedance is $Z(m) = am^2 + bm + c$ and the zeros are $m_1 = (-b + h)/2a$ and $m_2 = (-b - h)/2a$. Here m_1 and m_2 are real constants and the general solution is $y = c_1e^{m_1x} + c_2e^{m_2x}$.

Problem 6.282

Supposing that $a > 0$ and $b^2 - 4ac = -h^2$ where $h > 0$, solve the equation

$$a\frac{d^2y}{dx^2} + b\frac{dy}{dx} + cy = 0. \tag{6.2821}$$

Ans.: The impedance is $Z(m) = am^2 + bm + c$ and the zeros are $m_1 = -b/2a + ih/2a$ and $m_2 = -b/2a - ih/2a$. Here m_1 and m_2 are complex constants which are not real and the general solution is $y = c_1e^{m_1x} + c_2e^{m_2x}$.

Problem 6.283

Supposing that $a > 0$ and $b^2 - 4ac = 0$, solve the equation

$$a\frac{d^2y}{dx^2} + b\frac{dy}{dx} + cy = 0.$$

Ans.: The impedance is $Z(m) = am^2 + bm + c$ and the zeros are $m_1 = m_2 = -b/2a$. The general solution is $y = (c_1 + c_2x)e^{-(b/2a)x}$.

Problem 6.284

Find pairs of functions $x(t)$ and $y(t)$ satisfying the

$$\frac{dx}{dt} = -2y, \qquad \frac{dy}{dt} = -2x$$

system of equations. *Hint:* Differentiate the first equation and look around.

Ans.: $x = c_1e^{2t} + c_2e^{-2t}$

$y = -c_1e^{2t} + c_2e^{-2t}$.

Postscript: See what happens when you divide one of the given equations by the other.

Problem 6.285

Find pairs of functions $x(t)$ and $y(t)$ satisfying the

$$\frac{dx}{dt} = 2y, \qquad \frac{dy}{dt} = -2x$$

system of equations.

Ans.: $x = c_1 \cos 2t + c_2 \sin 2t$

$y = c_2 \cos 2t - c_1 \sin 2t$.

Problem 6.286

See whether you can make a good guess about the system

$$\frac{dx}{dt} = 2y, \qquad \frac{dy}{dt} = 2x$$

before you solve it.

Problem 6.287

Is the system of equations

$$\frac{d^2x}{dt^2} + y = 0, \qquad \frac{d^2y}{dt^2} + x = 0$$

too hot to handle?

Ans.: No. $x = c_1 \cos t + c_2 \sin t + c_3e^t + c_4e^{-t}$
$y = c_1 \cos t + c_2 \sin t - c_3e^t - c_4e^{-t}$.

Problem 6.291

Suppose that the earth is a homogeneous sphere of radius R and that a hole is drilled from a point on the surface to the center and through to the other side. It can then be shown that a particle in the hole is attracted toward the center of the earth by a force whose magnitude is proportional to the distance from the center. Using this fact and supposing that no other forces are present, show that the coordinate y of a particle dropped from rest into the hole at time $t = 0$ is

$$y = R \cos (g/R)^{\frac{1}{2}}t.$$

Using $R = 4{,}000 \times 5{,}280$ feet and $g = 32$ ft/sec², show that the particle will reappear at its starting point after 85 minutes. We can note that the 85 minutes is the time it would take a satellite to circle the earth just above the surface of the earth if the earth had no atmosphere; see Problem 2.54. Show that the speed at the center of the earth is 4.9 miles per second.

Problem 6.292

Everything is as in the previous problem except that the hole does not pass through the center of the earth. Show that the round trip still takes 85 minutes.

Problem 6.293

Suppose that the earth is a radially homogeneous sphere of radius R. Show that the equation

$$\frac{d^2x}{dt^2} + \frac{g}{R}\left(\frac{R^2}{R^2 + x^2}\right)^{\frac{3}{2}} x = 0$$

governs the motion of a particle sliding on a plane frictionless table tangent to the surface of the earth at a point O. Suppose that a particle starts from rest on a small table so that x is very small in comparison to R and $R^2/(R^2 + x^2)$ is essentially 1. Assuming (or proving) that a very small relative change in the force produces a small change in the motion during the first trip to O, show that the particle will slide to O in about 21 minutes. Note that the period of oscillation is about 85 minutes as in the previous problems.

Problem 6.294

A flexible chain 6 feet long is placed at rest with 5 feet stretched out on a slick horizontal table and the other foot hanging over the edge of the table. Show that, insofar as friction is negligible, the chain will slide off the table in such a way that the length of the part off the table t seconds later is

$$\frac{e^{at} + e^{-at}}{2},$$

where $a = \sqrt{g/6}$, until the chain flies off the table or the bottom of the chain hits the floor.

Problem 6.295

A flexible chain of length L is initially stretched out motionless on a frictionless tilted table with a segment of length a hanging over an edge of the table. The table makes an angle θ with the horizontal, where $-\pi/2 < \theta \leqq \pi/2$, the chain hanging over the highest edge of the table if $\theta > 0$ and the lowest edge if $\theta < 0$. Letting $y(t)$ denote the length of the part of the chain off the table at time t, show that

$$\frac{d^2y}{dt^2} - k^2 y = -g \sin \theta$$

where

$$k = \sqrt{\frac{g(1 + \sin \theta)}{L}}$$

and hence

$$y = \left[a - L\frac{\sin \theta}{1 + \sin \theta}\right]\frac{e^{kt} + e^{-kt}}{2} + L\frac{\sin \theta}{1 + \sin \theta}.$$

Note that when numerical values are assigned to the constants and the quantity in brackets is positive (or negative), we can use a table of values of $\cosh x$ to find times at which y is L (or zero).

6.3. Complex Numbers and Exponentials. In earlier sections, simple properties of complex numbers and exponentials have been used without definitions and proofs. We now need more information about these things. This section and the next give a connected account of the basic ideas and results needed in this book.

When z is a real number, the three formulas

$$e^z = 1 + z + \frac{z^2}{2!} + \frac{z^3}{3!} + \cdots \tag{6.31}$$

$$\cos z = 1 - \frac{z^2}{2!} + \frac{z^4}{4!} - \frac{z^6}{6!} + \cdots \tag{6.311}$$

$$\sin z = z - \frac{z^3}{3!} + \frac{z^5}{5!} - \frac{z^7}{7!} + \cdots \tag{6.312}$$

are given with or without proof in courses in elementary calculus and are proved in advanced calculus. The number e is defined by the first formula in

$$\lim_{n\to\infty}\left(1+\frac{1}{n}\right)^n = e = 2.71828\ 18284\ 59045 \tag{6.313}$$

and the numerical approximation is obtained by putting $z = 1$ in (6.31). The value of e correct to 2,010 places is given in "Mathematical Tables and Other Aides to Computation."*

Let i denote the so-called imaginary unit for which $i^2 = -1$. The number z defined by $z = x + iy$, where x and y are real, is called a *complex number* with *real part* x and *imaginary part* y. The notations $x = \text{Re}\, z$ and $y = \text{Im}\, z$ are sometimes used. When x_1, y_1, x_2, and y_2 are real, the numbers $z_1 = x_1 + iy_1$ and $z_2 = x_2 + iy_2$ are said to be equal if and only if $x_1 = x_2$ and $y_1 = y_2$. Thus, when x_1, y_1, x_2, and y_2 are real, the one equality $x_1 + iy_1 = x_2 + iy_2$ is equivalent to the two equalities $x_1 = x_2$ and $y_1 = y_2$. The laws governing addition and multiplication of complex numbers are the same as those applying to real numbers. For example,

$$(x_1 + iy_1) + (x_2 + iy_2) = (x_1 + x_2) + i(y_1 + y_2), \tag{6.32}$$

and

$$(x_1 + iy_1)(x_2 + iy_2) = x_1x_2 + i^2y_1y_2 + i(x_1y_2 + x_2y_1) \tag{6.321}$$

but this reduces to

$$(x_1 + iy_1)(x_2 + iy_2) = x_1x_2 - y_1y_2 + i(x_1y_2 + x_2y_1) \tag{6.322}$$

because $i^2 = -1$. In particular, $i^0 = 1$, $i^1 = i$, $i^2 = -1$, $i^3 = (i^2)i = -i$, $i^4 = (i^2)(i^2) = 1$, $i^5 = (i^4)i = i$, $i^6 = -1$, $i^7 = -i$, $i^8 = 1$, ... When x and y are real, the complex number $x + i0$ is the same as the real number x, and iy is called *pure imaginary*. Thus 0 is both real and pure imaginary. Without going into details (some are given in Chapter 7), we accept the fact that the series in (6.31), (6.311), and (6.312) are convergent even when z is a complex number and that the numbers to which the series converge are *defined* to be e^z, $\sin z$, and $\cos z$. Thus the formulas (6.31), (6.311), and (6.312) are valid for each real or complex z. For example, we could calculate $e^{i\pi/2}$ by calculating the number to which the series in (6.31) converges when $z = i\pi/2$.

We now prove the four Euler (1707–1783) formulas

$$e^{iz} = \cos z + i \sin z, \qquad e^{-iz} = \cos z - i \sin z, \tag{6.33}$$

$$\cos z = \frac{e^{iz} + e^{-iz}}{2}, \qquad \sin z = \frac{e^{iz} - e^{-iz}}{2i} \tag{6.331}$$

that are sometimes said to be the most remarkable formulas in mathe-

* Published by *Natl. Research Council, Div. Phys. Sci.*, vol. 4, pp. 14–15, 1950.

matics. Replacing z by iz in (6.31) gives

$$(6.332)\quad e^{iz} = 1 + \frac{iz}{1} + \frac{(iz)^2}{2!} + \frac{(iz)^3}{3!} + \frac{(iz)^4}{4!} + \cdots = \left(1 - \frac{z^2}{2!} + \frac{z^4}{4!} - \frac{z^6}{6!} + \cdots\right) + i\left(z - \frac{z^3}{3!} + \frac{z^5}{5!} - \frac{z^7}{7!} + \cdots\right).$$

From this, (6.311), and (6.312) we obtain the first formula in (6.33). Replacing z by $-z$ in the first formula gives $e^{-iz} = \cos(-z) + i \sin(-z)$, and this gives the second formula because (6.311) and (6.312) show that $\cos(-z) = \cos z$ and $\sin(-z) = -\sin z$. Solving (6.33) for $\cos z$ and $\sin z$ gives (6.331). Thus the four Euler formulas are proved. These formulas are important because they enable us to replace trigonometry by algebra and to replace manipulations with trigonometric functions by simpler manipulations with exponentials.

To interpret and make effective use of complex exponentials, we need the fundamental fact that the formula

$$(6.34)\qquad e^z e^w = e^{z+w}$$

is valid whenever z and w are complex numbers. This formula, which is more remarkable than it looks to be, shows that complex exponentials can be manipulated just like real ones. It can be proved in several ways. One who knows about change of order of summation in absolutely convergent double series (some do) and the binomial formula (many do) can see a proof in the formula

$$(6.341)\quad e^{z+w} = \sum_{n=0}^{\infty} \frac{(z+w)^n}{n!} = \sum_{n=0}^{\infty}\sum_{k=0}^{n} \frac{1}{n!}\frac{n!}{k!(n-k)!} z^{n-k}w^k = \sum_{k=0}^{\infty}\sum_{n=k}^{\infty} \frac{z^{n-k}}{(n-k)!}\frac{w^k}{k!} = \sum_{k=0}^{\infty}\frac{w^k}{k!}\sum_{n=0}^{\infty}\frac{z^n}{n!} = e^w e^z = e^z e^w.$$

Another proof of (6.34) depends upon the nontrivial facts that the formula $dz^n/dz = nz^{n-1}$ is valid for complex as well as for real variables, that (6.31) can be differentiated termwise to prove that $de^z/dz = e^z$, and that the formulas

$$(6.342)\qquad \frac{d}{dz}e^u = e^u\frac{du}{dz}, \qquad \frac{duv}{dz} = u\frac{dv}{dz} + v\frac{du}{dz}$$

are valid when u and v are differentiable function of z. Using these facts shows that

$$\frac{d}{dz}(e^z e^{w-z}) = e^z(-e^{w-z}) + e^{w-z}e^z = 0 \tag{6.343}$$

so that $e^z e^{w-z}$ must be independent of z. Since (6.31) shows that $e^0 = 1$, putting $z = 0$ shows that $e^z e^{w-z} = e^w$. Replacing w by $w + z$ gives (6.34). The following third proof of (6.34) is more elementary because it involves derivatives with respect to real variables. Let α and β be constants which may be complex, and let x and y be real. The formula

$$e^{\alpha x+\beta y}e^{-\alpha x} = e^{\beta y} \tag{6.344}$$

is valid because the left side is $e^{\beta y}$ when $x = 0$ and differentiation with respect to x (see Problem 6.363) shows that it is independent of x. Putting $y = 0$ in (6.344) shows that $e^{\alpha x}e^{-\alpha x} = 1$. Hence multiplying (6.344) by $e^{\alpha x}$ gives $e^{\alpha x+\beta y} = e^{\alpha x}e^{\beta y}$. Putting $x = y = 1$, $\alpha = z$, and $\beta = w$ gives (6.34).

Putting $w = -z$ in (6.34) shows that $e^z e^{-z} = 1$. This implies that $e^z \neq 0$ and $e^{-z} = 1/e^z$ for all complex as well as real values of z. Putting $w = z$ shows that $(e^z)^2 = e^{2z}$; and it follows easily that $(e^z)^k = e^{kz}$ whenever k is an integer. Putting $z = e^{i\theta}$ in the last formula and using the first Euler formula gives the *Demoivre* (1667–1754) *formula*

$$(\cos\theta + i\sin\theta)^k = \cos k\theta + i\sin k\theta. \tag{6.345}$$

Figure 2.503 illustrates the simple fact that each complex number $z = x + iy$ is representable in the form

$$z = x + iy = r(\cos\theta + i\sin\theta) = re^{i\theta} \tag{6.35}$$

where

$$r = |z| = (x^2 + y^2)^{\frac{1}{2}} \geqq 0 \tag{6.351}$$

and, when $r > 0$, θ is any one of the angles (of which two must differ by an integer multiple of 2π) for which

$$\cos\theta = x/r, \qquad \sin\theta = y/r. \tag{6.352}$$

In case $r = 0$ and hence $z = 0$, (6.35) holds with an arbitrarily selected θ. Whenever x, y, r, and θ appear in the context of these formulas, we tacitly assume that they are real and that $r \geqq 0$. From (6.34) we obtain

$$(r_1e^{i\theta_1})(r_2e^{i\theta_2}) = r_1r_2e^{i(\theta_1+\theta_2)}. \tag{6.353}$$

This shows that $|z_1z_2| = |z_1|\,|z_2|$, so that the absolute value of the product of two complex numbers is the product of the absolute values of the factors, and that one of the possible polar angles of the product is obtained by adding polar angles of the factors. When, as in Section 2.5, we think of complex numbers as being vectors, we can see that (6.353) is telling us that the result of multiplying $r_1e^{i\theta_1}$ by $r_2e^{i\theta_2}$ is to stretch the vector $r_1e^{i\theta_1}$ by the factor r_2 (the stretching being a contraction if $0 \leqq r_2 < 1$) and rotate the result through the angle θ_2.

When $z = x + iy$ use of (6.34) and the first Euler formula (6.31) gives the formula

$$e^z = e^{x+iy} = e^x e^{iy} = e^x(\cos y + i \sin y) \tag{6.354}$$

which shows how e^z depends upon the real and imaginary parts of z. Such applications as

$$e^{2\pi i} = 1, \qquad e^{\pi i} = -1, \qquad e^{i\pi/2} = i \tag{6.355}$$

are useful as well as spectacular.

Problem 6.361

By use of (6.34) and the Euler formulas, which we must now use freely, show that each solution of the equation

$$a\frac{d^2y}{dx^2} + b\frac{dy}{dx} + cy = 0, \tag{6.3611}$$

in which a, b, c are real constants for which $a > 0$ and $b^2 - 4ac = -h^2$ where $h > 0$, can be put in the forms

$$y = c_1e^{(-b/2a+ih/2a)x} + c_2e^{(-b/2a-ih/2a)x} \tag{6.3612}$$

and

$$y = e^{-(b/2a)x}[c_1e^{i(h/2a)x} + c_2e^{-i(h/2a)x}] \tag{6.3613}$$

and

$$y = e^{-(b/2a)x}\left[C_1 \cos\frac{h}{2a}x + C_2 \sin\frac{h}{2a}x\right] \tag{6.3614}$$

where C_1 and C_2 are real if and only if y is real. Show that

$$C_1 = c_1 + c_2, \qquad C_2 = i(c_1 - c_2), \qquad c_1 = \frac{C_1 - iC_2}{2}, \qquad c_2 = \frac{C_1 + iC_2}{2}$$

and hence that c_1 and c_2 are usually not real when y is real. *Remark:* It is not implied that we should always write the solutions of (6.3611) in the form (6.3614). When we are going to do something with the solutions, it is usually best, even when $k = 0$, to keep those formulas which involve terms of the form x^ke^{mx} to avoid manipulations involving such terms as $x^ke^{px} \cos gx$. It is sometimes worth while to know about trigonometric and even hyperbolic functions, but we must learn to keep them out of our work when we can do our chores much more simply with exponentials.

Problem 6.362

By use of the hyperbolic functions cosh z and sinh z for which

(6.3621) $$\cosh z = \frac{e^z + e^{-z}}{2}, \qquad \sinh z = \frac{e^z - e^{-z}}{2}$$

(6.3622) $$e^z = \cosh z + \sinh z, \qquad e^{-z} = \cosh z - \sinh z,$$

show that each real solution of the equation

(6.3623) $$a\frac{d^2y}{dx^2} + b\frac{dy}{dx} + cy = 0,$$

in which a, b, c are real constants for which $a > 0$ and $b^2 - 4ac = h^2$ where $h > 0$, can be put in the form

(6.3624) $$y = e^{-(b/2a)x}\left(C_1 \cosh \frac{h}{2a}x + C_2 \sinh \frac{h}{2a}x\right).$$

Remark: See the remark at the end of the preceding problem.

Problem 6.363

Supposing that $m = \alpha + i\beta$ where α and β are real, and that x is real, prove the chain-rule formula

(6.3631) $$\frac{d}{dx}e^{mx} = me^{mx}$$

by differentiating the members of the equation

$$e^{mx} = e^{\alpha x}(\cos \beta x + i \sin \beta x).$$

Problem 6.364

Prove (6.3631) again by replacing z by mx in (6.31) and differentiating the result with respect to x. (Theorem 7.24 on power series allows termwise differentiation of the series.)

Problem 6.365

Equations of the form

(6.3651) $$x^2\frac{d^2y}{dx^2} + ax\frac{dy}{dx} + by = 0,$$

in which a and b are constants and $x > 0$, arise occasionally and are called *Cauchy* (1789–1857) *linear equations;* too many equations are already named after Euler. The weakness of the equation lies in the fact that differentiating x^m knocks the exponent down 1 and multiplying by x puts it back. Show that x^m satisfies (6.3651) iff (if and only if)

(6.3652) $$m^2 + (a - 1)m + b = 0$$

so we catch two independent solutions unless we have bad luck with equal roots. That was easy, but let us recognize that (6.3652) might have unreal solutions. What is x^m if m is complex, and can we differentiate it? When $x > 0$, we have

$$x^m = e^{m \log x} \tag{6.3653}$$

by definition. (Note that this looks right because $x = e^{\log x}$). Differentiating by the chain rule gives

$$\begin{aligned} \frac{d}{dx} x^m &= \frac{d}{dx} e^{m \log x} = \frac{m}{x} e^{m \log x} \\ &= m e^{m \log x} e^{-\log x} = m e^{(m-1) \log x} \\ &= m x^{m-1} \end{aligned} \tag{6.3654}$$

and the country is saved. Solve the equation

$$x^2 \frac{d^2y}{dx^2} + x \frac{dy}{dx} + y = 0 \tag{6.3655}$$

to obtain the general solution

$$y_1 = c_1 \cos \log x + c_2 \sin \log x.$$

Maybe we should not be suspicious, but check $\cos \log x$ anyway. *Remark:* Persons who do not use complex numbers can avoid them by making the change of variable $x = e^t$ to convert (6.3651) to a linear equation with constant coefficients and fighting with the result. See Remark 6.876.

Problem 6.37

The *conjugate* of a complex number $z = x + iy$ is the number $\bar{z} = x - iy$ obtained by replacing i by $-i$. Prove that the conjugate of $e^{i\theta}$ is $e^{-i\theta}$, and that the conjugate of the product of two or more factors is the product of the conjugates of the factors. Prove that the conjugate of the sum of two or more terms is the sum of the conjugates of the terms. Prove that $z\bar{z} = |z|^2$.

Problem 6.38

Suppose that, as is true in most applications, the coefficients $a_0, a_1, \ldots, a_n$ in the polynomial $Z(m)$ in (6.23) are real. Prove that if k and ω are real and $\omega \neq 0$ and $Z(k + i\omega) = 0$, then $Z(k - i\omega) = 0$. In other words, the nonreal zeros of $Z(m)$ occur in conjugate pairs; if $-3 + 2i$ is a zero, then $-3 - 2i$ is another.

Problem 6.381

Prove that if $P(z)$ and $Q(z)$ are polynomials of degrees m and n for which $m < n$ and if $Q(z)$ has n distinct zeros $z_1, z_2, \ldots, z_n$, then $P(z)/Q(z)$ has a unique *partial fraction expansion* of the form

$$\frac{P(z)}{Q(z)} = \sum_{k=1}^{n} \frac{A_k}{z - z_k} \tag{6.3811}$$

and that the coefficient A_k can be calculated from the formula

$$A_k = \frac{P(z_k)}{Q'(z_k)}. \tag{6.3812}$$

Solution: If (6.3811) holds, we can multiply by $Q(z)$ and use the fact that $Q(z_k) = 0$ to obtain

$$P(z) = \sum_{j=1}^{n} A_j \frac{Q(z) - Q(z_k)}{z - z_j}.$$

Letting $z \to z_k$ gives $P(z_k) = A_k Q'(z_k)$. Under our hypotheses, there is a constant $a_0 \neq 0$ such that

$$Q(z) = a_0(z - z_1)(z - z_2) \cdots (z - z_n).$$

Differentiating this shows that $Q'(z_k)$ is the product obtained from the right side by omitting the factor $z - z_k$ and putting $z = z_k$ in the result. Hence $Q'(z_k) \neq 0$ and we get (6.3812). To prove that $P(z)/Q(z)$ has a partial fraction of the form (6.3812), it will be sufficient to prove that the polynomial $R(z)$ of degree $n - 1$ or less defined by

$$R(z) = \sum_{k=1}^{n} \frac{P(z_k)}{Q'(z_k)} \frac{Q(z) - Q(z_k)}{z - z_k} \tag{6.3813}$$

is $P(z)$. Observe that, when $1 \leqq j \leqq n$,

$$\lim_{z \to z_j} \frac{Q(z) - Q(z_k)}{z - z_k}$$

is 0 when $k \neq j$ and is $Q'(z_k)$ when $k = j$. Hence letting $z \to z_j$ in (6.3813) gives $R(z_j) = P(z_j)$. Thus $R(z) - P(z)$ is a polynomial of degree less than n which is zero for n different values of z. Therefore $R(z) - P(z)$ is identically zero and the conclusion follows. *Remark:* We will want to use this result later. In case $Q(z)$ has multiple zeros, $P(z)/Q(z)$ has a partial fraction expansion including terms of the form $B/(z - z_k)^p$ where $p > 1$, but we omit discussion of it.

Problem 6.382

Prove that, when $n > 0$, the functions

$$\cos^n x, 1, \cos x, \cos 2x, \ldots, \cos nx$$

are not independent by proving the first of the formulas

$$\cos^n x = \frac{1}{2^n} \sum_{k=0}^{n} \binom{n}{k} \cos (n - 2k)x \tag{6.3821}$$

$$\sin^n x = \frac{1}{(2i)^n} \sum_{k=0}^{n} (-1)^k \binom{n}{k} e^{i(n-2k)x}. \tag{6.3822}$$

Prove the second of the formulas and show that

$$\sin^5 x = \tfrac{1}{16}(10 \sin x - 5 \sin 3x + \sin 5x).$$

Hint: Use the Euler formulas and the binomial formula

$$(a + b)^n = \sum_{k=0}^{n} \binom{n}{k} a^k b^{n-k} = \sum_{k=0}^{n} \binom{n}{k} a^{n-k} b^k$$

in which $\binom{n}{k} = n!/k!(n - k)!$.

Problem 6.383

Use (6.3821) to show that

(6.3831) $$\frac{1}{\pi}\int_0^{\pi} \cos^{2n} x\, dx = \frac{(2n)!}{2^{2n}n!n!} \qquad n = 0, 1, 2, \ldots .$$

To show that this formula can be useful, we use it to obtain information about the Bessel function

(6.3832) $$J_0(x) = 1 - \frac{x^2}{2^2} + \frac{x^4}{2^2 4^2} - \frac{x^6}{2^2 4^2 6^2} - \frac{x^8}{2^2 4^2 6^2 8^2} + \cdots$$

which can be put in the form

(6.3833) $$J_0(x) = \sum_{k=0}^{\infty} (-1)^k \frac{x^{2k}}{(2k)!}\frac{(2k)!}{2^{2k}k!k!}.$$

It is simply impossible to look at these series and guess whether $|J_0(x)|$ will be large or small when x is large. To learn something, we use (6.3833) and (6.3831) to obtain

$$J_0(x) = \sum_{k=0}^{\infty} (-1)^k \frac{x^{2k}}{(2k)!}\frac{1}{\pi}\int_0^{\pi} \cos^{2k} t\, dt$$

so

$$J_0(x) = \frac{1}{\pi}\sum_{k=0}^{\infty} \int_0^{\pi} (-1)^k \frac{(x \cos t)^{2k}}{(2k)!}\, dt.$$

Changing the order of summation and integration can be proved legitimate and gives

$$J_0(x) = \frac{1}{\pi}\int_0^{\pi} \left[\sum_{k=0}^{\infty} (-1)^k \frac{(x \cos t)^{2k}}{(2k)!}\right] dt$$

and hence

(6.3834) $$J_0(x) = \frac{1}{\pi}\int_0^{\pi} \cos (x \cos t) dt.$$ $xJ_0'' + J_0' + xJ_0$

While this formula has other uses, we shall now be content with the observation that, when x is real, $|\cos (x \cos t)| \leqq 1$ and $|J_0(x)| \leqq 1$.

Problem 6.384

For what constant values of a and b does the function $u = e^{ax+by}$ satisfy the *Laplace equation*

(6.3841) $$\frac{\partial^2 u}{\partial x^2} + \frac{\partial^2 u}{\partial y^2} = 0?$$

Ans.: Those for which $b = \pm ia$. Use your result to show that, when a is a constant, the functions $e^{ax} \cos ay$ and $e^{ax} \sin ay$ satisfy (6.3841). Is it true that each linear combination of solutions of (6.3841) is also a solution of (6.3841)? Show that if $\phi_1(a)$ and $\phi_2(a)$ are functions for which the integral has derivatives equal to the integrals of the derivatives of the integrand (that is, if differentiation under the integral sign is permitted), then the function $u(x, y)$ defined by

$$u = \int_{-\infty}^{\infty} e^{ax}[\phi_1(a)e^{iay} + \phi_2(a)e^{-iay}]da \tag{6.3842}$$

is a solution of (6.3841). Evaluate (in terms of elementary functions) the integral for the case in which $\phi_2(a)$ is always 0 and $\phi_1(a)$ is 0 except where $0 \leqq a \leqq 1$ when $\phi_1(a) = 1$. *Ans.*: $u = 1$ when $x = y = 0$; otherwise $u = (e^{x+iy} - 1)/(x + iy)$. Separation of the real and imaginary parts of u gives

$$u = \frac{e^x(y \sin y + x \cos y) - x}{x^2 + y^2} + i\,\frac{e^x(x \sin y - y \cos y) + y}{x^2 + y^2}.$$

6.4. More about Complex Exponentials. Theorem 6.25 shows that if the impedance $Z(m)$ of the equation

$$a_0 \frac{d^n y}{dx^n} + a_1 \frac{d^{n-1}y}{dx^{n-1}} + \cdots + a_{n-1}\frac{dy}{dx} + a_n y = 0 \tag{6.41}$$

has n distinct zeros, then each solution of (6.41) is a linear combination of terms of the form e^{mx} where m is a constant. This is the usual case and the important case. Theorem 6.26 shows that, whether the zeros of $Z(m)$ are distinct or not, each solution of (6.41) is a linear combination of terms of the form x^pe^{mx} where p and m are constants and p is 0 or a positive integer. It is therefore important to know about functions of the form Cx^pe^{mx}, particularly when $p = 0$. This section gives information that is needed whenever (6.41) appears.

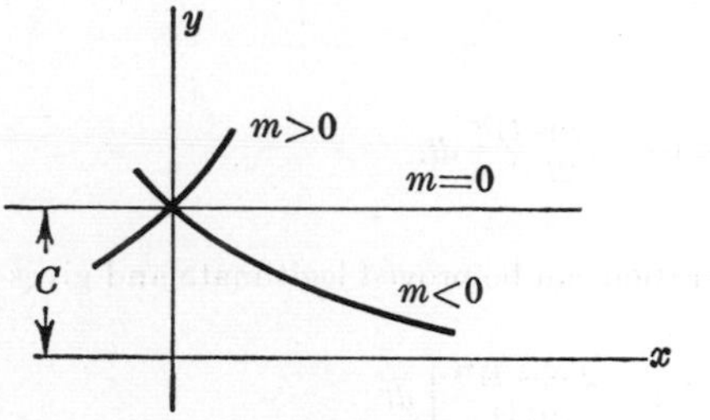

FIG. 6.42

In case m is real, the nature of the graph of $y = Ce^{mx}$ depends upon whether m is positive or zero or negative. Figure 6.42 shows three of these graphs for the case in which $C > 0$.

We come now to the case in which m is a nonzero pure imaginary number and set $m = i\omega$. Considering first the case in which $C > 0$ and $\omega > 0$, we use an Euler formula to obtain

$$y = Ce^{mx} = Ce^{i\omega x} = C(\cos \omega x + i \sin \omega x). \tag{6.43}$$

Thus $y = y_1 + iy_2$ where

$$y_1 = C \cos \omega x, \qquad y_2 = C \sin \omega x. \tag{6.431}$$

These are periodic functions of x having *amplitude* C, and both are said to be *sinusoidal;* in fact $e^{i\omega x}$ is said to be sinusoidal. In each case the *period* P is the amount that x must increase to make ωx increase from 0 to 2π. Thus $\omega P = 2\pi$ and $P = 2\pi/\omega$. The frequency ν (Greek letter nu) is the reciprocal of the period and $\nu = \omega/2\pi$, this being the number of complete oscillations or *cycles* per unit x. The number ω itself is called the *angular frequency*. The graphs of $y_1(x)$ and $y_2(x)$ are shown in Figs. 6.432 and 6.433.

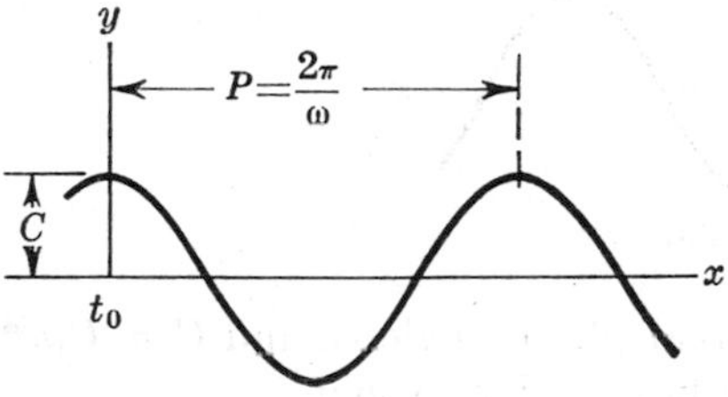

Fig. 6.432

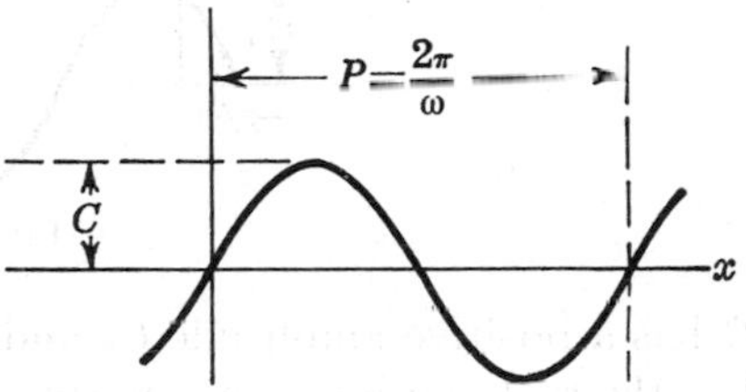

Fig. 6.433

The situation is not changed very much when $y = Ce^{i\omega x}$ when $\omega > 0$ and C is a nonzero complex constant which is not necessarily real and positive. As Fig. 2.503 shows, each nonzero constant C is uniquely representable in the form

$$C = C_0 e^{i\phi}$$

where $C_0 > 0$ and $-\pi < \phi \leqq \pi$. The constant C_0 is the *amplitude* of C, and the angle ϕ is the *phase* (or *phase angle*) of C. In case C is given in the form $C = c_1 + ic_2$, the amplitude C_0 is $(c_1^2 + c_2^2)^{\frac{1}{2}}$ and the phase ϕ is determined from the two formulas* $\cos\phi = c_1/C_0$ and $\sin\phi = c_2/C_0$. Thus the formula $y = Ce^{i\omega x}$ can be put in the form

$$(6.434) \qquad \begin{aligned} y &= C_0 e^{i\phi} e^{i\omega x} = C_0 e^{i(\omega x + \phi)} \\ &= C_0[\cos(\omega x + \phi) + i \sin(\omega x + \phi)]. \end{aligned}$$

and $y = y_1 + iy_2$ where

$$(6.435) \qquad y_1 = C_0 \cos(\omega x + \phi), \qquad y_2 = C_0 \sin(\omega x + \phi).$$

The formulas (6.435) are the same as (6.431) except for the *phase shift* ϕ. It is clear that $\sin(\omega x + \phi) = 0$ when $\omega x + \phi = 0$ and $x = -\phi/\omega$. The graph of $y = C_0 \sin(\omega x + \phi)$ is therefore as shown in Fig. 6.436; except for the phase shift, it is the same as the graph in Fig. 6.433. On account of the identity $\cos\theta = \sin(\theta + \pi/2)$, the graph of $\cos(\omega x + \phi)$ is the same except for a phase shift of $\pi/2$.

* Attempts to determine the angle ϕ from the single formula $\phi = \tan^{-1}(c_2/c_1)$ are defective because the value of the quotient c_2/c_1 does not (even when $c_1 \neq 0$) determine the quadrant in which ϕ lies.

We now consider $y = Ce^{mx}$ for the case in which C is a nonzero constant and m is a constant which is neither real nor pure imaginary. As above,

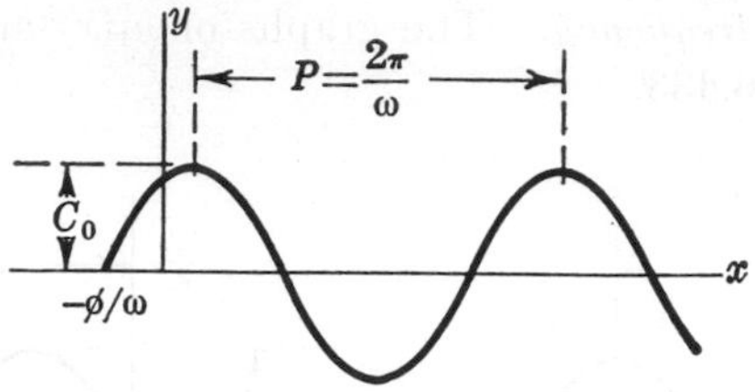

Fig. 6.436

C has a positive amplitude C_0 and a real phase angle ϕ, and $C = C_0e^{i\phi}$. Let the real and imaginary parts of m be k and ω so that

(6.44) $$m = k + i\omega$$

where neither k nor ω is 0. We then have

(6.441) $$\begin{aligned} y &= Ce^{mx} = C_0e^{i\phi}e^{(k+i\omega)x} \\ &= C_0e^{kx}e^{i(\omega x+\phi)} \\ &= C_0e^{kx}[\cos(\omega x + \phi) + i \sin(\omega x + \phi)] \end{aligned}$$

and $y = y_1 + iy_2$ where

(6.442) $$y_1 = C_0e^{kx} \cos(\omega x + \phi)$$
(6.443) $$y_2 = C_0e^{kx} \sin(\omega x + \phi).$$

The natures of the graphs of the functions in (6.442) and (6.443) depend violently upon whether $k > 0$ or $k < 0$. Supposing first that $k > 0$, we begin by sketching graphs of C_0e^{kx} and $-C_0e^{kx}$. These are the upper and lower dashed curves in Fig. 6.444. Completion of a sketch of the

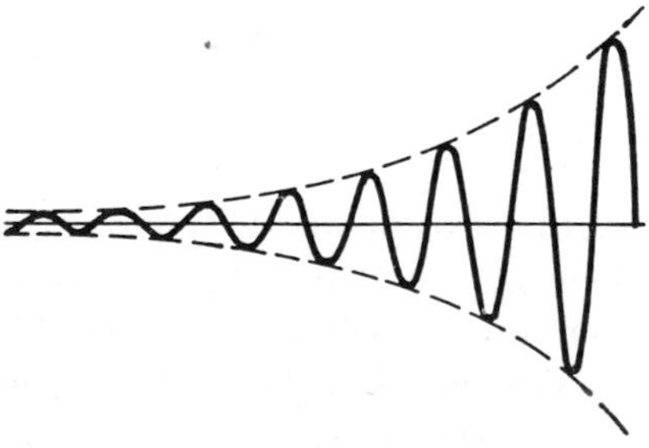

Fig. 6.444

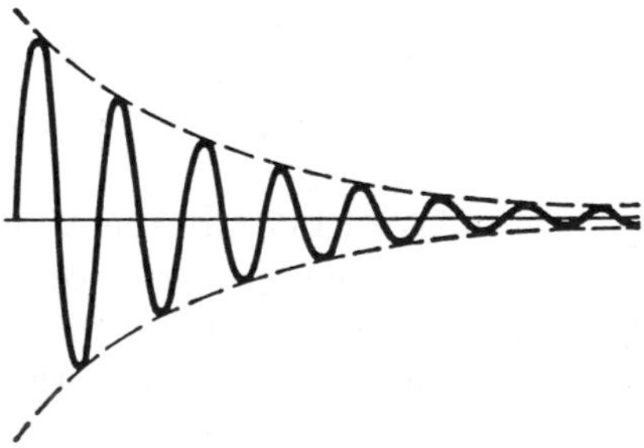

Fig. 6.445

graph of $y_1(x)$ is easily accomplished with the aid of the facts that $-1 \leqq \cos(\omega x + \phi) \leqq 1$, that $y_1(x) = c_0e^{kx}$ whenever $\cos(\omega x + \phi) = 1$, that $y_1(x) = 0$ whenever $\cos(\omega x + \phi) = 0$, and that $y_1(x) = -C_0e^{-kx}$

whenever $\cos(\omega x + \phi) = -1$. Except for a difference in phase of the sinusoidal part, the graph of $y_2(x)$ is the same as that of $y_1(x)$. When $k < 0$, the graphs of (6.442) and (6.443) have the form shown in Fig. 6.445, it being true in this case that $C_0 e^{kx} \to 0$ as $x \to \infty$.

The factor e^{kx} in (6.441), (6.442), and (6.443) is called a *damping factor* when $k < 0$ and a *negative damping factor* when $k > 0$. Thus the functions in (6.441), (6.442), and (6.443) are *damped sinusoids* when $k < 0$ and *negatively damped sinusoids* when $k > 0$. One way to emphasize the fact that a sinusoid is neither damped nor negatively damped is to say that it is a *pure sinusoid.* Of course damped and negatively damped sinusoids are not periodic, but it is nevertheless customary to say that they have frequencies, and that their frequencies are equal to the frequencies of their pure sinusoidal factors. When these sinusoids are outputs of homogeneous equations, their frequencies are said to be *natural frequencies* of the equations and of the things governed by the equations.

It is not difficult to extend the above discussion of functions of the form e^{mx} to functions of the form Cx^pe^{mx} where p is a positive integer and we make only a few remarks. In case $p = 1$ and $m = i\omega$ where $\omega \neq 0$, the function reduces to

$$y = Cxe^{i\omega x} = C_0xe^{i(\omega x+\phi)} \tag{6.45}$$

and $y = y_1 + iy_2$ where

$$y = C_0x \cos(\omega x + \phi), \qquad y_2 = C_0x \sin(\omega x + \phi). \tag{6.451}$$

These functions are negatively damped sinusoids with negative damping factor x. Their graphs lie between the graphs of C_0x and $-C_0x$, and they look much like the graph in Fig. 6.452.

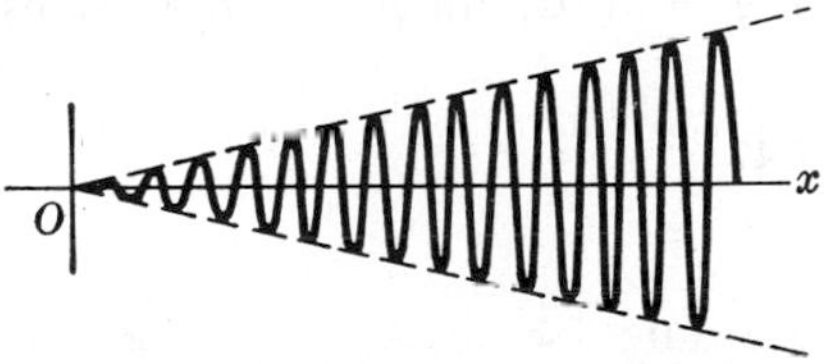

FIG. 6.452

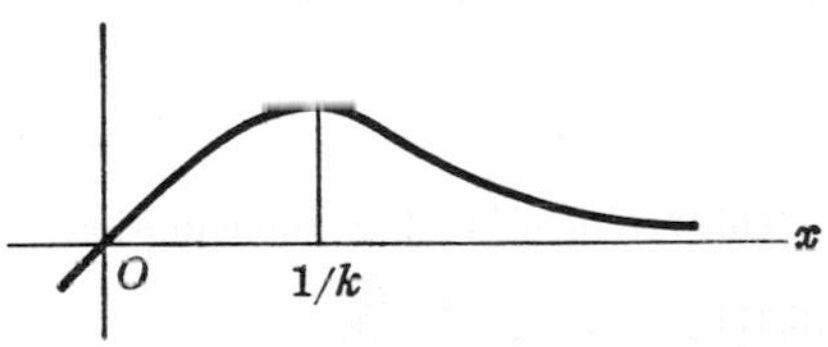

FIG. 6.453

Another case worthy of notice is that for which C and k are positive constants and $y = Cxe^{-kx}$. Here y is zero only once and attains the maximum value C/ke when $x = 1/k$. The graph is shown in Fig. 6.453.

In addition to information about individual functions of the form Cx^pe^{mx}, we sometimes want information about sums of two or more such terms. Suppose, for example, that the coefficients $a_0, a_1, \ldots, a_n$ in (6.101) are all real, and that one zero of the impedance $Z(m)$ is $k + i\omega$ where k is real and $\omega > 0$. Since the zeros of $Z(m)$ come in conjugate pairs, $k - i\omega$ will also be a zero of $Z(m)$. According to Theorem 6.25, the general solution of (6.401) will contain the terms in the right member of the equation

$$w = c_1 e^{(k+i\omega)x} + c_2 e^{(k-i\omega)x},$$

and will contain additional terms if $n > 2$. For some purposes, we want to restrict c_1 and c_2 to values for which w is real, and to obtain a formula for w which involves only real quantities. To investigate this matter, we put w in the form

$$(6.46) \qquad w = e^{kx}[c_1 e^{i\omega x} + c_2 e^{-i\omega x}] = e^{kx}[(c_1 + c_2) \cos \omega x + i(c_1 - c_2) \sin \omega x].$$

It follows that w is real for all values of x if and only if $(c_1 + c_2)$ is real and $(c_1 - c_2)$ is pure imaginary. If we set

$$c_1 + c_2 = A \quad \text{and} \quad i(c_1 - c_2) = B$$

where A and B are *real* constants, we obtain the formula

$$(6.461) \qquad w = e^{kx}[A \cos \omega x + B \sin \omega x]$$

which has the desired form. Sometimes it is desirable to introduce a nonnegative number C defined by $C = (A^2 + B^2)^{\frac{1}{2}}$ and, when $C > 0$, to put this in the form

$$(6.462) \qquad w = Ce^{kx}[(A/C) \cos \omega x + (B/C) \sin \omega x].$$

Letting ϕ be an angle for which $\cos \phi = B/C$, $\sin \phi = A/C$ gives the first of the formulas

$$(6.463) \qquad w = Ce^{kx} \sin (\omega x + \phi), \qquad w = Ce^{kx} \cos (\omega x + \psi),$$

and letting ψ be an angle for which $\cos \psi = A/C$, $\sin \psi = -B/C$ gives the second.

Problem 6.47

This problem involves the equation

$$(6.471) \qquad y'' + 2\delta y' + k^2 y = 0$$

and gives a summary of results of which some have already been obtained. We think of k as being a fixed positive number and consider separately the cases in which δ is a positive *damping constant* for which

(i) $\delta < k$; light damping;
(ii) $\delta = k$; critical damping;
(iii) $\delta > k$; heavy damping.

We consider only nontrivial outputs of (6.471), that is, outputs $y(x)$ which are not identically zero. The impedance of the given equation is $m^2 + 2\delta m + k^2$ and the zeros are

$$(6.472) \qquad m_1 = -\delta - (\delta^2 - k^2)^{\frac{1}{2}}, \qquad m_2 = -\delta + (\delta^2 - k^2)^{\frac{1}{2}}.$$

Show that, in case (i), each real nontrivial output $y(x)$ has the form $y = Ce^{-\delta x} \sin (\omega x + \phi)$ and that $y(x)$ has an infinite number of oscillations as shown in Fig. 6.445.

Now jump to case (iii) where $\delta > k$ and show that each real nontrivial output $y(x)$ has the form

$$y(x) = Ae^{-ax} + Be^{-bx}$$

where a and be are different positive constants and A and B are real constants not both zero. Prove the following facts: (a) $y(x)$ is transient. (b) If $A \geqq 0$ and $B \geqq 0$, then $y(x) > 0$ for each x; if $A \leqq 0$ and $B \leqq 0$, then $y(x) < 0$. (c) If $AB > 0$, then $y(x)$ is never 0. (d) If $AB < 0$, then $y(x) = 0$ iff

$$x = (b - a) \log [-B/A].$$

(e) The graph of the output must have one of the four forms shown in Fig. 6.473.

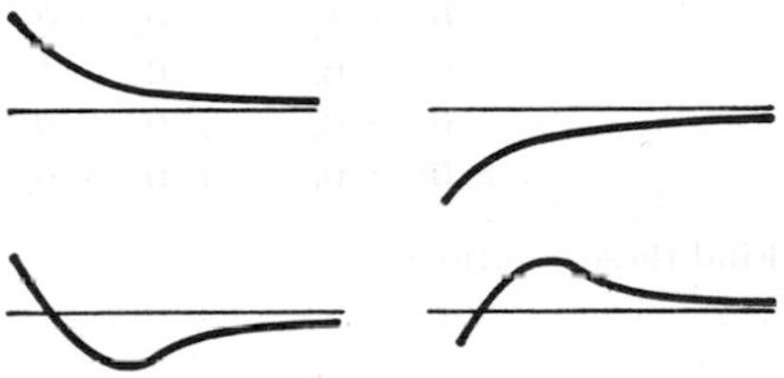

FIG. 6.473

The intermediate case (ii) can be only approximately attained with mechanical and electrical hardware, but let us suppose that $\delta = k$. Then the impedance of (6.471) becomes $(m + \delta)^2$ and $-\delta$ is a double zero. In this case, each output $y(x)$ has the form

$$y = (c_1x + c_2)e^{-\delta x}. \tag{6.474}$$

Show now that each such real nontrivial output has a graph looking like one of the top curves in Fig. 6.473 if $c_1 = 0$ and like one of the bottom curves if $c_2 \neq 0$. Note that the damping constant δ is now smaller than in case (iii) and that the output is not as severely restrained as it was in case (iii).

For understanding of the above three cases, it is helpful to see how we would look at them if we were building a seismograph. This apparatus contains a part bearing a needle which is always pushed toward a neutral position but which is shaken aside by earthquakes. We do not want heavy damping because this makes it too hard for the needle to get away from the neutral position to register a quake. We do not want light damping because this allows the needle to oscillate around the neutral position making it hard to tell when the next quake comes and how big it is. Critical damping is just right. There are other situations in which heavy damping is desirable. We must approve of it when it tames vibrations which otherwise would shake airplane engines out of their mountings. However we do not want heavy damping to smother the signals in transatlantic cables.

Problem 6.481

Show that each function which is equal to its first derivative must have the form $y = c_1e^x$; that each function which is equal to its second derivative must have the form $y = c_1e^x + c_2e^{-x}$; that each function which is equal to its third derivative must have the form

$$y = c_1e^x + c_2e^{-x/2} \cos \tfrac{1}{2} \sqrt{3}\, x + c_3e^{-x/2} \sin \tfrac{1}{2} \sqrt{3}\, x;$$

and that each function which is equal to its fourth derivative must have the form

$$y = c_1e^x + c_2e^{-x} + c_3 \cos x + c_4 \sin x.$$

Problem 6.482

According to Theorem 6.03, the equation

$$\frac{d^4y}{dx^4} - y = 0 \tag{6.4821}$$

has four solutions y_1, y_2, y_3, y_4 such that

$$\begin{array}{llll}
y_1(0) = 1, & y_1'(0) = 0, & y_1''(0) = 0, & y_1'''(0) = 0 \\
y_2(0) = 0, & y_2'(0) = 1, & y_2''(0) = 0, & y_2'''(0) = 0 \\
y_3(0) = 0, & y_3'(0) = 0, & y_3''(0) = 1, & y_3'''(0) = 0 \\
y_4(0) = 0, & y_4'(0) = 0, & y_4''(0) = 0, & y_4'''(0) = 1.
\end{array}$$

Find these solutions:

Ans.: $y_1 = \frac{1}{4}e^x + \frac{1}{4}e^{-x} + \frac{1}{2}\cos x.$
Ans.: $y_2 = \frac{1}{4}e^x - \frac{1}{4}e^{-x} + \frac{1}{2}\sin x.$
Ans.: $y_3 = \frac{1}{4}e^x + \frac{1}{4}e^{-x} - \frac{1}{2}\cos x.$
Ans.: $y_4 = \frac{1}{4}e^x - \frac{1}{4}e^{-x} - \frac{1}{2}\sin x.$

Problem 6.483

Using the results of the preceding problem, find the solution $y(x)$ of (6.4821) for which

$$y(0) = b_1, \qquad y'(0) = b_2, \qquad y''(0) = b_3, \qquad y'''(0) = b_4.$$

Ans.: $y(x) = \frac{1}{4}(b_1 + b_2 + b_3 + b_4)e^x + \frac{1}{4}(b_1 - b_2 + b_3 - b_4)e^{-x} + \frac{1}{2}(b_2 - b_4)\sin x + \frac{1}{2}(b_1 - b_3)\cos x.$

Problem 6.484

Suppose that the coefficients $a_0, a_1, \ldots, a_n$ in (6.251) are real. Prove that if $y(x)$ satisfies (6.251), then the real and imaginary parts of $y(x)$ both satisfy (6.251). Obtain and check (by differentiation) the conclusion to be drawn from the fact that $e^{i\omega x}$ satisfies the equation $y'' + \omega^2 y = 0$. What conclusion is drawn from the fact that $e^{-i\omega x}$ satisfies the same equation?

Problem 6.485

This problem requires proof of a modification of Theorem 6.25 which is sometimes useful. Let the coefficients $a_0, a_1, \ldots, a_n$ in (6.251) be real, and let the impedance $Z(m)$ have n distinct zeros of which some or all are not real. Prove that if $Z(m)$ has exactly q zeros with positive imaginary parts, then $2q \leq n$ and the number of real zeros of $Z(m)$ is exactly $n - 2q$. Prove that if the real zeros of $Z(m)$ are $m_1, m_2, \ldots, m_{n-2q}$ and if the zeros of $Z(m)$ with positive imaginary parts are $k_1 + i\omega_1, k_2 + i\omega_2, \ldots, k_q + i\omega_q$, then each real solution of (6.251) is representable in one and only one way in the form

$$y = \sum_{p=1}^{n-2q} c_p e^{m_p x} + \sum_{p=1}^{q} e^{k_p x}(A_p \cos \omega_p x + B_p \sin \omega_p x)$$

where the constants c_p, A_p, and B_p are real.

Problem 6.486

Observe that (1.41) reduces to

$$\frac{d^2y}{dt^2} + \frac{\sigma}{mL_0} y = 0$$

when $\delta = 0$ and $f(t) = 0$. This is the equation governing the undamped mechanical oscillator with 0 input. Show that each output has the form

$$y = C \sin \left(\sqrt{\frac{\sigma}{mL_0}}\, t + \phi \right)$$

where $C \geqq 0$. Suppose that $C > 0$. Show that the frequency ν is

$$\nu = \frac{1}{2\pi} \sqrt{\frac{\sigma}{mL_0}}.$$

State clearly how ν is affected when we double (*a*) the amplitude C; (*b*) the spring constant σ; (*c*) the mass m of the oscillating body; (*d*) the natural length L_0 of the spring. Show that the oscillating body passes through the neutral position with speed $C(\sigma/mL_0)^{\frac{1}{2}}$. Show that if, contrary to a proviso mentioned in connection with (1.46), we take an ordinary spring and make m sufficiently small, then the formula for the speed would yield a speed exceeding the speed of light. This implausible result contradicts the popular belief that objects do not travel with speeds exceeding that of light.

Problem 6.487

Observe that (1.41) reduces to

$$\frac{d^2y}{dt^2} + \frac{\delta}{m}\frac{dy}{dt} + \frac{\sigma}{mL_0} y = 0.$$

when $f(t) = 0$. Solve this equation, paying particular attention to the manner in which the nature of the solution depends upon the value of the positive damping constant δ. If a frequency exists, discuss the manner in which it depends upon δ. If it is possible to determine δ by measuring quantities that are more easily measured, tell how it can be done.

Problem 6.4881

It is very instructive to study the function

$$x(t) = A_1 \cos \omega_1 t + A_2 \cos (\omega_2 t + \phi) \tag{6.48811}$$

where A_1, A_2, ω_1, ω_2, ϕ are real constants for which $A_1 \geqq A_2 > 0$ and $\omega_2 \neq \omega_1$ but $\omega_2 - \omega_1$ is small in comparison to ω_1. In applications, t can be time and the two terms giving $x(t)$ can be audible outputs from two musical instruments that do not quite agree on the frequency of middle C or voltage outputs from two generators that are driven with slightly different speeds. Phenomena known as *beats* result. To study $x(t)$, introduce complex exponentials so that $x(t)$ is the real part of the function $z(t)$ defined by

$$z(t) = A_1 e^{i\omega_1 t} + A_2 e^{i(\omega_2 t + \phi)}. \tag{6.48812}$$

After putting this in the form

$$z(t) = e^{i\omega_1 t}[A_1 + A_2 e^{i((\omega_2-\omega_1)t+\phi)}],$$

all you have to do is appraise what you see. Denoting the last quantity in brackets by $R(t)e^{i\theta(t)}$, show that

$$R(t) = \{A_1^2 + 2A_1A_2 \cos [(\omega_2 - \omega_1)t + \phi] + A_2^2\}^{\frac{1}{2}}$$

and that this varies slowly between the extremes $A_1 - A_2$ and $A_1 + A_2$ as t increases. Show that $\theta(t)$ varies slowly as t increases. Show that

(6.48813) $$x(t) = R(t) \cos (\omega_1 t + \theta(t)).$$

Show finally that, when $A_1 = 5.5$ and $A_2 = 4.5$, the graph of $x(t)$ looks much like the graph that oscillates between the lower and upper dashed curves in Fig. 6.48814.

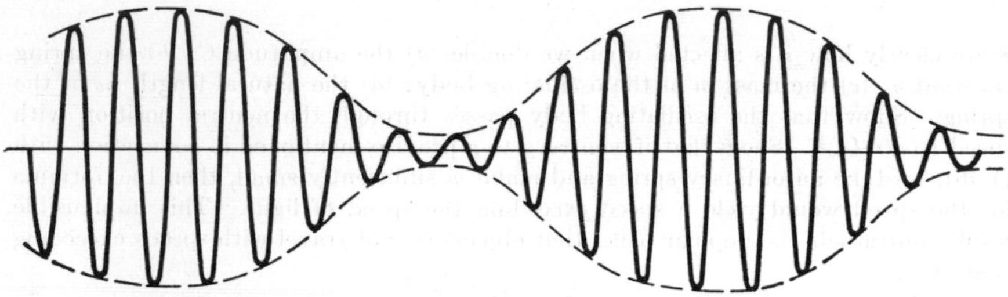

FIG. 6.48814

Problem 6.4882

Look at Fig. 6.445, which shows the graph of $y = e^{-ax} \sin bx$, and note that the relative maxima do not occur for values of x for which $\sin bx = 1$. Is the difference between two values of x for which $y(x)$ has consecutive relative maxima the same as the difference between two values of x for which $\sin bx$ has consecutive relative maxima? *Ans.:* Yes. The facts become clear when the derivative $y'(x)$ is expressed in the form

$$y'(x) = Ce^{-ax} \sin (bx + \phi).$$

Problem 6.489

Show that if $a > 0$, $b > 0$, and the damped sinusoid $y = e^{-ax} \sin bx$ has successive relative maxima $y_1, y_2, y_3, \ldots$, then

(6.4891) $$\frac{y_{n+1}}{y_n} = e^{-2\pi a/b}.$$

Suppose something which we can observe oscillates, in the above manner, very slowly about a zero point which we want to locate without waiting for the oscillations to damp down to negligible proportions. Taking some convenient reference point, we measure $y_1 + A$, $y_2 + A$, and $y_3 + A$. Show how to use (6.4891) to calculate A and the unknown zero point.

Problem 6.491

Is it true that if $\sin x$ is a solution of a homogeneous linear differential equation with real constant coefficients, then $\cos x$ must be another solution? Answer the same question for e^{ix} and e^{-ix}.

Problem 6.492

Theorem 6.03 neglected to say anything about the possibility of finding a solution of the equation

$$y'' + y = 0$$

whose graph passes through two preassigned points in the plane. Discuss this matter.

Problem 6.493

Perhaps we should look at an example which shows that we get in trouble if we suppose that we can apply our theory of linear differential equations to nonlinear ones. Show that the nonlinear equation

$$\frac{d^2y}{dx^2} - \epsilon\left[1 - y^2 - \left(\frac{dy}{dx}\right)^2\right]\frac{dy}{dx} + y = 0,$$

in which $\epsilon > 0$, is satisfied when $y = \sin(x + c)$ but not when $y = 2\sin x$ or $y = e^{ix}$

6.5. Transients; Stability. We shall be concerned with the following definition whose appropriateness becomes clear when we consider x to be time (measured, say, in seconds) and recognize the fact that a transient is a fleeting thing which fades out of significance as time passes.

DEFINITION 6.51. *A transient is a function, say y, of a real variable, say x, such that*

$$\lim_{x\to\infty} y(x) = 0. \tag{6.511}$$

In addition to having mathematical interest, the following theorem is very important in engineering. The equation (6.522) below, as well as any gadget that it governs, is said to be *stable* if its solutions are all transients. Hence the theorem gives a *stability criterion.*

THEOREM 6.52. *Let*

$$Z(m) = a_0m^n + a_1m^{n-1} + \cdots + a_{n-1}m + a_n \tag{6.521}$$

be the impedance of the linear homogeneous equation

$$a_0\frac{d^ny}{dx^n} + a_1\frac{d^{n-1}y}{dx^{n-1}} + \cdots + a_{n-1}\frac{dy}{dx} + a_ny = 0 \tag{6.522}$$

with constant coefficients for which $a_0 \neq 0$. In order that each solution of (6.522) be a transient, it is necessary and sufficient that each zero of $Z(m)$ have a negative real part.

To prove sufficiency, suppose that each zero of $Z(m)$ has a negative real part. Each solution y of (6.522) is a linear combination of terms of the form $x^p e^{-ax} e^{i\beta x}$ where $a > 0$. But

$$|x^p e^{-\alpha x} e^{i\beta x}| = \frac{x^p}{e^{\alpha x}} < \frac{x^p}{(\alpha x)^{p+1}/(p+1)!}, \tag{6.53}$$

and hence each term is a transient. Therefore y is a transient. To prove necessity, let each solution of (6.252) be a transient. If $\alpha + i\beta$ is a zero of $Z(m)$, then $e^{(\alpha+i\beta)x}$ must be a transient. Hence $\alpha < 0$ and the theorem is proved.

Electrical engineers have highly cultivated abilities for obtaining and using information about zeros of impedances.

Remark 6.54

The following is the *stability criterion of Hurwitz* (Adolf, 1859–1919). The zeros of the polynomial

$$Z(m) = a_0 m^n + a_1 m^{n-1} + \cdots + a_{n-1} m + a_n,$$

in which the a's are real constants and $a_0 > 0$, all have negative real parts if and only if the n determinants $\Delta_1, \Delta_2, \ldots, \Delta_n$ defined below are all positive. When a_k is defined to be 0 when $k < 0$ and when $k > n$, the first four of the determinants are $\Delta_1 = a_1$ and

$$\Delta_2 = \begin{vmatrix} a_1 & a_0 \\ a_3 & a_2 \end{vmatrix}; \ \Delta_3 = \begin{vmatrix} a_1 & a_0 & a_{-1} \\ a_3 & a_2 & a_1 \\ a_5 & a_4 & a_3 \end{vmatrix}; \ \Delta_4 = \begin{vmatrix} a_1 & a_0 & a_{-1} & a_{-2} \\ a_3 & a_2 & a_1 & a_0 \\ a_5 & a_4 & a_3 & a_2 \\ a_7 & a_6 & a_5 & a_4 \end{vmatrix}.$$

When $1 \leqq q \leqq n$, the first column of Δ_q contains the first q of the numbers $a_1, a_3, a_5, \ldots$ and the rows contain consecutive a's with decreasing subscripts.

Problem 6.55

Prove that the equation

$$y'' + a_1 y' + a_2 y = 0$$

with real constant coefficients is stable iff (if and only if) a_1 and a_2 are both positive. *Solution:* The two Hurwitz determinants are a_1 and $\begin{vmatrix} a_1 & a_0 \\ 0 & a_2 \end{vmatrix}$. These have values a_1 and $a_1 a_2$, and both are positive iff both $a_1 > 0$ and $a_2 > 0$. Can you prove this without the Hurwitz criterion?

Problem 6.56

For what real values of k are the solutions of the equation

$$y''' + 2y'' + ky' + 4y = 0.$$

all transients? *Ans.:* $k > 2$.

Problem 6.57

For what real values of k is the equation

$$y''' + (2 - k)y'' + (4 + k)y' + 5y = 0$$

stable? *Ans.:* $-3 < k < 1$.

Problem 6.58

Apply the Hurwitz criterion to show that the solutions of

$$y''' + y'' + y' + y = 0$$

are not all transients. Then solve the equation and verify the fact.

Problem 6.59

Prove that the equation

$$y^{(n)} + a_1 y^{(n-1)} + \cdots + a_{n-1}y' + a_n y = 0$$

with real constant coefficients cannot be stable if some of the coefficients are 0 or negative. *Hint:* If the equation is stable, the factors of its impedance must have the form $(m + m_k)$, where $m_k > 0$, or

$$[m - (-\alpha + i\beta)][m - (-\alpha - i\beta)]$$

where $\alpha > 0$. Find out what happens when such factors are multiplied to give polynomials in m.

Problem 6.591

Supposing that δ is real, give several good reasons why the equation

$$y'' + \delta y' + y = 0$$

is stable only when $\delta > 0$.

Problem 6.592

Let $y(x)$ be a real solution of the nonlinear van der Pol equation

$$\frac{d^2x}{dt^2} - \epsilon(1 - x^2)\frac{dx}{dt} + x = 0 \tag{6.5921}$$

in which $\epsilon > 0$. Over any short interval of time when the value of $x(t)$ is nearly a constant k, $x(t)$ should differ only a little from a solution of the linear equation

$$\frac{d^2x}{dt^2} - \epsilon(1 - k^2)\frac{dx}{dt} + x = 0.$$

Show that the latter equation is unstable when $|k| < 1$ and is stable when $|k| > 1$. Try to guess what happens when small oscillations build up and large oscillations die down as t increases. *Remark:* Of course (6.9521) is satisfied when $x(t)$ is identically zero, but this is a state of unstable equilibrium that can be upset by the slightest disturbance. We rarely see pencils standing upright on their sharpened tips.

6.6. Sinusoidal Inputs. For many reasons, some of which appear later in this chapter, it is important to know about the equations

$$(6.61)\qquad a_0\frac{d^ny}{dx^n} + a_1\frac{d^{n-1}y}{dx^{n-1}} + \cdots + a_{n-1}\frac{dy}{dx} + a_ny = E_0 \cos \omega x$$

$$(6.611)\qquad a_0\frac{d^ny}{dx^n} + a_1\frac{d^{n-1}y}{dx^{n-1}} + \cdots + a_{n-1}\frac{dy}{dx} + a_ny = E_0 \sin \omega x,$$

where $a_0, a_1, \ldots, a_n, E_0$, and ω are real constants for which $a_0 \neq 0$, $E_0 > 0$, $\omega \geqq 0$, and where real solutions are sought. Having reached a situation where it becomes irksome to write the left members of (6.61) and (6.611) as often as we need them, we again abbreviate them to the symbol L_ay which is discussed in Section 6.8. Thus, for example, (6.61) is abbreviated to $L_ay = E_0 \cos \omega x$. Since it is so much easier to work with complex exponentials instead of sines and cosines, we immediately write the equation

$$(6.612)\qquad L_ay = E_0e^{i\omega x}$$

which is equivalent to the two equations (6.61) and (6.611). If u and v are real solutions of (6.61) and (6.611), then the complex function $w = u + iv$ is a solution of (6.612). Conversely, if w is a solution of (6.612), then its real part is a solution of (6.61) and its imaginary part is a solution of (6.611). It follows that if we solve (6.612) we can get the solutions of (6.61) and (6.611) in a hurry. We therefore concentrate upon (6.612).

It will not complicate our work to attack the more general equation

$$(6.62)\qquad L_ay = E_0e^{\lambda x}$$

where λ can be $i\omega$ or any real or complex constant. Our previous experiences with complex exponentials suggest that we seek a solution of (6.62) of the form $Ae^{\lambda x}$. Substitution shows that this is a solution if and only if

$$(6.621)\qquad [a_0\lambda^n + a_1\lambda^{n-1} + \cdots + a_{n-1}\lambda + a_n]A = E_0.$$

The coefficient of A is the number $Z(\lambda)$ where $Z(m)$ is the familiar impedance polynomial of the homogeneous equation $L_ay = 0$. The number $Z(\lambda)$ is called the impedance of the nonhomogeneous equation $L_ay = E_0e^{\lambda x}$. Thus, for each fixed λ, the impedance of the nonhomogeneous equation $L_ay = E_0e^{\lambda x}$ is the number obtained by setting $m = \lambda$ in the impedance polynomial $Z(m)$ of the homogeneous equation $L_ay = 0$; this may sound complicated, but the applications are very simple. In case $Z(\lambda) = 0$, it is impossible to determine A so that (6.621) will hold, and our treatment of this case is postponed to Section 6.8. In the usual case in which $Z(\lambda) \neq 0$, the equations are satisfied when $A = E_0/Z(\lambda)$.

Thus, for the equation $L_a y = E_0 e^{\lambda x}$ with input $E_0 e^{\lambda x}$, a possible output is given by the very simple formula

$$(6.63) \qquad y = \frac{E_0 e^{\lambda x}}{Z(\lambda)}$$

or

$$(6.631) \qquad \text{Output} = \frac{\text{input}}{\text{impedance}}$$

whenever $Z(\lambda) \neq 0$. It follows from Theorem 6.04 that each output must be the sum of a solution of the homogeneous equation $L_a y = 0$ and the output in (6.63).

We now consider the following situation which occurs in many mechanical and electrical problems. Let all solutions of the homogeneous equation $L_a y = 0$ be transients and let $\lambda = i\omega$ where ω is real so that the equation to be solved is

$$(6.64) \qquad L_a y = E_0 e^{i\omega x}.$$

Each output of (6.64) then differs by a transient from the output

$$(6.65) \qquad y = \frac{E_0 e^{i\omega x}}{Z(i\omega)}$$

and this output is therefore called the *steady-state output* of (6.64). There is no danger that $Z(i\omega) = 0$ because, under our hypotheses, all of the zeros of $Z(m)$ have negative real parts. The most fundamental and important observation that can be made is the following: *The steady-state output due to a sinusoidal input is sinusoidal and has the same frequency as the input.*

It is easy to put (6.65) in a more informative form which gives the amplitude and phase of this output. Let $Z(i\omega) = u + iv$, let

$$Z_0 = (u^2 + v^2)^{\frac{1}{2}}$$

so that $Z_0 = |Z| > 0$, and let ϕ be the angle for which $-\pi < \phi \leqq \pi$ and

$$(6.651) \qquad \cos\phi = u/Z_0, \qquad \sin\phi = v/Z_0.$$

Then

$$(6.652) \qquad Z(i\omega) = Z_0(\cos\phi + i\sin\phi) = Z_0 e^{i\phi}.$$

This enables us to put (6.65) in the form

$$(6.66) \qquad y = \frac{E_0}{Z_0} e^{i(\omega x - \phi)}.$$

Finding the steady-state solution of the equation $L_a y = E_0 e^{i\omega x}$ is now a very simple matter; all we have to do is find the absolute value Z_0 and the phase angle ϕ of the impedance $Z(i\omega)$ and, dividing and subtracting in the right places, write the answer (6.66). Everybody should thoroughly understand that *we get the steady-state solution without finding the zeros of the impedance polynomial.* For this reason, problems in which only steady-state solutions are required are vastly easier than problems in which transients must be calculated.

Problem 6.67

This problem requires us to see how the above theory is related to the fundamental equation

$$L\frac{dI}{dt} + RI + \frac{Q}{C} = E_0e^{j\omega t} \tag{6.671}$$

in which L, R, and C real positive constants, E_0 and ω are real nonnegative constants, and j is used instead of i for the pure imaginary unit. The equation involves an L-R-C oscillator containing an inductor with inductance L, a resistor with resistance R, and a capacitor with capacitance C as in Fig. 6.672. When i is the current and q is

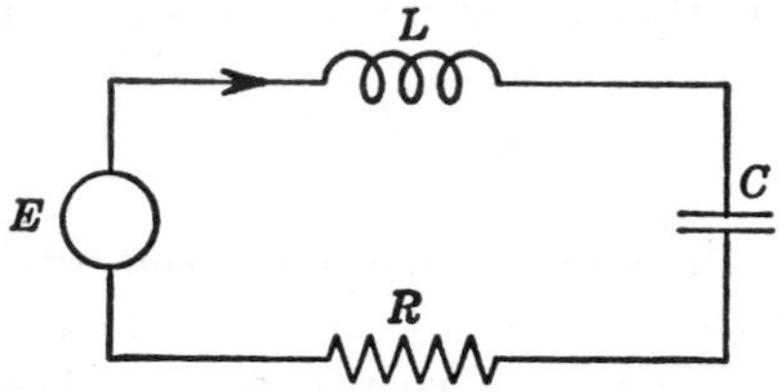

FIG. 6.672

the charge on the capacitor, the voltage drops across the inductor, resistor, and capacitor are $L\,di/dt$, Ri, and q/C. When an electromotive force or input E is applied, a Kirchhoff (1824–1877) law gives

$$L\frac{di}{dt} + Ri + \frac{q}{C} = E. \tag{6.673}$$

When $E = E_0 \cos \omega t$ or $E = E_0 \sin \omega t$, we can find i and q by finding the I and Q which satisfy (6.671) and then taking real or imaginary parts. In fact if we let

$$L\frac{di_1}{dt} + Ri_1 + \frac{q_1}{C} = E_0 \cos \omega t \tag{6.674}$$

$$L\frac{di_2}{dt} + Ri_2 + \frac{q_2}{C} = E_0 \sin \omega t \tag{6.6741}$$

and put $I = i_1 + ji_2$, $Q = q_1 + jq_2$, then multiplying (6.674) and (6.6741) by 1 and j and adding shows that I and Q satisfy (6.671). Thus I and Q are complex numbers but we may think of them as being a current and a charge. The current and charge are related by the formulas

$$I = \frac{dQ}{dt}, \qquad Q = Q_0 + \int_0^t I(s)ds, \tag{6.675}$$

and this relationship must be taken into account before we can solve (6.671). Because of the awkward constant that appears when we express Q in terms of I, it is simplest to put (6.671) in the form

$$L\frac{d^2Q}{dt^2} + R\frac{dQ}{dt} + \frac{Q}{C} = E_0e^{j\omega t}. \tag{6.676}$$

The impedance of this equation is

$$j\omega R - \left(\omega^2L - \frac{1}{C}\right) \tag{6.6761}$$

and hence the steady-state solution for the charge is

$$Q = \frac{E_0}{j\omega R - (\omega^2L - 1/C)}e^{j\omega t}. \tag{6.6762}$$

The two formulas above are much less familiar and important than the formulas involving I. In case $\omega = 0$, (6.6762) reduces to $Q = E_0C$ and $I = dQ/dt = 0$. Henceforth we suppose that $\omega > 0$. Differentiating (6.6762) then gives the very familiar formula

$$I = \frac{E_0}{R + j\left(\omega L - \dfrac{1}{\omega C}\right)}e^{j\omega t}. \tag{6.677}$$

Comparing this with (6.671) we see that when (6.671) is viewed as an equation involving I its impedance is

$$Z(j\omega) = R + j\left(\omega L - \frac{1}{\omega C}\right). \tag{6.678}$$

This familiar impedance of the L-R-C oscillator was called complex impedance when it was introduced because at the time electrical engineers had not yet converted to the habitual use of complex numbers. In Remark 6.873, after we have learned about operators, we will obtain (6.678) in a much better way and will show how electrical engineers really get their formulas for currents.

It is important to see that impedance behaves like a resistance in the sense that impedance and sinusoidal (or alternating) currents fit together like resistance and direct currents. When $E = E_0e^{j\omega t}$, we have $I = E/Z(j\omega)$ for alternating currents; and when E is a constant, we have $I = E/R$ for direct currents. It is easy to see from (6.677) that, for given values of R, E_0, ω, the amplitude of the output I is greatest when L and C are adjusted so that $LC = 1/\omega^2$. When L, C, and ω satisfy this condition, the oscillator is said to be *tuned* to the frequency ω, and the input is said to be in *resonance* with the oscillator. Note that the resonant frequency is equal to the natural frequency of the undamped fictitious oscillator obtained by setting $R = 0$.

Problem 6.68

The L-R-C oscillator of a radio receives inputs from N broadcasting stations. Discuss the relevance of the equation

$$L\frac{dI}{dt} + RI + \frac{Q}{C} = \sum_{k=1}^{N} E_ke^{j\omega_kt + \alpha_k}. \tag{6.681}$$

Show that the steady-state solution is

$$I = \sum_{k=1}^{N} \frac{E_k}{R + j\left(\omega_k L - \dfrac{1}{\omega_k C}\right)} e^{j\omega_k t + \alpha_k}. \tag{6.682}$$

The amplitude A_k of the output (current) due to the input from station k is

$$A_k = \frac{E_k}{|Z(j\omega_k)|} = \frac{E_k}{\left[R^2 + \left(\omega_k L - \dfrac{1}{\omega_k C}\right)^2\right]^{\frac{1}{2}}}. \tag{6.683}$$

It should be obvious to everyone that the radio will not produce satisfactory reception from station 44 unless the output due to the input from station 44 overwhelms the outputs due to the other inputs, that is, unless A_{44} is the giant in the crowd of numbers A_k. One way to make A_{44} large is to move the radio near station 44 or get a good aerial to make E_{44} large; persons who listen to automobile radios on long trips know about this, and everybody knows that this is not the whole story. Another way is to turn the knob on the radio which changes the capacitance C (or perhaps the inductance L) until

$$\omega_{44} L - \frac{1}{\omega_{44} C} = 0 \tag{6.684}$$

and the denominator in (6.683) is minimized. The latter operation is known as the operation of *tuning* the radio to station 44. Many questions can now be answered. For example, examination of the numbers A_k shows that if we want good reception from station 44, which is 200 miles away, we would not want to have $E_{45} \geqq E_{44}$ and ω_{45} too close to ω_{44}.

Problem 6.685

Find a particular solution of the equation

$$\frac{d^2y}{dx^2} + a^2 y = E_0 \sin \omega x$$

where $a > 0$, $\omega > 0$, and $a \neq \omega$, in two ways. First, solve

$$\frac{d^2y}{dx^2} + a^2 y = E_0 \frac{e^{i\omega x} - e^{i\omega x}}{2i}.$$

Then solve

$$\frac{d^2y}{dx^2} + a^2 y = E_0 e^{i\omega x}$$

and equate coefficients of i. Then think a little about the whole business.

Problem 6.691

Find the steady-state solution of the equation

$$a\frac{d^4y}{dx^4} + b\frac{d^3y}{dx^3} + c\frac{d^2y}{dx^2} + d\frac{dy}{dx} + ky = E_0 e^{i\omega t} \tag{6.6911}$$

in which a, b, c, d, and k are real constants not all zero. *Solution:* The impedance is $Z(i\omega) = a(i\omega)^4 + b(i\omega)^3 + c(i\omega)^2 + d(i\omega) + k = (a\omega^4 - c\omega^2 + k) + i(d\omega - b\omega^3)$; the absolute value of the impedance is

$$Z_0 = \sqrt{(a\omega^4 - c\omega^2 + k)^2 + (d\omega - b\omega^3)^2},$$

and the phase angle ϕ of the impedance is determined by the equations

$$\cos \phi = \frac{a\omega^4 - c\omega^2 + k}{Z_0}, \qquad \sin \phi = \frac{d\omega - b\omega^3}{Z_0}.$$

The steady-state solution of the equation is

$$y = \frac{E_0}{Z_0} e^{i(\omega x - \phi)}, \tag{6.6912}$$

and the steady-state solution of the equation obtained by replacing $e^{i\omega t}$ by $\cos \omega t$ is

$$y = \frac{E_0}{Z_0} \cos (\omega x - \phi). \tag{6.6913}$$

Problem 6.692

Suppose that a and k are positive in (6.6911). Show that, in the low-frequency case in which ω is near 0, the amplitude E_0/Z_0 in (6.6913) is near E_0/k and that the phase angle ϕ is near 0.

Problem 6.693

Suppose a is positive in (6.6911). Show that, in the high-frequency case in which ω is very great, the amplitude E_0/Z_0 in (6.6913) is near $E_0/(a\omega^4)$ in the sense that the ratio $[E_0/Z_0]/[E_0/(a\omega^4)]$ is near 1. Show also that the phase angle ϕ is near 0. In fact, it is not difficult to show that $\phi \to 0$ in such a way that $\omega\phi \to -b/a$ as $\omega \to \infty$.

Problem 6.694

To what extent would the work of the last three problems have to be changed to cover the equation

$$\alpha \frac{d^2y}{dx^2} + \beta \frac{dy}{dx} + \gamma y = E_0 \cos \omega t$$

in which α, β, and γ are real constants not all 0? What can be said about a similar equation of order 16?

Problem 6.695

Assuming that a and b are positive constants and that the E's are given constants, show that the steady-state solution of the equation

$$\frac{d^2y}{dx^2} + 2a \frac{dy}{dx} + by = \sum_{n=-N}^{N} E_n e^{inx} \tag{6.6951}$$

is

$$Y_N(x) = \sum_{n=-N}^{N} \frac{E_n}{\sqrt{(b - n^2)^2 + 4a^2n^2}} e^{i(nx - \phi_n)} \tag{6.6952}$$

where the phase angles ϕ_n are given by the formulas

$$\cos \phi_n = \frac{b - n^2}{\sqrt{(b - n^2)^2 + 4a^2n^2}}, \qquad \sin \phi_n = \frac{2an}{\sqrt{(b - n^2)^2 + 4a^2n^2}}. \tag{6.6953}$$

Show that, if $|n|$ is large, then ϕ_n is near $-\pi$. Show that if $\ldots E_{-2}, E_{-1}, E_0, E_1, E_2, \ldots$ is an infinite set of E's which is bounded, that is, if there is a constant B for which

$$|E_n| \leqq B \qquad n = 0, \pm 1, \pm 2, \ldots, \tag{6.6954}$$

then

$$\lim_{N \to \infty} Y_N(x) \tag{6.6955}$$

must exist.

Problem 6.696

A particle slides without friction in a long slender tube which rotates in a vertical plane about its center with constant angular velocity $\omega > 0$. Let $u(t)$ denote the displacement of the particle from the center at time t, and suppose the time origin to be so chosen that at time $t = 0$ the tube is horizontal. Show that

$$\frac{d^2u}{dt^2} - \omega^2 u = -g \sin \omega t$$

and that, if the initial velocity and displacement of the particle are $u(0) = A$ and $u'(0) = B$, then

$$u = \frac{1}{2}\left[A + \frac{B}{\omega} - \frac{g}{2\omega^2}\right] e^{\omega t} + \frac{1}{2}\left[A - \frac{B}{\omega} + \frac{g}{2\omega^2}\right] e^{-\omega t} + \frac{g}{2\omega^2} \sin \omega t.$$

Show that $u(t)$ is bounded if and only if $2A\omega^2 + 2B\omega = g$ and that $u(t)$ is periodic if and only if $A = 0$ and $2B\omega = g$.

6.7. Periodic Inputs; Harmonic Analysis.

As before, let

$$L_a y = a_0 \frac{d^n y}{dx^n} + a_1 \frac{d^{n-1} y}{dx^{n-1}} + \cdots + a_{n-1} \frac{dy}{dx} + a_n y \tag{6.71}$$

where the a's are constants and $a_0 \neq 0$. Suppose, as is true in many applications, that the solutions of the homogeneous equation $L_a y = 0$ are all transients. One of the most interesting and important problems of pure and applied mathematics is that of obtaining useful information about the steady-state output of the equation

$$L_a y = f(x) \tag{6.72}$$

where $f(x)$ is a given input having period h, that is,

$$f(x + h) = f(x). \tag{6.721}$$

The restrictions which $f(x)$ are required to satisfy are very light. We do not need, for example, to require that $f(x)$ be continuous. It is sufficient to require that the two integrals $\int_0^h f(t)dt$ and $\int_0^h |f(t)|^2dt$ exist. Partly to simplify the formulas which we write, and partly to suggest that our methods have many other applications, we define functions $\phi_0(x)$, $\phi_1(x)$, $\phi_{-1}(x)$, $\phi_2(x)$, $\phi_{-2}(x)$, . . . by the formula

$$\phi_k(x) = h^{-\frac{1}{2}}e^{i(2\pi/h)kx}. \tag{6.73}$$

The normalizing constant $h^{-\frac{1}{2}}$ is inserted so that the functions $\phi_k(x)$ constitute an *orthonormal set* over the interval $0 \leqq x \leqq h$, that is, the integral $\int_0^h \phi_j(x)\overline{\phi_k(x)}dx$ is 0 when $j \neq k$ and is 1 when $j = k$. The set is *complete;* information about these matters is given in Chapter 12. Because it is easy to write the steady-state output of the equation $L_ay = \phi_k(x)$, it will be easy to write a good approximation to the steady-state output of the equation $L_ay = f(x)$ if we can find constants c_0, c_{-1}, c_1, . . . , c_{-m}, c_m such that the sum

$$\sum_{k=-m}^{m} c_k\phi_k(x) \tag{6.731}$$

is a good approximations to $f(x)$. It is a standard procedure in pure and applied mathematics to consider the sum in (6.731) to be the best approximation to $f(x)$ when the c's are chosen such that

$$\int_0^h |f(x) - \sum_{k=-m}^{m} c_k\phi_k(x)|^2dx \tag{6.732}$$

is a minimum. In order to keep our discussion informative and reasonably brief, it is now necessary to give some results without proofs; some proofs and more information are given in Chapter 12. It is shown in (12.74) that

$$\int_0^h |f(x) - \sum_{k=-m}^{m} c_k\phi_k(x)|^2dx = \int_0^h |f(x)|^2dx - \sum_{k=-m}^{m} |b_k|^2 + \sum_{k=-m}^{m} |c_k - b_k|^2 \tag{6.733}$$

where the constants b_k are the *Fourier* (1768–1830) *coefficients* defined by the Euler (1707–1783) formula

$$b_k = \int_0^h f(x)\overline{\phi_k(x)}dx. \tag{6.74}$$

These coefficients are usually called a's instead of b's, but in our present situation the a's have been preempted by (6.71). It is very easy to see that the right side of (6.733) is a minimum when $c_k = b_k$. Hence the constants c_k in (6.731) should be chosen to be the Fourier coefficients b_k. The individual terms $b_k\phi_k(x)$ are called *harmonics* of $f(x)$. The combination $b_k\phi_k(x) + b_{-k}\phi_{-k}(x)$ is also called a harmonic of $f(x)$, and so also is each term in the right member of the formula

$$(6.741) \qquad b_k\phi_k(x) + b_{-k}\phi_{-k}(x) = A_k \cos \frac{2\pi}{h} kx + B_k \sin \frac{2\pi}{h} kx.$$

Putting $c_k = b_k$ in (6.733) gives the formula

$$(6.75) \qquad \int_0^h |f(x) - \sum_{k=-m}^{m} b_k\phi_k(x)|^2 dx = \int_0^h |f(x)|^2 dx - \sum_{k=-m}^{m} |b_k|^2.$$

The next and most remarkable fact is that the members of this equation converge to 0 as $m \to \infty$. Thus

$$(6.751) \qquad \lim_{m\to\infty} \int_0^h |f(x) - \sum_{k=-m}^{m} b_k\phi_k(x)|^2 dx = 0,$$

and the *Parseval* (?–1836) *formula*

$$(6.752) \qquad \sum_{k=-\infty}^{\infty} |b_k|^2 = \int_0^h |f(x)|^2 dx$$

holds.

Our next step is to replace the equation $L_a y = f$ by the equation

$$(6.76) \qquad L_a y_m = \frac{1}{h^{\frac{1}{2}}} \sum_{k=-m}^{m} b_k e^{i\omega_k x}$$

where

$$(6.761) \qquad \omega_k = (2\pi/h)k.$$

The numbers b_k, which are not necessarily real, can be put in the form

$$(6.762) \qquad b_k = A_k e^{i\alpha_k}$$

where $A_k \geqq 0$ and α_k is real. Thus (6.76) can be put in the form

$$(6.763) \qquad L_a y_m = \frac{1}{h^{\frac{1}{2}}} \sum_{k=-m}^{m} A_k e^{i(\omega_k x + \alpha_k)}.$$

The steady-state output of this input is

$$(6.764) \qquad y_m(x) = \frac{1}{h^{\frac{1}{2}}} \sum_{k=-m}^{m} \frac{A_k}{Z(i\omega_k)} e^{i(\omega_k x + \alpha_k)}.$$

This is an exceptionally useful formula. As m increases, $y_m(x)$ converges rapidly to the output $y(x)$ of $L_a y = f$, so that one who cares to do so can write

$$(6.765) \qquad y(x) = \frac{1}{h^{\frac{1}{2}}} \sum_{k=-\infty}^{\infty} \frac{A_k}{Z(i\omega_k)} e^{i(\omega_k x + \alpha_k)}.$$

An important point is that, in very many practical applications, $y_m(x)$ is a thoroughly satisfactory approximation to $y(x)$ when m is a positive integer as small as 1 or 2 or 3 or 4. This happy state of affairs is due partly to the tendency of the numbers A_k to decrease as $|k|$ increases, but it is due mostly to the tendency of $|Z(i\omega_k)|$ to increase very rapidly as $|k|$ increases. Specialists in applied mathematics feel injured when it is necessary to take m as large as 10 or 20. Another important point is that (6.764) and (6.765) give approximations to $y(x)$ that have very useful forms; they are simple sums of simple sinusoidal terms.

The remainder of this section can be read quite casually in a short course, and can profitably be studied for a long time in a long course. Everybody should read it in self-defense. Harmonic analysis is a very large subject, and the unwary can easily be filled with bread when they want cake or vice versa.

Remark 6.77

We now make some remarks about what are called Fourier series—in spite of the fact that they were discovered and used before the time of Fourier (1768–1830). Fourier solved many problems by use of these series, but he made no substantial contributions to their theory; the author regrets that statements about Fourier in the first edition of this book were misleading. So far as theory is concerned, Fourier's claim to fame rests on his revival of the false contention of d'Alembert (1717–1783) that the "Fourier series" of an arbitrary function converges to the function. When the constants b_k are defined by the Euler formula (6.74), the series

$$(6.771) \qquad \sum_{k=-\infty}^{\infty} b_k \phi_k(x) \quad \text{or} \quad \frac{1}{\sqrt{h}} \sum_{k=-\infty}^{\infty} b_k e^{i(2\pi/h)kx},$$

which looks simplest when $h = 2\pi$, is called the *Fourier series* of $f(x)$. It can be put in the forms

$$(6.7711) \qquad \frac{1}{\sqrt{h}} \left[b_0 + \sum_{k=1}^{\infty} (b_k e^{i(2\pi/h)kx} + b_{-k} e^{-i(2\pi/k)kx}) \right]$$

and

$$(6.7712) \qquad \frac{1}{2} A_0 + \sum_{k=0}^{\infty} \left(A_k \cos \frac{2\pi k}{h} x + B_k \sin \frac{2\pi k}{h} x \right).$$

The series is said to *converge* to $f(x)$ if

$$\lim_{n\to\infty} \sum_{k=-n}^{n} b_k\phi_k(x) = f(x). \tag{6.772}$$

The functions $S_n(x)$ defined by

$$S_n(x) = \sum_{k=-n}^{n} b_k\phi_k(x) \tag{6.773}$$

are called the *partial sums* of the series.

It is possible to spend a lifetime studying the old and difficult theory of convergence of Fourier series (many persons have done it) and still be unable to answer such fundamental questions as the following. Is it true that if $f(x)$ is a given continuous periodic function, then there must be at least one value of x for which the series converges? So much true (and some false) information about convergence of Fourier series is so interesting and so widely publicized that it is not always easy for specialists in applied mathematics to realize that this theory is rarely as useful in their field as information about (6.751). The main service of the old theory was to provide intensive interest in the subject which led to development of the more modern theory of orthonormal sets in which completeness plays a central role. To construct the newer theory is not a short task, but to use it is very easy. It is a fact that television sets can be turned on by persons who do not know enough about them to be able to make one. It is another fact that (6.764) can be used by persons who know relatively little about the mathematics that lies behind it. The formula (6.764) is so simple and straightforward that it can be used with equal success by those who do not know why it works and by those who think it works because Fourier series converge. All we have to do is calculate a few of the numbers in (6.764) from formulas by which they are defined and put them together. To be thoroughly informative, we must continue with some remarks about convergence of Fourier series. As a matter of fact, unless one is allowed to accept proof by intimidation and naïvely assume that convergent series of functions behave like uniformly convergent series of functions, it does very little good to know the bare fact that the Fourier series of a particular given function is convergent. Bare facts can be interesting, particularly when their importance is sometimes overemphasized, and we give some. We confine attention to the class F of functions $f(x)$ which have period h and are bounded and integrable (Riemann or Lebesgue) over each interval of length h. Each such f has a Fourier series with coefficients defined by the Euler formulas for them. It is not a simple matter to construct a function f in the class F whose Fourier series is not everywhere convergent; only clever or well-tutored mathematicians can do it. Each function f in the class F which a specialist in applied mathematics would dream up for use in his work has a Fourier series which converges everywhere and converges to

$$\lim_{h\to 0} \frac{f(x+h) + f(x-h)}{2} \tag{6.774}$$

wherever this limit exists and hence to $f(x)$ whenever $f(x)$ is continuous. In particular, this kind of convergence exists whenever $f(x)$ has period h and has bounded variation over $0 \leqq x \leqq h$. A function is said to have *bounded variation* (the name *finite variation* would be more sane) over the interval $0 \leqq x \leqq h$ if there is a constant M such that

$$\sum_{k=1}^{n} |f(x_k) - f(x_{k-1})| \leqq M \tag{6.7741}$$

whenever $x_0, x_1, \ldots, x_n$ are numbers for which

$$0 = x_0 < x_1 < x_2 < \cdots < x_{n-1} < x_n = h. \tag{6.7742}$$

Roughly speaking, we may say that a function has bounded variation over an interval if its graph does only a finite amount of wiggling over the interval. In a more particular sense, the above kind of convergence exists whenever $f(x)$ has period h and satisfies the classic conditions of Dirichlet (1805–1859). Roughly speaking, we may say that a function $f(x)$ satisfies the Dirichlet conditions if it is bounded and its graph has only a finite set of wiggles in each finite interval. This means that there is a constant M such that $|f(x)| \leqq M$, and the interval $0 \leqq x \leqq h$ can be cut into a finite set of subintervals such that, in each subinterval, $f(x)$ is either monotone increasing or monotone decreasing. A function is said to be *monotone increasing* (graph staying level or going up) over an interval $a < x < b$ if $f(x_1) \leqq f(x_2)$ whenever $a < x_1 < x_2 < b$.

As these remarks may have suggested, the facts and the importance of the facts relating to convergence of Fourier series were, for a long time, the subjects of violent controversies. For those with sufficient knowledge of the subject, the wars are now over. The Fourier series of bounded periodic functions (and many unbounded ones too) that occur in our work are surely convergent, but it would make no difference if they were not convergent; we can use them equally effectively whether they converge or do not converge.

Finally we give our attention to a much more difficult problem. We suppose that $f(x)$ is Riemann integrable over the interval $0 \leqq x \leqq h$ and has period h. We suppose also that the series in

$$f(x) = \sum_{k=-\infty}^{\infty} b_k \phi_k(x) \tag{6.7743}$$

converges everywhere to $f(x)$, and ask whether this hypothesis implies that the series must be the Fourier series of $f(x)$, that is, whether the numbers b_k must be the numbers defined by the Euler formulas (6.74). Riemann (1826–1866) was sane enough to realize that this is a very difficult problem and was brilliant enough to construct the Rieman theory of trigonometric series and to prove that the answer is affirmative.*

Problem 6.775

Let $f(x)$ be the function (or input) which has period 2π and has the values $f(x) = e^{-x}$ when $0 < x < 2\pi$. Sketch a graph of $f(x)$ and see how it fades between integer multiples of 2π and is rejuvenated at these multiples of 2π. Using (6.74) and (6.73) with $h = 2\pi$, show that the Fourier coefficients b_k of $f(x)$ are

$$b_k = \frac{1}{(2\pi)^{\frac{1}{2}}} \int_0^{2\pi} e^{-(1+ik)x}\,dx = \frac{1}{(2\pi)^{\frac{1}{2}}} \frac{1 - e^{-2\pi}}{1 + ik}.$$

Show that the Parseval formula (6.752) becomes

$$\frac{(1 - e^{-2\pi})^2}{2\pi} \sum_{k=-\infty}^{\infty} \frac{1}{1 + k^2} = \frac{1 - e^{-4\pi}}{2}.$$

To be thoroughly realistic we should recognize that there can be mistakes in calcula-

* An authoritative account of the matter is given by A. Zygmund (1900–) in "Trigonometrical Series," Warszawa-Lwow, Poland, 1933.

tions, and even in theories, and we should wonder whether this is really a correct formula. Show that it is correct iff

$$\sum_{k=-\infty}^{\infty} \frac{1}{1+k^2} = \pi \frac{1+e^{-2\pi}}{1-e^{-2\pi}}. \tag{6.7751}$$

For practical applications of our work, the important fact is that the terms for which $k = 0, 1, -1$, and -2 have a sum differing relatively little from the right side, and that the sum of the first few harmonics of $f(x)$ approximates $f(x)$ very nicely. One who wishes a proof of (6.7751) which does not involve Fourier series can put $s = 2\pi$ in (9.863) and read Problem 9.87.

Remark 6.776

Let $f(x)$ and $g(x)$ be two functions such that f, g, $|f|^2$, and $|g|^2$ are all integrable over $0 \leqq x \leqq h$ and let

$$f(x) \sim \sum_{k=-\infty}^{\infty} b_k \phi_k(x) \tag{6.7761}$$

where the series on the right is the Fourier series of f. It is then possible to prove that the series in

$$\int_0^h f(x)g(x)dx = \sum_{k=-\infty}^{\infty} b_k \int_0^h \phi_k(x)g(x)dx \tag{6.7762}$$

is convergent and the equality holds. Thus, whether the series in (6.7761) is convergent or not, we can multiply by $g(x)$ and integrate termwise to obtain the formula (6.7762) in which the series must be convergent. The proof goes quickly when the right methods are used. Use of (6.751) and the Schwarz inequality (9.791) gives

$$\lim_{n\to\infty} \int_0^h [f(x) - \sum_{k=-n}^{n} b_k\phi_k(x)]g(x)dx = 0$$

and the result follows. When we set $g(x) = \overline{\phi_n(x)}$, (6.7762) reduces to the formula (6.74) which defines the Fourier coefficient b_n. If we set $g(x) = \overline{f(x)}$, then (6.7762) reduces to the Parseval formula (6.752). If, in (6.7762), we replace $g(x)$ by $\overline{g(x)}$ and let the Fourier coefficients of $g(x)$ be denoted by $B_0, B_{-1}, B_1, \ldots$, we obtain the two-function Parseval equality

$$\int_0^h f(x)\overline{g(x)}dx = \sum_{k=-\infty}^{\infty} b_k\overline{B_k} \tag{6.7763}$$

which reduces to (6.752) when $g = f$. If $0 \leqq t \leqq h$ and we set $g(x) = 1$ when $0 \leqq x \leqq t$ and $g(x) = 0$ when $t < x \leqq h$, we obtain

$$\int_0^t f(x)dx = \sum_{k=-\infty}^{\infty} b_k \int_0^t \phi_k(x)dx. \tag{6.7764}$$

This proves that the Fourier series can be integrated termwise.

We have seen that (6.7761) implies (6.7762). If someone thinks that this is so because (i) the series in (6.7761) is convergent and (ii) convergent series can always be integrated termwise, his reasoning is faulty but his conclusion is correct.

Problem 6.777

A function $f(x)$ is said to be an *even function* if $f(-x) = f(x)$ and an *odd function* if $f(-x) = -f(x)$. For example, $x^2 + 1$ and other polynomials containing only even exponents are even; and $x^3 - 5x$ and other polynomials containing only odd exponents are odd. Show that if $f(x)$ is a function having period $2p$, its Fourier series with fundamental period $2p$ is

$$\sum_{k=-\infty}^{\infty} \left[\int_{-p}^{p} f(x) \frac{e^{-ik(\pi/p)x}}{\sqrt{2p}}\, dx\right] \frac{e^{ik(\pi/p)x}}{\sqrt{2p}}.$$

Show that if $f(x)$ is even, this reduces to

$$\frac{1}{p} \sum_{k=-\infty}^{\infty} \left[\int_{0}^{p} f(x) \cos \frac{k\pi}{p} x\, dx\right] e^{ik(\pi/p)x}$$

and to

$$\frac{1}{p}\int_0^p f(x)dx + \frac{2}{p} \sum_{k=1}^{\infty} \left[\int_0^p f(x) \cos \frac{k\pi}{p} x\, dx\right] \cos \frac{k\pi}{p} x.$$

This is a *cosine series.* Show that if $f(x)$ is odd, the series reduces to

$$\frac{1}{p} \sum_{k=-\infty}^{\infty} \left[i \int_0^p f(x) \sin \frac{k\pi}{p} x\, dx\right] e^{ik(\pi/p)x}$$

and to

$$\frac{2}{p} \sum_{k=1}^{\infty} \left[\int_0^p f(x) \sin \frac{k\pi}{p} x\, dx\right] \sin \frac{k\pi}{p} x.$$

This is a *sine series.*

Problem 6.778

Information about Bernoulli functions is given in Remark 9.78. In particular $B_1(x)$ is the saw function of period 1 which has the value $x - \frac{1}{2}$ when $0 < x < 1$. While importance of the matter does not shake the earth, we suppose that $B_1(0) = 0$. Draw a graph of $B_1(x)$, find out whether it is even or odd or neither, and find its trigonometric Fourier series with fundamental interval $-1 \leq x \leq 1$.

Ans.: See Remark 9.78.

Problem 6.779

With $B_1(x)$ defined as in the previous problem, $B_2(x)$ is defined by the formula

$$B_2(x) = c + \int_0^x B_1(t)dt$$

where c is chosen such that $\int_0^1 B_2(x)dx = 0$. Find $B_2(x)$ and its Fourier series over the interval $-1 \leqq x \leqq 1$. *Ans.:* See Remark 9.78.

Problem 6.78

This problem provides a summary of facts relating to natural frequencies and resonances in lightly damped oscillators (see Problem 6.47) governed by the equation

$$y'' + 2\delta y' + k^2 y = 0 \tag{6.781}$$

where $0 < \delta < k$. The ideas are both interesting and important. Show in an efficient way that each real nontrivial output of (6.781) has the form

$$y = Ce^{-\delta x} \cos (\alpha x + \beta) \tag{6.782}$$

where $\alpha = (k^2 - \delta^2)^{\frac{1}{2}}$, C is a positive amplitude, and β is a real phase angle. Note that if $\beta = -\pi/2$, then the pure sinusoidal part is $\sin \alpha x$. Note that, according to Section 6.4 (which should be read again if this sounds strange), $\alpha/2\pi$ is the natural frequency of (6.781).

This matter of natural frequencies is worth a lot of thought. Countless other examples are more or less similar to the following. Suppose that a heavy man (two or three small persons would serve the same purpose) steps on the front bumper of an automobile. The bumper will sag below its neutral position and, when the man steps off, the bumper will rise up to and above its neutral position and will oscillate about its neutral position. Automobile suspensions are designed so that the oscillations will damp out quite quickly, but nevertheless the oscillations will have a natural frequency which we may call $\alpha/2\pi$ even if we do not know its numerical value. Now suppose that the heavy man gets back onto the bumper and jumps up and down with frequency $\omega/2\pi$. In case ω is near α, a phenomenon will occur. After a few cycles, the bumper will be oscillating, the man will be pressing down on the bumper when it is going down, and the magnitudes of the oscillations will be built up, perhaps to unpleasant proportions. All this leads us to the important idea that inputs having frequencies near natural frequencies produce large outputs. In such situations, we say that *resonance* occurs. Of course it is not to be expected that a man jumping on an automobile bumper, with a frequency $\omega/2\pi$ at or near the natural frequency $\alpha/2\pi$, will be clever enough to produce a sinusoidal input. However his input will have harmonics that are sinusoids with frequencies $\omega/2\pi$, $2(\omega/2\pi)$, $3(\omega/2\pi)$, . . . and the first one or two or three of these will [see (6.765)] be responsible for nearly all of the output due to the whole input.

For reasons set forth in the above paragraph, it is important to know how the output of the equation

$$y'' + 2\delta y' + k^2 y = E_0 e^{i\omega x} \tag{6.783}$$

depends upon ω and to know about resonance. Let $\omega \geqq 0$. Show that each output of (6.783) differs by a transient from the steady-state output

$$y = \frac{E_0}{Z(i\omega)} e^{i\omega x} \tag{6.784}$$

where

$$Z(i\omega) = k^2 - \omega^2 + i2\delta\omega. \tag{6.785}$$

Show that if δ and k are fixed constants for which $0 < \delta < k$, then

(6.786) $$\frac{d}{d\omega}|Z(i\omega)|^2 = 4\omega[\omega^2 + 2\delta^2 - k^2].$$

Use this to show that if $0 < \delta < k/2^{\frac{1}{2}}$, then the amplitude of the output (6.784) is a maximum when $\omega = (k^2 - 2\delta^2)^{\frac{1}{2}}$. Show how this compares with α when δ/k is small. Show that if $k/2^{\frac{1}{2}} \leqq \delta < k$, then the above amplitude is a maximum when $\omega = 0$.

Problem 6.791

This problem involves outputs of undamped oscillators governed by the equation

(6.7911) $$y'' + k^2y = E_0e^{i\omega x}$$

where $k > 0$ and ω is real. Nontrivial outputs of the homogeneous equation are not transients but are sinusoids

(6.7912) $$y = C \sin (kt + \alpha)$$

of frequency $k/2\pi$. Supposing that $\omega \neq \pm k$, obtain the particular output

(6.7913) $$Y = \frac{E_0}{k^2 - \omega^2} e^{i\omega x}$$

in an efficient way. Note that this output is a pure sinusoid having the frequency of the input and discuss the manner in which its amplitude and phase depend upon ω. *Remark:* The case of resonant inputs for which $\omega = k$ will appear in Problem 6.871.

Problem 6.792

This problem illustrates an important method (the *eigenvalue method* or the *Fourier method*) of attacking partial differential equations. The heat equation in one space dimension is

(6.7921) $$a^2\frac{\partial^2 u}{\partial x^2} = \frac{\partial u}{\partial t}.$$

We seek solutions of this equation of the form

(6.7922) $$u = X(x)T(t).$$

Show that (6.7922) satisfies (6.7921) iff (if and only if)

(6.7923) $$\frac{X''(x)}{X(x)} = \frac{T'(t)}{a^2T(t)}.$$

Now comes a little argument that is very familiar to many scientists. The left side of the last equation is independent of t and the right side is independent of x; the two are equal; so they must be independent of both x and t and so must be a constant which we could call q but which we call $-\lambda^2$.* Equate the members of (6.7923) to

* For the applications we are going to make, calling the constant $-\lambda^2$ simplifies our work by eliminating radicals and unreal numbers that otherwise would appear, but it does not change the final results. The only way to discover this fact is to call the constant q and see what happens when we proceed.

$-\lambda^2$ and solve the resulting equations to discover that the function

$$u(x, t) = e^{-\lambda^2 a^2 t}(c_1 \cos \lambda x + c_2 \sin \lambda x) \tag{6.7924}$$

satisfies (6.7921) for each λ. Show that if this is 0 when $x = 0$ and when $x = L$, then $c_1 = 0$ and $\lambda = k\pi/L$ where k is an integer and obtain

$$u(x, t) = C_k e^{\frac{-k^2\pi^2 a^2}{L^2} t} \sin \frac{k\pi}{L} x. \tag{6.7925}$$

The sum of k of these things gives (1.371). It might be a good idea to read Remark 1.351 and Problem 1.37 again, and to note that more information about these matters appears in Chapter 12. Note that the k^2 in the exponent makes harmonics of higher order damp out with lightning rapidity as t increases from 0.

Problem 6.793

Work a little with the wave equation (1.362) and find out where (1.361) came from.

Problem 6.794

Find material in Section 1.1 which will show you that if u satisfies the heat equation in cylindrical coordinates, and if u is independent of ϕ and z, then

$$a^2 \left[\frac{\partial^2 u}{\partial \rho^2} + \frac{1}{\rho} \frac{\partial u}{\partial \rho} \right] = \frac{\partial u}{\partial t}. \tag{6.7941}$$

Show that the function

$$u = R(\rho) T(t) \tag{6.7942}$$

satisfies this equation iff there is a constant λ for which

$$\frac{R''(\rho) + \frac{1}{\rho} R'(\rho)}{R(\rho)} = \frac{T'(t)}{a^2 T(t)} = -\lambda \tag{6.7943}$$

and hence

$$T'(t) + \lambda a^2 T(t) = 0 \tag{6.7944}$$

$$\rho R''(\rho) + R'(\rho) + \lambda \rho R(\rho) = 0. \tag{6.7945}$$

The last equation is the Bessel (1784–1846) equation of order zero with parameter λ. We shall attack Bessel equations in the next chapter.

Remark 6.795

A horde of the classic equations and functions of mathematical physics arise from the Laplace, heat, and wave equations in the three brands of coordinates appearing in (1.171), (1.172), and (1.173). Parameters appear everywhere when u is allowed to depend upon t and all three space variables.

6.8. Operators. This section deals with the use of operators in solving linear equations of the form

$$a_0 \frac{d^n y}{dx^n} + a_1 \frac{d^{n-1} y}{dx^{n-1}} + \cdots + a_{n-1} \frac{dy}{dx} + a_n y = f(x). \tag{6.801}$$

Some of our work is meaningful when the coefficients $a_0, \ldots, a_n$ are functions of x, but we simplify matters by assuming that they are constants and that $a_0 \neq 0$. In the particularly important case in which the impedance of the homogeneous equation has distinct zeros and $f(x)$ is 0 or a sum of sinusoids, the results will be the same as the results we have previously obtained much more easily. However, the new results will cover cases in which the zeros of the impedance are not distinct. Moreover we do not require that the input $f(x)$ be 0 or constant or sinusoidal or periodic. All we require of $f(x)$ is that it be integrable (Riemann or Lebesgue) over each finite interval; we do not require that $f(x)$ be continuous. The output $y(x)$ which we obtain as a solution of the problem will then be continuous and have $n - 1$ derivatives that are continuous (absolutely continuous, in fact) and will satisfy the differential equation for each x for which f is continuous.

Let D denote the operator $\frac{d}{dx}$. The operator D applies (or is applicable) to each differentiable function $y(x)$, and the result of applying the operator D to such a function is the function

$$Dy = \frac{d}{dx} y = y'(x). \tag{6.802}$$

For example,

$$D \sin \omega x = \omega \cos \omega x, \qquad D(xe^{ax}) = (ax + 1)e^{ax}.$$

Thus D is an example of an operator which operates on a function $y(x)$ to produce a new function. All operators used in this book operate on functions.

Two operators E_1 and E_2 are said to be *equal*, and we write $E_1 = E_2$ if

$$E_1 y = E_2 y \tag{6.811}$$

for each y to which either E_1 or E_2 applies. An operator E is said to be the *sum* of two operators E_1 and E_2, and we write $E = E_1 + E_2$ if

$$Ey = E_1 y + E_2 y \tag{6.812}$$

for each y to which both E_1 and E_2 apply. An operator E is said to be the *product* of two operators E_1 and E_2, and we write $E = E_1 E_2$ if

$$Ey = E_1(E_2 y) \tag{6.813}$$

for each y such that E_2 applies to y and E_1 applies to $E_2 y$. We ordinarily write $E_1(E_2 y)$ in the simpler form $E_1 E_2 y$, EEy in the form $E^2 y$, and $EE^n y$ in the form $E^{n+1} y$.

The formula

$$D^2 y = DDy = \frac{d}{dx}\frac{d}{dx} y = \frac{d^2}{dx^2} y$$

and other similar formulas justify writing

$$(6.8131) \qquad D = \frac{d}{dx}, \qquad D^2 = \frac{d^2}{dx^2}, \quad \ldots, \quad D^n = \frac{d^n}{dx^n}.$$

It is convenient to regard a function $a(x)$, which may be a constant, as being an operator the effect of which is to multiply by $a(x)$.

Two operators E_1 and E_2 are said to *commute* (or to be *permutable*) if $E_1E_2 = E_2E_1$. Note that E_1E_2y is the function obtained by applying E_2 to y and then E_1 to the result, whereas E_2E_1y is the function obtained by applying E_1 to y and then E_2 to the result. According to the problems below, the operators $D - m_1$ and $D - m_2$ commute when m_1 and m_2 are constants; but the operators $D + x$ and $D - x$ do not commute.* An operator E is said to be *linear* if

$$(6.814) \qquad E(c_1y_1 + c_2y_2) = c_1Ey_1 + c_2Ey_2$$

whenever c_1 and c_2 are constants and E applies to both y_1 and y_2.

Problem 6.815

Prove that

$$(D - m)e^{mx} = 0.$$

Remark: It is a good idea to remember this.

Problem 6.816

Show that if m_1 and m_2 are constants, then each step in the computation

$$\begin{aligned}(D - m_1)(D - m_2)y &= \left(\frac{d}{dx} - m_1\right)\left[\left(\frac{d}{dx} - m_2\right)y\right] \\ &= \left(\frac{d}{dx} - m_1\right)\left[\frac{dy}{dx} - m_2y\right] \\ &= \frac{d}{dx}\left[\frac{dy}{dx} - m_2y\right] - m_1\left[\frac{dy}{dx} - m_2y\right] \\ &= \frac{d^2y}{dx^2} - m_2\frac{dy}{dx} - m_1\frac{dy}{dx} + m_1m_2y \\ &= [D^2 - (m_1 + m_2)D + m_1m_2]y\end{aligned}$$

is justified whenever $y(x)$ has two derivatives and hence that

$$(D - m_1)(D - m_2) = D^2 - (m_1 + m_2)D + m_1m_2.$$

Tell why $D - m_1$ and $D - m_2$ commute.

* One who is naïve with respect to the question of possible differences in consequences resulting from application of operators in different orders may profit by thinking a little about the operations of (i) insuring an automobile and (ii) driving the automobile into collision with that of a struggling lawyer.

Problem 6.817

Show that each step in the computation

$$\begin{aligned}(D + x)(D - x)y &= \left(\frac{d}{dx} + x\right)\left[\left(\frac{d}{dx} - x\right) y\right] \\ &= \left(\frac{d}{dx} + x\right)\left[\frac{dy}{dx} - xy\right] = \frac{d}{dx}\left[\frac{dy}{dx} - xy\right] + x\left[\frac{dy}{dx} - xy\right] \\ &= \frac{d^2y}{dx^2} - x\frac{dy}{dx} - y + x\frac{dy}{dx} - x^2y = \frac{d^2y}{dx^2} - (1 + x^2)y\end{aligned}$$

is justified when $y(x)$ has two derivatives and hence that

$$(D + x)(D - x) = D^2 - (1 + x^2).$$

Show that $(D - x)(D + x) = D^2 + (1 - x^2)$. Notice that

$$(D + x)(D - x) \neq (D - x)(D + x).$$

Problem 6.8171

The operator xD has applications. Prove the formulas

$$\begin{aligned}(xD)^2 &= xDxD = x^2D^2 + xD \\ (xD)^3 &= xDxDxD = x^3D^3 + 3x^2D^2 + xD.\end{aligned}$$

Obtain a formula for $(xD)^4$, and check it by applying the operators to the function $y = x^n$.

Problem 6.8172

Show that, if m_1 and m_2 are constants, then

$$(xD - m_1)(xD - m_2) = x^2D^2 + (1 - m_1 - m_2)xD + m_1m_2.$$

Tell why $xD - m_1$ and $xD - m_2$ commute.

Problem 6.818

If $f(x)$ has n derivatives and a is a constant, then

(6.8181) $$(D - a)^n f(x) = e^{ax}D^n e^{-ax} f(x);$$

to prove this we show easily that it holds when $n = 1$; and if it holds for a given n, then the computation

$$\begin{aligned}(D - a)^{n+1} f(x) &= (D - a)e^{ax}D^n e^{-ax} f(x) \\ &= e^{ax}D^{n+1}e^{-ax}f(x) + ae^{ax}D^n e^{-ax}f(x) - ae^{ax}D^n e^{-ax}f(x) = e^{ax}D^{n+1}e^{-ax}f(x)\end{aligned}$$

shows that it holds for the next greater value of n. Use formula (6.8181) to show that

(6.8182) $$(D - a)^n(c_1x^{n-1} + c_2x^{n-2} + \cdots + c_n)e^{ax} = 0.$$

Remark: This suddenly takes care of the worst case of multiple zeros of impedances. It shows that the equation $(D - a)^n y = 0$ has the solution

$$y = (c_0 + c_1x + c_2x^2 + \cdots + c_{n-1}x^{n-1})e^{ax},$$

and the solution must be the general solution because it is a linear combination of n independent solutions.

Problem 6.819

Use the remark of the previous problem to prove Theorem 6.26.

The operator L_a, which was defined in Section 6.08 and can now be put in the form

$$L_a = a_0D^n + a_1D^{n-1} + \cdots + a_{n-1}D + a_n, \tag{6.82}$$

applies to each function $y(x)$ having n derivatives, and for each such function

$$L_ay = a_0\frac{d^ny}{dx^n} + a_1\frac{d^{n-1}y}{dx^{n-1}} + \cdots + a_{n-1}\frac{dy}{dx} + a_ny. \tag{6.821}$$

The letter L is chosen to remind us continually that the operator is *linear*, that is,

$$L_a(c_1y_1 + c_2y_2) = c_1L_ay_1 + c_2L_ay_2, \tag{6.8211}$$

and the subscript a indicates that the operator depends on the a's. By use of the operator L_a, the linear equation (6.01) can be written in the convenient form

$$L_ay = f \tag{6.8212}$$

and the corresponding homogeneous equation in the convenient form

$$L_ay = 0. \tag{6.8213}$$

Thus one service of the operator L_a is to make a linear differential equation look very innocent; it will appear later that operators have more serious applications.

The operator L_a furnishes an important way of looking at the equation $L_ay = f$. Each function $y(x)$ having n derivatives is *carried* or *transformed* by the operator L_a into some function or other of x which may or may not be $f(x)$; and the solutions of $L_ay = f$ are those special functions $y(x)$ which happen to be transformed by L_a into the given function $f(x)$. It is sometimes said that an operator L_a *annihilates* a function $y(x)$ if L_a transforms $y(x)$ into the function which vanishes identically; the solutions of $L_ay = 0$ are then the functions $y(x)$ annihilated by L_a.

It is a fundamental fact that the operator L_a in (6.82) can be factored in the form

$$L_a = a_0(D - m_1)(D - m_2) \cdots (D - m_n) \tag{6.822}$$

where $m_1, m_2, \ldots, m_n$ are the zeros of the impedance of the equation $L_ay = 0$. When $n = 2$, this is a consequence of the result of Problem

6.816; and when $n > 2$, the result can be proved in the same way or by induction.

The equation $L_a y = f$ is identical with the equation (6.032) of Theorem 6.03, and it is therefore a consequence of Theorem 6.03 that there is a unique function $y(x)$ for which $L_a y = f$ and

$$y(x_0) = y'(x_0) = \cdots = y^{(n-1)}(x_0) = 0. \tag{6.823}$$

This particular solution of $L_a y = f$ is of great interest in both pure and applied mathematics and we denote it by the symbol $L_a^{-1}f$ or $(1/L_a)f$. Passage from the first to the second of the formulas

$$L_a y = f, \qquad y = \frac{1}{L_a} f = L_a^{-1} f \tag{6.824}$$

could look like a routine procedure, but it must be emphatically realized that the procedure is valid *only* when $y(x)$ is the solution of $L_a y = f$ for which (6.823) holds. Observe that

$$D^{-1}f = \int_{x_0}^{x} f(t)dt. \tag{6.825}$$

Discussion of the connection between the two operators L_a and L_a^{-1} will be greatly simplified after we have obtained an important formula (the Faltung formula) giving $L_a^{-1}f$ in terms of f. Meanwhile we make some remarks concerning the class F of continuous inputs f and the class Y of outputs y which have n continuous derivatives and satisfy (6.823). To each output y in the class Y, there corresponds exactly one input $L_a y$ in the class F, this input being calculable by substituting y into the formula $L_a y = f$. To each input f in the class F, there corresponds exactly one output in the class Y, and this is $L_a^{-1}f$. So long as we stay within the classes F and Y, the two operators L_a and L_a^{-1} are *inverse operators* because

$$L_a^{-1}L_a y = y, \qquad L_a L_a^{-1} f = f. \tag{6.826}$$

Both L_a and L_a^{-1} are linear operators. When we wish to solve differential equations, the operator L_a works the wrong way; it carries outputs into inputs. It is the inverse operator L_a^{-1} which works the right way; it carries inputs which we are given into outputs which we want to find. All this is very important, and we had better learn about L_a^{-1}. We will.

We now start on a systematic campaign to apply operators to solve nonhomogeneous linear differential equations having constant coefficients. The campaign begins with an attack upon the equation

$$a_0 \frac{dy}{dx} + a_1 y = f(x). \tag{6.83}$$

After dividing by a_0, we can put this in the form

(6.831) $$(D - m_1)y = f_1(x),$$

where $f_1(x) = f(x)/a_0$. Multiplying by the integrating factor e^{-m_1x} gives

$$\frac{d}{dx}e^{-m_1x}y = e^{-m_1x}f_1(x)$$

(check this by differentiation); and integration gives

$$e^{-m_1x}y = c_1 + \int_{x_0}^{x} e^{-m_1t}f_1(t)dt.$$

Hence

(6.832) $$y = c_1e^{m_1x} + e^{m_1x}\int_{x_0}^{x} e^{-m_1t}f_1(t)dt.$$

Thus (6.83) is solved. Putting $f_1 = 0$ shows that the first term in the right member of (6.832) is a solution of the homogeneous equation $(D - m_1)y = 0$, that is, $(D - m_1)e^{m_1x} = 0$; and putting $c_1 = 0$ shows that the last term is the solution of (6.831) for which $y(x_0) = 0$. Hence, according to the definition involving (6.824),

(6.833) $$\frac{1}{D - m_1}f_1 = e^{m_1x}\int_{x_0}^{x} e^{-m_1t}f_1(t)dt.$$

The campaign continues with an attack upon the equation

(6.84) $$a_0\frac{d^2y}{dx^2} + a_1\frac{dy}{dx} + a_2y = f(x).$$

Using the fact that L_a can be factored enables us to put this in the form

(6.841) $$(D - m_1)(D - m_2)y = f_1(x)$$

where $f_1(x) = f(x)/a_0$. Our next step is to recognize that this has the form

(6.842) $$(D - m_1)[(D - m_2)y] = f_1(x)$$

and make the very profound observation that we can find y in two steps by first finding the quantity in brackets and then finding y. This is very important because it reduces the task of solving (6.841) to the much simpler task of solving two linear equations of first order. When we look at (6.842) and think of $(D - m_2)y$ as being a single unknown function which we are seeking, we see that, except for the notation for the function we are seeking, (6.842) is identical with (6.831). This fact and the fact that (6.832) is the solution of (6.831) give

$$(D - m_2)y = c_1e^{m_1x} + e^{m_1x}\int_{x_0}^{x} e^{-m_1t}f_1(t)dt.$$

This completes the first step, and we start on the second. Multiplying by the integrating factor e^{-m_2x} gives

$$\frac{d}{dx} e^{-m_2x}y = c_1e^{(m_1-m_2)x} + e^{(m_1-m_2)x} \int_{x_0}^{x} e^{-m_1t}f_1(t)dt. \tag{6.843}$$

When we come to integrate this, we can see that formulas of different types result when $m_2 = m_1$ and $m_2 \neq m_1$. Taking first the case in which $m_2 = m_1$ and the equation which we are solving becomes

$$(D - m_1)^2y = f_1(x), \tag{6.8431}$$

we replace m_2 by m_1 in (6.843) and integrate to obtain

$$e^{-m_1x}y = c_1x + c_2 + \int_{x_0}^{x} du \int_{x_0}^{u} e^{-m_1t}f_1(t)dt. \tag{6.844}$$

Before solving for y, we simplify the iterated integral by making a change of the order of integration. Figure 6.845 shows the triangle in the (u, t)

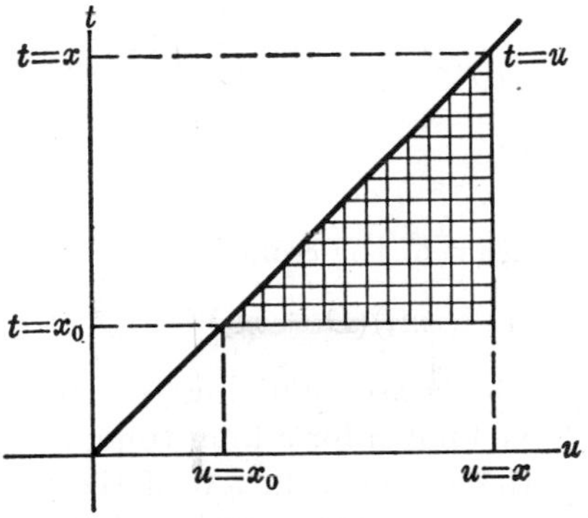

FIG. 6.845

plane covered by the integration, and inspection of the figure shows what the new limits of integration will be. The value I of the integral is found to be

$$I = \int_{x_0}^{x} dt \int_{t}^{x} e^{-m_1t}f(t)du = \int_{x_0}^{x} (x - t)e^{-m_1t}f_1(t)dt.$$

Putting this in (6.844) and solving for y gives

$$y = (c_1x + c_2)e^{m_1x} + e^{m_1x} \int_{x_0}^{x} (x - t)e^{-m_1t}f_1(t)dt. \tag{6.846}$$

Thus (6.8431) is solved. Putting $f_1 = 0$ shows that the first term in the right member is a solution of the homogeneous equation $(D - m_1)^2y = 0$, and everybody should see one or more reasons why it is the general solution. Putting $c_1 = c_2 = 0$ in (6.846) shows that the last term is the solution of (6.8431) for which $y(0) = y'(0) = 0$. Hence, according to the definition involving (6.824)

$$\text{(6.847)} \qquad \frac{1}{(D - m_1)^2} f_1 = e^{m_1 x} \int_{x_0}^{x} (x - t) e^{-m_1 t} f_1(t)\,dt.$$

We still have to find the solution of (6.841) when $m_2 \neq m_1$. In this case we integrate (6.843) and replace the constant $c_1/(m_1 - m_2)$ by a new c_1 to obtain

$$\text{(6.8471)} \qquad e^{-m_2 x} = c_1 e^{(m_1 - m_2)x} + c_2 + \int_{x_0}^{x} du \int_{x_0}^{u} e^{(m_1 - m_2)u} e^{-m_1 t} f_1(t)\,dt.$$

The change of order of integration used above shows that the integral has the value

$$\int_{x_0}^{x} dt \int_{t}^{x_0} e^{(m_1 - m_2)u} e^{-m_1 t} f_1(t)\,du.$$

Simplifying this by integrating with respect to u, putting the result in (6.8471), and solving for y give

$$\text{(6.8472)} \qquad y = c_1 e^{m_1 x} + c_2 e^{m_2 x} + \frac{e^{m_1 x}}{m_1 - m_2} \int_{x_0}^{x} e^{-m_1 t} f_1(t)\,dt + \frac{e^{m_2 x}}{m_2 - m_1} \int_{x_0}^{x} e^{-m_2 t} f_1(t)\,dt.$$

This is the general solution of the equation

$$\text{(6.8473)} \qquad (D - m_1)(D - m_2) y = f_1(x)$$

for the case in which $m_2 \neq m_1$. Putting $f_1 = 0$ in (6.8472) yields an elementary fact we have known for a long time; the sum of the first two terms on the right is the general solution of the homogeneous equation corresponding to (6.8473). It is easy to see that putting $c_1 = c_2 = 0$ in (6.8472) gives the solution of (6.8473) for which $y(x_0) = y'(x_0) = 0$. Hence, according to the definition involving (6.824)

$$\text{(6.848)} \qquad \frac{1}{(D - m_1)(D - m_2)} f_1 = \frac{1}{m_1 - m_2} \frac{1}{D - m_1} f_1 + \frac{1}{m_2 - m_1} \frac{1}{D - m_2} f_1.$$

From our definition of equality for operators, it follows that

$$\text{(6.849)} \qquad \frac{1}{(D - m_1)(D - m_2)} = \frac{1}{m_1 - m_2} \frac{1}{D - m_1} + \frac{1}{m_2 - m_1} \frac{1}{D - m_2}.$$

This is a remarkable fact for the following reason. If we forget that D is an operator and think of it as being an ordinary real or complex number, addition of the two terms on the right side produces a single quotient which is the left side. This is, of course, just another way of saying that the right side of (6.849) is the partial fraction expansion of the left side.

It is obvious that the methods which we have applied to equations of orders 1 and 2 could be applied to equations of order 3. The results already obtained would give us a formula for the quantity in brackets in the equation

$$(D - m_1)(D - m_2)[(D - m_3)y] = f, \tag{6.85}$$

and then solving a first order equation by use of an integrating factor would determine y. Three cases would arise. Usually m_1, m_2, and m_3 are distinct, but the cases in which $m_1 = m_2 \neq m_3$ and $m_1 = m_2 = m_3$ have at least theoretical interest.

The facts relating to solutions of the homogeneous equation $L_a y = 0$ are easiest to obtain. Little if any more work with special cases is required to enable us to guess the result of Theorem 6.26; it can be proved by induction without the aid of Problem 6.818.

We now return to consideration of solutions of the nonhomogeneous equation $L_a\, y = f$ satisfying (6.823) and give some results without proof. The formula

$$\frac{1}{(D - m)^k} f = e^{mx} \int_{x_0}^{x} \frac{(x - t)^{k-1}}{(k - 1)!} e^{-mt} f(t)\, dt \tag{6.86}$$

or

$$\frac{1}{(D - m)^k} f = \int_{x_0}^{x} \frac{(x - t)^{k-1}}{(k - 1)!} e^{m(x-t)} f(t)\, dt, \tag{6.861}$$

which has been proved when $k = 1, 2$, is valid when $k = 1, 2, \ldots$. The proof can be completed by induction. The formula

$$\frac{1}{D^k} f - \int_{x_0}^{x} \frac{(x - t)^{k-1}}{(k - 1)!} f(t)\, dt \tag{6.8611}$$

to which this reduces when $m = 0$ is often used. Partial fraction expansions, of which (6.849) is an example, can be obtained by solving more differential equations. However it is much easier to reverse the procedure so that the expansions are obtained first and then used to solve the equations. Since we are using complex numbers, and polynomials can always be factored into products of powers of linear factors as in (6.053), we can always represent L_a in the form

$$L_a = a_0(D - m_1)^{p_1}(D - m_2)^{p_2} \cdots (D - m_r)^{p_r} \tag{6.862}$$

where $p_1\, p_2, \ldots, p_r$ are positive integers and $p_1 + p_2 + \cdots + p_r = n$. It is then possible to generalize (6.849) by proving that there exist constants A_{jk} such that the partial fraction expansion

$$\frac{1}{L_a} = \sum_{j=1}^{r} \sum_{k=1}^{p_j} \frac{A_{jk}}{(D - m_j)^k} \tag{6.863}$$

is valid. This and (6.861) imply that

$$\frac{1}{L_a} f = \int_{x_0}^{x} \left[\sum_{j=1}^{r} \sum_{k=1}^{p_j} A_{jk} \frac{(x - t)^{k-1}}{(k - 1)!} e^{m_j(x-t)} \right] f(t)dt. \tag{6.864}$$

Letting y_0 be the function defined by

$$y_0(x) = \sum_{j=1}^{r} \sum_{k=1}^{p_j} A_{jk} \frac{x^{k-1}}{(k - 1)!} e^{m_j x} \tag{6.865}$$

puts (6.864) in the form

$$L_a^{-1} f = \int_{x_0}^{x} y_0(x - t) f(t)dt. \tag{6.87}$$

This is the *faltung formula;* other names will appear in Section 6.9.

This faltung formula is exceptionally interesting and important. It is a source of very much theoretical and numerical information. We shall return to (6.865) and (6.87) after we have done some chores; see Sections 6.9 and 9.9.

Problem 6.871

Supposing that k is a nonzero constant, find the general solution of the equation

$$(D - k)[(D + k)y] = E_0 e^{kx} \tag{6.8711}$$

by using integrating factors in such a way that the quantity in brackets is found first and then y is found. *Ans.:* $y = (E_0/2k)xe^{kx} + c_1 e^{kx} + c_2 e^{-kx}$.
Remark: In the interesting case in which $k = i\omega$, the given equation is the equation

$$\frac{d^2y}{dx^2} + \omega^2 y = E_0 e^{i\omega x} \tag{6.8712}$$

of an undamped harmonic oscillator with a *resonant input,* that is, an input whose frequency is the natural frequency of the oscillator. The first output in the answer then has the form

$$Y = \frac{E_0}{2i\omega} xe^{i\omega x} = \frac{E_0}{2\omega} xe^{i(\omega x - \pi/2)}. \tag{6.8713}$$

This and its real and imaginary parts are amplified sinusoids with amplification factor x. The graphs are similar to that in Fig. 6.452. Perhaps this is not the time for it, but the meaning of the $-\pi/2$ in the above equation should be explained.

Problem 6.872

By the method of the previous problem, find the general solution of the equation

$$(D - k)[(D - k)y] = E_0 e^{kx} \tag{6.8721}$$

Ans.: $y = (E_0/2)x^2e^{kx} + (c_0 + c_1x)e^{kx}$.

Remark 6.873

This remark involves a modification of the work on *L-R-C* oscillators in Problem 6.67. Electrical engineers like it because, when circuits are more complex and the Kirchhoff (1824–1887) laws lead to a system of equations involving assorted charges and currents and circuit parameters (inductances, resistances, and capacitances), it simplifies their work. We start with the equation

$$L\frac{dI}{dt} + RI + \frac{Q}{C} = E(t) \tag{6.8731}$$

where I and Q are related by the formulas

$$I = \frac{dQ}{dt}, \qquad Q = Q_0 + \int_{t_0}^{t} I(s)ds. \tag{6.8732}$$

This time we do not, as in Problem 6.67, find Q and differentiate to get I; it turns out to be much better to concentrate upon I all of the time. We are now using t instead of x for the independent variable, and Dy means dy/dt. With the aid of (6.825), we can put (6.862) in the form

$$I = DQ, \qquad Q = Q_0 + D^{-1}I$$

and hence put (6.861) in the form

$$\left(LD + R + \frac{1}{CD}\right) I = E(t) - \frac{Q_0}{C}. \tag{6.8733}$$

Now D is a derivative operator (which for some strange reason or no reason at all is called a *differential operator*) and D^{-1} is an integral operator. The linear operator Λ (we can hardly call it L) defined by

$$\Lambda = LD + R + \frac{1}{CD} \tag{6.8734}$$

is called an *integro-differential operator*. When I is, as usual, viewed as the unknown function, the above differential equations are really integro-differential equations. The impedance $Z(m)$ of the operator Λ is obtained by replacing D by m and is

$$Z(m) = Lm + R + \frac{1}{Cm} \tag{6.8735}$$

when $m \neq 0$. In particular, when j is the imaginary unit as in Problem 6.67,

$$Z(j\omega) = R + j\left(\omega L - \frac{1}{\omega C}\right). \tag{6.8736}$$

This gives the ordinary impedance of an *L-R-C* oscillator without fooling around as we did in Problem 6.67.

The steady-state solution of the equation

(6.8737) $$\left(LD + R + \frac{1}{LD}\right) I = E_0 e^{j\omega t}$$

is, when $\omega > 0$, obtained by dividing by the impedance; we replace D by $j\omega$ and divide to obtain

(6.8738) $$I = \frac{E_0}{Z(j\omega)} e^{j\omega t}.$$

All applications are left to electrical engineers who handle them extraordinarily well.

Problem 6.874

Look at the formulas (6.8473) and (6.8472). Show that for the important equation

(6.8741) $$\frac{d^2y}{dx^2} + a^2y = f(x)$$

with $a \neq 0$, we have $m_1 = ia$, $m_2 = -ia$, and the general solution becomes

(6.8742) $$y = c_1e^{iax} + c_2e^{-iax} + \frac{1}{a}\int_{x_0}^{x} \sin a(x - t)f(t)dt.$$

We must now look at this and think about our general theory. We have seen over and over again that the first two terms in the output constitute the general output when there is no input. Let us call the last term $Y(x)$ so that

(6.8743) $$Y(x) = \frac{1}{a}\int_{x_0}^{x} \sin a(x - t)f(t)dt.$$

This must be the output of (6.8741) for which $Y(x_0) = Y'(x_0) = 0$. If it must be, then it is. Look at (6.8743) and tell why $Y(x_0) = 0$. Show that

$$Y'(x) = \int_{x_0}^{x} \cos a(x - t)f(t)dt$$

and tell why $Y'(x_0) = 0$. Show that

$$Y''(x) = f(x) - a\int_{x_0}^{x} \sin a(x - t)f(t)dt$$

and tell why Y satisfies (6.8741). *Remark:* While you can prepare the way for finding $Y'(x)$ and $Y''(x)$ by expanding $\sin a(x - t)$ and $\cos a(x - t)$, it is much better to use formula (6.927).

Problem 6.875

Prove that if $a > 0$, if

(6.8751) $$\frac{d^2y}{dx^2} + a^2y = f(x) \qquad x > h,$$

and if

(6.8752) $$\int_h^{\infty} |f(x)|dx < \infty,$$

then there exist constants c_1 and c_2 such that, when $x > h$,

$$y(x) = c_1e^{iax} + c_2e^{-iax} + \epsilon(x) \tag{6.8753}$$

where

$$\epsilon(x) = \frac{1}{a}\int_x^\infty \sin a(t - x)f(t)dt. \tag{6.8754}$$

You may start with (6.8751) and derive (6.8753). You may differentiate (6.8753) and verify the fact. You may do both. Under the hypothesis (6.8752), $\epsilon(x)$ is a transient because $|\sin a(t - x)| \leqq 1$ and $|\epsilon(x)| < a^{-1}\int_x^\infty |f(t)|dt$. This gives a very easy proof of the following important fact. If $a > 0$ and if $y(x)$ and $f(x)$ are real functions satisfying (6.8751) and (6.8752), then $y(x)$ must be either a transient or the sum of a nontrivial sinusoid and a transient: there exist a constant C for which $C \geqq 0$, a real phase angle δ, and a transient $\epsilon(x)$ such that

$$y(x) = C \sin (ax + \delta) + \epsilon(x). \tag{6.8755}$$

This result has obvious applications to oscillators. The following example, which can easily be modified in various ways, illustrates a more subtle application. Let A be a real constant and let $y(x)$ be a function for which

$$\frac{d^2y}{dx^2} + \left[1 + \frac{A}{x^2}\right] y = 0 \tag{6.8756}$$

when $x > 0$. Then, as is easy to guess, $y(x)$ is bounded over the interval $x \geqq 1$. After putting this equation in the form

$$\frac{d^2y}{dx^2} + y = -\frac{A}{x^2}\, y(x) \tag{6.8757}$$

we can see that the right side is a function f for which (6.8752) holds with $h = 1$ and conclude that the representation (6.8755) is possible with $a = 1$. This is interesting for the following reason. Let $y(x)$ be any of the standard Bessel functions or any other solution of the Bessel equation (7.62) of real order α. Then Problem 7.884 shows that $\sqrt{x}\, y(x)$ satisfies an equation of the form (6.8756). Therefore there exist constants C and δ and a transient $\epsilon(x)$ such that

$$y(x) = \frac{C \sin (x + \delta) + \epsilon(x)}{\sqrt{x}}. \tag{6.8758}$$

Remark 6.876

Apart from the Cauchy linear equations of Problem 6.365, relatively few linear equations with nonconstant coefficients can be usefully factored. The next two problems involve Cauchy equations.

Problem 6.877

Use the identity in Problem 6.8172 to factor the operator in

$$(x^2D^2 + 3xD + 1)y = 0$$

and solve the equation. *Ans.*: $y = (c_1 + c_2 \log x)/x$.

Problem 6.878

Apply the method of the preceding problem to solve the equation

$$(x^2D^2 + xD + 1)y = 0.$$

Ans.: See Problem 6.365.

Problem 6.879

Show that the equation

$$\frac{d^2y}{dx^2} - (1 + x^2)y = 0$$

is equivalent to the equation

$$(D + x)(D - x)y = 0$$

and obtain the general solution

$$y = c_1e^{x^2/2} + c_2e^{x^2/2}\int_0^x e^{-t^2}\,dt.$$

See Problem 6.817.

Problem 6.8791

Use the formula (8.908) to show that

(6.87911) $$\frac{1}{(D - m)^k}f(x) = e^{\alpha x}\frac{1}{(D + \alpha - m)^k}e^{-\alpha x}f(x)$$

when m and α are constants and k is a positive integer.

Problem 6.8792

Show that if $m \neq i\omega$

$$\frac{1}{D - m}e^{i\omega x} = \frac{1}{i\omega - m}e^{i\omega x} - \frac{e^{(i\omega - m)x_0}}{i\omega - m}e^{mx}.$$

Show that, if ω is real and the real part of m is negative, then the second term on the right is a transient and the first term is the steady-state solution of

$$(D - m)y = e^{i\omega x}.$$

Problem 6.8793

Verify each step in the following solution: If m_1 and m_2 are different constants, $f(x)$ is continuous and $y(x)$ is the solution of

$$(D - m_1)(D - m_2)y = f(x)$$

for which $y(x_0) = y'(x_0) = 0$, then

$$y = \frac{1}{(D - m_1)(D - m_2)}f(x) = \frac{1}{m_1 - m_2}\left(\frac{1}{D - m_1} - \frac{1}{D - m_2}\right)f(x)$$

so that

$$y = \frac{1}{m_1 - m_2}e^{m_1x}\int_{x_0}^x e^{-m_1t}f(t)dt - \frac{1}{m_1 - m_2}e^{m_2x}\int_{x_0}^x e^{-m_2t}f(t)dt.$$

Remark: This is the easy way to obtain the answer; see (6.8472) and the theory centering around it.

Problem 6.8794

It can be shown that the formula

$$\frac{1}{L_aL_b} = \left(\frac{1}{L_a}\right)\left(\frac{1}{L_b}\right) = \left(\frac{1}{L_b}\right)\left(\frac{1}{L_a}\right) = \frac{1}{L_bL_a}$$

is valid when L_a and L_b are operators of the form (6.82) having constant coefficients. Using this fact and (6.87911), prove that

$$\frac{1}{(D-m_1)^{k_1}}\frac{1}{(D-m_2)^{k_2}}f(x) = e^{\alpha x}\frac{1}{(D+\alpha-m_1)^{k_1}(D+\alpha-m_2)^{k_2}}e^{-\alpha x}f(x).$$

Show that

$$\frac{1}{(D-2)(D-3)}x^ne^{2x} = e^{2x}\frac{1}{D(D-1)}x^n.$$

Use this formula to find the particular solution of the equation

$$(D-2)(D-3)y = x^3e^{2x}$$

for which $y(0) = y'(0) = 0$. *Ans.:* $y = -(\frac{1}{4}x^4 + x^3 + 3x^2 + 6x + 6)e^{2x} + 6e^{3x}$.
(See Example 6.896.)

Problem 6.8795

Assuming that $m_1, m_2, \ldots, m_n$ are n different numbers, use the method of partial fractions to find the solution of the equation

$$(D-m_1)(D-m_2)\cdots(D-m_n)y = f(x)$$

for which $y(x_0) = y'(x_0) = \cdots = y^{((n-1)}(x_0) = 0$. *Hint:* The easiest way to find constants $A_1, A_2, \ldots, A_n$ such that

$$\frac{1}{(D-m_1)(D-m_2)\cdots(D-m_n)} = \sum_{k=1}^{n}\frac{A_k}{(D-m_k)}$$

is to regard D temporarily as being a number rather than an operator, to multiply by the denominator on the left to obtain

$$\sum_{k=1}^{n} A_k\frac{(D-m_1)(D-m_2)\cdots(D-m_n)}{(D-m_k)} = 1,$$

and then, for each k, to let $D \to m_k$ to obtain

$$A_k = \left\{\frac{D-m_k}{(D-m_1)(D-m_2)\cdots(D-m_n)}\right\}_k \qquad k = 1, 2, \ldots, n$$

where $\{\quad\}_k$ means the result of canceling the factor $(D-m_k)$ from the numerator and denominator and setting $D = m_k$ in the result; for example,

$$A_3 = \frac{1}{(m_3 - m_1)(m_3 - m_2)(m_3 - m_4)(m_3 - m_5) \cdots (m_3 - m_n)}.$$

$$Ans.: \; y = \sum_{k=1}^{n} \left\{ \frac{D - m_k}{(D - m_1)(D - m_2) \cdots (D - m_n)} \right\}_k e^{m_k x} \int_{x_0}^{x} e^{-m_k t} f(t)\,dt.$$

Problem 6.8796

Considering the case in which m_1, m_2, E, and ω are real, $m_1 \neq 0$, $m_2 \neq 0$, and $m_1 \neq m_2$, find the solution $y(x)$ of the equation

$$(D - m_1)(D - m_2)y = E \cos \omega x$$

for which $y(0) = y'(0) = 0$. *Ans.:*

$$y(x) = E \frac{m_1}{(m_1 - m_2)(m_1^2 + \omega^2)} e^{m_1 x} + E \frac{m_2}{(m_2 - m_1)(m_2^2 + \omega^2)} e^{m_2 x} + \frac{E(m_1 m_2 - \omega^2) \cos \omega x}{(m_1^2 + \omega^2)(m_2^2 + \omega^2)} - \frac{E(m_1 + m_2)\omega \sin \omega x}{(m_1^2 + \omega^2)(m_2^2 + \omega^2)}.$$

Problem 6.8797

Considering the case in which m_1, E, and ω are real and $m_1 \neq 0$, find the solution $Y(x)$ of the equation

$$(D - m_1)^2 Y = E \cos \omega x$$

for which $Y(0) = Y'(0) = 0$. *Ans.:*

$$Y = \frac{E(\omega^2 - m_1^2)}{(m_1^2 + \omega^2)^2} e^{m_1 x} + \frac{E m_1}{m_1^2 + \omega^2} x e^{m_1 x} + \frac{E(m_1^2 - \omega^2) \cos \omega x}{(m_1^2 + \omega^2)^2} - \frac{2E m_1 \omega \sin \omega x}{(m_1^2 + \omega^2)^2}.$$

Problem 6.8798

Do you believe that the answers $y(x)$ and $Y(x)$ of the two previous problems should be nearly the same when m_2 is nearly m_1? The question can be settled by proving that, when m_1, E, ω, and x are fixed, $y(x)$ converges to $Y(x)$ as $m_2 \to m_1$.

6.88. Some Special Inputs; Method of Undetermined Coefficients. Let L_a be an operator with impedance $Z(m)$ as in preceding sections. In case $p = 0$ and q is not a zero of $Z(m)$, a particular solution of the equation

$$L_a Y = E_0 x^p e^{qx} \tag{6.881}$$

is obtained so quickly and easily as in (6.63) that this section should be ignored. One reason for interest in (6.881) lies in the fact that problems of the forms

$$L_a y = E_0 x^p e^{ax} \cos bx, \qquad L_a y = E_0 x^p e^{ax} \sin bx \tag{6.8811}$$

are easily converted to it by use of complex exponentials.

We turn now to the more tedious cases in which q is a zero of the impedance or p is a positive integer or both. When L_a has been factored, (6.881) can be solved by use of operators. There are other methods that can be used when $L_aY = 0$ has been solved, but these methods also require that L_a be factored. The *method of undetermined coefficients* which we are about to present has the advantage of working when L_a has not been factored. One who doubts that this is an advantage may try to find a particular solution of the equation

$$(D^5 + 40D^4 + D^3 + D^2 + 1)Y = x^2. \tag{6.8812}$$

It is a consequence of Problem 6.818 or Theorem 6.85 that

$$(D - q)^{p+1}x^pe^{qx} = 0.$$

It follows that if Y satisfies (6.881), then

$$(D - q)^{p+1}L_aY = 0. \tag{6.8813}$$

It may happen that $(D - q)$ is a factor of L_a. If so, we let r be the multiplicity of this factor. In any case we represent L_a in the form $(D - q)^rL_b$ where $r = 0$ and $L_b = L_a$ if $(D - q)$ is not a factor of L_a. Then

$$(D - q)^{r+p+1}L_bY = 0. \tag{6.8814}$$

It follows from Theorem 6.26 that Y must be the sum of the right member of the equation

$$Y = (A_0x^r + A_1x^{r+1} + \cdots + A_px^{r+p})e^{qx} \tag{6.882}$$

and other terms which satisfy the equation $L_ay = 0$. It follows that there exist constants $A_0, A_1, \ldots, A_p$ such that the function Y in (6.882) is a particular solution of (6.881). The process of substituting (6.882) in (6.881) and determining the coefficients so that (6.881) is satisfied is known as the *method of undetermined coefficients* for finding a particular solution of (6.881).

Several of the following problems contain introductory material which shows how the r in (6.882) is determined when the method is applied.

Problem 6.883

Thinking of the operator in the left member of the equation

$$(D^5 + 40D^4 + D^3 + D^2 + 1)Y = x^2$$

as being L_a, we obtain

$$D^3L_aY = 0.$$

Since D is not a factor of L_a, the given equation must have a solution of the form

$$Y = A + Bx + Cx^2.$$

Find Y. *Ans.*: $Y = x^2 - 2$.

Observe that it is easier to check the answer than to find it.

Problem 6.884

Thinking of the operator in the left member of the equation

$$(D^5 + 40D^4 + D^3 + D^2)Y = x^2$$

as being L_a, we obtain

$$D^3L_aY = 0.$$

But this time L_a has the factor D^2, and we conclude that the given equation must have a solution of the form

$$Y = Ax^2 + Bx^3 + Cx^4.$$

Note that $c_0 + c_1x$ satisfies the homogeneous equation $L_aY = 0$ so adding $c_0 + c_1x$ to the right side would increase our labor and would not be helpful. Find Y.

Ans.: $Y = -39x^2 - \frac{1}{3}x^3 + \frac{1}{12}x^4.$

Example 6.885

To find a particular output Y of the equation

$$(D - k)(D + k)Y = E_0e^{kx}$$

in which $k \neq 0$, we observe that $Z(k) = 0$ and our easy method of finding Y does not work. Applying the above theory (or, alternatively, applying $D - k$ to both sides of the equation and working things out in the special case) shows that there is a solution of the form

$$Y = Axe^{kx}$$

where A is an undetermined coefficient. Substituting in the given equation, which we can now put in the form

$$Y'' - k^2Y = E_0e^{kx}$$

gives $A = E_0/2k$ and the solution

$$Y = (E_0/2k)xe^{kx}.$$

This agrees with the result in Problem 6.871.

Example 6.886

For the equation

$$(D - 2)(D - 3)y = x^3e^{2x} \tag{6.8861}$$

the tentative particular solution formed in accordance with the above discussion has the form

$$Y = (A_1x + A_2x^2 + A_3x^3 + A_4x^4)e^{2x}.$$

Computation of $(D - 2)(D - 3)Y$ may be systematized as follows: For each $n = 1$, 2, 3, 4,

$$(D - 3)x^ne^{2x} = (nx^{n-1} - x^n)e^{2x}$$

so that

$$(D - 3)Y = [A_1 + (2A_2 - A_1)x + (3A_3 - A_2)x^2 + (4A_4 - A_3)x^3 - A_4x^4]e^{2x}.$$

For each $n = 0, 1, 2, 3, 4$,

$$(D - 2)x^ne^{2x} = nx^{n-1}e^{2x}$$

so that

$$(D-2)(D-3)Y = [(2A_2 - A_1) + 2(3A_3 - A_2)x + 3(4A_4 - A_3)x^2 - 4A_4x^3]e^{2x}.$$

This will be x^3e^{2x} if and only if $A_4 = -\frac{1}{4}$, $A_3 = -1$, $A_2 = -3$, and $A_1 = -6$; and accordingly

$$Y = -\tfrac{1}{4}(24x + 12x^2 + 4x^3 + x^4)e^{2x}.$$

The general solution of the homogeneous equation corresponding to (6.8861) is

$$c_1e^{2x} + c_2e^{3x},$$

and accordingly the general solution of (6.8861) is

$$y = -\tfrac{1}{4}(24x + 12x^2 + 4x^3 + x^4)e^{2x} + c_1e^{2x} + c_2e^{3x}$$

(see Example 6.896).

Problem 6.887

Find particular solutions of the following equations; if you are not sure your answers are correct, check them.

(*a*) $(D^2 + 1)y = e^{ax}$
(*b*) $(D^2 + 1)y = xe^{ax}$
(*c*) $(D^2 + 1)y = x^2e^{ax}$
(*d*) $(D^2 + 1)y = x$
(*e*) $(D^2 + 1)y = x \sin x$
(*f*) $(D^2 + 1)y = e^{-x} \sin x$
(*g*) $(D^2 + 1)y = xe^{-x} \sin x$
(*h*) $(D^2 + 4D + 4)y = e^{-x}$
(*i*) $(D^2 + 4D + 4)y = e^{-2x}$
(*j*) $Dy = x$
(*k*) $Dy = e^{ax} \sin bx$
(*l*) $Dy = x^2e^{ax} \cos bx$

6.89. Variation of Parameters. A special method of obtaining solutions of a nonhomogeneous equation $L_ay = f$, after the homogeneous equation $L_ay = 0$ has been solved, is known as the method of *variation of parameters*. This method is used in cases where the coefficients in the operator L_a are nonconstant functions of x as well as when they are constant. When $n = 2$, the method is equivalent to the methods in Problems 6.191 and 6.1918, but the details look quite different. The method provides a way of generalizing (6.1917) from equations of order 2 to equations of order n.

Let the equation to be solved have the form

(6.891) $$L_ay = (a_0D^n + a_1D^{n-1} + \cdots + a_{n-1}D + a_n)y = f$$

where the a's are continuous and $a_0 \neq 0$, and let the general solution of the homogeneous equation $L_ay = 0$ be

(6.892) $$y = c_1y_1(x) + c_2y_2(x) + \cdots + c_ny_n(x) \equiv \Sigma c_ky_k.$$

The stratagem of the method under discussion is that of replacing the constants (or parameters) $c_1, c_2, \ldots, c_n$ by functions $\gamma_1, \gamma_2, \ldots, \gamma_n$ of x and determining these functions in such a way that

$$y = \gamma_1 y_1(x) + \gamma_2 y_2(x) + \cdots + \gamma_n y_n(x) = \Sigma \gamma_k y_k \tag{6.893}$$

will be a solution of $L_a y = f$. The procedure is motivated by the optimistic principles that one should make one's work as simple as possible and that a set of n functions can be found which satisfies n conditions.

With the γ's as yet undetermined but assumed to have all the derivatives we want to use, let y be defined by (6.893). Then for each x

$$Dy = \Sigma \gamma_k y_k' + \Sigma \gamma_k' y_k$$

where primes denote derivatives with respect to x. To simplify further work, let the γ's be required to satisfy the condition $\Sigma \gamma_k' y_k = 0$. Then

$$D^2 y = \Sigma \gamma_k y_k'' + \Sigma \gamma_k' y_k'.$$

If $n > 2$, we simplify further work by demanding that $\Sigma \gamma_k' y_k' = 0$ and then obtain

$$D^3 y = \Sigma \gamma_k y_k''' + \Sigma \gamma_k' y_k''.$$

This procedure is continued until we have required

$$\Sigma \gamma_k' y_k^{(\nu)} = 0 \qquad \nu = 0, 1, \ldots, n-2 \tag{6.894}$$

and have obtained

$$D^\nu y = \Sigma \gamma_k y_k^{(\nu)} \qquad \nu = 0, 1, \ldots, n-1 \tag{6.8941}$$

$$D^n y = \Sigma \gamma_k y_k^{(n)} + \Sigma \gamma_k' y_k^{(n-1)}. \tag{6.8942}$$

We then find that

$$\begin{aligned} L_a y &= \sum_{\nu=0}^{n} a_{n-\nu} D^\nu y = \sum_{\nu=0}^{n} a_{n-\nu} \sum_{k=1}^{n} \gamma_k y_k^{(\nu)} + a_0 \sum_{k=1}^{n} \gamma_k' y_k^{(n-1)} \\ &= \sum_{k=1}^{n} \gamma_k \sum_{\nu=0}^{n} a_{n-\nu} y_k^{(\nu)} + a_0 \sum_{k=1}^{n} \gamma_k' y_k^{(n-1)} \\ &= \sum_{k=1}^{n} \gamma_k L_a y_k + a_0 \sum_{k=1}^{n} \gamma_k' y_k^{(n-1)} = a_0 \sum_{k=1}^{n} \gamma_k' y_k^{(n-1)}, \end{aligned}$$

the last step being justified by the fact that $L_a y_k = 0$ for each k. It thus appears that if the γ's satisfy the $n - 1$ equations (6.894) and the additional equation

$$\sum_{k=1}^{n} \gamma_k' y_k^{(n-1)} = \frac{f}{a_0}, \tag{6.8943}$$

then $L_a y$ will be f; *i.e.*, the function y defined by (6.893) will be a solution of $L_a y = f$. These equations are

$$\text{(6.895)} \quad \begin{cases} y_1\gamma_1' + y_2\gamma_2' + \cdots + y_n\gamma_n' = 0 \\ y_1'\gamma_1' + y_2'\gamma_2' + \cdots + y_n'\gamma_n' = 0 \\ \cdots\cdots\cdots\cdots\cdots\cdots\cdots\cdots \\ y_1^{(n-2)}\gamma_1' + y_2^{(n-2)}\gamma_2' + \cdots + y_n^{(n-2)}\gamma_n' = 0 \\ y_1^{(n-1)}\gamma_1' + y_2^{(n-1)}\gamma_2' + \cdots + y_n^{(n-1)}\gamma_n' = \dfrac{f}{a_0}. \end{cases}$$

As Chapter 16 will show, the determinant W of the coefficients of the unknown functions γ_k' is the Wronskian of $y_1, y_2, \ldots, y_n$ and hence is never zero. Therefore functions γ_k' and γ_k can be found which satisfy (6.895), and putting them in (6.893) gives the answer to our problem.

Example 6.896

To solve the equation

$$\text{(6.8961)} \qquad (D-2)(D-3)y = x^3e^{2x}$$

by the method of variation of parameters, we observe that the general solution of the homogeneous equation is

$$\text{(6.8962)} \qquad Y_1 = c_1e^{2x} + c_2e^{3x}.$$

The stratagem is to determine functions γ_1 and γ_2 such that

$$\text{(6.8963)} \qquad y = \gamma_1e^{2x} + \gamma_2e^{3x}$$

will be a solution of (6.8961). We find

$$\text{(6.8964)} \qquad Dy = 2\gamma_1e^{2x} + 3\gamma_2e^{3x} + (\gamma_1'e^{2x} + \gamma_2'e^{3x}).$$

Imposing the condition

$$\text{(6.8965)} \qquad \gamma_1'e^{2x} + \gamma_2'e^{3x} = 0$$

on the γ's we find

$$\text{(6.8966)} \qquad D^2y = 4\gamma_1e^{2x} + 9\gamma_2e^{3x} + 2\gamma_1'e^{2x} + 3\gamma_2'e^{3x}.$$

Since $(D-2)(D-3) = D^2 - 5D + 6$, we can multiply (6.8963), (6.8964), and (6.8966), respectively, by 6, -5, and 1 and then add to obtain

$$(D-2)(D-3)y = 2\gamma_1'e^{2x} + 3\gamma_2'e^{3x}.$$

Therefore (6.8963) will be a solution of (6.8961) if (6.8965) holds and

$$\text{(6.8967)} \qquad 2\gamma_1'e^{2x} + 3\gamma_2'e^{3x} = x^3e^{2x}.$$

Solving (6.8965) and (6.8967) for γ_1' and γ_2', we obtain

$$\text{(6.8968)} \qquad \gamma_1' = -x^3, \qquad \gamma_2' = x^3e^{-x}.$$

Integration gives

$$\gamma_1 = -\tfrac{1}{4}x^4 + c', \qquad \gamma_2 = -(x^3 + 3x^2 + 6x + 6)e^{-x} + c'',$$

and substitution in (6.8963) gives

$$y = -\tfrac{1}{4}(x^4 + 4x^3 + 12x^2 + 24x)e^{2x} + c_1e^{2x} + c_2e^{3x}$$

as the general solution of (6.8961) (see Example 6.886).

Problem 6.897

Solve, by the method of variation of parameters,

(a) $y'' + y = \sec x$ *Ans.:* $y = (c_1 + \log\cos x)\cos x + (c_2 + x)\sin x$
(b) $y'' + y = \cot x$ *Ans.:* $y = c_1\cos x + (c_2 + \log\tan\tfrac{1}{2}x)\sin x$

Problem 6.898

Derive the formula (6.1917) by the method of variation of parameters.

6.9. Faltungs. We begin by recalling a fact involving (6.87). To each operator L_a defined as usual by

$$L_a = a_0D^n + a_1D^{n-1} + \cdots + a_{n-1}D + a_n \tag{6.901}$$

there corresponds a function $y_0(x)$ defined by (6.865) such that the unique solution $y = L_a^{-1} f$ of the equation $L_ay = f$ for which

$$y(x_0) = y'(x_0) = y''(x_0) = \cdots = y^{(n-1)}(x_0) = 0 \tag{6.902}$$

has the form

$$y(x) = \int_{x_0}^{x} y_0(x - t)f(t)dt. \tag{6.91}$$

It often happens, outside as well as inside the theory of differential equations, that an input f and an output y are related by this important formula. The integral is called the *faltung* or *convolution* or *resultant* or *superposition integral* of y_0 and f. It is a good idea to have an understanding of rough ideas such as the following. If $y_0(s)$ is never very big and approaches 0 rapidly as s increases, then reasonable inputs never produce big outputs and the output at time x depends principally upon inputs in short intervals preceding x. In some situations, the function y_0 is completely known and finding the output corresponding to a given input is then merely a matter of evaluating an integral having a known integrand. This happy situation can arise, for example, when y_0 is given by (6.865) and we have enough information to enable us to get a useful formula or approximation for y_0. In other situations it is known that there is a function y_0 such that inputs f and outputs y are related by (6.91), but information about y_0 is meager or totally absent.

Our situation, in which $y_0(x)$ is defined by (6.865), is a curious one. In all except the simplest situations, it is very hard to get good quantitative information about $y_0(x)$ from (6.865). Sometimes it is quite impossible because good estimates of the coefficients in L_a are not known and there is no possibility of getting good estimates of the zeros of the impedance of L_a that are in (6.865). It turns out, however, that (6.865) is always very valuable. It tells us that the function $y_0(x)$ is an *entire function*. This means that, even when the variable x in (6.865) is regarded as a complex variable, $y_0(x)$ has derivatives of all orders for all values of x.

The fact that $y_0(x)$ is an entire function allows authorities on faltungs to draw very many important conclusions, and we pause to give a sample. Suppose that (6.91) holds and that y_1 is an output due to another input f_1. Then

(6.911) $$y(x) - y_1(x) = \int_{x_0}^{x} y_0(x - t)[f(t) - f_1(t)]dt.$$

Suppose that $x_0 < x_1$ and we are interested in values of x for which $x_0 \leqq x \leqq x_1$. The fact that $y_0(x)$ is entire in itself implies that it is bounded over each finite interval and that we can choose a constant B such that $|y_0(x - t)| \leqq B$ whenever $x_0 \leqq t \leqq x$ and $x_0 \leqq x \leqq x_1$. It then follows from (6.911) that

(6.912) $$|y(x) - y_1(x)| \leq \int_{x_0}^{x} B|f(t) - f_1(t)|dt$$

and hence

(6.913) $$|y(x) - y_1(x)| \leqq B \int_{x_0}^{x_1} |f(t) - f_1(t)|dt$$

whenever $x_0 \leqq x \leqq x_1$. Since B is a fixed constant, this tells us that if we take $f_1(x)$ close enough to $f(x)$ to make the last integral small enough (note that this does not require that $f_1(t)$ be near $f(t)$ everywhere), then the two outputs $y(x)$ and $y_1(x)$ will be nearly the same for all values of x in the interval $x_0 \leqq x \leqq x_1$. This shows that we change outputs very little when we make adjustments in inputs such as the following: (i) an input which starts at 0 when $t = 0$ rises continuously but very quickly to 5 and then stays 5 is replaced by an input which is 5 when $t \geqq 0$; and (ii) a periodic input is replaced by a sum of some of its harmonics. If $f_1(x), f_2(x), \ldots$ is a sequence of inputs for which

(6.914) $$\lim_{k\to\infty} \int_{x_1}^{x_2} |f(x) - f_k(x)|dx = 0,$$

then we can replace $f_1(x)$ by $f_k(x)$ in (6.913) and draw the conclusion that the sequence of outputs $y_1(x), y_2(x), \ldots$ converges to $y(x)$ uniformly over $x_0 \leqq x \leqq x_1$. Such information is very useful.

In the preceding paragraph, we have used the faltung formula to obtain proofs that small changes in inputs produce small changes in outputs. By use of the Faltung formula and the formula (6.865) defining $y_0(x)$ it is possible to prove that, when a finite interval $x_1 \leqq x \leqq x_2$ is specified, small changes in the coefficients $a_0, a_1, \ldots, a_n$ produce small changes in $y_0(x)$ and hence in the output due to a given input during that interval. This matter is important because in numerical applications to specific practical problems, one never quite knows what the coefficients are. For example, even resistors with gold bands have 5 per cent tolerances.

We now obtain some information about our function $y_0(x)$.

THEOREM 6.92. *The function $y_0(x)$ in* (6.865) *and* (6.91) *is the unique function for which*

(6.921) $$L_a y_0 = 0$$

and

(6.922) $$y_0(0) = y_0'(0) = \cdots = y_0^{(n-2)}(0) = 0, \qquad y^{(n-1)}(0) = \frac{1}{a_0}.$$

According to Theorem 6.03 there is a unique function $y_0(x)$ satisfying (6.921) and (6.922), and we must show that the function $y_0(x)$ defined by (6.865) is it. From (6.862) and (6.865), we see that $L_a y_0 = 0$. The rest of the proof is a little tricky. We start by letting f_0 be the function for which $f_0(x) = 1$ for all values of x and let

(6.923) $$F = \frac{1}{L_a} f_0$$

so that $L_a F = f_0$, *i.e.*,

(6.924) $$a_0 F^{(n)}(x) + a_1 F^{(n-1)}(x) + \cdots + a_{n-1}F'(x) + a_n F(x) = 1$$

and

(6.925) $$F(x_0) = F'(x_0) = \cdots = F^{(n-1)}(x_0) = 0$$

in accordance with the definition of $1/L_a$. Putting these functions in (6.91) gives

(6.926) $$F(x) = \int_{x_0}^{x} y_0(x - t)\,dt.$$

Everybody should know the formula

(6.927) $$\frac{d}{dx}\int_{a(x)}^{b(x)} G(x, t)\,dt = b'(x)G(x, b(x)) - a'(x)G(x, a(x)) + \int_{a(x)}^{b(x)} \frac{\partial}{\partial x} G(x, t)\,dt$$

or learn about it at the first opportunity from a textbook on advanced calculus. This is a standard formula for *differentiation of integrals;* indexes can probably tell you where it is in this and other books. The fact that y_0 is entire justifies application of this formula to (6.926) and we obtain

$$F'(x) = y_0(0) + \int_{x_0}^{x} y_0'(x - t)dt. \tag{6.928}$$

More differentiations give

$$F^{(k)}(x) = y^{(k-1)}(0) + \int_{x_0}^{x} y^{(k)}(x - t)dt \tag{6.929}$$

for each $k = 2, 3, \ldots$. We are now almost done. Putting $x = x_0$ in (6.928) and using (6.925) gives $y_0(0) = 0$. Similarly, for each $k = 2, 3, \ldots, n - 1$, putting $x = x_0$ in (6.929) and using (6.925) gives $y^{(k-1)}(0) = 0$. Finally, putting $k = n$ and $x = x_0$ in (6.929) gives $F^{(n)}(x_0) = y^{(n-1)}(x_0)$. But putting $x = x_0$ in (6.924) and using (6.925) gives $a_0F^{(n)}(x_0) = 1$. Hence $y^{(n-1)}(x_0) = 1/a_0$ and our proof of Theorem 6.92 is complete.

Theorem 6.92 puts us in an interesting situation. If, by some method which may be very laborious, we can calculate or approximate the function $y_0(x)$ in Theorem 6.92, then we can put this function in (6.91) and have a formula from which outputs due to given inputs can be calculated by evaluating integrals.

As we have remarked, it often happens, outside as well as inside the theory of differential equations, that an input f and an output y are related by the Faltung formula

$$y(x) = \int_{x_0}^{x} y_0(x - t)f(t)dt; \tag{6.93}$$

this is (6.91) brought up where we can see it. We now discuss a powerful method by which calculations or experiments are made to determine or approximate y_0 so that y_0 is available for other calculations. This method involves impulses, which are thoroughly discussed in Section 9.5. Physicists and engineers say they have an *impulse* when they have an input of large magnitude but small duration. Blows from a hammer and strokes of lightning provide examples. The exact nature of the input is both unknown and unimportant; the important thing is the integral of the input over the interval of its duration, this being the *magnitude* of the impulse. While other approximations can be used, it is often simplest and best to describe the input f_h of a unit impulse, in terms of an x_0 and small positive number h, by the formula

$$\begin{aligned} f_h(t) &= 0 & t &\leqq x_0 \\ f_h(t) &= h^{-1} & x_0 < t &\leqq x_0 + h \\ f_h(t) &= 0 & t &> x_0 + h. \end{aligned} \tag{6.931}$$

From (6.931) we see that the output $Y_h(x)$ due to the impulsive input f_h

is 0 when $x < x_0$ and is

$$Y_h(x) = \frac{1}{h}\int_{x_0}^{x_0+h} y_0(x - t)dt \tag{6.932}$$

when $x > x_0 + h$. Assuming that $y_0(s)$ is continuous, the mean value theorem of the integral calculus implies that

$$y_0(x - x_0) = \lim_{h\to 0} Y_h(x). \tag{6.933}$$

Hence we can determine $y_0(s)$ or an approximation to it by calculating the limit in (6.933) or by observing $Y_h(x)$ when h is a fixed small number and x increases.

Remark 6.94

Those who undertake to do more than the most ordinary things with integral transformations, of which the Faltung transformation is an example, should be or become authorities on Stieltjes (1856–1894) integrals. The *Stieltjes integral* in the right member of the equation

$$I = \int_a^b f(x)dg\,(x) \tag{6.941}$$

is said to exist and to have the value I if to each $\epsilon > 0$ there corresponds to a $\delta > 0$ such that

$$\left| I - \sum_{k=1}^{n} f(\xi_k)[g(x_k) - g(x_{k-1})] \right| < \epsilon \tag{6.942}$$

whenever $a = x_0 < x_1 < x_2 < \cdots < x_n = b$, $|x_{k+1} - x_k| < \delta$ for each k, and $x_{k-1} \leqq \xi_k \leqq x_k$ for each k. This definition shows that Stieltjes integrals are very simple generalizations of the Riemann integrals to which they reduce when $g(x) = x$. Many branches of pure and applied mathematics require knowledge of them. In terms of Stieltjes integrals, the Faltung formula (6.93) can be put in the form

$$y(x) = \int_0^x y_0(x - t)d\int_{x_0}^t f(s)ds. \tag{6.943}$$

This has the form

$$y(s) = \int_0^x y_0(x - t)dF\,(t) \tag{6.944}$$

where $F(t)$ is the absolutely continuous function $\int_{x_0}^t f(s)ds$. The next step is to extend the domain of (6.944) by allowing F to be any function having bounded variation over each finite interval. In one sense those who use (6.944) have the same advantage over those who use (6.93) that modern men who use the complete real number system have over their remote ancestors who floundered around with only rational numbers. Thus we need more mathematics for profound studies of faltungs. See Section 9.5

Problem 6.95

+ Should we expect faltungs to appear in formulas for outputs of differential equations whose coefficients are not constants? *Ans.:* No. According to (3.17), the critical output of the little equation

$$\frac{dy}{dx} + p(x)y = f(x)$$

is

$$y(x) = \int_{x_0}^{x} e^{-[P(x)-P(t)]}f(t)dt$$

where $P(x) = \int_{x_0}^{x} p(s)ds$. In case $p(x)$ is a constant h we have $P(x) = h(x - x_0)$ and we obtain the attractive faltung

$$y(x) = \int_{x_0}^{x} e^{-h(x-t)}f(t)dt.$$

In other cases, the best we can do is obtain the less informative formula

$$y(x) = \int_{x_0}^{x} K(x, t)f(t)dt$$

where the *kernel* $K(x, t)$ has values determined by x and t but not by $x - t$.

6.96. Systems of Equations. Systems containing two or more ordinary differential equations involving the same number of unknown functions occur frequently in mechanical and electrical problems. It is quite impossible to give rules for best attacks upon a system until we know what the system is and what we want to do with it. Suppose

$$\text{(6.961)} \qquad \begin{aligned} \frac{dy_1}{dx} &= a_{11}y_1 + a_{12}y_2 - f_1(x) \\ \frac{dy_2}{dx} &= a_{21}y_1 + a_{22}y_2 - f_2(x) \end{aligned}$$

where the a's are given constants and the f's are given functions. Sometimes it is desirable to put this system in the form

$$\text{(6.9611)} \qquad \begin{aligned} (a_{11} - D)y_1 + \qquad a_{12}y_2 &= f_1(x) \\ a_{21}y_1 + (a_{22} - D)y_2 &= f_2(x). \end{aligned}$$

This system and many others can be put in the form

$$\text{(6.962)} \qquad \begin{aligned} L_{11}y_1 + L_{12}y_2 &= f_1(x) \\ L_{21}y_1 + L_{22}y_2 &= f_2(x) \end{aligned}$$

where each of the L's is a linear operator of the form

$$\text{(6.9621)} \qquad a_0D^n + a_1D^{n-1} + \cdots + a_{n-1}D + a_n$$

in which n as well as $a_0, a_1, \ldots, a_n$ may be different for the different operators. Since the constant a_{12} in (6.9611) may be 0, we must admit the possibility that L_{12}, for example, may be the *null operator* for which all of the a's in (6.9621) are 0. Sometimes, but not always, it is a good idea to pause to recognize that each pair $y_1(x)$, $y_2(x)$ of functions satisfying (6.962) is the sum of a pair of functions satisfying the equations

$$\begin{aligned} L_{11}y_1 + L_{12}y_2 &= f_1(x) \\ L_{21}y_1 + L_{22}y_2 &= 0 \end{aligned} \tag{6.9622}$$

and a pair satisfying the equations

$$\begin{aligned} L_{11}y_1 + L_{12}y_2 &= 0 \\ L_{21}y_1 + L_{22}y_2 &= f_2(x). \end{aligned} \tag{6.9623}$$

Sometimes, but not always, the solutions of the homogeneous equations

$$\begin{aligned} L_{11}y_1 + L_{12}y_2 &= 0 \\ L_{21}y_1 + L_{22}y_2 &= 0 \end{aligned} \tag{6.9624}$$

are transients and we are not required to bother with them.

Before we go to work with useful systems, we can observe that strange things can happen in special cases. If L_{11}, L_{12}, L_{21}, and L_{22} are all null operators and $f_1(x)$ is never 0, then no pair of functions can satisfy (6.9622) and every pair satisfies (6.9624). If $L_{21} = L_{11}$, $L_{22} = L_{12}$, and $f_1(x)$ is never 0, then no pair can satisfy (6.9622). There can be no doubt that matrices and determinants are essential for general discussions of these matters, but simpler methods are preferred when solving specific numerical systems containing more than two equations.

We now try to pick up some ideas about problems of three different types. For simplicity, we confine attention to the simple systems written above. The ideas, however, are applicable to systems containing more equations. Moreover, some or all of the operators L_{rs} may be integro-differential operators like that in (6.8734).

TYPE A

Suppose that the solutions of (6.9624) are all transients, that

$$f_1(x) = E_1e^{i\omega_1x},$$

and that we are required to find the steady-state solution of (6.9622). Letting Z_{rs} be the impedance of the operator L_{rs}, we apply the operators L_{22} and $-L_{12}$ to the first and second equations in (6.9622) and add the results to eliminate y_2 and obtain

$$(L_{22}L_{11} - L_{12}L_{21})y_1 = E_1Z_{22}(i\omega_1)e^{i\omega_1x}.$$

The operator in the left member is the determinant of the operators in (6.9622). Letting Z be the impedance of this operator and supposing that $Z(i\omega_1) \neq 0$, we apply (6.65) to obtain the first of the formulas

$$y_1 = E_1\frac{Z_{22}(i\omega_1)}{Z(i\omega_1)}e^{i\omega_1x}, \qquad y_2 = E_1\frac{-Z_{21}(i\omega_1)}{Z(i\omega_1)}e^{i\omega_1x}. \tag{6.963}$$

A similar procedure gives the second. Substituting (6.963) in (6.9622) shows that the equations are satisfied. We can put the impedance and their quotients in polar form so we can see the amplitudes and phases of y_1 and y_2. It is important to observe that all this is done without finding the zeros of impedances. The result is significant. It shows that the outputs due to a single sinusoidal input of angular frequency ω_1 are, except for transients, sinusoids having the same frequency; but the amplitudes and phases depend upon the nature of the system. Problems involving periodic but nonsinusoidal inputs are usefully solved by replacing the inputs by sums of harmonics as in Section 6.7.

TYPE B

Problems of this type require us to find the general solution of the system (6.962). Of course this system reduces to the homogeneous system (6.9624) when $f_1 = f_2 = 0$. Two ponderous and powerful methods for solving problems of this type, the Heaviside and Laplace methods, will appear when we discuss problems of type C. We now discuss a much simpler method which sometimes works when the Laplace method does not and often brings results more quickly than any other method.

Assuming that y_1 and y_2 constitute a pair of functions satisfying (6.962) we can, as for problems of type A, apply operators and algebra to (6.962) to obtain the equations

$$(6.964)\qquad \begin{aligned} (L_{11}L_{22} - L_{12}L_{21})y_1 &= L_{22}f_1 - L_{12}f_2 \\ (L_{11}L_{22} - L_{12}L_{21})y_2 &= -L_{21}f_1 + L_{11}f_2, \end{aligned}$$

provided f_1 and f_2 are such that the right members exist. The operator L in the left members may be null, it may be a nonzero constant, or it may have the form L_a to which this chapter has been devoted. The first two possibilities are easily handled. In the third case, we put the system in the form

$$(6.9641)\qquad L_a y_1 = g_1, \qquad L_a y_2 = g_2$$

and conclude that

$$(6.9642)\qquad \begin{aligned} y_1(x) &= c_1u_1(x) + c_2u_2(x) + \cdots + c_nu_n(x) + Y_1(x) \\ y_2(x) &= d_1u_1(x) + d_2u_2(x) + \cdots + d_nu_n(x) + Y_2(x) \end{aligned}$$

where $u_1(x), u_2(x), \ldots, u_n(x)$ are independent solutions of the equation $L_a y = 0$ as in Theorem 6.26, where $Y_1(x)$ and $Y_2(x)$ are particular solutions of (6.9641) and where the c's and d's are constants. Thus, under the assumption that y_1 and y_2 satisfy (6.962), we obtain (6.9642). This does not imply that all of the pairs of functions defined by (6.9642) actually satisfy (6.962); we must substitute in (6.962) to find which ones of them do.* Our problem will then be solved. Examples 6.965 and 6.966 will show that this method, which we shall call the method involving (6.964), can sometimes be modified to simplify the work.

Example 6.965

We illustrate some points by considering the special system

$$\begin{aligned}(D+1)y_1 + Dy_2 &= 2e^x\\ Dy_1 + Dy_2 &= e^x.\end{aligned}$$

Of course everybody should eliminate y_2 by a simple subtraction and obtain $y_1 = e^x$. Then $Dy_2 = 0$ and $y_2 = c$. Thus each pair y_1, y_2 of solutions must have the form $y_1 = e^x$, $y_2 = c$. It is easily seen that each such pair satisfies the given system, and our problem is solved. Matters are not so simple when we blindly follow the ritual involving (6.964). For our example, (6.964) becomes

$$(D^2 + D - D^2)y_1 = e^x, \qquad (D^2 + D - D^2)y_2 = 0.$$

From this we draw the correct conclusion that each solution of our system has the form $y_1 = e^x + c_1$, $y_2 = c_2$. However substituting shows that this pair of functions satisfies the system of equations only when $c_1 = 0$ and we obtain the correct answer.

Example 6.966

Supposing that y_1, y_2 satisfy the system

$$\begin{aligned}Dy_1 + y_2 &= 0\\ y_1 + Dy_2 &= 0\end{aligned}$$

and eliminating y_2 give $(D^2 - 1)y_1 = 0$ and hence $y_1 = c_1e^x + c_2e^{-x}$. It is clearly unwise to obtain another differential equation and new constants involving y_2 when the first equation in the system says so clearly that $y_2 = -Dy_1$ and hence $y_2 = -c_1e^x + c_2e^{-x}$. Substitution shows that y_1, y_2 satisfy the system for each pair c_1, c_2 of constants.

Problem 6.967

Show that the homogeneous equations

$$\begin{aligned}(a_{11} - D)y_1 + \qquad a_{12}y_2 &= 0\\ a_{21}y_1 + (a_{22} - D)y_2 &= 0\end{aligned} \tag{6.9671}$$

corresponding to (6.961) and (6.9611) have nontrivial periodic solutions if and only if $a_{22} = -a_{11}$ and $a_{12}a_{21} \leqq -a_{11}^2$.

* As a matter of fact, it is a straightforward matter to solve problems with no more theory than this. What happens when we do the substituting can, in practical problems, be known after the substituting has been done. However a mathematical theory is often presumed to be very shabby when it tells us to substitute and see what will happen; it is presumed that a good theory should tell us what will happen when we substitute. After the following examples and problems, we shall give a much more satisfactory mathematical approach to homogeneous systems. Whether all this helps a particular individual when he solves a particular problem may depend upon the individual and upon the problem.

Problem 6.968

Supposing that the constants in (6.9671) are real, show that the solutions are all transients if and only if $a_{22} < -a_{11}$ and $a_{12}a_{21} < a_{11}a_{22}$.

The work involved in determining which ones of the tentative solutions (6.9642) actually satisfy (6.962) leads to the following fact. If the homogeneous system

$$\begin{aligned} L_{11}y_1 + L_{12}y_2 &= 0 \\ L_{21}y_1 + L_{22}y_2 &= 0 \end{aligned} \tag{6.97}$$

has any nontrivial solutions, then it has solutions of the form

$$y_1 = Ae^{mx}, \qquad y_2 = Be^{mx} \tag{6.971}$$

where A, B, and m are constants for which A and B are not both 0. This suggests that we can start solving (6.97) by seeking solutions of the form (6.971). This idea is exceptionally valuable. Letting Z_{rs} denote the impedance of L_{rs}, we see that (6.971) satisfies (6.97) if and only if

$$\begin{aligned} Z_{11}(m)A + Z_{12}(m)B &= 0 \\ Z_{21}(m)A + Z_{22}(m)B &= 0. \end{aligned} \tag{6.972}$$

Let $Z(m)$ denote the determinant of the coefficients of A and B in (6.972), so that

$$Z(m) = Z_{11}(m)Z_{22}(m) \qquad Z_{12}(m)Z_{21}(m), \tag{6.973}$$

and leave aside the trivial cases in which $Z(m)$ is independent of m so that $Z(m)$ is a polynomial in m of positive degree n having zeros m_1, m_2, $\ldots$, m_n. Remark 4.292 shows that equations (6.972) have nontrivial solutions for A and B if and only if m is one of the numbers m_k. In case $m = m_k$, the equations have a nontrivial solution, say A_k, B_k, for A and B. We can pause to note that this attack upon (6.97) brings significant results very quickly. In case $m_k = i\omega_k$, and perhaps even when $m_k = b_k + i\omega_k$ and $b_k < 0$, the functions

$$y_1 = A_ke^{m_kx}, \qquad y_2 = B_ke^{m_kx}$$

constitute a normal solution or *normal mode* of the system (6.97) and the number ω_k is a *normal* (angular) *frequency* of the system. In the terminology of classical astronomy, the equation $Z(m) = 0$, whose solutions are the normal frequencies, is the *secular equation* of the system. Now comes the awkward part of the story and the reason why details must be handled carefully. Whether A_k and B_k must satisfy a relation such as $A_k = 2B_k$ (as usually happens) or are arbitrary (as sometimes happens) depends upon the nature of the collection or *matrix* of numbers Z_{rs} in (6.972). It is necessary to know about theories of matrices and independence to talk intelligibly about this problem. For present purposes, we suppose that we are dealing with a special case and have discovered the facts about A_k and B_k; at least one of A_k and B_k is arbitrary and the other is expressed in terms of this arbitrary one whenever this is necessary. In case the zeros $m_1, m_2, \ldots, m_k$ of Z are distinct, we obtain the solutions

$$\begin{aligned} y_1(x) &= A_1e^{m_1x} + A_2e^{m_2x} + \cdots + A_ne^{m_nx} \\ y_2(x) &= B_1e^{m_1x} + B_2e^{m_2x} + \cdots + B_ne^{m_nx} \end{aligned} \tag{6.974}$$

of (6.97), and our work involving (6.964) shows that these are the only solutions. Each solution of (6.97) is then a sum of special solutions constituting normal modes. This is very important, and those who study engineering and classical or atomic physics find the reasons.

In case the zeros of $Z(m)$ are not distinct, the work involving (6.964) shows that functions of the form $x^pe^{m_kx}$, with $p > 0$, enter the game and the theory is completed with attention to these details. If, for example, $m_2 = m_1$, the first two terms of the right members of (6.974) would be $(A_1 + A_2x)e^{m_1x}$ and $(B_1 + B_2x)e^{m_1x}$ and the question of relations between these A's and B's would require an answer.

Remark 6.98

When the homogeneous system (6.97) corresponding to the system

$$\begin{aligned} L_{11}y_1 + L_{12}y_2 &= f_1(x) \\ L_{21}y_1 + L_{22}y_2 &= f_2(x) \end{aligned} \tag{6.981}$$

is solved by the method following (6.97), our work produces no information about solutions of (6.981). When f_1 and f_2 have enough derivatives, we can get our information by the method involving (6.964). While there are often better ways to solve problems, we give an example to illustrate the fact that the method of *variation of parameters* can be used to solve (6.981) when the corresponding homogeneous system has been solved. When the method is applied to systems of first-order equations, the application is simplified by the fact that the parameters need not (and cannot) be required to satisfy supplementary conditions such as the conditions (6.894) which appeared when the method was applied to a single equation of higher order.

To illustrate the fact that equations of higher order and systems of such equations can be reduced to systems of first-order equations, we start with the equation

$$y''(x) + y(x) = f(x) \tag{6.982}$$

where $f(x)$ is assumed to be integrable over each finite interval. On setting $y_1(x) = y(x)$ and $y_2(x) = y'(x)$ we obtain the system

$$\begin{aligned} y_1'(x) - y_2(x) &= 0 \\ y_1(x) + y_2'(x) &= f(x) \end{aligned} \tag{6.983}$$

which we proceed to solve by the method of variation of parameters. We readily find the general solution

$$\begin{aligned} y_1 &= c_1e^{ix} + c_2e^{-ix} \\ y_2 &= ic_1e^{ix} - ic_2e^{-ix} \end{aligned}$$

of the homogeneous system. The idea of the method is to replace the parameters c_1 and c_2 by functions $v_1(x)$ and $v_2(x)$ and to determine these functions so that

$$\begin{aligned} y_1 &= v_1e^{ix} + v_2e^{-ix} \\ y_2 &= iv_1e^{ix} - iv_2e^{-ix} \end{aligned} \tag{6.984}$$

will satisfy (6.983). Differentiation and substitution show that (6.983) is satisfied iff (if and only if)

$$\begin{aligned} v_1'e^{ix} + v_2'e^{-ix} &= 0 \\ v_1'e^{ix} - v_2'e^{-ix} &= -if(x) \end{aligned} \tag{6.985}$$

and hence, iff

$$\begin{aligned} v_1(x) &= c_1 - \frac{i}{2}\int_0^x f(t)e^{-it}\,dt \\ v_2(x) &= c_2 + \frac{i}{2}\int_0^x f(t)e^{it}\,dt \end{aligned}$$

and hence, iff

$$\begin{aligned} y_1 &= c_1e^{ix} + c_2e^{-ix} + \int_0^x f(t)\sin(x-t)dt \\ y_2 &= ic_1e^{ix} - ic_2e^{-ix} + \int_0^x f(t)\cos(x-t)dt. \end{aligned} \tag{6.986}$$

Thus this is the general solution of (6.983), and putting $c_1 = c_2 = 0$ gives the particular solution for which $y_1(0) = y_2(0) = 0$.

Finally, we remark that the method of variation of parameters is useful for obtaining approximations of solutions of equation systems containing small complicating *perturbations* that may be nonlinear. For example, suppose that, instead of (6.983), we have the system

$$\begin{aligned} y_1'(x) - y_2(x) &= 0 \quad + g_1(x, y_1, y_2) \\ y_1(x) + y_2'(x) &= f(x) + g_2(x, y_1, y_2) \end{aligned} \tag{6.987}$$

and we are interested in solutions over an interval over which $g_1(x, y_1, y_2)$ and $g_2(x, y_1, y_2)$ are very small in comparison to $y_1(x)$ and $y_2(x)$. Suppose that

$$\begin{aligned} y_1 &= F_1(x, c_1, c_2) \\ y_2 &= F_2(x, c_1, c_2) \end{aligned}$$

are solutions of the unperturbed system obtained by omitting g_1 and g_2. It may then be expected that solutions of (6.987) have the form

$$\begin{aligned} y_1 &= F_1(x, v_1(x), v_2(x)) \\ y_2 &= F_2(x, v_1(x), v_2(x)) \end{aligned}$$

where $v_1(x)$ and $v_2(x)$ vary slowly as x increases. In many important problems, of which the classic examples appear in astronomy, the slow variation of the v's makes it possible to obtain information about the v's and hence about the solutions of the given system. For this reason, the method of variation of parameters is much more important than one might think.

TYPE C

A problem of this type requires us to find the pair y_1, y_2 of functions satisfying the system (6.962) and prescribed initial conditions. One way to solve one of these problems is to find the general solution of the system (*i.e.* solve a problem of type B) and then determine the c's so that the initial conditions will be satisfied. It turns out that, even in quite simple cases, this method is unnecessarily tedious. There exist two more expeditious methods that use the initial conditions at the start of the process of obtaining the answers. One of these is the Heaviside (1850–1925) method which depends upon use of the operator D^{-1} and which appears in the first edition of this book. The other is the Laplace (1749–1827) transform method which appears in Chapter 9 of this edition. The Laplace transform method seems to have completely won the battle for attention because it is more interesting, it is easier to apply to routine problems, and (except for limitations that are usually more irksome than harmful) it is more versatile.

CHAPTER 7

USE OF SERIES

7.0. Introduction. There are several ways in which series are used in studies of differential equations. For example, series are used in Chapters 15 and 16 to obtain fundamental theorems about differential equations. Our work in this chapter deals largely with the problem of finding power series which represent solutions of differential equations. Anyone who happens to know the theory of functions of a complex variable will see that much of the work of this chapter applies to the case in which x is a complex variable as well as the case in which x is a real variable; but this fact need not disturb those who wish to regard x as a real variable.

7.1. Definitions and Fundamental Concepts. A series

$$u_1 + u_2 + u_3 + \cdots \tag{7.12}$$

is said to *converge* to y if

$$\lim_{n \to \infty} y_n = y \tag{7.13}$$

where

$$y_n = u_1 + u_2 + u_3 + \cdots + u_n \qquad n = 1, 2, \ldots . \tag{7.14}$$

If the series (7.12) converges to y, we write

$$y = u_1 + u_2 + u_3 + \cdots, \tag{7.15}$$

and we *always* understand (7.15) to mean that (7.13) holds where y_1, y_2, y_3, . . . are defined by (7.14). The sequence y_1, y_2, y_3, . . . is called the *sequence of partial sums* of the series (7.12).* If a series fails to converge, it is said to *diverge*.

* Just as an automobile mechanic may be expected to know the difference between a *steering wheel* and a *windshield wiper*, so also a scholar may be expected to know the difference between a *series* such as (7.12) and a *sequence* such as

$$y_1, y_2, y_3, \ldots .$$

The numbers that appear in the series are *terms* (terms are things that are added); the numbers that appear in a product are *factors* (factors are things that are multiplied); and the numbers that appear in the sequence are *elements* (not terms or factors) of the sequence.

If $y_1, y_2, \ldots$ is a given sequence, then it is easy to concoct a series $u_1 + u_2 + \cdots$ of which $y_1, y_2, \ldots$ is the sequence of partial sums; we have only to set

$$(7.16)\qquad u_1 = y_1, \qquad u_2 = y_2 - y_1, \qquad u_3 = y_3 - y_2, \qquad \ldots .$$

If the sequence $y_1, y_2, \ldots$ converges to y, then we can write either

$$(7.161)\qquad \lim_{n\to\infty} y_n = y_1 + (y_2 - y_1) + (y_3 - y_2) + \cdots$$

or

$$(7.162)\qquad y = y_1 + (y_2 - y_1) + (y_3 - y_2) + \cdots .$$

A series

$$(7.17)\qquad u_1 + u_2 + u_3 + \cdots$$

is said to be *dominated* by a series

$$(7.171)\qquad a_1 + a_2 + a_3 + \cdots$$

of constants if $|u_n| \leqq a_n$ for each $n = 1, 2, \ldots$. A fundamental theorem which justifies the *comparison test* for convergence is the following: *If $u_1 + u_2 + \cdots$ is dominated by a convergent series $a_1 + a_2 + \cdots$ of constants, then $u_1 + u_2 + \cdots$ is convergent.*

The following theorem gives criteria for convergence and divergence of series of nonzero terms. The criteria are known, collectively, as *the ratio test. If*

$$(7.18)\qquad \lim_{n\to\infty} \left|\frac{u_{n+1}}{u_n}\right| = \rho$$

and $\rho < 1$, then the series

$$(7.19)\qquad u_1 + u_2 + u_3 + \cdots$$

converges; if (7.18) *holds and $\rho > 1$, then the series* (7.19) *diverges.* More delicate ratio tests are given in books on series, but they need not concern us here.

7.2. Power Series. The series (6.31), (6.311), and (6.312) for e^x, $\cos x$, and $\sin x$ are *power series,* in particular, series in powers of x. A function $f(x)$ is represented as a *power series in* $(x - a)$ or a *Taylor* (1658–1731) *series* if

$$(7.21)\qquad f(x) = c_0 + c_1(x - a) + c_2(x - a)^2 + \cdots .$$

In case $a = 0$, so that

$$(7.22)\qquad f(x) = c_0 + c_1 x + c_2 x^2 + \cdots ,$$

the series is a *power series in* x and is sometimes called a *Maclaurin* (1698–1746) *series.*

In each case, the c's are constants. The series in (7.21) can be made to look like the series in (7.22) by introducing a new variable X defined by $X = x - a$. Most courses in elementary calculus contain some exercises (but very little theory) involving power series. Power series have many uses in pure and applied mathematics, and in particular they are often used in the solution of differential equations.

The three power series

$$1 + x + \frac{x^2}{2!} + \frac{x^3}{3!} + \cdots \tag{7.231}$$

$$1 + x + x^2 + x^3 + \cdots \tag{7.232}$$

$$1 + 1!x + 2!x^2 + 3!x^3 + \cdots \tag{7.233}$$

represent three types of power series in x. The first converges for all x. The second converges when $|x| < 1$ and diverges (that is, fails to converge) when $|x| > 1$. The third diverges for all $x \neq 0$. It is an interesting and important fact that, insofar as convergence properties are concerned, power series fall into three classes. The following facts are given without proof.

Some power series such as (7.231) converge for all x; these are the easiest to use. Some power series such as (7.233) diverge for each $x \neq 0$; these can be used only by specialists in series. Each other power series converges for some $x \neq 0$ and diverges for some $x \neq 0$; to each such series corresponds a positive number R, called the *radius of convergence* of the power series, such that the series converges when $|x| < R$ and the series diverges when $|x| > R$.

If the series *converges* for all x, it is convenient and customary to say that *the radius of convergence is infinite,* to write $R = \infty$, and to say that $|x| < R$ for each x. If the series diverges for all $x \neq 0$, it is convenient and customary to say that *the radius of convergence is* 0, to write $R = 0$, and to say that $|x| < R$ is satisfied for no x. This terminology is so constructed that *each power series has a radius of convergence R and the series is convergent when $|x| < R$.*

The following theorem, of which the best proofs are to be found in books on complex variables, is so important and useful that one should know it even though one does not know how to prove it:

THEOREM 7.24. *If $\Sigma c_n x^n$ converges when $|x| < R$ and*

$$f(x) = c_0 + c_1 x + c_2 x^2 + c_3 x^3 + \cdots \qquad |x| < R, \tag{7.241}$$

then $f(x)$ is differentiable and integrable when $|x| < R$ and the derivative and integral may be obtained by termwise differentiation and integration so that

$$f'(x) = 0 + c_1 + 2c_2 x + 3c_3 x^2 + \cdots \qquad |x| < R \tag{7.242}$$

and

$$\int_0^x f(t)dt = c_0x + \frac{c_1}{2}x^2 + \frac{c_2}{3}x^3 + \frac{c_3}{4}x^4 + \cdots \qquad |x| < R. \tag{7.243}$$

Another result which we need is given by the following:

THEOREM 7.25. *If* $R > 0$,

$$f_1(x) = c_0 + c_1x + c_2x^2 + c_3x^3 + \cdots \qquad |x| < R \tag{7.251}$$

and

$$f_2(x) = d_0 + d_1x + d_2x^2 + d_3x^3 + \cdots, \qquad |x| < R \tag{7.252}$$

then $f_1(x) = f_2(x)$ *when* $|x| < R$ *if and only if*

$$c_0 = d_0, \qquad c_1 = d_1, \qquad c_2 = d_2, \qquad \ldots . \tag{7.253}$$

Problem 7.26

Starting with the formula obtained by setting $x = -t^2$ in (6.31), prove that for each real x,

$$\int_0^x e^{-t^2}\,dt = x - \frac{1}{3}\frac{x^3}{1!} + \frac{1}{5}\frac{x^5}{2!} - \frac{1}{7}\frac{x^7}{3!} + \frac{1}{9}\frac{x^9}{4!} - \cdots .$$

Problem 7.27

Show that

$$\frac{1}{1+x} = 1 - x + x^2 - x^3 + x^4 - x^5 + \cdots,$$

the series being convergent when $|x| < 1$ and divergent when $|x| > 1$. Use this result, Theorem 7.24, and the fact that $\log 1 = 0$ to prove that

$$\log(1+x) = x - \frac{x^2}{2} + \frac{x^3}{3} - \frac{x^4}{4} + \cdots,$$

the series being convergent when $|x| < 1$ and divergent when $|x| > 1$.

7.3. Power-series Solutions. The best way to obtain an idea of the technique involved in solving differential equations by means of power series is to understand a simple example. Let us try to solve the equation

$$\frac{dy}{dx} = ky, \tag{7.31}$$

k being a constant, by trying to find constants $c_0, c_1, c_2, \ldots$ and a constant $R > 0$ such that the series

$$y = c_0 + c_1x + c_2x^2 + c_3x^3 + \cdots \tag{7.32}$$

will converge for $|x| < R$ to a solution $y = y(x)$ of (7.31). To attack the problem in an intelligent fashion, let us *assume* that $c_0, c_1, \ldots,$ and R represent constants for which (7.32) satisfies (7.31) when $|x| < R$.

Then from (7.32) we obtain

$$\frac{dy}{dx} = c_1 + 2c_2x + 3c_3x^2 + 4c_4x^3 + \cdots \qquad |x| < R$$

and

$$ky = kc_0 + kc_1x + kc_2x^2 + kc_3x^3 + \cdots \qquad |x| < R.$$

Therefore

$$c_1 = kc_0, \qquad 2c_2 = kc_1, \qquad 3c_3 = kc_2, \qquad 4c_4 = kc_3, \qquad \ldots .$$

These formules, which express c's in terms of c's with smaller subscripts, are *recursion formulas*. They imply that

$$c_1 = c_0k, \qquad c_2 = \frac{c_0k^2}{2!}, \qquad c_3 = \frac{c_0k^3}{3!}, \qquad \ldots .$$

Putting these expressions for the c's in (7.32) gives, when $|x| < R$,

$$y = c_0\left[1 + \frac{kx}{1} + \frac{(kx)^2}{2!} + \frac{(kx)^3}{3!} + \frac{(kx)^4}{4!} + \cdots\right]. \tag{7.33}$$

What we have shown so far is that, *if* (7.31) has a solution of the form (7.32), then $y(x)$ must have the form (7.33). The next step is to examine (7.33) to see whether it really does furnish a solution of (7.31). It can be shown (by the ratio test, for example) that the series in (7.33) converges for all x; we may take $R = \infty$ and show that (7.33) satisfies (7.31) for all x.

Thus we have obtained a solution of the differential equation in the form of a series. It happens that the series in (7.33) is the power-series expansion of c_0e^{kx}, and we may therefore present our solutions in the familiar form $y = c_0e^{kx}$. It is important to emphasize the fact that (7.33) would still be a solution of (7.31) if we were unable to see that the series in (7.33) converges to a familiar elementary function. Frequently one is unable to see that series solutions converge to familiar elementary functions for the simple reason that functions defined by power series are frequently not elementary functions.

Problem 7.34

Find the soultions of the following equations representable in the form $y = c_0 + c_1x + c_2x^2 + \cdots$:

(7.341) $\quad \dfrac{dy}{dx} = 2xy \qquad$ *Ans.:* $y = ce^{x^2}$

(7.342) $\quad x\dfrac{dy}{dx} = y \qquad$ *Ans.:* $y = cx$

(7.343) $\quad x^2\dfrac{dy}{dx} = y \qquad$ *Ans.:* $y = 0$

(7.344) $\quad \dfrac{dy}{dx} = x + y \qquad$ *Ans.:* $y = ce^x - 1 - x$

Problem 7.35

Find the solutions of (7.343) which are representable in the form

$$y = c_0 + c_1x^{-1} + c_2x^{-2} + c_3x^{-3} + \cdot \cdot \cdot . \qquad \textit{Ans.: } y = ce^{-1/x}.$$

Problem 7.36

Find the solutions of the equation

$$(1 + x^2)y' - y = 0 \tag{7.361}$$

having the form

$$y = c_0 + c_1x + c_2x^2 + c_3x^3 + c_4x^4 + \cdot \cdot \cdot . \tag{7.362}$$

Solution: Keeping the terms involving the same powers of x in vertical columns, we write

$$\begin{aligned} -y &= -c_0 - c_1x - c_2x^2 - c_3x^3 - c_4x^4 - \cdots \\ y' &= c_1 + 2c_2x + 3c_3x^2 + 4c_4x^3 + 5c_5x^4 + \cdots \\ x^2y' &= 0 + 0 + c_1x^2 + 2c_2x^3 + 3c_3x^4 + \cdots . \end{aligned}$$

The sum of these things will be 0 and (7.361) will be satisfied iff $c_0, c_1, c_2, \ldots$ satisfy the recursion formulas obtained by equating the sums of the coefficients of the various powers of x to 0. The recursion formulas are $c_1 = c_0$, $2c_2 = c_1$, and

$$c_n = \frac{1}{n}[c_{n-1} - (n-2)c_{n-2}] \qquad n \geqq 3.$$

The formula

$$y = c_0[1 + x + \tfrac{1}{2}x^2 - \tfrac{1}{6}x^3 - \tfrac{7}{24}x^4 + \cdot \cdot \cdot]$$

shows five terms of the answer, and more terms are easily calculated. It can be noticed that solving (7.361), as a linear equation of first order, gives the solution exp $(\tan^{-1} x)$, and that our work gives a very easy way of calculating the coefficients in the power-series expansion of this function. Some other ways are very tedious.

Problem 7.37

Find the power series solutions of the equation

$$(1 + x^2)y' + 2xy = 0.$$

Then solve the equation without use of series and find the power-series expansions of the solutions. Make everything agreeable.

Problem 7.38

Find the power-series solutions of the equation

$$y' - (1 + x + x^2 + x^3 + \cdot \cdot \cdot)y = 0$$

without making use of the fact that the coefficient of y is $(1 - x)^{-1}$. Then use this fact to solve the equation without use of series, and find the power-series expansions of the solutions. Make everything check so that problems do not browbeat us; we browbeat them.

Remark 7.39

It is a good idea to read Section 7.99 rather casually now and to consult it occasionally as we proceed. It assures us that the methods we are about to use will catch fish.

7.4. Some Equations of Second Order. The equations solved in Section 7.3 were of the first order. In this section we find power-series solutions of equations of second order, starting with

$$y'' + xy = 0. \tag{7.41}$$

Assuming that $y = c_0 + c_1x + c_2x^2 + \cdots$ is a solution of (7.41), we write

$$\begin{aligned} y'' &= 1\cdot 2c_2 + 2\cdot 3c_3x + 3\cdot 4c_4x^2 + 4\cdot 5c_5x^3 + \cdots \\ xy &= \quad 0 \quad + \quad c_0x + \quad c_1x^2 + \quad c_2x^3 + \cdots \end{aligned}$$

and equate the sums of the coefficients of the various powers of x to 0 to obtain

$$\begin{aligned} &1\cdot 2c_2 = 0, \quad 2\cdot 3c_3 = -c_0,\ 3\cdot 4c_4 = -c_1,\ 4\cdot 5c_5 = -c_2, \\ &5\cdot 6c_6 = -c_3,\ 6\cdot 7c_7 = -c_4,\ 7\cdot 8c_8 = -c_5,\ 8\cdot 9c_9 = -c_6,\ \ldots . \end{aligned}$$

These formulas, which express c's in terms of c's with smaller subscripts, are *recursion formulas,* and we have illustrated the fact that it is often a good idea to write more than a few of them. They imply that $c_2 = 0$, $c_5 = 0$, $c_8 = 0$, . . . and enable us to express the remaining c's in terms of c_0 and c_1 to obtain

$$\begin{aligned} y = c_0&\left(1 - \frac{x^3}{2\cdot 3} + \frac{x^6}{2\cdot 3\cdot 5\cdot 6} - \frac{x^9}{2\cdot 3\cdot 5\cdot 6\cdot 8\cdot 9} + \cdots\right) \\ &+ c_1\left(x - \frac{x^4}{3\cdot 4} + \frac{x^6}{3\cdot 4\cdot 6\cdot 7} - \frac{x^{10}}{3\cdot 4\cdot 6\cdot 7\cdot 9\cdot 10} + \cdots\right). \end{aligned} \tag{7.42}$$

Each series converges for all values of x, and (7.42) is the general solution of (7.41). It is no disgrace not to know whether the functions to which the series converge are elementary functions. However it is a disgrace not to see that they are impeccable functions of x whose values can be computed just as values of $\cos x$ and $\sin x$ are computed from their series expansions. In fact we could put (7.42) in the form

$$y = c_1 \operatorname{jos} x + c_2 \operatorname{jin} x$$

if we call the functions jos x and jin x.

Problem 7.43

Solve the equation $y'' = xy$.

Ans.: $y = c_0\left(1 + \dfrac{x^3}{2\cdot 3} + \dfrac{x^6}{2\cdot 3\cdot 5\cdot 6} + \dfrac{x^9}{2\cdot 3\cdot 5\cdot 6\cdot 8\cdot 9} + \cdots\right)$

$\qquad + c_1\left(x + \dfrac{x^4}{3\cdot 4} + \dfrac{x^7}{3\cdot 4\cdot 6\cdot 7} + \dfrac{x^{10}}{3\cdot 4\cdot 6\cdot 7\cdot 9\cdot 10} + \cdots\right).$

Problem 7.44

Solve the equation $y'' + y = 0$. You should recognize the series in your answer.

Problem 7.45

Solve $y'' - xy' - y = 0$.

$$Ans.: y = c_0\left(1 + \frac{x^2}{2} + \frac{x^4}{2\cdot 4} + \frac{x^6}{2\cdot 4\cdot 6} + \cdots\right) + c_1\left(x + \frac{x^3}{3} + \frac{x^5}{3\cdot 5} + \frac{x^7}{3\cdot 5\cdot 7} + \cdots\right).$$

If you look real hard at the coefficient of c_0, you may notice the connection between it and

$$e^{x^2/2} = 1 + \frac{x^2/2}{1!} + \frac{(x^2/2)^2}{2!} + \frac{(x^2/2)^3}{3!} + \cdots.$$

Information theory suggests a check.

Problem 7.46

Using the power-series expansion of $\sin x$, find the solution of

$$y'' + y = \sin x$$

for which $y(0) = y'(0) = 0$. After the result has been found, seek a neat way of checking it.

Problem 7.461

Find the solution of the equation

$$xy'' + y' + xy = 0$$

for which $y(0) = 1$, $y'(0) = 0$. *Ans.:* $J_0(x)$; see Problem 1.344.

Problem 7.462

Using the power-series expansion of $J_0'(x)$, which is to be obtained from (1.3441), find the power-series solution of the equation

(7.4621) $$xu'' + u' + xu = -2J_0'(x)$$

for which $u(0) = u'(0) = 0$. *Ans.:* The terms following $J_0(x) \log x$ in the right member of the formula

(7.4622) $$K_0(x) = J_0(x)\log x + \frac{1}{2^2}x^2 - \frac{1}{2^2 4^2}\left(1 + \frac{1}{2}\right)x^4 + \frac{1}{2^2 4^2 6^2}\left(1 + \frac{1}{2} + \frac{1}{3}\right)x^6 - \frac{1}{2^2 4^2 6^2 8^2}\left(1 + \frac{1}{2} + \frac{1}{3} + \frac{1}{4}\right)x^8 + \cdots.$$

Remark: We should see where this weird problem came from. The Bessel equation

(7.4623) $$xy'' + y' + xy = 0$$

of order 0 has the solution $J_0(x)$, and we sometimes need a solution independent of

$J_0(x)$. Supposing that $x > 0$, we can let

$$y = J_0(x) \log x + u \tag{7.4624}$$

and substitute in (7.4623) to find that y satisfies it iff (if and only if) u satisfies (7.4621). Hence, by solving the problem, we showed that $K_0(x)$ is a solution of the Bessel equation of order 0. It is clearly independent of $J_0(x)$ because $J_0(x) \to 1$ as $x \to 0$ and $K_0(x) \to -\infty$ as $x \to 0$ and neither can be a constant multiple of the other. It is a Bessel function of the second kind; $J_0(x)$ is of the first kind. The result is not weird. Everybody should see that it can be put in the form

$$K_0(x) = J_0(x) \log x \quad \sum_{k=1}^{\infty} \frac{(-1)^k}{k!k!} \left\{ \sum_{p=1}^{k} \frac{1}{p} \right\} \left(\frac{x}{2}\right)^{2k} \tag{7.4625}$$

and that (7.884) reduces to this when $\alpha = B = 0$. Each solution of the Bessel equation of order 0 has the form $c_1 J_0(x) + c_2 K_0(x)$.

Problem 7.463

Find all power-series solutions of the equation

$$xy'' + y' + a^2xy = 0.$$

$$\textit{Ans.: } y = c_0 \left(1 - \frac{a^2x^2}{2^2} + \frac{a^4x^4}{2^24^2} - \frac{a^6x^6}{2^24^26^2} + \frac{a^8x^8}{2^24^26^28^2} - \cdots\right).$$

Remark: The quantity in parentheses is $J_0(ax)$. In case $a^2 = -i$, it is customary to put it in the form

$$J_0(\sqrt{-i}\,x) = J_0(i\sqrt{i}\,x) = \operatorname{ber} x + i \operatorname{bei} x$$

where

$$\operatorname{ber} x = 1 - \frac{x^4}{2^24^2} + \frac{x^8}{2^24^26^28^2} - \cdots$$

$$\operatorname{bei} x = \frac{x^2}{2^2} - \frac{x^6}{2^24^26^2} + \frac{x^{10}}{2^24^26^28^210^2} - \cdots.$$

We should allow ber x and bei x to make us think of Bessel-real and Bessel-imaginary.

Problem 7.471

Find all of the power-series solutions of the equation

$$xy'' - y = 0. \tag{7.4711}$$

$$\textit{Ans.: } y = c_0 \left(x + \frac{x^2}{2} + \frac{x^3}{2^2 \cdot 3} + \frac{x^4}{2^2 \cdot 3^2 \cdot 4} + \cdots\right).$$

Problem 7.472

Find all of the power-series solutions of the equation

$$x^2y'' - y = 0. \qquad \textit{Ans.: } y = 0.$$

Problem 7.473

Confining attention to the interval $x > 0$, find two independent solutions of the equation

$$x^2y'' - 2y = 0 \tag{7.4731}$$

by finding two values of m and corresponding values of c_0, c_1, . . . such that the function

$$y = c_0x^m + c_1x^{m+1} + c_2x^{m+2} + \cdots$$

satisfies it. *Ans.*: x^2 and x^{-1}

Problem 7.474

The equation

$$(1 - x^2)y'' - 2xy' + 12y = 0$$

will turn out to be the Legendre (1752–1833) equation of order 3. It has solutions of the form

$$y = c_1x + c_3x^3 + c_5x^5 + \cdots .$$

Find them. *Ans.*: $y = cP_3(x)$ (see Problem 7.96).

Problem 7.475

For each $n = 0, 1, 2, \ldots$, the *Laguerre* (1834–1886) *equation*

$$xy'' + (1 - x)y' + ny = 0 \tag{7.4751}$$

has a polynomial solution $L_n(x)$ defined by

$$L_n(x) = e^x \frac{d^n}{dx^n}(x^ne^{-x})$$

so that

$$\begin{aligned}
L_0(x) &= 1 \\
L_1(x) &= -x + 1 \\
L_2(x) &= x^2 - 4x + 2 \\
L_3(x) &= -x^3 + 9x^2 - 18x + 6 \\
L_4(x) &= x^4 - 16x^3 + 72x^2 - 96x + 24.
\end{aligned}$$

These are the *Laguerre polynomials*. The *Laguerre functions* $\phi_n(x)$ defined by

$$\phi_n(x) = \frac{1}{n!} e^{-x/2}L_n(x) \tag{7.4752}$$

form a complete orthonormal set over the interval $0 \leqq x < \infty$; Chapter 12 tells about such things. The formulas

$$L_n(x) = \frac{e^x}{2n!}\int_0^\infty \left(\frac{u^2}{4}\right)^n e^{-u^2/4}J_0(u\sqrt{x})u\,du$$

and

$$\sum_{n=0}^{\infty} \frac{L_n(x)}{n!} t^n = \frac{e^{-xt/(1-t)}}{1-t}$$

are fertile sources of information. Check up on the first part of this story by finding the power-series solutions of (7.4751) when $n = 2$ and when $n = 3$.

Problem 7.476

This problem involves a constant a which is taken to be 1 in many modern applications but is often taken to be 2. For each $n = 0, 1, 2, \ldots$, the *Hermite* (1822–1901) *equation*

$$y'' - axy' + any = 0 \tag{7.4761}$$

has the polynomial solution $H_n(x)$ defined by

$$H_n(x) = (-1)^n e^{ax^2/2} \frac{d^n}{dx^n} e^{-ax^2/2}$$

so that

$$\begin{aligned}
H_0(x) &= 1 \\
H_1(x) &= ax \\
H_2(x) &= a^2x^2 - a \\
H_3(x) &= a^3x^3 - 3a^2x \\
H_4(x) &= a^4x^4 - 6a^3x^2 + 3a^2 \\
H_5(x) &= a^5x^5 - 10a^4x^3 + 15a^3x \\
H_6(x) &= a^6x^6 - 15a^5x^4 + 45a^4x^2 - 15a^3 \\
H_7(x) &= a^7x^7 - 21a^6x^5 + 105a^5x^3 - 105a^4x.
\end{aligned}$$

These are *Hermite polynomials.* The Hermite functions $\phi_n(x)$, defined by

$$\phi_n(x) = p_n H_n(x) e^{-ax^2/4}, \tag{7.4762}$$

where $p_0, p_1, \ldots$ are positive normalizing constants defined by

$$p_n = \frac{1}{\sqrt{\sqrt{\dfrac{2\pi}{a}}\, a^n n!}}$$

form a complete orthonormal set over the interval $-\infty < x < \infty$; Chapter 12 tells about such things. The formulas

$$H_{n+1}(x) = axH_n(x) - H_n'(x)$$

$$H_n(x) = \sum_{k \leqq n/2} (-1)^k \frac{n!}{k!(n-2k)!} \frac{a^{n-k}}{2^k} x^{n-2k}, \qquad \sum_{n=0}^{\infty} \frac{H_n(x)}{n!} t^n = e^{axt} e^{-at^2/2}$$

$$H_n(x) = \sqrt{\frac{a}{2\pi}} \int_{-\infty}^{\infty} (ax + iau)^n e^{-au^2/2}\, du$$

$$\phi_n(u) = \sqrt{\frac{a}{2}} \frac{i^n}{\sqrt{2\pi}} \int_{-\infty}^{\infty} \phi_n(x) e^{-iaux/2}\, dx$$

are fertile sources of information. Check up on the first part of this story by finding the power-series solutions of (7.4761) when $n = 2$ and when $n = 3$.

Problem 7.477

Let θ and x satisfy the conditions $0 \leqq \theta \leqq \pi$, $-1 \leqq x \leqq 1$, $x = \cos\theta$, and $\theta = \cos^{-1} x$. Let $T_0(x) = 1$ and, for each $n = 1, 2, 3, \ldots$, let

$$T_n(x) = 2^{1-n} \cos(n \cos^{-1} x) = 2^{1-n} \cos n\theta. \tag{7.4771}$$

Using the fact that $\cos n\theta$ is the real part of the members of the formula

$$e^{in\theta} = (e^{i\theta})^n = (\cos\theta + i\sin\theta)^n = (x + i\sqrt{1-x^2})^n$$

shows that, when $n > 0$,

(7.4772) $$T_n(x) = 2^{1-n}\left[x^n + \binom{n}{2}x^{n-2}(x^2-1) + \binom{n}{4}x^{n-4}(x^2-1)^2 + \cdots\right]$$

and hence that $T_n(x)$ is a polynomial in x of degree n. These polynomials are called *Tchebycheff* (1821–1894) *polynomials.* The first five of them are:

$$T_0(x) = 1, \qquad T_1(x) = x, \qquad T_2(x) = x^2 - \tfrac{1}{2}$$
$$T_3(x) = x^3 - \tfrac{3}{4}x, \qquad T_4(x) = x^4 - x^2 + \tfrac{1}{8}.$$

For each $n = 0, 1, 2, \ldots, T_n(x)$ has the form

(7.4773) $$x^n + c_1x^{n-1} + c_2x^{n-2} + \cdots + c_{n-1}x + c_n$$

where $c_1, c_2, \ldots, c_n$ are real constants. With the aid of (7.4771), it is easy to see that, when $n > 0$,

(7.4774) $$\max_{-1\leqq x\leqq 1} |T_n(x)| = 2^{1-n}$$

and that the maximum is attained when x has the $n + 1$ values $x_k = \cos(k\pi/n)$ for which $k = 0, 1, 2, \ldots, n$. One interest in these results arises from the fact that, for each n, $T_n(x)$ is the unique polynomial $p_n(x)$ of the form (7.4773) for which $\max_{-1\leqq x\leqq 1}|p_n(x)|$ assumes its minimum value. Thus the Tchebycheff polynomials are solutions of special *minimax* problems. Proof of this fact can be made to depend upon a study of the intersections of the graph of $T_n(x)$ and the graph of a polynomial $p_n(x)$ of the form (7.4773) which is assumed to satisfy the condition $\max_{-1\leqq x\leqq 1}|p_n(x)| \leqq 2^{1-n}$, with recognition of the fact that the degree of $T_n(x) - p_n(x)$ is, at most, $n - 1$. The Tchebycheff functions $\phi_0, \phi_1, \phi_2, \ldots$ defined by

(7.4775) $$\phi_n(x) = E_n(2/\pi)^{\frac{1}{2}}(1 - x^2)^{-\frac{1}{4}}\cos(n\cos^{-1}x),$$

where $E_0 = 1/\sqrt{2}$ and $E_n = 1$ when $n > 1$, form an orthonormal set over the interval $-1 \leqq x \leqq 1$. With the aid of (7.4771), it can be shown that $T_n(x)$ satisfies the *Tchebycheff differential equation*

(7.4776) $$(1 - x^2)y'' - xy' + n^2y = 0.$$

Check up on the last part of this story by solving (7.4776) for some small integer values of n. *Remark:* Of course (7.4776) has solutions independent of $T_n(x)$, and these are interesting.

Problem 7.48

Starting with $y = a_1x + a_2x^2 + \cdots$ and $z = b_1x + b_2x^2 + \cdots$, find functions $y(x)$ and $z(x)$ for which $y(0) = z(0) = 0$ and

$$y'(x) = y + z + x$$
$$z'(x) = y + z - x.$$

Ans.: $y = x^2/2$ and $z = -x^2/2$.

Note that more difficult problems could be solved by the same method.

Problem 7.49

The equation

$$y^{(4)} + y = 1$$

has a power-series solution for which $y(0) = y'(0) = y''(0) = y'''(0) = 0$ and $y^{(4)}(0) = 1$. Find it. *Ans.*: $y = \frac{x^4}{4!} - \frac{x^8}{8!} + \frac{x^{12}}{12!} - \frac{x^{16}}{16!} + \cdots$.

7.5. Nonlinear Equations. Power-series solutions of nonlinear differential equations play minor or nonexistent roles in the lives of most people, but we pause to look at the example

$$y'' = x^2 + y^2. \tag{7.51}$$

Assuming that

$$y = c_0 + c_1x + c_2x^2 + c_3x^3 + \cdots \tag{7.52}$$

is a solution of (7.51) for some range of values of x, we find

$$y'' = 1 \cdot 2c_2 + 2 \cdot 3c_3x + 3 \cdot 4c_4x^2 + 4 \cdot 5c_5x^3 + \cdots$$

and

$$x^2 + y^2 = c_0^2 + (c_0c_1 + c_1c_0)x + (1 + c_0c_2 + c_1c_1 + c_2c_0)x^2 + (c_0c_3 + c_1c_2 + c_2c_1 + c_3c_0)x^3 + (c_0c_4 + c_1c_3 + c_2c_2 + c_3c_1 + c_4c_0)x^4 + \cdots.$$

Equating coefficients of like powers of x, we obtain equations that determine $c_2, c_3, c_4, \ldots$ in terms of c_0 and c_1. Substituting these values in (7.52) gives

$$y = c_0 + c_1x + \tfrac{1}{2}c_0^2x^2 + \tfrac{1}{3}c_0c_1x^3 + \tfrac{1}{12}(1 + c_0^3 + c_1^2)x^4 + \tfrac{1}{12}c_0^2c_1x^5 + \tfrac{1}{360}(2c_0 + 5c_0^4 + 10c_0c_1^2)x^6 + \cdots. \tag{7.53}$$

We do not enter into the question of convergence of (7.53). A student who wishes to pursue a study of (7.53) may well pay attention firstly to the case in which $c_0 = c_1 = 0$ and accordingly $y(0) = y'(0) = 0$. In this case, many of the coefficients in (7.53) vanish.

The J. C. Adams method, which appears in Section 8.4, provides another method for obtaining the coefficients $c_0, c_1, c_2, \ldots$ in the power-series expansion (7.52) of the solution of (7.51) for which $y(0) = c_0$ and $y'(0) = c_1$. The method depends upon direct use of (7.51) and the Taylor (1685–1731) formula $c_n = y^{(n)}(0)/n!$ for the coefficients. Putting $x = 0$ in (7.51) gives $y''(0) = c_0^2$ and $c_2 = \frac{1}{2}c_0^2$. Differentiating (7.51) gives

$$y''' = 2x + 2yy'$$

and putting $x = 0$ gives $y'''(0) = 2c_0c_1$ and $c_3 = \frac{1}{3}c_0c_1$. Another differentiation gives

$$y^{(4)} = 2 + 2yy'' + 2y'y',$$

and putting $x = 0$ gives

$$y^{(4)}(0) = 2 + 2c_0c_0^2 + 2c_1^2$$

and

$$c_4 = \tfrac{1}{12}(1 + c_0^3 + c_1^2).$$

The results are agreeing with those in (7.53), and the process can be continued.

The right member of (7.51) is a relatively simple polynomial in x and y. We can undertake to use the Adams method to find power-series solutions of the equations $y' = f(x, y)$ and $y'' = g(x, y, y')$ when the functions f and g are analytic and hence are representable as sums of convergent power series in their arguments. However, even in simple cases, the method brings more complications than illuminations. Consider, for example, the Newton equation

$$y'' = f(y) \tag{7.54}$$

where we may suppose that $f(y) = b \sin y$ as in the pendulum equation (1.53). Starting with given numerical values $y(0) = c_0$ and $y'(0) = c_1$, we use (7.54) and formulas obtained by differentiating (7.54) to obtain the coefficients in

$$y(x) = y(0) + \frac{y'(0)}{1!}x + \frac{y''(0)}{2!}x^2 + \frac{y'''(0)}{3!}x^3 + \cdots \tag{7.541}$$

in terms of c_0 and c_1. Putting $x = 0$ in (7.54) gives $y''(0) = f(c_0)$. Differentiating (7.54) gives $y^{(3)} = f'(y)y'$ and $y^{(3)}(0) = f'(c_0)c_1$. Another differentiation gives

$$y^{(4)} = f'(y)y'' + f''(y)(y')^2,$$

which we can put in the form

$$y^{(4)} = f'(y)f(y) + f''(y)(y')^2,$$

and hence $y^{(4)}(0) = f'(c_0)f(c_0) + f''(c_0)c_1^2$. The next differentiation gives

$$y^{(5)} = [f'(y)]^2y' + f(y)f''(y)y' + 2f''(y)y'y'' + f'''(y)(y')^3,$$

which we can put in the form

$$y^{(5)} = [f'(y)]^2y' + 3f(y)f''(y)y' + f'''(y)(y')^3.$$

From this point on, complications increase very rapidly and about two more differentiations tempt us to feed the wastebasket and go to work on the next chapter.

Problem 7.55

We saw in Section 2.2 that $y(x) = \tan x$ is the unique function which satisfies the condition $y(0) = 0$ and

$$\frac{dy}{dx} = 1 + y^2 \qquad -\frac{\pi}{2} < x < \frac{\pi}{2}. \tag{7.551}$$

Let us use also the fact (which we do not prove here) that $\tan x$ can be represented in the form

$$\tan x = c_1x + c_3x^3 + c_5x^5 + c_7x^7 + \cdots, \tag{7.552}$$

the series being convergent when $|x| < \pi/2$. By determining the c's so that the right member of (7.552) satisfies (7.551), show that when $|x| < \pi/2$,

$$\tan x = x + \frac{1}{3}x^3 + \frac{2}{15}x^5 + \frac{17}{315}x^7 + \frac{62}{2{,}835}x^9 + \frac{1{,}382}{155{,}925}x^{11} + \cdots. \tag{7.553}$$

Problem 7.56

Use the result of the previous problem to obtain several terms of the power-series expansions of $\sec^2 x$ and $\log \cos x$.

Remark 7.57

It is often possible to use power series in a purely formal way to discover solutions of equations. Suppose functions $u(x, y)$ are sought for which the partial differential equation

$$x\frac{\partial u}{\partial x} + y\frac{\partial u}{\partial y} = 2u \tag{7.571}$$

holds. A function of the form

$$u = \sum a_{j,k}x^j y^k,$$

for which formal differentiation gives

$$x\frac{\partial u}{\partial x} = \sum ja_{j,k}x^j y^k, \qquad y\frac{\partial u}{\partial y} = \sum ka_{j,k}x^j y^k,$$

should satisfy (7.571) if

$$\sum (j + k - 2)a_{j,k}x^j y^k = 0$$

and hence if $a_{j,k} = 0$ when $j + k - 2 \neq 0$ or $j \neq 2 - k$. Thus functions of the form

$$u = \sum A_k x^{2-k}y^k = x^2 \sum A_k \left(\frac{y}{x}\right)^k$$

should satisfy (7.571). But since $\Sigma A_k(y/x)^k$ can, for different choices of the A's, represent many different functions of y/x, one may suspect that the function

$$u = x^2\phi\left(\frac{y}{x}\right) \tag{7.572}$$

will satisfy (7.571) for many different functions ϕ. Actually, it is easy to show that if ϕ is differentiable, then (7.572) satisfies (7.571) when $x \neq 0$. Do this. [According to Section 5.3 a function $f(x, y)$ which is homogeneous in x and y of degree 2 can be written in the form $x^2\phi(y/x)$.]

Problem 7.58

Use the formal method of Remark 7.57 to discover solutions of the equation

$$x\frac{\partial u}{\partial x} + y\frac{\partial u}{\partial y} = ku$$

where k is a constant. For what values of k do you obtain results? Check with Problem 2.18.

7.6. The Method of Frobenius. Three famous linear differential equations with nonconstant coefficients are

$$(x^2 - x)\frac{d^2y}{dx^2} + [(\alpha + \beta + 1)x - \gamma]\frac{dy}{dx} + \alpha\beta y = 0 \tag{7.61}$$

(hypergeometric)

$$x^2\frac{d^2y}{dx^2} + x\frac{dy}{dx} + (x^2 - \alpha^2)y = 0 \qquad \text{(Bessel)} \tag{7.62}$$

$$(1 - x^2)\frac{d^2y}{dx^2} - 2x\frac{dy}{dx} + \alpha(\alpha + 1)y = 0 \qquad \text{(Legendre)} \tag{7.63}$$

where the Greek letters represent constants. These equations are, as indicated by the names at the right, known as the *hypergeometric differential equation*, the *Bessel* (1784–1846) *differential equation of order* α, and the *Legendre* (1752–1833) *differential equation of order* α. This order α, which is sometimes but not always an integer in applications, does not refer to the orders of the derivatives; there is another sense in which each equation has order 2. Each is important because of its applications. Each is a linear differential equation of the second order with coefficients which are polynomials in the independent variable. Thus each equation has the form

$$Py'' + Qy' + Ry = 0 \tag{7.64}$$

where P, Q, and R are polynomials in x. As in Chapter 6, let

$$Ly = Py'' + Qy' + Ry \tag{7.65}$$

so that L is a linear operator and (7.64) may be written $Ly = 0$.

A standard method of seeking solutions of $Ly = 0$ is to seek to determine an exponent m (which may or may not be an integer) and a set of coefficients $c_0, c_1, c_2, \ldots$ such that $c_0 \neq 0$ and

$$y = x^m(c_0 + c_1x + c_2x^2 + \cdots) \tag{7.66}$$

will converge and be a solution of $Ly = 0$ for some range of values of x. This method is known as the *method of Frobenius* (1849–1917). In case m is 0 or a positive integer, the function (7.66) of Frobenius type is a power series in x; otherwise it is not. Whenever we have occasion to use an m which is -1 or $\frac{1}{2}$ or i or any other number which is neither 0 nor a positive integer, we simplify matters by supposing that $x > 0$. If r has one of the values $m, m + 1, m + 2, \ldots$, then

$$\begin{aligned} Lx^r &= Pr(r - 1)x^{r-2} + Qrx^{r-1} + Rx^r \\ &= [r(r - 1)P + rxQ + x^2R]x^{r-2}. \end{aligned} \tag{7.661}$$

If y is defined by (7.66), then

$$y = \sum_{n=0}^{\infty} c_nx^{m+n} \tag{7.662}$$

and

$$\begin{aligned} Ly &= \sum_{n=0}^{\infty} c_nLx^{m+n} \\ &= \sum_{n=0}^{\infty} c_n[(m + n)(m + n - 1)P + (m + n)xQ + x^2R]x^{m+n-2}. \end{aligned} \tag{7.663}$$

When the last series is expanded and coefficients of like powers of x

are collected, we obtain

$$Ly = A_0x^q + A_1x^{q+1} + A_2x^{q+2} + \cdots \tag{7.664}$$

where q is one of the exponents $m - 2, m - 1, m, m + 1, \ldots$; where the coefficients $A_0, A_1, A_2, \ldots$ are determined in terms of m and $c_0, c_1, c_2, \ldots$; and where $A_0 \neq 0$ unless special values are given to m or to the c's. The next step is to try to determine m so that the *indicial equation* $A_0 = 0$ is satisfied and then to try to determine the c's so that $A_1 = 0$, $A_2 = 0$, $A_3 = 0, \ldots$. If one succeeds in making these determinations of m and $c_0, c_1, c_2, \ldots$, then

$$y = x^m(c_0 + c_1x + c_2x^2 + \cdots) \tag{7.665}$$

is a solution of $Ly = 0$ for the range (if any) of values of x for which the series converges and $x > 0$ if m is neither 0 nor a positive integer.

In the following sections, we illustrate use of this method of Frobenius by finding solutions of the classic equations (7.61), (7.62), and (7.63).

Remark 7.666

One of our main tasks is to become thoroughly familiar with the summation symbol Σ and its uses. Each expression involving Σ can be written twice, once with use of Σ and once with use of the first few terms followed by the traditional three dots. The ability to make calculations like

$$\begin{aligned}\sum_{n=0}^{\infty}(a_nx^{-1} + b_n + c_nx)x^{m+n} &= \sum_{n=0}^{\infty} a_nx^{m+n-1} + \sum_{n=0}^{\infty} b_nx^{m+n} + \sum_{n=0}^{\infty} c_nx^{m+n+1}\\ &= \sum_{n=-1}^{\infty} a_{n+1}x^{m+n} + \sum_{n=0}^{\infty} b_nx^{m+n} + \sum_{n=1}^{\infty} c_{n-1}x^{m+n}\\ &= a_0x^{m-1} + (a_1 + b_0)x^m + \sum_{n=1}^{\infty}(a_{n+1} + b_n + c_{n-1})x^{m+n}\end{aligned}$$

is easily acquired and is very valuable. Everything depends upon the simple and fundamental fact that we can add an integer (positive or negative) to the index of summation wherever it appears after the Σ if we compensate for the deed by subtracting the same integer from the index on the Σ. For example,

$$\sum_{n=0}^{\infty}\frac{1}{(n+1)^2} = \sum_{n=1}^{\infty}\frac{1}{n^2}.$$

It is a good idea to solve each of the classic equations two or three times to become thoroughly familiar with the manner in which series and Σ are used in the process. Making these repetitions promotes familiarity with important things and can be more beneficial than solving many similar but unimportant problems.

7.7. The Hypergeometric Equation. Let Ly denote the left member of the equation

$$(7.71)\qquad (x^2 - x)\frac{d^2y}{dx^2} + [(\alpha + \beta + 1)x - \gamma]\frac{dy}{dx} + \alpha\beta y = 0$$

so that the hypergeometric equation becomes $Ly = 0$. We find that

$$(7.72)\qquad Lx^r = r(1 - \gamma - r)x^{r-1} + (\alpha + r)(\beta + r)x^r.$$

Hence, if y has the Frobenius form

$$(7.73)\qquad y = x^m \sum_{n=0}^{\infty} c_n x^n = \sum_{n=0}^{\infty} c_n x^{m+n} = c_0 x^m + c_1 x^{m+1} + c_2 x^{m+2} + \cdots$$

for some range of values of x, then

$$\begin{aligned}(7.74)\qquad Ly &= \sum_{n=0}^{\infty} c_n L x^{m+n} \\ &= \sum_{n=0}^{\infty} c_n[(m + n)(1 - \gamma - m - n)x^{m+n-1} \\ &\qquad\qquad + (\alpha + m + n)(\beta + m + n)x^{m+n}] \\ &= c_0 m(1 - \gamma - m)x^{m-1} \\ &\quad + \sum_{n=1}^{\infty} c_n(m + n)(1 - \gamma - m - n)x^{m+n-1} \\ &\qquad\qquad + \sum_{n=0}^{\infty} c_n(\alpha + m + n)(\beta + m + n)x^{m+n} \\ &= c_0 m(1 - \gamma - m)x^{m-1} \\ &\quad + \sum_{n=0}^{\infty} [-c_{n+1}(m + n + 1)(\gamma + m + n) \\ &\qquad\qquad + c_n(\alpha + m + n)(\beta + m + n)]x^{m+n}.\end{aligned}$$

The next step is to try to determine m such that the *indicial equation*

$$(7.741)\qquad c_0 m(1 - \gamma - m) = 0$$

holds and then to determine the c's such that

$$\begin{aligned}(7.742)\qquad (m + n + 1)(\gamma + m + n)c_{n+1} \\ = (\alpha + m + n)(\beta + m + n)c_n \qquad n = 0, 1, 2, \ldots .\end{aligned}$$

This is a *recursion formula* which, when the coefficient of c_{n+1} is not 0, determines c_{n+1} in terms of c_n. In this and other applications of the method of Frobenius, one phase of our work is ended and we can make a progress report when we have found the indicial equation and recursion formula.

If $\gamma \neq 0, -1, -2, -3, \ldots$, we can satisfy (7.741) by setting $m = 0$, let $c_0 = 1$, and determine $c_1, c_2, c_3, \ldots$ from (7.742) to obtain the series in the right member of the equation

$$(7.75)\quad F(\alpha, \beta, \gamma; x) = 1 + \frac{\alpha \cdot \beta}{\gamma \cdot 1} x + \frac{\alpha(\alpha + 1)\beta(\beta + 1)}{\gamma(\gamma + 1)1 \cdot 2} x^2 + \cdots + \frac{\alpha(\alpha + 1) \cdots (\alpha + n - 1)\beta(\beta + 1) \cdots (\beta + n - 1)}{\gamma(\gamma + 1) \cdots (\gamma + n - 1)1 \cdot 2 \cdots n} x^n + \cdots.$$

This series is known as the *hypergeometric series*. The function to which it converges is known as the *hypergeometric function*, and it is denoted by $F(\alpha, \beta, \gamma; x)$ as indicated in (7.75). If α or β is 0 or a negative integer, the function is a polynomial; otherwise the series is a power series with radius of convergence 1, as may be shown by the ratio test. Thus, if $\gamma \neq 0, -1, -2, \ldots$, then (7.75) defines a function satisfying the hypergeometric equation when $|x| < 1$.

Returning to (7.741) and (7.742) we see that if $\gamma \neq 1, 2, 3, \ldots$, we can satisfy (7.741) by setting $m = 1 - \gamma$, let $c_0 = 1$, and determine $c_1, c_2, c_3, \ldots$ from (7.742) to obtain

$$(7.76)\qquad x^{1-\gamma}F(\alpha - \gamma + 1, \beta - \gamma + 1, 2 - \gamma; x)$$

as a solution of the hypergeometric equation over the interval

$$0 < x < 1.$$

Thus, if γ is not an integer, we have found two independent functions, say $y_1(x)$ and $y_2(x)$, satisfying the hypergeometric equation $Ly = 0$ over the interval $0 < x < 1$; and accordingly each function satisfying $Ly = 0$ over the interval $0 < x < 1$ must (Theorem 6.04) be a linear combination of $y_1(x)$ and $y_2(x)$. Since $x = 0$ is a singular point of $Ly = 0$, Theorem 6.04 does not apply to the whole interval $-1 \leqq x \leqq 1$.

Whether γ is an integer or not, at least one of the two functions in (7.75) and (7.76) must be a solution of $Ly = 0$ over the interval $0 < x < 1$; let one be denoted by $y_1(x)$. It is easy to show that, for each sufficiently small positive number x_0, $y_1(x) \neq 0$ when $0 < x \leqq x_0$. Then using (6.1908), we find that each solution of $Ly = 0$ may be represented over the interval $0 < x \leqq x_0$ by the formula

$$(7.77)\qquad y(x) = cy_1(x) + c_2y_1(x) \int_{x_0}^{x} \frac{1}{s^{\gamma}(1 - s)^{\alpha+\beta-\gamma+1}[y_1(s)]^2}\, ds.$$

This is an important formula, and we give one of its applications. If x_0

and x are confined to a sufficiently small interval $0 < x < \delta$, the second term on the right can be put in the form

$$y_1(x) \int_{x_0}^{x} s^M \sum_{k=0}^{\infty} A_k s^k \, ds \tag{7.771}$$

where M and $A_0, A_1, A_2, \ldots$ are constants. In case $A_k \neq 0$ for a k which makes $M + k = -1$, integration of this term will yield a term which is a nonzero multiple of $\log x$. All other terms have integrals that are powers of x, and (7.771) boils down to

$$Cy_1(x) \log x + x^m(c_0 + c_1x + c_2x^2 + \cdots) \tag{7.772}$$

where $C, m, c_0, c_1, \ldots$ are constants. Note that $y_1(x)$ has the Frobenius form

$$x^m(c_0 + c_1x + c_2x^2 + \cdots) \tag{7.773}$$

and that the product of two such functions is another one with different constants. Note also that $\log x$ does not have an expansion of this form. It follows that if the hypergeometric equation (7.71) has a solution $y_1(x)$ of the Frobenius form but does not have two independent solutions of this form, then it must have a solution of the form

$$y_2 = y_1(x) \log x + u \tag{7.774}$$

where u has the Frobenius form. The same method and the same conclusion apply to the Bessel equation and to each other equation having a regular singular point at the origin (see Sections 7.8 and 7.99). This removes the mystery from Problem 7.462 and from some things that lie ahead, and, at the same time, Problem 7.462 shows a method for finding u.

Remark 7.781

We have observed that, except for special cases, the hypergeometric series (7.75) converges to a solution of the hypergeometric equation only when $|x| < 1$. Anyone who happens to know the theory of *analytic extension*, which is best known as a part of the theory of analytic functions of a complex variable, should see that analytic extension furnishes a solution for wider ranges of x. Anyone not so fortunate can form an idea of the meaning of this remark from the following example: For the equation

$$(x^2 - x)y'' + (3x - 1)y' + y = 0 \tag{7.7811}$$

we have $\alpha = \beta = \gamma = 1$. From (7.75) we see that

$$F(1, 1, 1; x) = 1 + x + x^2 + \cdots = \frac{1}{1 - x} \qquad |x| < 1. \tag{7.7812}$$

Therefore $1/(1 - x)$ satisfies (7.7811) when $|x| < 1$, and one may guess that the same is true for other values of $x \neq 1$. Substitution shows that the guess is correct.

Problem 7.782

Show that, for the special hypergeometric equation (7.7811), the formula (7.77) with $y_1(x) = 1/(1 - x)$ gives the general solution

$$y = c_1 \frac{1}{1-x} + c_2 \frac{\log x}{1-x}$$

involving elementary functions.

Problem 7.783

If A, B, C, D, E, and F are constants for which $A \neq 0$ and $B^2 - 4AC \neq 0$, the equation

$$(At^2 + Bt + C)\frac{d^2y}{dt^2} + (Dt + E)\frac{dy}{dt} + Fy = 0 \tag{7.7831}$$

can be transformed into a hypergeometric equation by a simple change of variable. Show that constants p and q can be determined such that $p \neq 0$ and that, when $t = px + q$, (7.7831) holds if and only if

$$(x^2 - x)\frac{d^2y}{dx^2} + (Gx + H)\frac{dy}{dx} + Iy = 0 \tag{7.7832}$$

where G, H, and I are appropriate constants. Then show that constants α, β, and γ can be determined so that (7.7832) takes the form

$$(x^2 - x)\frac{d^2y}{dx^2} + [(\alpha + \beta + 1)x - \gamma]\frac{dy}{dx} + \alpha\beta y = 0$$

of a hypergeometric equation. What conclusion can be drawn from this work?

Problem 7.784

Start applying the method of Frobenius to the equation (7.7831) and observe that the indicial equation and recursion formula are thoroughly unpleasant. Then abandon this work and solve (7.71) again, noting how the particular forms of the coefficients contribute to simplicities of the indicial equation and recursion formula. Gauss (1777–1855) discovered the advantages of putting equations in the form (7.71).

Remark 7.79

In the next section, we need the factorial function $\alpha!$, and we make some remarks because many students of differential equations are acquainted with the definition and properties of $\alpha!$ only when $\alpha = 0, 1, 2, 3, \ldots$. The familiar formula

$$\alpha! = 1 \cdot 2 \cdot 3 \cdots (\alpha - 1)\alpha$$

clearly makes sense only when α is a positive integer. When α is a positive integer, it is easy to see that

$$\begin{aligned}\alpha! &= \lim_{n\to\infty} \frac{1 \cdot 2 \cdot 3 \cdots \alpha(\alpha+1)(\alpha+2)\cdots(\alpha+n)}{(\alpha+1)(\alpha+2)\cdots(\alpha+n)} \\ &= \lim_{n\to\infty} \frac{n!n^\alpha}{(\alpha+1)(\alpha+2)\cdots(\alpha+n)} \frac{(n+1)(n+2)\cdots(n+\alpha)}{n^\alpha}\end{aligned}$$

and hence that

$$\alpha! = \lim_{n\to\infty} \frac{n!n^\alpha}{(\alpha+1)(\alpha+2)\cdots(\alpha+n)}. \tag{7.791}$$

This can be put in the form

$$\alpha! = \lim_{n\to\infty} \frac{n^\alpha}{\left(1+\frac{\alpha}{1}\right)\left(1+\frac{\alpha}{2}\right)\left(1+\frac{\alpha}{3}\right)\cdots\left(1+\frac{\alpha}{n}\right)}. \tag{7.792}$$

It is just one of the accidents of nature that the limits in (7.791) and (7.792) exist whenever α is a number (real or complex) which is not a negative integer. These formulas are used to define the *factorial function* $\alpha!$, which is the same as the *gamma function* $\Gamma(\alpha + 1)$ so that $\Gamma(\alpha + 1) = \alpha!$, when $\alpha \neq -1, -2, -3, \ldots$ This definition of $\alpha!$ was used by Gauss who had the habit of knowing how things should be done. The factorial function* is the most important nonelementary function of mathematical analysis.

The nature of the graph of $\alpha!$ versus α, for real α, is shown in Fig. 7.7921.

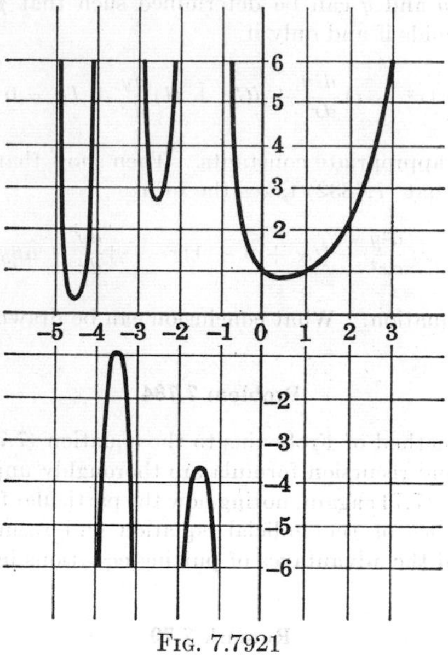

FIG. 7.7921

We now give, largely without proofs, some information and formulas. The factorial function $\alpha!$ is defined for each complex $\alpha \neq -1, -2, -3, \ldots$ and, when k is a positive integer, $|\alpha!| \to \infty$ as $\alpha \to -k$. Like the exponential function e^α, the factorial function $\alpha!$ is never 0. It is easy to use (7.971) to prove that

$$(\alpha + 1)! = \alpha!(\alpha + 1) \qquad \alpha \neq -1, -2, -3, \ldots \tag{7.793}$$

* Tables, graphs, and much information about this and other nonelementary functions are given in a book entitled "*Funktionentafeln* and Tables of Functions," by Jahnke (1861–1921) and Emde (1873–). This book, published by Teubner Verlagsgesellschaft, Leipzig, in several editions, gives the text in both German and English and gives references to other sources of information.

This is the *functional equation* of the factorial function. When $\gamma_1, \gamma_2, \gamma_3, \ldots$ are defined by

(7.794) $$\gamma_n = 1 + \frac{1}{2} + \frac{1}{3} + \cdots + \frac{1}{n} - \log n,$$

existence of the Euler constant gamma defined by

(7.795) $$\gamma = \lim_{n\to\infty} \gamma_n = 0.57721\ 56649\ 01532\ 86061$$

can be proved. This is, after π and e, the most important mathematical constant not appearing in elementary arithmetic. With the aid of the formula

$$n^\alpha = e^{\alpha \log n} = e^{\alpha\left[-\gamma_n+1+\frac{1}{2}+\frac{1}{3}+\cdots+\frac{1}{n}\right]}$$

we can put (7.792) in the form

(7.7951) $$\alpha! = e^{-\gamma\alpha} \lim_{n\to\infty} \frac{e^{\alpha/1}}{1+\frac{\alpha}{1}} \frac{e^{\alpha/2}}{1+\frac{\alpha}{2}} \frac{e^{\alpha/3}}{1+\frac{\alpha}{3}} \cdots \frac{e^{\alpha/n}}{1+\frac{\alpha}{n}}.$$

Persons who know about infinite products (things like infinite series except that we multiply factors instead of adding terms) prefer this formula because of the ease with which existence of the limit can be proved. If α is not an integer, we can replace α by $-\alpha$ and do some multiplying to obtain

(7.7952) $$\alpha!(-\alpha)! = \lim_{n\to\infty} \frac{1}{\left(1-\frac{\alpha^2}{1^2}\right)\left(1-\frac{\alpha^2}{2^2}\right)\cdots\left(1-\frac{\alpha^2}{n^2}\right)}.$$

From this and the famous nonelementary formula

(7.7953) $$\sin \pi\alpha = \lim_{n\to\infty} \pi\alpha \left(1-\frac{\alpha^2}{1^2}\right)\left(1-\frac{\alpha^2}{2^2}\right)\cdots\left(1-\frac{\alpha^2}{n^2}\right)$$

we obtain the formula

(7.7954) $$\alpha!(-\alpha)! = \frac{\pi\alpha}{\sin \pi\alpha}$$

which is valid when α is not an integer. It can be proved that

(7.796) $$\alpha! = \int_0^\infty e^{-x}x^\alpha\, dx$$

when α is a complex number with real part exceeding -1; this is the *Euler* (1707–1783) *gamma integral* which, depending upon circumstances, is used to give the value of the integral or to give a useful formula for $\alpha!$. It can be proved that

(7.7961) $$\int_0^1 x^\alpha(1-x)^\beta dx = \frac{\alpha!\beta!}{(\alpha+\beta+1)!}$$

when α and β are complex numbers with real parts exceeding -1; this is the *Euler beta integral.* The formulas

$$(7.7962)\qquad \left(-\frac{1}{2}\right)! = \sqrt{\pi}, \qquad \left(\frac{1}{2}\right)! = \frac{\sqrt{\pi}}{2},$$

are both interesting and important.

One who doubts that the information given above can be the source of much more information should see something. At least when $\alpha > -1$, taking logarithms of the members of (7.7951) gives the formula

$$(7.797)\qquad \log \alpha! = -\gamma\alpha + \sum_{k=1}^{\infty} \left[\frac{\alpha}{k} - \log\left(1 + \frac{\alpha}{k}\right)\right]$$

and differentiation gives

$$(7.7971)\qquad \Psi(\alpha) = \frac{d}{d\alpha} \log \alpha! = -\gamma + \sum_{k=1}^{\infty} \left[\frac{1}{k} - \frac{1}{k+\alpha}\right]$$

and

$$(7.7972)\qquad \Psi'(\alpha) = \frac{d^2}{d\alpha^2} \log \alpha! = \sum_{k=1}^{\infty} \frac{1}{(k+\alpha)^2}.$$

The function $\Psi(\alpha)$ is the *logarithmic derivative* of $\alpha!$, and the derivative of $\alpha!$ is obtained from the formulas

$$(7.7973)\qquad \frac{d}{d\alpha} \log \alpha! = \frac{1}{\alpha!}\frac{d\alpha!}{d\alpha}, \qquad \frac{d\alpha!}{d\alpha} = \alpha!\Psi(\alpha).$$

Some applications of these things are simple; it is easy to see that the graph of $\alpha!$ has slope $-\gamma$ at the point (0, 1) and has slope $1 - \gamma$ at the point (1, 1). It is not so easy to see that the minimum value of $\alpha!$ for $\alpha > 0$ occurs when $\alpha = 0.46163$ and is 0.88560.

Problem 7.798

Determine the values of α, β, and γ for which

$$F(\alpha, \beta, \gamma; x) = \frac{(\gamma-1)!}{(\alpha-1)!(\beta-1)!}\, y(x)$$

where

$$(7.7981)\qquad y = \sum_{k=0}^{\infty} \frac{(\alpha-1+k)!(\beta-1+k)!}{(\gamma-1+k)!\,k!} x^k.$$

Then do a little experimenting. See whether you can survive the operation of writing out the series in (7.75) and doing the differentiating and substituting necessary to show directly that $F(\alpha, \beta, \gamma; x)$ satisfies the hypergeometric equation (7.71). Finally, try showing that the above function y satisfies (7.71).

7.8. The Bessel Equation.

Let Ly denote the left member of the equation

$$(7.81)\qquad x^2\frac{d^2y}{dx^2} + x\frac{dy}{dx} + (x^2 - \alpha^2)y = 0$$

so that the Bessel equation of order α becomes $Ly = 0$. We find in this case

$$Lx^r = (r^2 - \alpha^2)x^r + x^{r+2}. \tag{7.82}$$

Hence, if y has the Frobenius form

$$y = x^m \sum_{n=0}^{\infty} c_n x^n = \sum_{n=0}^{\infty} c_n x^{m+n} \tag{7.83}$$

for some range of values of x, then

$$\begin{aligned} Ly &= \sum_{n=0}^{\infty} c_n L x^{m+n} = \sum_{n=0}^{\infty} c_n[\{(m+n)^2 - \alpha^2\}x^{m+n} + x^{m+n+2}] \\ &= c_0\{m^2 - \alpha^2\}x^m + c_1\{(m+1)^2 - \alpha^2\}x^{m+1} \\ &\qquad + \sum_{n=0}^{\infty} [\{(m+n+2)^2 - \alpha^2\}c_{n+2} + c_n]x^{m+n+2}. \end{aligned} \tag{7.831}$$

The next step is to try to determine m such that the *indicial equation*

$$c_0\{m^2 - \alpha^2\} = 0 \tag{7.832}$$

holds and then to determine the c's such that

$$c_1\{(m+1)^2 - \alpha^2\} = 0 \tag{7.833}$$

and

$$\{(m+n+2)^2 - \alpha^2\}c_{n+2} = -c_n \qquad n = 0, 1, 2, \ldots . \tag{7.834}$$

We can now report that the indicial equation and recursion formula have been found.

If α is not a negative integer, we can set $m = \alpha$, set $c_0 = 1/2^\alpha \alpha!$, set $c_1 = 0$, and then determine $c_2, c_3, \ldots$ from (7.834) to obtain the series in the right member of the equation

$$\begin{aligned} J_\alpha(x) = \frac{x^\alpha}{2^\alpha \alpha!}\Bigg[1 &- \frac{1}{1(\alpha+1)}\left(\frac{x}{2}\right)^2 + \frac{1}{1\cdot 2(\alpha+1)(\alpha+2)}\left(\frac{x}{2}\right)^4 \\ &- \cdots + (-1)^n \frac{1}{1\cdot 2 \cdots n(\alpha+1)(\alpha+2)\cdots(\alpha+n)}\left(\frac{x}{2}\right)^{2n} \\ &+ \cdots\Bigg]. \end{aligned} \tag{7.84}$$

The series in brackets converges for all values of x; the function on the right is called *Bessel's function of the first kind of order* α and is denoted by $J_\alpha(x)$ as in (7.84). Using the fundamental formula $\alpha!(\alpha+1) = (\alpha+1)!$, we can write (7.84) in the form

$$(7.85)\quad J_\alpha(x) = \left(\frac{x}{2}\right)^\alpha \left[\frac{1}{0!\alpha!} - \frac{1}{1!(\alpha+1)!}\left(\frac{x}{2}\right)^2 + \frac{1}{2!(\alpha+2)!}\left(\frac{x}{2}\right)^4 + \cdots + (-1)^n \frac{1}{n!(\alpha+n)!}\left(\frac{x}{2}\right)^{2n} + \cdots\right]$$

$$\alpha \neq -1, -2, -3, \ldots .$$

In particular,

$$(7.851)\quad J_0(x) = 1 - \frac{x^2}{2^2} + \frac{x^4}{2^2 4^2} - \frac{x^6}{2^2 4^2 6^2} + \frac{x^8}{2^2 4^2 6^2 8^2} - \cdots .$$

This is the most important Bessel function. The others are not used so often but, like the landing gear on an airplane, it is very convenient to have them when they are needed. The power-series expansion of $J_0(x)$ is the same as that in

$$\cos x = 1 - \frac{x^2}{1 \cdot 2} + \frac{x^4}{1 \cdot 2 \cdot 3 \cdot 4} - \frac{x^6}{1 \cdot 2 \cdot 3 \cdot 4 \cdot 5 \cdot 6} + \cdots$$

except that each odd integer in a denominator is replaced by the next greater integer.

The first of the formulas

$$(7.852)\quad J_\alpha(x) = \sum_{k=0}^{\infty} (-1)^k \frac{1}{k!(\alpha+k)!}\left(\frac{x}{2}\right)^{\alpha+2k}$$

$$(7.853)\quad xJ'_\alpha(x) = \sum_{k=0}^{\infty} (-1)^k \frac{\alpha+2k}{k!(\alpha+k)!}\left(\frac{x}{2}\right)^{\alpha+2k}$$

$$(7.854)\quad x\frac{d}{dx}\, xJ'_\alpha(x) = \sum_{k=0}^{\infty} (-1)^k \frac{(\alpha+2k)^2}{k!(\alpha+k)!}\left(\frac{x}{2}\right)^{\alpha+2k}$$

is merely another way of writing the definition (7.85) of $J_\alpha(x)$, and the others are obtained by differentiating and multiplying by x. In case α is a negative integer, we define $J_\alpha(x)$ by the same formula (7.852), but with the stipulation that those terms for which $\alpha + k$ is a negative integer are to be replaced by zero or omitted from the series. If n is a positive integer, then

$$(7.855)\quad J_{-n}(x) = \sum_{k=n}^{\infty} (-1)^k \frac{1}{k!(-n+k)!}\left(\frac{x}{2}\right)^{-n+2k}$$

$$= \sum_{k=0}^{\infty} (-1)^{n+k} \frac{1}{(n+k)!k!}\left(\frac{x}{2}\right)^{n+2k} = (-1)^n J_n(x)$$

so $J_{-n}(x)$ and $J_n(x)$ are not independent when x is an integer.

The definition (7.852) and the formulas following it can be used to derive numerous Bessel function identities. The principal ones are:

$$J'_\alpha(x) = \tfrac{1}{2}J_{\alpha-1}(x) - \tfrac{1}{2}J_{\alpha+1}(x) \tag{7.856}$$

$$J'_0(x) = -J_1(x) \tag{7.8561}$$

$$J_{\alpha+1}(x) = \frac{2\alpha}{x} J_\alpha(x) - J_{\alpha-1}(x) \tag{7.857}$$

$$\frac{d}{dx}[x^\alpha J_\alpha(x)] = x^\alpha J_{\alpha-1}(x), \qquad \frac{d}{dx}[x^{-\alpha} J_\alpha(x)] = -x^{-\alpha} J_{\alpha+1}(x) \tag{7.858}$$

$$J'_\alpha(x) = \frac{\alpha}{x} J_\alpha(x) - J_{\alpha+1}(x), \qquad J'_\alpha(x) = J_{\alpha-1}(x) - \frac{\alpha}{x} J_\alpha(x) \tag{7.8581}$$

$$J''_0(x) = \tfrac{1}{2}J_2(x) - \tfrac{1}{2}J_0(x) \tag{7.8582}$$

$$J_{\frac{1}{2}}(x) = \sqrt{\frac{2}{\pi}}\frac{\sin x}{\sqrt{x}}, \qquad J_{-\frac{1}{2}}(x) = \sqrt{\frac{2}{\pi}}\frac{\cos x}{\sqrt{x}}. \tag{7.8583}$$

Use of (7.857) and (7.8583) shows that if n is an odd integer, then $J_{(n/2)}(x)$ is an elementary function. For example

$$J_{\frac{3}{2}}(x) = \sqrt{\frac{2}{\pi}}\frac{1}{\sqrt{x}}\left(\frac{\sin x}{x} - \cos x\right). \tag{7.8584}$$

One who wishes to see how an identity can be discovered can start with (7.853), replace the numerator $\alpha + 2k$ by the sum of k and $\alpha + k$, break the series into the sum of two series, and simplify the result. Graphs of $J_0(x)$ and $J_1(x)$ for $x \geqq 0$ are shown in Fig. 7.859.

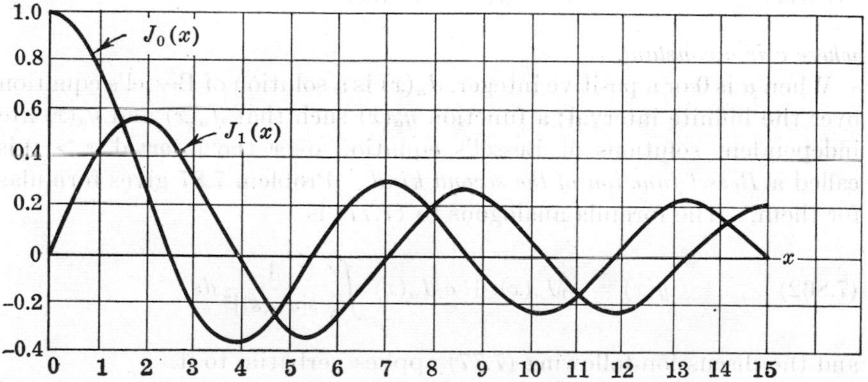

FIG. 7.859

Let $\alpha \geqq 0$. In case α is an integer, the functions $J_\alpha(x)$ and $J_{-\alpha}(x)$ are solutions of the Bessel equation of order α over the entire infinite interval $-\infty < x < \infty$, but they are not independent. In case α is not an integer, $J_\alpha(x)$ and $J_{-\alpha}(x)$ are both solutions of the Bessel equation of order α over the interval $x > 0$ but

$$\lim_{x \to 0} |J_{-\alpha}(x)| = \infty. \tag{7.8591}$$

Moreover $J_0(x) \to 1$ as $x \to 0$ and, when $\alpha > 0$, $J_\alpha(x) \to 0$ as $x \to 0$. When α is not an integer, this implies that $J_\alpha(x)$ and $J_{-\alpha}(x)$ must be independent, and accordingly we obtain the following result which we formulate as a theorem:

THEOREM 7.86. *If α is not an integer, then each function $y(x)$ satisfying Bessel's equation*

$$x^2 \frac{d^2y}{dx^2} + x\frac{dy}{dx} + (x^2 - \alpha^2)y = 0 \tag{7.8601}$$

over the interval $x > 0$ must have the form

$$y(x) = c_1 J_\alpha(x) + c_2 J_{-\alpha}(x) \tag{7.8602}$$

where c_1 and c_2 are constants.

If $\alpha \geqq 0$ and α is not an integer, then (7.8591) implies that $J_{-\alpha}(x)$ is not bounded over the interval $0 < x \leqq 1$. Since $J_\alpha(x)$ is bounded over the interval $0 < x \leqq 1$, this fact and Theorem 7.86 imply the conclusion of the following theorem for the case in which α is not an integer.

THEOREM 7.861. *If $\alpha \geqq 0$, then each function $y(x)$ which satisfies Bessel's equation over the interval $x > 0$ and which is bounded over the interval $0 < x \leqq 1$ must have the form*

$$y(x) = cJ_\alpha(x) \tag{7.8611}$$

where c is a constant.

When α is 0 or a positive integer, $J_\alpha(x)$ is a solution of Bessel's equation over the infinite interval; a function $y_\alpha(x)$ such that $J_\alpha(x)$ and $y_\alpha(x)$ are independent solutions of Bessel's equation over the interval $x > 0$ is called a *Bessel function of the second kind.* Problem 7.87 gives formulas for them. The formula analogous to (7.77) is

$$y(x) = c_1 J_\alpha(x) + c_2 J_\alpha(x) \int_{x_0}^{x} \frac{1}{s[J_\alpha(s)]^2}\, ds \tag{7.862}$$

and the discussion following (7.77) applies verbatim to it.

Bessel functions are often called *cylindrical harmonics;* they are used in problems in which there is radial symmetry about an axis. In many cases the axis is a wire or the axis of a cylinder or pipe. Scientific libraries contain books on Bessel functions and their applications. The Jahnke-Emde tables cited in Remark 7.79 devote 127 pages to Bessel functions, giving many graphs and tables.

Problem 7.87

This problem involves formulas for Bessel functions of the second kind. Show that, when $x > 0$, the function y defined by

$$y = J_\alpha(x) \log x + u \tag{7.871}$$

satisfies the Bessel equation of order α iff u satisfies the equation

$$x^2u'' + xu' + (x^2 - \alpha^2)u = -2xJ'_\alpha(x). \tag{7.872}$$

Putting $u = x^{-\alpha}v$ gives the more attractive equation

$$xv'' - (2\alpha - 1)v' + xv = -2x^\alpha J'_\alpha(x). \tag{7.873}$$

We suppose that α is 0 or a positive integer. There exist constants $c_0, c_1, c_2, \ldots$ such that the series in

$$v = c_0 + c_1x + c_2x^2 + \cdots$$

converges for all values of x (complex as well as real) and defines a function v satisfying (7.873) for all values of x. In case $\alpha > 0$, the constant $c_{2\alpha-2}$ must have the value $-1/(\alpha - 1)!2^{\alpha-1}$, and in every case the constant $c_{2\alpha}$ can have an arbitrary value A. All of the other c's are determined by these two and recursion formulas. Determining the c's and v, expressing y in terms of v, and calling the result $K_\alpha(B, x)$ give the formula

$$K_\alpha(B, x) = J_\alpha(x) \log x - \frac{1}{2}\sum_{k=0}^{\alpha-1} \frac{(\alpha - 1 - k)!}{k!}\left(\frac{x}{2}\right)^{-\alpha+2k} - \frac{1}{2}\sum_{k=0}^{\infty} \frac{(-1)^k}{k!(\alpha + k)!}\left\{B + \sum_{p=\alpha+1}^{\alpha+k} \frac{1}{p} + \sum_{p=1}^{k} \frac{1}{p}\right\}\left(\frac{x}{2}\right)^{\alpha+2k} \tag{7.874}$$

where $B = -2^{\alpha+1}\alpha!A$. In case $\alpha = 0$ and $B = 0$, this reduces to (7.4625) because there are no integers k or p for which $0 \leqq k \leqq -1$ or $1 \leqq p \leqq 0$.

For each value of the constant B, this is a Bessel function of the second kind which satisfies the Bessel equation of positive or zero integer order α. The effect of a change in the constant B is to add a multiple of $J_\alpha(x)$ to the right side. One way to use B is to make it equal to $1 + \frac{1}{2} + \cdots + \frac{1}{\alpha}$, this being 0 when $\alpha = 0$, to fill out the sum that follows it. Some useful determinations of B involve the *Euler constant* γ defined by (7.795). Note that $K_\alpha(B, x)$ depends upon B and that each Bessel function of the second kind and order α has the form $AK_\alpha(B, x)$ where A and B are constants for which $A \neq 0$. Different ones of these are useful for different purposes, and the museum of the SPC (*Society for the Promotion of Confusion*) contains a huge collection of notations that have been proposed for them.

Problem 7.875

Neglecting to require that α be an integer, the first edition of this book said that if $\alpha \geqq 0$, then $J_\alpha(x)$ is a solution of the Bessel equation over the interval $-\infty < x < \infty$. Using (7.8583) with $J_{\frac{1}{2}}(0) = 0$, discuss this matter.

Problem 7.881

Let $y(x)$ be a solution, for $x > 0$, of Bessel's equation

$$x^2y'' + xy' + (x^2 - \alpha^2)y = 0. \tag{7.8811}$$

Show that if $y = uv$ where $u(x)$ and $v(x)$ have two derivatives each, then

$$x^2uv'' + (2x^2u' + xu)v' + [x^2u'' + xu' + (x^2 - \alpha^2)u]v = 0.$$

Determine $u(x)$ so that the coefficient of v' is 0, and continue your work to show that the function $v(x)$ defined by

$$v(x) = \sqrt{x}\, y(x) \tag{7.8812}$$

is a solution of the differential equation

$$v'' + \left[1 + \frac{\frac{1}{4} - \alpha^2}{x^2}\right]v = 0. \tag{7.8813}$$

[This result can be used to determine properties of Bessel functions $y(x)$. If α and h are fixed, then when A is a large positive number the coefficients in (7.8813) differ very little over the interval $A \leqq x \leqq A + h$ from the coefficients in the equation

$$w'' + w = 0. \tag{7.8814}$$

A solution of (7.8814) over the interval $A \leqq x \leqq A + h$ must have the form

$$w = C \sin (x - x_0)$$

where C and x_0 are constants. Hence it is not surprising that, if $y(x)$ is a Bessel function, then the graph of $\sqrt{x}\, y(x)$ over the interval $A \leqq x \leqq A + h$ looks very much like a piece of a sine curve. The positive zeros of $\sqrt{x}\, y(x)$ and $y(x)$ are the same; each has an infinite set $z_1 < z_2 < z_3 < \cdots$ of them, and the distance $z_{n+1} - z_n$ between two consecutive zeros converges to π as $n \to \infty$. Some precise information about this matter is given in Problem 6.875.]

Problem 7.882

When $x > 0$, Bessel's equation of order α can be written in the form

$$\frac{d^2y}{dx^2} + \frac{1}{x}\frac{dy}{dx} + \left(1 - \frac{\alpha^2}{x^2}\right)y = 0. \tag{7.8821}$$

Show that if k is a constant not 0, then each solution $z(x)$ of the equation

$$\frac{d^2z}{dx^2} + \frac{1}{x}\frac{dz}{dx} + \left(k^2 - \frac{\alpha^2}{x^2}\right)z = 0 \tag{7.8822}$$

has the form $z = y(kx)$ where $y(x)$ satisfies (7.8821). [This means that each solution of (7.8822) has the form $z = y_\alpha(kx)$ where $y_\alpha(x)$ is a linear combination of Bessel functions.]

Problem 7.883

Considering positive values of x, show that if

$$\frac{d^2w}{dx^2} + \frac{a}{x}\frac{dw}{dx} + k^2w = 0, \tag{7.8831}$$

then an exponent α can be determined such that the function $z(x)$ defined by $z(x) = x^{-\alpha}w(x)$ satisfies (7.8822). [The value of α is $(1 - a)/2$. This means that each solution $w(x)$ of (7.8831) has, when $k \neq 0$, the form $w = x^\alpha y_\alpha(kx)$ where $y_\alpha(x)$ is a linear combination of Bessel functions.] By examining the case in which $a = 0$, $k = 1$, show that each linear combination of $\sin x$ and $\cos x$ must be a linear combination of $\sqrt{x}\, J_{\frac{1}{2}}(x)$ and $\sqrt{x}\, J_{-\frac{1}{2}}(x)$ [see (7.8583)].

Problem 7.884

This problem illustrates the fact that a more extensive batch of parameters increases the class of differential equations whose solutions are known to be expressible in terms of Bessel functions. Supposing that $y_\alpha(x)$ satisfies the Bessel equation of order α, let $x > 0$ and show that the function $u(x)$ defined by

$$u(x) = x^p y_\alpha(\lambda x^q), \tag{7.8841}$$

where p, λ, and q are real parameters with $\lambda \neq 0$ and $q \neq 0$, satisfies the equation

$$x^2 \frac{d^2u}{dx^2} + (1 - 2p)x \frac{du}{dx} + [\lambda^2 q^2 x^{2q} + (p^2 - \alpha^2 q^2)]u = 0$$

and conversely that if u satisfies this equation, then $y_\alpha(x)$ satisfies the Bessel equation. Many things can be done with this. For example, choosing the parameters so that $1 - 2p = 0$, $p^2 - \alpha^2 q^2 = 0$, and $2q - 2 = h$ shows that solutions of the equation

$$\frac{d^2u}{dx^2} + Ax^h u = 0 \tag{7.8842}$$

are expressible in terms of Bessel functions. Show that (7.8841) satisfies the equation

$$\frac{d^2u}{dx^2} + xu = 0 \tag{7.8843}$$

when $\alpha = \frac{1}{3}$, $p = \frac{1}{2}$, $\lambda = \frac{2}{3}$, and $q = \frac{3}{2}$. This shows that each solution of (7.8843) has the form

$$u = c_1 \sqrt{x}\, J_{\frac{1}{3}}(\tfrac{2}{3}x^{\frac{3}{2}}) + c_2 \sqrt{x}\, J_{-\frac{1}{3}}(\tfrac{2}{3}x^{\frac{3}{2}}). \tag{7.8844}$$

We solved the equation (7.8843) in Section 7.4, but we did not learn anything about the nature of its solutions. We now have a chance to learn about them. Since $J_{\frac{1}{3}}(x)$ is a Bessel function it must, according to Problem 6.875, have the form

$$J_{\frac{1}{3}}(x) = \frac{C \sin (x + \delta) + \epsilon(x)}{\sqrt{x}}$$

where C and δ are constants and $\epsilon(x)$ is a transient. Hence

$$\sqrt{x}\, J_{\frac{1}{3}}\left(\frac{2}{3}\, x^{\frac{3}{2}}\right) = \frac{C_1 \sin (\frac{2}{3}x^{\frac{3}{2}} + \delta) + \epsilon_1(x)}{x^{\frac{1}{4}}}$$

where C_1 is another constant and $\epsilon_1(x)$ is another transient. The last term in (7.8844) has this same form and hence u does also. This gives remarkable information about the manner in which u oscillates with rapidly increasing frequency and slowly decreasing amplitude.

Problem 7.891

Show that

$$J_\alpha(x) = \sum_{p=0}^{\infty} \frac{1}{(2p)!(\alpha + 2p)!}\left[1 - \frac{x^2}{4(2p+1)(\alpha+2p+1)}\right]\left(\frac{x}{2}\right)^{\alpha+4p}.$$

Use this to show that if $\alpha > -1$, then

(7.892) $$J_\alpha(x) > 0 \qquad 0 < x < 2\sqrt{\alpha+1}.$$

Problem 7.893

Note that the positive zeros of $J_\alpha(x)$ are the same as those of $x^\alpha J_\alpha(x)$ and $x^{-\alpha}J_\alpha(x)$. Use the Rolle theorem (the index will provide help if it is needed) and (7.858) to prove that if α is real, then the positive zeros of $J_\alpha(x)$ and $J_{\alpha+1}(x)$ interlace. This means that between each pair or positive zeros of $J_\alpha(x)$ there is a zero of $J_{\alpha+1}(x)$ and between each pair of positive zeros of $J_{\alpha+1}(x)$ there is a zero of $J_\alpha(x)$.

Remark 7.894

We should see how differential equations are used to work out some formulas, involving integrals of Bessel functions, that have important applications.

Let α be a real constant, and let $y(x)$ be a nontrivial solution of the Bessel equation of order α. Let $\lambda_1, \lambda_2, \lambda_3, \ldots$ be a sequence of distinct nonzero complex constants. Let a and b be real constants such that $0 \leqq a < b < \infty$ and integral in

(7.8941) $$\int_a^b x|y(\lambda_k x)|^2 dx = \frac{1}{B_k^2}$$

exists for each k, and let B_k be the positive number for which the equality holds. Let

(7.8942) $$\phi_k(x) = B_k\sqrt{x}\, y(\lambda_k x) \qquad x > 0.$$

These two formulas imply the first of the formulas

(7.89421) $$\int_a^b |\phi_k(x)|^2 dx = 1 \qquad k = 1, 2, \ldots$$

(7.89422) $$\int_a^b \overline{\phi_j(x)}\phi_k(x)dx = 0 \qquad j \neq k.$$

Our principal task is to learn about sequences $\lambda_1, \lambda_2, \ldots$ for which the whole set of formulas is valid. This is important because when the formulas are valid the functions $\phi_1, \phi_2, \ldots$ constitute an orthonormal set and we can apply the ideas and methods of Section 6.7 and Chapter 12. Putting $p = \frac{1}{2}$ and $q = 1$ in (7.8841) and the following formulas shows that the first of the two formulas

$$x^2\phi_k'' + [\lambda_k^2x^2 + (\tfrac{1}{4} - \alpha^2)]\phi_k = 0$$
$$x^2\bar\phi_j'' + [\bar\lambda_j^2x^2 + (\tfrac{1}{4} - \alpha^2)]\bar\phi_j = 0$$

is valid. The second is obtained from the first by replacing k and j and taking complex conjugates. One who has not seen things like this before is quite right in feeling that things are growing mysterious. He should read Chapter 12 sometimes and learn that our equations have the Sturm-Liouville form. We eliminate α from the two equations by multiplying the first by $\bar{\phi}_j$ and the second by $-\phi_k$ and adding. This gives

$$(\bar{\lambda}_j^2 - \lambda_k^2)\bar{\phi}_j\phi_k = \bar{\phi}_j\phi_k'' - \bar{\phi}_j''\phi_k.$$

We are very close to useful information when we observe that the right side of this equation is, when $x > 0$, the derivative $R'(x)$ of the function $R(x)$ defined by

$$R(x) = \overline{\phi_j(x)}\phi_k'(x) - \overline{\phi_j'(x)}\phi_k(x). \tag{7.8943}$$

Therefore when $0 < h < b$, so that h can be a if $a > 0$, we can integrate to obtain

$$(\bar{\lambda}_j^2 - \lambda_k^2)\int_h^b \overline{\phi_j(x)}\phi_k(x)dx = R(b) - R(h). \tag{7.8944}$$

In case $h = a$, the integral in this formula is the integral about which we are seeking information.

While (7.8944) has other applications, we confine our attention to the case in which $\alpha > -1$, $a = 0$, and $y = J_\alpha(x)$. In this case (7.8943) reduces to

$$R(x) = B_jB_kx[\lambda_k\overline{J_\alpha(\lambda_jx)}J_\alpha'(\lambda_kx) - \bar{\lambda}_j\overline{J_\alpha'(\lambda_jx)}J_\alpha(\lambda_kx)]$$

and $R(x) \to 0$ as $x \to 0$. Hence (7.8944) implies the familiar formula

$$\begin{aligned}(\bar{\lambda}_j^2 - \lambda_k^2)\int_0^b x\overline{J_\alpha(\lambda_jx)}J_\alpha(\lambda_kx)dx \\ = b\{\lambda_k\overline{J_\alpha(\lambda_jb)}J_\alpha'(\lambda_kb) - \bar{\lambda}_j\overline{J_\alpha'(\lambda_jb)}J_\alpha(\lambda_kb)\}.\end{aligned} \tag{7.8945}$$

It is very easy to see that the right member of this equation must be zero if the numbers $\lambda_1, \lambda_2, \ldots$ are chosen such that $J_\alpha(\lambda_pb) = 0$ for each $p = 1, 2, \ldots$ or such that $J_\alpha'(\lambda_pb) = 0$ for each $p = 1, 2, \ldots$. This information and very much more is contained in the following theorem.

THEOREM 7.8946. *Let $\alpha > -1$. If H_1 and H_2 are real constants not both* 0 *and if the numbers $\lambda_1b, \lambda_2b, \ldots$ are all zeros of the function*

$$H_1J_\alpha(z) + H_2zJ_\alpha'(z) \tag{7.89461}$$

then the right member of (7.8945) *is* 0. *Moreover each zero of* (7.89461) *having a nonzero real part must be real.*

To prove the first part of the theorem, we observe that if

$$H_1J_\alpha(\lambda_kb) + H_2\lambda_kbJ_\alpha'(\lambda_kb) = 0$$

for each $k = 1, 2, 3, \ldots$, then we can replace k by j and take conjugates to obtain

$$H_1\overline{J_\alpha(\lambda_jb)} + H_2\bar{\lambda}_jb\overline{J_\alpha'(\lambda_jb)} = 0.$$

For each pair j and k of positive integers, these two equations then have a nontrivial solution for H_1 and H_2. The determinant of the coefficients of H_1 and H_2 is the right member of (7.8945) and this must be 0. To prove the last part of the theorem, let z_0 be a zero of (7.89461) for which $z_0 = \sigma_0 + it_0$ and $\sigma_0 \neq 0$. Defining λ_p by the formula $\lambda_pb = z_0$ and setting $\lambda_j = \lambda_k = \lambda_p$ in (7.8945) then gives the formula

$$\sigma_0t_0\int_0^b x|J_\alpha(\lambda_px)|^2dx = 0.$$

Neither σ_0 nor the integral is 0 so $t_0 = 0$ and z_0 must be real. This completes the proof of the theorem. Using this theorem and the formula (7.8945) gives the following theorem.

Theorem 7.8947. *Let $\alpha > -1$. If H_1 and H_2 are real constants not both 0 and if the numbers $\lambda_1 b, \lambda_2 b, \ldots$ are distinct positive zeros of the function*

$$H_1 J_\alpha(z) + H_2 z J'_\alpha(z), \tag{7.89471}$$

then

$$\int_0^b x J_\alpha(\lambda_j x) J_\alpha(\lambda_k x)\,dx = 0 \tag{7.89472}$$

when $j \neq k$.

One who wishes to see a thoroughly transparent special case of this theorem may look at the case in which $\alpha = -\frac{1}{2}$, $H_2 = 0$, and

$$J_\alpha(x) = \sqrt{\frac{2}{\pi}}\frac{\cos x}{\sqrt{x}}, \qquad \lambda_k b = k\pi - \frac{\pi}{2}.$$

Theorem 7.8946 does not answer the question whether the function (7.89461) can have nonreal zeros of the form it, and we shall answer the question when $H_2 = 0$ by proving the following theorem.

Theorem 7.8948. *If $\alpha > -1$, the zeros of $J_\alpha(x)$ are all real.*

Let $\sigma + it$ be a zero of $J_\alpha(x)$. Theorem 7.8946 shows that if $\sigma \neq 0$, then $t = 0$ and the zero must be real. It is therefore sufficient to show that $J_\alpha(it) \neq 0$ when t is real and $t \neq 0$. From (7.85) or (7.852) we obtain

$$J_\alpha(it) = \left(\frac{it}{2}\right)^\alpha \sum_{k=0}^{\infty} \frac{1}{k!(\alpha + k)!}\left(\frac{t}{2}\right)^{2k}.$$

When t is real and $t \neq 0$, the first factor is not 0 and the second factor is positive because it is the limit of a sum of positive terms. The conclusion follows.

Finally we suppose that $\alpha > -1$ and $\lambda_k > 0$ and show a special trick that produces a derivation of the formula

$$2\lambda_k \int_0^b x[J_\alpha(\lambda_k x)]^2 dx = b^2\lambda_k[J'_\alpha(\lambda_k b)]^2 - bJ_\alpha(\lambda_k b)J'_\alpha(\lambda_k b) - b^2\lambda_k J_\alpha(\lambda_k b)J''_\alpha(\lambda_k b) \tag{7.8949}$$

which, in some circumstances, determines the normalizing constant B_k in (7.8941). Supposing that λ_j is real and $\lambda_j > \lambda_k$, we can put (7.8945) is the form

$$(\lambda_j + \lambda_k)\int_0^b xJ_\alpha(\lambda_j x)J_\alpha(\lambda_k x)\,dx = \frac{F(\lambda_j) - F(\lambda_k)}{\lambda_j - \lambda_k}$$

where

$$F(\lambda_j) = b\lambda_k J_\alpha(\lambda_j b)J'_\alpha(\lambda_k b) - b\lambda_j J_\alpha(\lambda_k b)J'_\alpha(\lambda_j b).$$

Since $F'(\lambda_k)$ is the right member of (7.8949), taking limits as $\lambda_j \to \lambda_k$ gives the result. In the important special case in which the numbers $\lambda_k b$ are zeros of $J_\alpha(x)$, (7.8581) enables us to put (7.8949) in the much more agreeable form

$$\int_0^b x[J_\alpha(\lambda_k x)]^2 dx = \frac{b^2}{2}[J'_\alpha(\lambda_k b)]^2 = \frac{b^2}{2}[J_{\alpha+1}(\lambda_k b)]^2 = \frac{b^2}{2}[J_{\alpha-1}(\lambda_k b)]^2.$$

7.9. The Legendre Equation. Let Ly denote the left member of the equation

$$(1 - x^2)\frac{d^2y}{dx^2} - 2x\frac{dy}{dx} + \alpha(\alpha + 1)y = 0 \tag{7.91}$$

so that the Legendre equation of order α becomes $Ly = 0$. One who has read Section 7.99 will see that the origin is a regular point of this equation, and that we can obtain two independent power-series solutions which do not explicitly involve the factor x^m appearing in the functions of Frobenius form. However it costs us very little to seek solutions of the Frobenius form, and we do it to see what will happen. We find that

$$(7.911) \qquad Lx^r = r(r-1)x^{r-2} + (\alpha - r)(\alpha + r + 1)x^r.$$

Hence, if

$$(7.912) \qquad y = x^m \sum_{n=0}^{\infty} c_n x^n = \sum_{n=0}^{\infty} c_n x^{m+n}$$

for some range of values of x, then

$$(7.913) \quad \begin{aligned} Ly &= \sum_{n=0}^{\infty} c_n L x^{m+n} \\ &= \sum_{n=0}^{\infty} c_n[(m+n)(m+n-1)x^{m+n-2} \\ &\qquad + (\alpha - m - n)(\alpha + m + n + 1)x^{m+n}] \\ &= c_0 m(m-1)x^{m-2} + c_1(m+1)mx^{m-1} \\ &\quad + \sum_{n=0}^{\infty} [(m+n+2)(m+n+1)c_{n+2} \\ &\qquad + (\alpha - m - n)(\alpha + m + n + 1)c_n]x^{m+n}. \end{aligned}$$

Putting $m = 0$ and letting c_0 and c_1 be constants different from 0 to which values may be assigned later, we find two independent solutions

$$(7.92) \quad y_1 = c_0\left[1 - \frac{(\alpha+1)\alpha}{2!}x^2 + \frac{(\alpha+1)(\alpha+3)\alpha(\alpha-2)}{4!}x^4 - \frac{(\alpha+1)(\alpha+3)(\alpha+5)\alpha(\alpha-2)(\alpha-4)}{6!}x^6 + \cdots\right]$$

and

$$(7.93) \quad y_2 = c_1\left[x - \frac{(\alpha+2)(\alpha-1)}{3!}x^3 + \frac{(\alpha+2)(\alpha+4)(\alpha-1)(\alpha-3)}{5!}x^5 - \frac{(\alpha+2)(\alpha+4)(\alpha+6)(\alpha-1)(\alpha-3)(\alpha-5)}{7!}x^7 + \cdots\right].$$

If α is not an integer, each of the series is an infinite series with radius of convergence equal to 1. The functions are called *Legendre functions.* The solution $y_1(x)$ is a polynomial if α is 0, an even positive integer, or an odd negative integer; and $y_2(x)$ is a polynomial if α is an odd positive integer or an even negative integer.

When α is 0 or a positive integer, one of the two functions in (7.92) and (7.93) is not a polynomial; the other is a polynomial of degree α which, when the constant is assigned a certain particular value, is called the *Legendre polynomial* of degree α and is denoted by $P_\alpha(x)$. The constants are so adjusted that, for each $\alpha = 0, 1, 2, \ldots,$

$$(7.94)\quad P_\alpha(x) = \frac{(2\alpha)!}{2^\alpha\alpha!\alpha!}\left[x^\alpha - \frac{\alpha(\alpha-1)}{2(2\alpha-1)}x^{\alpha-2} + \frac{\alpha(\alpha-1)(\alpha-2)(\alpha-3)}{2\cdot 4(2\alpha-1)(2\alpha-3)}x^{\alpha-4} - \frac{\alpha(\alpha-1)(\alpha-2)(\alpha-3)(\alpha-4)(\alpha-5)}{2\cdot 4\cdot 6(2\alpha-1)(2\alpha-3)(2\alpha-5)}x^{\alpha-6} + \cdots\right].$$

It is easy to see that

$$(7.941)\qquad \frac{(2\alpha)!}{2^\alpha\alpha!\alpha!} = \frac{1\cdot 3\cdot 5\cdots(2\alpha-1)}{\alpha!}\qquad \alpha = 1, 2, 3, \ldots .$$

Any adjustment of the constants different from the above would necessitate insertion of constant factors in the terms of the right member of the identity

$$(7.95)\qquad (1 - 2xt + t^2)^{-\frac{1}{2}} = P_0(x) + P_1(x)t + P_2(x)t^2 + \cdots$$

which holds when $|x|$ and $|t|$ are sufficiently small. It is a good exercise in the use of series to prove (7.95); the trick is to expand

$$\{1 + [t(t - 2x)]\}^{-\frac{1}{2}}$$

by the binomial formula, to pick out the coefficients of the various powers of t, and to see that they are the Legendre polynomials. The manipulations are easily justified when $|x| \leqq 1$ and $|t| \leqq \frac{4}{10}$, for in this case

$$|t^2 - 2xt| \leqq |t|^2 + |2xt| \leqq 0.16 + 0.8 = 0.96 < 1.$$

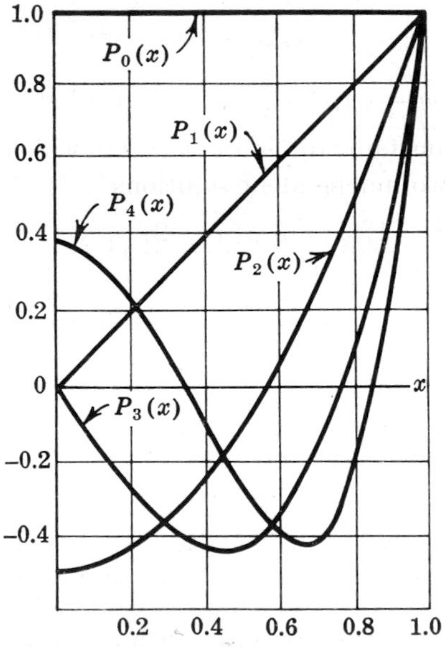

FIG. 7.951

Legendre functions and polynomials are often called *zonal functions* and *zonal harmonics*. They enter into many problems, in particular into many problems in which it is convenient to use spherical coordinates. The identity (7.95) is used with x defined by $x = \cos\theta$, θ being a spherical coordinate. Graphs of the first five Legendre Polynomials $P_0, P_1, \ldots, P_4$ are shown in Fig. 7.951.

Problem 7.96

Show that $P_0(x) = 1$; $P_1(x) = x$; $P_2(x) = (3x^2 - 1)/2$; $P_3(x) = (5x^3 - 3x)/2$; $P_4(x) = (35x^4 - 30x^2 + 3)/8$; $P_5(x) = (63x^5 - 70x^3 + 15x)/8$.

Problem 7.961

Show by means of formula (7.95) that for each $n = 0, 1, 2, \ldots$

$$P_n(1) = 1, \qquad P_n(-1) = (-1)^n. \tag{7.962}$$

Problem 7.97

Verify the *formula of Rodrigues* (1794–1851)

$$P_n(x) = \frac{1}{2^n n!} \frac{d^n}{dx^n} (x^2 - 1)^n \tag{7.971}$$

for a few values of n; if curiosity impels and ability permits, prove the formula.

Problem 7.98

Verify the formulas

$$\int_{-1}^{1} P_m(x)P_n(x)dx = 0 \qquad m \neq n \tag{7.981}$$

$$\int_{-1}^{1} [P_n(x)]^2 dx = \frac{2}{2n+1} \qquad n = 0, 1, 2, \ldots \tag{7.982}$$

for a few values of m and n.

Remark 7.983

The reason why (7.981) holds and an indication of reasons why the result is important are set forth in Chapter 12. When (7.981) has been established, we can obtain (7.982) by the following use of (7.95): From (7.95) we obtain

$$\frac{1}{1 - 2xt + t^2} = \sum_{m=0}^{\infty} \sum_{n=0}^{\infty} P_m(x)P_n(x)t^{m+n}. \tag{7.9831}$$

Integrating this over the interval $-1 \leqq x \leqq 1$ and using (7.981) give, after some reductions that are justified by rules for operating with series,

$$\sum_{n=0}^{\infty} \frac{2}{2n+1} t^{2n} = \sum_{n=0}^{\infty} \left\{ \int_{-1}^{1} [P_n(x)]^2 dx \right\} t^{2n}; \tag{7.9832}$$

and comparing the coefficients of the powers of t then gives (7.982). Another proof of (7.981) and (7.982) involves use of the formula of Rodrigues and integration by parts.

Everybody should know that Legendre polynomials are important and that, among other things, they can be used to solve a fundamental problem in polynomial approximation. Let f be a given function for which $f(x)$ and $|f(x)|^2$ are integrable over the interval $-1 \leqq x \leqq 1$, and let n be a given nonnegative integer. The problem is to determine the polynomial $p_n(x)$ of degree n or less for which the integral

$$\int_{-1}^{1} |f(x) - p_n(x)|^2 dx \tag{7.9833}$$

assumes its minimum value. The right way to attack this problem is to introduce the *normalized Legendre polynomials* $\phi_n(x)$ defined by

$$\phi_n(x) = \sqrt{\frac{2n+1}{2}}\, P_n(x). \tag{7.9834}$$

From (7.981) and (7.982), we obtain the fundamental fact that these functions ϕ_0, ϕ_1, ϕ_2, . . . form an orthonormal set over the interval $-1 \leqq x \leqq 1$. Since $P_n(x)$ and $\phi_n(x)$ are polynomials of degree n, it follows that there exist constants b_{jk} with $b_{kk} \neq 0$ such that $\phi_0(x) = b_{00}$,

$$\phi_1(x) = b_{10} + b_{11}x, \qquad \phi_2(x) = b_{20} + b_{21}x + b_{22}x^2, \; . \; . \; . \; .$$

It follows that, for each n, x^n is a linear combination of $\phi_0(x)$, $\phi_1(x)$, . . . , $\phi_n(x)$. Therefore each polynomial $p_n(x)$ of degree n or less is also a linear combination of $\phi_0(x)$, $\phi_1(x)$, . . . , $\phi_n(x)$. Hence we can put (7.9833) in the form

$$\int_{-1}^{1} \left|f(x) - \sum_{k=0}^{n} c_k\phi_k(x)\right|^2 dx. \tag{7.9835}$$

Since the functions ϕ_0, ϕ_1, . . . constitute a real orthonormal set, we can apply (12.74), which is given without proof in (6.733), to see that (7.9835) is a minimum iff c_k is the Fourier coefficient

$$a_k = \int_{-1}^{1} f(x)\phi_k(x)dx \qquad k = 0, 1, 2, \ldots \tag{7.9836}$$

of f. Thus the one and only solution of our problem is the sum of the first $n + 1$ terms of the Legendre expansion

$$a_0\phi_0(x) + a_1\phi_1(x) + a_2\phi_2(x) + \cdots \tag{7.9837}$$

of $f(x)$.

The good or poor old Maclaurin expansion

$$b_0 + b_1x + b_2x^2 + \cdots \tag{7.9838}$$

of $f(x)$, which exists and has coefficients b_k defined by $b_k = f^{(k)}(0)/k!$ when these derivatives exist, now has a devastating rival. The Maclaurin expansion has its virtues, but the poor fellow exists only for very special functions. Moreover if two functions $f_1(x)$ and $f_2(x)$ defined over $-1 \leqq x \leqq 1$ are such that $f_2(x) = f_1(x)$ when $-10^{-10} < x < 10^{-10}$, then $f_2(x)$ and $f_1(x)$ cannot have different Maclaurin expansions even though $f_2(x)$ and $f_1(x)$ may be very different over most of the interval $-1 \leqq x \leqq 1$. Hence, except in very special cases, the Maclaurin expansion is totally useless as a producer of useful polynomial approximations to given functions. On the other hand, the Legendre expansion is a hardy rock crusher that necessarily exists and necessarily has partial sums that produce the answers to our problem when $n = 0, 1, 2, \ldots$. Moreover the formula

$$\int_{-1}^{1} \left|f(x) - \sum_{k=0}^{n} a_k\phi_k(x)\right|^2 dx = \int_{-1}^{1} |f(x)|^2 dx - \sum_{k=0}^{n} |a_k|^2 \tag{7.9839}$$

is available for estimating the closeness of the approximations, and the statement involving (12.795) implies that the members of (7.9839) converge to 0 as $n \to \infty$. This is very solid information. The subject of polynomial approximation is very important, and everybody should realize that, even when $f(x)$ has a power-series expansion, best approximations to f are not obtained by taking partial sums of its power-series expansion.

Problem 7.984

Make calculations and draw figures which show how the simple function $\cos \pi x$ is approximated over the interval $-1 \leqq x \leqq 1$ by the first term of its Maclaurin series and by the first term of its Legendre series. Note that this problem can be solved without electronic computers.

Problem 7.985

Show that, if $Q_0(x)$ and $Q_1(x)$ denote, respectively, the functions in (7.93) and (7.92) when $\alpha = 0$, $c_1 = 1$ and when $\alpha = 1$, $c_0 = -1$, then

(7.9851) $$Q_0(x) = \frac{1}{2} \log \frac{1+x}{1-x} \qquad |x| < 1$$

and

(7.9852) $$Q_1(x) = \frac{x}{2} \log \frac{1+x}{1-x} - 1 \qquad |x| < 1.$$

Hint: In evaluating the series, use the fact that

$$x + \frac{x^3}{3} + \frac{x^5}{5} + \cdots = \int_0^x (1 + t^2 + t^4 + \cdots)dt,$$

and notice that the integrand is a geometric series.

7.99. Regular Points; Singular Points. Let the coefficients $P(x)$, $Q(x)$, and $R(x)$ in

(7.991) $$P(x)y'' + Q(x)y' + R(x)y = 0$$

be polynominals in x, as in (7.64), or be functions defined by power series

(7.992) $$P(x) = \sum_{k=0}^{\infty} p_k x^k, \qquad Q(x) = \sum_{k=0}^{\infty} q_k x^k, \qquad R(x) = \sum_{k=0}^{\infty} r_k x^k$$

having positive radii of convergence which may be infinite. In any case, we assume that the series all converge and define $P(x)$, $Q(x)$, and $R(x)$ when $|x| < \rho$, where ρ may be infinite. We do not assume that

$$P(0) = p_0 \neq 0$$

but we do assume that $p_k \neq 0$ for at least one k; otherwise (7.991) would not be an equation of order 2. Moreover we assume that p_0, q_0, and r_0 are not all 0; otherwise we would divide (7.991) by a power of x. We consider only power series in x; power series in $(x - x_0)$ are obtained by replacing x by $(x - x_0)$.

In case $P(0) \neq 0$, the origin is called a *regular point* or an *ordinary point* of the equation (7.991). In each such case there is a positive number ρ_1 such that $P(x) \neq 0$ when $-\rho_1 < x < \rho_1$. Theorem 6.04 then implies that (7.991) has two independent solutions $y_1(x)$ and $y_2(x)$ over this interval, and that each function which satisfies (7.991) over this interval must have the form

$$y(x) = c_1y_1(x) + c_2y_2(x). \tag{7.993}$$

It is not necessarily true that $y_1(x)$ and $y_2(x)$ have power-series expansions converging to them over the whole interval $-\rho_1 < x < \rho_1$. However the theory of analytic functions of a complex variable gives very useful information. The series in (7.992) converge and define functions $P(x)$, $Q(x)$, and $R(x)$ analytic over the circular disk of *complex* numbers x for which $|x| < \rho$. Since $P(0) \neq 0$, we can choose a positive number ρ_2 such that $\rho_2 \leq \rho$ and $P(x) \neq 0$ when $|x| < \rho_2$. It can be proved that $y_1(x)$ and $y_2(x)$ have power-series expansions converging to them over the complex disk $|x| < \rho_2$ and hence over the real interval $-\rho_2 < x < \rho_2$. All this shows that if the origin is a regular point of (7.991), then (7.991) has two independent solutions of the form $c_0 + c_1x + c_2x^2 + \cdots$ and we can seek solutions of this form with complete confidence that they exist. It can happen that the radii of convergence of the power-series solutions are not as large as we would like. For example, Theorem 6.04 tells us that the equation

$$(1 + x^2)y'' + y' + y = 0 \tag{7.994}$$

has two independent solutions over the whole interval $-\infty < x < \infty$, but we have no guarantee that the power series will converge when $|x| \geqq 1$ because $1 + x^2 = 0$ when $x = i$ and $|i| = 1$.

In case $P(0) = 0$, the origin is called a *singular point* of the equation (7.991). In this case, Theorem 6.04 and our other theorems fail to apply to an interval containing the origin. We can, however, choose a positive number ρ_1 such that $P(x) \neq 0$ when $0 < x < \rho_1$ and use Theorem 6.04 to see that there exist two independent solutions $y_1(x)$ and $y_2(x)$ over the interval $0 < x < \rho_1$. Sometimes we can find these solutions and use the information to tell whether the given equation has power-series solutions. For example, the equation

$$xy'' - y' = 0 \tag{7.995}$$

has the independent solutions $y_1(x) = 1$ and $y_2(x) = x^2$, and each of these is representable as power-series convergent for each x. Problem 7.471 shows that the equation

$$xy'' - y = 0 \tag{7.9951}$$

has a nontrivial power-series solution but does not have two independent ones. Problem 7.472 shows that the equation

$$x^2y'' - y = 0 \tag{7.9952}$$

has no nontrivial power-series solutions. A small clue to a significant result is provided by Problem 6.365 which shows that the Cauchy equation

$$x^2y'' + axy' + by = 0 \qquad x > 0 \tag{7.9953}$$

has two independent solutions of the form x^m, provided the equation (6.3652) has two different solutions for m, but that m need not be an integer and, in fact, need not be real.

The equations displayed in the above paragraph, as well as the hypergeometric and Bessel equations, are examples of equations having regular singular points at the origin. The equation (7.991), with coefficients given by (7.992) and satisfying the conditions stated there, is said to have a *regular singular point* at the origin if $p_0 = 0$ and, in addition, either (i) $p_1 \neq 0$ but q_0 and r_0 are not both 0 or (ii) $p_1 = 0$ but $p_2 \neq 0$, $q_0 = 0$, and $r_0 \neq 0$. In the terminology of the theory of analytic functions, this means that at least one of the quotients $Q(x)/P(x)$ and $R(x)/P(x)$ has a pole at the origin but that $Q(x)/P(x)$ does not have a pole of order exceeding 1 and $R(x)/P(x)$ does not have a pole of order exceeding 2. The following theorem guarantees that the method of Frobenius must produce results when it is applied to equations having regular singular points at the origin.

THEORM 7.996. *If the equation*

$$P(x)y'' + Q(x)y' + R(x)y = 0 \tag{7.9961}$$

described following (7.991) *has a regular singular point at the origin, then there exist constants* $m, c_0, c_1, \ldots$ *such that* $c_0 \neq 0$, *the series in*

$$y(x) = x^m(c_0 + c_1x + c_2x^2 + \cdots) \tag{7.9962}$$

has a positive radius of convergence R, *and the function* $y(x)$ *satisfies* (7.9961).

Sometimes, but not always, (7.9961) has two independent solutions of the Frobenius form (7.9962). In case (7.9961) has a nontrivial solution $y_1(x)$ of the Frobenius form but does not have two independent solutions of this form, it must have a solution of the form

$$y_2(x) = y_1(x) \log x + u(x) \tag{7.9963}$$

where $u(x)$ has the Frobenius form; see Section 7.7. In many applications, the constants $m, c_0, c_1, \ldots$ in (7.9962) are real, but this is not always so. One who is interested in this matter should apply the method of Frobenius to the honorable equation

$$x^2y'' + xy' + y = 0 \tag{7.9964}$$

and then read Problem 6.365.

Problem 7.997

Find out whether the method of Frobenius will produce nontrivial solutions of the equations

(a) $$x^3y'' + y' = 0$$
(b) $$x^3y'' + y = 0$$

which have irregular singular points at the origin.

Problem 7.9981

Let

$$Ly = P(x)y'' + Q(x)y' + R(x)y \tag{7.99811}$$

where $P(x)$, $Q(x)$, $R(x)$ are polynomials or have power-series expansions as in (7.992). Suppose the equation $Ly = 0$ has a nontrivial solution y_1 of the Frobenius form

$$x^m(c_0 + c_1x + c_2x^2 + \cdot \cdot \cdot) \tag{7.99812}$$

but does not have two independent solutions of this form. We should think about the method we have used in special cases to find a function u such that $Ly_2 = 0$ when y_2 is defined by

$$y_2 = y_1(x) \log x + u. \tag{7.99813}$$

Show that $Ly_2 = 0$ iff u satisfies a particular equation of the form

$$Lu = x^M(C_0 + C_1x + C_2x^2 + \cdot \cdot \cdot). \tag{7.99814}$$

Note that if no simpler method occurs to us, we seek u by the method of Frobenius.

Problem 7.9982

When we apply the method of Frobenius to the special hypergeometric equation (7.7811), we find that the indicial equation has a double root and we obtain only the solution in (7.7812). Apply the idea of Problem 7.9981 to obtain another solution.

Ans.: See Problem 7.782.

CHAPTER 8

NUMERICAL METHODS

8.0. Introduction. *Numerical methods* are methods by which evidence about numbers is used to obtain decimal approximations to the numbers. In our work, the evidence will consist of differential equations and supplementary conditions that are called *boundary conditions* or *initial conditions.* We begin with a single differential equation of first order, and give practically all of our attention to those methods that are most effectively adapted to solving equations of higher order and systems of equations.

Thus we begin with the general problem

$$y' = f(x, y), \qquad y(x_0) = y_0 \tag{8.01}$$

where $f(x, y)$ is a given function and x_0 and y_0 are given in decimal form. To simplify matters, we assume that $f(x, y)$ and the partial derivative $\partial f/\partial y$ are continuous over some rectangle $x_0 \leqq x \leqq a$, $b_1 \leqq y_0 \leqq b_2$ for which $x_0 < a$ and $b_1 < y_0 < b_2$ as in Fig. 8.02. It is then possible to

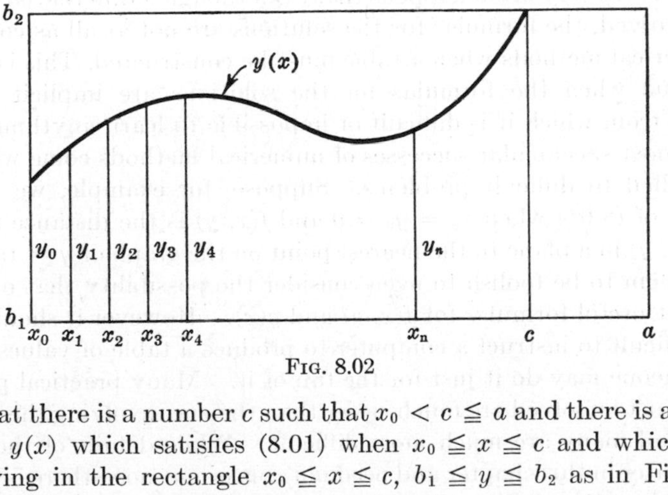

FIG. 8.02

prove that there is a number c such that $x_0 < c \leqq a$ and there is a unique function $y(x)$ which satisfies (8.01) when $x_0 \leqq x \leqq c$ and which has a graph lying in the rectangle $x_0 \leqq x \leqq c$, $b_1 \leqq y \leqq b_2$ as in Fig. 8.02. Having been given or having chosen a positive *tabular difference* h, we put $x_1 = x_0 + h$, $x_2 = x_1 + h$, $x_3 = x_2 + h$, . . . and put $y_k = y(x_k)$ for each $k = 1, 2, \ldots$ as in Fig. 8.02. Our fundamental problem is to find approximations as good as are desired to as many of the numbers y_1, y_2, y_3, . . . as are desired.

What we need are methods by which we can find an approximation to y_{n+1} when we have approximations to y_0, y_1, . . . , y_n. When such a method is in hand, we can use it with $n = 0$ to find y_1, then use it with $n = 1$ to find y_2, and so on. It turns out that there are methods by which y_{n-2} and y_{n-1} (and even earlier values) as well as y_n can be efficiently used in finding y_{n+1}. A method which employs y_{n-1} and y_n cannot be used until we have both y_0 and y_1. A method which employs y_{n-2}, y_{n-1}, and y_n cannot be used until we have y_0, y_1, and y_2. For this reason, a method which employs only y_n for the determination of y_{n+1} is called a *starting method*. We always need a starting method to get started. Sometimes the nature of the problems being solved and the computing equipment being used (pencils, slide rules, desk calculators, electronic computers, for example) is such that it is best to use a good starting method to obtain all of the required numbers y_1, y_2, . . . , y_p. Sometimes it is best to obtain one or more of y_1, y_2, . . . by a starting method and then switch to a *continuing method* which employs one or more of . . . , y_{n-2}, y_{n-1} as well as y_n.

It is sometimes thought that numerical methods are developed for the purpose of obtaining solutions of differential equations that cannot be solved by methods like those studied in earlier chapters of this book. This idea may be historically correct but, at least in modern times, it comes very short of giving the whole truth about applications of numerical methods. It very often happens that even though a differential equation can be solved, the formulas for the solutions are not at all as convenient as numerical methods when a table must be constructed. This is particularly true when the formulas for the solutions are implicit function jumbles from which it is difficult or impossible to learn anything.

The most spectacular successes of numerical methods come when they are applied to difficult problems. Suppose, for example, we wish the solution of (8.01) when $x_0 = y_0 = 0$ and $f(x, y)$ is the distance from the point (x, y) in a plane to the nearest point on the graph of $y = \tan x$. It would seem to be foolish to even consider the possibility that one might work out useful formulas for $f(x, y)$ and $y(x)$. However it should not be very difficult to instruct a computer to produce a table of values of $y(x)$, and someone may do it just for the fun of it. Many practical problems which must be solved are much easier than the one involving the graph of $\tan x$, and many are much more difficult. While details of the matter appear later in this chapter and need not concern us now, there is a special reason why very much attention should be given to the problem (8.01). A person who has learned the best methods for attacks upon (8.01) will find it surprisingly easy to make appropriate modifications of these methods to obtain methods for successful attacks upon equations and systems of equations of more complex types. These latter applications constitute our real goal because, in most fields of applications, equations of order 2 (and sometimes more) are much more prevalent and important than equations of order 1.

It is our purpose to present information needed by everyone interested in the application of numerical methods to differential equations. This chapter provides all of the material required for understanding and use of the methods that are almost universally considered to be the most useful for practical applications. The methods are used by operators of high-speed electronic digital computers as well as by those who must employ pencils or slide rules or modest desk calculators. Readers who solve problems only occasionally should be fixed for life by reading this chapter, solving a few problems with pencil and paper, and keeping the chapter available for reference. Readers who expect to solve more problems with less primitive equipment should supplement the reading and pencil work by solving many problems with the best available equipment. Finally, those who expect to devote substantial parts of their lives to numerical work should begin by learning the contents of this chapter as thoroughly as they learned their alphabets. The information and ideas provide a basis for deciding what kinds of mechanical hardware, electrical hardware, and theories are worthy of study, use, and development. In any case, the importance of knowing about the subject is steadily increasing as high-speed computers become more prevalent and extensive applications become commonplace.

8.1. A Standard Problem; Introduction of Differences. We shall test our methods by applying them to the problem

$$\frac{dy}{dx} = x + y, \qquad y(0) = 1 \tag{8.11}$$

which we shall call our standard problem. Thus (8.11) will serve as a target for numerical methods in the same way that a target towed by an airplane serves as a target for guns. It is obvious that the target (8.11) fails to expose a fundamental weakness in those methods that require the calculation of $f(x, y)$ for excessively many pairs of values of x and y. Such methods are inefficient when applied to cases in which these calculations are tedious. In spite of the fact that the following principle cannot be swallowed without reservations, it is worthy of notice because it is informative and constructive and does have many applications. *If a powerful* (*i.e.*, widely applicable) *method is effective* (*i.e.*, produces results as accurate as are needed) *and efficient* (*i.e.*, does not take too much time) *when applied to* (8.11), *then the method is a good one for use when the very simple* $x + y$ *of* (8.11) *is replaced by other functions of* x *and* y.

While other standard examples would serve the same purpose, it should be clear that (8.11) is selected because, among all nontrivial problems, it minimizes arithmetical chores. It is very definitely expected that students beginning their study of numerical methods with this chapter will solve key problems with no worldly equipment other than pencil (not pen), eraser, and paper. It is thoroughly reasonable that these problems should involve moderate amounts of additions and subtractions which everybody should either do with reasonable accuracy or learn to do with reasonable accuracy. An occasional requirement that something be multiplied or divided by 6 is reasonable. Rare divisions by 24 are allowed because the result can be obtained by divisions by 3 and 8. When (8.11) is used, the applications involve arithmetical operations no more complex than these. Moreover, maximum insight into relations among different methods is gained when nearly all of the applications involve the same problem.

Because of the above circumstances, we give information about (8.11) for later use. The function determined by (8.11) is

$$y = 2e^x - x - 1. \tag{8.12}$$

The National Bureau of Standards has published an excellent table of values of e^x and e^{-x}. With the aid of these tables, it is easy to calculate the values $y_n = y(x_n)$ when $x_n = 0, 0.1, 0.2, \ldots, 0.9, 1$. These values, correct to 11D (11 decimal* places or 11 significant figures, but only 10 after the decimal point) are given in Table 8.13. Too many D are less likely to be harmful than too few.

TABLE 8.13

$y(\ 0\ ) = 1.00000\ 00000$	$y(0.6) = 2.04423\ 76008$
$y(0.1) = 1.11034\ 18362$	$y(0.7) = 2.32750\ 54149$
$y(0.2) = 1.24280\ 55163$	$y(0.8) = 2.65108\ 18570$
$y(0.3) = 1.39971\ 76152$	$y(0.9) = 3.01920\ 62223$
$y(0.4) = 1.58364\ 93953$	$y(1.0) = 3.43656\ 36569$
$y(0.5) = 1.79744\ 25414$	

We now examine the more elaborate Table 8.14, in which the values of $y_n = y(x_n)$ in column 2 are rounded to 6D, to pick up some valuable ideas we will need later. The third column gives values of y'_n which is $y'(x_n)$ or $x_n + y_n$. The other columns contain *differences* that have many applications and will be needed later in this chapter. Column 4 contains the *first differences* (or differences of order 1) of the sequence y'_0, y'_1,

* We shall continually use the letter D to abbreviate "decimal places" or "decimals" or "decimal"; for example, the result of rounding 234.5678 to 6D is 234.568 and this approximation is used in 6D calculations.

TABLE 8.14

(1) x_n	(2) y_n	(3) y'_n	(4) $\nabla y'_n$	(5) $\nabla^2 y'_n$	(6) $\nabla^3 y'_n$	(7) $\nabla^4 y'_n$	(8) $\nabla^5 y'_n$
0	1.00000	1.00000	—	—	—	—	—
0.1	1.11034	1.21034	0.21034	—	—	—	—
0.2	1.24281	1.44281	0.23247	0.02213	—	—	—
0.3	1.39972	1.69972	0.25691	0.02444	0.00231	—	—
0.4	1.58365	1.98365	0.28393	0.02702	0.00258	0.00027	—
0.5	1.79744	2.29744	0.31379	0.02986	0.00284	0.00026	−0.00001
0.6	2.04424	2.64424	0.34680	0.03301	0.00315	0.00031	0.00005
0.7	2.32751	3.02751	0.38327	0.03647	0.00346	0.00031	0.00000
0.8	2.65108	3.45108	0.42357	0.04030	0.00383	0.00037	0.00006
0.9	3.01921	3.91921	0.46813	0.04456	0.00426	0.00043	0.00006
1.0	3.43656	4.43656	0.51735	0.04922	0.00466	0.00040	−0.00003

$y'_2, \ldots,$ defined by

$$\nabla y'_n = y'_n - y'_{n-1}. \tag{8.141}$$

The inverted delta is called *del.* Each item in column 4 is obtained by subtracting the number above the number to the left of it from the latter number.* Similarly, column 5 contains first differences of the sequence in the column to the left of it. These are *second differences,* or differences of order 2, of the sequence $y'_0, y'_1, y'_2, \ldots.$ Thus

$$\nabla^2 y'_n = \nabla y'_n - \nabla y'_{n-1}, \tag{8.142}$$

where ∇^2 is read "del squared," and

$$\nabla^2 y'_n = y'_n - 2y'_{n-1} + y'_{n-2}. \tag{8.143}$$

Similarly, for the *third differences,* or differences of order 3, we have $\nabla^3 y'_n = \nabla^2 y'_n - \nabla^2 y'_{n-1}$ and

$$\nabla^3 y'_n = y'_n - 3y'_{n-1} + 3y'_{n-2} - y'_{n-3}. \tag{8.144}$$

* Those who consider it awkward to make upside-down subtractions may take this occasion to learn the rarely explained art of subtraction. Consider the following example:

$$\begin{array}{ll} 1.776 & \\ 4.914 & 3.138. \end{array}$$

The ritual goes as follows. Only the digits in parentheses being written, we say that 6 and (8) are 14, 8 and (3) are 11, 8 and (1) are 9, 1 and (3) are 4. Thus, when 1 has been borrowed, we pay the penalty by adding 1 to the digit subtracted the next time so that we are adding all the time and everything runs smoothly.

In terms of the binomial coefficients which appear in the binomial formula

$$(8.145) \qquad (a+b)^p = \sum_{k=0}^{p} \frac{p!}{k!(p-k)!} a^{p-k}b^k = \sum_{k=0}^{p} \binom{p}{k} a^{p-k}b^k$$

we have

$$(8.146) \qquad \nabla^p y'_n = \sum_{k=0}^{p} (-1)^k \binom{p}{k} y'_{n-k} \qquad p = 1, 2, \ldots .$$

It is not a good idea to use this formula to calculate the entries in tables. It is much better to use repeated subtractions in such a way that the desired differences of lowest order are calculated first. The errors involved in rounding the correct values of y'_n to the number of decimal places given in column 3 of Table 8.14 are responsible for visible irregularities in columns 7 and 8 and for invisible irregularities in earlier columns. Nontrivial errors in calculating or copying calculated values of y'_n will produce violent irregularities in the differences of higher order. Computers know all about this and examine the differences to see whether errors have been made and to locate errors when they have been made. The following problems throw light upon these and other matters and give information needed by everyone concerned with the construction and enlightened use of tables.

Remark 8.147

It is a standard practice to use ∇ (del) for *backward differences* so that $\nabla w_n = w_n - w_{n-1}$, $\nabla^2 w_n = w_n - 2w_{n-1} + w_{n-2}$, . . . and to use Δ (delta) for *forward differences* so that $\Delta w_n = w_{n+1} - w_n$, $\Delta^2 w_n = w_{n+2} - 2w_{n+1} + w_n$, ... Only backward differences appear in this chapter, and we use the dels. Another scheme of honorable parentage employs deltas with exponents, as above, for forward differences and employs deltas with subscripts for backward differences so that $\Delta_1 w_n = w_n - w_{n-1}$, $\Delta_2 w_n = w_n - 2w_{n-1} + w_{n-2}$, . . . and $\Delta_p = \nabla^p$. For the benefit of those who prefer the subscript notation, a little tale must be told. The author considers the two schemes to be equally good and would like to use the subscript notation to accommodate a typewriter that has a delta but no del. However it seems to be necessary to use the dels to maintain peaceful relations with critics having violent preferences for the dels.

Problem 8.15

This problem involves several ideas. In comparison to the items in the earlier columns, the differences of higher order in the last columns of Table 8.14 are small and (except for strange fluctuations in the last decimal place in the last column) they change slowly and regularly as we go down a column. This is a very common situation when the tabular difference h is small enough to allow the table to show the nature of the function being differenced, and we should see another example. The entries in column 2 of Table 8.151 can be selected from tables of sines of angles measured in radians.

TABLE 8.151

x	$\sin x$	∇	∇^2	∇^3	∇^4
0	0.00000	—	—	—	—
0.1	0.09983	0.09983	—	—	—
0.2	0.19867	0.09884	−0.00099	—	—
0.3	0.29552	0.09685	−0.00199	−0.00100	—
0.4	0.38942	0.09390	−0.00205	−0.00096	0.00004
0.5	0.47943	0.09001	−0.00389	−0.00094	0.00002
0.6	0.56464	0.08521	−0.00480	−0.00091	0.00003
0.7	0.64422	0.07958	−0.00563	−0.00083	0.00008
0.8	0.71736	0.07314	−0.00644	−0.00081	0.00002
0.9	0.78333	0.06597	−0.00717	−0.00073	0.00008

Look at this table and check at least some of the differences, being careful to determine whether the signs are correct. It is not illegal to notice that the signs of the differences of the sine behave like the signs of the derivatives of the sine. In fact it is not difficult to show that if $w(x)$ has plenty of derivatives, then

$$\lim_{h\to 0} \frac{\nabla w_n}{h} = w'(x_n), \qquad \lim_{h\to 0} \frac{\nabla^2 w_n}{h^2} = w''(x_n), \quad \dots .$$

In many cases these formulas enable us to see why differences of high order should be small.

We now go on a little excursion to see that the things we are working with are useful for interpolation (including extrapolation). With or without a preliminary look at material in Section 8.5, employ (8.52) with $y'(x)$ replaced by $\sin x$, with $h = \frac{1}{10}$, with the items in the right member referring to items in the last row of Table 8.151, and with $\epsilon(x)$ replaced by zero, to obtain the approximation (or interpolation formula)

$$(8.152)\qquad \begin{aligned}\sin x = 0.78333 &+ 0.6597(x - 0.9)\\ &- 0.3585(x - 0.9)(x - 0.8)\\ &- 0.122(x - 0.9)(x - 0.8)(x - 0.7)\\ &+ 0.033(x - 0.9)(x - 0.8)(x - 0.7)(x - 0.6) + \cdots\end{aligned}$$

which is designed for use when $0.8 < x \leqq 1.0$. Within this range, (8.152) is almost accurate to 5D; if we want to be sure of 5D accuracy, we must start with a table accurate to more than 5D so that we can reduce rounding errors and replace the numbers in (8.152) by more accurate ones. The values

$$\sin 0.85 = 0.75128 \qquad \sin 0.95 = 0.81342$$
$$\sin 0.89 = 0.77707 \qquad \sin 1.00 = 0.84147$$

will serve as checks. Everyone should at least show that putting $x = 1$ in (8.152) gives for sin 1.00 the good approximation 0.84148. The error is 0.00001, and this must be regarded as being small because errors this big or bigger continually creep into 5D calculations with numbers between 0.1 and 10.0. It is often necessary to make 7D calculations to secure 5D accuracy in results. Proper respect for (8.152) can be obtained by comparing it with the result of applying linear interpolation (the brand used, for example, in elementary trigonometry books) to Table 8.151. The best we can do with linear interpolation is use the last two values of $\sin x$ in Table 8.151 to obtain the formula

$$\sin x = 0.78333 + 0.6597(x - 0.9) \tag{8.153}$$

which gives the approximation 0.84930 for sin 1. The error is 0.00783 and this is far from being a little rounding error.

Problem 8.16

Column 2 of Table 8.161 is a table of sines that contains an error, 0.56564 being present instead of sin 0.6 = 0.56464. This error produces errors in the boldface items of the table. Note that a superficial examination of column 2 in Table 8.161 does not reveal the error but that the violent fluctuations in the last columns cannot escape notice. Note also that these fluctuations begin in the row which contains the error. Look a little more at Table 8.161, compare it with the more agreeable Table 8.151, and proceed to the next problem.

TABLE 8.161

(1) x	(2) ?	(3) ∇	(4) ∇^2	(5) ∇^3	(6) ∇^4
0	0.00000	—	—	—	—
0.1	0.09983	0.09983	—	—	—
0.2	0.19867	0.09884	−0.00099	—	—
0.3	0.29552	0.09685	−0.00199	−0.00100	—
0.4	0.38942	0.09390	−0.00295	−0.00096	0.00004
0.5	0.47943	0.09001	−0.00389	−0.00094	0.00002
0.6	**0.56564**	**0.08621**	**−0.00380**	**+0.00009**	**0.00103**
0.7	0.64422	**0.07858**	**−0.00763**	**−0.00383**	**−0.00392**
0.8	0.71736	0.07314	**−0.00444**	**+0.00219**	**+0.00602**
0.9	0.78333	0.06597	−0.00717	**−0.00273**	**−0.00492**

Problem 8.17

Let the elements of a sequence $v_0, v_1, v_2, \ldots$ be $0, 0, \ldots, 0, q, 0, 0, \ldots$. Show that the difference table displaying the differences $\nabla^k v_n$ is Table 8.171. We may think of the sequence $v_0, v_1, \ldots$ as being the sequence of errors in a sequence having true values $w_0, w_1, \ldots$ so that the erroneous sequence $v_0 + w_0, v_1 + w_1, \ldots$ contains just one erroneous element. The items in Table 8.171 then show the amounts by which the items of the difference table, formed for the erroneous sequence, differ from the items of the difference table formed for the correct sequence. When q is a small rounding error, this explains the strange fluctuations in the last digits of the last columns of Tables 8.14 and 8.151. When q is larger, it explains the more violent fluctuations in

TABLE 8.171

v_n	∇v_n	$\nabla^2 v_n$	$\nabla^3 v_n$	$\nabla^4 v_n$	$\nabla^5 v_n$
. . . .					
0	0	0	0	0	0
q	q	q	q	q	q
0	$-q$	$-2q$	$-3q$	$-4q$	$-5q$
0	0	q	$3q$	$6q$	$10q$
0	0	0	$-q$	$-4q$	$-10q$
0	0	0	0	q	$5q$
0	0	0	0	0	$-q$

Table 8.161. Observe that an error q in the column headed by v_n produces errors of magnitude $|q|$, $|2q|$, $|3q|$, $|6q|$, and $|10q|$ respectively in special items in the columns headed by ∇, ∇^2, ∇^3, ∇^4, and ∇^5.

Problem 8.18

Sane persons should think a little about the consequences of having a rounding error in each element of the sequence being differenced. A little thought, in which Table 8.1801 plays a prominent role, shows that the resulting errors can never exceed the

TABLE 8.1801

	∇	∇^2	∇^3	∇^4	∇^5
q	—	—	—	—	—
$-q$	$-2q$	—	—	—	—
q	$2q$	$4q$	—	—	—
$-q$	$-2q$	$-4q$	$-8q$	—	—
q	$2q$	$4q$	$8q$	$16q$	—
$-q$	$-2q$	$-4q$	$-8q$	$-16q$	$32q$

errors produced when the rounding errors have the greatest possible magnitude q, say 0.00000 5, and alternate in sign. The error in ∇^4 could never exceed $|16q|$, and even a little knowledge of probability and statistics shows that it is usually substantially less.

Problem 8.181

Supposing that $x_n = n$ and $w_n = x_n^2$ when $0 \leqq n \leqq 8$, construct a table exhibiting the differences $\nabla^k w_n$. Construct the table for which $w_n = x_n^3$.

Problem 8.182

Suppose as in the previous problem that $x_n = n$ when $0 \leqq n \leqq 8$. Let $z_n = x_n^2$ when $0 \leqq n \leqq 4$ but $z_n = x_n^2 + 1$ when $5 \leqq n \leqq 8$. Thus $z_n = w_n$ except that z_5 involves a discrepancy which is inherited by z_6, z_7, z_8. Construct the difference table showing $\nabla^p z_n$. *Remark.* The fact that inherited errors disturb differences of higher order should be both discovered and remembered. This problem is a good test question for this section. If you solve it neatly and correctly, you get top score.

Problem 8.19

One who can devote a substantial amount of time to this chapter can profitably parallel work of the present and following sections by replacing our standard problem $y' = x + y$, $y(0) = 1$ by another. The problem

$$\frac{dy}{dx} = x - y, \qquad y(0) = 1 \tag{8.1901}$$

with the solution

$$y = 2e^{-x} + x - 1 \tag{8.1902}$$

would be a very good choice. The difference between (8.1901) and our standard problem is significant because, as x increases, the y in (8.1901) behaves much like a linear function while the solution of our standard problem behaves like an exponential function. The first step in an extensive study of (8.1901) would be to prepare, and keep for future reference, tables analogous to Tables 8.13 and 8.14. Since adequate tables of exponentials are not always in hand, we give a little table which is needed for the purpose.

TABLE 8.1903

x	e^{-x}	x	e^{-x}
0.1	0.90483 74180 36	0.6	0.54881 16360 94
0.2	0.81873 07530 78	0.7	0.49658 53037 91
0.3	0.74081 82206 82	0.8	0.44932 89641 17
0.4	0.67032 00460 36	0.9	0.40656 96597 41
0.5	0.60653 06597 13	1.0	0.36787 94411 71

Problem 8.191

The following is a sample list of equations of the form $y' = f(x, y)$ which, together with suitable conditions of the form $y(x_0) = y_0$, constitute reasonable problems for testing methods and computing equipment. Different problems result from different choices of numerical values of the constants that appear.

(*a*) $y' = ax + by$ (*b*) $y' = ax^{-1} + by^{-1}$
(*c*) $y' = x^2 + y^2$ (*d*) $y' = (x^2 - y^2)^{\frac{1}{2}}$
(*e*) $y' = \log (x^2 + y^2)$ (*f*) $y' = e^{-xy}$
(*g*) $y' = A \sin x \sin y$ (*h*) $y' = \sin x + \sin y$

8.2. The Euler-Cauchy Method. This elementary method is a starting method for the problem $y' = f(x, y)$, $y(x_0) = y_0$ which was used by Euler (1707–1783) and Cauchy (1785–1857). The names of Lipschitz (1832–1903) and Peano (1858–1932) are sometimes included because they used the method to prove existence and uniqueness theorems for the problem. It is not an efficient method, but it is very simple and has substantial theoretical interest. We study it to pick up ideas we need later. For this method, y_{n+1} is computed from the approximate formula

$$y_{n+1} = y_n + hf(x_n, y_n). \tag{8.21}$$

We now see how this formula can be obtained and discuss it. When $y' = f(x, y)$ holds, we have the exact formula

$$y_{n+1} - y_n = y(x_n + h) - y(x_n) = \int_{x_n}^{x_n+h} y'(t)\,dt$$

and hence

$$y_{n+1} = y_n + \int_{x_n}^{x_n+h} f(t, y(t))\,dt. \tag{8.22}$$

We obtain the approximation in (8.21) by replacing the integrand $f(t, y(t))$ by the computable value $f(x_n, y(x_n)) = f(x_n, y_n)$ which the integrand takes at the left end of the interval of integration where $t = x_n$. It is clear that there are two sources of error in the y_{n+1} computed from (8.21). In the first place, an error in y_n produces an inherited error. In the second place, an error is usually introduced when we replace $f(t, y(t))$ by $f(x_n, y_n)$. In all or nearly all sensible applications of the Euler-Cauchy and other methods, the graph of $f(t, y(t))$ over the interval $x_n \leqq t \leqq x_n + h$ looks much like a short line segment. Therefore, when we are replacing $f(t, y(t))$ by a constant, it would seem to be silly to use the value of $f(t, y(t))$ when t is at an end of the interval because it would be much better to use the value when t is at the middle of the interval. The difficulty lies in the fact that we do not know $y(x_n + h/2)$ and cannot calculate $f(x_n + h/2, y(x_n + h/2))$. The next two sections give methods for surmounting this difficulty and improving the Euler-Cauchy method.

When the Euler-Cauchy formula (8.21) is being applied, good computing technique requires that a table such as Table 8.24 be filled in or out as the calculations proceed. Table 8.24 shows results of applying the method to the standard problem

$$\frac{dy}{dx} = x + y, \qquad y(0) = 1 \tag{8.23}$$

with $h = \frac{1}{2}$. It could be expected that the results are crude, and comparison with Table 8.13 shows that they are. It should be expected that better results are obtained by taking smaller values of h, and this is true. Tables 8.241 and 8.242 give results for the same problem when $h = \frac{1}{4}$ and $h = \frac{1}{10}$ respectively.

To tabulate $y(0)$, $y(0.1)$, $y(0.2)$, . . . , $y(1.0)$ with $h = 0.01$ and $h = 0.001$ is child's play for a high-speed computer. These computers work fastest when they are instructed to record relatively few of the numbers they calculate. A computer which makes 10D calculations gave the estimate $y(1.0) = 3.40963$ when $h = 0.01$ and the estimate $y(1.0) = 3.43384$ when $h = 0.001$.

TABLE 8.24. $h = \frac{1}{2}$

x_n	y_n	$f(x_n, y_n)$	$hf(x_n, y_n)$
0.000	1.000	1.000	0.500
0.500	1.500	2.000	1.000
1.000	2.500	—	—

TABLE 8.241. $h = \frac{1}{4}$

x_n	y_n	$f(x_n, y_n)$	$hf(x_n, y_n)$
0.000	1.000	1.000	0.250
0.250	1.250	1.500	0.375
0.500	1.625	2.125	0.531
0.750	2.166	2.906	0.728
1.000	2.894	—	—

TABLE 8.242. $h = \frac{1}{10}$

x_n	y_n	$f(x_n, y_n)$	$hf(x_n, y_n)$
0.0	1.000	1.000	0.100
0.1	1.100	1.200	0.120
0.2	1.220	1.420	0.142
0.3	1.362	1.662	0.166
0.4	1.528	1.928	0.193
0.5	1.721	2.221	0.222
0.6	1.943	2.543	0.254
0.7	2.197	2.897	0.290
0.8	2.487	3.287	0.329
0.9	2.816	3.716	0.372
1.0	3.188	—	—

Problem 8.25

With the book closed, or at least with Tables 8.24, 8.241, and 8.242 covered, reproduce these tables. It is a good idea to reproduce the whole Table 8.242 to see how easily and quickly it can be done.

Problem 8.251

Using Tables 8.13, 8.24, 8.241, 8.242, and graph paper, sketch graphs of the solution of (8.11) and of the approximations which we have obtained. *Remark:* Sometimes graphs speak louder than tables.

Problem 8.252

In connection with (8.22), it was pointed out that we cannot replace the integrand $f(t, y(t))$ by the constant $f(x_n + h/2, y(x_n + h/2))$ because we cannot compute this constant. When x_n, y_n, and h are known, we can compute $f(x_n + h/2, y_n)$ and replace $f(t, y(t))$ in (8.22) by this to obtain the formula

$$y_{n+1} = y_n + hf(x_n + h/2, y_n) \tag{8.253}$$

which should (Why?) be a little better than (8.21). Check all this by using (8.253) instead of (8.21) to compute tables similar to Tables 8.24 and 8.241 and (if you think it will be good for you) Table 8.242.

8.26. Geometrical Considerations. This section deals with the psychological rather than logical development of our subject. It is designed to show why the Euler-Cauchy method gives crude approximations and to indicate that substantial improvements should be possible. The big improvement will come in the next section.

Let the curve C of Fig. 8.27 be a part of the graph of the solution $y(x)$

of $y' = f(x, y)$ which runs from the point P with known coordinates (x_n, y_n) to the point Q with coordinates $(x_n + h, Y)$ where $x_n + h$ is known but Y is unknown. It is our problem to obtain a number y_{n+1} which is a good approximation to Y. Let PA be, as it looks to be, the tangent to C at P. Since $f(x_n, y_n)$ is the slope of C at P, we see that $z_n = hf(x_n, y_n)$. From (8.21), we see that the Euler-Cauchy approximation to Y is $y_n + z_n$, and Fig. 8.27 indicates that this approximation is

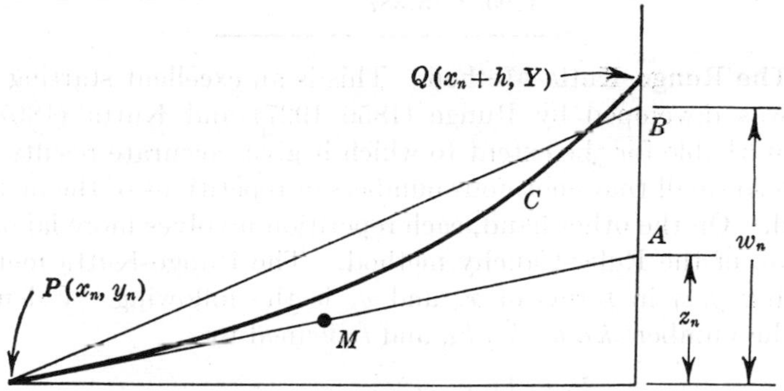

FIG. 8.27

very bad unless h is very much smaller than the h shown in the figure. While the simplicity of the operation can be admired, a bad approximation results from drawing a line through P with slope $f(x_n, y_n)$ and using $y_n + z_n$ to approximate Y. Since the midpoint M of the segment PA is much nearer the center of the arc C than P is, it should be much better to draw the line PB whose slope is the value of $f(x, y)$ at M and then use $y_n + w_n$ to approximate Y. Since $z_n = hf(x_n, y_n)$ and the coordinates of M are $(x_n + h/2, y_n + z_n/2)$, all this suggests that we should set

$$z_n = hf(x_n, y_n) \tag{8.28}$$

and use the y_{n+1} of the formula

$$y_{n+1} = y_n + hf\left(x_n + \frac{h}{2}, y_n + \frac{z_n}{2}\right) \tag{8.29}$$

to approximate Y. The approximation method based upon (8.28) and (8.29) is a starting method.

Problem 8.291

For the standard problem $y' = x + y$, $y(0) = 1$, use (8.28) and (8.29) with $h = \frac{1}{4}$ to obtain all of the entries in Table 8.2911. Note that the results in Table 8.2911 are very much better than those in Table 8.241, and that they are almost respectable.

TABLE 8.2911

x_n	y_n	z_n
0.00	1.000	0.250
0.25	1.312	0.390
0.50	1.782	0.570
0.75	2.455	0.801
1.00	3.387	—

8.3. The Runge-Kutta Method. This is an excellent starting method which was developed by Runge (1856–1927) and Kutta (1867–1944). It is remarkable for the extent to which it gives accurate results without taking h so small that enormous numbers of repetitions of the method are required. On the other hand, each repetition involves more labor than a repetition of the Euler-Cauchy method. The Runge-Kutta method for estimating y_{n+1} in terms of x_n and y_n is the following. Calculate, in order, the numbers k_1, k_2, k_3, k_4, and k defined by

$$\begin{aligned} k_1 &= hf(x_n, y_n) \\ k_2 &= hf\left(x_n + \frac{h}{2}, y_n + \frac{k_1}{2}\right) \\ k_3 &= hf\left(x_n + \frac{h}{2}, y_n + \frac{k_2}{2}\right) \\ k_4 &= hf(x_n + h, y_n + k_3) \\ k &= \frac{1}{6}(k_1 + 2k_2 + 2k_3 + k_4) \end{aligned} \tag{8.31}$$

and then set

$$y_{n+1} = y_n + k. \tag{8.32}$$

The excellence of the method is partially revealed by the fact that if $f(x, y)$ is independent of y, say $f(x, y) = g(x)$, then the number k in (8.31) becomes the famous *Simpson* (1710–1761) *rule* value of the integral of $g(x)$ over the interval $x_n \leqq x \leqq x_n + h$. Theoretical investigations of its derivations and properties indicate that it should be very good. Perhaps its best recommendation is the great success with which it is widely used in practice. After some problems, we shall give some results obtained with the aid of an electronic computer.

Problems

The following problems all involve applications of the Runge-Kutta method to the standard problem $y' = x + y$, $y(0) = 1$. An instruction to keep 5D, for example, is an instruction to keep five decimal places (four after the decimal point) and to ignore rounding errors; it does not require keeping enough D to be sure of 5D accuracy in the computed results. Some of these problems involve calculations designed to test the usefulness of the following fact. In appropriate circumstances, *the error $E(h)$ resulting from a single application of the Runge-Kutta method has the order of h^5.* This means that there is a nonzero constant L such that the first formula in

$$\text{(8.331)} \qquad \lim_{h\to 0} \frac{E(h)}{h^5} = L, \qquad \lim_{h\to 0} \frac{E(h/2)}{(h/2)^5} = L, \qquad \lim_{h\to 0} \frac{E(h/2)}{E(h)} = \frac{1}{32}$$

holds. The first formula implies the other two. If, in the latter problems, we keep less than 11D, then the rounding errors are so great that they interfere with studies of $E(h)$.

Problem 8.332

Keeping 5D, use $h = 1$ to estimate $y(1)$. *Ans.:* 3.4167.

Problem 8.333

Keeping 5D, use $h = 0.5$ to estimate $y(0.5)$ and then, with the aid of this estimate, $y(1.0)$. *Ans.:* 1.7969 and 3.4347.

Problem 8.334

Keeping 11D, use $h = 0.1$ to estimate $y(0.1)$ and find the error E_1 in this estimate. Then use your estimate of $y(0.1)$ and $h = 0.1$ to estimate $y(0.2)$ and find the error E_2 in this estimate. Try to guess how E_1 and E_2 should compare. *Ans.:* The estimates are $y(0.1) = 1.11034\,16667$ and $y(0.2) = 1.24280\,51417$. The errors are $E_1 = 0.00000\,01695$ and $E_2 = 0.00000\,03746$, and E_2 is roughly double E_1.

Problem 8.335

Keeping 11D, use $h = 0.2$ to estimate $y(0.2)$ and find the error E_3 in this estimate. If (8.341) is to be very useful, the errors E_3 and E_1 should come close to satisfying the condition $E_3/32 = E_1$. What do the figures say? *Ans.:* The estimate is $y(0.2) = 1.24280\,00000$ and $E_3 = 0.00000\,55163$. Moreover $E_3/32$ is roughly E_1.

Problem 8.336

Keeping 11D, use $h = 0.05 = \frac{1}{20}$ to estimate $y(0.05)$ and then $y(0.1)$. Find the error E_4 in the last estimate. Guess how E_4 compares with E_1, and then find out. *Ans.:* While you should not need the result, you can check your intermediate result with the 11D value

$$y(0.05) = 1.05254\,21928.$$

Your estimates should be $y(0.05) = 1.05254\,21875$ and $y(1.0) = 1.11034\,18251$. It turns out that $E_4 = 0.00000\,00111$ and $E_1/16 = 0.00000\,00106$.

Problem 8.337

Show that applying the Runge-Kutta method to the problem

$$y' = ay, \qquad y(0) = 1,$$

whose solution is $y = e^{ax}$, gives $y_{n+1} = ry_n$ and hence $y_n = r^n$ where

$$r = 1 + ah + \tfrac{1}{2}(ah)^2 + \tfrac{1}{6}(ah)^3 + \tfrac{1}{24}(ah)^4.$$

Note that r is a good approximation to e^{ah} when ah is small. The exact value of y_n is e^{ahn} and the relative error in the Runge-Kutta estimate is therefore

$$\frac{|e^{ahn} - r^n|}{e^{ahn}} = \left|1 - \left(\frac{r}{e^{ah}}\right)^n\right|.$$

Discuss the behavior of the relative error in the following circumstances:

i. $ah = 0.1$ and n increases
ii. $ah = -0.1$ and n increases
iii. $ahn = 20$, h decreases, and n increases
iv. $ahn = -20$, h decreases, and n increases

Remark: As your results indicate, it is usually necessary to use small tabular differences h, and to keep many D in the calculations, in order to obtain respectable tables covering long ranges of values of x. For such operations, high-speed computers are a necessity.

8.34. The Runge-Kutta Method (Continued). Previous problems have involved applications of the Runge-Kutta method to the problem

$$(8.35)\qquad y' = x + y, \qquad y(0) = 1.$$

We now examine some further applications that are made much more easily with a high-speed computer than by hand. For each of several values of h, the Runge-Kutta estimates of $y(0.1)$, $y(0.2)$, . . . , $y(1.0)$ were obtained with a high-speed electronic digital computer (IBM) which can make 8D calculations and tabulate 8D results.*

When $h = 0.1$, the results agree so completely with those in the 6D Table 8.14 that Table 8.14 simply is not exact enough to tell how good the results are. Comparing the results with the more exact 11D Table 8.13 shows that the errors vary from 0.00000 01 when $x = 0.1$ to 0.00000 38 when $x = 1.0$. This seems very gratifying, but we can ask how we could know that the results are correct to even 2D or 3D if we did not have our tables available for comparison. It seems that the best way to find out is to repeat the calculation with a smaller value of h. Using $h = 0.05$ gives results agreeing so closely with those obtained when $h = 0.1$ that the discrepancies vary from 0.00000 01 when $x = 0.1$ to 0.00000 39 when $x = 1.0$. This agreement is taken to be a guarantee that no one of

* Some acknowledgements must be made. The author's son, Palmer Wright Agnew, when he was a junior in high school, carried through all of the programming and operating of the computer and its appurtenances which were required to obtain most of our results. Other and more extensive calculations, which were made later, confirmed them. The author is also indebted to Richard Lesser, director of the Cornell Computing Center, and to Robert J. Walker of the Cornell Mathematics Department for valuable information and advice.

the estimates contains an error much greater than 0.00000 4. Of course the guarantee is not absolute because of the remote possibility that the errors in one case happen to match the errors in the other case and that, from the 6D standpoint, the sets of results are seriously and equally wrong. The probability of being seriously injured by this eventuality may be at least as great as the probability of dipping a cup of fresh water from the ocean because all the molecules of salt happen to be elsewhere.

It seems desirable to pause and adopt a principle. Whenever the accuracy of calculations by the Runge-Kutta method or any other method can be conveniently and economically guaranteed in the manner described above, we shall never propose use of other checks upon the accuracy of the calculations. Therefore, whenever we propose use of ways of determining whether good methods are going astray, it is on the basis of the assumption that the calculations will not be checked in the painless manner described above.

It is now appropriate to give a little thought to the result of making h smaller and smaller. It is easy to see that, when we are making 8D calculations, we should not take h too small. Suppose, to take an extreme case, we are applying (8.31) and (8.32) and have, correct to 8D,

$$y_n = 1.11034\ 18,$$

and suppose further that h is so small that the value of the k in (8.31) and (8.32) turns out to be

$$k = 0.00000\ 00123\ 45678.$$

When we compute the 8D sum of y_n and k to obtain our y_{n+1}, we obtain, correct to 8D, $y_{n+1} = y_n$. Thus, rounding errors completely destroy the usefulness of the calculation. It is clear that the prohibition against small values of h is more severe when we make 3D or 4D calculations, and would remain if our equipment were used in such a way that it actually or effectively makes 50D calculations. Henceforth our remarks apply to the 8D case. If we choose h such that the k turns out to be

$$k = 0.00000\ 23456\ 789,$$

then the rounding error is less serious. Whether an accumulation of such errors would be injurious depends partly upon the extent to which the errors nullify themselves by having opposite signs. These considerations show very clearly that the true merit of a numerical method depends partly upon the extent to which rounding errors influence results of applying the method. In particular, it takes very much more than theorems involving (8.331) to establish the high merit of the Runge-Kutta method.

Table 8.36 shows, for each of several values of h and for 8D calculations, the errors in the Runge-Kutta estimates of $y(0.5)$ and $y(1.0)$ for the standard problem (8.35). The table shows that the errors decrease very nicely as h decreases to about 2^{-5} and that smaller values of h produce accumulated rounding errors that seriously affect the accuracy of the estimates.

TABLE 8.36

h	Error in $y(0.5)$	Error in $y(1)$
$1 = 1.0$	—	$-0.01989\ 70$
$2^{-1} = 0.5$	$-0.00056\ 75$	$-0.00187\ 12$
$2^{-2} = 0.25$	$-0.00004\ 36$	$-0.00014\ 38$
$2^{-3} = 0.125$	$-0.00000\ 30$	$-0.00001\ 00$
$2^{-4} = 0.0625$	$-0.00000\ 03$	$-0.00000\ 09$
$2^{-5} = 0.03125$	$-0.00000\ 01$	$-0.00000\ 05$
$2^{-6} = 0.01562\ 5$	$-0.00000\ 03$	$-0.00000\ 11$
$2^{-7} = 0.00781\ 25$	$-0.00000\ 06$	$-0.00000\ 21$
$2^{-8} = 0.00390\ 625$	$-0.00000\ 12$	$-0.00000\ 43$
$2^{-9} = 0.00195\ 312$	$-0.00000\ 23$	$-0.00000\ 85$
$2^{-10} = 0.00097\ 656$	$-0.00000\ 48$	$-0.00001\ 65$
$2^{-11} = 0.00048\ 828$	$-0.00000\ 96$	$-0.00003\ 34$
$2^{-12} = 0.00024\ 414$	$-0.00001\ 94$	$-0.00006\ 69$
$2^{-13} = 0.00012\ 207$	$-0.00003\ 94$	$-0.00013\ 53$
$2^{-14} = 0.00006\ 104$	$-0.00007\ 94$	$-0.00027\ 34$
$2^{-15} = 0.00003\ 052$	$-0.00015\ 89$	$-0.00054\ 59$
$2^{-16} = 0.00001\ 526$	$-0.00031\ 70$	$-0.00109\ 25$

8.4. J. C. Adams Method. This is a starting method which was used and perhaps originated by John Couch Adams (1819–1892). Its use for the problem

$$y'(x) = f(x, y), \qquad y(x_0) = y_0 \tag{8.41}$$

is restricted to cases in which $f(x, y)$ is a function for which

$$y''(x) = \frac{\partial f}{\partial x} + \frac{\partial f}{\partial y} y'(x) \tag{8.42}$$

and derivatives of higher order exist and have manageable expressions and, moreover, $y(x)$ is closely approximated by a few terms of its Taylor series so that we can calculate $y(x_n + h)$ from the formula

$$y(x) = y(x_n) + \frac{y'(x_n)}{1!}(x - x_n) + \frac{y''(x_n)}{2!}(x - x_n)^2 + \cdots. \tag{8.43}$$

The method of Adams consists in calculating $y_{n+p} = y(x_n + ph)$ when $p = 1$, and perhaps also for more values of p, by setting $x = x_n + ph$ in (8.43).

Since this method involves an elementary idea which speaks for itself, we conclude with a remark. For the standard problem (8.11) and with $x_n = x_0 = 0$ and $y_n = y_0 = 1$, (8.43) reduces to

$$(8.44) \qquad y(x) = 1 + \frac{x}{1} + 2\left(\frac{x^2}{2!} + \frac{x^3}{3!} + \frac{x^4}{4!} + \cdots\right).$$

It is amusing to notice that the quantity in parentheses is $e^x - x - 1$ and hence that (8.44) reduces to the known solution $y = 2e^x - x - 1$ of the problem.

8.45. Errors. Suppose we start with a problem $y' = f(x, y)$, $y(x_0) = y_0$ and make 5D calculations. We like to think of x_0 and y_0 as being correct, but in case the initial condition is $y(0) = \pi$, we would set $y_0 = 3.1416$ and start off with a rounding error. Except in the most trivial cases, the best 5D values of $y_0, y_0', y_1, y_1', \ldots, y_n, y_n'$ contain rounding errors. Even if we had a simple exact formula into which we could substitute the exact values of some of these numbers to obtain the exact value of y_{n+1}, substitution of the 5D values would produce an error in the computed y_{n+1}. This error might be ameliorated by rounding y_{n+1} to 5D, but it is sometimes aggravated (sometimes on frustrating close decisions) and we cannot be sure that our computed 5D value of y_{n+1} is correct to 5D. Thus, even with exact formulas, we can drift astray in our calculations. Rounding errors and evil consequences of rounding errors are inevitable and persistent. Contributions to the chaos occur when y_{n+1} is computed by a numerical method which employs one or more approximate formulas, this being particularly true when the formulas are not very good ones. We should try to get an idea whether errors made in calculating some of the numbers y_k tend to mushroom into larger errors in the numbers y_{n+1} calculated later or tend to fade away. The following remarks, which throw some light upon this matter, need not be taken too seriously.

It is possible to present a theoretical indication that there is some validity in the principle that a numerical method which fares well when applied to the standard problem $y' = x + y$, $y(0) = 1$ will also fare well when applied to a wide class of practical problems. Suppose that $y(x)$ is the solution of the problem $y' = x + y$, $y(x_0) = y_0$ which we want to solve and that $Y(x)$ is the solution of the problem $y' = x + y$, $y(x_0) = Y_0$ where Y_0 is a good approximation to y_0 and we could therefore hope that $Y(x)$ is a good approximation to $y(x)$. Since $y(x)$ and $Y(x)$ are both solutions of the equation $y' = x + y$, there must be constants c_1 and c_2 such that

$$y(x) = c_1e^x - x - 1, \qquad Y(x) = c_2e^x - x - 1.$$

The discrepancy between $y(x)$ and $Y(x)$ is therefore

$$(8.46) \qquad |y(x) - Y(x)| = |c_2 - c_1|e^x$$

and, provided $c_2 \neq c_1$, this discrepancy grows at an exponential rate as x increases. Thus, for our standard problem, the effects of a single initial discrepancy are magnified at a rate as great as one normally finds in applied mathematics. It can be expected that the effects of many discrepancies will be more pronounced. A sequence of rounding errors in $y_1, y_2, y_3, \ldots$ may be random enough to delay their inevitable evil consequences. But a steady stream of larger or equally small systematic errors will certainly mushroom into much larger errors before the calculations have gone very far. The practical consequences of a rapid growth of discrepancies are more injurious in some problems than in others; they are most injurious when $y(x)$ tends rapidly to 0 as x increases and the discrepancies seriously interfere with the determination of the order of magnitude of $y(x)$. The only way to cope with an awkward situation of the latter type is to use a good method with a small tabular difference h and keep many D in the calculations. Such situations never occur in test problems involving equations of the type $y' = ax + by$ where a and b are nonzero constants. Problem 1.382(c) shows that each solution of the equation has the form

$$y = ce^{bx} - \frac{a}{b}x - \frac{a}{b^2}$$

so $|y(x)| \to \infty$ as $x \to \infty$.

The main reason for calling attention to the forementioned ideas is the following. They show very clearly that we need good methods which will not materially augment the chaos produced by rounding errors. For example, when the solution $y(x)$ is to be tabulated over a long range, it may be necessary to use a good method and make 8D calculations at the start in order to secure 2D or 3D accuracy at the end.

8.5. Continuing Methods. We continue our discussion of the problem

$$y'(x) = f(x, y), \qquad y(x_0) = y_0 \tag{8.51}$$

and recall that a continuing method is a method for approximating y_{n+1} and y'_{n+1} when y_k and y'_k have already been approximated for some range $n - q \leqq k \leqq n$ and are available for use in calculations. For present purposes, as well as for many other purposes in numerical analysis, polynomial approximations constitute the principal tool by means of which results are obtained. Our first step is to recognize a vague but nevertheless valuable principle which has been known to computers for centuries and has been steadily used to obtain information about a function $w(x)$ when its values have been calculated or observed for a few values of x. For many applications, our statements and formulas would be better if $w(x)$ were written in place of $y'(x)$, but we use $y'(x)$ so the formulas that arise will be precisely the formulas we want to use. If $y'(x)$ is a decent function, if p is a small positive integer (say $2 \leqq p \leqq 30$), and if h is a positive number which is not too large, then the function $y'(x)$ is closely approximated over the whole interval $x_{n-p} \leqq x \leqq x_{n+1}$ by the unique polynomial $P(x)$ of degree p or less whose graph passes through the $p + 1$ points $(x_n, y'_n), (x_{n-1}, y'_{n-1}), \ldots, (x_{n-p}, y'_{n-p})$ on the graph of $y'(x)$. The polynomial $P(x)$ is an *interpolation polynomial*, and the conditions it must satisfy are

$$(8.511) \qquad P(x_k) = y'(x_k) = y'_k \qquad n - p \leqq k \leqq n.$$

Newton (1642–1727) was smart enough to give a formula for this polynomial $P(x)$ which is exceptionally useful for calculations involving $P(x)$ when x is near x_n. The formula is somewhat like the Taylor (1685–1731) power-series formula but is certainly less frightening because it contains only a finite set of terms.

Let $\epsilon(x) = y'(x) - P(x)$ so that $\epsilon(x)$ is the error term which shows how much $y'(x)$ differs from the approximating polynomial $P(x)$, and the left side of (8.52) is $P(x)$. The Newton formula, which is often called an *interpolation formula*, is then

$$(8.52) \quad y'(x) - \epsilon(x) = y'_n + \frac{\nabla y'_n}{1!h}(x - x_n) + \frac{\nabla^2 y'_n}{2!h^2}(x - x_n)(x - x_{n-1}) + \frac{\nabla^3 y'_n}{3!h^3}(x - x_n)(x - x_{n-1})(x - x_{n-2}) + \frac{\nabla^4 y'_n}{4!h^4}(x - x_n)(x - x_{n-1})(x - x_{n-2})(x - x_{n-3}) + \cdots.$$

The differences appearing here are precisely those defined in connection with Table 8.14. The right side of (8.52) is not, as the terminal dots indicate, an infinite series; it is a finite sum of $p + 1$ terms, the last term being

$$(8.521) \qquad \frac{\nabla^p y'_n}{p!h^p}(x - x_n)(x - x_{n-1}) \cdots (x - x_{n-p+1}).$$

It is easy to see that the right side of (8.52) really is a polynomial $P(x)$ of degree p or less according as $\nabla^p y'_n \neq 0$ or $\nabla^p y'_n = 0$. To prove that $P(x) = y'(x_k) = y'_k$ and hence that $\epsilon(x) = 0$ when $x = x_k$ and $n - p \leqq k \leqq n$ requires more effort. The start is easy. Clearly $P(x_n) = y'_n$ because, when $x = x_n$, all of the terms except the first are 0. When $x = x_{n-1} = x_n - h$, all of the terms except the first two are 0 and

$$P(x_{n-1}) = y'_n - \nabla y'_n = y'_n - (y'_n - y'_{n-1}) = y'_{n-1}.$$

Similarly it is easy to see that

$$\begin{aligned} P(x_{n-2}) &= y'_n - 2\nabla y'_n + \nabla^2 y'_n \\ P(x_{n-3}) &= y'_n - 3\nabla y'_n + 3\nabla^2 y'_n - \nabla^3 y'_n \\ P(x_{n-4}) &= y'_n - 4\nabla y'_n + 6\nabla^2 y'_n - 4\nabla^3 y'_n + \nabla^4 y'_n, \end{aligned}$$

and so forth, but it is no fun to expand the differences in the right members to show that $P(x_{n-k}) = y'_{n-k}$. It is more fun to notice that, by use of formulas such as

$$(1 - \nabla)^3 = 1 - 3\nabla + 3\nabla^2 - \nabla^3,$$

we can put the above equations in the form

$$P(x_{n-k}) = (1 - \nabla)^k y'_n.$$

Hence it is sufficient to prove that

$$(1 - \nabla)^k y'_n = y'_{n-k}.$$

It is easy to see that this formula holds when $k = 1$, and we complete the proof by induction by observing that if it holds for a particular k then

$$\begin{aligned}(1 - \nabla)^{k+1} y'_n &= (1 - \nabla)^k[(1 - \nabla)y'_n] \\ &= (1 - \nabla)^k y'_{n-1} \\ &= y'_{n-1-k} = y'_{n-k-1}\end{aligned}$$

so it holds when k is replaced by $k + 1$. This completes the proof that the right member of (8.52) is the required polynomial $P(x)$.

It must not be forgotten that the graph of $P(x)$ passes through $p + 1$ of the points . . . (x_{n-1}, y'_{n-1}), (x_n, y'_n). It is a very good idea to draw several figures and think about this. In case $p = 0$, we have $P(x) = y'_n$ and $|\epsilon(x)|$ shows how much $y'(x)$ differs from this constant. In case $p = 1$, the polynomial $P(x)$ contains two terms, its graph is a line through two points, and now $|\epsilon(x)|$ represents the distance measured vertically from a point on the graph of $y'(x)$ to a point on the interpolating line. In case $p = 2$, $P(x)$ contains three terms and interpolating parabolas are involved. In case $p = 3$, $P(x)$ contains four terms and interpolating cubics are involved. The truly remarkable feature of (8.52) is that adding another term is equivalent to adding another interpolation point and that, in many practical applications, $\epsilon(x)$ is quite negligible when p is 3 or 4 or 5 or 6 or 7. In much of our work, it is a good idea to think of p as being 6 or 7. For each fixed p, there are many other expressions for the polynomial $P(x)$, but the right member of (8.52) is by far the best one for our purposes.

The most useful continuing methods, as well as many others, depend upon a few basic formulas obtained by integrating the Newton formula (8.52) over the intervals $x_{n+1-k} \leqq x \leqq x_{n+1}$ for which k is a small positive integer. To derive these formulas, it is necessary to integrate several polynomials, and this can take considerable time even when it is done efficiently. Most readers would profit very little by making any of the calculations required to obtain formulas (8.53) to (8.557); it is better to spend time reading about the formulas and using them when they are useful. However we do show how all of the formulas can be obtained, and the same methods can be used to obtain many more formulas. We concentrate upon the useful ones. Using the first of the formulas

$$(8.522)\qquad \int_{x_i}^{x_j} y'(x)dx = y_j - y_i, \qquad \epsilon_j = \int_{x_j}^{x_{j+1}} \epsilon(x)dx,$$

defining epsilons by the second, and remembering that $x_{j+1} = x_j + h$ for each j, we can show that integrating (8.52) over the interval $x_{n+1-k} \leqq x \leqq x_{n+1}$ gives the ponderous formula

$$(8.53)\quad y_{n+1} = \epsilon_{n-k+1} + \epsilon_{n-k+2} + \cdots + \epsilon_n + y_{n+1-k}$$
$$+ kh\Big[y'_n + \left(-\frac{k}{2} + 1\right)\frac{\nabla y'_n}{1} + \left(\frac{k^2}{3} - \frac{3k}{2} + 2\right)\frac{\nabla^2 y'_n}{2}$$
$$+ \left(-\frac{k^3}{4} + 2k^2 - \frac{11k}{2} + 6\right)\frac{\nabla^3 y'_n}{6} + \left(\frac{k^4}{5} - \frac{5k^3}{2} + \frac{35k^2}{3} - 25k + 24\right)\frac{\nabla^4 y'_n}{24}$$
$$+ \left(-\frac{k^5}{6} + 3k^4 - \frac{85k^3}{4} + 75k^2 - 137k + 120\right)\frac{\nabla^5 y'_n}{120}$$
$$+ \left(\frac{k^6}{7} - \frac{7k^5}{2} + 35k^4 - \frac{735k^3}{4} + \frac{1624k^2}{3} - 882k + 720\right)\frac{\nabla^6 y'_n}{720} + \cdots \Big].$$

The most useful formula, obtained by setting $k = 2$ in (8.53), is

$$(8.54)\quad y_{n+1} = \epsilon_{n-1} + \epsilon_n + y_{n-1} + h[2y'_n + \tfrac{1}{3}(\nabla^2 y'_n + \nabla^3 y'_n + \nabla^4 y'_n + \nabla^5 y'_n) - \tfrac{1}{90}\nabla^4 y'_n - \tfrac{1}{45}\nabla^5 y'_n + \cdots].$$

One reason for the usefulness of this formula lies in the fact that it is equivalent to the formula

$$(8.541)\quad y_{n+1} = \epsilon_{n-1} + \epsilon_n + y_{n-1} + \frac{h}{3}\left[6y'_n + \nabla^2 y'_{n+1} - \frac{1}{30}\nabla^4 y'_n - \frac{1}{15}\nabla^5 y'_n + \cdots\right]$$

because of the identity

$$(8.542)\qquad \nabla^2 y'_n + \nabla^3 y'_n + \nabla^4 y'_n + \nabla^5 y'_n = \nabla^2 y'_{n+1} - \nabla^6 y'_n$$

which can be obtained by adding the four identities

$$\nabla^{k+1} y'_{n+1} = \nabla^k y'_{n+1} - \nabla^k y'_n$$

for which $k = 2, 3, 4, 5$. Putting $\nabla^2 y'_{n+1} = y'_{n+1} - 2y'_n + y'_{n-1}$ in (8.541) gives

$$(8.543)\quad y_{n+1} = y_{n-1} + \frac{h}{3}[y'_{n+1} + 4y'_n + y'_{n-1}] + \left\{\epsilon_{n-1} + \epsilon_n + h\left[-\frac{1}{90}\nabla^4 y'_n - \frac{1}{45}\nabla^5 y'_n + \cdots\right]\right\}.$$

The famous *Simpson* (1710–1761) *formula* is obtained by neglecting the quantity in braces.

The next most useful formula, obtained by setting $k = 4$ in (8.53), is

$$(8.55)\quad y_{n+1} = \epsilon_{n-3} + \epsilon_{n-2} + \epsilon_{n-1} + \epsilon_n + y_{n-3} + h[4y'_n - 4\nabla y'_n + \tfrac{8}{3}\nabla^2 y'_n + \tfrac{14}{45}\nabla^4 y'_n + \tfrac{14}{45}\nabla^5 y'_n + \cdots].$$

Putting $\nabla y'_n = y'_n - y'_{n-1}$ and $\nabla^2 y'_n = y'_n - 2y'_{n-1} + y'_{n-2}$ in (8.55) gives the formula

$$(8.551)\quad y_{n+1} = y_{n-3} + \frac{4h}{3}(2y'_n - y'_{n-1} + 2y'_{n-2}) + \left\{\epsilon_{n-3} + \epsilon_{n-2} + \epsilon_{n-1} + \epsilon_n + h\left[\frac{14}{45}\nabla^4 y'_n + \frac{14}{45}\nabla^5 y'_n + \cdots\right]\right\}.$$

Putting $k = 1$ in (8.53) gives the formula

$$(8.552)\quad y_{n+1} = \epsilon_n + y_n + h[y'_n + \tfrac{1}{2}\nabla y'_n + \tfrac{5}{12}\nabla^2 y'_n + \tfrac{3}{8}\nabla^3 y'_n + \tfrac{251}{720}\nabla^4 y'_n + \tfrac{95}{288}\nabla^5 y'_n + \cdots],$$

and putting $k = 3$ gives the formula

$$(8.553)\quad y_{n+1} = \epsilon_{n-2} + \epsilon_{n-1} + \epsilon_n + y_{n-2} + h[3y'_n - \tfrac{3}{2}\nabla y'_n + \tfrac{3}{4}\nabla^2 y'_n + \tfrac{3}{8}\nabla^3 y'_n + \tfrac{27}{80}\nabla^4 y'_n + \tfrac{51}{160}\nabla^5 y'_n + \cdots].$$

The formula

$$(8.554)\quad y_{n-1} = \epsilon_{n-2} + y_{n-2} + h[y'_n - \tfrac{3}{2}\nabla y'_n + \tfrac{5}{12}\nabla^2 y'_n + \tfrac{1}{24}\nabla^3 y'_n + \tfrac{11}{720}\nabla^4 y'_n + \tfrac{11}{1440}\nabla^5 y'_n + \cdots]$$

can be obtained by comparing (8.54) and (8.553). Expressing the differences of order 1, 2, 3 in terms of the numbers y'_k gives the formula

$$(8.555)\quad y_{n-1} = y_{n-2} + \frac{h}{24}[-y'_n + 13y'_{n-1} + 13y'_{n-2} - y'_{n-3}] + \left\{\epsilon_{n-2} + h\left[\frac{11}{720}\nabla^4 y'_n + \frac{11}{1440}\nabla^5 y'_n + \cdots\right]\right\}.$$

Finally, we record the *Weddle** (1817–1853) *formula*. Combining the results of putting $k = 1$ and $k = 6$ in (8.53) or, alternatively, integrating (8.52) over the interval $x_{n-6} \leqq x \leqq x_n$, gives

$$(8.556)\quad y_n = y_{n-6} + \frac{3h}{10}[20y'_n - 60\nabla y'_n + 90\nabla^2 y'_n - 80\nabla^3 y'_n + 41\nabla^4 y'_n - 11\nabla^5 y'_n + \nabla^6 y'_n] + \left\{\sum_{k=n-6}^{n-1}\epsilon_k - \frac{h}{140}\nabla^6 y'_n + \cdots\right\}.$$

When the differences in brackets are expressed in terms of the numbers y'_k, this becomes

$$(8.557)\quad y_n = W_n + \left\{\sum_{k=n-6}^{n-1}\epsilon_k + \frac{h}{140}\nabla^6 y'_n + \cdots\right\}$$

* Weddle rhymes with "meddle."

where

$$(8.558) \qquad W_n = y_{n-6} + \frac{3h}{10}[y'_n + 5y'_{n-1} + y'_{n-2} + 6y'_{n-3} + y'_{n-4} + 5y'_{n-5} + y'_{n-6}].$$

The approximate formula

$$(8.559) \qquad y_n = W_n$$

is the Weddle formula.

Undertaking to tell in a few words what has been done and can be done with these formulas is somewhat like undertaking to tell in a few words what has been done and what can be done with the tools in a carpenter shop. The important fact is that our tools are the very best tools, not inferior products cheaply constructed for small boys. It is very easy to start using the tools and, after a few remarks, we shall turn to problems. In each of the formulas, the terminal dots represent only a finite set of unwritten terms involving differences of order greater than those written. The formulas are exact, like the formula $\pi = \pi$; approximate formulas, like $\pi = 3.1416$, are obtained from these formulas by neglecting small terms in them. When the formulas are being usefully employed, the last terms written are negligible or nearly so, and the epsilons and unwritten terms are negligible in the sense that neglecting the sum of all of them does not produce errors of unallowed magnitude. The formula (8.54) is more attractive than (8.552). Also, when the numbers ϵ_n and ϵ_{n-1} are neglected as they always are in computations,* it is usually more accurate because the function $\epsilon(x)$ usually has opposite signs over adjacent intervals determined by the points $x_{n-p}, \ldots, x_{n-1}, x_n$ and hence $|\epsilon_{n-1} + \epsilon_n|$ is less than $|\epsilon_n|$.

Problem 8.56

Make a copy of all of the part of Table 8.14 which lies above the line containing the item for which $x_n = 0.6$. If you are writing on paper which is narrow and long, turn it sideways before copying the table. Suppose that a starting method has been applied to the problem

$$y' = x + y, \qquad y(0) = 1$$

and has given the data needed to make this table. Suppose that we wish to speed up progress by switching from the starting method to a continuing method. Our next step is to calculate y_n when $x_n = 0.6$ and we can do this by using (8.54) with $x_n = 0.5$. Observe that $y_{n-1} = 1.58365$ (not 1.79744 because this is y_n and not y_{n-1}), $y'_n = 2.29744$, $\nabla y'_n = 0.31379$, $\nabla^2 y'_n = 0.02986$, $\nabla^3 y'_n = 0.00284$, $\nabla^4 y'_n = 0.00026$, and $\nabla^5 y_n = -0.00001$. Use these values and (8.54) with $h = \frac{1}{10}$ to calculate y_n when $x_n = 0.6$. Then fill in all of the next row of your table. If sudden jumps (more violent than rounding errors could produce) appear in the columns, then either (i) a mistake has been made in the calculations or (ii) the continuing method is not good

* Sometimes, even in theoretical treatments of our subject, the epsilons are neglected so completely that they are both unwritten and unmentioned.

enough to keep accuracy of about 6D in y_{n+1}. When you are satisfied that your calculations are correct, look at the row in Table 8.14 for which $x = 0.6$. Then fill in another row of your table.

Problem 8.561

If you do not fully understand the calculations of the previous problem, start afresh and do them all over again.

Problem 8.57

Suppose that a starting method is applied to the problem $y' = x + y$, $y(0) = 1$ to obtain the values in Table 8.571.

TABLE 8.571

x_n	y_n	y'_n	$\nabla y'_n$	$\nabla^2 y'_n$	$\nabla^3 y'_n$	$\nabla^4 y'_n$	$\nabla^5 y'_n$
0	1.000	1.000					
0.2	1.243	1.443	*				
0.4	1.584	1.984	*	*			
0.6	2.044	2.644	*	*	*		
0.8	—	—	—	—	—	—	
1.0	—	—	—	—	—	—	—

Fill in the items of the table where the asterisks appear. Then, using $h = 0.2$, fill in the last two rows with the aid of (8.54) and the principle that you omit those terms whose values you do not know. Then look at all of your work and try to decide whether your values of $y(0.8)$ and $y(1.0)$ should (except for minor rounding errors) be correct to 4D (3D after the decimal point). Finally, check with Table 8.14.

Problem 8.58

The Weddle formula (8.559) is one of the world's best detectors of errors. We play a little game. Suppose that the values of $y(x)$ and $y'(x)$ in Table 8.14 were not obtained from a table of exponentials but have been worked out by use of approximate formulas quite different from the Weddle formula. We would like to know about the accuracy of the numbers y_n and y'_n in the first seven rows of the table. Now your work starts. Apply the Weddle formula to Table 8.14 with $y_n = 2.04424$ and show that $W_n = 2.04423\,76$. Thus W_n rounds to y_n and, moreover, Table 8.13 shows that W_n agrees to 8D with the 11D value of y_n. Do you think it likely that this close agreement between y_n and W_n would appear if the error in calculating y_n from y_{n-6} were more serious than a minor rounding error? Do you think it likely that y_n could fare so well under the Weddle check if there were a nontrivial error in the 6D values of the numbers $y_{n-5}, \ldots, y_{n-1}$ which were used in calculating y_n? *Ans.*: The answers are *no*, and you should now see a use for Weddle formula.

Problem 8.581

Apply the Weddle formula (8.559) to Table 8.14 with $y_n = 3.43656$ and show that $W_n = 3.43656\,52$. What does this indicate? *Ans.*: It indicates that if y_{n-6} is correct, then $y_{n-5}, \ldots, y_n$ are correct except for rounding errors. *Remark:* Nearly all of the small discrepancy between W_n and y_n is due to the rounding error in y_{n-6}.

Problem 8.582

The solution of the problem $y' = -y$, $y(0) = 1$ is $y(x) = e^{-x}$. Find how far the Weddle formula (8.559) will go in confirming correctness of the values from $y(0) = 0$ to $y(0.6) = 0.54881\ 16360\ 94$ in Table 8.1903. Keep all 12D to try to eliminate significance of rounding errors. *Ans.:* $W_n = 0.54881\ 16202\ 59$.
Remark: In those rare cases where better agreement is desired, the tabular difference h should be reduced.

Problem 8.583

From Table 8.242, copy the first seven sets of values of x_n, y_n, y'_n. Does the Weddle formula (8.559) with $y_n = 1.943$ indicate that these values are correct to 4D? *Ans.:* No. We find that $W_n = 2.019$ and doubt is cast upon the correctness of the second digit of y_n.

Problem 8.584

Sometimes we want to apply a critical test to calculations involving a tabular difference h which is larger than we expect to find in useful tables. This may put a strain upon the best test. Suppose we have started calculating $J_0(x)$ and have obtained Table 8.5841 by calculations of dubious accuracy. What does the Weddle test (8.559) say about the calculations? *Solution:* It says that if you want more accuracy, you better keep more D in your calculations. Using (8.558) with $y_n = -0.2601$ gives *Ans.:* $W_n = -0.260045$.
Remark: The items in Table 8.5841 can be selected from tables of Bessel functions.

TABLE 8.5841

x	$J_0(x)$	$J'_0(x)$
0.0	1.0000	0.0000
0.5	0.9385	−0.2423
1.0	0.7652	−0.4401
1.5	0.5118	−0.5579
2.0	0.2239	−0.5767
2.5	−0.0484	−0.4971
3.0	−0.2601	−0.3391

There is no dearth of easily constructed test problems of nature. Tables giving $\sin x$ and $\cos x$ in radian measure provide plenty.

Remark 8.585

As a check formula, the Weddle formula (8.559) has three virtues. It is exceptionally accurate, being more accurate than any of the other approximate formulas we will use. It is easily applied because W_n is easily calculated even with a pencil. Finally, it is essentially different from all other approximate formulas which we use so that results of applying the check are always thoroughly meaningful.

The Simpson formula, while less accurate than the Weddle formula, is accurate enough to be a useful check formula, but it is disqualified because all of our continuing methods are, in one way or another, too closely related to it. We cannot decide that neglected quantities are negligible by comparing the results obtained from two approximate formulas that neglect the same quantities. The formula

$$(8.586)\quad 11(y_n - y_{n-3}) + 27(y_{n-1} - y_{n-2}) = h[3(y_n' + y_{n-3}') + 27(y_{n-1}' + y_{n-2}')]$$

is a very accurate formula which is not disqualified. It involves only four rows and includes all values of y and y' in these rows. If the discrepancy between the members of (8.586) does not exceed ten times the allowable error in y_n', there is strong evidence that the four rows do not contain damaging uninherited errors.

Problem 8.59

Persons who have a desk calculator and time at their disposal can obtain valuable experience in numerical analysis in the following way: Select a problem from the list in Problem 8.191. Use the Runge-Kutta method (8.32) to obtain y_1, y_1', y_2, y_2', y_3, y_3'. Start a table of differences and use the method of Problem 8.57 to obtain y_4, y_4', y_5, y_5', y_6, y_6'. Then check the whole business by applying the Weddle check (8.559). Then, whether the results agree or not, repeat these calculations carrying more or fewer D. Then, with what would seem to be a sensible number of D, make new calculations with the tabular difference h double or half what it was before. Work with this problem until you have it thoroughly whipped. After this valuable experience, whip more problems and get more valuable experience. What you learn will help you in more ways than you can possibly predict.

8.6. The Milne Method. This is a very popular continuing method, originated by W. E. Milne (1890–), for the problem $y' = f(x, y)$, $y(x_0) = y_0$. The method depends upon three approximation formulas and, after seeing what the method is, we shall discuss the formulas and the method. The Milne formulas are

$$(8.61)\qquad y_{n+1} = y_{n-3} + \frac{4h}{3}(2y_n' - y_{n-1}' + 2y_{n-2}')$$

$$(8.62)\qquad y_{n+1}' = f(x_{n+1}, y_{n+1})$$

$$(8.63)\qquad y_{n+1} = y_{n-1} + \frac{h}{3}(y_{n+1}' + 4y_n' + y_{n-1}').$$

Perhaps we should recognize that these formulas, and the exact formulas from which they are derived, were known long before the time of Milne. However we shall call them the Milne formulas when we use them in the way that Milne* proposed that they should be used.

The Milne method, which is applicable when y_k and y_k' have been approximated for $k = n - 3, n - 2, n - 1, n$, is the following. First, calculate y_{n+1} from (8.61). Then insert this estimate of y_{n+1} in (8.62) to obtain y_{n+1}'. Then calculate y_{n+1} from (8.63). If the two estimates of y_{n+1} possess satisfactory agreement (even rounding errors can bring disagreement in the last digit kept) assume that the last estimate of y_{n+1} is correct and proceed to the next step. In case satisfactory agreement fails to

* W. E. Milne, *Amer. Math. Monthly*, vol. 33, pp. 455–460, 1926.

appear, take the occasion to find and correct all mistakes that have been made in calculations. In case satisfactory agreement refuses to appear, either decrease h or apply the Milne check formula which we shall describe presently.*

Seeing where the Milne formulas come from provides an understanding of the Milne method as well as other methods. If, in the exact formula (8.551) we neglect the batch of epsilons and differences of order 4 and more, we obtain the first Milne formula (8.61). If we could know that the things we neglected in (8.551) really are negligible, that we made no mistakes in calculating y_{n+1} from (8.61), and that rounding errors have not hurt us too much, then we would have an approximation to y_{n+1} that satisfies us. We would then use (8.62) to calculate y'_{n+1} and be ready for the next step, provided no mistakes were made in calculating y'_{n+1}. The whole situation makes it desirable to check the calculated values of y_{n+1} and y'_{n+1} by substituting them in a formula which contains both of them and has parentage quite different from that of (8.61). The exact formula (8.543) is a suitable parent formula. In fact, the third Milne formula (8.63) is the Simpson formula which comes from (8.543) by neglecting the batch of epsilons and differences of order 4 and more, this batch being different from the batch neglected in obtaining (8.61) from (8.551). Of course agreement to 10D of the values of y_{n+1} computed from (8.61) and (8.63) does not *prove* that the values are correct to 10D; it proves that the sum of the terms neglected in (8.551) is nearly the same as the sum of the terms neglected in (8.543), but it does not prove that the sums are near 0. It is possible to construct artificial examples where the sums are nearly equal and injuriously different from 0, but nobody expects to encounter such things in practical work and the possibility is systematically ignored. The assumption that the neglected sums are 0 whenever they are equal is, of course, equivalent to the Milne assumption that the two calculated values of y_{n+1} are correct whenever they agree.

* The numbers that actually appear when the Milne method is being applied are

$$y_{n+1,1} = e_1 + y_{n-3} + \frac{4h}{3}(2y'_n - y'_{n-1} + 2y'_{n-2}) \tag{8.631}$$

$$y'_{n+1,1} = e_2 + f(x_{n+1}, y_{n+1,1}) \tag{8.632}$$

$$y_{n+1,2} = e_3 + \frac{h}{3}(y'_{n+1,1} + 4y'_n + y'_{n-1}) \tag{8.633}$$

where e_1, e_2, e_3 are rounding errors and the numbers on the left are defined by these formulas. Usefulness of the method depends on the closeness with which $y_{n+1,1}$ and $y_{n+1,2}$ approximate the exact y_{n+1} determined by the problem $y' = f(x, y)$, $y(x_{n-3}) = y_{n-3}$. If $y_{n+1,1}$ and $y_{n+1,2}$ could always be identical with y_{n+1}, the method would give perfect continuations. Remarks similar to this apply to methods other than the Milne method.

We now discuss matters relating to a formula known as the Milne check formula. Let $y_{n+1,1}$ and $y_{n+1,2}$ denote the approximations to y_{n+1} which are calculated from the Milne formulas (8.61) and (8.63), and let

$$E_n = y_{n+1,2} - y_{n+1,1}. \tag{8.64}$$

According to Milne, it is desirable to calculate and record the discrepancies E_n and watch them so that suspicious jumps and fluctuations can indicate that mistakes in calculation have been made. Further, according to Milne, if E_n is not negligible then either a mistake has been made while calculating or $\nabla^4 y'_n$ is so large that $y_{n+1,1}$ and $y_{n+1,2}$ disagree. Thus Milne cheerfully blames $\nabla^4 y'_n$ for discrepancies that occur. (Problems 8.653 and 8.654 bear upon this point.) If we assume that the discrepancies between the Milne estimates $y_{n+1,1}$, $y_{n+1,2}$ and the correct y_{n+1} are due almost wholly to $\nabla^4 y'_n$, and if we neglect rounding errors and the error involved in replacing y'_{n+1} by $y'_{n+1,1}$ in (8.63), then comparisons of (8.61) with (8.551), and (8.63) with (8.543), give the approximate formulas

$$y_{n+1} - y_{n+1,1} = \tfrac{14}{45} h\nabla^4 y'_n, \qquad y_{n+1} - y_{n+1,2} = -\tfrac{1}{90} h\nabla^4 y'_n. \tag{8.641}$$

Subtraction gives the approximate formula

$$E_n = \tfrac{29}{90} h\nabla^4 y'_n. \tag{8.642}$$

This and the last formula in (8.641) give the approximate formula

$$|y_{n+1,2} - y_{n+1}| = \frac{|E_n|}{29} \tag{8.643}$$

which is known as the *Milne check formula*. When this formula is applied, the application runs as follows. If the difference between $y_{n+1,1}$ and $y_{n+1,2}$ is not negligible, calculate $|E_n|/29$. If this is negligible, assume that $y_{n+1,2}$ is correct, recalculate y'_{n+1} with this new value of y_{n+1}, and proceed to the next step. Applications of the Milne check formula are made very quickly. If we are willing to neglect 0.00001, we assume that $y_{n+1,2}$ is correct when $|E_n| < 0.00029$.

When the Milne method is being applied, it is often a very good idea to use the Weddle formula (8.559) (which is more accurate than any of the Milne formulas) as a check when seven pairs of values of y_n and y'_n have been obtained. This may reveal gross errors that can be corrected. It may show that another start with a smaller h is required to produce the desired accuracy. It may guarantee that the seven pairs are at least as accurate as we want. The Weddle formula is so easy to apply that it may be worth while to apply it frequently. Of course the frequency can depend upon how far we must go and upon the seriousness of the consequences of ending at a place remote from our destination.

Problem 8.65

For the standard problem $y' = x + y$, $y(0) = 1$, copy the starting values $y(0)$, $y(0.1)$, $y(0.2)$, and $y(0.3)$ to 6D from Table 8.13. Then use the Milne method to approximate $y(0.4)$, $y(0.5)$, and $y(0.6)$. Then apply the Weddle check (8.559).

Problem 8.651

For the standard problem $y' = x + y$, $y(0) = 1$, copy the starting values $y(0)$, $y(0.2)$, $y(0.4)$, and $y(0.6)$ to 6D from Table 8.13. Use the Milne method with $h = 0.2$ to find $y(0.8)$, $y(1.0)$, and $y(1.2)$. Then apply the Weddle check (8.559).

Problem 8.652

For the standard problem $y' = x + y$, $y(0) = 1$, copy the starting values $y(0)$, $y(0.3)$, $y(0.6)$, and $y(0.9)$ to 6D from Table 8.13. Use the Milne method with $h = 0.3$ to find three more rows and then apply the Weddle check (8.559). Note that, for hand or desk calculator use, it is a convenience to have h a simple multiple of 3.

Problem 8.653

A perfectly respectable function $g(x)$ and a value x_0 of x may be such that $g'(x_0) = 0$ and $g''(x_0) \neq 0$. Analogously, a perfectly respectable function $y'(x)$ and a set $x_1, x_2, \ldots, x_n$ of values of x may be such that $\nabla^4 y_n' = 0$ while $\nabla^5 y_n' \neq 0$. Can use of the Milne check formula be justified in this case? *Solution:* No, but under appropriate conditions a weaker check formula is available. If $\nabla^4 y_n' = 0$, if the descrepancies between the Milne estimates $y_{n+1,1}$ and $y_{n+1,2}$ and the correct y_{n+1} are due almost wholly to $\nabla^5 y_n'$, and if the error involved in replacing y_{n+1} by $y_{n+1,1}$ in (8.63) is negligible, then comparison of (8.61) with (8.551) and (8.63) with (8.543) gives

$$y_{n+1} - y_{n+1,1} = \tfrac{14}{45} h\nabla^5 y_n', \qquad y_{n+1} - y_{n+1,2} = -\tfrac{1}{45} h\nabla^5 y_n'.$$

Subtraction and use of the last of these formulas give

$$E_n = \frac{15}{45} h\nabla^5 y_n', \qquad |y_{n+1} - y_{n+1,2}| = \frac{E_n}{15}.$$

Problem 8.654

Sometimes, when neither of $\nabla^4 y_n'$ and $\nabla^5 y_n'$ is negligible, information can be gleaned from the approximate formulas

$$y_{n+1} - y_{n+1,1} = \frac{h}{90}[28\nabla^4 y_n' + 28\nabla^5 y_n']$$

$$y_{n+1} - y_{n+1,2} = \frac{h}{90}[-\nabla^4 y_n' - 2\nabla^5 y_n'].$$

Can it happen that use of a Milne check is absurd because $|y_{n+1} - y_{n+1,2}| \geq |E|$? *Ans.:* Of course, as when $\nabla^4 y_n' + \nabla^5 y_n' = 0$, but this rarely happens. *Remark:* When the Milne method is being applied to our standard example $y' = x + y$ with h small enough to make the method come close to working, $\nabla^5 y_n'$ is always small in comparison to $\nabla^4 y_n'$ and this cannot happen.

Remark 8.655

When we apply the Milne method, we do not calculate the differences $\nabla^4 y_n'$ and $\nabla^5 y_n'$. Hence we are never aware of occurrences of the circumstances considered in the two preceding problems.

Problem 8.656

Suppose that we start calculations with a small value of h to ensure 5D accuracy in our computed results. Suppose further that, after the process is well under way, we discover that everything is going nicely but slowly because h is small. We want to speed our progress by doubling the h we have been using. What shall we do? *Hint:* Derive a new table from Table 8.13 by eliminating the items y_n for which n is odd. Consult this table for a clue to the answer.

Problem 8.657

Suppose that we start calculations with a value of h small enough to ensure 5D accuracy. Suppose further that everything goes well for a while but that, because of the nature of $f(x, y)$, the errors creep up to unallowed magnitudes. How would we know that things are getting out of hand? *Ans.:* When differences are being computed as a part of the method being used or are specially computed for the purpose, we can look at them and see when they cease to be negligible. When the Milne method or some variant of it is being used, the danger signals are flashed by the failure of two computed values of y_{n+1} to possess satisfactory agreement.

Problem 8.658

What do we do when the difficulty of the previous problem runs into us? *Ans.:* We continue, by the same or another method but with a value of h half as large as before.

Problem 8.659

How can we decrease h? *Ans.:* Many ways. We can start from (x_n, y_n) with a starting method. We can use information we have and an interpolation formula, like (8.62), for example, to help us fill in as many of the blank spaces as we need in a table which (in terms of the new h) looks like Table 8.6591.

TABLE 8.6591

y_n	y_n'
2.04424	2.64424
*	*
2.65108	3.45108
*	*
3.43656	4.43656

We then have the material to continue our continuing method with the smaller h. Unless the application of starting methods involves too much work, we keep our routines free from additional complications even when the complications involve bright and even useful ideas. In each given situation, we simply do the best we can. *Remark:* The ideal is a high-speed computer and a prepared set of instructions which, when fed into the computer, force the computer to decide when shifting of h is desirable and to make the shifts automatically whenever they are desirable. Such enlightened instruments exist, the Runge-Kutta method being employed to provide new starting values whenever h is shifted.

Problems 8.66

These are more problems for persons having a desk calculator and time at their disposal. Read Problem 8.59. Solve problems of the same nature, with use of the method of Problem 8.57 replaced by use of the Milne method.

8.67. Milne Starting Method; Successive Approximations. To avoid misunderstandings, we remark that the *Milne method* which we have described and the *Milne starting method* which we are about to describe are different things and that confusion arises when one thing is called by the name of another. They were designed for use together, but the former is very often used when the latter is not. Of course it is not illegal to use the latter and not the former. The Milne starting method for the problem

$$y' = f(x, y), \qquad y(x_0) = y_0 \tag{8.671}$$

employs a convenient little ritual to determine approximations to the six numbers $y_k, y'_k (k = -1, 1, 2)$ so that we will have the eight numbers $y_k, y'_k (k = -1, 0, 1, 2)$ and therefore will have the material needed to start a continuing method. The ritual involves successive approximation with the aid of the approximate formulas

$$\begin{aligned} y_{-1} &= y_1 - \frac{h}{3}[y'_{-1} + 4y'_0 + y'_1] \\ y_0 &= y_0 \\ y_1 &= y_0 + \frac{h}{24}[-y'_{-1} + 13y'_0 + 13y'_1 - y'_2] \\ y_2 &= y_0 + \frac{h}{3}[y'_0 + 4y'_1 + y'_2]. \end{aligned} \tag{8.68}$$

These formulas are obtained from (8.543) and (8.555) by neglecting all epsilons and all differences of orders 4 and more.

We now see how the ritual goes and how the results should be tabulated. First, calculate y'_0 from the formula $y'_0 = f(x_0, y_0)$. Then use y_0, y_0, y_0, y_0 and y'_0, y'_0, y'_0, y'_0 as the first approximations to y_{-1}, y_0, y_1, y_2 and $y'_{-1}, y'_0, y'_1, y'_2$. These first approximations are denoted by the a's and b's with superscript 1 in Table 8.681. Put these a's and b's into (8.68) to obtain the second approximations $a_{-1}^{(2)}, \ldots, a_2^{(2)}$ to $y_{-1}, \ldots, y_2$, and then put these approximations into the formula

$$y'_k - f(x_k, y_k) \qquad k = -1, 0, 1, 2 \tag{8.682}$$

TABLE 8.681

y_{-1}	y_0	y_1	y_2	y'_{-1}	y'_0	y'_1	y'_2
$a_{-1}^{(1)}$	$a_0^{(1)}$	$a_1^{(1)}$	$a_2^{(1)}$	$b_{-1}^{(1)}$	$b_0^{(1)}$	$b_1^{(1)}$	$b_2^{(1)}$
$a_{-1}^{(2)}$	$a_0^{(2)}$	$a_1^{(2)}$	$a_2^{(2)}$	$b_{-1}^{(2)}$	$b_0^{(2)}$	$b_1^{(2)}$	$b_2^{(2)}$
$a_{-1}^{(3)}$	$a_0^{(3)}$	$a_1^{(3)}$	$a_2^{(3)}$	$b_{-1}^{(3)}$	$b_0^{(3)}$	$b_1^{(3)}$	$b_2^{(3)}$
. . .	. . .	. . .	. . .	. . .	. . .	. . .	. . .

to obtain the second approximations $b_{-1}^{(2)}, \ldots, b_2^{(2)}$ to $y'_{-1}, \ldots, y'_2$. Continue putting approximations alternately into (8.68) and (8.682) to record new rows until two consecutive rows agree to the desired number of D and then stop.

The Milne starting method has a feature which is appealing when calculations are made with pencil and paper. Large errors are easily noticed, and small ones do not matter much because they only delay (or perhaps sometimes speed) the approach to the final result and do not change the final result. It is easy to acquire the knack of picking the right places in the tables from which to select numbers for substitution in (8.68), and, for pencil work, division by 24 is easily accomplished by dividing by 8 and 3. Watching the rapid convergence can be interesting.

Problem 8.69

Apply the Milne starting method to the problem $y' = x + y$, $y(0) = 1$ with $h = 0.1$ to approximate $y(-0.1)$, $y(0)$, $y(0.1)$, and $y(0.2)$. Keep 6D. *Solution:* Except perhaps for minor rounding errors, rows 6 and 7 agree to 6D and row 7 is correct to 6D. See Table 8.13 and the modest table

$$y(-0.1) = 0.90967\ 48361.$$

Problem 8.691

The lopsidedness of (8.68) slowed the convergence of the approximations to y_{-1}. Find out whether this situation is improved by modifying the previous problem to find $y(-0.2)$, $y(-0.1)$, $y(0)$, $y(0.1)$, and $y(0.2)$ with the aid of the symmetric formulas

$$\begin{aligned} y_{-2} &= y_0 - \frac{h}{3}[y'_{-2} + 4y'_{-1} + y'_0] \\ y_{-1} &= y_0 - \frac{h}{24}[-y'_{-2} + 13y'_{-1} + 13y'_0 - y'_1] \\ y_0 &= y_0 \\ y_1 &= y_0 + \frac{h}{24}[-y'_{-1} + 13y'_0 + 13y'_1 - y'_2] \\ y_2 &= y_0 + \frac{h}{3}[y'_0 + 4y'_1 + y'_2]. \end{aligned} \tag{8.692}$$

Solution: The rate of convergence is improved. In this case, rows 5 and 6 agree to 6D and the results are correct to 6D. To 10D,

$$y(-0.2) = 0.83746\ 15062.$$

Problem 8.693

We embark on a pencil-and-paper project involving the problem $y' = x - y$, $y(0) = 1$ (note the negative sign) which appears with a table in Problem 8.19. Keeping 6D, use the symmetric formulas (8.692) with $h = 0.1$ to find $y(-0.2)$, $y(-0.1)$, $y(0)$, $y(0.1)$, and $y(0.2)$. This gives more information than is needed to start the Milne method, and gives us a chance to find out whether we can make some calculations jibe. Write your first four pairs of values of y_n and y'_n in vertical columns as usual, and find out whether application of the Milne method to these will yield the fifth pair. If so, use the Milne method to find two more pairs and then apply the Weddle formula (8.559) to check everything. *Remark:* This is a very significant problem because if chaos appears you live in a chaotic world and if orderliness appears you live in an orderly world. *Solution:* You should find an orderly world. Except for close decisions on rounding errors, rows 5 and 6 of your tables for y_k and y'_k should agree to 6D and rows 6 should be, respectively,

1.24281	1.11034	1.00000	0.90968	0.83746
−1.44281	−1.21034	−1.00000	−0.80968	−0.63746

Use of the first Milne formula (8.61) should give you the estimate $y_{n+1} = 0.83747$ and use of (8.63) then gives $y_{n+1} = 0.83746$. The Milne method, without or with use of the Milne check formula, then instructs us to use the estimate $y_{n+1} = 0.83746$. This visibly agrees with the original fifth y. The remaining calculations should be equally satisfying.

Problem 8.694

These are more problems for persons having a desk calculator and time at their disposal. Read Problem 8.59 again. Solve problems of the same nature, using the Milne starting method (8.68) or, if you want a little variety, (8.692), and then the Milne method.

8.7. Summary and an Example.

As we near the end of our discussion of the problem

$$y' = f(x, y), \qquad y(x_0) = y_0, \tag{8.71}$$

we should recognize that different methods of attack are in use because different ones are useful in different cases. If advice is to be given, the following is perhaps as good as any and better than most. Start with the Runge-Kutta method and continue with the Milne method unless the nature of $f(x, y)$ or the natures of the equipment used and the results required suggest that another attack would be equally good or better. It is often true that there is a fallacy in the argument that more complicated methods are preferable because, for a given h, they give more accurate results. The fact is that, very often, reducing h to $h/2$ and using the Runge-Kutta-Milne scheme gives still more accurate results with much less labor. This fact is analogous to and closely related to the fact that formulas more complicated than the Simpson formula are rarely used to obtain numerical approximations to integrals.

We conclude our discussion of (8.71) with a positive recommendation of a procedure to be followed in those cases where it takes all day to calculate $f(x, y)$ when x and y are given. A method which requires 30 such calculations is then much better than a method which requires 50, and the effort involved in making a few additions and subtractions is quite trivial. In particular, the method should give maximum information about accuracy of our results so that we will not waste much time on a method and a value of h which will give results correct to 3D or 10D when we want results correct to 5D. It will serve our purpose to attack the standard problem.

$$y'(x) = x + y, \qquad y(0) = 1 \tag{8.72}$$

with the pretense that it takes H hours to calculate $y'(x)$ from (8.72) whenever x and y are given. We work $11H$ hours (why not $12H$?) to employ the Runge-Kutta method with $h = 0.05$ to calculate $y(0.05)$ and $y(0.1)$, and with $h = 0.1$ to calculate $y(0.1)$. Our work (see Problem 8.336) convinces us that $y(0.1) = 1.11034$ correct to 6D. We can remember that we calculate $y'(0)$ and take H hours to calculate $y'(0.1)$. Then, after a simple subtraction, we have the numerical items in the first two rows of Table 8.73.

TABLE 8.73

x_n	y_n	y'_n	$\nabla y'_n$	$\nabla^2 y'_n$	$\nabla^3 y'_n$	$\nabla^4 y'_n$	$\nabla^5 y'_n$
0	1.00000	1.00000	—	—	—	—	—
0.1	1.11034	1.21034	0.21034	—	—	—	—
0.2	(1.24207)	(1.44207)	(0.23173)	(0.02139)	—	—	—
	(1.24278)	(1.44278)	(0.23244)	(0.02210)	—	—	—
	1.24280	1.44280	0.23246	0.02212	—	—	—
0.3	(1.39964)	(1.69964)	(0.25684)	(0.02438)	—	—	—
	1.39971	1.69971	0.25691	0.02445	0.00233	—	—
0.4	(1.58363)	(1.98363)	(0.28392)	(0.02701)	—	—	—
	1.58364	1.98364	0.28393	0.02702	0.00257	0.00024	—
0.5	1.79743	2.29743	0.31379	0.02986	0.00284	0.00027	0.00003

Further applications of the Runge-Kutta method would take too much time so we employ the approximation

$$y_{n+1} = y_{n-1} + h[2y'_n + \tfrac{1}{3}(\nabla^2 y'_n + \nabla^3 y'_n + \nabla^4 y'_n + \nabla^5 y'_n) - \tfrac{1}{90}\nabla^4 y'_n - \tfrac{1}{45}\nabla^5 y'_n + \cdots] \tag{8.74}$$

and the identity

$$\nabla^2 y'_n + \nabla^3 y'_n + \nabla^4 y'_n + \nabla^5 y'_n = \nabla^2 y'_{n+1} - \nabla^6 y'_n. \tag{8.75}$$

The approximation comes from (8.54) by omitting the epsilons which never seem to injure us, and (8.75) is (8.542). Our use of (8.74) is based upon the principle that we get information about y_{n+1} by feeding in all of the information we have and, subject to whatever compensations may be necessary, neglecting those terms whose values we do not know. At the start, items that are placed in the table may be subject to nontrivial improvement and we put parentheses around these items as soon as it is discovered that they are to be improved. As usual, a unit error in the last digit retained is not taken very seriously; if it must be taken seriously, we keep more D in our calculations.

When we start with $n = 1$, $x_n = 0.1$, $y_{n-1} = 1$, $y'_n = 1.21034$, $h = 0.1$ and wish to compute y_{n+1} from (8.74), we are quite short of information. Nevertheless, in accordance with our principle, we do the best we can and compute the approximation

$$y_{n+1} = y_{n-1} + h[2y'_n] = 1.24207. \tag{8.76}$$

We insert this in Table 8.73, compute y'_{n+1} (total now $13H$ hours), and compute the differences in this row to $\nabla^2 y'_{n+1} = 0.02139$. From (8.75) we see that this is, except for a term which we neglect, the quantity in parentheses in (8.74). Hence, with more information than before, we put what we know into (8.74) to obtain the improved estimate $y_{n+1} = 1.24278$. Inserting this in the table and calculating y'_{n+1} (total $14H$ hours) we obtain a new and improved set of differences ending with $\nabla^2 y_{n+1} = 0.02210$. Another improvement (total $15H$ hours) gives the row ending with $\nabla^2 y'_{n+1} = 0.02212$. It clearly makes little sense to compute y_{n+1} again to take account of the increase of 0.00002 in $\nabla^2 y'_{n+1}$ because rounding errors in y'_{n-2}, y'_{n-1}, and y'_n can produce errors about as large as 0.00002 in $\nabla^2 y'_{n+1}$ and besides, because of the factors $\frac{1}{3}$ and h, a change of 0.00002 in the quantity in parentheses in (8.74) produces a negligible change in the computed value of y_{n+1}. Thus, if the things we neglected in our calculations really are negligible, the items in the last row for which $x_n = 0.2$ should not contain errors greater than 2 in the last decimal place and the errors in y_n and y'_n should be less than 1 in the last decimal place. The first two rows for which $x_n = 0.2$ have served their purpose and may be obliterated or ignored.

Coming to the case $n = 2$, $x_n = 0.2$, $y_{n-1} = 1.11034$,

$$y'_n = 1.44280, \ldots,$$

we find our situation greatly improved because we now know the value of $\nabla^2 y'_n$. Putting all known terms in (8.74) gives the estimate

$$y_{n+1} = 1.39964$$

and we fill in (total $16H$ hours) the row to $\nabla^2 y'_{n+1} = 0.02438$. Putting this new information in (8.74), with the aid of (8.75) as before, gives the new estimate $y_{n+1} = 1.39971$, and (total $17H$ hours) we fill in the next row to $\nabla^3 y_{n+1} = 0.00233$. We see that the increase in $\nabla^2 y_{n+1}$ is only 0.00007, and to correct for this would increase y_{n+1} so little that we do not bother with it.

Coming now to the case $n = 3$, $x_n = 0.3$, $y_{n-1} = 1.44280$,

$$y_n' = 1.69971, \ldots,$$

we find our situation further improved by the fact that we know both $\nabla^2 y_n'$ and $\nabla^3 y_n'$. Putting our information in (8.74) gives $y_{n+1} = 1.58363$, and we fill in (total $18H$ hours) the row to $\nabla^2 y_{n+1}'$. Using this with (8.74) and (8.75) as before gives $y_{n+1} = 1.58364$ and we fill in (total 19 H hours) the new row to $\nabla^4 y_n' = 0.00024$. No corrections are needed here.

Coming now to the case $x_n = 0.4$, $y_{n-1}' = 1.39971$, $y_n' = 1.98364, \ldots,$ we see that our situation has improved to the point where a single substitution in (8.75) gives $y_{n+1} = 1.79743$ and (after $20H$ hours) we obtain the row, ending with $\nabla^5 y_{n+1}' = 0.00003$, which needs no corrections. It is now clear that our starting troubles are over, and that we can continue production of new rows with just one calculation of y_n' (H hours) per row. After $22H$ hours, we have seven rows and we pause. The difference table indicates that the differences which we have neglected really are negligible and that our results should be correct except for the omnipresent minor rounding errors. It is, however, an elementary principle of the theory of information that a hard-won mass of apparently correct information should be given a supplementary check when this can be done with practically no effort. Hence we apply the Weddle check (8.559). Strange things do sometimes happen; in case there is unsatisfactory agreement and no error can be found, it is always possible to bisect the tabular difference h and start all over again to see what is the root of the difficulty. Assuming that the Weddle check indicates that everything is in order, we continue to pause while we decide whether to proceed with the above method or switch to another method, presumably the Milne method.

Everybody should be able to participate in controversies involving the desirability of switching to the Milne method when a solution is well started as in Table 8.14 or Table 8.73. Suppose first that the epsilons which we have neglected really are negligible. Using the more accurate one of the Milne formulas is then equivalent to using the formula obtained by omitting some of the terms of (8.74). There are two ways to find out whether neglected terms really are negligible and whether mistakes are being made in calculations. One way is to continue Table 8.73 by use of (8.74) so one can see the neglected differences and decide whether they are negligible, and to spot an error as soon as it has been made by observing the resulting interruption in the trends of the columns of the difference table. Another way is to apply the Milne method. There is an obvious advantage in continuing Table 8.73 with the aid of (8.74); if we are in a situation where terms neglected by the Milne method are not negligible, we can see that they are not negligible and can take them into account in our calculations. If there is any advantage in the Milne method, it probably arises from the fact that it is easier to use (8.61) than to calculate a row of differences in Table 8.73. When an instrument no more enlightened than a modest desk calculator is being employed, there is much to be said in favor of the view that it is best to perform the subtractions required to find the differences and use (8.74) so that we have all of the information provided by the difference table and all the freedom of action provided by (8.74). However, when long runs of calculations are required, there can be no doubt that the Milne method should be used when it goes smoothly and more rapidly.

When methods are to be selected for programming for electronic computers, controversies can still rage. It is quite possible to program (8.74) and claim that this is best because it enables the computer to take account of differences of orders 4 and 5 and give accurate results for values of h for which the Milne method would not work. This argument would deserve serious consideration when the method is being applied in a case where $f(x, y)$ is such that even an electronic marvel would require a long time to calculate $f(x, y)$ with x and y given. However, except for these special applications, differences of higher order are by no means as useful to electronic brains as they are to human brains. When high-speed methods are being employed, there is much to be said in favor of avoiding the subtractions and storages which differences require and using the Milne method with h small enough to give the desired accuracy.

Problem 8.77

For this problem prepare a copy of the first six lines of Table 8.14 and, on another sheet of paper, a copy of the first three columns of the first six lines of the same table. These are starting values for the standard problem $y' = x + y$, $y(0) = 1$. Let A denote the process of using (8.74) to fill in another row of your first table, and let B denote the process of using the Milne method to fill in another row of your second table. Apply A and B alternately until you thoroughly understand them both and decide which you like best.

Problem 8.78

These are more problems for persons having a desk calculator and time at their disposal. Start with a problem $y' = f(x, y)$, $y(x_0) = y_0$ such that several minutes are required to calculate $f(x, y)$ when x and y are given in decimal form. Employ the method described in connection with Table 8.73 to obtain $y_1, y_1', \ldots, y_6, y_6'$, and then apply the Weddle check (8.559). Choices of appropriate problems depend upon the skill of the person making the calculations and upon the selection of tables available to him. The problem

$$y' = \frac{1}{x} + \frac{1}{y}, \qquad y(1) = 1$$

is too simple to genuinely meet the requirements but might be used. The problem

$$y' = \left(\frac{y^2}{1 + x^2y^2}\right)^{\frac{1}{2}}$$

would be just right for those who know and want to practice the standard best method for finding square roots on desk calculators. Other problems can be selected from the parts of Problem 8.191.

8.8. Systems of First-order Equations. To introduce our problem, we think a little about an island containing large populations of foxes, rabbits, and clover. The foxes eat rabbits, and the rabbits eat clover. Let x be time measured in years, and let $y_1(x)$ and $y_2(x)$ be the fox and rabbit populations which are so large that we are not injured by supposing that $y_1(x)$ and $y_2(x)$ change continuously with time and have nice derivatives. We suppose there is always so much clover that we do not have to worry about rabbit food. It makes sense to suppose that the fox population $y_1(x)$ changes at a rate $y_1'(x)$ which depends upon and is a function of $y_1(x)$ [which determines the number of potential parents], of $y_2(x)$ [which determines the food supply] and of x [which determines the calendar dates]. Similarly it makes sense to suppose that the rabbit population $y_2(x)$ changes at a rate $y_2'(x)$ which is a function of $y_2(x)$ [potential parents] of $y_1(x)$ [potential rabbit eaters] and of x. Thus there should be functions $f_1(x, y_1, y_2)$ and $f_2(x, y_1, y_2)$ such that

$$(8.81) \qquad y_1' = f_1(x, y_1, y_2), \qquad y_2' = f_2(x, y_1, y_2).$$

If we know these functions, and know that b_1 and b_2 are the fox and rabbit populations at some time $x = x_0$, so that

$$(8.811) \qquad y_1(x_0) = b_1, \qquad y_2(x_0) = b_2,$$

we have the problem of determining or approximating the fox and rabbit populations $y_1(x)$ and $y_2(x)$ at later times. It is genuinely interesting to determine the manner in which the fox population increases when there are relatively many rabbits and then how it whittles down its own food supply so that the fox population decreases, etc., etc. Solutions of appropriate differential equations reveal cycles that are familiar to biologists and others in situations where predators, parasites, germs, and such things appear.

It could be expected that it would be exceedingly difficult to describe methods for obtaining approximations to solutions of the problem consisting of the system (8.81) of differential equations satisfying the initial conditions (8.811). It turns out, however, that it is very easy when we approach the problem in the right way. We suppose that, where m may be 2 or any greater integer, we are given m equations

$$y'_k = f_k(x, y_1, y_2, \ldots, y_m) \qquad k = 1, 2, \ldots, m \tag{8.82}$$

in m unknown functions $y_1(x), y_2(x), \ldots, y_m(x)$, and m initial conditions

$$y_k(x_0) = b_k \qquad k = 1, 2, \ldots, m. \tag{8.821}$$

Our task is completed very quickly with the aid of vectors. We think of $U_1, U_2, \ldots, U_m$ as being m independent unit vectors and set

$$Y(x) = \sum_{k=1}^{m} U_k y_k(x) \tag{8.83}$$

so that $Y(x)$ is a vector which determines and is determined by its numerical components $y_k(x)$. Differentiating (8.83) with respect to x gives

$$Y'(x) = \sum_{k=1}^{m} U_k y'_k(x) \tag{8.831}$$

so that $Y'(x)$ is another vector having numerical components $y'_k(x)$. Since Y determines and is determined by its numerical components, we can use the notation

$$f_k(x, Y) = f_k(x, y_1, y_2, \ldots, y_m) \qquad k = 1, 2, \ldots, m \tag{8.832}$$

and define the vector $F(x, Y)$ by the first formula in

$$F(x, Y) = \sum_{k=1}^{m} U_k f_k(x, Y) = \sum_{k=1}^{m} U_k y'_k(x). \tag{8.833}$$

Use of (8.832) and (8.82) then gives the last part of (8.833). Comparing (8.831) and (8.833) gives the first formula in

$$Y' = F(x, Y), \qquad Y(x_0) = Y_0. \tag{8.84}$$

From (8.83) we obtain $Y(x_0) = \Sigma U_k y_k(x_0)$ and on letting Y_0 denote the vector

$$Y_0 = \sum_{k=1}^{m} U_k b_k \tag{8.841}$$

and using (8.821) we obtain the second formula in (8.84).

Two observations are now very important. In the first place, the single vector differential equation in (8.84) is completely equivalent to the whole system (8.82) of differential equations, and the single vector initial condition in (8.84) is completely equivalent to the whole system (8.821) of initial conditions. In the second place, (8.84) looks exactly like the problem $y' = f(x, y)$, $y(x_0) = y_0$ treated in earlier sections of this chapter and we can employ all of the methods which apply to the problem $y' = f(x, y)$, $y(x_0) = y_0$. The only difference is that when we apply our methods to (8.84) which involves vectors, our calculations all involve vectors and we must keep track of all m components instead of just one as in the simpler case. Our theory and our discussion are now completely finished. Only the applications remain.

Problem 8.85

Think about the application of the Runge-Kutta method to approximate Y_{n+1} when we have

$$Y' = F(x, Y), \qquad Y(x_n) = Y_n. \tag{8.851}$$

Write the following formulas by obtaining them from the above theory and not merely copying them. Displaying the numerical components which we need for computations, we have

$$Y(x) = \sum_{j=1}^{m} U_j y_j(x) \tag{8.852}$$

$$Y'(x) = \sum_{j=1}^{m} U_j f_j(x, Y) \tag{8.853}$$

$$Y_0 = \sum_{j=1}^{m} U_j b_j. \tag{8.854}$$

The Runge-Kutta formulas (8.31) and (8.32) then become (where K_1, K_2, K_3, K_4, and K are vectors)

$$\begin{aligned} K_1 &= h \sum_{j=1}^{m} U_j f_j(x_n, Y_n) \\ K_2 &= h \sum_{j=1}^{m} U_j f_j \left(x_n + \frac{h}{2}, Y_n + \frac{K_1}{2}\right) \\ K_3 &= h \sum_{j=1}^{m} U_j f_j \left(x_n + \frac{h}{2}, Y_n + \frac{K_2}{2}\right) \\ K_4 &= h \sum_{j=1}^{m} U_j f_j(x_n + h, Y_n + K_3) \\ K &= \tfrac{1}{6}[K_1 + 2K_2 + 2K_3 + K_4] \end{aligned} \tag{8.855}$$

and

$$Y_{n+1} = Y_n + K. \tag{8.856}$$

Remark: Table 8.857 shows how we can usefully record the m known components of a given vector Y_n and the m components of each of the vectors K_1, K_2, K_3, K_4, and K that are used in the process of calculating the m components of Y_{n+1}. The numerical values of the m components of Y_n are filled in first. These items, together with the numerical values of x_n and h, enable us to use the first formula in (8.855) to calculate and fill in the m components of K_1. This gives us the information needed to calculate and fill in the m components of K_2, and so on. In order to calculate the six vectors K_1, K_2, K_3, K_4, K, and Y_{n+1} we must calculate the m components of each, and this requires $6m$ calculations of which $4m$ involve determinations of numerical values of numbers of the form $f_j(x, Y)$ or $f_j(x, y_1, y_2, \ldots, y_n)$. When m is large, many

TABLE 8.857

	U_1	U_2	. . .	U_m
Y_n	*	*		*
K_1	*	*		*
K_2	*	*		*
K_3	*	*		*
K_4	*	*		*
K	*	*		*
Y_{n+1}	*	*		*

calculations are involved, but we can be cheerful. In the first place, $6m$ and $4m$ are not nearly as big as $6m^m$ and $4m^m$, and in the second place, we expect high-speed electronic computers to do the chores. In order to see how the formulas are used, and to see that they can be applied in frightfully complex situations, it should be sufficient to observe the following. It is a straightforward process to approximate the first numerical component of K_2 when $m = 4$, $x_n = 0.45$, $h = 0.05$,

$$f_1(x, Y) = \frac{x + y_1 + y_2y_3 + \sin y_4}{1 + x^2 + y_1^2 + y_2^2 + y_3^2 + y_4^2},$$

and we have learned that

$$Y_n = U_1(1.234) + U_2(2.345) + U_3(3.456) + U_4(4.567)$$

and

$$K_1 = U_1(0.123) + U_2(0.234) + U_3(0.345) + U_4(0.456).$$

With the aid of high-speed electronic computers, it is possible to handle systems of equations that one would not dream of attacking with more primitive weapons. These computers have been programmed to handle systems involving up to 30 or more unknown functions. Of course the unit vectors that have been very helpful to us do not go into computers; the different numerical components are kept in their places by storing them in different storage locations.

Problem 8.86

Think about application of the Milne method to approximate Y_{n+1} when

(8.861) $$Y' = F(x, Y)$$

and Y_{n-3}, Y_{n-2}, Y_{n-1}, and Y_n have been approximated. Write the following formulas by obtaining them from the above theory and not merely copying them. The Milne method is the following. First, calculate Y_{n+1} from the formula

$$(8.862) \qquad Y_{n+1} = Y_{n-3} + \frac{4h}{3}(2Y'_n - Y'_{n-1} + 2Y'_{n-2}).$$

Then calculate Y'_{n+1} from the formula

$$(8.863) \qquad Y'_{n+1} = F(x_{n+1}, Y_{n+1}).$$

Then calculate Y_{n+1} from the formula

$$(8.864) \qquad Y_{n+1} = Y_{n-1} + \frac{h}{3}(Y'_{n+1} + 4Y'_n + Y'_{n-1}).$$

If the components of the two estimates of Y_{n+1} agree to the desired number of D, assume that the components of the vectors Y_{n+1} and Y'_{n+1} are all correct and proceed to the next step. Otherwise, decrease h. When we write the vector equations in forms which display their components so that we can make calculations, we could introduce a double subscript notation whereby $y_j(x_k)$ is denoted by y_{jk}. However we shun this notation which might sometimes be "un-understood" or even misunderstood and write simply

$$(8.865) \qquad Y_k = Y(x_k) = \sum_{j=1}^{n} U_j y_j(x_k)$$

and

$$(8.866) \qquad Y'_k = Y'(x_k) = \sum_{j=1}^{n} U_j f_j(x_k, Y_k).$$

Equating components of the vectors in the members of (8.862), (8.863), and (8.864) then gives, for each $j = 1, 2, \ldots, m$,

$$(8.867) \qquad y_j(x_{n+1}) = y_j(x_{n-3}) + \frac{4h}{3}[2y'_j(x_n) - y'_j(x_{n-1}) + 2y'_j(x_{n-2})]$$

$$(8.868) \qquad y'_j(x_{n+1}) = f_j(x_{n+1}, y_1(x_{n+1}), y_2(x_{n+1}), \ldots, y_m(x_{n+1}))$$

$$(8.869) \qquad y_j(x_{n+1}) = y_j(x_{n-1}) + \frac{h}{3}[y'_j(x_{n+1}) + 4y'_j(x_n) + y'_j(x_{n-1})].$$

Remark: The remarks at end of the previous problem apply here. There exist basic computer programs, into which an operator can insert as many as 30 or more functions f with their initial values, which instruct electronic computers to start solutions with the Runge-Kutta method and continue with the Milne method.

Problem 8.87

When we presented the theory of systems of differential equations, the system of equations came first and the vectors were manufactured to give a single vector equation equivalent to the system. This problem is a special one which illustrates the familiar fact that the system of equations and the vector equation very often come in the reverse order. Let

$$Q = e^{it} = \cos t + i \sin t \tag{8.871}$$

so Q is a point which starts when $t = 0$ at the point $(1, 0)$ and travels around the unit circle with unit speed. Let a pursuing point $z = x + iy$ start at the origin and travel so that its speed is always $\frac{1}{2}$ and it is always headed toward Q. Show that z is a function of t for which

$$\frac{dz}{dt} = \frac{1}{2}\frac{e^{it} - z}{|e^{it} - z|}, \qquad z(0) = 0, \tag{8.872}$$

so the motion of z is governed by one equation. Use this to show that

$$\frac{dx}{dt} + i\frac{dy}{dt} = \frac{1}{2}\frac{\cos t - x}{D} + i\frac{1}{2}\frac{\sin t - x}{D} \tag{8.873}$$

where

$$D = [(\cos t - x)^2 + (\sin t - y)^2]^{\frac{1}{2}}. \tag{8.874}$$

Observe that if we set $y_1 = x(t)$, $y_2 = y(t)$, $U_1 = 1$ and $U_2 = i$, then (8.873) takes the form

$$\sum_{k=1}^{2} U_k \frac{dy_k}{dt} = \sum_{k=1}^{2} U_k f_k(t, y_1, y_2). \tag{8.875}$$

This looks like all other vector differential equations except that the independent variable is now t instead of x. Observe that in this case we obtained the vector equation before (not after) obtaining the system

$$\frac{dx}{dt} = \frac{1}{2}\frac{\cos t - x}{D}, \qquad \frac{dy}{dt} = \frac{1}{2}\frac{\sin t - y}{D} \tag{8.876}$$

$$x(0) = 0, \qquad y(0) = 0 \tag{8.877}$$

of differential equations and initial conditions involving the numerical components (or coordinates) about which we seek information. *Remark:* In problems of this nature, numerical methods are usually required to obtain tables and graphs of $x(t)$ and $y(t)$. Sometimes it is easier to find how x and y are related to each other than to t; this amounts to saying that it may be easier to determine the path of a railroad train than to determine the times at which it will occupy the various points on the path. The simplicities of the formula $Y'(t) = F(t, Y)$ or $z'(t) = F(t, z)$ show us how to attack the problem. The complexities in the formulas involving the numerical components (or coordinates) must be coped with when the numerical results are being obtained.

Problem 8.88

Let $y_1(x)$ and $y_2(x)$ be two functions of x for which

$$y_1'(x) = x + y_1(x) + y_2(x), \qquad y_1(0) = 1 \tag{8.881}$$

$$y_2'(x) = x + y_1(x) - y_2(x), \qquad y_2(0) = 0. \tag{8.882}$$

Keeping 5D and letting $h = 0.1$, use the Runge-Kutta method to obtain $y_1(x)$ and $y_2(x)$ when $x = 0.1$, 0.2, and 0.3. Then use the Milne method to obtain the results when $x = 0.4$, 0.5, and 0.6. Then apply the Weddle check (8.559) to your values of $y_1(x)$ and $y_2(x)$. Note the necessity of using $y_1'(x_k)$ or $y_2'(x_k)$ in place of y_k' in the Weddle formula. *Ans.:* See Table 8.883.

TABLE 8.883

x_n	$y_1(x_n)$	$y_1'(x_n)$	$y_2(x_n)$	$y_2'(x_n)$
0.0	1.0000	1.0000	0.0000	1.0000
0.1	1.1157	1.3210	0.1053	1.1104
0.2	1.2658	1.6886	0.2228	1.2430
0.3	1.4562	2.1101	0.3539	1.4023
0.4	1.6899	2.5940	0.5041	1.5858
0.5	1.9774	3.1496	0.6722	1.8052
0.6	2.3226	3.7888	0.8662	2.0564

8.9. Equations and Systems of Equations of Order 2 or More. As we shall see, equations of order 2 or more and systems of such equations can be quickly and easily reduced to systems of first-order equations to which methods of the previous section apply. Consider, for example, the nonlinear equation

$$a\frac{d^2y}{dx^2} + b\frac{dy}{dx} + c\sin y = E(x) \tag{8.91}$$

together with the initial conditions $y(x_0) = b_1$ and $y'(x_0) = b_2$. Provided $a \neq 0$, this equation is easily put in the form

$$y'' = f(x, y, y'). \tag{8.92}$$

The trick is to define two functions $y_1(x)$ and $y_2(x)$ by the formulas

$$y_1(x) = y(x), \qquad y_2(x) = y'(x). \tag{8.921}$$

The equation (8.92) then becomes equivalent to the two equations

$$y_1'(x) = y_2(x), \qquad y_2'(x) = f(x, y_1(x), y_2(x)) \tag{8.922}$$

and the initial condition becomes

$$y_1(x_0) = b_1, \qquad y_2(x_0) = b_2. \tag{8.923}$$

But the system (8.922) is only a special case of the system

$$\frac{dy_k}{dx} = f_k(x, y_1, y_2) \qquad k = 1, 2 \tag{8.924}$$

treated in the previous section.

For a second example, suppose we have two unknown functions $y(x)$ and $z(x)$ satisfying the equations

$$y''(x) = g_1(x, y, y', z, z', z'') \tag{8.93}$$

and

$$z'''(x) = g_2(x, y, y', z, z', z'') \tag{8.931}$$

and the initial conditions $y(x_0) = b_1$, $y'(x_0) = b_2$, $z(x_0) = b_3$, $z'(x_0) = b_4$, and $z''(z_0) = b_5$. Even when g_1 and g_2 are complicated functions of their arguments, this system of equations does not scare us. We simply throw the whole system into the form

$$y_k'(x) = f_k(x, y_1, y_2, y_3, y_4, y_5) \qquad k = 1, 2, \ldots, 5 \tag{8.932}$$

by setting $y_1 = y$, $y_2 = y'$, $y_3 = z$, $y_4 = z'$ and $y_5 = z''$.

8.94. The Three-body Problem. We conclude with some remarks about a famous problem that requires nontrivial use of numerical methods. With reference to a stationary rectangular coordinate system, three bodies B_1, B_2, B_3 of masses m_1, m_2, m_3 are, at time t_0, placed at distinct points

$$(x_k(t_0), y_k(t_0), z_k(t_0)) \qquad k = 1, 2, 3 \tag{8.941}$$

with velocity components

$$(x_k'(t_0), y_k'(t_0), z_k'(t_0)) \qquad k = 1, 2, 3. \tag{8.942}$$

All of the masses, coordinates, and velocity components are given in decimal form. With no forces acting upon these bodies except their mutual attractions which obey the Newton inverse square law, the bodies are allowed to go their merry ways. We are required to give numerical values of the coordinates and velocity components at later times.

We are entitled to suppose that the units of time, distance, mass, and force are so related that the standard vector formulas $F = ma$ and $F = mMr/|r|^3$ are valid when a is the acceleration of a body of mass m and $|r|$ is the magnitude of the vector r running from a body of mass m to another body of mass M. Note that $r/|r|$ is a unit vector in the direction of r. Let r_1, r_2, and r_3 be the vectors running from the origin to the three bodies as in Fig. 8.95. The acceleration of B_1 is then d^2r_1/dt^2, and the

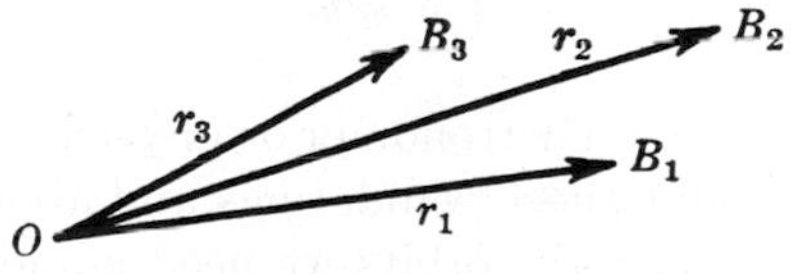

FIG. 8.95

vectors running from B_1 to B_2 and from B_1 to B_3 are $r_2 - r_1$ and $r_3 - r_1$. The motion of B_1 is then governed by the vector equation

$$m_1 \frac{d^2r_1}{dt^2} = \frac{m_1m_2}{|r_2 - r_1|^3}(r_2 - r_1) + \frac{m_1m_3}{|r_3 - r_1|^3}(r_3 - r_1), \tag{8.96}$$

and the motions of B_2 and B_3 are governed by two similar equations.

Equating the x components of (8.96) gives

$$(8.97)\quad \frac{d^2x_1}{dt^2} = \frac{m_2(x_2 - x_1)}{[(x_2 - x_1)]^2 + (y_2 - y_1)^2 + (z_2 - z_1)^2]^{3/2}} + \frac{m_3(x_3 - x_1)}{[(x_3 - x_1)^2 + (y_3 - y_1)^2 + (z_3 - z_1)^2]^{3/2}}.$$

This is one of a set of nine similar equations which, together with the initial conditions, determine the nine coordinates and nine components of velocities at later times. It is a routine matter to follow our procedure to go to work to tabulate the 18 functions. We are now in a realm where we do not expect to solve problems in a few minutes. If it takes all day to write the 18 equations and to get squared away to start calculations, so be it. If the problem is important, we do the required chores and use the best equipment available to make the calculations.

Suppose, for example, B_1, B_2, B_3 have masses 1, 2, 3 and start from rest at time $t = 0$, as shown in Fig. 8.98, at vertices of a cube whose sides have unit length. It is clear that the bodies would start wandering into the

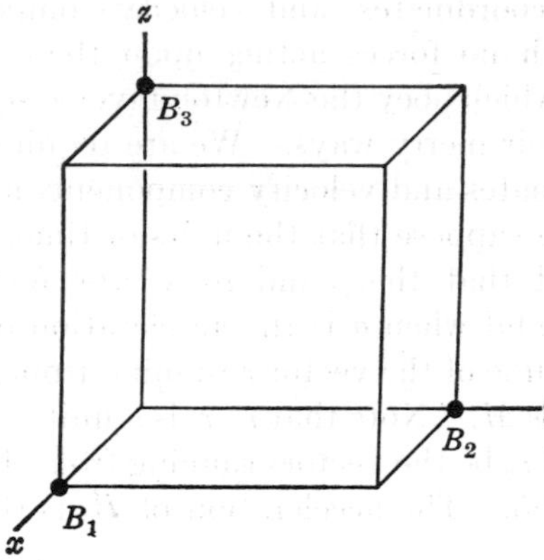

FIG. 8.98

interior of the cube. A good astronomer or physicist might know enough to tell us a little bit about these wanderings and about the possibility of collisions. But to compute the orbits we need numerical methods.

Numerical methods have many accomplished and many potential applications. Whether a prospected application is judged to be feasible depends partly upon the problem and partly upon the judge who must decide whether and how the problem can be solved. This chapter will have served its purpose if its readers become good judges.

CHAPTER 9

LAPLACE TRANSFORMS

9.0. Introduction. This chapter contains an account of Laplace (1749–1827) transforms and their applications. The parts preferred by applied mathematicians and the parts preferred by pure mathematicians are well mixed together so each must peer into the garden of the other. We begin with some history. It seems that Laplace transforms, like many other things bearing names of other persons, are inventions of Euler (1707–1783). In any case, Euler used the transforms to solve differential equations when Laplace was -7 years old, and he did it very neatly. For a long time after Euler, Laplace transforms played a minor role in works on differential equations. This is probably due to the fact that, in those days, there was relatively little demand for numerical results for problems of the relatively special, but now very important, types that can be successfully attacked with the aid of Laplace transforms. Another factor, which could have been recognized by those who set the styles, is that Laplace transforms do not provide a satisfactory basis for development of a good clean general theory of linear differential equations with constant coefficients. The transforms can be applied only in cases where all of the functions involved are defined over the whole semi-infinite interval $x \geqq 0$ and, for example, cannot be applied when one of these functions grows too steadily and rapidly as $x \to \infty$. These limitations, which are ordinarily more irksome than harmful in applied mathematics, are not required when the Heaviside method is employed.

In more recent times, Laplace transforms have not been rejected because of the things they cannot do; they have become very popular because of the things that they *can* do. They have vast numbers of applications and produce results that it would be difficult or practically impossible to obtain by other methods.

9.1. Fundamental Formulas. A function $g(x)$, defined over the infinite interval $x > 0$, will be called *decent* if it is integrable (Riemann or Lebesgue) over each finite interval $0 \leqq x \leqq a$ and if there is a real constant b such that $e^{-bx}g(x) \to 0$ as $x \to \infty$. (Functions satisfying the latter condition are said to have *exponential order* over the positive real axis.) For example, all inputs and outputs of the form $x^k e^{mx}$ with $k > -1$ are decent, but $1/x$ behaves too badly near the origin and exp x^2 grows too rapidly to be decent. To each decent function $g(x)$ there corresponds a *Laplace transform* $G(s)$ defined by

$$G(s) = \int_0^\infty e^{-sx} g(x)dx \tag{9.11}$$

whenever s is a complex number (which may of course be real) having a real part sufficiently great. Moreover it can be proved that the integral

$$\int_0^\infty |e^{-sx} g(x)|dx \tag{9.111}$$

will exist and the manipulations which we wish to perform are valid when the real part of s is sufficiently great; see Theorem 9.717.

If m is a complex constant and $g_1(x) = e^{mx}$, then

$$\begin{aligned} G_1(s) &= \int_0^\infty e^{-sx} e^{mx}\, dx = \int_0^\infty e^{-(s-m)x}\, dx \\ &= \frac{-1}{s-m} e^{-(s-m)x}\Big]_0^\infty = \frac{1}{s-m} \end{aligned} \tag{9.12}$$

provided the real part of s exceeds that of m so that $e^{-(s-m)x} \to 0$ as $x \to \infty$. Observe that validity of (9.12) is a consequence of the formula

$$\begin{aligned} \int_0^\infty [u(x) + iv(x)]dx &= \lim_{a\to\infty} \int_0^a [u(x) + iv(x)]dx \\ &= \lim_{a\to\infty} [U(x) + iV(x)]_0^a = [U(x) + iV(x)]_0^\infty \end{aligned} \tag{9.121}$$

where U and V are real functions whose derivatives are u and v.

Usefulness of Laplace transforms in solving differential equations depends upon the following fact. If $g(x)$ is decent and has a decent derivative $g'(x)$ and we put

$$\phi(s) = \int_0^\infty e^{-sx} g'(x)dx, \tag{9.13}$$

then integration by parts with

$$\begin{aligned} u &= e^{-sx} & dv &= g'(x)dx \\ du &= -se^{-sx}\, dx & v &= g(x) \end{aligned}$$

gives

$$\phi(s) = -g(0) + s \int_0^\infty e^{-sx} g(x)dx \tag{9.131}$$

where the last integral is the Laplace transform of the original function $g(x)$. Repeated use of this result gives the fundamental collection of formulas of which the first five are

$$(9.14)\qquad \begin{aligned} \int_0^\infty e^{-sx}y(x)dx &= Y(s) \\ \int_0^\infty e^{-sx}y'(x)dx &= sY(s) - y(0) \\ \int_0^\infty e^{-sx}y''(x)dx &= s^2Y(s) - sy(0) - y'(0) \\ \int_0^\infty e^{-sx}y'''(x)dx &= s^3Y(s) - s^2y(0) - sy'(0) - y''(0) \\ \int_0^\infty e^{-sx}y^{(4)}(x)dx &= s^4Y(s) - s^3y(0) - s^2y'(0) - sy''(0) - y'''(0), \end{aligned}$$

and more are easily written.

For application to integro-differential equations, in which $D^{-1}y$ appears with the meaning

$$(9.141)\qquad D^{-1}y = \int_0^x y(t)dt$$

as in (6.825) with $x_0 = 0$, we need the formulas

$$(9.15)\qquad \int_0^\infty e^{-sx}D^{-k}y(x)dx = \frac{1}{s^k}\int_0^\infty e^{-sx}y(x)dx \qquad k = 1, 2, 3, \ldots,$$

which are easily obtained by integration by parts.

Another collection of important formulas

$$(9.16)\qquad G^{(k)}(s) = (-1)^k \int_0^\infty e^{-sx}x^k g(x)dx \qquad k = 0, 1, 2, \ldots$$

is obtained by differentiating (9.11) with respect to s. These formulas and earlier ones provide the basis for applications of Laplace transforms to linear equations in which the coefficients are polynomials in the independent variable.

The equivalent formulas

$$(9.17)\qquad \frac{\alpha!}{(s-m)^{\alpha+1}} = \int_0^\infty e^{-sx}x^\alpha e^{mx}\,dx,$$

$$(9.171)\qquad \frac{1}{(s-m)^\beta} = \frac{1}{(\beta-1)!}\int_0^\infty e^{-sx}x^{\beta-1}e^{mx}\,dx$$

turn out to be exceptionally useful. The first holds when α, m, and s are complex numbers (which may of course be real) for which the real part of α exceeds -1 and the real part of s exceeds that of m. It gives the Laplace transform of $x^\alpha e^{mx}$ and, because m can be complex, enables us to handle functions such as $x^\alpha e^{ax}\sin bx$. The second, which is obtained from the first by setting $\beta = \alpha + 1$, holds when β, m, and s are complex numbers for which the real part of β is positive and the real part of s exceeds that of m. It shows that $(s-m)^{-\beta}$ is the Laplace transform of the function $x^{\beta-1}e^{mx}/(\beta - 1)!$. It is possible to prove (9.17) when α is a positive integer by differentiating the members of (9.12) α times with respect to s. A more sophisticated approach to (9.17) starts with the *Euler gamma integral formula*

$$\alpha! = \int_0^\infty e^{-y}y^\alpha\,dy \tag{9.172}$$

which holds whenever α is a complex number having real part greater than -1. When $s > 0$, putting $y = sx$ in (9.172) gives

$$\frac{\alpha!}{s^{\alpha+1}} = \int_0^\infty e^{-sx}x^\alpha\,dx. \tag{9.173}$$

Replacing s by $s - m$ then gives (9.17). Principles of the theory of analytic functions of a complex variable then imply that (9.17) holds whenever α, m, and s are complex numbers for which the real part of α exceeds -1 and the real part of s exceeds that of m.

When we apply Laplace transforms to the equation (9.181) below, we will want to use Laplace transforms of all of the functions y, y', y'', . . . , $y^{(n)}$, and f. When we are interested in a particular equation involving a decent function f which possesses a Laplace transform, we are not injured by the requirement that f possess a transform; but if the particular y which we are seeking should be such that one or more of y, y', y'', . . . , $y^{(n)}$ fails to have a transform, it would be awkward to assume that they have transforms. Hence we need the following theorem.

THEOREM 9.18. *If $f(x)$ is decent and a_0, a_1, . . . , a_n are constants for which $a_0 \neq 0$, then each solution $y(x)$ of the equation*

$$a_0\frac{d^ny}{dx^n} + a_1\frac{d^{n-1}y}{dx^{n-1}} + \cdots + a_ny = f(x) \tag{9.181}$$

is decent and, moreover, y', y'', . . . , $y^{(n)}$ are decent.

LEMMA 9.182. *If $g(x)$ and its first k derivatives are decent and if*

$$(D - m)u = g, \tag{9.183}$$

then u and its first $k + 1$ derivatives are decent.

Our first step is to show that the lemma implies the theorem. Supposing that f is decent and (9.181) holds we obtain, as in Chapter 6,

$$(D - m_1)(D - m_2)(D - m_3)\ .\ .\ .\ (D - m_n)y = f.$$

On setting

$$(D - m_2)(D - m_3)\ .\ .\ .\ (D - m_n)y = g_1,$$

we see from the lemma that g_1 and g_1' are decent. On setting

$$(D - m_3)(D - m_4)\ .\ .\ .\ (D - m_n)y = g_2$$

we see from the lemma that g_2, g_2', and g_2'' are decent. Continuing this process shows that $y, y', y'', \ldots, y^{(n)}$ are all decent and gives the conclusion of the theorem. To prove the lemma, we solve (9.183) by use of the integrating factor e^{-mx} to obtain

$$u(x) = e^{mx}\left[c + \int_0^x e^{-mt}g(t)dt\right].$$

Now e^{mx} and each of its derivatives is bounded over each finite interval and is decent. In order to show that u and its first $k + 1$ derivatives are decent, it is therefore sufficient to show that the function $v(x)$ defined as

$$v(x) = \int_0^x e^{-mt}g(t)dt$$

has the same property. With the aid of the formula

$$v'(x) = e^{-mx}g(x)$$

and the hypothesis that $g, g', \ldots, g^{(k)}$ are decent, it is easy to show that $v, v', \ldots, v^{(k+1)}$ are decent and the lemma is proved.

Problem 9.19

If

$$F(s) = \int_0^\infty e^{-sx}f(x)dx$$

and $a > 0$, show that

$$\frac{1}{a}F\left(\frac{s}{a}\right) = \int_0^\infty e^{-sx}f(ax)dx.$$

Problem 9. 191

If $f(x) = 0$ when $x < 0$ and

$$F(s) = \int_0^\infty e^{-sx}f(x)dx,$$

then whenever $x_0 > 0$, we can multiply by e^{-sx_0} to obtain

$$e^{-sx_0}F(s) = \int_0^\infty e^{-s(x+x_0)}f(x)dx$$

and

$$e^{-sx_0}F(s) = \int_{x_0}^\infty e^{-sx}f(x - x_0)dx.$$

Finally, since $f(x - x_0) = 0$ when $x < x_0$, we obtain

$$e^{-sx_0}F(s) = \int_0^\infty e^{-sx}f(x - x_0)dx.$$

This is the exponential-shift formula for Laplace transforms. Sketch graphs which show what this means. Show how to determine α and m in (9.17) to obtain a function of which $1/s^2$ is the Laplace transform; then find and graph a function of which e^{-s}/s^2 is the Laplace transform.

Problem 9.192

Prove that the Laplace transform of the faltung

(9.1921)
$$\int_0^x f(x-t)g(t)dt$$

of two decent functions f and g is the product of the Laplace transforms of f and g.
Solution: The change of order of integration being justified by the Fubini (1879–1943) theorem, we find that

(9.1922)
$$\begin{aligned}\int_0^\infty e^{-sx}dx \int_0^x f(x-t)g(t)dt &= \int_0^\infty dt \int_t^\infty e^{-sx}f(x-t)g(t)dx \\ &= \int_0^\infty dt \int_0^\infty e^{-s(x+t)}f(x)g(t)dx \\ &= \left[\int_0^\infty e^{-st}g(t)dt\right]\left[\int_0^\infty e^{-sx}f(x)dx\right]\end{aligned}$$

provided the real part of s is sufficiently great. The easiest way to prove the equalities is to start at the end and work backward.

Problem 9.193

Note that the result of Problem 9.192 can be stated in the following way. If F and G are Laplace transforms of f and g and if

(9.1931)
$$H = FG,$$

then H is the Laplace transform of the faltung h defined by

(9.1932)
$$h(x) = \int_0^x f(x-t)g(t)dt.$$

Use this to show that if

(9.1933)
$$H(s) = (s-m_1)^{-p}(s-m_2)^{-q}$$

where m_1, m_2, p, q are constants for which p and q have positive real parts, then

(9.1934)
$$h(x) = \frac{e^{m_1x}}{(p-1)!(q-1)!}\int_0^x (x-t)^{p-1}t^{q-1}e^{(m_2-m_1)t}dt.$$

In particular, use the first of the formulas

$$H_1(s) = \frac{1}{(s-1)\sqrt{s}}, \qquad h_1(x) = \frac{e^x}{\sqrt{\pi}}\int_0^x \frac{e^{-t}}{\sqrt{t}}\,dt$$

to obtain the second. Show finally that the substitution $u = \sqrt{2t}$ gives the formula

$$h_1(x) = 2e^x\left[\frac{1}{\sqrt{2\pi}}\int_0^{\sqrt{2x}} e^{-u^2/2}\,du\right]$$

involving the tabulated probability integral in brackets.

Problem 9.194

Note that (9.1933) and (9.1934) become particularly simple when $m_1 = m_2 = 0$. Use this idea, and the fact that $H(x)$ cannot be the Laplace transform of two different continuous functions, to show that

$$\int_0^x (x - t)^a t^b \, dt = \frac{a!b!}{(a + b + 1)!} x^{a+b+1} \tag{9.1941}$$

when a and b are constants whose real parts exceed -1 and $x > 0$. The integrals in (9.1941) and

$$\int_0^1 (1 - t)^a t^b \, dt = \frac{a!b!}{(a + b + 1)!} \tag{9.1942}$$

are *beta integrals*, and the formulas are useful. Show that putting $a = b = \frac{1}{2}$ gives $(\frac{1}{2})! = \sqrt{\pi}/2$ and putting $a = b = -\frac{1}{2}$ gives $(-\frac{1}{2})! = \sqrt{\pi}$.

Problem 9.195

Find out whether existence of $\int_0^\infty e^{-sx} g(x) dx$ when $s > 0$ implies that $g(x)$ is decent. *Solution:* See the remark following Problem 9.771.

9.2. Linear Equations with Constant Coefficients. In Chapter 6, we learned that it is very easy to find the steady-state solution of equation (9.21) which follows when the solutions of the homogeneous equation are all transients and the input is a sinusoid or a sum of sinusoids. To find the general solution of the equation is much more difficult because this requires knowledge of the zeros of the impedance. Experience shows that, except in the simplest cases, it is far from a pleasant task to start with the general solution and determine the constants to obtain the particular solution satisfying particular given initial conditions. It is easy to tell how to do it, but it takes a long time to do it. It is too much to expect that Laplace transforms can eliminate the problem of finding zeros of impedances, but they do in many cases provide the best method for solving the following problem.

Suppose that $y(x)$ is the particular solution of the equation

$$(a_0 D^n + a_1 D^{n-1} + \cdots + a_{n-1} D + a_n) y(x) = f(x) \tag{9.21}$$

which satisfies the conditions

$$y^{(r)}(0) = k_r \qquad 0 \leqq r \leqq n - 1. \tag{9.22}$$

Our problem is to determine $y(x)$ for those cases in which the functions $f, y, y', \ldots, y^{(n)}$ are decent functions or at least possess Laplace transforms.

We outline the steps involved in using Laplace transforms to solve this problem. Let $Y(s)$ and $F(s)$ be the Laplace transforms of $y(x)$ and

$f(x)$ so that

$$(9.23) \qquad Y(s) = \int_0^\infty e^{-sx} y(x)dx, \qquad F(s) = \int_0^\infty e^{-sx} f(x)dx.$$

With the aid of formulas (9.14), we find that taking the Laplace transforms of the members of (9.21) gives the equation

$$(9.24) \qquad Z(s)Y(s) - P(s) = F(s)$$

where $Z(s)$ is the impedance of the operator L_a in (9.21) and $P(s)$ is a polynomial in s, of degree $n - 1$ or less whose coefficients are determined by use of (9.14) and (9.22). This is the *subsidiary equation* of the problem, and we can now see the possibility of finding $Y(s)$ and $y(s)$.

In very many useful applications, $F(s)$ is the quotient of polynomials in s, say $F(s) = F_1(s)/F_2(s)$, and (9.24) becomes

$$(9.241) \qquad Y(s) = \frac{F_1(s) + F_2(s)P(s)}{F_2(s)Z(s)}.$$

Usually the zeros of $Z(s)$ are distinct, the zeros of $F_2(s)$ are distinct and different from the zeros of $Z(s)$, and the degree of the numerator in (9.241) is less than that of the denominator. The next step is the one and only step in the whole process which may be onerous. This involves finding the zeros of the polynomial $F_2(s)Z(s)$ and using partial fractions to put (9.241) in the form

$$(9.242) \qquad Y(s) = \frac{B_1}{s - m_1} + \frac{B_2}{s - m_2} + \cdots + \frac{B_N}{s - m_N}.$$

Use of (9.12) shows that $Y(s)$ and the function $y(x)$ defined by

$$(9.25) \qquad y(x) = B_1 e^{m_1 x} + B_2 e^{m_2 x} + \cdots + B_N e^{m_N x}$$

have the same Laplace transform. It can be proved that two different continuous functions cannot have the same Laplace transform; see Section 9.7. Therefore (9.25) gives the answer to our problem.

Appropriate modifications of the above steps produce results when $F_2(s)Z(s)$ has multiple zeros. Even when $F(s)$ is not a quotient of polynomials, it may still be possible to put (9.24) in the form

$$(9.26) \qquad Y(s) = \sum_{k=1}^{n} \frac{A_k}{s - m_k} + \sum_{k=1}^{n} \frac{B_k}{s - m_k} F(s)$$

and determine $y(x)$ by use of tables of Laplace transforms or otherwise. In later sections, we shall see some examples of partial fraction expansions that are not finite sums but are infinite series.

The last of the following problems illustrates the fact that not all problems involve numerical calculations and that sometimes considerable juggling is required to put transforms in their most informative forms.

Problem 9.27

Use Laplace transforms to find the functions satisfying the following simple equations and conditions

(*a*) $\dfrac{dy}{dx} = x;\ y(0) = 1$ *Ans.:* $y = 1 + \dfrac{x^2}{2}$

(*b*) $\dfrac{dy}{dx} + y = 1;\ y(0) = 1$ *Ans.:* $y = 1$

(*c*) $\dfrac{d^2y}{dx^2} + k^2y = 0,\ y(0) = a,\ y'(0) = b$

$$Ans.:\ y = \left(\frac{a}{2} + \frac{b}{2ik}\right)e^{ikx} + \left(\frac{a}{2} - \frac{b}{2ik}\right)e^{-ikx} = a\cos kx + \frac{b}{k}\sin kx$$

(*d*) $\dfrac{d^2y}{dx^2} - (p+q)\dfrac{dy}{dx} + pqy = e^{rx},\ y(0) = a,\ y'(0) = b$

where p, q, and r are different constants.

$$Ans.:\ y = Ae^{px} + Be^{qx} + Ce^{rx}$$

$$\text{where } A = \frac{(b-aq)(p-r)+1}{(p-q)(p-r)}$$

$$B = \frac{(b-ap)(q-r)+1}{(q-p)(q-r)}$$

$$C = \frac{1}{(r-p)(r-q)}.$$

Problem 9.28

Differentiation shows that if $n \geqq 2$ and $y(x) = \cos^{2n} x$ when $0 \leqq x \leqq \pi/2$ and $y(x) = 0$ when $x \geqq \pi/2$, then $y''(x)$ is continuous and

$$y''(x) + y(x) = f(x),\ y(0) = 1,\ y'(0) = 0 \tag{9.281}$$

where

$$f(x) = (4n^2 - 2n)\cos^{2n-2} x - (4n^2 - 1)\cos^{2n} x \tag{9.282}$$

when $0 \leqq x \leqq \pi/2$ and $f(x) = 0$ when $x \geqq \pi/2$. It is clear that if the function $y(x)$ satisfying (9.281) were unknown and we were to try to find it by use of Laplace transforms, we would need a formula for the transform $G_{2k}(s)$ of the function $g_{2k}(x)$ for which $g_{2k}(x) = \cos^{2k} x$ when $0 \leqq x \leqq \pi/2$ and $g_{2k}(x) = 0$ when $x \geqq \pi/2$. Show that

$$G_{2k}(s) = \frac{1}{2^{2k}} \sum_{j=0}^{2k} \binom{2k}{j} \frac{1 - (-1)^{k-j}e^{-s\pi/2}}{s - i(2k - 2j)}.$$

Show that equating the Laplace transforms of the members of (9.281) gives the subsidiary equation

$$(1 + s^2)Y(s) = s + (4n^2 - 2n)G_{2n-2}(s) - (4n^2 - 1)G_{2n}(s).$$

Remark: It is easy to divide by $(1 + s^2)$ to obtain an expression for $Y(s)$, but it is not so easy to show in a straightforward way that this expression can be reduced to $G_{2n}(s)$.

9.3. Integro-differential Equations. The familiar equation

$$L\frac{dI}{dt} + RI + \frac{Q}{C} = f(t) \tag{9.31}$$

governing L-R-C oscillators can be handled in various ways. For example, if $f(t)$ is differentiable, it is possible to differentiate with respect to t to obtain an equation involving I and its derivatives. One may always replace I by Q', and I' by Q'' to obtain an equation involving Q and its derivatives. It seems that in all or almost all practical problems, it is most convenient to use the relation

$$Q(t) = Q(0) + \int_0^t I(\alpha)d\alpha = Q_0 + D^{-1}I$$

to put (9.31) in the form

$$\left(LD + R + \frac{1}{CD}\right) I = f(t) - \frac{Q_0}{C}, \tag{9.32}$$

for which the impedance is

$$Z(s) = Ls + R + \frac{1}{Cs}. \tag{9.33}$$

The application of Laplace transforms to (9.32) differs only a little from the outline of Section 9.2.

9.4. Systems of Equations. The most spectacular successes of Laplace transforms appear in their applications to electrical networks. Applications of *Kirchhoff* (1824–1887) *laws* give systems of equations of which the system

$$\begin{cases} \Lambda_1 u + \Lambda_2 v = f_1 \\ \Lambda_3 u + \Lambda_4 v = f_2 \end{cases} \tag{9.41}$$

is a very modest sample. For our purpose, we may consider f_1 and f_2 to be given functions and consider Λ_1, Λ_2, Λ_3, and Λ_4 to be four given operators which may be like the integro-differential operator in (9.32) or may have the form L_a appearing inside or outside electrical engineering. The problem is to find functions u and v satisfying the system of equations and prescribed initial conditions.

Taking Laplace transforms gives two equations which are linear in the transforms U and V of u and v, the coefficients being the impedances of the operators. In many important cases, everything is reduced to the algebra involved in finding U and V and expressing them as sums of terms (often partial fractions) which are recognizable as Laplace transforms.

We selected a system containing two equations in two unknown functions only as a matter of convenience; the same remarks apply when there are n equations in n unknown functions. Theories of independence and matrices form the basis of the theory of such systems. That a general theory must deal with some awkward cases is shown by the following example. If, in the system (9.41), we have $\Lambda_1 = \Lambda_3$ and $\Lambda_2 = \Lambda_4$ but $f_1 \neq f_2$, then the system has no solutions. It is, by the way, absurd to claim that problems without solutions never occur in practical work. Nobody should be so practical that he never tries to do anything without knowing in advance that it can be done.

Problem 9.42

Find the functions u and v for which

$$\frac{du}{dx} + u + \frac{dv}{dx} + v = 1$$

$$2\frac{du}{dx} + u + \frac{dv}{dx} = 0$$

and $u(0) = 1$, $v(0) = 0$. *Ans.*: $u = e^{-x}$, $v = 1 - e^{-x}$.

Problem 9.43

The equation

$$y(x) = Af(x) + \int_0^x g(t)f(x - t)dt,$$

which appears in (3.9905) with different notation, arises in many problems. It usually happens that all of the functions, those that are sought as well as those that are known, are decent functions possessing Laplace transforms. Show that, in this case, the equation is equivalent to

$$Y(s) = AF(s) + F(s)G(s).$$

Remark: This clearly provides a possible way of finding F or G and hence f or g when the other functions are given functions of such natures that calculations can be managed.

9.5. Laplace-Stieltjes Transforms; Dirac Functions; Impulses. Remark 6.94 applies here. Ordinary Laplace transforms (9.11) are adequate for problems involving ordinary inputs, but Laplace-Stieltjes transforms substantially increase the class of inputs that can be cleanly handled.

The best and most versatile treatments of Laplace transforms employ the Laplace-Stieltjes transform of $g_1(x)$ defined by

$$G(x) = \int_0^\infty e^{-sx}\, dg_1(x) = \lim_{b\to\infty} \int_0^b e^{-sx}\, dg_1(x) \tag{9.51}$$

when $g_1(x)$ has bounded variation over each finite interval $0 \leqq x \leqq b$ and the limit exists. In case $g(x)$ possesses an ordinary Laplace transform, the Laplace-Stieltjes transform of the *cumulative function* $g_1(x)$ defined by

$$g_1(x) = \int_0^x g(t)dt \tag{9.52}$$

is the same as the Laplace transform of $g(x)$; that is,

$$\int_0^\infty e^{-sx}d\int_0^x g(t)dt = \int_0^\infty e^{-sx}g(x)dx. \tag{9.521}$$

Laplace-Stieltjes transforms provided an excellent method for introducing and using impulses. An ordinary physical input $f(x)$ of large magnitude but short duration may be such that, for some fixed small positive h, we have $f(x) = 0$ when $x < 0$ and when $x > h$ but nevertheless $\int_0^h f(x)dx = 1$. Corresponding to $f(x)$ there is the cumulative function $f_1(x)$ defined by

$$f_1(x) = \int_0^x f(t)dt. \tag{9.53}$$

In case $f(x) \geqq 0$, and in some other cases as well, smallness of h is a guarantee that (within the class of functions having bounded variation) $f_1(x)$ is a good approximation to the *unit-step function* or *Heaviside* (1850–1925) *unit function* $H(x)$ which is 0 when $x < 0$ and is 1 when $x > 0$. The Laplace transform $F(s)$ of $f(x)$ is then closely approximated by the Laplace-Stieltjes transform of $H(x)$, *provided s is not too large.* It is the Laplace-Stieltjes point of view that gives us a chance to see what we are doing and to estimate the effects of errors resulting from uses of approximations. One who knows a little bit about Stieltjes integrals can calculate the latter transform in a flash. It is the function F_H for which $F_H(s) = 1$ for all values of s.

There is nothing illogical about postulating existence of the *Dirac* (1902–) *delta function* $\delta(x)$ whose cumulative function is $H(x)$ and constructing definitions of integrals in such a way that $\delta(x)$ can be used. We do this and call $\delta(x)$ a *unit impulse.* The most satisfactory way to make the necessary modifications in the definitions of integrals is to introduce Stieltjes integrals, and those who dwell in intellectual communities where this matter cannot be ignored should learn about Stieltjes integrals defined by (6.942). The fundamental definition

$$\int_{-\infty}^\infty f(x)\delta(x - x_0)dx = \int_{-\infty}^\infty f(x)dH\,(x - x_0) \tag{9.531}$$

justifies all ordinary calculations involving $\delta(x)$; *the integrals exist and have the value $f(x_0)$ provided f is continuous at x_0.* It seems to be an incontrovertible fact that it is often easier to employ the formula

$$\int_{-\infty}^\infty f(x)\delta(x - x_0)dx = f(x_0) \tag{9.532}$$

than to construct and use cumulative functions and Laplace-Stieltjes integrals, and that many problems involving impulses can be solved without use of the more potent machinery. It must be emphasized that the integrals in (9.531) and (9.532) are not Riemann integrals. Persons who know about Riemann integrals, and fail to realize that there are other kinds of integrals, fall into three classes. A few keep quiet. The rest express weak reasons for strong opinions that Dirac functions are (or are not) reliable mathematical tools.

There may be some truth in the old Chinese proverb that says a picture is worth a thousand words. If so, we should have a pictorial representation of the Dirac function $a_0\delta(x - \lambda_0)$, whose cumulative function is the Heaviside function $a_0H(x - \lambda_0)$, when a_0 and λ_0 are real constants. In Fig. 9.533, the heavy vertical line bearing an arrowhead represents the

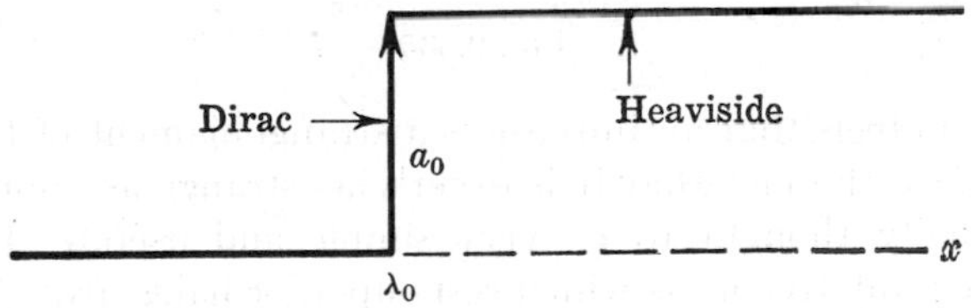

FIG. 9.533

Dirac function and the heavy horizontal lines constitute the graph of the Heaviside function, both functions being *unit functions* when $a_0 = 1$.

It must be emphasized that the pictorial representation of the delta function is not an ordinary graph of an ordinary function. It is easy to amplify Fig. 9.533 to produce Fig. 9.534 which shows the sum

$$g(x) = a_0\delta(x - \lambda_0) + a_1\delta(x - \lambda_1) + a_2\delta(x - \lambda_2)$$

of three Dirac functions and the cumulative function

$$g_1(x) = a_0H(x - \lambda_0) + a_1H(x - \lambda_1) + a_2H(x - \lambda_2)$$

which is a sum of three Heaviside functions. The Dirac functions furnish the risers and the cumulative Heaviside sum furnishes the treads of a staircase; we go upstairs when $a_k > 0$ and downstairs when $a_k < 0$.

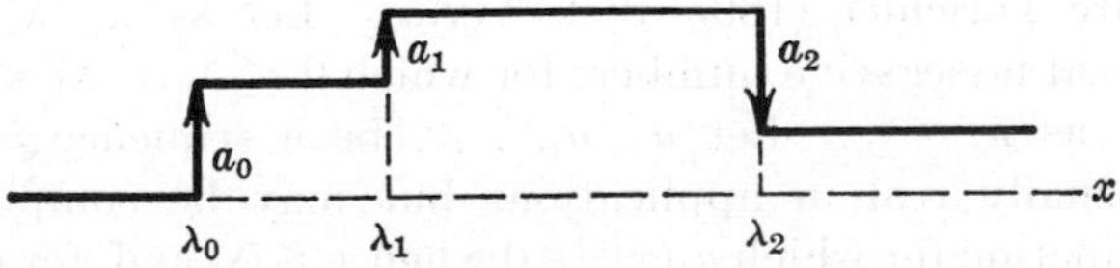

FIG. 9.534

The positions of the treads determine the positions of the risers and vice versa. When $0 \leqq \lambda_0 < \lambda_1 < \lambda_2$, the first member of the formula

$$\int_0^\infty e^{-sx}g(x)dx = \int_0^\infty e^{-sx}\,dg_1(x) = \sum_{k=0}^{2} a_ke^{-\lambda_ks}$$

is the Laplace transform of $g(x)$, the middle member is the Laplace-Stieltjes transform of $g_1(x)$, and each one of these is equal to the last member. When we want pictorial representations of Dirac functions alone, without showing the cumulative function, we can slide the arrows of Fig. 9.534 up or down (but not sideways) so that they all start at points on the x axis.

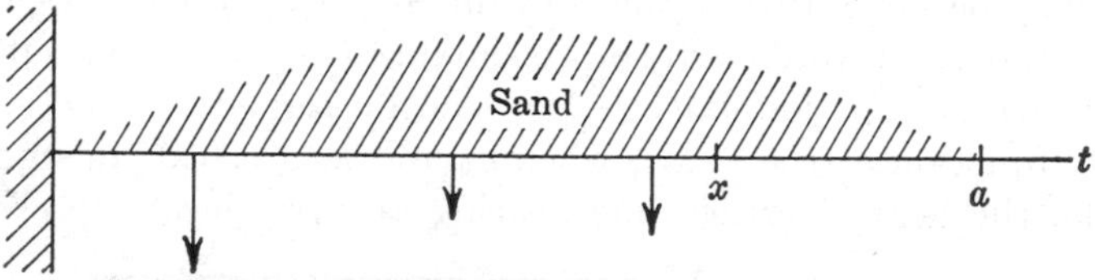

FIG. 9.535

Anyone who feels that an impulse is a strange figment of the imagination should face the fact that it is exactly as strange as another figment that is normally thought to be very simple and useful. Let $g_1(x)$ be the total or cumulative mass which rests upon or hangs from the beam of Fig. 9.535 over the interval $0 \leqq t \leqq x$. The mass function $g_1(x)$ is important; for example, when $p \geqq 0$, the number M_p defined by

$$M_p = \int_0^a x^p \, dg_1(x)$$

is the pth moment, about the left end of the beam, of the mass attached to the interval $0 \leqq t \leqq a$. The physical assumption that there can be a distribution of mass whose mass function $g_1(x)$ is $H(x - x_0)$ implies the absurd but very simple and useful conclusion that we can suspend a body from the beam by a hook so slender that the whole force on the beam is concentrated at a single point x_0. The absurdity of the assumption and conclusion becomes apparent when we realize that the suspended body would be in a precarious position if the hook happened to be attached to the beam at a place where no atoms or molecules are present.

We now discuss an important class of functions whose Laplace-Stieltjes transforms are Dirichlet (1805–1859) series. Let $\lambda_0, \lambda_1, \lambda_2, \ldots$ be a sequence of real nonegative numbers for which $0 \leq \lambda_0 < \lambda_1 < \lambda_2 < \cdots$ and $\lambda_n \to \infty$ as $n \to \infty$. Let $a_0, a_1, \ldots$ be a sequence of constants which are usually real in applications but may be complex. Let g_1 be the step function for which $g_1(x) = 0$ when $x \leqq \lambda_0$ and, for each $n > 0$,

$$g_1(x) = a_0 + a_1 + \cdots + a_{n-1} \tag{9.54}$$

when $\lambda_{n-1} < x \leqq \lambda_n$. Thus $g_1(x) = a_0$ when $\lambda_0 < x \leqq \lambda_1$ and

$$g_1(x) = a_0 + a_1$$

when $\lambda_1 < x \leqq \lambda_2$, and so on. When the numbers a_n are real, it is easy to sketch a schematic graph of $g_1(x)$, as in Fig. 9.534, and see that the function makes a jump of magnitude a_n in a little interval including λ_n. Thus $g_1(x)$ is the function which is closely approximated by the cumulative function $g_2(x)$ of each function $g(x)$ which is 0 except that for each n there is a physically realizable impulse of magnitude a_n in a short interval following λ_n. Sometimes, but by no means always, interest in $g_1(x)$ depends upon this fact. The Laplace-Stieltjes transform of $g_1(x)$ is

$$G(s) = \sum_{n=0}^{\infty} a_n e^{-\lambda_n s}. \tag{9.55}$$

Sometimes, but by no means always, $G(s)$ is thought of as the Laplace transform of the series $\Sigma a_n\ \delta(x - \lambda_n)$ of Dirac functions. The series in (9.55) is called a *Dirichlet series* with exponents $\lambda_0, \lambda_1, \ldots$, and our work shows that all Dirichlet series are representable as Laplace transforms. In case $a_0 = \lambda_0 = 0$ and $\lambda_n = \log n$ when $n = 1, 2, \ldots$, the formula reduces to

$$G(s) = \sum_{n=1}^{\infty} \frac{a_n}{n^s} \tag{9.56}$$

and the series is called an ordinary Dirichlet series. In case $a_n = 1$, this reduces to the *Riemann zeta function*

$$\zeta(s) = \sum_{n=1}^{\infty} \frac{1}{n^s}. \tag{9.561}$$

In case h is a positive constant and $\lambda_n = nh$ for each $n = 0, 1, 2, \ldots$, (9.55) reduces to

$$G(s) = \sum_{n=0}^{\infty} a_n e^{-nhs} \tag{9.562}$$

and this is a power series in e^{-hs}. In case $a_n = 1$ for each n, (9.562) reduces to

$$G(s) = \frac{1}{1 - e^{-hs}}. \tag{9.563}$$

This is the Laplace-Stieltjes transform* of the special staircase function, stair hx having risers of height 1 on the lines for which $x = 0, h, 2h, \ldots$.

It is the Laplace transform of the function $\sum_{n=0}^{\infty} \delta(x - nh)$ which is 0 except for unit impulses at the times $0, h, 2h, \ldots$.

* The theory of Stieltjes integrals and Laplace transforms, with emphasis upon Laplace Stieltjes transforms, is expounded in a book by D. V. Widder (1898–), "The Laplace Transform," Princeton University Press, Princeton, N.J., 1941.

Problem 9.57

Find the Laplace (not Laplace-Stieltjes) transform of the staircase function stair x for which stair $x = 0$ when $x \leqq 0$, and stair $x = n$ when n is a positive integer and $n - 1 < x \leqq n$. *Ans.:* $\dfrac{1}{s(1 - e^{-s})}$.

Problem 9.581

The formula

$$\int_a^b f(x)dg\,(x) = f(x)g(x)\Big]_a^b - \int_a^b g(x)df\,(x) \tag{9.5811}$$

for *integration by parts* is valid whenever either of the two integrals exists. The formula

$$\int_a^b g(x)df\,(x) = \int_a^b g(x)f'(x)dx \tag{9.5812}$$

is valid whenever $g(x)$ has bounded variation and $f'(x)$ is continuous over $a \leqq x \leqq b$. Use these facts and the fact that putting $h = 1$ in (9.561) gives

$$\int_0^\infty e^{-sx}d \text{ stair } x = \frac{1}{1 - e^{-s}}$$

to derive the answer to Problem 9.57. *Solution:* Since stair $0 = 0$, integrating by parts and using (9.5812) gives

$$\int_0^b e^{-sx}d \text{ stair } x = e^{-sb} \text{ stair } b + s\int_0^b e^{-sx} \text{ stair } x\, dx.$$

Letting $b \to \infty$ and dividing by s gives the result.

Problem 9.582

Sketch graphs of $f(x)$ and its cumulative function $f_1(x)$ when

$$f(x) = 1 - \delta(x) - \delta(x-1) - \delta(x-2) - \delta(x-3) - \cdots.$$

Tell how $f(x)$ might be described if x is time (measured in any old units) and $f(x)$ is the signed magnitude of a force which pulls a unit mass in the direction of a positive y axis. Find the Laplace transform $Y(s)$ of the function $y(x)$ for which $y(0) = y'(0) = 0$ and

$$\frac{d^2y}{dx^2} = f(x). \quad \textit{Ans.}\text{ (partial): } Y(s) = \frac{1}{s^2}\left(\frac{1}{s} - \frac{1}{1 - e^{-s}}\right).$$

Problem 9.583

Discuss the equation

$$\frac{d^2y}{dx^2} + a^2y = E_0[\delta(x) + \delta(x-1) + \delta(x-2) + \cdots].$$

Problem 9.584

If you happen to know about hammers and nails, sketch a reasonably realistic graph showing, as a function of the time, the magnitude of the force exerted upon a nail by a hammer when the nail is being driven into a plank. Do not overlook the fact that the force is 0 most of the time.

Problem 9.585

If you happen to know about *L-R-C* oscillators, sketch a reasonably realistic graph showing, as a function of the time, the charge on one side of a capacitor when a spark jumps to it once each second.

Remark 9.591

The Dirac function $\delta(x)$ is not an ordinary function, but (9.531) gives the possibility of using it. We now postulate existence of a function $\delta'(x)$, which we can call a generalized derivative of $\delta(x)$, and construct a definition of a new kind of integral to go with it. When $f(x)$ is an ordinary function having a continuous derivative at x_0, and when $a < x_0 < b$, where a may be $-\infty$ and b may be $+\infty$, the value of the integral in the left member of the formula

$$\text{(9.5911)} \qquad \int_a^b f(x)\delta'(x - x_0)dx = -f'(x_0)$$

is, by definition, the number obtained by formal integration by parts with

$$f(a)\delta(a - x_0) = 0$$

and $f(b)\delta(b - x_0) = 0$. Setting $u = f(x)$, $dv = \delta'(x - x_0)$, $du = f'(x)$, $v = \delta(x - x_0)$ and using the definition then shows that the integral has the value

$$-\int_a^b f'(x)\delta(x - x_0)dx.$$

But (9.531) implies that this is $-f'(x_0)$, and it follows that (9.5911) is a valid formula. In particular, setting $a = 0$, $b = \infty$, and $f(x) = e^{-sx}$ gives the formula

$$\text{(9.5912)} \qquad \int_0^\infty e^{-sx}\delta'(x - x_0)dx = se^{-sx_0}$$

which is valid for each complex s when x_0 is real and positive. The remarks following (9.531) apply here.

9.6. Equations whose Coefficients are Polynomials in the Independent Variable. We illustrate the application of Laplace transforms to equations of this type by considering an example.

Supposing that $f(x)$ is a given function having a Laplace transform, we seek a (or the) solution $y(x)$ of the equation

$$\text{(9.61)} \qquad xy''(x) + y'(x) + xy(x) = f(x)$$

for which y, y', and y'' possess Laplace transforms and $y(0)$ and $y'(0)$ have prescribed numerical values for which we do not introduce supplementary notation. In case $f(x)$ is identically 0, (9.61) reduces to the Bessel equation of order 0.

To start applying Laplace transforms to (9.61), we let $Y(s)$ and $F(s)$ be the transforms of $y(x)$ and $f(x)$ and copy, from the list (9.14), the formulas

$$\int_0^\infty e^{-sx}y(x)dx = Y(s) \tag{9.621}$$

$$\int_0^\infty e^{-sx}y'(x)dx = sY(s) - y(0) \tag{9.622}$$

$$\int_0^\infty e^{-sx}y''(x)dx = s^2Y(s) - sy(0) - y'(0). \tag{9.623}$$

The second of these formulas gives the transform of the second term in (9.61), but the others need modification. Formulas for transforms of $xy(x)$ and $xy''(x)$ can be obtained by going back to (9.16), but it is much easier to differentiate (9.621) and (9.623) with respect to s. This gives

$$\int_0^\infty e^{-sx}xy(x)dx = -Y'(s) \tag{9.624}$$

and

$$\int_0^\infty e^{-sx}xy''(x)dx = -s^2Y'(s) - 2sY(s) + y(0). \tag{9.625}$$

With the aid of (9.625), (9.622), and (9.624), we see that taking transforms of the members of (9.61) gives

$$(1 + s^2)Y'(s) + sY(s) = -F(s). \tag{9.63}$$

This ends one phase of the attack. We have obtained a linear differential equation whose coefficients are polynomials in s, and we can see that this always happens when we take transforms of the members of a linear differential equation in which the coefficients are polynomials in the independent variable. Moreover we can see that special properties of the special equation (9.61) are responsible for the failure of $y(0)$ and $y'(0)$ to appear in (9.63).

Solving the first-order linear equation (9.63) by use of an integrating factor gives

$$Y(s) = \frac{c}{\sqrt{1+s^2}} - \frac{1}{\sqrt{1+s^2}}\int_{s_0}^{s} \frac{F(t)}{\sqrt{1+t^2}}\,dt \tag{9.64}$$

where c is a constant which depends upon s_0 and upon the solution of (9.61) with which we started. This formula is just complicated enough to suggest that persons who work extensively with these things should be on very good terms with tables of integrals and tables of Laplace transforms.

We conclude by showing that it is sometimes possible to use power series to find functions when their transforms are known. We seek information about the function whose Laplace transform is the left member of the identity

$$\frac{c}{\sqrt{1+s^2}} = \frac{c}{s}\left(1 + \frac{1}{s^2}\right)^{-\frac{1}{2}}. \tag{9.65}$$

We suppose that $s > 1$ and expand the right member by use of the binomial formula (or by the Taylor formula) to obtain

$$\frac{c}{\sqrt{1+s^2}} = c\sum_{k=0}^{\infty}(-1)^k \frac{(2k)!}{2^{2k}k!k!}\frac{1}{s^{2k+1}}. \tag{9.651}$$

Using (9.17) with $m = 0$ gives

$$\frac{c}{\sqrt{1+s^2}} = c\sum_{k=0}^{\infty}\int_0^\infty e^{-sx}(-1)^k \frac{x^{2k}}{2^{2k}k!k!}\,dx. \tag{9.652}$$

It can be proved that it is possible to interchange the order of summation and integration so that, semifinally,

$$\frac{c}{\sqrt{1+s^2}} = c\int_0^\infty e^{-sx}\sum_{k=0}^{\infty}(-1)^k \frac{x^{2k}}{2^{2k}k!k!}\,dx.$$

On setting $c = 1$ and noticing that the above series is precisely the series (7.851) which defines $J_0(x)$, we obtain our final formula

$$\frac{1}{\sqrt{1+s^2}} = \int_0^\infty e^{-sx}J_0(x)\,dx. \tag{9.66}$$

This proves that the left side of (9.66) is the Laplace transform of $J_0(x)$.

As is easy to guess, Laplace transforms prove to be most useful in studies of functions when the transforms are simpler than the functions. Sinusoids, including damped ones, and $J_0(x)$ are shining examples of functions having simple transforms.

Problem 9.67

Look at all of Section 9.6 with the hypothesis that $f(x)$ is identically zero and the equation being studied is the Bessel equation of order 0. Does the work show that each solution of this equation has the form $cJ_0(x)$? *Ans.:* No. It shows that each solution $y(x)$ for which y, y', and y'' possess Laplace transforms must have the form $cJ_0(x)$. This result is to be expected because each solution independent of $J_0(x)$ behaves like $\log x$ as $x \to 0$.

Problem 9.681

Show that if y is a solution of the Bessel equation

$$x^2y''(x) + xy'(x) + (x^2 - \alpha^2)y(x) = 0 \tag{9.6811}$$

of order α which possesses a Laplace transform $Y(s)$, then

$$(1 + s^2)Y''(s) + 3sY'(s) + (1 - \alpha^2)Y(s) = 0. \tag{9.6812}$$

In case $\alpha = 0$, show that this can be written in the form

$$\frac{d}{ds}[(1 + s^2)Y'(s) + sY(s)] = 0$$

and solved as (9.63) was solved. In case $\alpha = 1$, find $Y'(s)$ and then $Y(s)$, show that

$$Y(s) = \frac{c_1\sqrt{1+s^2} - c_2 s}{\sqrt{1+s^2}}, \tag{9.6813}$$

and show that $c_2 = c_1$ if $Y(s) \to 0$ as $s \to \infty$; see Problem 9.792. *Remark:* In order to determine the constants to obtain transforms of the special functions $J_\alpha(x)$, we must use some quantitative information about the functions $J_\alpha(x)$. See the next problem.

Problem 9.682

Formula (9.66) gives the Laplace transform of $J_0(x)$, formula (7.858) says that $J_0'(x) = -J_1(x)$, we have a ritual for finding the transform of $y'(x)$ when we know the transform of $y(x)$, and we know that $J_0(0) = 1$. Employ these ideas to obtain the formula

$$\int_0^\infty e^{-sx}J_\alpha(x)dx = \frac{(\sqrt{1+s^2} - s)^\alpha}{\sqrt{1+s^2}} \tag{9.6821}$$

when $\alpha = 0$ and when $\alpha = 1$. Our next task is to prove by induction that the formula is valid when $\alpha = 0, 1, 2, 3, \ldots$. Supposing that α_0 is a fixed positive integer and that (9.6821) holds when $\alpha = 0, 1, \ldots, \alpha_0$, use the identity

$$J_{\alpha+1}(x) = J_{\alpha-1}(x) - 2J_\alpha'(x) \tag{9.6822}$$

which comes from (7.856) to prove that (9.6821) holds when $\alpha = \alpha_0 + 1$; matters are simplified by the fact that $J_\alpha(0) = 0$ when $\alpha > 0$. *Remark:* Bad tables, and even some good ones, give formulas such as (9.6821) without specifying the set of values of the parameter for which the formula is valid. The compiler of the table may be ignorant or negligent, but in either case the person using the table is left ignorant. Sometimes it is not easy to find out whether a formula such as (9.6821) is valid when $\alpha = \frac{1}{2}$.

Problem 9.69

The *exponential-integral* function $E(x)$ defined by

$$E(x) = \int_x^\infty \frac{e^{-u}}{u}du = \int_1^\infty \frac{e^{-vx}}{v}dv$$

has a simple Laplace transform. Find it. *Ans.:* $\dfrac{\log(1+s)}{s}$.

9.7. Existence and Uniqueness Theorems. The functions $\tan^2 x$ and $\exp x^2$ have no Laplace transforms; if one of them is called $g(x)$, then there is no s for which the integral defining $G(s)$ exists. The following theorem shows that if $g(x)$ is such that $G(s)$ exists for at least one s, then there must be a whole half plane of complex numbers s for which $G(s)$ exists.

THEOREM 9.71. *If the integral in*

$$G(s) = \int_0^\infty e^{-sx} g(x)dx \tag{9.711}$$

exists when $s = s_0$, then it also exists whenever the real part of s exceeds that of s_0.

Let

$$G_h(s) = \int_0^h e^{-sx} g(x)dx. \tag{9.712}$$

The hypothesis means that the limit in

$$G(s) = \lim_{h\to\infty} G_h(s) \tag{9.713}$$

exists when $s = s_0$. To obtain the conclusion, we suppose that s is a complex number (which may be real) having a real part exceeding that of s_0. Then

$$G_h(s) = \int_0^h e^{-(s-s_0)x} e^{-s_0x} g(x)dx. \tag{9.714}$$

Integrating by parts with

$$u = e^{-(s-s_0)x} \qquad dv = e^{-s_0x} g(x)dx$$

$$du = -(s - s_0)e^{-(s-s_0)x}\, dx \qquad v(x) = \int_0^x e^{-s_0t} g(t)dt$$

gives

$$G_h(s) = e^{-(s-s_0)h} v(h) + (s - s_0) \int_0^h e^{-(s-s_0)x} v(x)dx. \tag{9.715}$$

Since $v(x)$ is a continuous function of x for which $v(x) \to 0$ as $x \to 0$ and $v(x) \to G(s_0)$ as $x \to \infty$, it is easy to see that letting $h \to \infty$ in (9.715) gives

$$G(s) = (s - s_0) \int_0^\infty e^{-(s-s_0)x} v(x)dx \tag{9.716}$$

and shows that $G(s)$ exists. This proves Theorem 9.71 and, in addition, gives useful formulas.

The simple character of the function $v(x)$ in (9.716) makes (9.716) a very fruitful source of information about $G(s)$. For example, it is possible to use (9.716) with $s_0 = 0$ to prove that the formula

$$\lim_{s\to 0+} \int_0^\infty e^{-sx} g(x)dx = \int_0^\infty g(x)dx \tag{9.7161}$$

is valid whenever the integral on the right exists. The proof depends upon the fact that if

$$\lim_{x\to\infty} v(x) = \lim_{x\to\infty} \int_0^x g(t)dt = \int_0^\infty g(t)dt = I,$$

then to each $\epsilon > 0$ there corresponds a number M such that $|v(x) -$

$I| < \epsilon/2$ when $x \geqq M$. Using (9.716) with $s_0 = 0$ then gives

$$|G(s) - I| \leqq s \int_0^M |v(x) - I|dx + s \int_M^\infty e^{-sx} \frac{\epsilon}{2} dx$$

when $s > 0$, and we can choose a δ such that $|G(s) - I| < \epsilon$ when $0 < s < \delta$. It is also possible to use (9.716) to prove that if $G(s_0)$ exists, then

$$\lim_{s \to \infty} \int_0^\infty e^{-sx} g(x) dx = 0 \tag{9.7162}$$

and

$$\frac{d^k}{ds^k} \int_0^\infty e^{-sx} g(x) dx = \int_0^\infty e^{-sx}(-x)^k g(x) dx \tag{9.7163}$$

when the real part of s exceeds that of s_0 and $k = 1, 2, 3, \ldots$. These ideas and facts have swarms of applications. For example, since the integral in the first formula in

$$\int_0^\infty \frac{\sin x}{x} dx = \frac{\pi}{2}, \qquad \int_0^\infty e^{-sx} \frac{\sin x}{x} dx = \frac{\pi}{2} - \tan^{-1} s \tag{9.7164}$$

exists, the first formula is a consequence of the second which holds when $s > 0$. To prove the second formula, let $G(s)$ denote its left member. Then

$$G'(s) = -\int_0^\infty e^{-sx} \sin x \, dx = \operatorname{Im} \int_0^\infty e^{-(s+i)x} dx = \frac{1}{1 + s^2}.$$

The result follows from this and the fact that $G(s) \to 0$ as $s \to \infty$.

THEOREM 9.717. *If $g(x)$ is decent, in the sense of Section* 9.1, *then the integrals in* (9.11) *and* (9.111) *exist when $s = \sigma + it$ and $\sigma > b$.*

To prove this we need the following fact which we shall not prove. If $f(x)$ is integrable over each finite subinterval of an infinite interval I and is dominated by a function $F(x)$, *i.e.*, $|f(x)| \leqq F(x)$, integrable over I, then $f(x)$ is integrable over I. Choose x_0 such that $|e^{-bx} g(x)| < 1$ when $x > x_0$. Our hypotheses imply that $e^{-sx} g(x)$ and $|e^{-sx} g(x)|$ are integrable over each finite interval and are dominated by the integrable function $F(x)$ which is $|e^{-sx} g(x)|$ when $0 \leqq x \leqq x_0$ and is $e^{-(\sigma - b)x}$ when $x \geqq x_0$. The conclusion of Theorem 9.717 follows.

Theorem 9.72 is a uniqueness theorem which implies that two different continuous functions $f_1(x)$ and $f_2(x)$ cannot have the same Laplace transform. If $f_1(x)$ and $f_2(x)$ are not assumed to be continuous, it is not possible to prove that $f_1(x) = f_2(x)$ everywhere because $f_1(x)$ and $f_2(x)$ might differ for a finite set of values of x (or even for an infinite set) and still have identical transforms. It is, however, easy to modify the proof to show that $f_1(x) = f_2(x)$ almost everywhere and that $f_1(x) = f_2(x)$ wherever both functions are continuous; this is a theorem of Lerch (1860–1922).

THEOREM 9.72. *If two functions $f_1(x)$ and $f_2(x)$ are continuous when $x \geqq 0$ and if, for some real constant a, the integrals in*

(9.721) $$\int_0^\infty e^{-sx} f_2(x)dx = \int_0^\infty e^{-sx} f_1(x)dx$$

exist and are equal when $s = a, a + 1, a + 2, \ldots$, then $f_1(x) = f_2(x)$ when $x \geqq 0$.

To prove the theorem, let

(9.722) $$g(x) = f_2(x) - f_1(x).$$

Then

(9.723) $$\int_0^\infty e^{-(a+n)x} g(x)dx = 0, \qquad n = 0, 1, 2, \ldots.$$

Integrating by parts with

(9.724) $$u = e^{-nx} \qquad dv = e^{-ax}g(x)dx$$

(9.725) $$du = -ne^{-nx}\,dx \qquad v(x) = \int_0^x e^{-at}g(t)dt$$

shows that

(9.726) $$\int_0^\infty e^{-nx} v(x)dx = 0 \qquad n = 1, 2, \ldots$$

where $v(x)$ is a continuous function of x for which $v(x) \to 0$ as $x \to 0$ and $v(x) \to 0$ as $x \to \infty$. It will be sufficient to prove that $v - 0$ [*i.e.*, $v(t) = 0$ for each t] because then (9.725) will imply that $g = 0$ and (9.722) will imply that $f_2 = f_1$.

To prove that $v = 0$, we throw (9.926) into a simpler form by making a change of the variable of integration. Putting $e^{-x} = t$, $x = \log t^{-1}$, and letting $u(0) = u(1) = 0$ and $u(t) = v(\log t^{-1})$ when $0 < t < 1$, we see that $u(t)$ is continuous over $0 \leqq t \leqq 1$ and

(9.727) $$\int_0^1 t^{n-1}u(t)dt = 0 \qquad n = 1, 2, \ldots.$$

The fact that $u = 0$ and hence $v = 0$ is now seen to be a consequence of the following theorem.

THEOREM 9.73. *If $u(t)$ is continuous over $0 \leqq t \leqq 1$ and*

$$\int_0^1 t^n u(t)dt = 0 \qquad n = 0, 1, 2, \ldots,$$

then $u(t) = 0$ when $0 \leqq t \leqq 1$.

This is one of the fundamental theorems of mathematical analysis. There is no easy way to prove it. The standard and most informative proof depends upon important theorems on *trigonometric* and *polynomial approximation* which are not quickly proved. These theorems are worthy of notice.

THEOREM 9.74. *If $f(x)$ is continuous over $a \leqq x \leqq a + h$ and if $f(a) = f(a + h)$, then to each positive number ϵ there corresponds a trigonometric polynomial*

$$(9.741) \qquad T(x) = \sum_{k=-n}^{n} c_k e^{i(2\pi/h)kx}$$

such that

$$(9.742) \qquad |f(x) - T(x)| < \epsilon \qquad a \leqq x \leqq a + h.$$

This theorem looks simplest when $h = 2\pi$ and a is $-\pi$ or 0. Of course $T(x)$ can always be expressed in terms of cosines and sines by use of the Euler formula, but our grandfathers did this much more frequently than we do. The following is the *Weierstrass* (1815–1897) *approximation theorem.*

THEOREM 9.75. *If $f(x)$ is continuous over $a \leqq x \leqq b$, then to each $\epsilon > 0$ there corresponds a polynomial*

$$P(x) = a_0 + a_1x + \cdots + a_nx^n$$

such that

$$(9.751) \qquad |f(x) - P(x)| < \epsilon \qquad a \leqq x \leqq b.$$

Theorem 9.74 is the basic one of these theorems; the others are easily derived from it. The partial sums $S_n(x)$, defined in (6.773), of the Fourier series of $f(x)$ do not always, even when n is large, approximate $f(x)$ closely enough to allow them to serve as $T(x)$ in (9.741) and (9.742). However the *Fejér* (1880–) *arithmetic mean*

$$(9.752) \qquad \sigma_N(x) = \frac{1}{N+1} \sum_{n=0}^{N} S_n(x)$$

always does when N is sufficiently great. This just happens to be another situation where averages smooth out kinks, and anybody who is really allergic to kinks can use these averages instead of the partial sums of Fourier series.

We use Theorem 9.75 to prove the following theorem which includes Theorem 9.73

THEOREM 9.76. *If $f(x)$ is continuous over $a \leqq x \leqq b$ and*

$$\int_a^b x^n f(x)dx = 0 \qquad n = 0, 1, 2, \ldots,$$

then $f(x) = 0$ when $a \leqq x \leqq b$.

We may suppose that $f(x)$ is real; otherwise we treat the real and imaginary parts separately. Let $\epsilon > 0$ and choose a polynomial $P(x)$

such that (9.751) holds. Then

$$\int_a^b [f(x)]^2 dx = \int_a^b f(x)[f(x) - P(x)]dx$$
$$\leqq \int_a^b |f(x)|\epsilon\, dx = \epsilon \int_a^b |f(x)|dx.$$

Hence $\int_a^b [f(x)]^2 dx = 0$ and the result follows.

Problem 9.771

Supposing that $f(x)$ is integrable over $0 \leqq x \leqq h$ and has period h, prove that

$$\int_0^\infty e^{-sx} f(x)dx = \frac{1}{1 - e^{-hs}} \int_0^h e^{-sx} f(x)dx$$

when $s = \sigma + it$ and $\sigma > 0$. *Remark:* A solution will appear in Section 9.8. A little lesson in mathematics comes from consideration of the case in which $h = 1$ and $f(x) = h^{-\frac{1}{2}}$ when $0 < x \leqq 1$. The above integrals exist, but there is no s for which $e^{-sx}f(x) \to 0$ as $x \to \infty$.

Problem 9.772

Derive the formula

$$\int_0^\infty e^{-sx}|\sin \omega x|dx = \frac{\omega}{s^2 + \omega^2} \frac{e^{\pi s/2\omega} + e^{-\pi s/2\omega}}{e^{\pi s/2\omega} - e^{-\pi s/2\omega}}$$

involving fully rectified sinusoids. To each real function $f(x)$ there corresponds the semirectified function $f^+(x)$ for which $f^+(x) = f(x)$ when $f(x) \geqq 0$ and $f^+(x) = 0$ when $f(x) \leqq 0$. Tell how to calculate

$$\int_0^\infty e^{-sx} \sin^+ \omega x\, dx$$

without (and then with) the aid of the formula

$$f^+(x) = \tfrac{1}{2}[|f(x)| + f(x)].$$

Problem 9.773

Letting $q(x)$ denote the *square-wave* function of period h for which $q(x) = 1$ when $0 < x < h/2$ and $q(x) = -1$ when $h/2 < x < h$, show that

$$\int_0^\infty e^{-sx} q(x)dx = \frac{1}{s} \frac{1 - e^{-hs/2}}{1 + e^{-hs/2}} = \frac{1}{s} \tanh \frac{hs}{4}.$$

Problem 9.774

The *Bernoulli* (James, 1654–1705) *function* $B_1(x)$, which appears with other Bernoulli functions in the Euler-Maclaurin summation formula, is the *saw function* which has period 1 and has the values $x - \frac{1}{2}$ when $0 < x < 1$. Show that

$$\int_0^\infty e^{-sx} B_1(x)dx = \frac{1}{s^2} - \frac{1}{2s} - \frac{1}{s(e^s - 1)} = \frac{1}{s^2} - \frac{1}{2s} \frac{e^{s/2} + e^{-s/2}}{e^{s/2} - e^{-s/2}} = \frac{1}{s^2} - \frac{1}{2s} \coth \frac{s}{2}.$$

Problem 9.775

Using material from Problems 9.58 and 9.744, show that

$$\int_0^\infty e^{-sx}\,dB_1(x) = \frac{1}{s} - \frac{1}{2}\frac{e^{s/2}+e^{-s/2}}{e^{s/2}-e^{-s/2}}. \tag{9.7751}$$

Remark: The right side is the Laplace-Stieltjes transform of $B_1(x)$. With the aid of Dirac functions, we can build up a function f whose cumulative function is 0 when $x \leq 0$ and is $B_1(x)$ when $x > 0$. In fact $f(x) = H(x) + f_2(x)$ where $f_2(x)$ is 0 except for an impulse of magnitude $-\frac{1}{2}$ when $x = 0$ and impulses of magnitude -1 when $x = 1, 2, 3, \ldots$.

Problem 9.776

Find the Laplace transform $Y(s)$ of the function $y(x)$ for which $y(0) = y'(0) = 0$ and

$$\frac{d^2y}{dx^2} + k^2y = f(x)$$

where $f(x)$ is the function, of the previous problem, whose cumulative function is $B_1(x)$. *Solution:* Since the Laplace transform of f is the Laplace-Stieltjes transform of $B_1(x)$, taking Laplace transform gives

$$(s^2+k^2)Y(s) = \frac{1}{s} - \frac{1}{2}\frac{e^{s/2}+e^{-s/2}}{e^{s/2}-e^{-s/2}}$$

and dividing by $s^2 + k^2$ gives the answer.

Remark 9.78

The *Bernoulli functions* $B_0(x)$, $B_1(x)$, $B_2(x)$, . . . may be defined as those functions of period 1 for which $B_0(x) = 1$; $B'_{n+1}(x) = B_n(x)$ when $n = 0, 1, 2, \ldots$ and $0 < x < 1$; $\int_0^1 B_n(x)dx = 0$ when $n = 1, 2, \ldots$; $B_1(0) = 0$; and $B_n(x)$ is continuous when $n > 1$. Thus $B_1(x)$ is the saw function of Problem 9.774, and it is not difficult to show that

$$B_1(x) = \frac{-2}{2\pi}\left[\frac{\sin 2\pi x}{1} + \frac{\sin 4\pi x}{2} + \frac{\sin 6\pi x}{3} + \cdots\right]$$
$$B_2(x) = \frac{2}{(2\pi)^2}\left[\frac{\cos 2\pi x}{1^2} + \frac{\cos 4\pi x}{2^2} + \frac{\cos 6\pi x}{3^2} + \cdots\right]$$
$$B_3(x) = \frac{2}{(2\pi)^3}\left[\frac{\sin 2\pi x}{1^3} + \frac{\sin 4\pi x}{2^3} + \frac{\sin 6\pi x}{3^3} + \cdots\right]$$
$$B_4(x) = \frac{-2}{(2\pi)^4}\left[\frac{\cos 2\pi x}{1^4} + \frac{\cos 4\pi x}{2^4} + \frac{\cos 6\pi x}{3^4} + \cdots\right]$$
$$B_5(x) = \frac{-2}{(2\pi)^5}\left[\frac{\sin 2\pi x}{1^5} + \frac{\sin 4\pi x}{2^5} + \frac{\sin 6\pi x}{3^5} + \cdots\right], \text{ etc.,}$$

the signs being determined such that $B'_{n+1}(x) = B_n(x)$. The *Bernoulli numbers* are defined by $B_0 = 1$, $B_1 = \lim_{x\to 0} B_1(x) = -\frac{1}{2}$, and $B_n = n!B_n(0)$ when $n > 1$. It can be proved by induction that, when $0 < x < 1$,

$$n!B_n(x) = \binom{n}{0}B_0x^n + \binom{n}{1}B_1x^{n-1} + \cdots + \binom{n}{n-1}B_{n-1}x + \binom{n}{n}B_n. \tag{9.781}$$

These are *Bernoulli polynomials*, and the Bernoulli functions are periodic extensions of them. Using the fact that $B_n(x)$ is continuous and $B_n(1) = B_n(0)$ when $n \geqq 2$ gives the formula

$$\binom{n}{0} B_0 + \binom{n}{1} B_1 + \binom{n}{2} B_2 + \cdots + \binom{n}{n} B_n = \binom{n}{n} B_n \tag{9.782}$$

from which $B_2, B_3, \ldots$ can be calculated. It can be shown that $B_0 = 1$, $B_1 = -\frac{1}{2}$, $B_2 = \frac{1}{6}$, $B_3 = 0$, $B_4 = -\frac{1}{30}$, $B_5 = 0$, $B_6 = \frac{1}{42}$, $B_7 = 0$, $B_8 = -\frac{1}{30}$, $\ldots$ and that $|B_{2n}|$ is very large when n is large. Putting $x = 0$ in the trigonometric formulas for $B_2(x), B_4(x), \ldots$ gives the famous formulas

$$\sum_{n=1}^{\infty} \frac{1}{n^2} = \frac{\pi^2}{6}, \qquad \sum_{n=1}^{\infty} \frac{1}{n^4} = \frac{\pi^4}{90}, \qquad \ldots, \tag{9.783}$$

but as usual the value of $\Sigma(1/n^3)$ remains unrevealed. Many applications are based upon the formula

$$\frac{te^{xt}}{e^t - 1} = \sum_{n=0}^{\infty} B_n(x)t^n \tag{9.784}$$

which holds when $0 < x < 1$ and $|t| < 2\pi$, the left side being defined to be 1 when $t = 0$. Putting $x = 0$ in (9.784) gives the more elementary formula

$$\frac{t}{2} \frac{e^{t/2} + e^{-t/2}}{e^{t/2} - e^{-t/2}} = \sum_{k=0}^{\infty} \frac{B_{2k}}{(2k)!} t^{2k} \tag{9.7841}$$

and putting $t = 2iz$ gives

$$z \cot z = \sum_{k=0}^{\infty} (-1)^k \frac{2^{2k}B_{2k}}{(2k)!} z^{2k}. \tag{9.7842}$$

Using the formula $z \tan z = z \cot z - 2z \cot 2z$ gives

$$\tan z = \sum_{k=1}^{\infty} (-1)^{k-1} \frac{2^{2k}(2^{2k} - 1)B_{2k}}{(2k)!} z^{2k-1}. \tag{9.7843}$$

Problem 9.785

Using only the properties of $B_n(x)$ given in the first sentence of Remark 9.78 to obtain a formal derivation of (9.784). *Solution:* To avoid bothering with partial derivatives, let t be fixed and let

$$y(x) = \sum_{n=0}^{\infty} B_n(x)t^n.$$

Then

$$y'(x) = \sum_{n=1}^{\infty} B_n'(x)t^n = t \sum_{n=1}^{\infty} B_{n-1}(x)t^{n-1} = ty(x)$$

so

$$\frac{d}{dx}\, e^{-xt}y(x) = 0, \qquad y(x) = c(t)e^{xt}$$

where $c(t)$ is a constant that may depend upon the fixed t. Thus

$$c(t)e^{xt} = \sum_{n=0}^{\infty} B_n(x)t^n.$$

When $t \neq 0$, integrating over $0 \leqq x \leqq 1$ gives

$$c(t)(e^t - 1)/t = 1$$

and (9.784) follows. When $t = 0$, the integration gives $c(0) = 1$. The result follows.

Problem 9.786

When the integral in the right member of the formula

$$f_2(s) = \int_0^\infty \frac{f_0(x)}{x+s}\, dx$$

exists, it is called the *Stieltjes transform* of $f_0(x)$. Show that if $f_0(x)$ and $|f_0(x)|$ are integrable over the infinite interval $x > 0$, then the Laplace transform of $f_0(x)$ has a Laplace transform which is the Stieltjes transform of $f_0(x)$. *Remark:* Stieltjes used the more general transformation

$$G(x) = \int_0^\infty \frac{1}{x+s}\, dg(x)$$

in his work on continued fractions. For information about these matters, see Widder* and books on continued fractions.

Remark 9.79

In the remaining problems and remarks of this section, we dip a little deeper into the world's mathematical storehouse than we normally do.

Problem 9.791

The Riemann-Lebesgue theorem says that if $\int_{-\infty}^{\infty} f(x)dx$ and $\int_{-\infty}^{\infty} |f(x)|dx$ exist and u is real, then

$$\lim_{|u|\to\infty} \int_{-\infty}^{\infty} f(x)e^{iux}\, dx = 0.$$

Use this to show that if $f(x)$ is decent, if $F(s)$ is the Laplace transform of $f(x)$, and if $s = \sigma + it$, then

$$\lim_{|t|\to\infty} F(\sigma + it) = 0$$

for each sufficiently great σ. Use the latter result to show that e^{-s} cannot be the Laplace transform of a decent function.

* D. V. Widder, "The Laplace Transform," Princeton University Press, Princeton, N.J., 1941.

Problem 9.792

A theorem (known as the *Lebesgue criterion of dominated convergence* for taking limits under integral signs) says that if the integral

$$\int_{-\infty}^{\infty} \phi(u, x)dx$$

exists when $u \geqq u_0$, if

$$\lim_{u\to\infty} f(u, x) = 0$$

for each x, and if there is a function $\psi(x)$ such that $\psi(x) \geqq 0$,

$$|\phi(u, x)| \leqq \psi(x)$$

when $u \geqq u_0$, and

$$\int_{-\infty}^{\infty} \psi(x)dx$$

exists, then

$$\lim_{u\to\infty} \int_{-\infty}^{\infty} \phi(u, x)dx = 0.$$

Use this to show that, when F is the function of the previous problem,

$$\lim_{\sigma\to\infty} F(\sigma + it) = 0$$

for each t. If knowledge and ability permit, prove that this holds uniformly in t.

Remark 9.793

When σ is fixed and is large enough to make the integral exist, the function of t in

(9.7931) $$\frac{1}{\sqrt{2\pi}} F(\sigma + it) = \frac{1}{\sqrt{2\pi}} \int_0^{\infty} e^{-itx}e^{-\sigma x}f(x)dx$$

is the *Fourier* (1768–1830) *transform* of the function $\phi(x)$ which is $e^{-\sigma x}f(x)$ when $x > 0$ and is 0 when $x < 0$. One who is fortunate enough to know about the *Fourier transform inversion formulas*

(9.7932) $$\begin{cases} \psi(t) = \dfrac{1}{\sqrt{2\pi}} \displaystyle\int_{-\infty}^{\infty} e^{-itx}\phi(x)dx \\ \phi(x) = \dfrac{1}{\sqrt{2\pi}} \displaystyle\int_{-\infty}^{\infty} e^{itx}\psi(t)dt \end{cases}$$

can see the possibility of inverting (9.7931) to obtain

(9.7933) $$\phi(x) = \frac{1}{2\pi} \int_{-\infty}^{\infty} e^{itx}F(\sigma + it)dt$$

when $-\infty < x < \infty$ and

(9.7934) $$f(x) = \frac{1}{2\pi} \int_{-\infty}^{\infty} e^{(\sigma+it)x}F(\sigma + it)dt$$

when $x > 0$. This formula, which is often written in the form

(9.7935) $$f(x) = \frac{1}{2\pi i} \int_{\sigma-i\infty}^{\sigma+i\infty} e^{sx}F(s)ds$$

and in other forms which look quite different, is the *Mellin* (1854–1933) *formula* which expresses functions in terms of their Laplace transforms.

Studies of these things can be very interesting and profitable. It is easy to tell how these studies should be conducted. Simply spend a year or two making a study of Fourier transforms in which studies of Lebesgue integration, convergence in mean (or in L_2), the inversion formulas (9.7932), and the Parseval (–1836) formula

$$\int_{-\infty}^{\infty} |\psi(x)|^2 dx = \int_{-\infty}^{\infty} |\phi(x)|^2 dx \tag{9.7936}$$

play central roles. Spend another or the same year or two studying the theory of analytic functions of a complex variable. This puts us in a position where we do not have to drive nails with saws or cut off beams with hammers, as people do when they attack the formulas with inadequate equipment.

Remark 9.794

In the next section we will need the *Schwarz* (1843–1921) *inequality*

$$\int_a^b |F(x)G(x)| dx \leqq \sqrt{\int_a^b |F(x)|^2 dx} \sqrt{\int_a^b |G(x)|^2 dx} \tag{9.7941}$$

which holds whenever the integrals on the right side exist. This is an exceptionally potent weapon. There are many occasions on which persons who know and think of using this formula can shine while their less fortunate brethren flounder. Proof of the inequality can be eked out of the fact that

$$\int_a^b [|F(x)|^2 + \lambda |G(x)|]^2 dx \geqq 0$$

whenever λ is real.

9.8. Periodic Inputs. As in Section 6.7, let $f(x)$ be a function, having period h, for which the two integrals $\int_0^h f(x)dx$ and $\int_0^h |f(x)|^2 dx$ exist. We would like to know whether we can make the Laplace transform method work when f is not one of those cooperative functions whose transforms appear in tables. Without yet knowing why, we grind out the Fourier coefficients of f defined by (6.74) and obtain the Fourier series in

$$f(x) \sim \sum_{k=-\infty}^{\infty} b_k \phi_k(x) \tag{9.81}$$

where

$$\phi_k(x) = \frac{1}{h^{\frac{1}{2}}} e^{i(2\pi/h)kx}. \tag{9.811}$$

As we know, Laplace transforms of sinusoids are simple fractions. If we could multiply the members of (9.81) by e^{-sx}, then integrate over the infinite interval, then interchange the order of integration and summation, and then equate the results, we would obtain the formula

$$F(s) = \sum_{k=-\infty}^{\infty} \frac{b_k}{\sqrt{h}} \frac{1}{s - i(2\pi/h)k} \tag{9.82}$$

for the Laplace transform F of f. If all this can be done, we will have something reasonable to work with because the right side of (9.82) is nothing but a glorified partial fraction expansion of $F(s)$. The crucial fact is that the representation (9.82) makes it possible to obtain a similar representation of $F(s)/(s - m_k)$.

What we are going to do can be stated very simply. We are going to show that, whether the series in (9.81) converges or not, we can operate on (9.81) in the manner described above to obtain (9.82) whenever $s = \sigma + it$ and $\sigma > 0$; *the series in* (9.82) *converges to* $F(s)$ *over the whole half-plane to the right of the pure imaginary axis.* If the given function f has honorable engineering parentage, the series in (9.81) will surely converge to $f(x)$ and there is no difficulty in obtaining the formula

$$\int_0^\infty e^{-sx} f(x)dx = \int_0^\infty \sum_{k=-\infty}^{\infty} b_k e^{-sx}\phi_k(x)dx, \tag{9.83}$$

but this does not help us. The formula that we must prove is

$$\int_0^\infty e^{-sx} f(x)dx = \sum_{k=-\infty}^{\infty} \int_0^\infty b_k e^{-sx}\phi_k(x)dx, \tag{9.84}$$

and we cannot get from (9.83) to (9.84) without proving that it is possible to change the order of integration and summation, that is, to integrate the series termwise.

From our hypotheses and (9.811), we see that $f(x)$ and the partial sums

$$S_n(x) = \sum_{k=-n}^{n} b_k\phi_k(x) \tag{9.841}$$

of the Fourier series of $f(x)$ have period h and are integrable over each interval of length h. To obtain information applicable to $f(x)$, $S_n(x)$, and $f(x) - S_n(x)$, we suppose that $g(x)$ is any function which has period h and is integrable over $0 \leqq x \leqq h$. Then, for each $a > 0$, we can let m be the greatest integer for which $mh < a$ and write

$$\int_0^a e^{-sx}g(x)dx = \int_0^{mh} e^{-sx}g(x)dx + \epsilon(a) \tag{9.842}$$

where

$$\epsilon(a) = \int_{mh}^{a} e^{-sx}g(x)dx.$$

But, because $g(x)$ has period h,

$$|\epsilon(a)| \leqq \int_{mh}^{(m+1)h} e^{-\sigma x}|g(x)|dx$$
$$\leqq \int_{mh}^{(m+1)h} e^{-mh\sigma}|g(x)|dx = e^{-mh\sigma}\int_0^h |g(x)|dx.$$

Therefore $\epsilon(a) \to 0$ as $a \to \infty$ and hence $m \to \infty$. Again using periodicity of $g(x)$ gives

$$\int_0^{mh} e^{-sx}g(x)dx = \sum_{k=0}^{m-1}\int_{kh}^{(k+1)h} e^{-sx}g(x)dx$$
$$= \sum_{k=0}^{m-1}\int_0^h e^{-s(x-kh)}g(x)dx = \sum_{k=0}^{m-1}(e^{-hs})^k\int_0^h e^{-sx}g(x)dx$$

so

$$\lim_{m\to\infty}\int_0^{mh} e^{-sx}g(x)dx = \frac{1}{1-e^{-hs}}\int_0^h e^{-sx}g(x)dx.$$

These results and (9.842) show that $g(x)$ possesses a Laplace transform and

(9.843) $$\int_0^\infty e^{-sx}g(x)dx = \frac{1}{1-e^{-hs}}\int_0^h e^{-sx}g(x)dx.$$

This shows that $f(x)$ and $S_n(x)$ possess Laplace transforms. Our next step is to apply (9.843) with $g(x)$ replaced by $f(x) - S_n(x)$. Let

$$\epsilon_n = \int_0^h e^{-sx}[f(x) - S_n(x)]dx.$$

Use of the Schwarz inequality (9.7941) gives

$$|\epsilon_n|^2 \leqq \left[\int_0^h e^{-2\sigma x}dx\right]\left[\int_0^h |f(x) - S_n(x)|^2dx\right]$$

and use of (6.751) then shows that $\epsilon_n \to 0$ as $n \to \infty$. This shows that

$$\lim_{n\to\infty}\int_0^\infty e^{-sx}[f(x) - S_n(x)]dx = 0$$

and we are almost done. This can be put in the form

(9.844) $$\int_0^\infty e^{-sx}f(x)dx = \lim_{n\to\infty}\int_0^\infty e^{-sx}\sum_{k=-n}^{n} b_k\phi_k(x)dx.$$

Now we have the integral of a finite sum of integrable functions so we can interchange the order of summation and integration to obtain the desired result (9.84).

Problem 9.86

The formulas in Remark 9.775 show that

$$B_n(x) = Re \frac{-1}{i^n} \frac{2}{(2\pi)^n} \sum_{k=1}^{\infty} \frac{e^{2k\pi ix}}{k^n} \tag{9.861}$$

when $n = 1, 2, \ldots$. The Laplace transform of a function f is sometimes denoted by $\hat{f}$ (read "f hat," because f wears a hat). Show that, when s is real and positive,

$$\hat{B}_n(s) = Re \frac{-1}{i^n} \frac{2}{(2\pi)^n} \sum_{k=1}^{\infty} \frac{1}{k^n} \frac{s + 2k\pi i}{s^2 + 4k^2\pi^2}.$$

Show that

$$\hat{B}_1(s) = -2 \sum_{k=1}^{\infty} \frac{1}{s^2 + 4k^2\pi^2}. \tag{9.862}$$

Observe that this formula for $\hat{B}_1(s)$ looks very different from the one found in Problem 9.774. Show that equating the two gives the identity

$$\frac{e^{s/2} + e^{-s/2}}{e^{s/2} - e^{-s/2}} = \frac{2}{s} + 4s \sum_{k=1}^{\infty} \frac{1}{s^2 + 4k^2\pi^2}. \tag{9.863}$$

This nontrivial identity can be used to obtain very many others. Show that

$$\lim_{s \to 0+} \hat{B}_n(s) = -B_{n+1}(0) = \frac{-B_{n+1}}{(n+1)!}.$$

Problem 9.87

Letting $q(x)$ denote the square-wave function of Problem 9.773, show that

$$q(x) = \frac{4}{\pi} \left[\sin \frac{\pi}{h/2} x + \frac{1}{3} \sin \frac{3\pi}{h/2} x + \frac{1}{5} \sin \frac{5\pi}{h/2} x + \cdots \right].$$

Thus $q(x)$ is the imaginary part of the function $r(x)$ in

$$r(x) = \frac{4}{\pi} \sum_{k=0}^{\infty} \frac{1}{2k+1} e^{i[2(2k+1)\pi/h]x}. \tag{9.871}$$

Show that

$$\hat{r}(s) = \frac{4}{\pi} \sum_{k=0}^{\infty} \frac{1}{2k+1} \frac{s + i[2(2k+1)\pi/h]}{s^2 + 4(2k+1)^2\pi^2/h^2}$$

and hence that

$$\hat{q}(s) = \frac{8}{h} \sum_{k=0}^{\infty} \frac{1}{s^2 + 4(2k+1)^2\pi^2/h^2}. \tag{9.872}$$

Show that equating this to the result obtained in Problem 9.773 and then setting $h = 2$ gives the identity

$$\frac{e^{s/2} - e^{-s/2}}{e^{s/2} + e^{-s/2}} = 4s \sum_{k=0}^{\infty} \frac{1}{s^2 + (2k+1)^2\pi^2}. \tag{9.873}$$

Remark: The two formulas (9.863) and (9.873) are not unrelated to each other and to other interesting things. One who wishes to derive some formulas and tie various things together can show that these formulas are, respectively, equivalent to

$$\pi z \cot \pi z = 1 - 2z^2 \sum_{k=1}^{\infty} \frac{1}{k^2 - z^2} \tag{9.874}$$

$$\pi \tan \frac{\pi z}{2} = \sum_{k=0}^{\infty} \frac{4z}{(2k+1)^2 - z^2} \tag{9.875}$$

and that the second of these formulas can be derived from the first by using the identity

$$\pi z \tan \pi z = \pi z \cot \pi z - 2\pi z \cot 2\pi z$$

and replacing z by $z/2$. From the famous infinite product expansion

$$\sin \pi z = \pi z \prod_{k=1}^{\infty} \left(1 - \frac{z^2}{k^2}\right), \tag{9.876}$$

where the right side means

$$\lim_{n\to\infty} \pi z \left(1 - \frac{z^2}{1^2}\right)\left(1 - \frac{z^2}{2^2}\right) \cdots \left(1 - \frac{z^2}{n^2}\right),$$

we can obtain (9.874) by taking logarithms and differentiating. It is possible to obtain (9.876) from (9.874) by reversing the process. By starting with the definition (7.7922) of $z!$, it is easy to write an expression for $z!(-z)!$ and use (9.876) to prove that

$$z!(-z)! = \frac{\pi z}{\sin \pi z} \tag{9.877}$$

when z is not an integer; see Remark 7.792. Putting $z = \frac{1}{2}$ shows that

$$\left(\frac{1}{2}\right)! = \frac{\sqrt{\pi}}{2}, \qquad \left(-\frac{1}{2}\right)! = \sqrt{\pi}. \tag{9.878}$$

Putting $z = \frac{1}{2}$ in (9.876) shows that

$$\lim_{n\to\infty} \binom{2n}{n} \frac{\sqrt{n}}{2^{2n}} = \frac{1}{\sqrt{\pi}}. \tag{9.879}$$

This shows that when $2n$ coins are tossed, the probability of getting exactly n heads and n tails is of the order of $1/\sqrt{n\pi}$ when n is large.

9.9. Faltungs. The approach to the faltung (or convolution or resultant or superposition integral) formula in (6.87) and (6.91) by way of Laplace transforms is very direct. However the approach is tainted by the fact that we must assume that all functions are such that they possess Laplace transforms. The problem is that of finding the solution of the equation

$$a_0 \frac{d^n y}{dx^n} + a_1 \frac{d^{n-1} y}{dx^{n-1}} + \cdots + a_{n-1} \frac{dy}{dx} + a_n y = f(x) \tag{9.91}$$

for which

$$y(0) = y'(0) = \cdots = y^{(n-1)}(0) = 0. \tag{9.911}$$

To simplify matters, we suppose that the zeros $s_1, s_2, \ldots, s_n$ of the impedance $Z(s)$ of the operator L_a in (9.91) are distinct and hence that there exist constants $A_1, A_2, \ldots, A_n$ for which

$$\frac{1}{Z(s)} = \sum_{k=1}^{n} \frac{A_k}{s - s_k}. \tag{9.912}$$

Because of (9.911), taking Laplace transforms of the members of (9.91) gives $Z(s)Y(s) = F(s)$ and hence

$$Y(s) = \left(\sum_{k=1}^{n} \frac{A_k}{s - s_k} \right) F(s). \tag{9.913}$$

The sum in parentheses is the Laplace transform of the function $y_0(x)$ defined by

$$y_0(x) = \sum_{k=1}^{n} A_k e^{s_k x} \tag{9.914}$$

and $F(s)$ is the Laplace transform of $f(x)$. It follows from Problem 9.193 that the product of the two transforms is the transform of the right member of the equation

$$y(x) = \int_0^x y_0(x - t) f(t)\, dt. \tag{9.92}$$

Hence (9.92) follows from (9.913). In case the zeros of $Z(s)$ are not distinct, the right side of (9.914) must be replaced by the less attractive right side of (6.865), and (9.92) follows in the same way.

Proof of Theorem 6.92 by use of Laplace transforms is exceedingly simple. Because of (6.922), taking Laplace transforms of (6.921) gives

$$Z(s)Y_0(s) - 1 = 0 \tag{9.93}$$

where $Y_0(s)$ is the Laplace transform of $y_0(x)$. Thus the transform of $y_0(x)$ is $1/Z(s)$ and the result follows.

Finally, Laplace transforms show very simply that $y_0(x)$ is the solution of (9.91) for which $f(x)$ is a unit impulse and (9.911) holds. Taking Laplace transforms gives $Z(s)Y(s) = 1$ and it follows that $y(x) = y_0(x)$.

Problem 9.94

Let $T(y)$ be the time required for a bead, starting from rest at a point $P(x, y)$ in a vertical plane, to slide without friction down a curve C to the origin. Let $s(u)$ be the distance, measured along C, from the origin to the point Q with ordinate u. If $0 < u < y$, then the speed of the bead when it reaches Q is $\sqrt{2g(y-u)}$ and the time required to traverse a short arc of length Δs is roughly $\Delta s/\sqrt{2g(y-u)}$. It follows that

$$T(y) = \int_0^y \frac{s'(u)}{\sqrt{2g(y-u)}}\,du. \tag{9.941}$$

The *Abel* (1802–1829) *mechanical problem* is the problem of finding $s(u)$, and perhaps more orthodox equations of the curve C, when $T(y)$ is a given function. Show that (9.941) has the form

$$h(y) = \int_0^y (y-u)^{-p} g'(u)\,du \tag{9.942}$$

where $p = \frac{1}{2}$. Let $H(s)$ and $G(s)$ be the Laplace transforms of h and g. With the aid of Problem 9.192, show that

$$G(s) = \frac{1}{(-p)!}\, s^{-p} H(s).$$

Show that s^{-p} is the Laplace transform of $u^{p-1}/(p-1)!$ and use Problem 9.193 to show that

$$g(y) = \frac{1}{(-p)!(p-1)!}\int_0^y (y-u)^{p-1} h(u)\,du. \tag{9.943}$$

This is the result of solving (9.942) for $g(y)$. Using the fact that $(-\frac{1}{2})! = \sqrt{\pi}$, show that the result of solving (9.941) for $s(y)$ is

$$s(y) = \frac{1}{\pi\sqrt{2g}}\int_0^y (y-u)^{-\frac{1}{2}} T(u)\,du. \tag{9.944}$$

For the tautochrone (equal time) problem, $T(y)$ is a given constant, say A. Show that, in this case,

$$s(y) = \frac{2A}{\pi\sqrt{2g}}\sqrt{y}$$

and

$$1 + \left(\frac{dx}{dy}\right)^2 = [s'(y)]^2 = \frac{a}{y} \tag{9.945}$$

where a is a constant depending upon A. Finally, separate the variables, simplify the result by means of the substitution $y = 2a \sin^2 \frac{1}{2}\theta$, and obtain

$$x = a(\theta + \sin\theta), \qquad y = a(1 - \cos\theta). \tag{9.946}$$

These are parametric equations of a cycloid, one arch of which is the curve which furnishes the solution of the tautochrone problem. This cycloid is the path traced by the point initially at the bottom of the circle with center at $(0, a)$ and radius a when this circle rolls to and fro, without slipping, under its upper horizontal tangent.

CHAPTER 10

BENDING OF BEAMS

10.0. Introduction. In order to design beams to support specified loads, it is necessary to have appropriate formulas. These formulas are obtained by means of differential equations. The simplest problems lead to complicated differential equations which cannot be solved by simple methods. One either finds approximations to solutions of the equations or replaces the equations by simpler approximate equations which can be more easily solved. In the following discussion, the complicated differential equations are replaced by approximate equations having the form $y''(x) = f(x)$. When the values of $y(x_0)$ and $y'(x_0)$ are known for some value x_0 of x, determination of $y'(x)$ and then $y(x)$ is accomplished by methods of the calculus set forth in Chapter 2. The problems may be described as problems in *elastic stability*.

A beam of uniform cross section (which may, for example, be an I beam or a beam having a rectangular cross section) may be regarded as being composed of many small fibers running the length of the beam. When the beam is bent, the fibers in one part of the beam are stretched and those in the other part of the beam are compressed. Between these parts there is a *neutral surface* of fibers which are neither stretched nor compressed. Let I be the moment of inertia of the area of a given cross section of the beam, computed with reference to the line (say AB) in which this cross section intersects the neutral surface. Let E denote Young's modulus (see Section 1.4) for the material constituting the beam.

In ordinary circumstances, the beam remains relatively straight after bending. It may then be assumed that two near-by cross sections of the straight beam are, when the beam is bent, deformed into two plane sections of the bent beam and that the extensions of these sections intersect at the center of curvature of the fibers lying between the sections. It is then possible to use fundamental principles of geometry, physics, and calculus to show that the tensile and compressive forces acting on a given cross section of the beam have a moment about AB equal to EI/R where R is the radius of curvature of the fibers at the cross section. This moment EI/R tends to straighten the beam. When the beam is bent in static equilibrium, this moment EI/R must be balanced by the total moment M (about AB) of all other forces acting upon one of the two segments into which the cross section separates the beam. Thus $EI/R = M$. When one of the fibers of the bent beam lies in an xy plane we can use the standard formula for $1/R$ to put the equation of the fiber in the form

$$EI \frac{\dfrac{d^2y}{dx^2}}{\left[1 + \left(\dfrac{dy}{dx}\right)^2\right]^{\frac{3}{2}}} = M. \tag{10.1}$$

When the beam is, at all of its points, nearly parallel to the x axis, so that dy/dx is near 0 and the denominator in (10.1) is near 1, it is standard practice to replace (10.1) by the approximate equation

$$EI \frac{d^2y}{dx^2} = M. \tag{10.2}$$

The quantity EI is a measure of the ability of the beam to resist bending; it is called the *flexural rigidity* of the beam. Many textbooks in physics and engineering, particularly books on strength of materials, present these matters in greater detail and provide many problems, of which the following are typical.*

Problem 10.3

A *cantilever beam* of length l is placed on the interval $0 \leqq x \leqq l$ of a horizontal x axis. The end at $x = 0$ is clamped so that it remains horizontal, and the beam is allowed to sag under the load of:

(i) a single weight W at the free end
(ii) a uniform weight w per unit length
(iii) both (i) and (ii)

Find in each case an approximation to the equation of the beam, and find how much the free end sags below the clamped end. *Ans.:*

(i) $y = -\dfrac{W[3lx^2 - x^3]}{6EI}$; Sag $= \dfrac{Wl^3}{3EI}$

(ii) $y = -\dfrac{w[6l^2x^2 - 4lx^3 + x^4]}{24EI}$; Sag $= \dfrac{wl^4}{8EI}$

(iii) y = sum of y's in (i) and (ii); Sag $= \dfrac{l^3[8W + 3wl]}{24EI}$.

* For the theory of oscillation of vibrating beams, see Theodor von Kármán (1881–) and M. A. Biot (1905–), "Mathematical Methods in Engineering," McGraw-Hill Book Company, Inc., New York, 1940.

Problem 10.4

A beam of length $2l$ has its ends resting on supports at the same horizontal level and is loaded with:

(i) a single weight W at the center
(ii) a uniform weight w per unit length
(iii) both (i) and (ii)

Taking the x axis horizontal and the origin at the center of the bent beam, find in each case an approximation to the equation of the beam, and find how much the center sags below the ends. *Ans.:*

$$\text{(i)}\quad y = \frac{W[3lx^2 - |x|^3]}{12EI}; \qquad \text{Sag} = \frac{Wl^3}{6EI}$$

$$\text{(ii)}\quad y = \frac{w[6l^2x^2 - x^4]}{24EI}; \qquad \text{Sag} = \frac{5wl^4}{24EI}$$

$$\text{(iii)}\quad y = \text{sum of } y\text{'s in (i) and (ii)}; \qquad \text{Sag} = \frac{l^3[4W + 5wl]}{24EI}.$$

Problem 10.5

A horizontal beam of length $2l$ has its ends supported at the points $(-l, 0)$ and $(l, 0)$ of an xy plane. Let a be a number for which $0 < a < l$, and let the beam be allowed to sag under the load of a single weight W placed on the beam at the point $(a, 0)$. Find an approximation to the equation of the beam and to the coordinates of the lowest point on the beam. At what point on the beam should the weight be placed in order to obtain a maximum value for the slope of the beam at the point upon which the weight rests? *Ans.:* It is found that (10.2) becomes the first of the formulas

$$\text{(10.51)} \qquad \frac{2lEI}{W}\frac{d^2y}{dx^2} = (l - a)(l + x), \qquad \frac{2lEI}{W}\frac{d^2y}{dx^2} = (l + a)(l - x)$$

when $-l \leqq x \leqq a$ and the second when $a \leqq x \leqq l$. It follows that the formula

$$\text{(10.52)} \qquad \frac{2lEI}{W}\frac{d^2y}{dx^2} = l^2 - ax - l|a - x|$$

holds over the whole interval $-l \leq x \leq l$. Hence constants c_1 and c_2 exist such that

$$\text{(10.53)} \qquad \frac{12lEI}{W}y = 3l^2x^2 - ax^3 - l|a - x|^3 + c_1x + c_2.$$

The fact that $y = 0$ when $x = l$ and when $x = -l$ gives two equations to solve for c_1 and c_2. The results are

$$\text{(10.54)} \qquad c_1 = -2al^2 - a^3, \qquad c_2 = 3a^2l^2 - 2l^4.$$

Considering separately the cases in which $-l \leqq x \leqq a$ and $a \leqq x \leqq l$, we substitute in (10.53) to find that the equation of the beam is

$$\text{(10.55)} \qquad y = \frac{W(l-a)}{12lEI}[(l + x)^3 - (3l^2 + 2al - a^2)(l + x)] \qquad -l \leqq x \leqq a$$

$$= \frac{W(l+a)}{12lEI}[(l - x)^3 - (3l^2 - 2al - a^2)(l - x)] \qquad a \leqq x \leqq l.$$

It is possible to obtain the equation (10.55) of the beam in a different way. From (10.51), it is seen that four constants c_1, c_2, c_3, and c_4 exist such that

$$\frac{12lEI}{W}\,y = (l - a)[(l + x)^3 + c_1(l + x) + c_2] \qquad -l \leqq x \leqq a$$

and

$$\frac{12lEI}{W}\,y = (l + a)[(l - x)^3 + c_3(l - x) + c_4] \qquad a \leqq x \leqq l.$$

Upon determining the four constants so that $y(-l) = y(l) = 0$ and so that $y(x)$ and $y'(x)$ are continuous at $x = a$, we obtain (10.55).

Differentiation of (10.55) gives

$$\text{(10.56)} \qquad \begin{aligned} \frac{dy}{dx} &= \frac{W(l - a)}{12lEI}[\;\;3(l + x)^2 - (3l^2 + 2al - a^2)] \qquad && -l \leqq x \leqq a \\ &= \frac{W(l + a)}{12lEI}[-3(l - x)^2 + (3l^2 - 2al - a^2)] && a \leqq x \leqq l. \end{aligned}$$

As (10.51) shows, $y''(x) > 0$ over $-l < x < l$, and it follows that the x coordinate of the lowest point of the beam is the unique value of x in the interval $-l \leqq x \leqq l$ for which $y'(x) = 0$. This coordinate, say x_0, is found to be

$$\text{(10.57)} \qquad x_0 = \sqrt{l^2 + \tfrac{1}{3}a(2l - a)} - l.$$

Since $0 < x_0 < a$, substitution in the first part of (10.55) shows that the y coordinate of the lowest point of the beam is

$$\text{(10.58)} \qquad y_0 = -\frac{W(l - a)(l + a)(3l - a)}{18lEI}\sqrt{l^2 + \tfrac{1}{3}a(2l - a)}.$$

The sag and slope of the beam at the point on which the weight rests are given by the simpler formulas

$$\text{(10.59)} \qquad -y(a) = \frac{W}{6lEI}(l^2 - a^2)^2, \qquad y'(a) = \frac{Wa}{3lEI}(l^2 - a^2).$$

The slope of the beam at the point upon which the weight rests depends upon a. Use of ordinary rules for obtaining the maximum value of a function shows that this slope is a maximum when $a = \sqrt{3}\,l/3 = .577l$, that is, when the weight is a little more than halfway from the center to the end of the beam. *Remark:* Even those unaccustomed to making connections between equations and physical phenomena should find it easy to place a weight upon a flexible bar of wood or metal and to see that (10.57) seems to give the distance from the center to the lowest point of the bar. It is especially interesting to see what happens when the weight is placed near an end of the bar.

CHAPTER 11

SERIES EXPANSIONS OF OPERATORS

11.1. Introduction. This brief chapter contains several very interesting ideas. Readers are hereby warned that some of the ideas are more interesting than useful and that one who reads it is in danger of mixing pleasure with business.

11.2. Series Expansions of Operators. When operators commute, the algebra of the operators is so much like the algebra of real numbers that we may wonder whether we can do anything with series of operators. We begin with a simple question. By using the fact that

$$\frac{1}{1-x} = 1 + x + x^2 + \cdots$$

if and only if $|x| < 1$ we see that, if m is a constant not 0, then the first of the two formulas

$$\text{(11.21)} \qquad \frac{1}{D-m} \overset{?}{=} -\frac{1}{m}\frac{1}{1-D/m} \overset{?}{=} -\frac{1}{m} - \frac{D}{m^2} - \frac{D^2}{m^3} - \frac{D^3}{m^4} - \cdots$$

and

$$\text{(11.22)} \qquad \frac{1}{D-m} \overset{?}{=} \frac{1}{D}\frac{1}{1-m/D} \overset{?}{=} \frac{1}{D} + \frac{m}{D^2} + \frac{m^2}{D^3} + \frac{m^3}{D^4} + \cdots$$

is valid when D is a constant for which $|D/m| < 1$, and the second is valid when D is a constant for which $|m/D| < 1$; the question is whether or not these are *operational identities*, that is, identities when D is an operator.*

We look first at (11.21) and the question whether or not

$$\text{(11.23)} \qquad \frac{1}{D-m} f \overset{?}{=} -\frac{f}{m} - \frac{Df}{m^2} - \frac{D^2f}{m^3} - \frac{D^3f}{m^4} - \cdots.$$

The operator on the left applies to a function $f(x)$ if it is continuous. The operator on the right applies to each function $f(x)$, having derivatives of all orders, for which the series converges. Let us try $f = x^3$. Assuming that (11.23) is correct when $f = x^3$, we obtain immediately

$$\text{(11.231)} \qquad \frac{1}{D-m} x^3 = -\frac{x^3}{m} - \frac{3x^2}{m^2} - \frac{6x}{m^3} - \frac{6}{m^4}.$$

Letting $y(x)$ denote the right member of (11.231) we can show easily that

$$(D - m)y = x^3.$$

* There is, of course, the possibility of trying to replace D by a more general operator L or L^{-1}.

However it is not true that $y(x_0) = 0$ unless by accident x_0 is one of the roots of the cubic equation $y(x) = 0$. It thus appears that the expansion in the last member of (11.21) serves in some cases to furnish quickly a solution of $(D - m)y = f$. But (11.21) is not an operational identity since the last member does not ordinarily furnish the particular solution of $(D - m)y = f$ for which $y(x_0) = 0$. Hence, except for the following problem, we disregard (11.21).

Problem 11.232

Determine whether or not the following steps, which purport to find the particular solution of the equation $(D - 2)(D - 3)y = x^3e^{2x}$ for which

$$y(0) = y'(0) = 0,$$

are correct:

$$\begin{aligned} y &= \frac{1}{(D-2)(D-3)} x^3e^{2x} = \frac{1}{D-3} x^3e^{2x} - \frac{1}{D-2} x^3e^{2x} = e^{2x}\frac{1}{D-1} x^3 - e^{2x}\frac{1}{D} x^3 \\ &= e^{2x}[-1 - D - D^2 - \cdots]x^3 - e^{2x}D^{-1}x^3 = e^{2x}[-x^3 - 3x^2 - 6x - 6] - \tfrac{1}{4}e^{2x}x^4. \end{aligned}$$

Show that the result does not agree with Problem 6.8794, but that it does provide an easy way of obtaining a particular solution of the given equation.

Problem 11.24

By use of algebraic manipulations such as those in (11.22) and the fact that the binomial formula

$$(1 + z)^r = 1 + \frac{r}{1} z + \frac{r(r-1)}{1 \cdot 2} z^2 + \frac{r(r-1)(r-2)}{1 \cdot 2 \cdot 3} z^3 + \cdots$$

is valid when r is real and $|z| < 1$, prove that

$$\frac{D^{\sigma-1}}{(D-m)^\sigma} = \frac{1}{D} + \frac{\sigma}{1}\frac{m}{D^2} + \frac{\sigma(\sigma+1)}{1 \cdot 2}\frac{m^2}{D^3} + \frac{\sigma(\sigma+1)(\sigma+2)}{1 \cdot 2 \cdot 3}\frac{m^3}{D^4} + \cdots \tag{11.241}$$

and

$$\frac{1}{(D-m)^\sigma} = \frac{1}{D^\sigma} + \frac{\sigma}{1}\frac{m}{D^{\sigma+1}} + \frac{\sigma(\sigma+1)}{1 \cdot 2}\frac{m^2}{D^{\sigma+2}} + \frac{\sigma(\sigma+1)(\sigma+2)}{1 \cdot 2 \cdot 3}\frac{m^3}{D^{\sigma+3}} + \cdots \tag{11.242}$$

are algebraic identities when σ is a positive integer, m and D are numbers, and $|D| > |m|$. To what do (11.241) and (11.242) reduce when $\sigma = 1$?

We now prove that

$$\frac{1}{D-m} = \frac{1}{D} + \frac{m}{D^2} + \frac{m^2}{D^3} + \cdots \tag{11.3}$$

is an operational identity by evaluating the result of applying the operator on the right to a function f and observing that the result is $(D - m)^{-1}f$. Multiplying (6.8611) by m^{k-1} gives, for each $k = 1, 2, 3, \ldots,$

$$\frac{m^{k-1}}{D^k} f = \int_{x_0}^{x} \frac{[m(x-t)]^{k-1}}{(k-1)!} f(t)\,dt.$$

Addition gives

$$\sum_{k=1}^{n} \frac{m^{k-1}}{D^k} f = \int_{x_0}^{x} \left[\sum_{k=1}^{n} \frac{\{m(x-t)\}^{k-1}}{(k-1)!} \right] f(t)dt.$$

We are now prepared to use the fact that

$$\lim_{n\to\infty} \sum_{k=1}^{n} \frac{\{m(x-t)\}^{k-1}}{(k-1)!} = e^{m(x-t)}.$$

Whether we assume that $f(x)$ is continuous or that $f(x)$ merely satisfies the more general conditions set forth after (6.801), it follows* that

$$\lim_{n\to\infty} \int_{x_0}^{x} \sum_{k=1}^{n} \frac{[m(x-t)]^{k-1}}{(k-1)!} f(t)dt = \int_{x_0}^{x} e^{m(x-t)} f(t)dt.$$

Therefore,

(11.31) $$\sum_{k=1}^{\infty} \frac{m^{k-1}}{D^k} f = \int_{x_0}^{x} e^{m(x-t)} f(t)dt.$$

The right side of (11.31) is familiar; it is, by (6.833), simply $(D-m)^{-1}f$. Thus

$$(D-m)^{-1}f = \sum_{k=1}^{\infty} m^{k-1}D^{-k}f,$$

and the identity (11.3) is established.

There are many other ways of arriving at the identity (11.3). One method is that of *successive approximations* used in the proof of Picard's theorem in Chapter 15; in fact, the identity is a corollary of Picard's theorem.

Another interesting method is the method of *successive substitution*. To illustrate this method, let

(11.4) $$y = (D-m)^{-1}f.$$

Then $(D-m)y = f$ and $y(x_0) = 0$ so that $Dy = f + my$ and

(11.41) $$y = D^{-1}f + mD^{-1}y.$$

Substituting the right member for the last y gives

(11.42) $$y = D^{-1}f + mD^{-1}[D^{-1}f + mD^{-1}y] = D^{-1}f + mD^{-2}f + m^2D^{-2}y.$$

Substituting the right member of (11.41) for the last y in (11.42) gives

$$y = D^{-1}f + mD^{-2}f + m^2D^{-3}f + m^3D^{-3}y.$$

By continuing the process, we obtain for each $n = 1, 2, 3, \ldots$

$$y = D^{-1}f + mD^{-2}f + \cdots + m^{k-1}D^{-k}f + R_k(x)$$

* The fact that the limit of the integral is the integral of the limit is the crucial fact involved; this point is considered in the proof of Picard's theorem in Chapter 15.

where

$$R_k(x) = m^k D^{-k} y = m \int_{x_0}^{x} \frac{m^{k-1}(x-t)^{k-1}}{(k-1)!} y(t)dt.$$

It can be shown, by methods such as those used in Chapter 15, that $R_k(x)$ converges* to 0. Therefore,

$$y = D^{-1}f + mD^{-2}f + m^2D^{-3}f + \cdots.$$

Comparing this result with (11.4) we obtain again the identity (11.3).

Problem 11.51

Assuming that $y(x)$ is the function for which $y(0) = 1$ and

$$\frac{dy}{dx} = y$$

show that (when $x_0 = 0$)

$$y = 1 + D^{-1}y,$$

and use the method of successive substitution to find $y(x)$.

Problem 11.52

Assuming that $y(x)$ is the function for which $y(0) = 1$, $y'(0) = 0$, and

$$\frac{d}{dx}\left(x\frac{dy}{dx}\right) + xy = 0$$

show that (when $x_0 = 0$)

$$x\frac{dy}{dx} = -D^{-1}(xy)$$
$$y = 1 - D^{-1}[x^{-1}D^{-1}(xy)],$$

and use the method of successive substitution to find $y(x)$. Show that your solution should be Bessel's function $J_0(x)$.

Problem 11.53

Show that if $y(x)$ is a continuous function for which $y(0) = 0$ and

(11.531) $$\frac{dy}{dx} - y = \log x \qquad x > 0$$

then use of the identity (11.3) gives

(11.532) $$y(x) = (e^x - 1)\log x - \Phi(x)$$

where

$$\Phi(x) = x + \frac{x^2}{2!}\left(1+\frac{1}{2}\right) + \frac{x^3}{3!}\left(1+\frac{1}{2}+\frac{1}{3}\right) + \frac{x^4}{4!}\left(1+\frac{1}{2}+\frac{1}{3}+\frac{1}{4}\right) + \cdots.$$

Tell why Cauchy rather than Riemann integrals must be used. Show, by direct methods not involving (11.3), that, if $y(x)$ is defined for $x > 0$ by (11.532), then

* The convergence is uniform over each finite interval in which (11.4) holds.

$y(x) \to 0$ as $x \to 0$ and $y(x)$ satisfies (11.531). Solve (11.531) by use of the integrating factor e^{-x}, and use your result with (11.532) to obtain the formula

$$\int_0^x e^{-t} \log t \, dt = (1 - e^{-x}) \log x - e^{-x} \Phi(x).$$

Hint: By use of the fact that $t^n \log t \to 0$ as $t \to 0$ when $n = 1, 2, 3, \ldots$, it can be shown by integration by parts that when $x > 0$

$$\int_0^x t^n \log t \, dt = \frac{x^{n+1}}{n+1} \log x - \frac{x^{n+1}}{(n+1)^2} \qquad n = 0, 1, 2, \ldots .$$

We now give a straightforward derivation of an expansion of $(D - m)^{-\sigma}$ when σ is a positive integer. Replacing k by σ in (6.861) gives

$$\frac{1}{(D - m)^\sigma} f = \int_{x_0}^x \frac{(x - t)^{\sigma - 1}}{(\sigma - 1)!} e^{m(x-t)} f(t) dt.$$

By use of the formula

$$e^{m(x-t)} = \sum_{k=0}^{\infty} \frac{m^k (x - t)^k}{k!}$$

and, as before, of the methods of Chapter 15, it can be shown that the integral of the series is the series of integrals; thus

$$(D - m)^{-\sigma} f = \sum_{k=0}^{\infty} \frac{(k + \sigma - 1)! m^k}{k!(\sigma - 1)!} \int_{x_0}^x \frac{(x - t)^{k+\sigma-1}}{(k + \sigma - 1)!} f(t) dt,$$

and use of (6.8611) gives

$$(D - m)^{-\sigma} f = \sum_{k=0}^{\infty} \frac{(k + \sigma - 1)!}{k!(\sigma - 1)!} \frac{m^k}{D^{k+\sigma}} f.$$

Therefore,

$$\frac{1}{(D - m)^\sigma} = \frac{1}{D^\sigma} + \frac{\sigma}{1} \frac{m}{D^{\sigma+1}} + \frac{\sigma(\sigma + 1)}{1 \cdot 2} \frac{m^2}{D^{\sigma+2}} + \cdots . \tag{11.6}$$

Thus we have proved the operational identity that corresponds to the algebraic identity (11.242). If $\sigma = 1$, (11.6) becomes (11.3).

When the operators in (11.6) are applied to a function $f(x)$ of the types we are considering, it is possible to use uniform convergence of all the series involved to justify differentiating $\sigma - 1$ times with respect to x; in this way we obtain the operational identity

$$\frac{D^{\sigma-1}}{(D - m)^\sigma} = \frac{1}{D} + \frac{\sigma}{1} \frac{m}{D^2} + \frac{\sigma(\sigma + 1)}{1 \cdot 2} \frac{m^2}{D^3} + \cdots , \tag{11.61}$$

which corresponds to the algebraic identity (11.241).

We are now able to expand the reciprocal L^{-1} of each operator of the form

$$L = a_0(D - m_1)^{\sigma_1}(D - m_2)^{\sigma_2} \cdots (D - m_k)^{\sigma_k},$$

in which $k > 0$ and the σ's are positive integers, into a power series in D^{-1}. In the first place, L^{-1} may be represented in either one of the two forms

$$\sum \frac{A}{(D-m)^\sigma}, \qquad \sum \frac{AD^{\sigma-1}}{(D-m)^\sigma};$$

these are finite sums representing the two kinds of partial-fraction expansions. In the next place, each individual fraction is given as a power series in D^{-1} by one of the formulas (11.6) and (11.61). Therefore L^{-1} must be representable in the form

$$\frac{1}{L} = \sum_{n=1}^{\infty} \frac{B_n}{D^n} = B_1 \frac{1}{D} + B_2 \frac{1}{D^2} + B_3 \frac{1}{D^3} + \cdots. \tag{11.7}$$

Either one of the two partial-fraction expansions of L^{-1} may be used to obtain this expansion of L^{-1}. A contribution (which may be 0) to each B_n is made by the coefficient of D^{-k} in the expansion of each partial fraction.

Problem 11.81

Use the formula

$$\frac{1}{1+D^4} = \frac{1}{D^4} - \frac{1}{D^8} + \frac{1}{D^{12}} - \frac{1}{D^{16}} + \cdots,$$

to show that the solution of $(D^4 + 1)y = 1$, for which

$$y(1) = y'(1) = y''(1) = y'''(1) = 0,$$

is

$$y = \frac{(x-1)^4}{4!} - \frac{(x-1)^8}{8!} + \frac{(x-1)^{12}}{12!} - \frac{(x-1)^{16}}{16!} + \cdots.$$

Remark: Finding the solution of $(D^4 + 1)y = 1$ for which

$$y(1) = 1,\ y'(1) = 2,\ y''(1) = 3,\ y'''(1) = 4,$$

is more tedious.

Problem 11.82

Obtain the first terms of the expansion in powers of D^{-1} of

$$[(D-m_1)^3(D-m_2)]^{-1}.$$

Remark 11.9

In concluding this chapter on series expansions of operators, it is interesting to look at operators *defined* by series. For example, let the operator e^{hD} be defined by

$$e^{hD} = 1 + hD + \frac{h^2D^2}{2!} + \frac{h^3D^3}{3!} + \cdots$$

where h is a constant. If $f(x)$ has derivatives of all orders, then

$$e^{hD}f = f(x) + \frac{h}{1} f'(x) + \frac{h^2}{2!} f''(x) + \frac{h^3}{3!} f'''(x) + \cdots,$$

provided that the series on the right converges. The right member reminds one of the formula*

$$f(x+h) = f(x) + \frac{h}{1} f'(x) + \frac{h^2}{2!} f''(x) + \frac{h^3}{3!} f'''(x) + \cdots$$

which holds when $f(x)$ is an *analytic function,* that is, a function such that its Taylor series converges to it. Thus, if $f(x)$ is an analytic function,

$$e^{hD}f(x) = f(x+h).$$

We can now point out an essential difference between the operator p of Heaviside and the operator D: A fundamental property of the operator p is that the equation

$$e^{hp}f(x) = f(x+h)$$

holds for each function $f(x)$ and, in particular, for the discontinuous Heaviside unit function.

Problem 11.91

Show that, when D and a are properly restricted numbers,

$$(D^2 + a^2)^{-\frac{1}{2}} = \frac{1}{D} - \frac{2!a^2}{2^2 1!1!}\frac{1}{D^3} + \frac{4!a^4}{2^4 2!2!}\frac{1}{D^5} - \frac{6!a^6}{2^6 3!3!}\frac{1}{D^7} + \cdots + (-1)^n \frac{(2n)!a^{2n}}{2^{2n}n!n!}\frac{1}{D^{2n+1}} + \cdots$$

is an algebraic identity. Taking the equality as the definition of the operator on the left, show that

$$\frac{1}{\sqrt{D^2+a^2}} f = \int_{x_0}^{x} J_0(ax - at)f(t)dt$$

where J_0 is Bessel's function of order 0 (see Section 7.8). Using this result, show that

$$\frac{1}{\sqrt{D^2+a^2}}\frac{1}{\sqrt{D^2+a^2}} f = \int_{x_0}^{x} f(t)dt \int_{t}^{x} J_0(ax - au)J_0(au - at)du.$$

Is there any connection between this formula and the formula

$$\frac{1}{D^2+a^2} f = \frac{1}{a}\int_{x_0}^{x} \sin a(x-t)f(t)dt$$

which was obtained in Problem 6.874?

* Doubtless this formula would look more familiar if x and h were interchanged in the formula, but obviously the names of the numbers are not significant.

CHAPTER 12

EIGENVALUES, FOURIER SERIES, AND PARTIAL DIFFERENTIAL EQUATIONS

12.0. Introduction. This chapter is designed to give an introduction to and to set forth relations among several important concepts such as *exact linear equation, integrating factor, adjoint equation, Lagrange's formula, Green's formula, self-adjoint operator, eigenvalue* (characteristic value) *and eigenfunction* (characteristic function), *Sturm-Liouville equation and system, orthonormal set, completeness,* and *Fourier series in general as well as in trigonometric and complex exponential functions.* In Section 12.9, we show how these concepts are used in the Fourier method of solving boundary-value problems involving partial differential equations.

These concepts appear in many phases of science, and it is not unlikely that the reader has been mystified by one or more of them in courses in mathematics, physics, chemistry, or engineering. It is impossible to give in this book or in any other single book a thorough treatment of these concepts which adequately covers their theory and applications.* However, it is possible to set forth fundamental definitions of, properties of, and relations among these concepts in a few pages. We proceed.

12.1. Exact Linear Equations. The linear equation

$$\frac{d^2y}{dx^2} + x\frac{dy}{dx} + y = \sin x \tag{12.11}$$

may be written in the form

$$\frac{d}{dx}\left\{\frac{dy}{dx} + xy\right\} = \sin x. \tag{12.12}$$

* In fact, it is impossible to give a reasonably short list of references to works which, collectively, are adequate. One who wishes to make a serious study of these concepts and their applications may find plenty of references by consulting the subject index at the end of a volume of *Mathematical Reviews.* This periodical, giving abstracts of current mathematical literature, is published by the American Mathematical Society, Providence, R.I. An excellent way to accumulate references is to look up books and papers to which references are made by *Mathematical Reviews,* to look up books and papers to which references are made in the books and papers already found, and to continue the process until one has an abundance of references. The results will amaze a person who is unfamiliar with the scope of scientific literature.

These equations hold if and only if

$$\frac{dy}{dx} + xy = c_1 - \cos x; \tag{12.121}$$

thus the problem of solving (12.11) is reduced to the simpler problem of solving the first-order linear differential equation (12.121). By use of the operator D, (12.11) and (12.12) can be written, respectively,

$$(D^2 + xD + 1)y = \sin x, \qquad D(D + x)y = \sin x. \tag{12.13}$$

We see that the differential equation (12.13) and the operator $D^2 + xD + 1$ are *exact* in accordance with the following definition:

DEFINITION 12.14. *A differential equation*

$$(a_0D^n + a_1D^{n-1} + \cdots + a_{n-1}D + a_n)y = f \tag{12.141}$$

and the operator

$$L_a = a_0D^n + a_1D^{n-1} + \cdots + a_{n-1}D + a_n \tag{12.142}$$

are said to be exact if there exists an operator

$$L_b = b_0D^{n-1} + b_1D^{n-2} + \cdots + b_{n-2}D + b_{n-1} \tag{12.143}$$

of order one less than the order of L_a *such that* $L_a = DL_b$.

Thus, to say that an operator is exact means merely that it can be factored (see Section 6.8) in a simple special way. The following theorem furnishes an easy method of determining whether a given second-order operator is exact:

THEOREM 12.15. *If* a_0, a_1, *and* a_2 *are functions of* x *for which* $a_0''(x)$ *and* $a_1'(x)$ *exist, then the equation*

$$a_0y'' + a_1y' + a_2y = f \tag{12.151}$$

and the operator

$$L_a = a_0D^2 + a_1D + a_2 \tag{12.152}$$

are exact if and only if

$$a_0'' - a_1' + a_2 = 0. \tag{12.153}$$

Suppose first that (12.151) and (12.152) are exact. Then functions $b_0(x)$ and $b_1(x)$ exist such that

$$a_0D^2 + a_1D + a_2 = D(b_0D + b_1),$$

that is, such that

$$a_0\frac{d^2y}{dx^2} + a_1\frac{dy}{dx} + a_2y = \frac{d}{dx}\left(b_0\frac{dy}{dx} + b_1y\right) \tag{12.154}$$

for each function $y(x)$ having two derivatives. Considering in turn the functions $y = 1$ and $y = x$, we see that the derivatives b_1' and b_0' must exist. Hence the right member of (12.154) can be written in the form

$$b_0 \frac{d^2y}{dx^2} + (b_0' + b_1) \frac{dy}{dx} + b_1'y.$$

Hence, we can set in turn $y = 1$, $y = x$, and $y = x^2$ to obtain

$$a_2 = b_1', \qquad a_1 = b_0' + b_1, \qquad a_0 = b_0.$$

Therefore,

$$a_1' = b_0'' + b_1' = a_0'' + a_2,$$

and consequently (12.153) holds.

Suppose now that (12.153) holds; we are required to show that (12.151) and (12.152) are exact. Using (12.153) we obtain, when $y(x)$ has two derivatives,

$$\begin{aligned} a_0 \frac{d^2y}{dx^2} + a_1 \frac{dy}{dx} + a_2 y &= a_0 \frac{d^2y}{dx^2} + a_1 \frac{dy}{dx} + (a_1' - a_0'')y \\ &= \left(a_0 \frac{d^2y}{dx^2} - a_0''y\right) + \left(a_1 \frac{dy}{dx} + a_1'y\right) = \frac{d}{dx}\left[\left(a_0 \frac{dy}{dx} - a_0'y\right) + a_1 y\right] \\ &= \frac{d}{dx}\left[a_0 \frac{dy}{dx} + (a_1 - a_0')y\right] \end{aligned}$$

so that

$$a_0D^2 + a_1D + a_2 = D[a_0D + (a_1 - a_0')]$$

and therefore (12.151) and (12.152) are exact. This proves Theorem 12.15.

Problem 12.16

Show that, if a_0, a_1, and a_2 are constants, then

$$a_0D^2 + a_1D + a_2$$

is exact if and only if $a_2 = 0$.

Problem 12.17

State and prove a theorem analogous to Theorem 12.15 which applies to linear operators of order 4.

12.2. Integrating Factors and Adjoint Equations. In this section, we use $\bar{w}$ to denote the congugate $u - iv$ of a complex number $w = u + iv$ in which u and v are real. Insofar as real solutions of differential equations with real coefficients are concerned, the bars have no significance since $\bar{w} = w$ when w is real.

A function $\mu(x)$ is called an *integrating factor* of an equation $Ly = f$ and of the operator L if the equation $\mu Ly = \mu f$ and the operator μL are exact. We confine our attention to differential equations and operators of the second order.

THEOREM 12.21. *If a_0, a_1, and a_2 are continuous functions of x for which a_0'' and a_1' exist, then $\mu(x)$ is an integrating factor of the equation*

$$a_0y'' + a_1y' + a_2y = f \tag{12.211}$$

if and only if

$$(12.212) \qquad a_0\mu'' + (2a_0' - a_1)\mu' + (a_0'' - a_1' + a_2)\mu = 0.$$

By Theorem 12.15 the equation

$$(a_0\mu)y'' + (a_1\mu)y' + (a_2\mu)y = \mu f$$

is exact if and only if

$$(12.213) \qquad (a_0\mu)'' - (a_1\mu)' + (a_2\mu) = 0;$$

and (12.212) is merely an expanded form of (12.213). This proves Theorem 12.21.

The equation (12.212) can be written in the form

$$(12.214) \qquad \bar{a}_0\bar{\mu}'' + (2\bar{a}_0' - \bar{a}_1)\bar{\mu}' + (\bar{a}_0'' - \bar{a}_1' + \bar{a}_2)\bar{\mu} = 0.$$

Hence, Theorem 12.21 can be stated in the following form:

THEOREM 12.22. *Under the hypothesis of Theorem 12.21, a function μ is an integrating factor of the equation*

$$(12.221) \qquad a_0y'' + a_1y' + a_2y = f$$

if and only if $\bar{\mu}$ is a solution of the equation

$$(12.222) \qquad \bar{a}_0y'' + (2\bar{a}_0' - \bar{a}_1)y' + (\bar{a}_0'' - \bar{a}_1' + \bar{a}_2)y = 0.$$

The equation (12.222) is called the *adjoint* (or *adjoint equation*) of (12.221). The adjoint of an operator is often indicated by an asterisk superscript which is commonly called a *star*. Thus, if L denotes the operator

$$(12.23) \qquad L = a_0D^2 + a_1D + a_2,$$

then the *adjoint* (or *adjoint operator*) is†

$$(12.24) \qquad L^* = \bar{a}_0D^2 + (2\bar{a}_0' - \bar{a}_1)D + (a_0'' - \bar{a}_1' + \bar{a}_2).$$

Problem 12.241

Prove that the adjoint of the adjoint of the operator L in (12.23) is L itself; that is $L^{**} = L$. Find whether the formula

$$(L_1 + L_2)^* = L_1^* + L_2^*$$

is correct when L_1 and L_2 are second-order operators.

The most obvious connection between the operators L and L^* lies in the fact that the integrating factors of $Ly = f$ are the conjugates of the solutions of $L^*y = 0$. An important connection between L and L^* is set

† In case the a's are real, the bars may naturally be omitted; but, when the a's are not real, omission of the bars leads to confusion.

forth in the following theorem which is one of various theorems known as *Lagrange's theorem.*†

THEOREM 12.25. If

$$L = a_0D^2 + a_1D + a_2$$

where a_0, a_1, *and* a_2 *are functions of* x *for which* a_0'' *and* a_1' *exist and if* $y_m(x)$ *and* $y_n(x)$ *are two functions each having two derivatives, then*‡

$$(12.26) \quad y_m\overline{L^*y_n} - \bar{y}_nLy_m = \frac{d}{dx}[a_0(y_m\bar{y}_n' - y_m'\bar{y}_n) - (a_1 - a_0')y_m\bar{y}_n].$$

The simplest way to prove this theorem is to expand both sides of (12.26) [using (12.23) and (12.24) in the left-hand member] and to show that the terms all cancel. A formula obtained by integrating *Lagrange's formula* (12.26) is one of various formulas known as Green (George, 1793–1841) formulas.

12.27. Self-adjoint Operators. An operator L is called *self-adjoint* if $L^* = L$. If a_0, a_1, and a_2 are real, the conditions for $L^* = L$ are

$$a_0 = a_0, \qquad a_1 = 2a_0' - a_1, \qquad a_2 = a_0'' - a_1' + a_2,$$

and these three conditions are satisfied if and only if $a_1 = a_0'$. Therefore, each self-adjoint linear operator of the second order with real coefficients has the form

$$(12.28) \qquad L = a_0(x)D^2 + a_0'(x)D + a_2(x).$$

This can of course be written in the form $L = D(a_0D) + a_2$. For this operator, $L^* = L$ and $\overline{Ly} = L\bar{y}$ so that Lagrange's formula (12.26) becomes

$$(12.29) \qquad y_mL\bar{y}_n - \bar{y}_nLy_m = \frac{d}{dx}[a_0(y_m\bar{y}_n' - y_m'\bar{y}_n)].$$

The fact that (12.29) is simpler than (12.26) shows why self-adjoint operators are more tractable than others.

Problem 12.291

Show that, if $a_0(x)$, $a_1(x)$, and $a_2(x)$ are real continuous functions of x for which $a_0''(x)$ and $a_1'(x)$ exist, then a factor $\nu(x)$ makes the operator

$$a_0(x)\nu(x)D^2 + a_1(x)\nu(x)D + a_2(x)\nu(x)$$

† Joseph Louis Lagrange (1736–1813) was a great French mathematician who is best known for his work in analytical mechanics.

‡ It is somewhat absurd to call two functions by the names $y_m(x)$ and $y_n(x)$; names such as $y_1(x)$ and $y_2(x)$ would seem more appropriate. However, this notation results in formulas written exactly the way we want to use them later.

self-adjoint if and only if $\nu(x)$ is a solution of the first-order equation

$$a_0(x)\nu' + [a_0(x) - a_1(x)]\nu = 0.$$

Problem 12.292

Derive (12.29) directly from (12.28) without use of (12.26).

12.3. Eigenvalue Problems.

Differential equations of the form $Ly = \lambda y$, in which L is a linear operator and λ is a parameter, arise in many problems. It is often true that special solutions, called *eigenfunctions* or *characteristic functions*, are required which are not identically 0 and which satisfy one or more supplementary conditions pertinent to the problem being solved. In important cases, eigenfunctions exist only for special values of the parameter λ; these values of λ are called *eigenvalues* or *characteristic values*. If λ_n is an eigenvalue and y_n is a solution of $Ly = \lambda_n y$ which is not identically 0 and which satisfies the supplementary conditions, then y_n is called an *eigenfunction belonging to* λ_n. It is customary to think of the differential equation and the supplementary conditions together as constituting a *system;* the eigenvalues and eigenfunctions are then *eigenvalues and eigenfunctions of the system.*

It is impossible to indicate in a paragraph the role which eigenvalues play in science, but we can see clearly the meaning of the equation $Ly = \lambda y$. Though certain functions may be drastically changed when the operator L is applied to them, the eigenfunctions enjoy a very special status; *an eigenfunction* y_n *belonging to* λ_n *is merely multiplied by* λ_n. Moreover, if $y_1, y_2, \ldots, y_n$ are eigenfunctions belonging to $\lambda_1, \lambda_2, \ldots, \lambda_n$, respectively, and

$$g = c_1y_1 + c_2y_2 + \cdots + c_ny_n,$$

then linearity of L implies that

$$Lg = c_1\lambda_1y_1 + c_2\lambda_2y_2 + \cdots + c_n\lambda_ny_n;$$

thus an expression for Lg is quickly obtained when g is a given linear combination of eigenfunctions. It is a more significant observation that it is easy to write out a solution of the equation

$$Ly = c_1y_1 + c_2y_2 + \cdots + c_ny_n \tag{12.31}$$

when $\lambda_k \neq 0$ for each k; a solution is

$$y = \frac{c_1}{\lambda_1}y_1 + \frac{c_2}{\lambda_2}y_2 + \cdots + \frac{c_n}{\lambda_n}y_n. \tag{12.32}$$

In case the supplementary conditions are linear (that is, such that they are satisfied by each linear combination of functions which satisfy them), then not only is (12.32) a solution of (12.31); (12.32) *is a solution of* (12.31) *which satisfies the supplementary conditions.*

These considerations indicate that it should be useful to know what functions g can be expressed as linear combinations of eigenfunctions, either exactly or approximately in some sense satisfying to an applied mathematician who is always ready to use good approximations. The following sections consider an important class of eigenvalue problems.

12.33. Sturm-Liouville Equations. We consider here the case in which L is a second-order operator,

$$L = a_0(x)D^2 + a_1(x)D + a_2(x),$$

and x lies in an open interval $a < x < b$ over which $a_0(x)$, $a_1(x)$, and $a_2(x)$ are real and continuous and $a_0(x)$ is not zero. For example, with the Bessel operator $L = x^2D^2 + xD + (x^2 - \alpha^2)$ we can take $a = 0$, $b = 1$; likewise for the self-adjoint operator $\mathfrak{L} = xD^2 + D + (x - \alpha^2/x)$ we can take $a = 0$, $b = 1$. In case $a_0(x) = 1 - x^2$ while $a_1(x)$ and $a_2(x)$ are continuous, we can take $a = -1$, $b = 1$.

The equation $Ly = \lambda y$ is then

$$a_0(x)\frac{d^2y}{dx^2} + a_1(x)\frac{dy}{dx} + a_2(x)y = \lambda y. \tag{12.34}$$

Having seen (Section 12.27) that self-adjoint operators are more tractable than others, we introduce the factor

$$p(x) = \frac{A}{a_0(x)} \exp \int_{x_0}^{x} \frac{a_1(t)}{a_0(t)}\,dt$$

in which x_0 is a point of the interval $a < x < b$ and A is a conveniently chosen constant such that $p(x) > 0$, and set

$$q(x) = a_0(x)p(x), \qquad r(x) = a_2(x)p(x)$$

to obtain the *Sturm-Liouville equation*

$$\frac{d}{dx}[q(x)y'] + r(x)y = \lambda p(x)y, \tag{12.35}$$

in which the operator

$$\mathfrak{L} \equiv D(qD) + r \equiv qD^2 + q'D + r \tag{12.36}$$

is self-adjoint.* In case L is self-adjoint, we may take $p(x) = 1$ so that the operators L and $\mathfrak{L}$ are identical.

* The equation (12.35), which may of course be written in the form

$$q(x)\frac{d^2y}{dx^2} + q'(x)\frac{dy}{dx} + [-\lambda p(x) + r(x)]y = 0,$$

is known as a Sturm (1803–1855) Liouville (1809–1882) equation of second order. Theorem 6.04 guarantees existence of solutions over $a < x < b$ for each λ.

Now let λ_m and λ_n be two numbers and let $y_m(x)$ and $y_n(x)$ be two functions such that, when $a < x < b$,

$$Ly_m = \lambda_m y_m, \qquad Ly_n = \lambda_n y_n$$

or (what amounts to the same thing)

$$\mathcal{L}y_m = \lambda_m p y_m, \qquad \mathcal{L}y_n = \lambda_n p y_n.$$

Since $\mathcal{L}$ is self-adjoint, we can substitute in the Lagrange formula (12.29) to obtain, when $a < x < b$,

$$(12.37) \qquad (\lambda_m - \bar{\lambda}_n) p y_m \bar{y}_n = \frac{d}{dx}[q(y_m \bar{y}_n' - y_m' \bar{y}_n)].$$

The two members of (12.37) are certainly (why?) continuous over the open interval $a < x < b$; but they may either be or fail to be continuous over the closed interval $a \leqq x \leqq b$. We can (why?) integrate (12.37) over $x_1 \leqq x \leqq x_2$ when $a < x_1 < x_2 < b$ and then let $x_1 \to a$ and $x_2 \to b$ to obtain (see Section 13.6 on Cauchy integrals)

$$(12.38) \quad (\bar{\lambda}_n - \lambda_m) \int_a^b p(x) y_m(x) \bar{y}_n(x)\,dx = \lim_{x \to b} [q(x)\{y_m(x)\bar{y}_n'(x) - y_m'(x)\bar{y}_n(x)\}] - \lim_{x \to a} [q(x)\{y_m(x)\bar{y}_n'(x) - y_m'(x)\bar{y}_n(x)\}]$$

whenever the limits on the right exist. In case the functions

$$p(x),\ q(x),\ y_m(x),\ y_m'(x),\ y_n(x),\ y_n'(x)$$

are continuous over $a \leqq x \leqq b$, (12.38) can be written in the form

$$(12.39) \quad (\bar{\lambda}_n - \lambda_m) \int_a^b p(x) y_m(x) \bar{y}_n(x)\,dx = q(b)[y_m(b)\bar{y}_n'(b) - y_m'(b)\bar{y}_n(b)] - q(a)[y_m(a)\bar{y}_n'(a) - y_m'(a)\bar{y}_n(a)],$$

the integral on the left now being a Riemann integral with a continuous integrand.

Conditions under which the second member of (12.38) is 0 are of great interest; one obvious fact is that vanishing of the second member implies that the integral in (12.38) must be 0 unless $\lambda_m = \bar{\lambda}_n$.

12.4. Sturm-Liouville Systems. A *Sturm-Liouville system* is a system composed of (i) a Sturm-Liouville equation

$$(12.41) \qquad \frac{d}{dx}[q(x)y'(x)] + r(x)y(x) = \lambda p(x)y(x)$$

and (ii) a set of supplementary conditions on $p(x)$, $q(x)$, $r(x)$, and $y(x)$ which, among other things, implies that each pair of functions $y_m(x)$ and $y_n(x)$ satisfying the conditions imposed upon $y(x)$ is a pair for which the right-hand member of (12.38) is 0.

One important system is composed of (12.41) and the conditions that $p(x)$ be positive and $r(x)$ be continuous over $a < x < b$; that $p(x)$, $q(x)$, $y(x)$, and $y'(x)$ be continuous over $a \leqq x \leqq b$; that $q(x)$ be positive over $a \leqq x \leqq b$; and that

$$A_1 y(a) + A_2 y'(a) = 0, \qquad B_1 y(b) + B_2 y'(b) = 0 \tag{12.42}$$

where A_1 and A_2 are real constants not both 0 and likewise B_1 and B_2 are real constants not both 0. The special case in which (12.42) takes the form

$$y(a) = y(b) = 0 \tag{12.43}$$

and that in which (12.42) takes the form

$$y'(a) = y'(b) = 0 \tag{12.44}$$

frequently occur.

Another type of system is just like the preceding except that the function $q(x)$ satisfies the additional condition $q(a) = q(b)$ and (12.42) is replaced by the so-called *periodic boundary condition*

$$y(a) = y(b), \qquad y'(a) = y'(b). \tag{12.45}$$

For each of these systems, an *eigenvalue of the system* is a value of λ for which a function $y_\lambda(x)$ not identically 0 over $a < x < b$ exists which satisfies (12.41) and the specified supplementary conditions; the function $y_\lambda(x)$ is an *eigenfunction belonging to* λ.

Formulation of satisfactory supplementary conditions when $q(a) = 0$ or $q(b) = 0$ or both is a more delicate matter. The footnote below* contains a discussion of this point more easily understood after a preliminary reading of this chapter.

It is easy to see that the eigenvalues must be real. If $\lambda_m = \alpha + i\beta$ is an eigenvalue with eigenfunction $y_m(x) = u(x) + iv(x)$, then $\lambda_n = \alpha - i\beta$

* When the coefficient $q(x)$ in (12.41) is such that $q(a) = 0$ or $q(b) = 0$ or both, it sometimes happens that some or all [except the function $y(x) \equiv 0$] of the functions $y(x)$ which satisfy the differential equation over the interval $a < x < b$ fail to be such that $y(x)$ and $y'(x)$ have limits as $x \to a$ and as $x \to b$. In such cases the formula (12.39) and such conditions as (12.42) cannot be used; to obtain supplementary conditions which yield a satisfactory Sturm-Liouville system, it is necessary to formulate conditions on $y(x)$ in such a way that the right-hand member of (12.38) may be used. We do not go into details in this matter; the essential point is that the conditions are so formulated that each eigenfunction satisfies (12.41) over the interval $a < x < b$; that, if $y_m(x)$ and $y_n(x)$ are two eigenfunctions, then the right-hand member of (12.38) is 0; that, if $y_n(x)$ is an eigenfunction belonging to λ, then $\bar{y}_n(x)$ is an eigenfunction belonging to $\bar{\lambda}$; and that, if $y_n(x)$ is an eigenfunction, then $p(x)|y_n(x)|^2$ has a Cauchy integral (Section 13.6) over $a \leqq x \leqq b$, the value of the integral being positive.

must be an eigenvalue with eigenfunction

$$y_n(x) = u(x) - iv(x).$$

The equation (12.38) is in this case

$$2\beta \int_a^b p(x)[u^2(x) + v^2(x)]dx = 0.$$

Since the integral is not 0, β must be 0 and the eigenvalue λ_m must be real.

It thus appears that if $y_m(x)$ and $y_n(x)$ are eigenfunctions belonging to λ_m and λ_n, respectively, then

$$(12.46) \qquad (\lambda_m - \lambda_n) \int_a^b p(x) y_m(x) \bar{y}_n(x) dx = 0.$$

If $\lambda_m \neq \lambda_n$, this implies that the integral must be 0. In this case, we can write (12.46) in the form

$$(12.47) \qquad \int_a^b \{\sqrt{p(x)}\, y_m(x)\}\{\sqrt{p(x)}\, \bar{y}_n(x)\} dx = 0.$$

Thus we are led to the developments of the next sections.

12.5. Orthonormal Sets. Two functions $\phi(x)$ and $\psi(x)$ are said to be *orthogonal* over an interval $a \leqq x \leqq b$ if

$$(12.51) \qquad \int_a^b \phi(x)\bar{\psi}(x) dx = 0.$$

One function $\phi(x)$ is said to be *normal* (or *normalized*) if

$$(12.52) \qquad \int_a^b |\phi(x)|^2 dx = 1.$$

A set of functions

$$\phi_1(x),\ \phi_2(x),\ \phi_3(x),\ \ldots$$

is said to form a *normal and orthogonal set of functions*, or, briefly, an *orthonormal set*, over an interval $a \leqq x \leqq b$ if

$$(12.53) \qquad \int_a^b \phi_m(x)\bar{\phi}_n(x) dx = 0 \qquad m \neq n$$

$$= 1 \qquad m = n.$$

A set $\psi_1(x), \psi_2(x), \ldots$ is said to form an *orthogonal set* over $a \leqq x \leqq b$ if

$$\int_a^b \psi_m(x)\bar{\psi}_n(x) dx = 0 \qquad m \neq n.$$

It is clear that each orthonormal set is an orthogonal set and that an orthogonal set may fail to be orthonormal.

Each Riemann integrable function $\psi(x)$ for which $\int_a^b |\psi(x)|^2 dx \neq 0$ can be normalized by multiplication by an appropriate constant Q. Thus, if we set

$$\phi(x) = Q\psi(x),$$

then

$$\int_a^b |\phi(x)|^2dx = |Q|^2 \int_a^b |\psi(x)|^2dx;$$

and $\phi(x)$ will be normal if we set

$$Q = \left[\int_a^b |\psi(x)|^2dx\right]^{-\frac{1}{2}}.$$

Suppose now $\lambda_1, \lambda_2, \lambda_3, \ldots$ is an infinite set of different eigenvalues of a Sturm-Liouville system and that $y_1(x), y_2(x), \ldots$ is an infinite set of eigenfunctions such that $y_n(x)$ belongs to λ_n for each $n = 1, 2, 3, \ldots$. Let

$$\phi_n(x) = Q_n \sqrt{p(x)}\, y_n(x) \tag{12.54}$$

where Q_n is the constant,

$$Q_n = \left[\int_a^b p(x)|y_n(x)|^2dx\right]^{-\frac{1}{2}}. \tag{12.541}$$

Then obviously

$$\int_a^b |\phi_n(x)|^2dx = 1 \qquad n = 1, 2, 3, \ldots \tag{12.55}$$

so that the set

$$\phi_1(x),\ \phi_2(x),\ \phi_3(x),\ \ldots \tag{12.56}$$

is normal. If $m \neq n$, we can use (12.54) and (12.46) to obtain

$$\int_a^b \phi_m(x)\bar{\phi}_n(x)dx = Q_mQ_n \int_a^b p(x)y_m(x)\bar{y}_n(x)dx = 0;$$

hence the set (12.56) must be orthogonal. The set of functions

$$\psi_n(x) = \sqrt{p(x)}\, y_n(x)$$

is orthogonal but is not normal unless by accident or design the functions $y_n(x)$ were so chosen that the integral in (12.541) is 1.

Thus we have shown that *if* $y_1(x), y_2(x), \ldots$ *is a set of eigenfunctions, of a Sturm-Liouville system, belonging to distinct eigenvalues* $\lambda_1, \lambda_2, \ldots,$ *then the functions*

$$\phi_n(x) = Q_n \sqrt{p(x)}\, y_n(x) \qquad n = 1, 2, \ldots \tag{12.57}$$

constitute an orthonormal set.

In cases in which $p(x) = 1$ for all x, the functions $Q_ny_n(x)$ themselves constitute an orthonormal set; in case $p(x)$ is not always 1, the functions $y_n(x)$ are said to be *orthogonal with weight function* $p(x)$.

Problem 12.581

Verify each of the following assertions: The operator

$$L = -D^2$$

is a self-adjoint linear operator of the second order with real coefficients. The equation $D^2y = -\lambda y$ together with the boundary conditions $y(0) = y(\pi) = 0$ constitutes a Sturm-Liouville system. The eigenvalues (and the only eigenvalues) are $\lambda_1 = 1^2$, $\lambda_2 = 2^2$, $\lambda_3 = 3^2$, . . . ; the eigenfunctions (and the only eigenfunctions) are $y_1 = c_1 \sin x$, $y_2 = c_2 \sin 2x$, $y_3 = c_3 \sin 3x$, . . . where $c_1 \neq 0$, $c_2 \neq 0$, $c_3 \neq 0$, ... In this example, $p(x) = 1$ for all x, and the functions $y_n(x)$ are orthogonal. Since

$$\int_0^\pi \sin^2 nx\, dx = \frac{1}{2}\int_0^\pi (1 - \cos 2nx)dx = \frac{\pi}{2} \qquad n = 1, 2, 3, \ldots,$$

the functions

$$\phi_n(x) = \sqrt{\frac{2}{\pi}} \sin nx \qquad n = 1, 2, 3, \ldots$$

constitute an orthonormal system over $0 \leqq x \leqq \pi$.

Problem 12.582

Establish the formula

$$\int_0^\pi \left(\sqrt{\frac{2}{\pi}} \sin mx\right)\left(\sqrt{\frac{2}{\pi}} \sin nx\right) dx = 0 \qquad m \neq n$$

by a method simpler than that used in the previous problem.

Problem 12.583

Show that if, in Problem 12.581, the boundary conditions $y(0) = y(\pi) = 0$ are replaced by the so-called *periodic boundary conditions*

$$y(0) = y(2\pi), \qquad y'(0) = y'(2\pi),$$

then the eigenvalues become $0, 1^2, 2^2, 3^2, \ldots$ and the corresponding eigenfunctions become

$$\alpha_n e^{inx} + \beta_n e^{-inx} \qquad n = 0, 1, 2, \ldots$$

or

$$A_n \cos nx + B_n \sin nx \qquad n = 0, 1, 2, \ldots.$$

Except in the case $n = 0$, there are two independent eigenfunctions belonging to each eigenvalue. Show that nevertheless if we set

$$\phi_n(x) = \frac{1}{\sqrt{2\pi}} e^{inx} \qquad n = 0, \pm 1, \pm 2, \ldots$$

then

$$\int_0^{2\pi} \phi_m(x)\overline{\phi_n(x)}dx = 0 \quad m \neq n; \qquad = 1 \quad m = n. \tag{12.5831}$$

Show also that if we set

$$\phi_0(x) = \frac{1}{\sqrt{2\pi}}$$

$$\phi_{2n}(x) = \frac{\cos nx}{\sqrt{\pi}} \qquad n = 1, 2, 3, \ldots$$

$$\phi_{2n-1}(x) = \frac{\sin nx}{\sqrt{\pi}} \qquad n = 1, 2, 3, \ldots$$

then (12.5831) holds.

12.6. Existence of Eigenvalues and Completeness of Orthonormal Sets. For the Sturm-Liouville systems in Problems 12.581 and 12.582, it was easy to show existence of an infinite set of nonnegative real eigenvalues and, in fact, to find them. These eigenvalues led to orthonormal sets having an important property, completeness, which we shall discuss presently.

We give now without proof an indication of results which are of great interest in pure and applied mathematics; accurate statements of the results are too involved to be given here.

Under quite general conditions, all eigenvalues of a Sturm-Liouville system are real and nonnegative. There is an infinite set of eigenvalues; and these eigenvalues can be named $\lambda_1, \lambda_2, \lambda_3, \ldots$ in such a way that

$$0 \leqq \lambda_1 < \lambda_2 < \lambda_3 < \lambda_4 < \cdots \tag{12.61}$$

and $\lambda_n \to \infty$ as $n \to \infty$. The eigenfunctions belonging to an eigenvalue λ_n are in some cases simply nonzero constant multiples of a single eigenfunction, say $y_n(x)$; in other cases they are linear combinations, with coefficients not both 0, of two independent eigenfunctions, say $y_n(x)$ and $Y_n(x)$. In the latter case it is always possible to choose the independent eigenfunctions $y_n(x)$ and $Y_n(x)$ in such a way that each eigenfunction belonging to λ_n is a linear combination of $y_n(x)$ and $Y_n(x)$ and moreover the two functions $y_n(x)$ and $Y_n(x)$ are *orthogonal with weight function* $p(x)$ in the sense that

$$\int_a^b [\sqrt{p(x)}\, y_n(x)][\sqrt{p(x)}\, \bar{Y}_n(x)]dx = 0.$$

For each n, let Q_n be a constant such that the function

$$Q_n \sqrt{p(x)}\, y_n(x) \tag{12.62}$$

is normal; and, for values of n for which $Y_n(x)$ is present, let R_n be a constant such that the function

$$R_n \sqrt{p(x)}\, Y_n(x) \tag{12.63}$$

is normal. Let the functions in (12.62) and (12.63) be denoted in some order by*

$$(12.64) \qquad \phi_1(x), \phi_2(x), \phi_3(x), \ldots .$$

These functions always form an orthonormal set over the interval $a \leqq x \leqq b$.

The most useful theorems involving Sturm-Liouville systems are those which show that, under conditions which we cannot set forth here, the orthonormal set (12.64) is *complete.* It is possible to define *complete orthonormal set* in several equivalent ways which appear to be quite different.

The next section involves ideas upon which all modern theories of orthonormal sets are based; see also Section 12.99.

12.65. Use of Lebesgue Integrals. The simplest discussions of orthonormal sets are those in which the integrals used are Lebesgue integrals. We neither assume knowledge of nor use Lebesgue integrals, but this is no reason why a student should not be interested in the subject. If a function $f(x)$ is Riemann integrable over an interval $a \leqq x \leqq b$, then it is Lebesgue integrable over the same interval and the integrals are equal. However, there are functions not Riemann integrable which are Lebesgue integrable. The definition of the Lebesgue integral is more complicated than that of the Riemann integral because it requires a working knowledge of *Lebesgue measure;* but those who understand both integrals find the Lebesgue integral much the easier to work with because it has many useful properties which the Riemann integral lacks.

An orthonormal set of functions

$$\phi_1(x), \phi_2(x), \phi_3(x), \ldots ,$$

which may be continuous but in any case must be *measurable,* is said to be *complete* if there exists no function $\phi_0(x)$ such that the set of functions

$$\phi_0(x), \phi_1(x), \phi_2(x), \ldots$$

is an orthonormal set. This simple definition, based on Lebesgue integration, says that an orthonormal set is complete if no new function can be added. Of course, it implies that the set obtained by removing one or more functions from a complete set is not complete. It can be shown that this definition of completeness is equivalent to the definition given in the next section; that is, if a set is complete in one sense, then it is also complete in the other sense.

It is possible to define an orthonormal set $\phi_1(x), \phi_2(x), \ldots$ of continuous functions to be *complete with respect to continuous functions* if there is no *continuous* function $\phi_0(x)$ such that the set $\phi_0(x), \phi_1(x), \ldots$ is an orthonormal set; but this property of orthonormal sets is by no means so strong as the property of completeness and serves no useful purpose in our theory.

One who knows the appropriate mathematics finds it very easy to prove that a definition of completeness equivalent to that given in the next section is obtained by

* In some cases it is convenient to denote the functions by $\phi_0, \phi_{-1}, \phi_1, \phi_{-2}, \phi_2, \ldots$, but after all it makes no difference how the functions are named; the important thing is that none be lost.

replacing the condition that $f(x)$ be Riemann integrable by (i) the condition that $f(x)$ be continuous, or (ii) the condition that $f(x)$ have two continuous derivatives, or (iii) the condition that $f(x)$ and $|f(x)|^2$ have Cauchy integrals, or (iv) the condition that $f(x)$ be measurable and $|f(x)|^2$ be Lebesgue integrable. The term *closed* is sometimes used in place of the term *complete.*

12.7. Completeness of Orthonormal Sets. An orthonormal set

$$\phi_1(x),\ \phi_2(x),\ \phi_3(x),\ \ldots \tag{12.71}$$

is said to be *complete* if, corresponding to each function $f(x)$ which is Riemann integrable* over $a \leqq x \leqq b$ and each $\epsilon > 0$, there exist an index n and constants $c_1, c_2, \ldots, c_n$ such that

$$\int_a^b \left| f(x) - \sum_{k=1}^{n} c_k\phi_k(x)\right|^2 dx < \epsilon. \tag{12.72}$$

The meaning of this definition may perhaps be made apparent by the following statement: If the orthonormal set is complete, then when $f(x)$ and ϵ are given it is possible to find a linear combination of the ϕ's which is so close to $f(x)$ so much of the time that the integral in (12.72) is less than ϵ.

When $f(x)$ is fixed, the value of the integral in (12.72) depends only on $c_1, c_2, \ldots, c_n$. As we shall see, an attempt to discuss the integral is facilitated by defining constants $a_1, a_2, a_3, \ldots$ by the formula

$$a_k = \int_a^b f(x)\bar{\phi}_k(x)dx \qquad k = 1, 2, \ldots; \tag{12.73}$$

these constants are called the *Fourier coefficients* of the function $f(x)$. Using the simple formula $|z|^2 = z\bar{z}$ to expand the integrand in (12.72), and using (12.73) and the orthonormality of the ϕ's, we obtain

$$\begin{aligned} &\int_a^b |f(x) - \sum_{k=1}^{n} c_k\phi_k(x)|^2 dx \\ &= \int_a^b \left[f(x) - \sum_{k=1}^{n} c_k\phi_k(x)\right]\left[\bar{f}(x) - \sum_{l=1}^{n} \bar{c}_l\bar{\phi}_l(x)\right] dx \\ &= \int_a^b |f(x)|^2 dx - \sum_{l=1}^{n} \bar{c}_l \int_a^b f(x)\bar{\phi}_l(x)dx \\ &\quad - \sum_{k=1}^{n} c_k \int_a^b \bar{f}(x)\phi_k(x)dx + \sum_{k=1}^{n}\sum_{l=1}^{n} c_k\bar{c}_l \int_a^b \phi_k(x)\bar{\phi}_l(x)dx \end{aligned} \tag{12.74}$$

* It should be recognized that each Riemann integrable function $f(x)$ is bounded and such that $|f(x)|^2$ is integrable, and that each bounded function $f(x)$ having at most a finite set of discontinuities is such that $f(x)$ and $|f(x)|^2$ are both integrable.

$$= \int_a^b |f(x)|^2 dx + \sum_{k=1}^n [-\bar{c}_k a_k - c_k \bar{a}_k + c_k \bar{c}_k]$$

$$= \int_a^b |f(x)|^2 dx - \sum_{k=1}^n |a_k|^2 + \sum_{k=1}^n |c_k - a_k|^2.$$

Since $|c_k - a_k|$ is never negative and is 0 only when $c_k = a_k$, this shows that the integral is a minimum when $c_k = a_k$ for each k; in other words, $c_1\phi_1(x) + \cdots + c_n(x)$ is the best approximation to $f(x)$ in the sense of *least squares* and in the sense of *approximation in mean* when the c's are the Fourier coefficients of $f(x)$. This type of approximation is held in highest esteem by all experts in the theorey of approximation. If

$$\int_a^b |f(x) - \sum_{k=1}^n c_k\phi_k(x)|^2 dx$$

is "small" then the function

$$\sum_{k=1}^n c_k\phi_k(x)$$

is regarded as a "good" approximation to $f(x)$.

Setting $c_k = a_k$ in (12.74) gives the important formula

$$\int_a^b |f(x) - \sum_{k=1}^n a_k\phi_k(x)|^2 dx = \int_a^b |f(x)|^2 dx - \sum_{k=1}^n |a_k|^2 \qquad n = 1, 2, 3, \ldots \tag{12.75}$$

which holds whether the orthonormal set is complete or not. Since the left side of (12.75) is never negative, we obtain

$$\sum_{k=1}^n |a_k|^2 \leqq \int_a^b |f(x)|^2 dx \qquad n = 1, 2, 3, \ldots . \tag{12.751}$$

Thus the partial sums of the series

$$|a_1|^2 + |a_2|^2 + |a_3|^2 + \cdots$$

are bounded, and since the terms are nonnegative, the series must converge. Using (12.751) we obtain the inequality

$$\sum_{k=1}^\infty |a_k|^2 \leqq \int_a^b |f(x)|^2 dx \tag{12.76}$$

which is known as *Bessel's inequality;* it holds whether the orthonormal set is complete or not.

When the orthonormal set is complete, the estimate in (12.76) can be strengthened by removal of the inequality sign. To be precise, we state and prove the following theorem:

THEOREM 12.77. *If $\phi_1(x)$, $\phi_2(x)$, . . . is a complete orthonormal set over $a \leqq x \leqq b$, if $f(x)$ is Riemann integrable over $a \leqq x \leqq b$, and if the constants*

$$a_n = \int_a^b f(x)\bar{\phi}_n(x)dx \qquad n = 1, 2, 3, \ldots$$

are the Fourier coefficients of $f(x)$, then the Parseval equality

$$\sum_{n=1}^{\infty} |a_n|^2 = \int_a^b |f(x)|^2dx \tag{12.78}$$

holds.

To prove this theorem, let the hypotheses be satisfied. Let $\epsilon > 0$. Then an integer n and constants $c_1, c_2, \ldots, c_n$ exist such that (12.72) holds. Using the equality (12.74) we obtain

$$\left\{\int_a^b |f(x)|^2\,dx - \sum_{k=1}^{n} |a_k|^2\right\} + \left\{\sum_{k=1}^{n} |c_k - a_k|^2\right\} < \epsilon.$$

The second quantity in braces is nonnegative. Therefore

$$\int_a^b |f(x)|^2dx - \sum_{k=1}^{n} |a_k|^2 < \epsilon$$

and hence

$$\sum_{k=1}^{n} |a_k|^2 > \int_a^b |f(x)|^2dx - \epsilon$$

so that

$$\sum_{k=1}^{\infty} |a_k|^2 > \int_a^b |f(x)|^2dx - \epsilon. \tag{12.781}$$

Since (12.781) holds for each $\epsilon > 0$, it follows that

$$\sum_{k=1}^{\infty} |a_k|^2 \geqq \int_a^b |f(x)|^2dx;$$

and this, together with Bessel's inequality (12.76), establishes the desired Parseval equality (12.78).

We state without proof the following facts: *The orthonormal set*

$$\sqrt{\frac{2}{b}}\sin\frac{n\pi x}{b} \qquad n = 1, 2, 3, \ldots \tag{12.791}$$

is complete over the interval $0 \leqq x \leqq b$. *The orthonormal set*

$$\sqrt{\frac{1}{b}}, \quad \sqrt{\frac{2}{b}}\cos\frac{n\pi x}{b} \qquad n = 1, 2, 3, \ldots \tag{12.792}$$

is complete over the interval $0 \leqq x \leqq b$. *The orthonormal set*

$$\sqrt{\frac{1}{2b}}\, e^{in(\pi/b)x} \qquad n = 0, \pm 1, \pm 2, \ldots \tag{12.793}$$

is complete over the interval $-b \leqq x \leqq b$. *The orthonormal set*

$$\sqrt{\frac{1}{2b}}, \quad \sqrt{\frac{1}{b}}\cos\frac{n\pi x}{b}, \quad \sqrt{\frac{1}{b}}\sin\frac{n\pi x}{b} \qquad n = 1, 2, 3, \ldots \tag{12.794}$$

is complete over the interval $-b \leqq x \leqq b$. *The orthornormal set of normalized Legendre polynomials* $\bar{P}_n(x)$ *defined by*

$$\bar{P}_n(x) = \sqrt{\frac{2n+1}{2}}\, P_n(x) \qquad n = 0, 1, 2, \ldots \tag{12.795}$$

(see Section 7.9) *is complete over the interval* $-1 \leqq x \leqq 1$.

12.8. Fourier Series. Let $\phi_1(x)$, $\phi_2(x)$, . . . be an orthonormal set over $a \leqq x \leqq b$, let $f(x)$ be Riemann integrable over $a \leqq x \leqq b$, and, as in Section 12.7, let

$$a_k = \int_a^b f(x)\bar{\phi}_k(x)\,dx \qquad k = 1, 2, 3, \ldots \tag{12.81}$$

be the Fourier coefficients of $f(x)$. Then the infinite series

$$a_1\phi_1(x) + a_2\phi_2(x) + a_3\phi_3(x) + \cdots \tag{12.82}$$

is called the *Fourier series* (or *Fourier expansion* or *Fourier development* or *orthogonal series*, etc.) of $f(x)$. It is customary and convenient to write

$$f(x) \sim a_1\phi_1(x) + a_2\phi_2(x) + a_3\phi_3(x) + \cdots \tag{12.83}$$

where the [$\sim$] means merely that the series on the right is the Fourier series of $f(x)$.

The sequence

$$\sum_{k=1}^{n} a_k\phi_k(x) \qquad n = 1, 2, 3, \ldots \tag{12.84}$$

which appeared in (12.75) is, of course, the sequence of partial sums of the Fourier series. We recall from Section 12.7 the formula

$$\int_a^b \left|f(x) - \sum_{k=1}^{n} a_k\phi_k(x)\right|^2 dx = \int_a^b |f(x)|^2 dx - \sum_{k=1}^{n} |a_k|^2, \tag{12.85}$$

which holds whether the set $\phi_n(x)$ is complete or not, and the Parseval equality

$$\int_a^b |f(x)|^2 dx = \sum_{k=1}^{\infty} |a_k|^2, \tag{12.86}$$

which holds when the set $\phi_n(x)$ is complete.

The three formulas (12.81), (12.85), and (12.86) alone constitute a very useful theory of expansion of functions into Fourier series. Starting with a given function $f(x)$, one uses (12.81) to compute Fourier coefficients $a_1, \ldots, a_n$; the aim is to get enough a's to make the right-hand member of (12.85) small enough to suit one's purpose. If the orthonormal set is complete and one knows that it is complete, then by use of (12.86) one can tell in advance that the aim can be realized. If one does not know whether or not the set is complete, one can try to realize the aim; if one succeeds, then the goal is attained whether the orthonormal set be complete or incomplete. The coefficients $a_1, a_2, \ldots, a_n$ having been computed to make the right-hand member of (12.85) "small," the formula (12.85) shows that the partial sum (12.84) is a "good" approximation to $f(x)$, and one uses the formula

$$f(x) = \sum_{k=1}^{n} c_k\phi_k(x)$$

which is usually incorrect but sufficiently accurate for many practical purposes.

The convergence theory of Remark 6.77 is not as relevant as it is sometimes thought to be.

12.9. Partial Differential Equations. Many problems in mathematical physics are solved by finding a function of two or more variables which satisfies a partial differential equation and supplementary conditions called *boundary conditions* (or *initial conditions*). Frequently, one of the independent variables represents a time coordinate, and the others represent space coordinates.

We give a brief discussion of the *Fourier method* or *eigenvalue method* of finding such functions. The equation

$$A\frac{\partial^2 u}{\partial x^2} + B\frac{\partial u}{\partial x} + C\frac{\partial^2 u}{\partial y^2} + D\frac{\partial u}{\partial y} + Eu = 0, \tag{12.91}$$

in which A and B are functions of x and C, D, and E are functions of y, is sufficiently complicated for significant illustration of the method. In case $A = C = 1$ and $B = D = E = 0$, this becomes the *Laplace equation;* in case $A = 1$, $C = -a^2$, and $B = D = E = 0$, it becomes the *wave equation;* and in case $A = a^2$, $D = -1$, $B = D = E = 0$, it becomes the *heat equation.* Other determinations of the functions A, B, C, D, E yield other important equations. Different boundary conditions correspond to different problems.

The procedure of the Fourier method is as follows: First determine functions $u_1(x, y)$, $u_2(x, y)$, . . . of the form

$$u_n(x, y) = X_n(x)Y_n(y) \tag{12.92}$$

such that, for each n, $u_n(x, y)$ satisfies the differential equation (12.91) and *some* of the boundary conditions; then determine constants A_1, A_2, . . . such that the series

$$A_1u_1(x, y) + A_2u_2(x, y) + A_3u_3(x, y) + \cdots$$

represents the required function $u(x, y)$ satisfying the differential equation (12.91) and *all* the boundary conditions. This Fourier (or eigenvalue) method appeared briefly in special cases in Problems 6.792, 6.793, and 6.794. We simplify our discussion by referring to the functions in (12.92) as *components* of $u(x, y)$.

The first step can be described in simple language: we seek components of the required solution. A function of the form

$$u_0(x, y) = X(x)Y(y),$$

where X is a function of x alone and Y is a function of y alone, will satisfy (12.91) if and only if

$$AX''Y + BX'Y + CXY'' + DXY' + EXY = 0 \tag{12.921}$$

where primes on X and Y mean, respectively, ordinary x and y derivatives. When neither X nor Y vanishes in the range of values of x and y considered, (12.921) holds if and only if

$$A\frac{X''}{X} + B\frac{X'}{X} = -\left(C\frac{Y''}{Y} + D\frac{Y'}{Y} + E\right). \tag{12.922}$$

Since the first member is independent of y and the second member is independent of x, it can be shown that (12.922) holds if and only if its members are constant, say $-\lambda$, so that

$$AX'' + BX' = -\lambda X \tag{12.923}$$

$$CY'' + DY' + EY = \lambda Y. \tag{12.924}$$

In case X or Y has zeros, these equations may be obtained by another and more tedious method. The two equations (12.923) and (12.924) have the forms $L_1X = -\lambda X$ and $L_2Y = \lambda Y$ where L_1 and L_2 are second-order operators of the familiar type,* and accordingly we now have

* Many of the important ordinary differential equations, including those of Bessel and Legendre, arise from partial differential equations in this way.

equations of the form considered in Section 12.3. If they are not self-adjoint, we can introduce factors as in Section 12.33 to make them self-adjoint. In many important applications of the Fourier method, the function $u_0(x, y) = X(x)Y(y)$ will satisfy some (but not all) of the boundary conditions which $u(x, y)$ must satisfy if $X(x)$ satisfies a set of linear boundary conditions which, together with the equation $L_1X = \lambda X$, constitute an eigenvalue problem of the Sturm-Liouville type of Section 12.4. It then often happens that the Sturm-Liouville system has an infinite set of eigenvalues $\lambda_1, \lambda_2, \lambda_3, \ldots$ and an infinite set of eigenfunctions $X_1(x), X_2(x), \ldots$ such that the functions

$$\sqrt{p(x)}\, X_n(x) \qquad n = 1, 2, 3, \ldots \tag{12.925}$$

form a complete orthonormal set over some interval $a \leqq x \leqq b$. Here $p(x)$ is, as in Section 12.33, the factor introduced into $L_1X = \lambda X$ to make it self-adjoint.

The next step is to get the solutions for each n of the equation $L_2Y = \lambda_n Y$, that is, of equation (12.924) when $\lambda = \lambda_n$. In case $C \equiv C(y) \not\equiv 0$ while C, D, E are continuous, the solutions have the form

$$Y_n(y) = \alpha_n U_n(y) + \beta_n V_n(y) \tag{12.93}$$

where α_n and β_n are constants and $U_n(y)$ and $V_n(y)$ are two independent solutions of $L_2Y = \lambda_n Y$. The components of the solution we are seeking are then of the form

$$X_n(x)[\alpha_n U_n(y) + \beta_n V_n(y)] \qquad n = 1, 2, 3, \ldots . \tag{12.94}$$

Since the differential equation (12.91) and the boundary conditions satisfied by the components are linear, it follows that the sum $S_N(x, y)$ defined by

$$S_N(x, y) = \sum_{n=1}^{N} X_n(x)[\alpha_n U_n(y) + \beta_n V_n(y)] \tag{12.95}$$

satisfies them for each positive integer N. In case $C \equiv C(y) = 0$ for all y while $D(y) \not\equiv 0$, the first-order equation $L_2y = \lambda_n y$ would have solutions of the form $Y_n(y) = \alpha_n U_n(y)$ and (12.95) would take the form

$$S_N(x, y) = \sum_{n=1}^{N} \alpha_n X_n(x) U_n(y). \tag{12.951}$$

It should now be observed that, however N and $\alpha_1, \alpha_2, \ldots, \beta_1, \beta_2, \ldots,$ are determined, $S_N(x, y)$ satisfies the differential equation (12.91) and *some* of the boundary conditions which $u(x, y)$ must satisfy. In a properly formulated problem to which the Fourier method applies, it turns out that $S_N(x, y)$ is a good approximation to the function $u(x, y)$

we are seeking provided that N is sufficiently great and the constants $\alpha_1, \alpha_2, \ldots$ and $\beta_1, \beta_2, \ldots$ are suitably determined.

These constants are often determined by use of such boundary conditions as we now describe. Let the points x, y for which $a \leqq x \leqq b$ and $y = y_0$ form a part of the boundary of the region R in the interior of which $u(x, y)$ is to satisfy the differential equation. Let the values of the required function $u(x, y)$ on this part of the boundary be $f(x)$. It is not necessary to assume that $f(x)$ is continuous or that it is bounded. It is enough to assume that $f(x)$ has at most a finite set of discontinuities in the interval $a \leqq x \leqq b$ and that

$$\int_a^b |f(x)|^2 dx$$

exists as a Cauchy integral. The condition

$$u(x, y_0) = f(x) \qquad a \leqq x \leqq b \tag{12.96}$$

is a sensible boundary condition provided that it is coupled with an assumption which yields a suitable connection between the values of $u(x, y)$ when (x, y) is a point of the region R and the values when (x, y) is a point of the boundary. An assumption that $u(x, y)$ is continuous at all points of the boundary would make the condition sensible provided that $f(x)$ is continuous. If $f(x)$ is not continuous, more finesse must be used in formulating a satisfactory boundary condition. There are reasons why the condition

$$\lim_{y \to y_0} \int_a^b |f(x) - u(x, y)|^2 dx = 0 \tag{12.961}$$

is the "best" condition to impose to make sure that the function $u(x, y)$ does not make a sudden and absurd jump from its values on the boundary to its values inside the region.* Indeed the condition (12.961) is so good that, when it is combined with (12.96), it becomes the more significant of the two conditions. In many problems, one can use (12.961) as the boundary condition, leaving (12.96) out of consideration.

* Suppose one is required to find a function $u(x, y)$ such that

$$\frac{\partial^2 u}{\partial x^2} + \frac{\partial^2 u}{\partial y^2} = 0$$

at all points (x, y) inside the square with opposite vertices at $(0, 0)$ and $(1, 1)$, and such that $u(x, y)$ is zero at all points of the boundary except that $u(x, 0) = x^2$ when $0 \leqq x \leqq \frac{1}{2}$. Obviously the function $u_1(x, y)$ which vanishes identically, except that $u_1(x, 0) = x^2$ when $0 \leqq x \leqq \frac{1}{2}$, meets the requirement. A practical problem would be so formulated that one is required to find a function $u(x, y)$ for which the function of x, obtained by assigning a fixed small positive value to the y in $u(x, y)$, is in some sense or other a good approximation to the function $u(x, 0)$.

We are now ready to do some optimistic supposing and concluding which lead to determinations of the α's and β's. Suppose that the series

$$\sum_{n=1}^{\infty} X_n(x)[\alpha_n U_n(y) + \beta_n V_n(y)], \tag{12.97}$$

whether convergent or divergent, represents the solution $u(x, y)$ of our problem in the sense that

$$\lim_{N\to\infty} \int_a^b |u(x, y) - \sum_{n=1}^{N} X_n(x)[\alpha_n U_n(y) + \beta_n V_n(y)]|^2 dx = 0. \tag{12.971}$$

Setting $y = y_0$ in this formula and using (12.96) give

$$\lim_{N\to\infty} \int_a^b |f(x) - \sum_{n=1}^{N} [\alpha_n A_n + \beta_n B_n] X_n(x)|^2 dx = 0 \tag{12.972}$$

where, to simplify writing, we have put $A_n = U_n(y_0)$ and $B_n = V_n(y_0)$. Upon assuming that the weight function $p(x)$ is bounded as well as positive over $a \leqq x \leqq b$, it can be shown that (12.972) implies

$$\lim_{N\to\infty} \int_a^b |\sqrt{p(x)}\, f(x) - \sum_{n=1}^{N} [\alpha_n A_n + \beta_n B_n] \sqrt{p(x)}\, X_n(x)|^2 dx = 0.$$

Since the functions $\sqrt{p(x)}\, X_n(x)$, which we could call $\phi_n(x)$, constitute a complete orthonormal set, this formula holds if and only if the coefficients $[\alpha_n A_n + \beta_n B_n]$ are the Fourier coefficients of the function $\sqrt{p(x)}\, f(x)$. Thus the formula holds if and only if

$$\alpha_n A_n + \beta_n B_n = \int_a^b \{\sqrt{p(x)}\, f(x)\}\{\sqrt{p(x)}\, \bar{X}_n(x)\} dx$$

or

$$\alpha_n A_n + \beta_n B_n = \int_a^b f(x) p(x) \bar{X}_n(x) dx. \tag{12.973}$$

For the simpler problem in which $C \equiv C(y) \equiv 0$ and the β's are absent the equations serve to determine the α's, provided, of course, that $A_n = U_n(y_0) \neq 0$. In case $C \neq 0$, another boundary condition would appear in the formulation of the problem and would be used to assist in the determination of the α's and β's. In some problems the extra boundary condition takes the form

$$\left.\frac{\partial u}{\partial y}\right|_{y=y_0} = g(x)$$

where the left-hand side denotes the value of $\partial u/\partial x$ when $y = y_0$, and this leads to equations

$$\alpha_n A'_n + \beta_n B'_n = \int_a^b g(x)p(x)\bar{X}_n(x)dx \tag{12.974}$$

where $A'_n = U'_n(y_0)$ and $B'_n = V'_n(y_0)$; the two equations (12.973) and (12.974) then determine the α's and β's. In problems of other types, other methods are used to determine the α's and β's, but it is characteristic of the Fourier method that Fourier series enter into the solution.

Having determined the α's and β's, applied mathematicians obtain many useful results by using

$$S_N(x, y) = \sum_{n=1}^{N} X_n(x)[\alpha_n U_n(y) + \beta_n V_n(y)] \tag{12.98}$$

as an approximation to the solution $u(x, y)$ of the problem. The problem involved in showing why this can be true involves mathematical analysis which we cannot present here; in particular, it is impossible to construct an adequate general theory without using Lebesgue integration.

Each of the following problems is not carefully formulated since there is no requirement that the values of the function $u(x, y)$ at interior points of the region where the differential equation holds must be related in some sensible way to the values of $u(x, y)$ at points of the boundary. To formulate satisfactory requirements, and to ask that students verify that their alleged solutions satisfy the requirements, would make the problems entirely too difficult for this book. Actually, many books more advanced than this one ignore these difficulties. A student in a first course in differential equations should be content if he can apply the procedure outlined in this chapter to obtain the functions $u(x, y)$ which are presented as answers to the problems.

Problem 12.981

Use the Fourier method to find a function $u(x, y)$ such that

$$\frac{\partial^2 u}{\partial x^2} = a^2 \frac{\partial u}{\partial y} \qquad 0 < x < \pi;\ y > 0$$

$$u(0, y) = u(\pi, y) = 0 \qquad y > 0$$

$$u(x, 0) = f(x) \qquad 0 < x < \pi,$$

where a is a positive constant and $f(x)$ is a given function of the type considered above.

$$Ans.: u(x, y) = \sum_{n=1}^{\infty} c_n e^{-(n^2/a^2)y} \sin nx \qquad 0 \leqq x \leqq \pi;\ y > 0,$$

where

$$c_n = \frac{2}{\pi}\int_0^{\pi} f(x) \sin nx\, dx \qquad n = 1, 2, 3, \ldots .$$

Discuss completely the special case in which the function $f(x)$ has the form

$$f(x) = \sum_{k=1}^{N} E_k \sin kx.$$

Remark: If x is the distance of a point from one end of a rod with initial temperature $f(x)$, if the ends of the rod are maintained at temperature 0, and if no heat escapes from the rod except at the ends, then $u(x, y)$ is the temperature at time $y > 0$ of the point of the rod with abscissa x.

Problem 12.982

Use the Fourier method to find approximations to a function $u(x, y)$ such that

$$\begin{aligned} \frac{\partial^2 u}{\partial x^2} + \frac{\partial^2 u}{\partial y^2} &= 0 & 0 < x, y < \pi \\ u(0, y) = u(\pi, y) &= 0 & 0 < y < \pi \\ u(x, \pi) &= 0 & 0 < x < \pi \\ u(x, 0) &= f(x) & 0 < x < \pi, \end{aligned}$$

where $f(x)$ is a given function of the type considered above. *Ans.:*

$$S_N(x, y) = \sum_{n=1}^{N} c_n[e^{n(\pi-y)} - e^{-n(\pi-y)}] \sin nx$$

where

$$c_n = \frac{2}{\pi} \frac{1}{e^{n\pi} - e^{-n\pi}} \int_0^\pi f(x) \sin nx \, dx \qquad n = 1, 2, 3, \ldots .$$

Discuss completely the special case in which the function $f(x)$ has the form

$$f(x) = \sum_{k=1}^{n} E_k \sin kx.$$

Remark: This problem has several important physical meanings.

Problem 12.983

Use the Fourier method to find approximations to a function $u(x, y)$ such that

$$\begin{aligned} \frac{\partial^2 u}{\partial x^2} &= a^2 \frac{\partial^2 u}{\partial y^2} & 0 < x < a;\ y > 0 \\ u(0, y) = u(\pi, y) &= 0 & y > 0 \\ u(x, 0) &= f(x) & 0 < x < \pi \\ u_y(x, 0) &= g(x) & 0 < x < \pi, \end{aligned}$$

where u_y means $\partial u/\partial y$ and $f(x)$ and $g(x)$ are given functions of the type considered above. *Ans.:*

$$S_N(x, y) = \sum_{n=1}^{N} [\alpha_n \cos any + \beta_n \sin any] \sin nx$$

where

$$\alpha_n = \frac{2}{\pi} \int_0^\pi f(x) \sin nx \, dx, \qquad \beta_n = \frac{2}{an\pi} \int_0^\pi g(x) \sin nx \, dx \qquad n = 1, 2, \ldots .$$

12.99. The Lebesgue Space L_2. We conclude this chapter with a brief introduction to geometric ideas which are often useful in physics (including quantum mechanics) and elsewhere. A thorough knowledge of Lebesgue (1875–1941) measure and integration is required for a full understanding of the results and proofs. However it should be clear to everyone that the ideas serve to show that some manipulations with functions (which may otherwise seem to be quite mysterious and complicated) are analogous to simple manipulations with real numbers or with ordinary vectors in Euclid space of two or three dimensions. Let n be a positive integer and let E be a measurable set in Euclid space of n dimensions. For example, we can let $n = 1$ and let E be one of the intervals $0 \leqq x \leqq 1$, $0 \leqq x < \infty$, $-\infty < x < \infty$. For another example we can let $n = 3$ and let E be all of three-dimensional space. In the latter case, we think of x as being an ordered set (x_1, x_2, x_3) of three real numbers which are the rectangular coordinates of a point in the three-dimensional space.

We now introduce the *Lebesgue space* L_2 which is, apart from Euclid spaces, the most important linear vector metric complete space. A *point* or *vector* in the space L_2 is a function $f(x)$ which is defined almost everywhere over E, is measurable over E, and is such that the integral in

(12.9901) $$\|f\| = \left[\int_E |f(x)|^2 dx\right]^{\frac{1}{2}}$$

exists as a Lebesgue integral. The nonnegative number $\|f\|$ is called the *length* of f. It can be proved that if f and g are two points (or vectors) in L_2, then the number (f, g) defined by

(12.9902) $$(f, g) = \int_E f(x)\overline{g(x)}dx$$

exists. This number (f, g) is called the *scalar product* of f and g; in ordinary vector analysis, the scalar product of two vectors f and g is often called the *dot product* and is denoted by $f \cdot g$. In each case, two vectors are orthogonal if and only if their scalar product is 0. The Schwarz inequality (9.7941) can now be put in the form

(12.9903) $$|(f, g)| \leq \|f\| \, \|g\|;$$

it says that the absolute value of the scalar product of f and g cannot exceed the product of the lengths of f and g. It can be proved that if f and g are points (or vectors) in L_2 and c_1 and c_2 are constants, then $c_1 f + c_2 g$ is in L_2 and

(12.9904) $$\|c_1 f + c_2 g\| \leqq |c_1| \, \|f\| + |c_2| \, \|g\|.$$

The *distance* between two points f and g is defined to be $\|f - g\|$, and it follows from (2.9904) that the *triangle inequality*

$$\|f + g\| \leqq \|f\| + \|g\| \tag{12.99041}$$

holds.

It can be proved that if $f_1, f_2, f_3, \ldots$ is a sequence of points of L_2 for which the first of the relations

$$\lim_{m,n\to\infty} \|f_m - f_n\| = 0, \qquad \lim_{n\to\infty} \|f - f_n\| = 0 \tag{12.9905}$$

holds, then there exists an f in L_2 such that the second one holds. This is the Riesz (1880–1956)-Fischer (1875–) theorem and it shows that the space L_2 is complete. When integrals less potent than Lebesgue integrals are used in (12.9901), the conclusion of the Riesz-Fischer theorem is invalid; this is perhaps the principal reason why applied mathematicians need Lebesgue integrals.

Suppose now that

$$\phi_1, \phi_2, \phi_3, \ldots$$

is an orthonormal set in L_2 and that f is in L_2. Using the notation and terminology involving (12.9902), we see that the Fourier coefficients of f are the numbers (f, ϕ_k) defined by

$$(f, \phi_k) = \int_E f(x)\bar{\phi}_k(x)dx \tag{12.9906}$$

and that these are the scalar products of f and the functions ϕ_k. When we think of f and the ϕ's as being vectors, we can think of $(f, \phi_k)\phi_k$ as being the component of the vector f in the direction of the vector ϕ_k. The Fourier expansion

$$(f, \phi_1)\phi_1 + (f, \phi_2)\phi_2 + (f, \phi_3)\phi_3 + \cdots$$

of a vector f is (except that there are more terms) completely analogous to the expansion of an ordinary vector f in Euclid space of three dimensions in terms of three orthonormal vectors ϕ_1, ϕ_2, ϕ_3. The coefficients are scalar products in both cases. The equality (12.75) can now be put in the form

$$\left\|f - \sum_{k=1}^{m} (f, \phi_k)\phi_k\right\|^2 = \|f\|^2 - \sum_{k=1}^{m} |(f, \phi_k)|^2.$$

In case the orthonormal set is complete, the members of this equality converge to 0 as $m \to \infty$ and the Parseval equality becomes

$$\|f\|^2 = \sum_{k=1}^{\infty} |(f, \phi_k)|^2.$$

This Parseval equality says that the square of the length of f is equal to the sum of the squares of the lengths of the components of f in the directions of the vectors in the orthonormal set, and this sounds exactly like a statement about ordinary vectors in Euclid space. It can be proved that, as our notation suggests, each complete orthonormal set contains a countably infinite set of elements that can be denoted by $\phi_1, \phi_2, \ldots$. The Riesz-Fischer theorem implies that if $a_1, a_2, \ldots$ is a sequence of constants for which $\sum_{k=1}^{\infty} |a_k|^2$ is convergent, then there must be an f in L_2 for which $(f, \phi_k) = a_k$, that is, there must be an f in L_2 having the numbers $a_1, a_2, \ldots$ for its Fourier coefficients.

The above geometric ideas provide a very simple way of attacking the problem of orthonormalization. This problem is the following. We suppose that $\psi_1, \psi_2, \ldots$ constitute a finite or infinite set of points (or vectors) in L_2. We suppose also that the set is not orthonormal but is independent in the sense that if n is a positive integer and $c_1, c_2, \ldots, c_n$ are constants, then

$$\|c_1\psi_1 + c_2\psi_2 + \cdots + c_n\psi_n\| \neq 0$$

unless $c_1 = c_2 = \cdots = c_n = 0$. The problem is that of determining an orthonormal set $\phi_1, \phi_2, \ldots$ such that, for each $n = 1, 2, \ldots$, the span (see Section 6.1) of $\phi_1, \phi_2, \ldots, \phi_n$ is the same as the span of $\psi_1, \psi_2, \ldots, \psi_n$. We begin by setting

$$\phi_1 = \psi_1/\|\psi_1\|.$$

The next step is to start with ψ_2, subtract the component of ψ_2 in the direction of ϕ_1 to obtain the vector $\psi_2 - (\psi_2, \phi_1)\phi_1$ orthogonal to ϕ_1, and then normalize this by dividing by its length to obtain

$$\phi_2 = \frac{\psi_2 - (\psi_2, \phi_1)\phi_1}{\|\psi_2 - (\psi_2, \phi_1)\phi_1\|}.$$

The next step is to start with ψ_3, subtract the components of ψ_3 in the directions of ϕ_1 and ϕ_2 to obtain a vector orthogonal to ϕ_1 and ϕ_2, and then normalize this to obtain

$$\phi_3 = \frac{\psi_3 - (\psi_3, \phi_1)\phi_1 - (\psi_3, \phi_2)\phi_2}{\|\psi_3 - (\psi_3, \phi_1)\phi_1 - (\psi_3, \phi_2)\phi_2\|}.$$

In general, after $\phi_1, \phi_2, \ldots, \phi_{n-1}$ have been determined, we start with ψ_n, subtract the components of ψ_n in the directions of $\phi_1, \phi_2, \ldots, \phi_{n-1}$ to obtain a vector orthogonal to $\phi_1, \phi_2, \ldots, \phi_{n-1}$, and then normalize this to obtain

$$\phi_n = \left[\psi_n - \sum_{k=1}^{n-1} (\psi_n, \phi_k)\phi_k\right] \Big/ \left\|\psi_n - \sum_{k=1}^{n-1} (\psi_n, \phi_k)\phi_k\right\|.$$

The process of obtaining the above orthonormal functions $\phi_1, \phi_2, \ldots$ is known as the *Schmidt* (Erhardt, 1876–) *orthonormalization process*, and many persons find it worth while to pay careful attention to all of the geometric and analytic details.

Problem 12.991

Think enough about pertinent matters to realize that the following statements are true. The functions $\psi_0, \psi_1, \ldots$ defined by $\psi_n(x) = x^n$ are independent over $-1 \leqq x \leqq 1$, and applying the Schmidt process to them must produce the normalized Legendre polynomials in (7.9834). The functions $\psi_0, \psi_1, \ldots$ defined by $\psi_n(x) = x^n e^{-x}$ are independent over the interval $x > 0$, and applying the Schmidt process to them must produce the normalized Laguerre functions in (7.4752). The functions $\psi_0, \psi_1, \ldots$ defined by $\psi_n(x) = x^n \exp(-ax^2/4)$ are independent over the interval $-\infty < x < \infty$, and applying the Schmidt process to them must produce the normalized Hermite functions in (7.4762). Then use the ideas to derive the first three or four normalized Legendre polynomials.

CHAPTER 13

LIMITS, DERIVATIVES, INTEGRALS

13.0. Introduction. This chapter contains a connected account of definitions and fundamental facts, involving limits, derivatives, and integrals, that are needed in studies of differential equations. Because of improvements in elementary calculus textbooks, it is now expected that students will know much of this material when they start the study of differential equations, but we still make it available for reference.

13.1. Limits. A function $f(x)$ is said to have a *limit* L as x approaches a, and we write

$$\lim_{x \to a} f(x) = L \tag{13.11}$$

if to each $\epsilon > 0$ corresponds a $\delta > 0$ such that $|f(x) - L| < \epsilon$ when $x \neq a$ and $|x - a| < \delta$.

One should understand thoroughly this definition and its geometrical significance.* Let us consider the meaning of the fact that

$$\lim_{x \to 0} (1 + x)^{1/x} = e, \tag{13.12}$$

where $e = 2.71828\,18284\,59045 \ldots$. Let, when $x > -1$ and $x \neq 0$,

$$f(x) = (1 + x)^{1/x}. \tag{13.13}$$

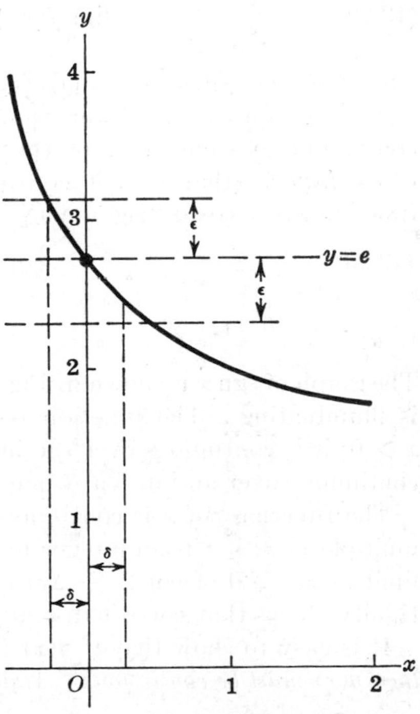

FIG. 13.14

A part of the graph of $f(x)$ is shown in Fig. 13.14. The assertion (13.12) means that when a positive number ϵ is first assigned, then it is possible to find a positive number δ such that

* It is correct to say that (13.11) means "$f(x)$ is near L when x is near a" if this vague phrase is understood to be a technical phrase meaning that to each $\epsilon > 0$ corresponds a $\delta > 0$ such that $|f(x) - L| < \epsilon$ when $x \neq a$ and $|x - a| < \delta$.

$|f(x) - e| < \epsilon$, that is,

$$e - \epsilon < f(x) < e + \epsilon, \tag{13.15}$$

for each x for which $x \neq 0$ and $-\delta < x < \delta$. Figure 13.14 shows a given positive ϵ, and a positive δ which meets the requirement.

13.2. Derivatives and Continuity. If $y(x)$ is a function of x, then

$$\frac{dy}{dx} = \lim_{\Delta x \to 0} \frac{y(x + \Delta x) - y(x)}{\Delta x} \tag{13.21}$$

when the limit exists. This definition of derivative is used in the elementary calculus to obtain the familiar formulas for derivatives of powers, logarithms, trigonometric functions, inverse trigonometric functions, and products and quotients of differentiable functions.

A function $f(x)$ is *continuous at a point* x if

$$\lim_{\Delta x \to 0} f(x + \Delta x) = f(x). \tag{13.22}$$

The functions $f_1(x) = x^2$ and $f_2(x) = \sin x$ are examples of functions continuous for all x. A function is *continuous over an interval* if it is continuous at each point of the interval. An example of a function *discontinuous* (that is, not continuous) at $x = 0$ is furnished by the function sgn x (read "signum x") defined by the formula

$$\begin{aligned} \operatorname{sgn} x &= 1 \qquad && x > 0 \\ &= 0 && x = 0 \\ &= -1 && x < 0. \end{aligned} \tag{13.23}$$

The graph of sgn x is shown in Fig. 2.0901, and the discussion given there is illuminating. The function is continuous over the infinite interval $x > 0$; it is continuous over the infinite interval $x < 0$; but it fails to be continuous over an interval when the interval contains the point $x = 0$.

The function cot x is continuous for each x different from an integer multiple of π; if x is an integer multiple of π, then neither cot x nor the limit as $\Delta x \to 0$ of cot $(x + \Delta x)$ exists and hence the criterion for continuity shows that cot x is discontinuous.

It is easy to show that *if $y(x)$ is differentiable* [that is, if $y'(x)$ exists], *then $y(x)$ must be continuous.* Indeed, if

$$\lim_{\Delta x \to 0} \frac{y(x + \Delta x) - y(x)}{\Delta x} = y'(x), \tag{13.24}$$

then

$$\lim_{\Delta x \to 0} [y(x + \Delta x) - y(x)] = \lim_{\Delta x \to 0} \frac{y(x + \Delta x) - y(x)}{\Delta x} \Delta x = y'(x) \cdot 0 = 0$$

so that $\lim y(x + \Delta x) = y(x)$, and $y(x)$ is continuous.

If every blonde whom you have seen happens to have had blue eyes, you may blithely (and incorrectly) assume that all blondes have blue eyes—until you meet a brown-eyed blonde. Likewise, if your elementary calculus dealt only with functions which are differentiable wherever they are continuous, you may blithely (and incorrectly) assume that functions are differentiable wherever they are continuous—until you meet an exception which rectifies your ideas. No mathematician can be really sophisticated until he knows that Weierstrass (1815–1897) gave an example of a continuous function which is nowhere differentiable. The example of Weierstrass is too complicated to be given here, but we shall give a classic example of a continuous function $g(x)$ for which $g'(0)$ fails to exist. Let

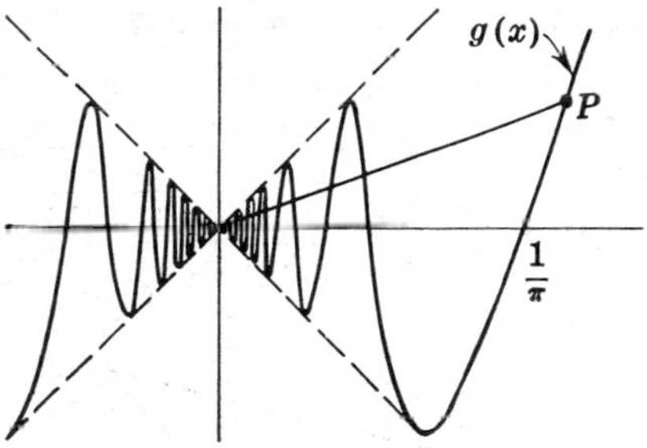

FIG. 13.25

$$g(x) = 0 \qquad x = 0 \tag{13.26}$$
$$= x \sin \frac{1}{x} \qquad x \neq 0.$$

Since $|g(x)| \leqq x$ for all x, $g(x) = x$ when $x = 1/(2n\pi + \pi/2)$, and $g(x) = -x$ when $x = 1/(2n\pi - \pi/2)$, it is easy to show that $g(x)$ is continuous and the graph of $g(x)$ is as shown in Fig. 13.25. When $\Delta x \neq 0$,

$$\frac{\Delta g}{\Delta x} = \frac{g(0 + \Delta x) - g(0)}{\Delta x} \tag{13.27}$$

is the slope of the line OP. We see that $\Delta g/\Delta x$ is $+1$ for a sequence of values of Δx converging to 0 and that $\Delta g/\Delta x$ is -1 for another sequence of values of Δx converging to 0. Hence there is no number $g'(0)$ such that (13.27) converges to $g'(0)$ as $\Delta x \to 0$, and therefore $g'(0)$ does not exist. Another continuous function $h(x)$ for which $h'(0)$ fails to exist is $h(x) = |x|$.

We have seen that continuous functions need not be differentiable. A student who wishes an exercise involving continuity and differentiability may wish to show that the function $f(x)$ defined by $f(0) = 0$ and

$$f(x) = x^2 \sin \frac{1}{x} \qquad x \neq 0 \tag{13.28}$$

is differentiable for all x but that $f'(x)$ is not continuous at $x = 0$.

13.3. Applications of the Mean-value Theorem of the Differential Calculus. The following *mean value theorem*, or *law of the mean*, of the differential calculus is mentioned in most elementary calculus textbooks and is proved in all advanced calculus textbooks that live up to their names.

THEOREM 13.31. *If $f(x)$ is continuous over $a \leqq x \leqq b$ and $f'(x)$ exists over $a < x < b$, then there is at least one point x_0 such that $a < x_0 < b$ and*

$$\frac{f(b) - f(a)}{b - a} = f'(x_0). \tag{13.311}$$

We shall not give a proof of this theorem here. The geometric interpretation of (13.311) is shown in Fig. 13.312: the tangent to the graph of $y = f(x)$ at the point x_0 is parallel to the chord joining the points $(a, f(a))$ and $(b, f(b))$. If the hypotheses of Theorem 13.31 hold and $f(a) = f(b) = 0$, the formula (13.311) becomes $f'(x_0) = 0$. This gives the following theorem of Rolle (1652–1719).

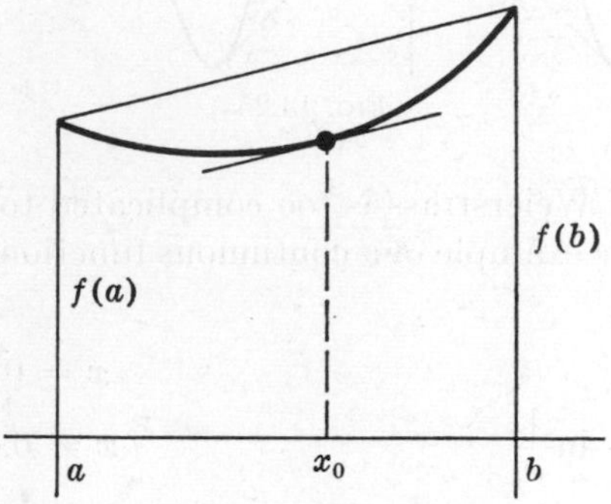

FIG. 13.312

ROLLE'S THEOREM 13.32. *If $f(x)$ is continuous over $a \leqq x \leqq b$, if $f(a) = f(b) = 0$, and if $f'(x)$ exists over $a < x < b$, then there is at least one point x_0 such that $a < x_0 < b$ and $f'(x_0) = 0$.*

One of the reasons why Theorem 13.31 is important is that it can be used to give a simple proof of the following theorem.

THEOREM 13.33. *If $f'(x) = 0$ over $a \leqq x \leqq b$, then $f(x)$ is constant over $a \leqq x \leqq b$.*

Assuming Theorem 13.31, we prove Theorem 13.33. Since $f'(x) = 0$ over $a \leqq x \leqq b$, it follows that $f'(x)$ and $f(x)$ are continuous over $a \leqq x \leqq b$. Let x be fixed such that $a < x \leqq b$. By Theorem 13.31 there must exist a point x_0 such that $a < x_0 < x$ and

$$\frac{f(x) - f(a)}{x - a} = f'(x_0). \tag{13.331}$$

But $f'(x_0) = 0$. Therefore $f(x) = f(a)$. Thus $f(x) = f(a)$ when $a < x \leqq b$, and Theorem 13.33 follows.

The same proof gives the following slightly stronger theorem which is often used.

THEOREM 13.34. *If $f(x)$ is continuous over $a \leqq x \leqq b$ and $f'(x) = 0$ over $a < x < b$, then $f(x)$ is constant over $a \leqq x \leqq b$.*

We can now make an application of Theorem 13.33 to obtain the following theorem pertaining to the differential equation $y' = f(x)$.

THEOREM 13.35. *If $y_1(x)$ is a solution of $y' = f(x)$ over $a \leqq x \leqq b$, then each function $y(x)$ which is a solution of $y' = f(x)$ over $a \leqq x \leqq b$ must have the form*

$$y = y_1(x) + c \qquad a \leqq x \leqq b \tag{13.351}$$

where c is a constant.

If $y_1(x)$ and $y(x)$ are two functions such that $y_1'(x) = f(x)$ and

$$y'(x) = f(x)$$

over $a \leqq x \leqq b$ and we put $g(x) = y(x) - y_1(x)$, then

$$g'(x) = y'(x) - y_1'(x) = f(x) - f(x) = 0$$

so that, by Theorem 13.33, $g(x)$ must be a constant c and hence (13.351) holds. This proves Theorem 13.35.

Example 13.4

It should be observed that Theorem 13.35 does not assert that the equation $y' = f(x)$ has any solutions. Whether the equation $y' = f(x)$ has any solutions depends upon $f(x)$. The equation $y' = 3x^2$ does have solutions; in fact, $y = x^3 + c$ is a solution for each constant c.

We shall now find out whether or not the differential equation

$$\frac{dy}{dx} = \text{sgn } x \tag{13.41}$$

has any solutions. If $y(x)$ satisfies (13.41) when $x > 0$, then $y'(x) = 1$ and therefore (why?) c_1 exists such that $y = x + c_1$ when $x > 0$. If $y(x)$ satisfies (13.41) when $x < 0$, then $y'(x) = -1$ and therefore c_2 exists such that $y = -x + c_2$ when $x < 0$. Figure 13.42 exhibits the graph of a function $y(x)$ which satisfies the equation $y' =$ sgn x for $x \neq 0$. If $y(x)$ satisfies $y' =$ sgn x for all x, then $y(x)$ must be continuous; therefore c_1 and c_2 must be equal, and $y(x)$ must have the form

$$y = |x| + c$$

where c is the common value of c_1 and c_2. The graph of $y = |x| + c$ is shown in Fig. 13.43. Since $y'(0)$ does not exist, it is not true that $y'(0) =$ sgn 0; accordingly,

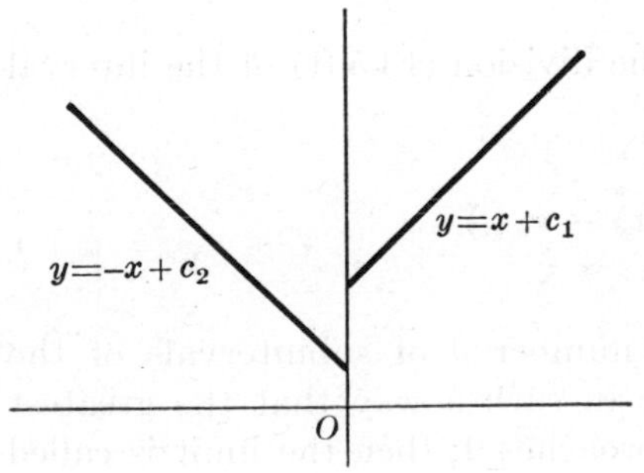

FIG. 13.42

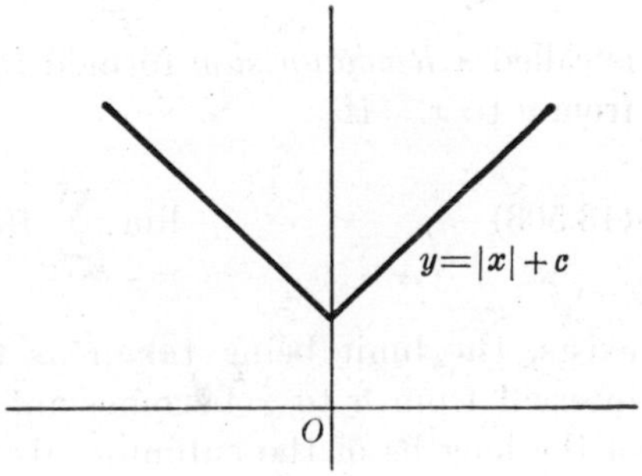

FIG. 13.43

we must conclude that $y(x)$ does not satisfy $y' = \operatorname{sgn} x$ for all x. We have shown (a) that if $y(x)$ satisfies $y' = \operatorname{sgn} x$ for all x, then $y(x) = |x| + c$ where c is a constant and (b) that the function $|x| + c$ fails to satisfy $y' = \operatorname{sgn} x$ for all x. We deduce from (a) and (b) that there is no function $y(x)$ satisfying for all x the differential equation $y' = \operatorname{sgn} x$. The best we can do is find a function which is continuous over $-\infty < x < \infty$ and satisfies $y'(x) = \operatorname{sgn} x$ when $x \neq 0$.

This example shows that if $f(x)$ is not continuous, then there may fail to be a function $y(x)$ such that $y'(x) = f(x)$. We shall show by means of the Riemann (definite) integral that if $f(x)$ is continuous, then a function $y(x)$ must exist such that $y'(x) = f(x)$. We shall then know, among other things, that there is a function whose derivative is $\sqrt{1 + x^2}\, e^{-x}$. One answer will turn out to be

$$\int_0^x \sqrt{1 + t^2}\, e^{-t}\, dt.$$

13.5. Riemann Integrals. We proceed to define the Riemann integral of a function $f(x)$. This integral, which as we shall see is defined as a limit of certain sums, is sometimes called a definite integral; but many other kinds of integrals are also definite integrals, and the term *Riemann integral* is preferable. Throughout this section, all integrals are Riemann integrals.

Let $f(x)$ be a function defined over an interval $a \leqq x \leqq b$, and let x be fixed such that $a < x \leqq b$. Let n be a positive integer. Let the interval from a to x be subdivided into n subintervals by points $x_1, x_2, \ldots, x_{n-1}$ so that

$$a = x_0 < x_1 < x_2 < x_3 < \cdots < x_{n-1} < x_n = x. \tag{13.501}$$

For each $k = 1, 2, \ldots, n$, the length of the kth subinterval is $x_k - x_{k-1}$. Let t_k be a point such that $x_{k-1} \leqq t_k \leqq x_k$. The number

$$\sum_{k=1}^{n} f(t_k)(x_k - x_{k-1}) \tag{13.502}$$

is called a *Riemann sum* formed for the division (13.501) of the interval from a to x. If

$$\lim \sum_{k=1}^{n} f(t_k)(x_k - x_{k-1}) \tag{13.503}$$

exists, the limit being taken as the number n of subintervals of the interval from a to x becomes infinite in such a way that the greatest of the lengths of the subintervals approaches 0; then the limit is called the *Riemann integral* of $f(x)$ over the interval (a, x) and we write*

$$(13.51)\qquad \int_a^x f(t)dt = \lim \sum_{k=1}^{n} f(t_k)(x_k - x_{k-1}).$$

If the limit does not exist, one says that the function is not integrable (that is, not Riemann integrable) over the interval.

It should be completely and thoroughly understood that the left member of (13.51) is merely a symbol to represent the number which is the limit in the right member of (13.51). The symbol

$$(13.511)\qquad \int_a^x f(x)dx$$

is commonly used in elementary-calculus books, but in more advanced work it is customary to choose a "dummy" variable of integration different from the letters used to represent the end points of the interval of integration. The left member of (13.51) would mean the same thing if t were replaced by u or y or α or ϕ or any other letter. Only a, x, f, and d are to be avoided.

The definition of the Riemann integral is completed by defining

$$(13.52)\qquad \int_a^x f(t)dt$$

to be 0 when $x = a$ and to be

$$(13.521)\qquad -\int_x^a f(t)dt$$

when $x < a$ and the latter integral exists.

All information obtained about Riemann integrals must be derived from their definitions as limits of Riemann sums. A careful consideration of the definitions is required to prove that if $f(x)$ is integrable over an interval with end points at a and b, where a may be either less or greater than b, and if c lies between a and b, then all three integrals

$$(13.522)\qquad \int_a^b f(t)dt = \int_a^c f(t)dt + \int_c^b f(t)dt$$

* The precise meaning of (13.51) is the following: To each $\epsilon > 0$ corresponds a $\delta > 0$ such that

$$\left| \int^x f(t)\,dt - \sum_{k-1}^{n} f(t_k)(x_k - x_{k-1}) \right| < \epsilon$$

for each division $a = x_0 < x_1 < \cdots < x_n = x$ of the interval (a, x) for which

$$|x_k - x_{k-1}| < \delta \qquad k = 1, 2, \ldots, n$$

and each choice of the points $t_1, \ldots, t_n$ for which $x_{k-1} \leqq t_k \leqq x_k$ when $k = 1, 2, \ldots, n$. A geometric interpretation of Riemann sums and integrals is given in Section 13.8.

exist and the equality holds. One of the simplest and most useful properties of Riemann integrals is embodied in the following theorem which is known as the *mean-value theorem of the integral calculus.*

THEOREM 13.53. *If $f(x)$ is integrable over an interval with end points a and b, where a may be either less or greater than b, and if m and M are constants such that*

$$m \leqq f(x) \leqq M \tag{13.531}$$

over the interval, then

$$m \leqq \frac{1}{b-a}\int_a^b f(t)dt \leqq M. \tag{13.532}$$

To prove this we consider first the case in which $a < b$. With the notation used in defining integrals, we have

$$m \leqq f(t_k) \leqq M \qquad k = 1, 2, \ldots, n \tag{13.533}$$

so that

$$m(x_k - x_{k-1}) \leqq f(t_k)(x_k - x_{k-1}) \leqq M(x_k - x_{k-1}) \tag{13.534}$$

and addition gives

$$m(b - a) \leqq \sum_{k=1}^{n} f(t_k)(x_k - x_{k-1}) \leqq M(b - a). \tag{13.535}$$

The first and last members of (13.535) are constants independent of n. Letting $n \to \infty$ in such a way that the greatest of the numbers $x_k - x_{k-1}$ approaches 0, we obtain

$$m(b - a) \leqq \int_a^b f(t)dt \leqq M(b - a) \tag{13.536}$$

since the middle term of (13.535) must converge to the middle term of (13.536). Dividing (13.536) by $(b - a)$ gives (13.532) for the case in which $a < b$. If $b < a$, we can write the inequality obtained by interchanging a and b in (13.532) and then interchange a and b to obtain (13.532). This proves Theorem 13.53.

An important theorem (which most elementary-calculus books do not prove and which we shall not prove here) is the following.

THEOREM 13.54. *If $f(x)$ is continuous over the interval $a \leqq x \leqq b$, then*

$$\int_a^x f(t)dt \tag{13.541}$$

exists when $a \leqq x \leqq b$.

A function is said to be *bounded* over an interval if there is a constant B such that $|f(x)| \leqq B$ for each point x of the interval. The following theorem, which is stronger than Theorem 13.54, is often useful.

THEOREM 13.542. *If $f(x)$ is bounded and is continuous except at a* *finite number of points in the interval $a \leqq x \leqq b$, then*

$$\int_a^x f(t)dt \tag{13.543}$$

exists when $a \leqq x \leqq b$.

Modern students of mathematical analysis know that (13.543) exists for a bounded function $f(x)$ if and only if the points of the interval $a \leqq x \leqq b$ at which $f(x)$ is not continuous form a set having Lebesgue measure 0; but proof, discussion, and use of this more profound result lie beyond a first course in differential equations.

The answer to the question whether the equation $y' = f(x)$ must have a solution when $f(x)$ is continuous is given by the following theorem, which is known as the *fundamental theorem of the calculus* and which furnishes a connection between the processes of integration and differentiation.

THEOREM 13.55. *If $f(x)$ is continuous over the interval $a \leqq x \leqq b$ and*

$$F(x) = \int_a^x f(t)dt \qquad a \leqq x \leqq b, \tag{13.551}$$

then

$$F'(x) = f(x) \qquad a \leqq x \leqq b. \tag{13.552}$$

The following theorem, which is stronger than Theorem 13.55, is often useful.

THEOREM 13.56. *If $f(x)$ is bounded and is continuous except at a finite number of points in the interval from a to b and*

$$F(x) = \int_a^x f(t)dt, \tag{13.561}$$

then $F(x)$ is continuous over $a \leqq x \leqq b$ and $F'(x) = f(x)$ for each x for which $f(x)$ is continuous.

We prove Theorem 13.56 and hence also at the same time the weaker Theorem 13.55. Our hypothesis and Theorem 13.542 imply that the integral in (13.561) exists when $a \leqq x \leqq b$. Let B be a constant such that

$$-B \leqq f(x) \leqq B \qquad a \leqq x \leqq b. \tag{13.562}$$

Using (13.561) and (13.522), we obtain

$$F(x + \Delta x) - F(x) = \int_a^{x+\Delta x} f(t)dt - \int_a^x f(t)dt = \int_x^{x+\Delta x} f(t)dt, \tag{13.563}$$

and dividing by Δx gives

$$\frac{F(x + \Delta x) - F(x)}{\Delta x} = \frac{1}{\Delta x}\int_x^{x+\Delta x} f(t)dt. \tag{13.564}$$

Using (13.562) and the law of the mean (Theorem 13.53), we obtain

$$-B \leqq \frac{F(x + \Delta x) - F(x)}{\Delta x} \leqq B. \tag{13.565}$$

Multiplying (13.565) by Δx and letting $\Delta x \to 0$, we see that

$$\lim_{\Delta x \to 0} F(x + \Delta x) = F(x). \tag{13.566}$$

This proves continuity of $F(x)$. Now let x be a point at which $f(x)$ is continuous; it remains for us to show that $F'(x) = f(x)$. Let $\epsilon > 0$, and choose $\delta > 0$ such that

$$f(x) - \epsilon < f(t) < f(x) + \epsilon \qquad |t - x| < \delta. \tag{13.567}$$

Then, when $|\Delta x| < \delta$, we can use the law of the mean (Theorem 13.53) to obtain

$$f(x) - \epsilon < \frac{1}{\Delta x}\int_x^{x+\Delta x} f(t)dt < f(x) + \epsilon \qquad 0 < |\Delta x| < \delta. \tag{13.568}$$

Therefore, because of (13.564),

$$-\epsilon < \frac{F(x + \Delta x) - F(x)}{\Delta x} - f(x) < \epsilon \qquad 0 < |\Delta x| < \delta. \tag{13.569}$$

This means, by definition of limit, that

$$\lim_{\Delta x \to 0} \frac{F(x + \Delta x) - F(x)}{\Delta x} = f(x)$$

and hence, by definition of derivative, that $F'(x) = f(x)$. This completes the proofs of Theorems 13.55 and 13.56.

Combining Theorems 13.34 and 13.55 and using the obvious fact that the derivative of a constant is 0, we obtain the following fundamental theorem.

THEOREM 13.57. *If $f(x)$ is continuous over an interval I containing a point a, then each solution of the differential equation*

$$\frac{dy}{dx} = f(x) \tag{13.571}$$

over the interval I must have the form

$$y = \int_a^x f(t)dt + c \tag{13.572}$$

where c is a constant; moreover, (13.572) *is a solution of* (13.571) *over I for each constant c.*

From the last theorem we obtain immediately the familiar formula used for the evaluation of integrals of continuous functions $f(x)$. If $\phi(x)$ is any function (obtained from whatever source) whose derivative is $f(x)$, then c exists such that

$$\phi(x) = \int_a^x f(t)dt + c. \tag{13.573}$$

Setting $x = a$, we find that $c = \phi(a)$. Hence, using the familiar notation

$$\phi(t)\Big]_a^x = \phi(x) - \phi(a), \tag{13.574}$$

we obtain the familiar formula

$$\int_a^x f(t)dt = \phi(t)\Big]_a^x = \phi(x) - \phi(a) \tag{13.575}$$

which is often used to evaluate integrals.

In many problems (such as the electric-circuit problem discussed in Section 3.9) one needs not only Theorem 13.56 but also the following converse theorem.

THEOREM 13.58. *If $f(x)$ is bounded over an interval $a \leqq x \leqq b$ and is continuous except at a finite number of points in the interval, then each function $y(x)$ which is continuous over $a \leqq x \leqq b$ and such that*

$$\frac{dy}{dx} = f(x) \tag{13.581}$$

for each x for which $f(x)$ is continuous must have the form

$$y(x) = \int_a^x f(t)dt + c \qquad a \leqq x \leqq b \tag{13.582}$$

where c is a constant.

Proof of Theorem 13.58 is not difficult. Let the points of discontinuity $x_1, x_2, \ldots, x_n$ be named so that $x_1 < x_2 < x_3 < \cdots < x_n$. By Theorem 13.56 the function $y_1(x)$ defined by

$$y_1(x) = \int_a^x f(t)dt$$

is one continuous function such that $y_1'(x) = f(x)$ except at the points $x_1, x_2, x_3, \ldots, x_n$. If $y(x)$ is another such function and we set $Y(x) = y(x) - y_1(x)$, we see that $Y(x)$ is continuous and that $Y'(x) = 0$ except perhaps at the points $x_1, x_2, \ldots, x_n$. It follows from Theorem 13.34 that $Y(x)$ must be a constant c over $a \leqq x \leqq x_1$, a constant c_1 over $x_1 \leqq x \leqq x_2$, a constant c_2 over $x_2 \leqq x \leqq x_3$, and so on. The conditions $Y(x_1) = c$ and $Y(x_1) = c_1$ imply that $c = c_1$; likewise $c = c_1 = c_2 = \cdots$, and hence $Y(x)$ is the constant c over the entire interval $a \leqq x \leqq b$. Thus $y(x) - y_1(x) = c$ over $a \leqq x \leqq b$, and this gives our result (13.582).

Problem 13.591

Explain carefully what the left member of the equality

$$\int_4^5 x^2\,dx = \frac{1}{3}x^3\Big]_4^5 = \frac{61}{3}$$

is, and tell why the equality holds.

Problem 13.592

Prove that if a and x are both positive or both negative, then

$$\int_a^x \frac{1}{t}\,dt = \log |t| \Big]_a^x = \log |x| - \log |a|.$$

You may use the fact that if $f(x)$ is differentiable and $f(x) > 0$, then the derivative with respect to x of $\log f(x)$ is $f'(x)/f(x)$.

Problem 13.593

Let $f(x) = 1$ when the greatest integer less than or equal to x is even (*i.e.*, $0, -2, 2, -4, 4, \ldots$), and let $f(x) = -1$ when the greatest integer less than or equal to x is odd (*i.e.*, $-1, 1, -3, 3, \ldots$). The function $f(x)$ may be described as the function with period 2 which is 1 when $0 \leqq x < 1$ and is -1 when $1 \leqq x < 2$. Draw graphs of $f(x)$ and

$$y(x) = \int_0^x f(t)dt.$$

Show that $y(x)$ is continuous and that $y'(x) = f(x)$ except when x is an integer.

Problem 13.594

A particle of unit mass is placed at rest at the origin of a horizontal x axis at time $t = 0$. During the first half of each minute it is pushed toward the right by a constant unit force, and during the second half of each minute it is pushed toward the left by a constant unit force. Where is the particle at the end of 10 minutes? [For the benefit of anyone whose knowledge of mechanics is fragmentary or untrustworthy, we remark that if $x(t)$ is the displacement of a particle of mass m moving under the action of a horizontal force $f(t)$ which is positive or negative according as the force pushes toward the right or left, then $x(t)$ is continuous and has a continuous derivative $x'(t)$. Moreover, by a fundamental law of Newton, $x''(t) = d^2x/dt^2$ exists for each value of t for which $f(t)$ is continuous and $f(t) = mx''(t)$.] Draw graphs of $x(t)$, $x'(t)$, and $x''(t)$.

13.6. Cauchy Integrals. A function $f(x)$ can have a Riemann integral over an interval $a \leqq x \leqq b$ only when the interval is finite and the function $f(x)$ is bounded over $a \leqq x \leqq b$. If $f(x)$ is defined over $a \leqq x \leqq b$ except perhaps at a single point c where $a \leqq c \leqq b$ and if for each h such that $h > 0$ and $c - h > a$ the Riemann integral

$$\int_a^{c-h} f(t)dt$$

exists, we define

$$\int_a^c f(t)dt = \lim_{h \to 0+} \int_a^{c-h} f(t)dt \tag{13.61}$$

when the limit exists. Similarly we define

$$\int_c^b f(t)dt = \lim_{h \to 0+} \int_{c+h}^b f(t)dt \tag{13.62}$$

when the limit exists. If the limits in (2.41) and (2.42) both exist, we define

$$(13.63)\qquad \int_a^b f(t)dt = \lim_{h\to 0+}\int_a^{c-h} f(t)dt + \lim_{h\to 0+}\int_{c+h}^b f(t)dt.$$

We also define

$$(13.64)\qquad \int_a^\infty f(t)dt = \lim_{h\to\infty}\int_a^h f(t)dt$$

$$(13.65)\qquad \int_{-\infty}^a f(t)dt = \lim_{h\to-\infty}\int_h^a f(t)dt$$

$$(13.66)\qquad \int_{-\infty}^\infty f(t)dt = \lim_{a\to-\infty}\int_a^\infty f(t)dt,$$

in case the limits exist. The integrals in the left members of (13.61) to (13.66) are called *Cauchy integrals* or *improper integrals.* The author prefers the first alternative since he sees no reason why defamatory terminology should be applied to useful integrals. The term *infinite integral* is sometimes used, but many persons object violently to this term.

A more abstruse integral, known as the *Cauchy principal-value integral,* is defined by

$$(13.67)\qquad \int_a^b f(t)dt = \lim_{h\to 0+}\left[\int_a^{c-h} f(t)dt + \int_{c+h}^b f(t)dt\right]$$

when the integrals on the right exist as Riemann or Cauchy integrals and the limit on the right exists. The important point to notice here is that the integral in (13.67) can exist when neither of the two separate limits in the right member of (13.63) exists. For an example, see Problem 13.68.

Problem 13.68

Draw graphs of $f(x) = 1/x$ and

$$(13.681)\qquad y(x) = \int_{-2}^x \frac{1}{t}\,dt$$

for those values of x between -2 and 2 for which the functions are defined. Pay careful attention to the kind or kinds of integral you use. Is $y'(x) = f(x)$?

13.7. Indefinite Integrals. The symbol

$$(13.71)\qquad \int f(x)dx$$

is used to denote a function of x whose derivative is $f(x)$; the function is called an *indefinite integral* of $f(x)$. For example, x^3 and $x^3 + 1{,}776$ are both indefinite integrals of $3x^2$, and each indefinite integral of $3x^2$ has the form $x^3 + c$ where c is a constant.

If $f(x)$ is continuous, then for each constant a the function

$$(13.72)\qquad \int_a^\infty f(t)dt$$

is *an* indefinite integral of $f(x)$. It is not necessarily true that each indefinite integral of $f(x)$ can be represented in the form (13.72); for if $f(x) = \cos x$ so that

$$\int_a^x \cos t\,dt = \sin t\Big]_a^x = \sin x - \sin a, \tag{13.73}$$

then it is impossible to choose a such that (13.73) is the indefinite integral $(\sin x - 10)$ of $\cos x$. However, each indefinite integral of $f(x)$ can be represented in the form

$$\int_a^x f(t)dt + c.$$

13.74. Elementary Functions; Integration. The so-called *elementary functions* include powers, roots, exponentials, logarithms, trigonometric and inverse trigonometric functions, and finite combinations of these obtained by addition, subtraction, multiplication, and division. For example, x^3, e^x, $(1 + x^2)^{\frac{1}{2}}$, $\log \sin x$, and

$$(1 + \log x)x^4e^{-x^2} \cos \frac{x^2 - 1}{x^2 + 1} \tag{13.75}$$

are elementary functions of x.

A considerable part of a course in elementary calculus is devoted to the following problem which is there called the *problem of integration:* Given an elementary function $f(x)$, find an elementary function $y(x)$ such that $y' = f(x)$ or

$$\int f(x)dx = y(x). \tag{13.76}$$

The techniques for finding $y(x)$ include, among others, integration by parts, change of variable, separation of quotients into partial fractions, remembering results of differentiation, guessing, and use of integral tables.

If, $f(x)$ being given, say $f(x) = x \sin x$, a student is unable to find an elementary function $y(x)$ for which (13.76) holds, he says, "I cannot integrate $f(x)$." Only this hypothetical student of the calculus can say whether a blind faith in his calculus teacher led him to believe his "teacher could integrate everything." Just as a lass may walk through the grass and, seeing no snakes, believe that there are no snakes, so also a student may pass through elementary calculus and, seeing only elementary functions having elementary functions for integrals, believe that each elementary function necessarily has an elementary function for an integral. Assuming that students who would be unduly shocked by discovery of presence of snakes have not ventured into a study of differential equations, we mention three examples of functions which are not elementary functions:

$$\int_0^x \sqrt{1 - k^2 \sin^2 t}\,dt \tag{13.761}$$

(13.762) $$\int_0^x \frac{\sin t}{t}\,dt$$

(13.763) $$\frac{2}{\sqrt{\pi}}\int_0^x e^{-t^2}\,dt.$$

These integrals are important because of their physical and other applications. Values of all three functions have been tabulated, the tables being used just as tables of logarithms and trigonometric functions are used.

Even when $f(x)$ is a given elementary function and x is restricted to an interval $a \leqq x \leqq b$ over which $f(x)$ is continuous, it is often true that one simply does not know whether the function $y(x)$ defined by

(13.77) $$y(x) = \int_a^x f(t)dt$$

is an elementary function. If one can "integrate $f(x)$" by finding an elementary function $F(x)$ such that $F'(x) = f(x)$ or $F(x) = \int f(x)dx$, then of course $y(x) = F(x) - F(a)$ and accordingly $y(x)$ is an elementary function. However, a mere failure to find such an elementary function $F(x)$ does not of itself imply that such a function $F(x)$ cannot be found or that $y(x)$ is not an elementary function. As one may suspect, the problem of showing that functions are not elementary is a difficult one; in fact, little is known about the matter. There is an obvious advantage in knowing that the functions in (13.761), (13.762), and (13.763) are not elementary; one does not waste time in trying to express the integrals as elementary functions.

We are now in a position to emphasize the result of Theorems 13.56 and 13.58. If $f(x)$, whether an elementary function or not, is bounded over an interval $a \leqq x \leqq b$ containing a point x_0 and if $f(x)$ is continuous except at a finite number of points of the interval, then for each constant c the function

(13.771) $$y(x) = \int_{x_0}^x f(t)dt + c \qquad a \leqq x \leqq b$$

is, whether an elementary function of x or not, a continuous function of x such that $y'(x) = f(x)$ wherever $f(x)$ is continuous; and, moreover, different values of the constant c give all the functions $y(x)$ with the properties. If one is so fortunate as to find, in an integral table or otherwise, an elementary function $F(x)$ equal to $\int f(x)dx$, then [see (13.575)] the formula

(13.772) $$y(x) = F(x) - F(a) + c$$

gives $y(x)$ as an elementary function. If one is not so fortunate, one can always use the methods of the following sections to find approximations to $y(x)$.

Problem 13.781

Prove that

$$|x| = \int_0^x \text{sgn } t\, dt. \tag{13.7811}$$

[The signum function was defined in (13.23).] One who feels that (13.7811) is a foolish formula should be impressed by knowledge that (13.7811) and the Dirichlet formula (2.0903) can be used to show that

$$|x| = \frac{1}{\pi}\int_{-\infty}^{\infty} \frac{1 - \cos xt}{t^2}\, dt. \tag{13.7812}$$

Such formulas are useful.

Problem 13.782

Using the rule for differentiating a function of a function of x, show that if

$$y = 2\int_0^{\sqrt{x}} e^{-t^2}\, dt + c \qquad x > 0 \tag{13.7821}$$

then

$$\frac{dy}{dx} = \frac{e^{-x}}{\sqrt{x}} \qquad x > 0. \tag{13.7822}$$

Can you show that if (13.7822) holds, then (13.7821) must hold?

13.8. Integrals and Areas. The following discussion applies to a function $f(x)$ which is positive and continuous over an interval $a \leqq x \leqq b$. Let x be fixed such that $a < x \leqq b$, and let

$$a = x_0 < x_1 < x_2 < \cdot \cdot \cdot < x_n = x$$

be a division of the interval from a to x as in (13.501). If

$$x_{k-1} \leqq t_k \leqq x_k,$$

then the product $f(t_k)(x_k - x_{k-1})$ is the area of a rectangle of height $f(t_k)$ standing on the interval from x_{k-1} to x_k on the x axis. Hence, the Riemann sum

$$\sum_{k=1}^{n} f(t_k)(x_k - x_{k-1}) \tag{13.81}$$

is the sum of the areas of such rectangles (see Fig. 13.82).

Everyone should have at least a vague feeling that if n is large and the greatest of the numbers $x_k - x_{k-1}$ is small, then the Riemann sum (*i.e.*, the sum of the areas of the rectangles) should be nearly equal to the area of the portion of the plane which lies above the x axis, under the curve whose equation is $y = f(x)$, and between the lines with abscissas a and x. It is in accordance with this feeling that the area of the region in question is defined* to be the limit of the Riemann sums (*i.e.*, the limit of the sum of areas of rectangles). The area in question depends on x and may be denoted by $A(x)$. Since $A(x)$ and the definite integral are both (by definition) equal to the limit of Riemann sums, we have

$$A(x) = \int_a^x f(t)dt. \tag{13.83}$$

In case the graph of $f(x)$ lies below the x axis, the integral in (13.83) is not the area of the region bounded by the curve, the x axis, and the two

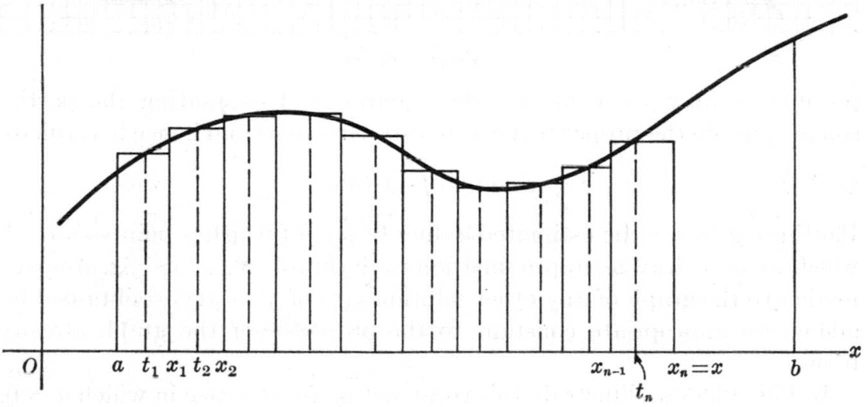

FIG. 13.82

lines with abscissas a and x; the integral is the negative of that area. In case the graph of $f(x)$ is sometimes above and sometimes below the x axis, the integral is a sum of areas and the negatives of areas.

In elementary calculus, the connection between integrals and areas is often represented as being important because it enables one to find areas by evaluating integrals. Apart from the solution of problems in calculus books (a worthy pursuit), one seldom finds areas by evaluating integrals. The real importance of the connection between integrals and areas lies in the fact that it enables one to obtain approximate values of integrals by estimating areas.

13.84. Graphical Solutions. The connection between integrals and areas furnishes a practical method of constructing graphs of solutions of $y' = f(x)$ when $f(x)$ is given. Let the graph of $f(x)$ be drawn on closely ruled graph paper (see Fig. 13.85), and let a convenient value of a be selected. Then for each of several judiciously spaced values of x it is

* We may recall that, even in elementary plane geometry, the area of a circle is *defined* to be the limit of areas of polygons.

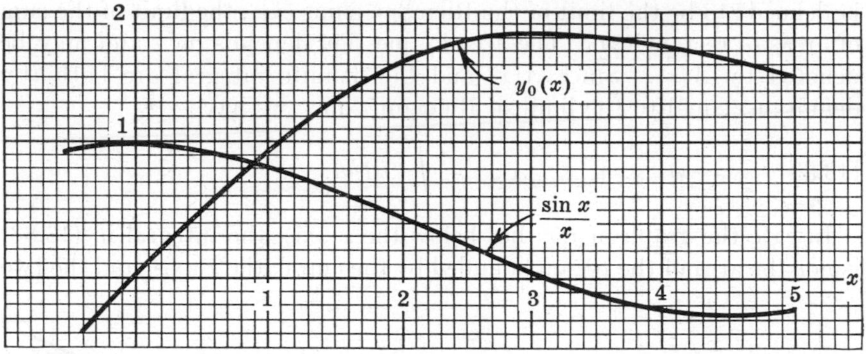

FIG. 13.85

possible (simply by counting the squares, and estimating the partial squares, inside the proper regions) to estimate areas and hence to estimate

(13.86) $$y_a(x) \equiv \int_a^x f(t)dt.$$

Plotting against x the estimated values of $y_a(x)$ furnishes points through which we may draw an approximation to the graph of $y_a(x)$. An approximation to the graph of any other solution $y(x)$ of $y' = f(x)$ is obtained by adding an appropriate constant to the ordinates of the graph already found.

In Fig. 13.85 we illustrate this construction for the case in which $a = 0$, $f(0) = 1$, and $f(x) = (\sin x)/x$ when $x \neq 0$. Values of $(\sin x)/x$ used in construction of the graph may be found by use of a table of sines and by division. However, it is simpler to use tables giving values of $(\sin x)/x$; such a table may be found in the Jahnke-Emde work cited in Remark 7.79. In fact this book contains a table of values of

$$y_0(x) = \int_0^x \frac{\sin t}{t}\, dt.$$

The *graphical*, or *square-counting*, method of solving $y' = f(x)$ can sometimes be applied even when one does not have a formula for the function $f(x)$. If one can determine by measurements (which may be based on physical, chemical, biological, or other experiments) the values of $f(x)$ for enough values of x to permit construction of the graph (or an approximation to the graph) of $f(x)$, then the graphical method yields an approximate solution of $y' = f(x)$ which may be sufficiently accurate for practical purposes.

Problem 13.87

Draw carefully on graph paper a graph of the function

(13.871) $$f(x) = \frac{1}{1 + x^4}$$

for $0 \leqq x \leqq 3$, and use the method of this section to obtain an approximation to the graph of

$$y(x) = \int_0^x f(t)dt \tag{13.872}$$

for $0 \leqq x \leqq 3$.

13.9. Other Methods of Evaluating Integrals. There are "integrating machines" (planimeters and integraphs) by means of which areas of regions can be found by pushing a point tracer of the apparatus around the boundaries of the regions. Some graph paper is carefully made with uniform known weight per unit area so that areas of regions may be found by cutting them out and weighing them.

An obvious way to obtain an approximate value of

$$\int_a^x f(t)dt, \tag{13.91}$$

when the integral exists as a Riemann integral, is to compute the Riemann sum

$$S_n = \sum_{k=1}^{n} f(a + k\,\Delta t)\Delta t \tag{13.92}$$

where $\Delta t = (x - a)/n$, for a large value of n. (Why?) A better method of approximating the integral is to compute

$$\begin{aligned} T_n = [\tfrac{1}{2}f(a) + f(a + \Delta t) + f(a + 2\,\Delta t) + \cdots \\ + f(a + \overline{n-1}\,\Delta t) + \tfrac{1}{2}f(a + n\,\Delta t)]\Delta t \end{aligned} \tag{13.93}$$

where $\Delta t = (x - a)/n$. The sum T_n is the sum of areas (or negatives of areas) of trapezoids; with this hint a student should be able to see why this *trapezoidal formula* (13.93) is appropriate.

A still better method is to compute U_n by the *Simpson* (1710–1761) *formula*

$$\begin{aligned} U_n = \tfrac{1}{3}[f(a) + 4f(a + \Delta t) + 2f(a + 2\,\Delta t) + 4f(a + 3\,\Delta t) \\ + 2f(a + 4\,\Delta t) + \cdots + 4f(a + \overline{n-1}\,\Delta t) + f(a + n\,\Delta t)]\Delta t \end{aligned} \tag{13.94}$$

where n is even and $\Delta t = (x - a)/n$. The right member is the sum of areas (or negatives of areas) partially bounded by parabolas; details may be found in many calculus books. For equal values of n, U_n is ordinarily a much closer approximation to the integral than S_n or T_n. Simpson's formula is often used. Its excellence is illustrated by obtaining the numerical value of

$$\int_0^1 \frac{1}{1 + t^2}\,dt = \tan^{-1} t\,\Big]_0^1 = \frac{\pi}{4}. \tag{13.95}$$

Taking $n = 4$, we find

$$(13.96) \qquad \begin{aligned} U_4 &= \tfrac{1}{12}[f(0) + 4f(\tfrac{1}{4}) + 2f(\tfrac{1}{2}) + 4f(\tfrac{3}{4}) + f(1)] \\ &= \tfrac{1}{12}[1 + \tfrac{64}{17} + \tfrac{8}{5} + \tfrac{64}{25} + \tfrac{1}{2}] = 0.78539\,2157. \end{aligned}$$

Using this value of U_4 as an approximation for the integral and hence for $\pi/4$, we obtain the approximate value

$$(13.961) \qquad \pi \sim 3.14156\,8628.$$

The value of π, correct to 16D, is

$$(13.962) \qquad \pi = 3.14159\,26535\,89793.$$

Thus very little effort was needed to obtain π correct to five digits, and few computations in applied mathematics require as much accuracy as this.

Problem 13.97

Use the formula

$$\int_0^{\frac{1}{2}} \frac{1}{1+t^2}\,dt = \tan^{-1} t\Big]_0^{\frac{1}{2}} = \tan^{-1}\frac{1}{2}$$

and Simpson's formula to compute $\tan^{-1}\frac{1}{2}$. (The value of $\tan^{-1}\frac{1}{2}$ is about 0.46364 76 radian.)

CHAPTER 14

THE HEAT EQUATION

14.0. Derivation of the Heat Equation. In this short chapter we employ fundamental principles of mathematics and classical physics* to obtain a completely rigorous derivation of the heat equation

$$a^2\left(\frac{\partial^2 u}{\partial x^2} + \frac{\partial^2 u}{\partial y^2} + \frac{\partial^2 u}{\partial z^2}\right) = \frac{\partial u}{\partial t}. \tag{14.1}$$

The work is extremely important, partly because of the intrinsic importance of (14.1) itself, and partly because variants of the method produce other important results involving ordinary and partial derivatives.

In order to see what mathematical and physical assumptions we use to obtain (14.1), we start with a very general situation. Let $u(x, y, z, t)$ be the temperature at time t at the point $P(x, y, z)$ in the interior of a body which can be a chunk of copper or an oak plank or a potato being baked in an oven. We assume that u and the partial derivatives

$$\frac{\partial u}{\partial t}, \frac{\partial u}{\partial x}, \frac{\partial^2 u}{\partial x^2}, \frac{\partial u}{\partial y}, \frac{\partial^2 u}{\partial y^2}, \frac{\partial u}{\partial z}, \frac{\partial^2 u}{\partial z^2} \tag{14.2}$$

all exist and are all continuous functions of the four variables x, y, z, t. Our derivation of (14.1) will be based upon the results of calculating, by two different methods, the number q of calories of heat which must be added to the rectangular solid S of Fig. 14.3 in order to change its temperature from $u(x, y, z, t_0)$ to $u(x, y, z, t_0 + \Delta t)$. The solid S has opposite

* By this we mean that we shall ignore all of the interesting and important molecular and statistical theories of matter and thermodynamics. When we say that we shall obtain a rigorous derivation of (14.1), we do not mean that (14.1) is actually "true" and that we shall prove it. We mean that (14.1) is a logical consequence of some assumptions that we shall make and that this fact will be proved. It is not asserted (and it is not true) that the assumptions are in exact agreement with molecular phenomena. It is, however, true that our assumptions and formulas are honorable ones that are continually depended upon to give useful approximations.

It can be added that the literature of mathematics, physics, and engineering contains many derivations of (14.1) that are much too brief to be intelligible. The saving of a few printed pages or lines is economical for authors and printers, but it is not so good for readers.

vertices at the points

$$P_0 = P_0(x_0, y_0, z_0), \qquad Q_0 = Q_0(x_0 + \Delta x, y_0 + \Delta y, z_0 + \Delta z)$$

and has edges parallel to the rectangular x, y, z axes.

Our first calculation of q depends upon the notion of specific heat. By definition, the *specific heat* of a body is the number σ of calories of heat required to raise 1 gram of the material from temperature u_0 to $u_0 + 1$ on the centigrade scale. We suppose that σ is a constant independent of

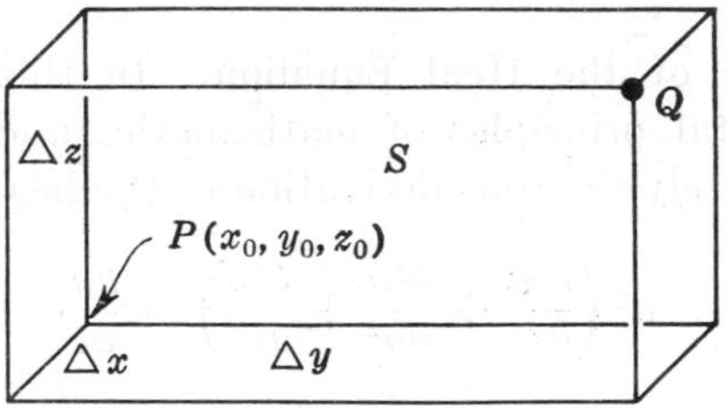

FIG. 14.3

x, y, z, t, and u_0; this could prevent application of our formulas to our potato because the chemical and thermal properties of the potato change as the baking progresses. The solid S has volume $\Delta x \Delta y \Delta z$ cc (cubic centimeters). We suppose that its density ρ (mass per cc) is a constant independent of x, y, z, t, and u. The number of calories of heat required to change the temperature of S from a constant u_1 to a constant u_2 is then

$$\sigma\rho[u_2 - u_1]\Delta x \Delta y \Delta z.$$

We now write the quantity $p(x, y, z)$ defined by

$$p(x, y, z) = \sigma\rho[u(x, y, z, t_0 + \Delta t) - u(x, y, z, t_0)]\Delta x \Delta y \Delta z$$

and look at it. If the temperatures in brackets are kind enough to be independent of x, y, and z, then $p(x, y, z)$ is q. In every case q lies between the minimum and maximum of $p(x, y, z)$ when x, y, z are coordinates of a point P in S, and there is therefore a point (x_1, y_1, z_1) in S such that

$$q = \sigma\rho[u(x_1, y_1, z_1, t_0 + \Delta t) - u(x_1, y_1, z_1, t_0)]\Delta x \Delta y \Delta z.$$

The mean value theorem (Theorem 13.31) then implies existence of a number t_1 between t_0 and $t_0 + \Delta t$ such that

$$q = \sigma\rho u_t(x_1, y_1, z_1, t_1)\Delta x \Delta y \Delta z \Delta t \tag{14.4}$$

where $u_t(x_1, y_1, z_1, t_1)$ is the value of $\partial u/\partial t$ when $x = x_1$, $y = y_1$, $z = z_1$, and $t = t_1$.

Our second calculation of q depends upon more assumptions and upon the notion of inner thermal conductivity. We assume that q is the number of calories of heat gained by the body S due to flow of heat through the boundary of S from time t_0 to time $t_0 + \Delta t$. This implies, for example, that no heat is gained or lost within S by freezing or thawing or chemical action. Thus

$$q = q_1 + q_2 + q_3 \tag{14.5}$$

where q_1 is the number of calories of heat gained by S due to flow of heat over the two parts of the boundary perpendicular to the x axis, and q_2 and q_3 are gains due to flows over the parts of the boundary perpendicular to the y and z axes. To calculate the quantity q_1, we write the quantity $P_1(y, z, t)$ defined by

$$p_1(y, z, t) = k_1[u_x(x_0 + \Delta x, y, z, t) - u_x(x_0, y, z, t)]\Delta y \Delta z \Delta t \tag{14.6}$$

and look at it. If $u_x(x_0, y, z, t)$ is independent of y, z, and t, then

$$k_1 u_x(x_0 + \Delta x, y, z, t)\Delta y \Delta z \Delta t \tag{14.61}$$

is the number of calories of heat gained by S, due to flow over the part of its boundary for which $x = x_0 + \Delta x$, when k_1 is the *inner thermal conductivity* of the body in the direction of the x axis. Again we simplify matters by supposing that k_1 is a constant independent of x, y, z, u, u_x, and t. The quantity (14.61) is the product of k_1, the temperature gradient, the area of the face of S under consideration, and the time interval Δt. If, in addition, $u_x(x_0, y, z, t)$ were independent of y, z, and t, then $p_1(y, z, t)$ would be q_1. In every case q_1 lies between the minimum and maximum values of $p_1(y, z, t)$ when $y_0 \leqq y \leqq y_0 + \Delta y$, $z_0 \leqq z \leqq z_0 + \Delta z$ and $t_0 \leqq t \leqq t_0 + \Delta t$, and we can therefore choose y_2, z_2, and t_2 such that

$$q_1 = k_1[u_x(x_0 + \Delta x, y_2, z_2, t_2) - u_x(x_0, y_2, z_2, t_2)]\Delta y \Delta z \Delta t.$$

Applying the mean value theorem (Theorem 13.31) shows that there is a number x_2 for which $x_0 < x_2 < x_0 + \Delta x$ and

$$q_1 = k_1 u_{xx}(x_2, y_2, z_2, t_2)\Delta x \Delta y \Delta z \Delta t. \tag{14.62}$$

Analogous calculations give

$$q_2 = k_2 u_{yy}(x_3, y_3, z_3, t_3)\Delta x \Delta y \Delta z \Delta t \tag{14.63}$$
$$q_3 = k_3 u_{zz}(x_4, y_4, z_4, t_4)\Delta x \Delta y \Delta z \Delta t \tag{14.64}$$

where k_2 and k_3 are the inner conductivities in the directions of the y and z axes. Using (14.5) and our formulas for q, q_1, q_2, and q_3 gives

$$k_1 u_{xx}(x_2, y_2, z_2, t_2) + k_2 u_{yy}(x_3, y_3, z_3, t_3) + k_3 u_{zz}(x_4, y_4, z_4, t_4) = \sigma \rho u_t(x_1, y_1, z_1, t_1).$$

Because of the assumption that the derivatives in (14.2) are all continuous, we can take limits as Δx, Δy, Δz, Δt all approach 0 to obtain

$$k_1 u_{xx} + k_2 u_{yy} + k_3 u_{zz} = \sigma \rho u_t \tag{14.65}$$

where the arguments of the functions are all (x_0, y_0, z_0, t_0). If we suppose that the given body is isotropic (which eliminates the oak plank) then k_1, k_2, and k_3 have a common value k and we can set $a^2 = k/\sigma\rho$ to obtain (14.1).

Problem 14.71

Describe circumstances under which the heat equation (14.1) reduces to the Laplace equation

$$\frac{\partial^2 u}{\partial x^2} + \frac{\partial^2 u}{\partial y^2} + \frac{\partial^2 u}{\partial z^2} = 0. \tag{14.711}$$

Hint: Look at (14.1).

Problem 14.72

All good scientists learn, at some time or other, that the gravitational or electrical potential $u_1(x, y, z)$ at the point (x, y, z) due to a unit mass or charge at the point (x_1, y_1, z_1) is given by the formula

$$u_1(x, y, z) = \frac{k_1}{\sqrt{(x - x_1)^2 + (y - y_1)^2 + (z - z_1)^2}} + k_2 \tag{14.721}$$

where k_1 is a constant that depends upon the units used and k_2 is a constant which is 0 provided $u_1(x, y, z)$ is "0 at infinity;" that is, $u_1(x, y, z)$ is near 0 whenever at least one of x, y, or z is large. Moreover these scientists learn that potential functions satisfy the Laplace equation (14.711). Show that $u_1(x, y, z)$ does.

CHAPTER 15

PICARD'S METHOD OF APPROXIMATING SOLUTIONS OF $y' = f(x, y)$; EXISTENCE THEOREMS

15.1. Introduction. Earlier parts of this book have presented special methods by which the differential equation

$$\frac{dy}{dx} = f(x, y) \tag{15.11}$$

can be solved when $f(x, y)$ has certain special forms. In this chapter we prove the *Picard* (1856–1941) *theorem* on existence of solutions of differential equations of the form (15.11). The method of proof is the *Picard method of successive approximations.* In some cases, this method furnishes an excellent practical method for obtaining formulas for approximations to solutions.

In Sections 15.2 and 15.3 we give the fundamental ideas of the Picard method; and in Sections 15.4, 15.5, and 15.6 we give and discuss applications. In Section 15.7 we give Picard's theorem with some comments. In Section 15.8 we prove Picard's theorem and thereby show that the Picard method will always furnish solutions of $y' = f(x, y)$ when $f(x, y)$ belongs to a certain class of functions.

15.2. The Picard Method. Postponing discussion of the vital question whether or not the method really produces results, we outline the Picard method of finding a function $y = y(x)$ such that $y(a) = b$ and

$$\frac{dy}{dx} = f(x, y) \tag{15.21}$$

for all values of x in an interval containing the point $x = a$. Thus we propose to outline the Picard method of finding a solution of (15.21) whose graph passes through the point (a, b) of an xy plane.

The first step is to select a function $y_1(x)$. We shall discuss later the effect of choosing different functions $y_1(x)$. There is a reason why it may be desirable to choose $y_1(x)$ such that $y_1(a) = b$, but even this is not essential. An easy way to solve the problem of selecting a function $y_1(x)$ is to set $y_1(x) = b$ for all x, but in any case choice of $y_1(x)$ must be made by the solver.

Having selected $y_1(x)$, we next determine $y_2(x)$ such that $y_2(a) = b$ and

$$\frac{d}{dx} y_2(x) = f(x, y_1(x)). \tag{15.22}$$

Having determined $y_2(x)$, we next determine $y_3(x)$ such that $y_3(a) = b$ and

$$\frac{d}{dx} y_3(x) = f(x, y_2(x)). \tag{15.23}$$

Proceeding in this manner, we obtain a sequence of functions

$$y_1(x),\ y_2(x),\ y_3(x),\ \ldots$$

such that $y_n(a) = b$ and

$$\frac{d}{dx} y_n(x) = f(x, y_{n-1}(x)) \qquad n = 2, 3, 4, \ldots. \tag{15.24}$$

A person with foresight and optimism can now recognize the possibility of being able to obtain a solution of the problem in the form $y(x) = \lim y_n(x)$. If it can be shown that a function $y(x)$ exists such that

$$\lim_{n\to\infty} y_n(x) = y(x), \qquad \lim_{n\to\infty} \frac{d}{dx} y_n(x) = \frac{d}{dx} y(x),$$
$$\lim_{n\to\infty} f(x, y_n(x)) = f(x, y(x)),$$

then we can let $n \to \infty$ in (15.24) to obtain

$$\frac{d}{dx} y(x) = f(x, y(x));$$

and since $y_n(a) = b$ when $n > 1$, $y(a) = b$. It thus appears that, if all goes well, we come out with a function $y(x)$ having the desired properties. Everyone should see the fundamental idea involved in Picard's method and should admire the idea; it is a good idea.

15.3. Introduction of Integrals. Our first step in developing the good idea to show that, in important cases, the functions $y_2(x)$, $y_3(x)$, . . . about which we have talked so glibly really exist. In fact, by use of Theorem 2.03, we are able to obtain formulas for these functions.

In case $f(x, y_1(x))$ is a continuous function of x, the unique function $y_2(x)$ for which $y_2(a) = b$ and (15.22) holds is

$$y_2(x) = b + \int_a^x f(t, y_1(t))dt.$$

In case $f(x, y_2(x))$ is a continuous function of x, the unique function $y_3(x)$ for which $y_3(a) = b$ and (15.23) holds is

$$y_3(x) = b + \int_a^x f(t, y_2(t))dt.$$

This process can be continued to show that if the functions $f(x, y_n(x))$ are all continuous functions of x, then the function $y_n(x)$ is given in terms of $y_{n-1}(x)$ by the *recursion formulas*

$$(15.31) \qquad y_n(x) = b + \int_a^x f(t, y_{n-1}(t))dt \qquad n = 2, 3, 4, \ldots .$$

This formula for $y_n(x)$ suggests another way of handling the question whether or not the sequence $y_1(x), y_2(x), \ldots$ converges to a solution of the differential equation. *If* a function $y(x)$ exists such that

$$(15.32) \qquad \lim_{n\to\infty} y_n(x) = y(x),$$

if we can let $n \to \infty$ in (15.31) to obtain

$$(15.33) \qquad y(x) = b + \int_a^x f(t, y(t))dt,$$

and *if* $f(x, y(x))$ is continuous, then, by the fundamental theorem of the calculus, $y'(x) = f(x, y(x))$; and (15.33) implies $y(a) = b$. Thus, if all goes well, we find that the function $y(x)$ in (15.32) has the desired properties.*

15.4. An Application of Picard's Method. In this section we apply Picard's method to find a function $y(x)$ satisfying the boundary condition $y(0) = 0$ and the differential equation

$$(15.41) \qquad \frac{dy}{dx} = x + y.$$

This equation is linear and can be quickly solved by elementary methods. To solve the problem by Picard's method, let $y_1(x) = 0$. For each $n = 2, 3, \ldots$ the function $y_n(x)$ is the unique function for which

$$y_n(0) = 0, \qquad y_n'(x) = x + y_{n-1}(x)$$

or

$$(15.42) \qquad y_n(x) = \int_0^x [t + y_{n-1}(t)]dt.$$

Using this *recursion formula,* we obtain

$$y_2(x) = \int_0^x [t + 0]dt = \frac{x^2}{2}$$

$$y_3(x) = \int_0^x \left[t + \frac{t^2}{2}\right] dt = \frac{x^2}{2} + \frac{x^3}{3!}$$

$$y_4(x) = \int_0^x \left[t + \frac{t^2}{2!} + \frac{t^3}{3!}\right] dt = \frac{x^2}{2!} + \frac{x^3}{3!} + \frac{x^4}{4!}.$$

* It may interest the reader to know that equation (15.33) is called an *integral equation.* The method of successive approximations which we are using is a standard method of solving integral equations.

It is very easy to prove by mathematical induction that

$$y_n(x) = \frac{x^2}{2!} + \frac{x^3}{3!} + \cdots + \frac{x^n}{n!} \qquad n = 2, 3, 4, \ldots. \tag{15.43}$$

In this application of Picard's method, it was very easy to get simple formulas for the *approximating functions* $y_1(x)$, $y_2(x)$, $y_3(x)$, ... It happens that it is easy to do more. Using the fundamental formula

$$e^x = 1 + x + \frac{x^2}{2!} + \frac{x^3}{3!} + \frac{x^4}{4!} + \cdots$$

we find that

$$e^x - 1 - x = \frac{x^2}{2!} + \frac{x^3}{3!} + \frac{x^4}{4!} + \cdots. \tag{15.44}$$

Since the sequence $y_2(x)$, $y_3(x)$, . . . is the sequence of partial sums of the series in (15.44), the sequence does converge and $\lim y_n(x) = y(x)$ where

$$y(x) = e^x - 1 - x.$$

That $y(x)$ is indeed a function for which $y(0) = 0$ and (15.41) holds is easily verified.

It is now time to consider the manner in which the functions $y_2(x)$, $y_3(x)$, . . . represent approximations to $y(x)$. The facts can be obtained either by drawing graphs or by such inequalities as the following. If $|x| \leqq 1$, then

$$\begin{aligned} |y(x) - y_5(x)| &= \left|\frac{x^6}{6!} + \frac{x^7}{7!} + \frac{x^8}{8!} + \cdots\right| \leqq \frac{1}{6!} + \frac{1}{7!} + \frac{1}{8!} + \cdots = \frac{1}{6!}\left[1 + \frac{1}{7}\right. \\ &\left. + \frac{1}{7 \cdot 8} + \frac{1}{7 \cdot 8 \cdot 9} + \cdots\right] < \frac{1}{720}\left[1 + \frac{1}{7} + \frac{1}{7^2} + \frac{1}{7^3} + \cdots\right] = \frac{7}{4{,}320}. \end{aligned}$$

The function $y_2(x)$ is, for many purposes, a good approximation to $y(x)$ in a small interval containing $x = 0$; the function $y_3(x)$ is a better approximation to $y(x)$ in the small interval and is a good approximation over a larger interval; the function $y_4(x)$ is a still better approximation over small intervals and is a good approximation over still larger intervals; and so on. The function $y_5(x)$ is a very good approximation to $y(x)$ when $|x| \leqq \frac{1}{2}$; is a good approximation when $|x| \leqq 1$; is a fair approximation when $|x| \leqq 3$; and is a very bad approximation when $x = 10$. It happens in the present case that the approximating functions $y_n(x)$ are exceptionally near the solution $y(x)$ when x is near 0 but that for each n the approximations are exceptionally bad when x is larger than n. In many applications, one fixes his attention on an interval in which he is interested and then chooses an approximating function $y_n(x)$ suitable for that interval. When the length of the interval is increased, it is often necessary to increase n.

Problem 15.45

Solve the above problem by the Picard method, starting with the function $y_1(x) = 1$.

Problem 15.46

Find the solution of $y' = y$ for which $y(1) = 1$.

15.5. A Significant Application of Picard's Method. In this section, we apply the Picard method to find a function $y(x)$ satisfying the condition $y(0) = 0$ and the nonlinear differential equation

$$\frac{dy}{dx} = 1 + y^2. \tag{15.51}$$

The solution is $\tan x$. Our purpose is to learn about the Picard method by seeing how the successive approximations behave. Letting $y_1(x) = 0$ and defining $y_2(x)$, $y_3(x)$, . . . by the formulas

$$y_n(x) = \int_0^x [1 + \{y_{n-1}(t)\}^2]dt \qquad n = 2, 3, \ldots \tag{15.52}$$

we find that

$$y_2(x) = \int_0^x 1\, dt = x$$

$$y_3(x) = \int_0^x (1 + t^2)dt = x + \frac{1}{3}x^3$$

$$y_4(x) = x + \tfrac{1}{3}x^3 + \tfrac{2}{15}x^5 + \tfrac{1}{63}x^7$$

$$y_5(x) = x + \frac{1}{3}x^3 + \frac{2}{15}x^5 + \frac{17}{315}x^7 + \frac{38}{2{,}835}x^9 + \frac{134}{51{,}927}x^{11} + \frac{4}{12{,}285}x^{13} + \frac{1}{59{,}535}x^{15}$$

$$y_6(x) = x + \frac{1}{3}x^3 + \frac{2}{15}x^5 + \frac{17}{315}x^7 + \frac{62}{2{,}835}x^9 + \frac{1{,}142}{115{,}925}x^{11} + \cdots + \frac{1}{59{,}535 \cdot 59{,}535 \cdot 31}x^{31}.$$

The parts of the graphs of the functions $y_3(x)$, . . . , $y_6(x)$ which lie near the origin are nearly coincident. For values of x more remote from 0, the graphs are widely separated. Taking $x = 10$ to make computation easy, we see by use of the last terms in the formulas for $y_2(x)$, $y_3(x)$, . . . that $y_2(10) = 10$, $y_3(10) > 10^2$, $y_4(10) > 10^5$, $y_5(10) > 10^{10}$, $y_6(10) > 10^{19}$. These considerations may lead one to guess that for values of x in some interval about $x = 0$ the sequence $y_1(x)$, $y_2(x)$, . . . converges to a function $y(x)$ satisfying the required conditions and that, for values of x remote from 0, the sequence does not converge.

The facts, as far as we can guess what they are, agree very nicely with the known fact that the given equation has solution $y = \tan x$ over the interval $-\pi/2 < x < \pi/2$ but has no solution over a larger interval. The first five terms of $y_6(x)$ agree with the first five terms of the power-series expansion [see (7.55)]

$$(15.53) \qquad x + \frac{1}{3}x^3 + \frac{2}{15}x^5 + \frac{17}{315}x^7 + \frac{62}{2{,}835}x^9 + \frac{1{,}382}{155{,}925}x^{11} + \cdots$$

of $\tan x$, and accordingly $y_6(x)$ is for many purposes a very good approximation to $y(x)$ over intervals extending well beyond the interval $-1 \leqq x \leqq 1$ but with end points not too close to $-\pi/2$ and $\pi/2$.

The refusal of the sequence $y_n(x)$ to converge for larger values of x (in fact when $|x| \geqq \pi/2$) is quite appropriate. The sequence $y_n(x)$ cannot converge over $-10 \leqq x \leqq 10$ to a function $y(x)$ satisfying the equation $y' = 1 + y^2$ over that interval because (see Remark 2.26) no such function exists.

Problem 15.54

Find a few of the Picard approximations to the function $y(x)$ satisfying the condition $y(0) = 0$ and the differential equation

$$\frac{dy}{dx} = 1 + x^2 + y^2.$$

Problem 15.55

Show without solving the differential equations that if $y_1(x)$ and $y_2(x)$ are, respectively, solutions of

$$\frac{dy}{dx} = 1 + y^2, \qquad \frac{dy}{dx} = 1 + x^2 + y^2$$

over an interval $0 \leqq x < a$ and if $y_1(0) = y_2(0) = 0$, then

$$0 \leqq y_1(x) \leqq y_2(x) \qquad 0 \leqq x < a.$$

What can you do with your answer?

15.6. Existence and Uniqueness Theorems. As the above examples indicate, the Picard method sometimes yields formulas for approximations to functions $y(x)$ satisfying an equation of the form $y' = f(x, y)$ and a condition of the form $y(a) = b$. As a method for obtaining a table of numerical values of $y(x)$, however, the Picard method rarely compares favorably with the Runge-Kutta and Milne methods of Chapter 8. To obtain numerical values of several Picard approximations to solutions equations much less complicated than the equation

$$(15.61) \qquad \frac{dy}{dx} = \frac{1 + xy^4}{1 + x^2y^2}\sin xy^2,$$

it would be necessary to resort to a formula for approximate integration, presumably the Simpson (1710–1761) method. This could be done, but the prospect is not appealing.

The main service of the Picard method is to provide proofs of theorems. Before stating the Picard theorem, we try to put ourselves into a position to understand it by looking at two simpler theorems which it implies.

THEOREM 15.62. *Let $f(x, y)$ and $\partial f/\partial y$ be continuous over a rectangle containing the point (a, b) in its interior. Then there is a positive number h for which the following is true. There is a function $y(x)$ for which $y(a) = b$ and*

$$\frac{dy}{dx} = f(x, y) \tag{15.621}$$

when $a - h < x < a + h$. Moreover if two functions satisfy the condition $y(a) = b$ and satisfy (15.621) when $a - h < x < a + h$, they must have equal values when $a - h < x < a + h$.

This theorem has a virtue; it is relatively short and easy to understand. But some theorems possessing this virtue are not as good as they might be because they take too much (have unnecessarily strong hypotheses) and give too little (have unnecessarily weak conclusions). We may want to know about solutions of $y' = f(x, y)$ when f does not possess a continuous $\partial f/\partial y$. In this case Theorem 15.62 takes too much and cannot be applied. It may happen, however, that there is a constant A such that

$$|f(x, y) - f(x, \eta)| \leqq A|y - \eta| \tag{15.63}$$

whenever (x, y) and (x, η) are points in the rectangle. The condition (15.63) is called a Lipschitz (1832–1903) condition. It requires that for each fixed x the resulting function of y have difference quotients bounded by A, but does not require that the function of y be differentiable. For example, the function

$$f(x, y) = 1 + x + |\sin y| \tag{15.631}$$

satisfies (15.63), with $A = 1$, over the whole plane but $\partial f/\partial y$ fails to exist when $y = 0$. On the other hand if $f(x, y)$ possesses a partial derivative $f_y(x, y)$ which is continuous over R, then we can apply the law of the mean to obtain

$$f(x, y) - f(x, \eta) = f_y(x, \eta_1)(y - \eta),$$

where η_1 is properly chosen between y and η; and choosing A such that $|f_y(x, y)| \leqq A$, when (x, y) is a point of the rectangle, shows that (15.63) must hold. All this shows that the following theorem is better than Theorem 15.62.

Theorem 15.64. *Let $f(x, y)$ be continuous and satisfy the Lipschitz condition* (15.63) *over a rectangle containing the point* (a, b) *in its interior. Then there is a positive number h for which the following is true. There is a function $y(x)$ for which $y(a) = b$ and*

$$\frac{dy}{dx} = f(x, y) \tag{15.641}$$

when $a - h < x < a + h$. Moreover if two functions satisfy the condition $y(a) = b$ and satisfy (15.641) *when $a - h < x < a + h$, they must have equal values when $a - h < x < a + h$.*

Now we discuss the conclusions of the theorems. The part of the conclusion which says that there is a function $y(x)$ for which (15.641) holds when $a - h < x < a + h$ gives an *existence theorem.* The last part of the theorem gives a *uniqueness theorem;* there may be many different functions $y(x)$ which satisfy (15.641) over the whole infinite interval $-\infty < x < \infty$, but they must all agree when $a - h < x < a + h$. It is obvious that we should like a theorem which gives solid information about the sizes of intervals over which solutions must exist and be unique. The Picard theorem of the next section gives such information. One reason for interest in the Picard theorem lies in the fact that it gives a *constructive* proof of existence of solutions by telling precisely how they can be found.

Example 15.65

Without preconceived notions about the facts, we undertake to see what we can conclude from the hypothesis that $y(x)$ is defined over some interval I of values of x containing the point $x = 1$, that

$$\frac{dy}{dx} = 2|y|^{\frac{1}{2}} \tag{15.651}$$

when x is in I, and that $y(1) = 1$. Over each subinterval I_1 of I over which $y(x) > 0$, we have $\frac{1}{2}y^{-\frac{1}{2}}(dy/dx) = 1$ so, for some constant c, $y^{\frac{1}{2}} = x - c$ and $y = (x - c)^2$.

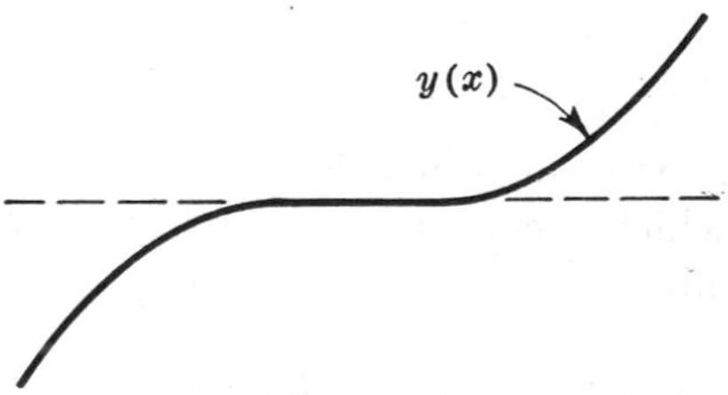

Fig. 15.652

Since $y(1) = 1$, we see that $c = 0$ and hence $y = x^2$ when x is in I. We must investigate the possibility that there may be a subinterval I_2 of I over which $y(x) < 0$. Over such a subinterval, we have $-\frac{1}{2}(-y)^{-\frac{1}{2}}(dy/dx) = -1$ so, for some constant c_1, $(-y)^{\frac{1}{2}} = -x + c_1$ and $y = -(x - c_1)^2$ with $x < c_1$ because (15.651) shows that

$dy/dx \geqq 0$. It turns out that I might be the whole infinite interval $-\infty < x < \infty$ with, for some constant c_1 which is 0 or negative, $y(x) = -(x - c_1)^2$ when $x \leqq c_1$; with $y(x) = 0$ when $c_1 \leqq x \leqq 0$, and with $y(x) = x^2$ when $x \geqq 0$. Moreover I might be the whole infinite interval $-\infty < x < \infty$ with $y(x) = 0$ when $x \leqq 0$ and $y(x) = x^2$ when $x \geqq 0$. Fig. 15.652 shows a graph.

The conclusions to be drawn from all this are the following. If I contains only nonnegative values of x, then there is a unique function (one and only one function) which is defined over I and which satisfies the equation (15.651) and the condition $y(1) = 1$. If I contains negative and positive values of x, then there are many functions $y(x)$ which are defined over I and which satisfy the equation (15.651) and the condition $y(1) = 1$, but in every case $y(x)$ has the unique value x^2 when x is in I and $x \geqq 0$. This enables us to assert that, *so far as the interval* $x \geqq 0$ *is concerned*, there is a unique function $y(x)$ satisfying (15.651) and the condition $y(1) = 1$.

Observe that if

$$f(x, y) = 2|y|^{\frac{1}{2}}$$

then, when y and η are both positive,

$$|f(x, y) - f(x, \eta)| = \frac{2}{|y|^{\frac{1}{2}} + |\eta|^{\frac{1}{2}}} |y - \eta|$$

and hence that there certainly is no constant A such that the Lipschitz condition (15.63) holds over a rectangle which contains a point on the x axis in its interior.

15.7. The Picard Theorem. As the preceding sections imply, the following Picard theorem is genuinely important.

THEOREM 15.71. *Let $f(x, y)$ be a continuous function of x and y over a region R containing the point (a, b) in its interior, and let M be a constant such that*

$$(15.72) \qquad |f(x, y)| < M$$

for each point (x, y) of R. Let $x_1 \leqq x \leqq x_2$ be an interval of the x axis such that R includes the region T consisting of the two triangles (shaded in Fig. 15.76) bounded by the lines $x = x_1$, $x = x_2$, and the two lines through (a, b) with slopes M and $-M$. Let A be a constant such that

$$(15.73) \qquad |f(x, y) - f(x, \eta)| \leqq A|y - \eta|$$

when (x, y) and (x, η) are two points of T. Let $y_1(x)$ be a continuous function of x such that the points $(x, y_1(x))$ for which $x_1 \leqq x \leqq x_2$ all lie in the region R. Let

$$(15.74) \qquad y_n(x) = b + \int_a^x f(t, y_{n-1}(t))dt \qquad n = 2, 3, 4, \ldots .$$

Then the sequence $y_1(x)$, $y_2(x)$, . . . converges uniformly over the interval $x_1 \leqq x \leqq x_2$ to a function $y(x)$ satisfying the conditions $y(a) = b$ and

$$(15.75) \qquad \frac{dy}{dx} = f(x, y) \qquad x_1 < x < x_2.$$

The graph over the interval $x_1 < x < x_2$ *of this solution lies in the region* T. *This solution* $y(x)$ *is unique in the sense that if* $Y(x)$ *satisfies the conditions* $Y(a) = b$ *and* $Y'(x) = f(x, y)$ *when* $x_1 < x < x_2$, *then* $Y(x) = y(x)$ *when* $x_1 < x < x_2$. *Finally, all of the different functions* $y_1(x)$ *that may be used at the start of the Picard method yield this unique solution.*

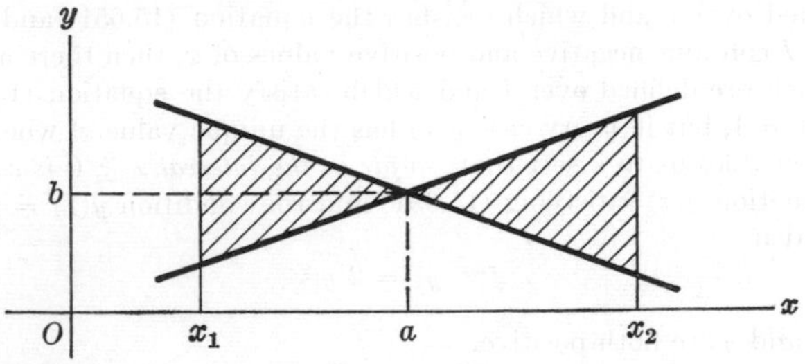

FIG. 15.76

We can make the process of determining the solution $y(x)$ completely explicit by putting $y_1(x) = b$ when $x_1 < x < x_2$.

The hypotheses of this theorem are satisfied in many important cases. If $f(x, y)$ is continuous at (a, b), then there necessarily exist a constant M and a region R (for example, a rectangle) containing the point (a, b) in its interior such that (15.72) holds for all points (x, y) of R. It is then possible to draw through (a, b) two lines of slopes $-M$ and M and then to determine x_1 and x_2 such that the shaded region T described in the theorem is a subset of R. Then, provided (15.73) holds, we have an interval $x_1 \leqq x \leqq x_2$ over which the conclusions of the theorem are valid. Very often, as is clearly the case when

$$\frac{dy}{dx} = \sin x + \sin y, \tag{15.77}$$

we can take x_1 and x_2 as remote from a as we please and conclude that there is a unique function $y(x)$ for which $y(a) = b$ and (15.77) holds when $-\infty < x < \infty$.

15.8. Proof of Picard's Theorem. In proving Picard's theorem, we use the notation of the statement of the theorem. Moreover, we shall consider only values of x for which $x_1 \leqq x \leqq x_2$. Our first step is to prove the following lemma.

LEMMA 15.81. *If* $y_{n-1}(x)$ *is continuous and* $(x, y_{n-1}(x))$ *is a point of the region* R, *then the function* $y_n(x)$ *defined by*

$$y_n(x) = b + \int_a^x f(t, y_{n-1}(t))dt \tag{15.82}$$

is continuous and $(x, y_n(x))$ *is a point of the region* T.

Our hypotheses imply that the integrand in (15.82) is continuous and hence that the right-hand member of (15.82) defines a continuous function $y_n(x)$ such that $y_n'(x) = f(x, y_{n-1}(x))$. From (15.82) we obtain

$$|y_n(x) - b| = \left|\int_a^x f(t, y_{n-1}(t))dt\right|$$
$$\leqq \left|\int_a^x |f(t, y_{n-1}(t))|dt\right| \leqq M\left|\int_a^x dt\right| = M|x - a|.$$

This implies that $y_n(a) = b$ and that if $x \neq a$ then the slope of the line joining (a, b) to $(x, y_n(x))$ is neither greater than M nor less than $-M$. Hence, the graph of $y_n(x)$ lies in the region T, and Lemma 15.81 is proved.

Since the graph of $y_1(x)$ lies in the region R and T is a subset of R, it follows from repeated application of Lemma 15.81 that the graphs of $y_2(x), y_3(x), \ldots$ over the interval $x_1 \leqq x \leqq x_2$ all lie in the region T.

We now show that the sequence $y_n(x)$ converges by showing that the series

(15.83) $$y_1(x) + [y_2(x) - y_1(x)] + [y_3(x) - y_2(x)] + \cdots$$

converges. For this it is sufficient to show that the series

(15.831) $$[y_3(x) - y_2(x)] + [y_4(x) - y_3(x)] + [y_5(x) - y_4(x)] + \cdots$$

converges. Subtracting (15.74) from the equation obtained by replacing n by $n + 1$ in it, we get

(15.84) $$y_{n+1}(x) - y_n(x) = \int_a^x [f(t, y_n(t)) - f(t, y_{n-1}(t))]dt.$$

If $n \geqq 3$ and t lies within the range of integration in (15.84), then the points $(t, y_n(t))$ and $(t, y_{n-1}(t))$ lie in the region T and we can apply (15.73) to obtain

(15.841) $$|f(t, y_n(t)) - f(t, y_{n-1}(t))| \leqq A|y_n(t) - y_{n-1}(t)|.$$

Using (15.84) and (15.841) we obtain

(15.85) $$|y_{n+1}(x) - y_n(x)| \leqq A\left|\int_a^x |y_n(t) - y_{n-1}(t)|dt\right| \qquad n > 2.$$

Choose a constant B such that

(15.86) $$|y_3(x) - y_2(x)| \leqq B \qquad x_1 \leqq x \leqq x_2.$$

Setting $n = 3$ in (15.85) and using (15.86), we obtain

(15.87) $$|y_4(x) - y_3(x)| \leqq BA\left|\int_a^x dt\right| = BA|x - a|.$$

Setting $n = 4$ in (15.85) and using (15.87), we obtain

$$(15.88) \qquad |y_5(x) - y_4(x)| \leqq BA^2 \left| \int_a^x (t-a)dt \right| = \frac{BA^2|x-a|^2}{2!}.$$

This process gives, as may be proved by induction,

$$(15.89) \qquad |y_{n+3}(x) - y_{n+2}(x)| \leqq \frac{BA^n|x-a|^n}{n!} \qquad n = 0, 1, 2, \ldots.$$

Let C be equal to the greater of the numbers $x_2 - a$ and $a - x_1$ so that $|x - a| \leqq C$ when $x_1 \leqq x \leqq x_2$. Then (15.89) gives

$$(15.90) \qquad |y_{n+3}(x) - y_{n+2}(x)| \leqq \frac{B(AC)^n}{n!}.$$

Using (15.90) we see that the series (15.831) is dominated by the series of constants

$$(15.901) \qquad B + B\frac{AC}{1!} + B\frac{(AC)^2}{2!} + B\frac{(AC)^3}{3!} + \cdots.$$

This series is convergent; in fact, it converges to Be^{AC}. Therefore, by the comparison test, the series (15.831) is convergent. Thus we have proved that there is a function $y(x)$ such that

$$(15.91) \qquad y(x) = \lim_{n\to\infty} y_n(x)$$

and

$$(15.92) \quad y(x) = y_1(x) + [y_2(x) - y_1(x)] + [y_3(x) - y_2(x)] + \cdots.$$

Since the point $(x, y_n(x))$ lies in the region T when $n \geqq 2$ and $x_1 \leqq x \leqq x_2$, it follows that the point $(x, y(x))$ lies in the region T when $x_1 \leqq x \leqq x_2$; thus the graph over the interval $x_1 \leqq x \leqq x_2$ of $y(x)$ lies in the region T. In particular, $y(a) = b$.

To show that $y(x)$ satisfies the differential equation, it will be sufficient to show that $y(x)$ is continuous and

$$(15.93) \qquad y(x) = b + \int_a^x f(t, y(t))dt;$$

for in this case (by the fundamental theorem of the calculus) the right-hand member has a derivative which is $f(x, y(x))$, and the same must therefore be true of the left-hand member.

From (15.92) we obtain for each $n > 2$ and each x in the interval $x_1 \leqq x \leqq x_2$

$$y(x) = \{y_1(x) + [y_2(x) - y_1(x)] + \cdots + [y_n(x) - y_{n-1}(x)]\} \\ + \{[y_{n+1}(x) - y_n(x)] + [y_{n+2}(x) - y_{n+1}(x)] + \cdots\}$$

so that, because of (15.90),

$$\begin{aligned}|y(x) - y_n(x)| &\leqq |y_{n+1}(x) - y_n(x)| + |y_{n+2}(x) - y_{n+1}(x)| + \cdots \\ &\leqq B\left[\frac{(AC)^{n-2}}{(n-2)!} + \frac{(AC)^{n-1}}{(n-1)!} + \frac{(AC)^n}{n!} + \cdots\right].\end{aligned}$$

Since the series (15.901) converges, it follows that to each $\epsilon > 0$ corresponds an index N such that

$$B\left[\frac{(AC)^{n-2}}{(n-2)!} + \frac{(AC)^{n-1}}{(n-1)!} + \frac{(AC)^n}{n!} + \cdots\right] < \epsilon \qquad n > N$$

and therefore

$$|y(x) - y_n(x)| < \epsilon \qquad x_1 \leqq x \leqq x_2;\, n > N.$$

This means that $y_n(x)$ converges *uniformly* over $x_1 \leqq x \leqq x_2$ to $y(x)$; and since $y_n(x)$ is continuous for each n, this implies (as is shown in advanced calculus) that $y(x)$ must be continuous.

To prove (15.93), we observe that if $n > N \geqq 1$, then

$$\begin{aligned}(15.94)\quad &\left|y(x) - b - \int_a^x f(t, y(t))dt\right| \\ &= \left|y(x) - y_{n+1}(x) + \int_a^x [f(t, y_n(t)) - f(t, y(t))]dt\right| \\ &\leqq |y(x) - y_{n+1}(x)| + \left|\int_a^x A|y_n(t) - y(t)|dt\right| \\ &\leqq \epsilon + \epsilon A|x - a| \leqq \epsilon(1 + AC)\end{aligned}$$

where A and C are fixed constants previously defined. If the first member of (15.94) were a number $P \neq 0$, we could obtain a contradiction of (15.94) by choosing ϵ to be a positive number less than $P/(1 + AC)$; hence, the left-hand member of (15.94) must be zero, and (15.93) is proved. This completes the "existence" part of the proof of Picard's theorem.

We prove that, insofar as the interval $x_1 \leqq x \leqq x_2$ is concerned, there is only one function $Y(x)$ such that $Y(a) = b$ and

$$(15.95)\qquad Y'(x) = f(x, Y(x)) \qquad x_1 \leqq x \leqq x_2$$

by proving that each such function must be equal, when $x_1 \leqq x \leqq x_2$, to the function $y(x)$ just obtained by the Picard method.

Our first step is to prove that the graph of $Y(x)$ must lie in the region T. Using (15.95) and the facts that $Y(a) = b$ and

$$|f(a, b)| < M,$$

we obtain

$$(15.951)\qquad |Y'(a)| = |f(a, b)| < M.$$

This implies existence of a positive number δ such that

$$(15.952) \qquad |Y(x) - Y(a)| < M|x - a| \qquad 0 < |x - a| \leqq \delta.$$

We can now show that

$$(15.953) \qquad |Y(x) - Y(a)| < M(x - a) \qquad a < x \leqq x_2.$$

If (15.953) fails to hold, then (15.952) and continuity of $Y(x)$ imply that there must be a least value of x greater than $a + \delta$, say ξ, such that

$$(15.954) \qquad |Y(\xi) - Y(a)| \geqq M(\xi - a).$$

But by the law of the mean there must be a point ξ_1 between a and ξ such that

$$(15.955) \qquad Y(\xi) - Y(a) = Y'(\xi_1)(\xi - a).$$

Hence,

$$(15.956) \qquad |f(\xi_1, Y(\xi_1))| = |Y'(\xi_1)| \geqq M,$$

and this is a contradiction of (15.72) since $(\xi_1, Y(\xi_1))$ is a point of the region T. Thus (15.953) holds, and a similar proof shows that

$$(15.957) \qquad |Y(a) - Y(x)| < M(a - x) \qquad x_1 \leqq x < a.$$

But (15.953), (15.957), and the fact that $Y(a) = b$ together imply that

$$|Y(x) - b| \leqq M|x - a| \qquad x_1 \leqq x \leqq x_2,$$

and this in turn implies that the graph of $Y(x)$ over the interval $x_1 \leqq x \leqq x_2$ must lie in the region T.

We can now use (15.93) and the equation resulting from replacing $y(x)$ by $Y(x)$ in it to obtain

$$(15.96) \qquad |y(x) - Y(x)| = \left|\int_a^x [f(t, y(t)) - f(t, Y(t))]dt\right| \leqq A\left|\int_a^x |y(t) - Y(t)|dt\right|.$$

Let D be the maximum value for $x_1 \leqq t \leqq x_2$ of $|y(t) - Y(t)|$. Then use of (15.96) gives

$$(15.961) \qquad |y(x) - Y(x)| \leqq AD|x - a|.$$

Using (15.961) in the last member of (15.96) gives

$$|y(x) - Y(x)| \leqq \frac{DA^2|x - a|^2}{2!},$$

and iteration of this process gives

$$|y(x) - Y(x)| \leqq \frac{DA^n|x - a|^n}{n!} \qquad n = 1, 2, 3, \cdots.$$

Thus, if $x_1 \leqq x \leqq x_2$ and C is, as before, the greater of the numbers $x_2 - a$ and $a - x_1$, then

$$|y(x) - Y(x)| \leqq \frac{D(AC)^n}{n!}. \tag{15.962}$$

Since the right-hand member of (15.962) can be made arbitrarily small by taking n sufficiently great (observe that the right-hand member is the general term of the convergent series for De^{AC}), it follows that the left-hand member of (15.962) must be 0 and that

$$Y(x) = y(x) \qquad x_1 \leqq x \leqq x_2.$$

This completes proof of the "uniqueness" part of Picard's theorem.

That all different functions $y_1(x)$ which may be used at the start of Picard's method must yield the same solution is a consequence of the fact that each yields a solution and that there is just one solution over $x_1 \leqq x \leqq x_2$. This completes the proof of Picard's theorem (Theorem 15.71).

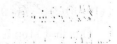

CHAPTER 16

APPROXIMATIONS TO SOLUTIONS AND EXISTENCE THEOREMS FOR EQUATIONS OF HIGHER ORDER AND FOR SYSTEMS OF EQUATIONS

16.0. Introduction. In this chapter, we apply the Picard method of successive approximations to obtain constructive proofs of existence and uniqueness theorems for differential equations and for systems of differential equations. In particular, we shall obtain proofs of Theorems 6.03 and 6.04, the fundamental theorems on linear differential equations.

The developments will be somewhat strange. We shall show that it is possible to solve the simplest problems by solving problems which seem to be much more general and difficult. It then turns out to be easiest to solve the most difficult problem. The reason for all this can be seen when everything is finished. The most difficult problem will be formulated in such a way that we can attack it by the Picard method and by other approximation methods.

16.1. Linear Equations. In this section, we show that the problem of finding a function $y(x)$ satisfying equations (16.12) and (16.13) below can be reduced to the problem of finding one of a set of functions which satisfies a system of equations, and that proof of Theorem 16.11 can be reduced to proof of a theorem involving a system of equations. Theorem 16.11 is essentially a restatement of Theorem 6.03 since (6.032) can, when $a_0(x) \neq 0$, be thrown into the form (16.12) by division by $a_0(x)$.

THEOREM 16.11. *If $a_1(x)$, $a_2(x)$, . . . , $a_n(x)$, and $f(x)$ are continuous over an interval I, then corresponding to each point x_0 of I and each set of constants k_1, k_2, . . . , k_n there is one and only one function $y(x)$, satisfying the differential equation*

$$(16.12)\qquad \frac{d^ny}{dx^n} + a_1(x)\frac{d^{n-1}y}{dx^{n-1}} + \cdots + a_{n-1}(x)\frac{dy}{dx} + a_n(x)y = f(x)$$

over the interval I, for which

$$(16.13)\qquad y(x_0) = k_1,\ y'(x_0) = k_2,\ \ldots,\ y^{(n-1)}(x_0) = k_n.$$

Our first step is to define n functions $y_1(x)$, $y_2(x)$, . . . , $y_n(x)$ in terms of $y(x)$ by the formulas

$$y_1(x) = y(x),\ y_2(x) = y'(x),\ y_3(x) = y''(x),\ \ldots,\ y_n(x) = y^{(n-1)}(x). \tag{16.14}$$

It is easy to see that (16.12) can then be written in the form

$$y_n'(x) + a_1 y_n(x) + a_2 y_{n-1}(x) + \cdots + a_{n-1} y_2(x) + a_n y_1(x) = f(x).$$

Hence, if $y(x)$ satisfies (16.12) and (16.13) and $y_1, y_2, \ldots, y_n$ are defined by (16.14), then

$$\begin{cases} y_1'(x) = y_2(x) \\ y_2'(x) = y_3(x) \\ \cdots\cdots\cdots \\ y_{n-1}'(x) = y_n(x) \\ y_n'(x) = -a_n y_1(x) - a_{n-1} y_2(x) - \cdots - a_1 y_n(x) + f(x) \end{cases} \tag{16.15}$$

and

$$y_1(x_0) = k_1,\ y_2(x_0) = k_2,\ \ldots,\ y_n(x_0) = k_n. \tag{16.16}$$

Conversely, if $y_1(x), y_2(x), \ldots, y_n(x)$ is a set of n functions satisfying the system of differential equations (16.15) and the boundary conditions (16.16), then the function $y(x)$ defined by $y(x) = y_1(x)$ satisfies (16.12) and (16.13).

Thus we have transformed the problem of finding a function satisfying the linear nth-order differential equation (16.12) and the n boundary conditions (16.13) into the problem of finding the first of a set of n functions $y_1, y_2, \ldots, y_n$ satisfying the system (16.15) of n linear first-order equations and the n boundary conditions (16.16). Therefore, since special choices of the functions in the right-hand member of (16.22) reduce the system (16.22) to the system (16.15), we can (and shall) prove Theorem 16.11 by proving Theorem 16.21.

16.2. Systems of Linear Equations. In this section we show that the system of equations (16.22) of the following theorem has a property which turns out to be very useful when we apply the Picard method of successive approximations to the system.

THEOREM 16.21. *If the coefficients $a_{m,k}(x)$ and the functions $\phi_k(x)$ in the system of equations*

$$\begin{cases} y_1' = a_{1,1}y_1 + a_{1,2}y_2 + \cdots + a_{1,n}y_n + \phi_1 \\ y_2' = a_{2,1}y_1 + a_{2,2}y_2 + \cdots + a_{2,n}y_n + \phi_2 \\ \cdots\cdots\cdots\cdots\cdots\cdots\cdots\cdots \\ y_n' = a_{n,1}y_1 + a_{n,2}y_2 + \cdots + a_{n,n}y_n + \phi_n \end{cases} \tag{16.22}$$

are continuous when x is in an interval I, if x_0 is a point of I, and if k_1,

$k_2, \ldots, k_n$ *are constants, then there is one and only one set of n functions*

$$y_1(x),\ y_2(x),\ \ldots,\ y_n(x)$$

satisfying the system of equations (16.22) *over the interval I, for which*

$$y_1(x_0) = k_1,\ y_2(x_0) = k_2,\ \ldots,\ y_n(x_0) = k_n. \tag{16.23}$$

If we set, for each $m = 1, 2, \ldots, n$,

$$f_m(x, y_1, y_2, \ldots, y_n) = a_{m,1}(x)y_1 + \cdots + a_{m,n}(x)y_n + \phi_m(x), \tag{16.24}$$

then it can be shown easily that the function $f_m(x, y_1, \ldots, y_n)$ satisfies the useful condition (16.25) which is analogous to that in Picard's theorem (Theorem 15.71). In case the interval I is not a finite closed interval, let I_1 be a finite closed subinterval of I; otherwise, let $I_1 = I$. Let A_{mk} denote the maximum value of $|a_{m,k}(x)|$ for x in the interval I_1, and let A denote the greatest of the numbers A_{mk} so that $|a_{m,k}(x)| \leqq A$ when x is in I_1. When x is in I_1 and $y_1, \ldots, y_n$ and $\eta_1, \ldots, \eta_n$ are any two sets of n numbers,

$$\begin{aligned} |f_m(x, y_1, \ldots, y_n) &- f_m(x, \eta_1, \ldots, \eta_n)| \\ &= |a_{m,1}(x)(y_1 - \eta_1) + a_{m,2}(x)(y_2 - \eta_2) + \cdots + a_{m,n}(x)(y_n - \eta_n)| \\ &\leqq |a_{m,1}(x)|\,|y_1 - \eta_1| + |a_{m,2}(x)|\,|y_2 - \eta_2| + \cdots + |a_{m,n}(x)|\,|y_n - \eta_n| \\ &\leqq A(|y_1 - \eta_1| + |y_2 - \eta_2| + \cdots + |y_n - \eta_n|). \end{aligned} \tag{16.25}$$

Because of the estimate (16.25) we can (and shall) prove Theorem 16.21 by proving a still more general theorem (Theorem 16.31 of the next section).

16.3. Systems of Equations Which Are Not Necessarily Linear. In this section we state and comment briefly upon the following theorem; in the next section we point out important applications; and in Section 16.5 we prove the theorem.

THEOREM 16.31. *If the functions* $f_1, \ldots, f_n$ *in the system of equations*

$$\begin{cases} y_1' = f_1(x, y_1, y_2, \ldots, y_n) \\ y_2' = f_2(x, y_1, y_2, \ldots, y_n) \\ \cdots\cdots\cdots\cdots\cdots\cdots \\ y_n' = f_n(x_1, y_1, y_2, \ldots, y_n) \end{cases} \tag{16.32}$$

are continuous in a region R defined by

$$|x - x_0| \leqq r_0,\ |y_1 - k_1| \leqq r_1,\ \ldots,\ |y_n - k_n| \leqq r_n \tag{16.33}$$

and for each $m = 1, 2, \ldots, n$ *the function* f_m *satisfies the condition*

$$(16.34)\quad |f_m(x, y_1, \ldots, y_n) - f_m(x, \eta_1, \ldots, \eta_n)| \leqq A(|y_1 - \eta_1| + |y_2 - \eta_2| + \cdots + |y_n - \eta_n|)$$

when $x, y_1, \ldots, y_n$ *and* $x, \eta_1, \ldots, \eta_n$ *are in* R, *then there is an interval* I *containing* x_0 *such that there is one and only one set of* n *functions*

$$(16.35)\qquad y_1(x), y_2(x), \ldots, y_n(x),$$

satisfying the system (16.32) *over the interval* I, *for which*

$$(16.36)\qquad y_1(x_0) = k_1,\ y_2(x_0) = k_2, \ldots, y_n(k_0) = k_n.$$

For the case of the system (16.22) *in which the f's are defined by* (16.24), *the interval* I *may be taken to be the interval over which the functions* $a_{m,k}(x)$ *and* $\phi_m(x)$ *are continuous.*

This theorem does not, except for the case (16.22), tell anything about the extent of the interval I containing x_0 over which there exists one and only one set of functions (16.35) satisfying (16.32) and (16.36). In some cases the interval I is relatively short; in other cases it is the entire interval $-\infty < x < \infty$. It is the duty of one who applies the method of successive approximations to a particular problem to find the extent of the interval I for that problem.

16.4. Equations of Order Greater than 1. The previous chapter dealt with equations of the form $y' = f(x, y)$. By use of Theorem 16.31 we obtain existence theorems for equations of the types

$$\frac{d^2y}{dx^2} = f\left(x, y, \frac{dy}{dx}\right), \quad \frac{d^3y}{dx^3} = f\left(x, y, \frac{dy}{dx}, \frac{d^2y}{dx^2}\right).$$

To show this, let n be an integer greater than 1 and consider the differential equation

$$(16.41)\qquad \frac{d^ny}{dx^n} = f\left(x, y, \frac{dy}{dx}, \frac{d^2y}{dx^2}, \ldots, \frac{d^{n-1}y}{dx^{n-1}}\right)$$

and the boundary conditions

$$(16.42)\qquad y(x_0) = k_1,\ y'(x_0) = k_2, \ldots, y^{(n-1)}(x_0) = k_n.$$

It is easy to see that if $y(x)$ satisfies (16.41) and (16.42) and we set $y_1 = y, y_2 = y', \ldots, y_n = y^{(n-1)}$, then the functions $y_1, y_2, \ldots, y_n$ satisfy the system of differential equations

$$(16.43)\qquad y_1' = y_2,\ y_2' = y_3, \ldots, y_{n-1}' = y_n,\ y_n' = f(x, y_1, \ldots, y_n)$$

and the boundary conditions

$$(16.44)\qquad y_1(x_0) = k_1,\ y_2(x_0) = k_2, \ldots, y_n(x_0) = k_n;$$

and, conversely, that if $y_1, y_2, \ldots, y_n$ satisfy (16.43) and (16.44), then the function $y(x)$ defined by $y(x) = y_1(x)$ satisfies (16.41) and (16.42). The system composed of (16.43) and (16.44) is a special form of the system composed of (16.32) and (16.36).

For example, one seeks a function $y(x)$ satisfying the equation

$$\frac{d^2y}{dx^2} + a_1(x, y)\frac{dy}{dx} + a_2(x, y) = 0 \tag{16.45}$$

and the boundary conditions

$$y(x_0) = k_1, \qquad y'(x_0) = k_2 \tag{16.46}$$

by seeking a pair of functions $y_1(x)$ and $y_2(x)$ which satisfy the system of equations

$$\begin{aligned} \frac{dy_1}{dx} &= y_2 \\ \frac{dy_2}{dx} &= -a_1(x, y_1)y_2 - a_2(x, y_1) \end{aligned} \tag{16.47}$$

and the conditions

$$y_1(x_0) = k_1, \qquad y_2(x_0) = k_2. \tag{16.48}$$

Problem 16.49

Show that if we set

$$x = t, \qquad y_1 = \theta(t), \qquad y_2 = \theta'(t), \qquad y_3 = r(t), \qquad y_4 = r'(t),$$

then the system composed of the two equations

$$\begin{aligned} \frac{d^2\theta}{dt^2} &= -\frac{g}{r}\sin\theta \\ \frac{d^2r}{dt^2} &= g\cos\theta - \frac{E}{ml}(r - l) + r\left(\frac{d\theta}{dt}\right)^2 \end{aligned}$$

takes the form

$$\begin{aligned} y_1' &= y_2 \\ y_2' &= -\frac{g\sin x}{y_3} \\ y_3' &= y_4 \\ y_4' &= g\cos x - \frac{E}{ml}(x - l) + y_3y_2^2 \end{aligned}$$

and that this system has the form (16.32). In appropriate circumstances, these equations govern two-dimensional cavortings of a body attached to the bottom of a spring which is suspended from the ceiling. The problem of finding $\theta(t)$ and $r(t)$ is sometimes called the *elastic pendulum problem*.

16.5. Proof of Theorem 16.31. In spite of the fact that Theorem 16.31 involves a system of n equations whereas Theorem 15.71 involves a single equation, the proof of Theorem 16.31 is somewhat simpler than that of Theorem 15.71; this situation is possible because Theorem 15.71 gives precise information about a special region T whereas no such special region is involved in Theorem 16.31.

The proof of Theorem 16.31 uses the method of successive approximations used in proof of Theorem 15.71. We start with the set of n functions $y_{1,0}, y_{2,0}, \ldots, y_{n,0}$ defined by the formulas

$$(16.51) \qquad y_{1,0}(x) = k_1,\ y_{2,0}(x) = k_2,\ \ldots,\ y_{n,0}(x) = k_n;$$

we could start with other functions, but we make the simple choice (16.51). Further sets of n functions

$$(16.52) \qquad y_{1,q}(x),\ y_{2,q}(x),\ \ldots,\ y_{n,q}(x) \qquad q - 1, 2, 3, \ldots$$

are defined, for x in a certain range $|x - x_0| \leqq r$ to be determined below, by induction by the *recursion formulas*

$$(16.53) \qquad \begin{cases} y_{1,q}(x) = k_1 + \int_{x_0}^{x} f_1(t, y_{1,q-1}(t), \ldots, y_{n,q-1}(t))dt \\ \cdot \quad \cdot \quad \cdot \quad \cdot \quad \cdot \quad \cdot \quad \cdot \quad \cdot \quad \cdot \quad \cdot \\ y_{n,q}(x) = k_n + \int_{x_0}^{x} f_n(t, y_{1,q-1}(t), \ldots, y_{n,q-1}(t))dt. \end{cases}$$

Let M be a constant such that

$$(16.531) \qquad |f_m(x, y_1, y_2, \ldots, y_n)| \leqq M \qquad m = 1, 2, \ldots, n$$

when (16.33) holds, and let r be the least of the numbers r_0, r_1/M, $r_2/M, \ldots, r_n/M$. Let x be confined to the interval I of points for which $|x - x_0| \leqq r$. The formulas

$$(16.54) \qquad |y_{m,q}(x) - k_q| \leqq r_m \qquad m = 1, 2, \ldots, n$$

hold when $q = 0$. Assuming that the formulas (16.54) hold when q is replaced by $(q - 1)$, we find by use of (16.53) that

$$\begin{aligned} |y_{m,q}(x) - k_q| &= \left|\int_{x_0}^{x} f_m(t, y_{1,q-1}(t), \ldots, y_{n,q-1}(t))dt\right| \\ &\leqq \left|\int_{x_0}^{x} M\,dt\right| = M|x - x_0| \leqq Mr \leqq r_m. \end{aligned}$$

This proves by induction that (16.54) holds for each $q = 0, 1, 2, \ldots$. Therefore we can use the recursion formulas (16.53) and the condition (16.34) to obtain for each $m = 1, 2, \ldots, n$ and $q = 1, 2, 3, \ldots$

$$\begin{aligned} (16.55) \quad & |y_{m,q+1}(x) - y_{m,q}(x)| \\ & \leqq \left|\int_{x_0}^{x} |f_m(t, y_{1,q}(t), \ldots, y_{n,q}(t)) - f_m(t, y_{1,q-1}(t), \ldots, y_{n,q-1}(t))|dt\right| \\ & \leqq \left|\int_{x_0}^{x} A[|y_{1,q}(t) - y_{1,q-1}(t)| + \cdots + |y_{n,q}(t) - y_{n,q-1}(t)|]dt\right|. \end{aligned}$$

Let B be a constant such that

(16.56) $$|y_{m,1}(x) - y_{m,0}(x)| \leqq B \qquad m = 1, 2, \ldots, n.$$

Using (16.56) and (16.55) with $q = 1$, we find that

(16.57) $$|y_{m,2}(x) - y_{m,1}(x)| \leqq BAn|x - x_0| \quad m = 1, 2, \ldots, n.$$

Using (16.57) and (16.55) with $q = 2$, we find that the formula

(16.571) $$|y_{m,q}(x) - y_{m,q-1}(x)| \leqq \frac{B(An|x - x_0|)^q}{q!} \qquad m = 1, 2, \ldots, n$$

holds when $q = 2$. It being assumed that (16.571) holds for a fixed q, the same procedure proves it for $q + 1$. Therefore, the inequality

(16.572) $$|y_{m,q}(x) - y_{m,q-1}(x)| \leqq \frac{B(Anr)^q}{q!} \qquad q = 2, 3, \ldots$$

holds for each $m = 1, 2, \ldots, n$.

For each fixed m the inequalities (16.572) are, except for differences in notation, the same as the inequalities (15.90); accordingly it follows exactly as in Section 15.8 that for each m the sequence

$$y_{m,0}(x),\ y_{m,1}(x),\ y_{m,2}(x), \ldots$$

converges uniformly to the function $y_m(x)$ defined by the series

$$y_m(x) = y_{m,0}(x) + [y_{m,1}(x) - y_{m,0}(x)] + [y_{m,2}(x) - y_{m,1}(x)] + \cdots$$

when $|x - x_0| \leqq r$. It follows by arguments used in Section 15.8 that y_m is continuous for each m, that $x, y_1, y_2, \ldots, y_m$ satisfy (16.33), and that

(16.58) $$y_m(x) = k_m + \int_{x_0}^{x} f_m(t, y_1(t), \ldots, y_n(t))dt$$

when $|x - x_0| \leqq r$. From (16.58) we see that $y_m(x_0) = k_m$ so that the boundary conditions (16.36) are satisfied, and using the fundamental theorem of the calculus we see that the system (16.32) of differential equations is satisfied. Proof of uniqueness of the solution proceeds as in Section 15.8; we shall not repeat the arguments.

For the case of the system (16.22) in which the f's are defined by (16.24), the foregoing proof can be simplified and the conclusion strengthened. If I_1 is a bounded closed interval over which the functions $a_{m,k}(x)$ and $\phi_m(x)$ are continuous, then the approximations $y_{m,q}(x)$ as defined by (16.53) exist for each x in the whole interval I_1. The inequality $|x - x_0| \leqq r$ and the inequalities (16.54) are not required. The condition (16.34) having been established in (16.25), we can use (16.34) with (16.53) to obtain (16.55) for each x in I_1 and proof proceeds without further change for the whole interval I_1. This completes the proof of Theorem 16.31.

16.6. Use of Vector Spaces. With the aid of the simplest ideas involving linear vector metric spaces, the statement and proof of Theorem 16.31 can be made to appear much simpler. Let $U_1, U_2, \ldots, U_n$ be n independent unit vectors. An ordered set $w_1, w_2, \ldots, w_n$ of n numbers (scalars) then determines a *vector* W defined by

$$W = w_1U_1 + w_2U_2 + \cdots + w_nU_n.$$

Let the length $\|W\|$ of W be defined by

$$\|W\| = |w_1| + |w_2| + \cdots + |w_n|.$$

This is not the good old Euclid (*c.* 330 B.C.–275 B.C.) formula, but it is better for our purpose. Finding the n functions $y_1(x), \ldots, y_n(x)$ in Theorem 16.31 is then equivalent to finding the vector function

$$Y(x) = \sum_{k=1}^{n} y_k(x)U_k.$$

If we set $f_k(x, Y) = f_k(x, y_1, y_2, \ldots, y_n)$ and

$$F(x, Y) = \sum_{k=1}^{n} f_k(x, Y)U_k,$$

then the system (16.32) of equations becomes the vector equation

$$Y'(x) = F(x, Y).$$

The boundary conditions (16.36) become the vector condition

$$Y(x_0) = K.$$

The hypothesis (16.34) becomes

$$\|F(x, Y) - F(x, \mathrm{H})\| \leqq A\|Y - \mathrm{H}\|$$

where H is the capital Greek eta. The Picard approximations are defined by the formula

$$Y_q(x) = K + \int_{x_0}^{x} F(t, Y_{q-1}(t))dt.$$

It is a good idea to know how vectors can be used to convert problems involving systems of scalar equations into single vector equations. Methods applicable to a single scalar equation can then be applied to the vector equation. See sections 8.8 and 8.9.

16.7. Linear Equations. We now develop some properties of solutions of the linear differential equation

$$(16.71)\qquad a_0\frac{d^ny}{dx^n} + a_1\frac{d^{n-1}y}{dx^{n-1}} + \cdots + a_{n-1}\frac{dy}{dx} + a_ny = f,$$

x being restricted to an interval I in which the functions $a_0(x), \ldots, a_n(x)$ and $f(x)$ are continuous and $a_0(x) \neq 0$. In particular, we shall obtain a proof of Theorem 6.04.

Let (16.71) be abbreviated in the form $Ly = f$, and let the corresponding homogeneous equation be written $Ly = 0$. Since the equations $Ly = 0$ and $Ly = f$ can be thrown into the form (16.12) by division by $a_0(x)$ and a slight change of notation, we can apply Theorem 16.11 to $Ly = 0$ and $Ly = f$. Let x_0 be a point of I.

Let $Y_1(x), Y_2(x), \ldots, Y_n(x)$ be the special solutions of $Ly = 0$ which satisfy, respectively, the boundary conditions

$$(16.72) \quad \begin{cases} Y_1(x_0) = 1, \; Y_1'(x_0) = 0, \; Y_1''(x_0) = 0, \; \ldots, \; Y_1^{(n-1)}(x_0) = 0 \\ Y_2(x_0) = 0, \; Y_2'(x_0) = 1, \; Y_2''(x_0) = 0, \; \ldots, \; Y_2^{(n-1)}(x_0) = 0 \\ Y_3(x_0) = 0, \; Y_3'(x_0) = 0, \; Y_3''(x_0) = 1, \; \ldots, \; Y_3^{(n-1)}(x_0) = 0 \\ \cdots\cdots\cdots\cdots\cdots\cdots\cdots\cdots\cdots\cdots \\ Y_n(x_0) = 0, \; Y_n'(x_0) = 0, \; Y_n''(x_0) = 0, \; \ldots, \; Y_n^{(n-1)}(x_0) = 1. \end{cases}$$

This system of solutions of $Ly = 0$ is called a *fundamental system* of solutions. These solutions are independent over the interval I; to prove this, let $c_1, c_2, \ldots, c_n$ be constants such that

$$(16.73) \qquad c_1Y_1(x) + c_2Y_2(x) + \cdots + c_nY_n(x) = 0$$

when x is in I. Then we can set $x = x_0$ in (16.73) to obtain $c_1 = 0$; differentiate (16.73) once and set $x = x_0$ to obtain $c_2 = 0$; differentiate again and set $x = x_0$ to obtain $c_3 = 0$; and continue the process to obtain $c_1 = c_2 = \cdots = c_n = 0$ and thus establish independence. It is also easy to show that each solution of $Ly = 0$ must be a linear combination of $Y_1, Y_2, \ldots, Y_n$. If $y(x)$ is a solution of $Ly = 0$ and we define $d_1, d_2, \ldots, d_n$ by the formulas

$$d_1 = y(x_0), \; d_2 = y'(x_0), \; d_3 = y''(x_0), \; \ldots, \; d_n = y^{(n-1)}(x_0)$$

and set

$$(16.731) \qquad \tilde{y}(x) = d_1Y_1(x) + d_2Y_2(x) + \cdots + d_nY_n(x),$$

then $y(x)$ and $\tilde{y}(x)$ are two solutions of $Ly = 0$ which are, together with their first $n - 1$ derivatives, equal when $x = x_0$; accordingly, by Theorem 16.11, $y(x) = \tilde{y}(x)$ and it follows that *each solution* $y(x)$ *of* $Ly = 0$ *can be represented in the form*

$$(16.74) \quad y(x) = y(x_0)Y_1(x) + y'(x_0)Y_2(x) + \cdots + y^{(n-1)}(x_0)Y_n(x).$$

Thus we have shown that each solution of $Ly = 0$ is a linear combination of functions in the fundamental set.

Now let $y_1(x), y_2(x), \ldots, y_n(x)$ denote any set, independent or not, of n solutions of $Ly = 0$. Making use of (16.74), we obtain

$$(16.75)\quad \begin{cases} y_1(x) = y_1(x_0)Y_1(x) + y_1'(x_0)Y_2(x) + \cdots + y_1^{(n-1)}(x_0)Y_n(x) \\ y_2(x) = y_2(x_0)Y_1(x) + y_2'(x_0)Y_2(x) + \cdots + y_2^{(n-1)}(x_0)Y_n(x) \\ \cdots\cdots\cdots\cdots\cdots\cdots\cdots\cdots\cdots\cdots \\ y_n(x) = y_n(x_0)Y_1(x) + y_n'(x_0)Y_2(x) + \cdots + y_n^{(n-1)}(x_0)Y_n(x). \end{cases}$$

The solutions $y_1, \ldots, y_n$ are independent if and only if the identity $c_1y_1 + \cdots + c_ny_n = 0$ implies $c_1 = c_2 = \cdots = c_n = 0$. But

$$\sum_{m=1}^{n} c_m y_m(x) = \sum_{m=1}^{n} c_m \sum_{k=1}^{n} y_m^{(k-1)}(x_0)Y_k(x)$$
$$= \sum_{k=1}^{n} \left[\sum_{m=1}^{n} c_m y_m^{(k-1)}(x_0) \right] Y_k(x);$$

and since $Y_1, \ldots, Y_k$ are independent, it follows that $\Sigma c_m y_m(x) = 0$ over I if and only if the sums in brackets all vanish. Thus $y_1, y_2, \ldots,$ y_n are independent over I if and only if the system of algebraic equations

$$(16.751)\quad \begin{cases} c_1y_1(x_0) + c_2y_2(x_0) + \cdots + c_ny_n(x_0) = 0 \\ c_1y_1'(x_0) + c_2y_2'(x_0) + \cdots + c_ny_n'(x_0) = 0 \\ \cdots\cdots\cdots\cdots\cdots\cdots\cdots\cdots\cdots\cdots \\ c_1y_1^{(n-1)}(x_0) + c_2y_2^{(n-1)}(x_0) + \cdots + c_ny_n^{(n-1)}(x_0) = 0 \end{cases}$$

is satisfied only when $c_1 = c_2 = \cdots = c_n = 0$, and therefore if and only if the determinant of the coefficients of the c's is different from 0. Thus we obtain the following:

Theorem 16.76. *A set of n solutions $y_1(x), \ldots, y_n(x)$ of $Ly = 0$ is independent over I if and only if*

$$\begin{vmatrix} y_1(x_0) & y_2(x_0) & \cdots & y_n(x_0) \\ y_1'(x_0) & y_2'(x_0) & \cdots & y_n'(x_0) \\ \cdots & \cdots & \cdots & \cdots \\ y_1^{(n-1)}(x_0) & y_2^{(n-1)}(x_0) & \cdots & y_n^{(n-1)}(x_0) \end{vmatrix} \neq 0.$$

This determinant is called the Wronskian of $y_1, y_2, \ldots, y_n$ and is denoted by $W(y_1, y_2, \ldots, y_n; x_0)$. Since the point x_0 could be taken to be any point of the interval I over which $a_0(x), \ldots, a_n(x)$ are continuous and $a_0(x) \neq 0$, it follows that *if $y_1, \ldots, y_n$ are dependent over I, their Wronskian $W(y_1, y_2, \ldots, y_n; x)$ vanishes for all x in I and if $y_1, \ldots,$ y_n are independent over I, their Wronskian $W(y_1, y_2, \ldots, y_n; x)$ is different from 0 for all x in I.*

We can now prove that if $y_1, y_2, \ldots, y_n$ are independent solutions of $Ly = 0$, then each solution $y(x)$ of $Ly = 0$ can be written in the form

$$(16.77) \qquad y(x) = c_1y_1(x) + c_2y_2(x) + \cdots + c_ny_n(x).$$

We have seen in (16.74) that $y(x)$ is a linear combination of $Y_1(x), \ldots,$ $Y_n(x)$. But the hypothesis that $y_1, \ldots, y_n$ are independent implies that $W(y_1, y_2, \ldots, y_n; x) \neq 0$, and hence using (16.75) we see that $Y_1, \ldots, Y_n$ are linear combinations of $y_1, \ldots, y_n$; our result follows.

This proves all the results of Theorem 6.04 which pertain to the homogeneous equation $Ly = 0$. The results pertaining to the equation $Ly = f$ follow from (i) Theorem 6.03 which shows that $Ly = f$ must have at least one solution, (ii) linearity of L which implies that if Y_1 and Y_2 are two solutions of $Ly = f$ then $L(Y_2 - Y_1) = 0$, and (iii) the known character of solutions of $Ly = 0$.

Problem 16.78

If $y_1 = e^{m_1x}, y_2 = e^{m_2x}, \ldots, y_n = e^{m_nx}$ where $m_1, m_2, \ldots, m_n$ are complex constants, prove that

$$W(y_1, \ldots, y_n; x) = e^{(m_1+m_2+\cdots+m_n)x}\Delta$$

where Δ is the *Vandermonde* (1735–1796) *determinant*

$$\Delta = \begin{vmatrix} 1 & 1 & \cdots & 1 \\ m_1 & m_2 & \cdots & m_n \\ m_1^2 & m_2^2 & \cdots & m_n^2 \\ \cdots & \cdots & \cdots & \cdots \\ m_1^{n-1} & m_2^{n-1} & \cdots & m_n^{n-1} \end{vmatrix},$$

and that

$$\Delta = (m_2 - m_1)(m_3 - m_1) \cdots (m_n - m_1)(m_3 - m_2) \cdots (m_n - m_2) \cdots (m_n - m_{n-1}),$$

the right-hand member containing all factors of the form $m_p - m_q$ where $p > q$. What conditions must $m_1, \ldots, m_n$ satisfy to ensure independence of $y_1, \ldots, y_n$?

Problem 16.781

Show that the derivative with respect to x of the Wronskian $W(y_1, \ldots, y_n; x)$ of n functions each having n derivatives is given by the formula

$$W'(y_1, \ldots, y_n; x) = \begin{vmatrix} y_1 & y_2 & y_3 & \cdots & y_n \\ y_1' & y_2' & y_3' & \cdots & y_n' \\ \cdots & \cdots & \cdots & \cdots & \cdots \\ y_1^{(n-2)} & y_2^{(n-2)} & y_3^{(n-2)} & \cdots & y_n^{(n-2)} \\ y_1^{(n)} & y_2^{(n)} & y_3^{(n)} & \cdots & y_n^{(n)} \end{vmatrix}.$$

Problem 16.782

Prove that, if

$$Ly = a_0y^{(n)} + a_1y^{(n-1)} + \cdots + a_{n-1}y' + a_ny$$

where $a_0(x), a_1(x), \ldots, a_n(x)$ are continuous and $a_0(x) \neq 0$ over an interval I and $y_1(x), y_2(x), \ldots, y_n(x)$ are n solutions of $Ly = 0$, then for each x in I

$$W(y_1, \ldots, y_n; x)Ly = (-1)^n a_0(x)\Delta \tag{16.783}$$
$$W'(y_1, \ldots, y_n; x)Ly = (-1)^{n+1} a_1(x)\Delta \tag{16.784}$$

where Δ is the determinant

$$\Delta = \begin{vmatrix} y & y_1 & y_2 & \cdots & y_n \\ y' & y_1' & y_2' & \cdots & y_n' \\ y'' & y_1'' & y_2'' & \cdots & y_n'' \\ \cdot & \cdot & \cdot & \cdots & \cdot \\ y^{(n)} & y_1^{(n)} & y_2^{(n)} & \cdots & y_n^{(n)} \end{vmatrix}$$

with $(n + 1)$ functions of x in each row and column. Show that if t is a point in the interval I and we put $y(x) = (x - t)^n/n!$ in (16.784) and set $x = t$ in the result, we obtain

$$W'(y_1, \ldots, y_n; t)a_0(t) = -a_1(t)W(y_1, \ldots, y_n; t).$$

Use this result to show that

$$W(y_1, \ldots, y_n; x) = C \exp\left[-\int_{x_0}^{x} \frac{a_1(t)}{a_0(t)}\, dt\right]. \tag{16.79}$$

This is *Abel's formula for the Wronskian* of n solutions of $Ly = 0$; the case $n = 2$ was treated in Section 6.1 by a different method. Can you obtain (16.79) by a less (or more) elaborate method?

POSTSCRIPT

When the author received the last of the original page proofs for this book, he noticed that the last half of this page was blank and was informed that the next page would be blank. This circumstance gives us an opportunity to look at a little intellectual puzzle that is "added in proof."

As some readers of this book already know, and as some others will learn, the Laplace equation

$$\frac{\partial^2 u}{\partial x^2} + \frac{\partial^2 u}{\partial y^2} = 0 \tag{17.1}$$

plays a fundamental role in the theory of analytic functions of a complex variable. According to some authors and teachers, a real function $u(x, y)$ is a *harmonic function* if it satisfies the Laplace equation (17.1). According to other authors and teachers, a real function $u(x, y)$ is a *harmonic function* if

$$u, \frac{\partial u}{\partial x}, \frac{\partial u}{\partial y}, \frac{\partial^2 u}{\partial x^2}, \frac{\partial^2 u}{\partial y^2} \tag{17.2}$$

are all continuous and $u(x, y)$ satisfies the Laplace equation (17.1). To solve our puzzle, we must decide whether these definitions really are different. The crucial question is whether each real function u satisfying the Laplace equation must be such that the functions in (17.2) are all continuous.

The scandalous fact is that a function u can satisfy the Laplace equation over the whole x, y plane and nevertheless be discontinuous at the origin. An infamous example of a function which proves this is the function for which $u(0, 0) = 0$ and, when $z = x + iy$ and $z \neq 0$, $u(x, y)$ is the real part of i/z^2. It is easy to show that

$$u(x, y) = \frac{2xy}{(x^2 + y^2)^2} \tag{17.3}$$

when x and y are not both zero. When $z = x + iy \neq 0$, u is the real part of the analytic function i/z^2 and it follows from the theory of these analytic functions that u must satisfy the Laplace equation. This fact may also be proved by differentiating (17.3) to obtain

$$\frac{\partial^2 u}{\partial x^2} = 24xy \frac{x^2 - y^2}{(x^2 + y^2)^2}, \qquad \frac{\partial^2 u}{\partial y^2} = 24xy \frac{y^2 - x^2}{(x^2 + y^2)^2}. \tag{17.4}$$

When $z = x + iy = 0$, the derivatives in (17.1) turn out to be zero because $u(x, y) = 0$ when $x = 0$ and when $y = 0$. Thus the Laplace equation is satisfied in this case also. Therefore the Laplace equation is satisfied over the whole plane. However when $x \neq 0$, we have $u(x, x) = 1/2x^2$, and this implies that $u(x, y)$ cannot be continuous at the origin.

In the theory of functions of a complex variable and elsewhere, a *region* R is defined to be an open connected set. It is always understood that a real function $u(x, y)$ which is harmonic over a region R is a very well-behaved function, so well-behaved, in fact, that it is the real part of a function analytic over the region. It is therefore incorrect to call a function harmonic over a region R merely because it satisfies the Laplace equation over R; it is necessary to add a requirement that implies that the functions in (17.2) are continuous.

On pages 409 and 411 it was pointed out that it is not always easy to write complete and sensible formulations of boundary-value problems involving partial differential equations. The example of this section throws another burden upon us. When the differential equation involved is the Laplace equation, it is not enough to require that the function u satisfy the Laplace equation over the given region. It is necessary to impose the additional requirement that the functions in (17.2) be continuous over the region.

INDEX

$$D(qD)+z$$

$$(D(qD)y+zy,\ z) = (y,\ D(qD)z+zz)$$

$$(D(qD)y, z) + (zy, z) = (y, D(qD)z) + (y, zz)$$

$$\int_\alpha^\beta (qy')'\bar{z}\,dx + \cancel{\int zy\bar{z}} = \int y\,(q\bar{z}')'\,dx + \cancel{\int y\bar{z}z}$$

$$\int \bar{z}\,d(qy') \qquad \int y\,d(q\bar{z}')$$

$$\bar{z}qy'\Big|_\alpha^\beta - \cancel{\int qy'\bar{z}'} \qquad qy\bar{z}'\Big|_\alpha^\beta - \cancel{\int q\bar{z}'y'\,dx}$$

$$q(x)\,z(x)\,y'(x)\Big|_\alpha^\beta = q(x)\,y(x)\,z'(x)\Big|_\alpha^\beta$$

$$q(\beta)z(\beta)y'(\beta) - q(\alpha)z(\alpha)y'(\alpha) = q(\beta)y(\beta)z'(\beta) - q(\alpha)y(\alpha)z'(\alpha)$$

$$y'' + \alpha^2 y = \cancel{\delta(t)}\ h(t)$$

$$y''+\alpha^2 y = \begin{cases} 0 & \alpha\epsilon\nu \\ 1 & \partial\alpha. \end{cases}$$

$$\cancel{c_1\cos\alpha t + c_2\sin\alpha t}$$

$$s^2Y + \alpha^2 Y = 1$$

$$Y = \frac{1}{s^2+\alpha^2}$$

$$\frac{1}{s(s^2+\alpha^2)} = \frac{\frac{1}{\alpha^2}}{s} + \frac{Bs+C}{s^2+\alpha^2}$$